BURNING BRITAIN

BRITAIN

THE HISTORY

OF UK PUNK

1980–1984

IAN GLASPER

PM

Burning Britain: The History of UK Punk 1980–1984
Ian Glasper
First published in the UK by Cherry Red
This edition © 2014 PM Press
All rights reserved. No part of this book may be transmitted by any means without
permission in writing from the publisher.

ISBN: 978–1–60486–748–0
Library of Congress Control Number: 2013956922

Cover by John Yates / www.stealworks.com
Interior design by briandesign

10 9 8 7 6 5 4 3 2 1

PM Press
PO Box 23912
Oakland, CA 94623
www.pmpress.org

Printed in the USA by the Employee Owners of Thomson-Shore in Dexter, Michigan.
www.thomsonshore.com

CONTENTS

The 1983 lineup of Grantham's English Dogs
(Pic: Mike Stone)

PREFACE TO THE PRESENT EDITION

When I wrote *Burning Britain* back in 2002–2003, I was writing it for myself. I was literally just writing the book that I wanted to see on my own bookshelves, so it was very gratifying when it chimed with so many people around the world, and I was touched that so many people instantly related with my own instinctive feeling that the early Eighties was *the* defining era for their own punk rock experience. No one's right or wrong here. It all comes down to when you were born and at what point in your life you got knocked sideways by your first punk rock song.

I'm also thrilled that the book seems to have genuine legs and, on the strength of grassroots recommendation alone, has been translated into various languages and keeps finding new enthusiastic audiences around the world – all testament of course to the eternal appeal of good honest punk music.

When *Burning Britain* was published in 2004, I was quite aware that, whilst about as good an account of the early Eighties punk scene as it could be, it wasn't quite complete, and there were certain bands that I'd been forced to skip over, and certain individuals I needed to talk to that I didn't, due to the inevitable time and financial constraints and having to meet an ever-looming publishing deadline.

Ten years on, this PM Press edition has given me the opportunity to include some of those bands that weren't given their proper due first time around – Infa-Riot, The Blood, Ultra Violent, Subculture, Red London, The Actives and Soldiers Of Destruction – and also to expand the current sections on Chaos UK, The Destructors and English Dogs with brand new additional interviews with key members that I couldn't locate in time ten years ago. I've also updated the discographies with some of the major releases since the book was first published. It's still not perfect, but then this isn't a fairytale and nothing ever is, is it? But it's still the most comprehensive account of that period you'll find anywhere . . . and even more so now.

So, sit back and relax with your favourite scratchy UK82 7" and enjoy this extra content that now complements *Burning Britain*. And remember, punk rock is an attitude, and as long as someone, somewhere, carries that attitude in their heart and soul, *punk rock will never die*.

Ian Glasper
2014

I WOULD LIKE TO THANK THE FOLLOWING PEOPLE FOR THEIR ASSISTANCE, SUPPORT AND ADVICE:

Mark Brennan and all at Captain Oi!; Simon Edwards and Shane Baldwin; Iain McNay, Matt, Alex and all at Cherry Red; Tim Wright, Welshy, Spike, Pete Don't Care, Rebecca Pollard (Punk and Oi In The UK), James Sherry, Steve (Art Of The State), Joel McIver and all at Record Collector; Des, Nosh and Nicky; Silv, Dave and Renn; Ben Williams; Mobs and all of Stampin' Ground; Simon Rockaway, Beddis, Pig and Payney; Albert Mudrian and Adam at Feral House; Richard White and Suicide Watch; Seany Rotten, Josh Upstart, Sean Forbes, Stu Decay (Sheffield), Tony Mottram and family; Mick Mercer, Carol Clerk, Chris Berry, Lyndon Henstridge, Deek Allan, Ian Armstrong, Jim (Intimidation); Jonathon Selzer, Damien and all at Terrorizer; Daz (remember 'Speed Hippy'?) and Jennie Russell-Smith; Michael and Andy of Therapy?; Sean McGhee and Martyn Cockbain; Steve and all at Plastic Head, and everyone else that made things happen behind the scenes. A thousand apologies to anyone I've forgotten.

And of course, all the bands and labels that have put up with me the last two years, for their co-operation and wonderful stories.

Likewise my family and friends for their patience during this long haul. Not least of all my wife, Jo, and daughter, Amy.

Oh, and punk rock because...well, just because.

This book is respectfully dedicated to the memory of my good friend Dean Uzell, who gave me so much encouragement during its early stages, but is sadly no longer with us. Rest in peace, mate.

Ian Glasper, May 2004

TITLE PAGE: Monkey of The Adicts (Picture: Tony Mottram)

ABOVE: Dead Wretched guitarist, Paul 'Baz' Harding

I n late 1980 I was just thirteen years old, and listening to everything from Adam And The Ants and Killing Joke to the Stray Cats and Shakin' Stevens, but when my cousin, Antony 'Mobs' Mowbray played me the 'Decontrol' single by Discharge, my whole perspective on music – and ultimately life, the universe and everything – changed. All the confused teen angst, all the rebellious cool, all the pent-up frustration and energy I was feeling… all seemed to be encapsulated in the incredible roar that emanated from those seven inches of crackling vinyl. My world was turned on its head… or rather it was turned on its feet and suddenly a lot of things fell into place for the very first time. Such is the power of music, I still get goose bumps whenever I hear 'Decontrol'.

So, I'm not even going to pretend that I was around to witness the first wave of punk come crashing down like a tidal wave on a bloated washed-up music scene back in 1976 – just check my birth certificate and do the maths – but when the second wave rose up ominously from the gutter and usurped the coveted crown from the preening poseurs I was stood in the front row rubbing my hands with glee.

The tender age of ten was far too young to appreciate the filth and the fury of The Sex Pistols, but four years later, during those most formative early teens, a tentacle reached out from the underground, snaked subversively through my bedroom window and touched me on the shoulder. It doesn't matter where you are, who you are, or how old you are when it happens, all that matters is that when the spirit of punk rock grabs a hold of you, it never ever lets go.

Of course, I'd seen the media coverage, and heard folk either scoffing or tutting in outrage at Malcolm McLaren's brilliantly orchestrated Jubilee antics, but it had all pretty much passed me by, until one day I suddenly started to wonder about the intriguing names painted amateurishly on the backs of some of my older friends' leather jackets. Names like Discharge and The UK Subs, names to be whispered in awe after night had fallen, names to be conjured with, a whole new world to be explored…

The soundtrack to our teens usually sets the rhythm that moves us for the rest of our lives, and mine was one long primal scream of distorted guitars, pounding drums and desperately hollered vocals. Yes, a lot of it was played badly, and most of it was badly produced (by today's over-clinical standards, at least), but there was no denying the urgency of these bands. And with no lengthy world tours undertaken to promote each release, they could also be incredibly prolific in a short period of time, sometimes amassing a sizable catalogue in the space of a few years. What they lacked in finesse, they made up for with sheer enthusiasm.

Youthful naiveté was often misinterpreted as genuine rebellion, but that the hell? It felt both exhilarating and liberating.

I was still living with my ever-patient parents when I fell in love with hardcore punk, watching the world from inside a protective bubble, so the harsh realities of the street that fuelled the fire in the bellies of these ferocious bands was something I could only imagine, but I felt their intensity and sensed their genuine angst, and somehow related to it and equated it to my own circumstances. It was only several years later when I was unemployed and living with no safety net in a bedsit that I realised the timeless truth of those profoundly simplistic lyrics that had so touched me previously.

Punk rock means a thousand different things to a thousand different people, but all that really matters is what it means to you. So, ladies and gentlemen, without further ado, never mind the bollocks, here's what I call real punk rock…

IAN GLASPER

OPPOSITE: Blitz, one of several bands instrumental in blurring the dividing line between the punk and skinhead genres

DISCLAIMER

Please note that there are deliberately no anarcho punk bands included in this book. Not because I didn't dig those bands (quite the opposite, in fact; I loved them!), but because it essentially seemed to be a whole different scene. My next book is about all those great bands like The Subhumans, Crass and Conflict, and the hundreds of other bands launched in their wake, but for now I decided not to confuse the issue by including them here. In fact, several bands originally interviewed for this book (The Disrupters, No Choice, Self Abuse, Reality and Contempt, to name but a few) have been 'held over' for that next tome. This may seem like a controversial and fractious decision to some, but it's one that's purely based on logistical constraints, namely time and space.

Likewise, I have only included a few skinhead bands, the ones that had most crossover appeal to fans of punk, but again, that was a whole separate scene, and best explored properly by someone who knows a lot more about it than me.

Another potential debating point is the whole phrase 'Second Wave'... was the punk scene of the early Eighties really the second wave? Or the third? But let's not get too pedantic here; it's a moot point and all depends upon individual interpretation.

The discographies are not meant to be exhaustive, but rather crucial bullet points tracking the career of a particular band. I really wanted to avoid this becoming little more than a reference volume full of anal listings of every song that ever appeared on every compilation album ever! The 'At A Glance' choice of release is intended for the reader who may be new to that band and just needs a 'one stop' purchase to get a decent overview of their output.

Good unseen photos from the period are elusive to say the least, but I think we've done all right, and wherever possible we've tried to ascertain who took the photograph and credit them accordingly. However, almost all the pictures are over twenty years old now and came from personal collections of the bands, so this has often been impossible.

Lastly, a book like this is bound to provoke a few angry thoughts along the lines of, 'What about such-and-such band? Why aren't they included?' and, 'Why's he raving about that album? It was shit!' All I can say is, I did my best to cover, with integrity and honesty, every band of merit from the chosen era, but one or two noteworthy bands were either untraceable or unwilling/unable to appear.

So, this is the real story of that criminally overlooked scene, in the words of the bands and labels that created it. I just pointed a torch into a few dark corners on their behalf.

A COUNTRY FIT FOR HEROES ...

By the end of the Seventies, the initial thrill of punk rock began to dissipate as quickly as it had amassed. Johnny Rotten had left the Pistols, Sid Vicious was dead, and The Clash were about to reveal their 'Sandinista!' triple album that sounded very different to the manic energy of 'White Riot'. Major labels had already picked over the carcass, salvaging what they thought was still marketable, and the sensationalist media frenzy had subsided to a contemptuous whimper. What began as a glorious shakedown of traditional values and industry bullshit was eventually turned on its head, and its essence leeched away by greed, boredom and excess – the very things that inspired it in the first place.

But seeds had been sown, and punk fans everywhere had already heard the call and been inspired to take up weapons – well, guitars and drums – to continue the fight.

"Yes, certainly by 1978 or 1979, the words 'punk rock' had become taboo with the media," agrees Gavin Gritton from Anti-Establishment. "Some groups like Adam And The Ants and The Police had used it as a bandwagon to move onto other things and become famous.

**Fleetwood's formidable One Way System
(Pic: Tony Mottram)**

"The second wave of punks were the kids who like ourselves had missed out on punk the first time around, who were less pretentious and proud to be punk for the youth culture side of it. The climate at the time included football terrace culture and teenage rebellion against outraged parents..."

"In the mid-Seventies, music had got so progressive and indulgent, that something had to give way," reckons Steve Arrogant from Special Duties. "The first wave of punk bands were all very musically accomplished; they could already play their instruments when punk came along, and they developed the original sound. The second wave was more genuine though; the influences of the second wave were the first wave. You had punk rock fans learning to play instruments just so they could be in punk rock bands. The first punk bands just kinda stumbled into it, whereas the second wave was only influenced by other punk bands."

"It all seemed much more hardcore," agrees Chris Taylor from The Mau Maus. "Kids coming off the streets trying to follow in the footsteps of their heroes. It gave bands like us, with limited musical ability, a chance to do something we enjoyed and believed in."

"Musically the waves were like gears on a car," adds Major Accident's Con Larkin. "Basically, the higher the number, the faster the music. The second wave also took it from the art schools and into the council estates."

Yes, as well as sounding different, the second wave bands looked different and had a whole new agenda to rage against. Amidst the backdrop of a derelict urban wasteland, rebellion against the expectations of parents gradually became rebellion against the state and all its henchmen. Unemployment was rife, opportunities non-existent, with so-called job creation schemes proving as ineffectual as they were patronising... Thatcherism was shading our green and pleasant land the very unpleasant grey shades of despair.

The police force, showing their true colours on picket lines and demonstrations, seemed increasingly concerned with oppression rather than protection, and the government was callously ignoring the plight of industry at home to concentrate on futile conquests overseas. Everybody was terrified of either a nuclear strike or meltdown, and soon there would be pitched battles on the streets when social tensions reached boiling point. And with such desperate times breeding equally desperate teenagers, the new punk bands took all

Peter And The Test Tube Babies – and audience! – in typically defiant mood (Pic: Tony Mottram)

that intensity and frustration and distilled it into some of the most potent and influential music ever. And if the record companies didn't want to know, they just started their own labels and put out their music themselves. It was the dawning of an angry age.

"Yeah, I think the first wave benefited, to an extent, from major record companies," says Mick McGee, from Mayhem. "They were actually signed to major labels, and although it didn't go well for all the bands concerned, especially The Pistols, they made money and they got their music distributed. They had some major exposure, but I don't think the executives really knew what they were dealing with. What we were involved in afterwards was much more independent. As someone once said, if you robbed three phone boxes you could almost set up your own record company, and that was what we were relying on. That gave access to upcoming bands to actually get their records heard."

"At the time, having been heavily influenced by various first wave bands, I was initially unmoved by many of the second wave bands," offers John Finch of Lunatic Fringe. "I could at first see little merit in, for example, The UK Subs, and felt that bands such as The Exploited were a godsend to critics of punk everywhere (with their 'Swastikas are a symbol of punk' first Sounds interview), irretrievably harming the movement. However, as the relevance and musical direction of most of the earlier bands was becoming diluted, I became more appreciative of the energy and political openness typical of many of the newer bands. Looking back, there was a crucial difference though; the first wave was an umbrella which could include bands of vastly differing influences and musical styles, whereas second wave bands were moving towards a much more uniform (some would say entrenched) sound and look. Broadly speaking, this to me is where punk music as a clearly defined musical sub-category, rather than a loose movement, began."

"If the first wave of punk was a breath of fresh air then the second wave was like a kick in the balls," claims Karl Morris of Xtract. "It was brutal, fast and very aggressive; I think it was more oriented towards the working classes and really did belong to youth subculture. Leather, studs, spiky hair, ripped jeans and Docs… definitely, and defiantly, no art school influences in this scene."

SO, LET'S MEET THE BANDS...

The Violators from New Mills, Derbyshire, a band that challenged many of the preconceptions of how second wave punk was 'meant' to sound and look (Pic: Tony Mottram)

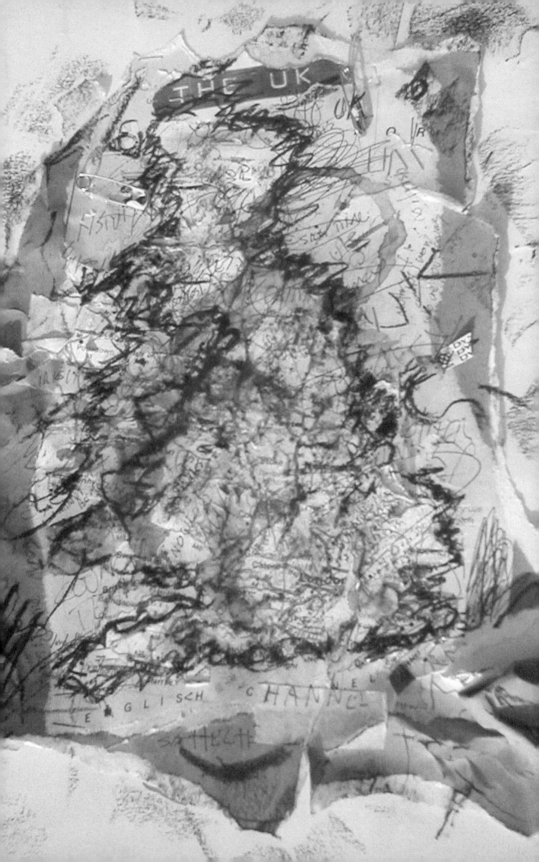

CHAPTER ONE

THE SOUTHWEST

VICE SQUAD

O utside of London, Bristol probably boasted the greatest number of signed punk bands in any one city – due no doubt in part to the presence of the prolific Riot City label as well as some particularly miserable areas of social squalor – and leading the charge was Vice Squad. A breakneck punk band who took the nail of disenfranchised West Country youth and hit it smack on its bored vacuous head, Vice Squad first appeared on the scene with a track, 'Nothing', for a regional

compilation album, 'Avon Calling' (Heartbeat Records, 1979). They actually formed the year before, with Beki Bondage on vocals, Dave Bateman on guitar, Mark Hambly on bass, and Shane Baldwin drumming, and played their first gig at the Bristol University Anson Rooms on April 12th 1979, supporting The X-Certs and Crisis. Shane has fond memories of those bad old days.

"The album got good reviews; a photo of us playing at the Summit Youth Club in Kingswood even appeared in Sounds (an influential music paper of the period), and John Peel played our track a lot on his show. So we were more than pleased! By this time, Dave and I had been trying

for a couple of years, with no success at all, to get a band going (they were previously in the TV Brakes with Ian Minter and Tim Clench), so it was definitely a big thrill when we got our copies of 'Avon Calling'. However, I couldn't help noticing that as well as sounding quite puny compared to the other more accomplished bands on the record, it even looked puny if you held it up to the light... it took up far less grooves than the other tracks.

"Sounds called our contribution 'rabid minimalism', which I had to look up in a

The original Vice Squad
L-R: Beki Bondage, Dave Bateman, Shane Baldwin, Mark Hambly

dictionary, but that about sums it up. Actually, now it's one of my favourite Vice Squad tracks..."

OPPOSITE: Beki Bondage
'... punk's first real pin-up...'

After that, things started to move pretty quickly for the band. John Peel picked up on them most enthusiastically, and was no doubt very instrumental in helping their growing profile.

"I thought it was a bit strange that Peel was so keen on our track," ponders a bemused Shane, "because there were much more established and capable bands on the record, like Glaxo Babies, Joe Public and The X-Certs. I spoke to John for the first time a few years ago, pointing out that we were much more 'basic' than the other bands, and he said, 'Well, basic is what I like'. I chose to take that as a compliment!

"And yes, he was always a staunch supporter; always played our records and we did two sessions for his show, which was a great honour. My dad was a big Peel fan and listened to the show every night, so that gave me a big kick.

"Things started to move quickly after 'Avon Calling', that's true, but they also ground to a halt pretty quickly as well. We supported The Damned and The Ruts at the Locarno, and picked up a bit of a following, but within months, after a lot of crowd trouble, we were banned from most local venues."

That didn't stop the band from helping launch Riot City Records with Heartbeat's Simon Edwards at the helm and going on to create a veritable punk classic as their debut 7". Even today, despite its thin production, 'Last Rockers' still sends a wicked thrill down the spine. The tantalising guitar intro that ushers in the ensuing chaos, Beki's scathing vocal delivery, and those sombre backing vocals… possibly more luck than judgement, but the band had hit upon a winning formula.

Surprisingly though, that initial deal was some time coming, even after the critical praise heaped upon 'Nothing'.

"After 'Avon Calling' we thought that Simon would immediately give us a singles deal at the very least," recalls Shane. "But for a long time he wasn't that keen. After the early bright start things nose-dived quite dramatically, and we only played six gigs in the whole of 1980. After much nagging though, he came to see us at the last of those, a 'Rock Against Thatcher' benefit at Trinity Church, after which he cautiously offered to put out a single, where he would pay for the manufacturing and we had to cough up for the studio costs. It wasn't exactly the record deal of our dreams, but totally understandable seeing as he'd recently lost his Heartbeat licensing deal with Cherry Red.

"The only person we knew with money was our friend Bill White, who owned a cafe, and he loaned us the cash, interest-free, on the sole condition that he was given a credit on all future releases. It was a generous offer, and of course we stuck to it and paid him back as soon as we were able."

It was a good call for Simon Edwards, because 'Last Rockers' sold well over twenty thousand copies and spent almost forty weeks in the then-important Independent Charts, reaching the giddy heights of No. 7, almost unheard of for a debut punk single. The follow-up, four months later in May '81, 'Resurrection', was equally successful, actually reaching No. 4, and the band did a tour with the UK Subs as well as their first session for John Peel. It was almost inevitable a major label would soon snap them up, and sure enough, before the year was out, the band's debut album was in the racks, with the EMI logo adorning its back cover – much to the horror of some DIY punk purists.

"We expected some flak when we chose to sign with EMI, but to be honest, we never expected it to be quite as bad as it was," sighs Shane. "In some ways it still mystifies me. When we're talked about now, it's always one of the first things mentioned, whereas it never seems to crop up with anything written about The (Cockney) Rejects or The (Angelic) Upstarts, who were already on the label when we joined. I don't regret it though; it was an opportunity to move into a completely different sphere, a whole new experience.

"Even Simon Edwards, who was understandably hopping mad when we left Riot City, has since admitted that we just had to seize that chance while it was going. The simple fact is that, for most of the bands who were up in arms about us signing to a major label, the argument was purely academic – nobody ever offered them a similar deal."

Although Shane is philosophical about the label the band chose for themselves, he remains less than flattering about that first album.

"It's just awful and I'm thoroughly ashamed of it! When Mark Brennan at Captain Oi! reissued the album recently he asked me what I thought we should do with it, meaning what bonus tracks to use etc. I suggested we take the fucking thing into the middle of a field and bury it, but he didn't find that idea very helpful..."

Harsh words indeed, but enough fans of the band rushed out and bought 'No Cause For Concern' for it to narrowly miss entering the Top Thirty of the National album charts. The poorly recorded but best-selling 'Out Of Reach' EP followed, but it wasn't until the summer of '82 and the far more confident-sounding second album, 'Stand Strong, Stand Proud', that the band had a record they were truly proud of.

"It's a little known fact that EMI wanted us to do 'Stand Strong...' at Abbey Road Studios," reveals Beki. "But the band – mainly Dave – talked me out of doing it! They said they'd use session musicians etc. I can't believe how naïve I was in those days; they even showed us round the studio where The Beatles recorded and bought us lunch there... but I let myself believe it wouldn't be a good idea!"

The preceding EP of the same name was even granted the accolade Single of the Week in Sounds, and the band celebrated with several dates in Holland and tours of the USA and Canada. A time fondly remembered by Shane Baldwin.

"The tour of America and Canada in 1982 was definitely the highlight of what we sometimes refer to, laughingly, as our 'career'. We started in California, and over six weeks drove from coast to coast, ending up, obviously, in New York. We got to play with the likes of Social Distortion, Youth Brigade, Battalion Of Saints, Black Flag and Bad Brains, and also linked up with fellow Brits, Chron Gen and Discharge, so it was quite an experience.

"The best bit for me was when we played the 9.30 Club in Washington DC. One of my favourite bands, Lords Of The New Church, were playing down the road on the same night, and as we had to play two sets, we went to see them during our break. They returned the compliment and came over for our last show. I'm not ashamed to admit that I got a kick out of that.

"Another thrill was when we arrived in New York. We stayed at the Iroquois Hotel, a famous rock'n'roll dive, and as we drove up we joked that the first thing we would see there would be The Clash, who always mentioned the place in interviews. And sure enough, as we pulled over, there they were, stood outside waiting for a taxi. Chelsea, Lou Reed and Brian Brain from PiL were also staying there, so we thought it the coolest place in the world, if a little dingy.

"At one point during that tour Mark said to me, 'Well, whatever else happens from now on, the bastards can't take this away from us.' And he was right!"

But contrary to all external signs, things were afoot in the Vice Squad camp and soon after the 'State of The Nation' EP that the band released upon returning from the USA, Beki announced her decision to leave for pastures new. Her powerful voice had been a major factor in shaping the band's distinct sound, and with her striking looks and dominatrix overtones, she had already become punk's first real pin-up, adorning the bedroom walls of a thousand spotty adolescents the length and breadth of the nation. For many fans, she WAS Vice Squad, and her departure was greeted with incredulous outrage.

"I didn't get on particularly well with the rest of the band as I was a teenage girl and they were teenage boys and at that age the sexes can be pretty unpleasant to each other," explains Beki, of her decision to leave. "One of the managers we had at the time was particularly fond of winding me up, which included driving past an abattoir to wave at his friends 'working' inside, and I decided that he wasn't going to make money out of me anymore and I left shortly after.

"I read something Shane wrote that said I left because I already knew EMI would give me another deal if I left Vice Squad, but I'm sorry to admit that I wasn't sussed enough to be that calculating. The irony of all this is that with CJD, foot and mouth disease, and mass starvation in the third world, not to mention all the other unpleasant by-products of the meat industry, I can see that I was right to believe in Animal Rights, and I still do.

"Still, the split was years ago and it's fair to say that people change and that ex-manager could well be a very nice person these days. To be honest, I hate being asked this question as the answer's likely to cause bad feeling and it's all water under the bridge and rather petty after all… but you did ask!"

Beki went on to front Ligotage and then Beki And The Bombshells, and her departure was to sound the death knell for the original incarnation of Vice Squad. Soon after, they were dropped by EMI, but undeterred recruited a young Clifton punkette by the name of Lia who was given the unenviable task of filling Beki's rather large (speaking metaphorically, of course) shoes.

"Actually, Lia was in her twenties when she joined the band and they were going to say she was sixteen," adds Beki. "She only lasted about six months because you just don't put up with being gobbed on and whatever when you're in your twenties. When I said that I was leaving the band one of the managers even said that they were going to recruit another girl and say that she was my sister and call her 'Belinda Bondage'!

"I thought Lia had a really good voice, but I'm surprised that they took on a relatively mature woman as there was no way she would put up with the abuse I had, and let's face it, the early incarnation of Vice Squad always attracted nutters! I'd like to meet her one day and talk about how she found life in the band; I bet we'd have quite a lot in common!"

Lia had formerly been known as Jools, singing for Affairs Of The Heart, the musical project of Steve Street and Martin 'Merv' Woolford, who between them ran Bristol's SAM Studios. The band even released a single on Heartbeat during the summer of 1983, a cover of 'Waterloo Sunset' by The Kinks.

The new Vice Squad, which now also comprised manager Mark 'Sooty' Byrne on second guitar, signed to Anagram, and did a David Jensen session for Radio One. There then followed three singles; late '83's 'Black Sheep', which spent two months in the Indies and achieved a respectable No. 13 position, '84's 'You'll Never Know', and their early '85 cover of The Sweet's 'Teenage Rampage', which barely managed to trouble the Indie Top Fifty.

The rather splendid third album 'Shot Away', despite its overly electronic drum sound and some disturbing pseudo-hard rock tendencies, is arguably the most complete sounding release by the Eighties incarnation of the band, and the atmospheric 'New Blood' comes across particularly well as a potent reworking of that magical 'Last Rockers' vibe. But soon after its release, the band split up altogether, and the record failed miserably to chart.

Vice Squad 2004 Clockwise from left: Tony Piper, Paul Rooney, Michael Giaquinto, Beki '… we've finally been accepted as the definitive version of Vice Squad…'

"That album died on its arse, to be honest," admits Shane. "By then we'd already achieved everything we'd set out to with that line-up, and it had all begun to fall apart. In fact, we'd split up even before the reviews started appearing in the magazines. Mark left halfway through the recording of the album, and his replacement was Jon Chilcott, from The Crazy Trains, who played on the rest of the tracks and the final Vice Squad tour. I suppose it just died a natural death, and we all moved on. Dave, Jon and I even launched another band, Sweet Revenge, but that's a whole other story."

In 1997, Beki reformed Vice Squad, with members of The Bombshells - Paul Rooney on guitar, Stilton on bass, and Pumpy on drums. Since then they have released a further five accomplished albums, and toured both extensively and successfully. They were even part of the huge Social Chaos tour that criss-crossed the USA in 1999 and appeared on tribute albums to both Metallica and Nirvana.

"I didn't actually 'reform' the band as I didn't get the original members back together," corrects Beki. "I was being asked over and over again if I'd play the old songs. I couldn't escape the past - mainly because record companies kept re-releasing the old material. In the end I was persuaded to do the Holidays In The Sun festival in 1997 as Vice Squad by a punk called Dougie who I met at The Goldsmiths Tavern in New Cross. I told the promoter I'd only do it if I could use the band I already had. This band, The Bombshells, had played every dodgy pub and club with me for the last ten years, and it seemed only fair that they should play the bigger shows like H.I.T.S.

"But I have to say that it didn't really work out in the end, so Michael (Giaquinto – bass) and Tony (Piper – drums) joined in late '99/early 2000 and this is by far the best band that I've ever worked with. We played H.I.T.S. in '97,'98 and '99 and gradually turned things round for Vice Squad, but since I got this line-up we've gone from strength to strength. Last year at H.I.T.S. 2003, we spent hours and hours signing autographs and having photos taken after the show. I am constantly told how much people love the new band which is gratifying after years of hard work. We've finally been accepted as the definitive version of Vice Squad; I should also point out that the current line-up has far outstripped the first incarnation in terms of touring and recorded output! Five studio albums, one EP, numerous compilation tracks in Europe and USA… and we've headlined several European festivals, three European tours and three coast to coast American tours too!

"The old VS members hadn't played for years, had got married, had kids or got other jobs. In other words, they would not have been able to dedicate themselves to a band the way that you have to, to stand a chance of succeeding. Also, the knackered Transit van, 'Bertha', that we were using to take us, the PA and backline to gigs was in serious need of repairs, and the fee for doing H.I.T.S. meant that I could afford to get it fixed. Without the van the band and I couldn't work.

"I didn't have any qualms about using the Vice Squad name as I thought of it in the first place and people associated me with it so much that it actually stopped me getting another record deal for years! And I always made it very clear that it was a new band with no original members except for myself."

Almost bringing everything full circle then, there was a new Vice Squad 'Best Of' CD – the appallingly named 'Bang To Rights' – released two years ago, once again on EMI, which compiles old and new songs from both eras of the band's existence. It tied up a lot of loose ends rather nicely, and even paved the way for future Vice Squad releases on the label.

"EMI own the recordings of the old songs so they could release them whenever and however they wanted," explains Beki when asked whether she insisted upon the inclusion of some of her newer songs. "There are far smaller companies than EMI releasing stuff of ours which they don't own, so I couldn't have insisted on EMI doing anything. They included the new tracks because they thought they were better than the old ones and as we have three albums on release from 1998, 1999 and 2000 it made sense to include tracks from these albums on any new 'Best Of' collection. In actual fact, there are ten new tracks and nine old tracks.

"We mastered the new tracks and cleaned up and re-mastered the old ones at Abbey Road. Ron Hill, the engineer, told us that the old master tapes had to be 'baked' in order for us to play and re-master them. This is done at a low temperature over several days, but I couldn't get past the image of these tapes cooking away on Regulo 8 in a gas oven and being burned to a crisp, so we were quite relieved when they arrived in one piece! I brought the new songs to Abbey Road on a tiny DAT whereas the old tapes turned up in big metal canisters looking like nuclear waste or something! Anyway, needless to say, the old stuff sounds better than it has before due to the wonders of modern technology.

"There are so many shoddy releases out at the moment claiming to be the 'best of' Vice Squad that we were worried that people wouldn't be interested in 'Bang To Rights' but thankfully they were and we had very positive feedback from it."

So positive in fact, Vice Squad have recently headlined another full, sell-out US tour, and their brand new studio album, 'Rich And Famous', appeared through EMI in September 2003. A convincing collection of great songs, drawing influence from power pop, hard rock, thrash metal and even some uptempo ska, 'Rich And Famous' ably demonstrates that Vice Squad aren't content to let the grass grow under them stylistically. And Beki's voice, not to mention her lyrical prowess, seems to grow in range and power with every new release, cementing her reputation as a genuine punk rock icon.

And rightfully so; Vice Squad were there from the very inception of that second wave of UK punk rock. They've provided us with some wonderful music over the years, and the fact that Beki is still out there working the clubs and keeping the name alive is testament to both her gritty determination and the timeless power of the band's songs.

SELECT DISCOGRAPHY:
7"s:
'Last Rockers' (Riot City, 1981)
'Resurrection' (Riot City, 1981)
'Out Of Reach' (EMI/Zonophone, 1982)
'Stand Strong Stand Proud' EP (EMI/Zonophone, 1982)
'State Of The Nation' EP (EMI/Zonophone, 1982)
'Black Sheep' (Anagram, 1983)
'You'll Never Know' (Anagram, 1984)
'Teenage Rampage' (Anagram, 1985)

12"s:
'Tour Issue' (Riot City, 1982)
'Black Sheep' (Anagram, 1983)
'You'll Never Know' (Anagram, 1984)

LPs:
'No Cause For Concern' (EMI/Zonophone, 1981)
'Stand Strong Stand Proud' (EMI/Zonophone, 1982)
'Shot Away' (Anagram, 1985)
'Get A Life' (Rhythm Vicar, 1998)
'Resurrection' (Rhythm Vicar, 1999)
'Lo Fi Life' (Sudden Death, 2000)
'Rich And Famous' (EMI, 2003)

AT A GLANCE:

No such thing for Vice Squad, I'm afraid. 'Bang To Rights', the aforementioned latest collection for EMI nicely compiles the highlights of 'Beki's Vice Squad', both past and present, but barely even acknowledges the Lia era, which did actually produce some fine moments as well. 'The Very Best Of', in Anagram's Punk Collectors Series, covers the whole of the Eighties Vice Squad period, but opts to ignore Beki's current line-up. For the best representation of that, you would be advised to pick up 'Rich And Famous', the new album and the one that Beki maintains she is most proud of.

CHAOTIC DISCHORD

C haotic Dischord were actually the ugly offspring of Vice Squad. Members of the Beki-fronted Squad by day turned into a sneering, spitting Mr. Hyde at night. Formed with the help of some roadies, more as a joke than anything else, and perpetrated originally to expose the pointlessness of the generic noise that many of the second wave punk bands were gravitating towards, it was to be especially ironic when the band became one of Riot City's best-selling acts. In fact, their signing to the label in the first place was all part of an elaborate hoax...

"Chaotic Dischord were myself ('Evo Stix') on drums, Dave Bateman ('Pox') on guitar, and Vice Squad roadies Igor ('Ampex') on bass and Bambi ('Ransid') on vocals," reveals Vice Squad's Shane. "We weren't impressed with some of the more 'crusty' bands that Simon Edwards was signing to Riot City, and an argument ensued, during which we claimed that we could knock out something along the same lines 'in ten minutes'.

"He laughed that off, but when we had some spare time at the end of a Vice Squad recording session, we had a go, strictly within that time limit, and ended up with 'Glue Accident'. Surprisingly, it sounded quite authentic, so we sent it, via a girlfriend of Dave's in Swindon (for that all-important non-Bristol post mark), to Simon, who was advertising for bands to be included on his 'Riotous Assembly' compilation.

"To cut a long story short, he fell for it, and we told him that, despite musical differences, Vice Squad were friends of ours, and we would only deal with them. We managed to keep up the subterfuge for quite a while, and by the time he found out, though he wasn't best pleased, we were selling serious numbers of records, so we carried on. We ended up releasing two EPs, a proper album, a mini album, and a live album for Riot City, plus later releases for Not Very Nice. Our first album, 'Fuck Religion, Fuck Politics, Fuck The Lot of You!', was actually one of the best selling UK punk albums of 1983!"

The elusive Chaotic Dischord
L–R: 'Ransid', 'Ampex', 'Evo', 'Pox'
Note Ampex's home–made 'I Hate Chaos UK' T–shirt!

The band were a total hoot, rehashing half-baked cliché punk riffs, with Ransid spewing out a diatribe of juvenile obscenities over all the feedback. They were unashamedly awful, yet somehow strangely relevant as a brutal parody of the intensely noisy thrash that was so popular at the time. Even if the unruly time signatures and the band's blatant disregard for writing decent tunes assaulted your sensibilities, the self-effacing humour displayed by some of their song titles and the sheer energy captured during their impromptu recording sessions helped them worm their way into the minds and hearts of many more people than just the local glue crew.

"We had a lot of fun with the press, they really didn't know what to make of it," laughs Shane. "It was especially delicious when (respected US hardcore fanzine) Maximum Rock'n'Roll gave us great reviews, 'cos they really hated Vice Squad. There were a few red faces there when the truth came out, but Tim (Yohannon, the editor) got his own back by saying that we were better as our joke band than the real one. God rest his soul!

"The only journalist that actually saw through it all was Attila The Stockbroker, who was working for Sounds as John Opposition, but he gave 'Fuck Religion...' five stars anyway. What a nice chap!"

The band's best moment remains to this day their Riot City debut, the 'Fuck The World' EP, three bursts of irreverent noise, all ushered in by an hilarious sample that could have been lifted straight from (popular youth comedy programme) 'The Young Ones'. Subsequent releases saw the joke starting to wear dangerously thin, although the band did do exceptionally well to release a 'Live In New York' album despite never doing a single show in their whole career. In fact, the closest they came to a stage was when Ransid kept ringing venues and booking shows "Just to piss people off."

As if one Chaotic Dischord wasn't enough, there were actually two in existence for a short period. An almost totally different band released an album charmingly entitled 'Fuck Off You Cunt, What A Load of Bollocks', which came packaged in sexual artwork so gross, it ended up being released in a white gatefold sleeve, with the intended cover inside, so as to avoid offending Joe Public. Of course, this was a clever marketing ploy to ensure a few extra sales, and rumours about the inclusion of a free glue bag helped fuel the controversy, but Shane is adamant that this was never a real Chaotic Dischord release.

"When Beki left Vice Squad, Igor chose to go with her. He then asked if he could still be in Dischord, and being mature, reasonable, sensible adults, we said, 'Nah, fuck off!' So, more or less as a spoiler, he and Beki put out what I regard as a bogus Dischord album. It didn't hurt us any, and I don't really know what it was like because I've never heard it, but people tell me that it's rude but just not funny. And if that's true then they missed the point somewhat."

The natural end of Chaotic Dischord should surely have been when Riot City closed its doors, but their respectable sales helped ensure that there were still some poor, deluded fools out there more than willing to finance more releases, and never ones to turn down some easy money the band obliged by bashing out three more albums for Not Very Nice. However nothing they recorded could recapture their early bluster, and instead of being funny, these later releases were just painful and dull. It was the end – thankfully – of something that should have remained as a one-off joke.

"I wouldn't dispute that allegation at all," admits Shane. "Of course it was a joke, and we were actually quite disturbed when so many people took it seriously!

"But there was no real 'demise of the band'... because there was never really a band in the first place. After the first album Dischord was just me, Dave and Bambi, plus whoever happened to be in the studio at the time. When Riot City folded there was still demand for another album, so we put out the 'Now That's What I Call A Fuckin' Racket!' on Not Very Nice Records. It was a compilation of old tracks, plus a few unreleased Sex Aids songs, released purely to squeeze out the last few drops of cash, and we assumed that that was the end. But someone at our distributors, Revolver, offered to stump up the cash for more Not Very Nice releases, and we put out 'Goat Fuckin' Virgin Killerz From Hell' and 'Very Fuckin' Bad' for them in the late Eighties.

"By then we were all quite bored with it all, though we kept threatening to record more anyway... until Bambi's tool hire firm took off," recalls Shane, before adding in true Dischord fashion, "He became a successful businessman and I haven't heard from the cunt since!"

SELECT DISCOGRAPHY:
7"s:
'Fuck The World' (Riot City, 1982)
'Never Trust A Friend' (Riot City, 1983)

12"s:
'Don't Throw It All Away' (Riot City, 1983)

LPs:
'Fuck Religion, Fuck Politics, Fuck The Lot Of You' (Riot G ty, 1983)
'Live In New York' (Riot City, 1984)
'Fuck Off You Cunt, What A Load Of Bollocks' (Synd cate, 198 4)
'Now That's What I Call A Fuckin' Racket, Volume One' (Not Very Nice, 1985)
'Goat Fuckin' Virgin Killerz From Hell' (Not Very Nice, 1986)
'Very Fuckin' Bad' (Not Very Nice, 1988)

AT A GLANCE:
'Their Greatest Fuckin' Hits' (Anagram, 1994) is as good a place to start as any for anyone foolhardy enough to want to find out more, although the US CD reissue of 'Now...' (Punkcore, 2001) also contains the 'Live In New York' album for good measure, thirty-three tracks in total. Whether that makes it a more desirable collection is open to debate!

SEX AIDS

The aforementioned Sex Aids were another side project of the seemingly tireless male contingent of Vice Squad. They released just the one single for Riot City in 1983, 'Back On The Piss Again', and although it was light-hearted and mildly enjoyable, the band was never pursued beyond that initial drunken get-together. They did record the song 'Cliff' for the 'Riotous Assembly' compilation, but it was left off the final cut of the record due to its libellous nature, and eventually turned up in the Chaotic Dischord set.

"Well, The Sex Aids were essentially the same band as Chaotic Dischord anyway," explains Shane. "Dave and I used to drink in two pubs in Hanham called The Swan and The Maypole, and joined an informal drinking club that we dubbed 'The No Hopers'. Originally, the idea was that we would release a single under that name, but none of our worthy comrades could actually play an instrument, so the four of us took care of that and the rest of the rabble joined in on backing vocals. The only real difference was that Igor did the lead vocal. Come to think of it, I can't remember what Bambi actually did!

"I think we used the Sex Aids name because in yet another conglomerate (with, if I remember correctly, yet another girlfriend of Dave's, Jane, on guitar), we had submitted a song called 'Lady Diana, Married To A Spanner' for possible inclusion on one of the Oi! albums. It was so bad it was turned down, but at least it got mentioned in Sounds, which made the name marginally more marketable for Riot City."

One other 'Vice Squad roadies spin-off' band who appeared on 'Riotous Assembly' (with 'Fun Wars') was the Dead Katts. Shane produced the song for the band, and seems to think he may have even played at least one show with them.

"Loads of people came and went in that band," he says, hinting yet again at the bewilderingly incestuous music scene of the time. "But it was basically Igor, Bambi, Mitch and Flea. I can't even remember who did what, other than Mitch played guitar and Flea played drums… although at one point, Bambi actually played drums. It was nearly as bad as his singing!"

By ruthlessly sending up their noisy neighbours, Chaotic Dischord were unwittingly mirroring the changing tastes in punk rock. With the scene veering ever nearer to extremities, there was no room for subtlety; only the most gratuitous uproar could satisfy those thrill-seeking punkers looking desperately for the ultimate expression of their own suppressed slow-burning aggression.

DISORDER

D isorder epitomised this violent disregard for musical tradition, and pushed the proverbial envelope right off the edge of the table plummeting towards oblivion. The band formed in Bristol in 1980, its initial incarnation comprising Steve Allen on guitar, Steve Curtis on vocals, Nick Peters on bass, and Virus on drums, but by 1981, Steve Robertson had replaced Nick, and this was the line-up that recorded the first two Disorder EPs, 'Complete Disorder' and 'Distortion To Deafness'.

After approaching Riot City Records with their demo, label boss Simon Edwards decided to set up Disorder Records with them, and unfettered by any sort of external label interference they were able to release some of the most uncompromising music ever committed to vinyl.

"When Disorder came to me with their demo, we decided that Riot City wasn't the right label for their music," explains Simon. "So we thought, 'Fuck it' and started another label just for them! I loved the band and thought they were really good... they were out there, wild, just didn't give a damn... they were exciting, loud, extreme and above all humorous!"

Astonishingly chaotic, those early EPs were rabid tirades against the establishment, drenched in howling feedback and propelled by runaway tin-pot drums, setting new standards – or lack thereof, some might argue – in belligerent punk music. This unique Disorder sound was to terrorise music lovers for the next twenty years… and then some.

Their third bassist Taf, who joined the band in 1982, in time to record the 'Mental Disorder' single and the eight-track 'Perdition' 12", was to be the sole constant member in a bewildering string of line-up changes over the next two decades. He still remembers vividly how he became fascinated with punk rock in the first place:

"I used to deliver newspapers when I was fifteen. I saw a lot of articles about punk rock, and I liked the style, thought it was very exciting. I went to see bands like The Clash and a lot of those other punk bands and thought I could do better. I wanted some

Bassist Taf of Disorder, a Bristol band that 'epitomised a violent disregard for musical tradition...'

attention, I wasn't satisfied with just being a member of the audience anymore; I wanted to be involved and contribute something too.

"Also, I was sixteen years old and I wanted a hire purchase agreement on a moped, but my mum wouldn't sign the agreement for me! She didn't want me to have a moped, so I opted to buy a bass guitar and amplifier and join a punk band instead. That'll show her… she should have let me have a moped!"

It may indeed have been safer for all concerned. Taf's first recorded output with the band is still their most potent and focused. 'Perdition' may have been aptly titled for anyone who preferred a little melody with their listening experience, but for anyone who yearned for a quick easy fix of abrasive punk, it was the ultimate high. The pounding toms and gurgling bass grounded the sound firmly in the gutter whilst the dinniest guitar imaginable assaulted the senses with a barb wire lash of mutilated power chords.

Recorded at Cave Studios in July '82, it wasn't all manic speed either. Although 'Stagnation' opens proceedings at a jaunty pace, such thrashy tracks contrast neatly with the ominous rumblings of the sprawling 'Remembrance Day'. And the relentless 'Life' also appeared on the 'UK/DK' video documentary, 'a film about punks and skinheads' by Christopher Collins and Ken Lawrence, alongside the likes of The Varukers and The Exploited, not to mention fellow Bristolians Vice Squad and Chaos UK.

"Our sound was more distorted and more metallic than most punk bands that went before us," he recalls, trying to pinpoint what set Disorder apart from the rest of the baying pack. "Now you've got lots of bands who use that sound. Also, our lyrics tend to be quite ambiguous… a lot of times we just sing about something that's happened or happening, without really telling the listener what the solution is. Take the song 'More Than Fights'… if you read the lyrics you can't really make out if it is for or against violence, and the thing is that it is neither. Unlike some other bands such as Crass, for example, Disorder have never told people what to do or how to live in our lyrics."

The 'Mental Disorder' EP was another highlight for the band, where they further honed their virulent thrash attack, whilst addressing the subject of mental health institutions in songs such as the suitably deranged 'Rampton Song'.

"The ex-bass player Steve Robertson had had a few episodes with the mental health authorities," reckons Taf. "And Boobs, the ex-vocalist, has been right through the system, too. We basically just seemed to attract an audience that included quite a few headcases, and because we socialise with the audience at our gigs, and get to meet all these nutters, it has been very influential on our lyrics!"

Boobs, the band's second singer, took over full-time from Steve Curtis after he provided additional vocals for a show at Bristol's Granary Club. Chaos from Chaos UK also played bass at that show, just before Taf joined. He also stood in for Taf on bass whilst the bassist moved to fill the guitar slot for a single show in Paris in 1984.

Another Chaos UK member, drummer Pottsy, then took over behind the kit from Virus for the first two Disorder albums, 'Under The Scalpel Blade', recorded during April '84 at SAM Studios, and 'Live In Oslo', recorded on May 24th 1985 at Oslo's Blitz Club. Although apparently recorded on a Sony Walkman, and then remastered back in Bristol at SAM, 'Live In Oslo' sounds far better than it has any right to, and features the band careening through a 'greatest hits' set as though their lives depend upon it.

'Under The Scalpel Blade', meanwhile, opens with the maddening whir of a spinning bit ushering in the barrage of noise that is 'Driller Killer'. Elsewhere there is the obligatory stab at dumb humour ('The Rhino Song') and the traditional Bristol ode to excessive alcohol consumption with the track 'Bent Edge' – a crude response to the 'straightedge' movement that was growing in popularity in the States at the time. This album even bore the legend 'Make Homebrew, Not War' proudly across its inlay.

Similarly to their friends and frequent touring partners, Chaos UK, Disorder has been in a state of constant flux since day one. The whole seemingly always greater than its individual parts, with members coming and going at an often ridiculous rate, and friends of the band sometimes standing in at the last minute for AWOL musicians. This is a problem that has plagued Disorder to this very day.

"Various different reasons, I suppose," sighs an exasperated Taf, before letting forth a stream of consciousness rant. "A lot to do with drinking, I have to admit, but also trouble with the police, marriage break ups, depression... somebody's girlfriend leaves him so he says, 'Right I'm fucking off to China or somewhere'... and it's two days before a fifty date, three month European tour and you need a new guitarist... then the drummer slips a disc, and you're off on tour with a drummer who's never played in a punk band before and a bass player who is trying to learn the guitar riffs in the back of a van on the way to your first gig in Sweden! Then, after two weeks on tour, the guitarist starts pining for the Fjords and takes the band's tour vehicle and drives back to Norway leaving the other band members stranded in Holland with no guitarist or car to get to the next gig, so then you have to play guitar yourself and get the drummer's girlfriend to learn the bass lines quickly in the toilet twenty-five minutes before you go on stage... etc., etc., etc.!

"And now (most recent guitarist) Yaga has decided that she and Ade the drummer have to make some babies, so they have just left the band...I don't know, really I don't!"

Somehow Taf managed to keep the band together, relocating it to Norway in 1986 (after he married a Norwegian girl) and recording a fine split album with Kafka Process entitled 'One Day Son, All This Will Be Yours'. Many more crazy tours were undertaken, many more members came and went, and many more records were released on various underground labels around the world, some of them good... some of them bad.

1989's 'Violent World', recorded at Bootleg Studios in Oslo, and featuring Kenneth Egen on drums, alongside Steve and Taf, is not as nihilistic as the title might suggest. As well as including a hilarious – not to mention outrageous – cover of Dolly Parton's 'Jolene', it actually features some of the band's best lyrics. From the pacifist plea of the title track, to the anti-misogyny message of 'Every Eight Seconds' and the sly scene commentary of 'Gods Are Born In The USA', 'Violent World' stands as possibly the band's best realised work to date.

"And my least favourite album is the 'Senile Punks...' one, because on the studio tracks the drummer was so pissed up that he couldn't play, and it really annoys me that it is not the right drumming to the songs. Another thing was that we recorded it and sent it to Slovakia for release, but suddenly it was released on a Czech Republic record label called Bastards Records! We didn't know anything about it, but Martin Valasek had actually sold the rights to Bastards, when he didn't even own the recording in the first place – he just ripped us off. So that fucking album still pisses me off.

"Another one is a bootleg live album that's going about of Disorder live in London; it's totally unofficial, so don't buy it. The record label didn't even send me one single free copy. That's not fair."

Despite it all, Disorder are still with us today, and sounding as good as ever on their latest album, (the rather appropriate) 'We're Still Here'. Over the years, many people may have dismissed them as a joke band, stereotypical drunken crusty punks that preferred revelling in their own self-destructive inebriation to actually rehearsing their music, but the fact that they have long out-lived many of their peers suggests that there is a lot more to Disorder than meets the eye.

"People only said that because they were jealous of what we had," claims Taf, in closing. "We did have a good time, that's true. We always had that family atmosphere; all our friends wanted to come to our gigs with us, so we usually took about eighteen people in our van every time, and we all got pissed and sniffed glue and had a laugh. We used to take the piss out of all the po-faced anarchists up in London too!

"But we did care about our music; we used to practice twice a week, and we spent ten days in the studio recording 'Perdition', five days doing the six tracks for 'Mental Disorder'... so we really did care about how we sounded. Although the guitars do tend to go a bit out of tune when you fall over! And yes, we revelled in it! So what?"

SELECT DISCOGRAPHY:

7"s:
'Complete Disorder' EP (Disorder Records, 1981)
'Distortion To Deafness' EP (Disorder, 1981)
'Mental Disorder' EP (Disorder, 1982)
'More Noize' EP (FFP, 1988)
'Pain, Headache, Depression' (Trujaca Fala, 1994)

12"s:
'Perdition' (Disorder, 1982)
'Complete Disorder: The Singles' (Disorder, 1984)

LPs:
'Under The Scalpel Blade' (Disorder, 1984)
'Live In Oslo' (Disorder, 1985)
'One Day Son, All This Will Be Yours' (Disorder, 1986) – split LP with Kafka Process
'Violent World' (Disorder, 1989)
'Masters Of The Glueniverse' (Desperate Attempt, 1991) – split LP w/ Mushroom Attack
'The Rest Home For Senile Old Punks Presents...' (Bastards, 1991)
'Sliced Punx On Meathooks' (Anagram, 1997) – CD only
'We're Still Here' (H.G. Fact, 2002)

AT A GLANCE:
If you want proof that the band can still cut it today, check out 'We're Still Here', their latest for Japanese label, H.G. Fact, which is as chaotic and noisy as anything they've released previously. Anyone wanting a good introduction to the band though should start with Anagram's 'The Best Of Disorder', which features twenty-five cuts from all their best releases and a ruthlessly comprehensive discography.

CHAOS UK

Formed in Portishead in 1979, Chaos UK, much like their partners in crime, Disorder, were the epitome of the 'noise not music' mentality... yet ironically managed to pen some great tunes in amongst all the mayhem. Having undergone a bewildering array of line-up changes over the years, vocalist Chaos - the band's original bassist – has somehow steered them through thick and thin, gaining a large following around the world in the process. And Chaos UK are still thrashing it out with the best of them to this very day.

"I always liked music, and got into punk around 1976," says Andy Farrier, the band's original guitarist. "I loved bands like The Adverts and The Damned, and The Pistols brought a whole new attitude that made you wanna get up and have a go. So I just taught myself to play guitar!

"There used to be a lot of little local bands, but none of them were too serious. I remember there was a band called The Pubix, who just did covers and stuff, of bands like The Pistols, but none of it ever went anywhere...

"One day I had a knock on my door, and there was Adie (Adrian Rice, aka 'Chaos'). I'd never seen him before in my life, and he just turned up on my doorstep and said, 'Are you Andy? I wanna join your band!' And it just went from there.

"We couldn't find a proper drummer, so Pottsy (aka Richard Potts) from Damage Department, who was a great drummer, came and helped us out. And Simon (Greenham) was one of my mates from work, who played bass in The Pubix, and he joined as singer.

"We rehearsed in a factory where I worked and all our mates used to come along and jam. I wrote most of the riffs, and we'd all work on it then, with Simon and Adie coming up with most of the lyrics. Songs just evolved out of these jams we were having. 'Four Minute Warning' was written in a pub one Saturday afternoon on the back of a dirty serviette! Although as usual Pottsy was nowhere to be found!"

Chaos UK, 1980
L–R: Pottsy, Simon, Chaos, Andy
(Pic: Simon Edwards)

It wasn't long before the band were taking themselves more seriously, and, as with several other Bristol punk bands, the release of the 'Avon Calling' compilation on Heartbeat was the catalyst to go in and do their own demo.

"We thought, 'If Vice Squad can do it, why can't we? Let's do our own tape!' We were so naïve; we went into a local studio and made a terrible noise for a few hours. It was awful, really badly produced, so we decided we had to do it properly. We all saved up a bit of money – about twenty quid each or something – and went into Cave Studios for a day. We took all our mates in with us, and we had a great laugh; it was a brilliant day.

"And to be honest, that's all it was – a laugh. It was just for us, so we were very dubious about sending it out to any labels or anything. But we played the tape to Simon Edwards at Riot City and he liked it, and he put it out as our first EP. Originally we thought it was going to go on some kind of 'Avon Calling, Volume 2', but that never happened.

"Before we had the interest off Simon, we were going to put that first demo out ourselves as a flexi-disc, but it worked out too expensive. We got as far as getting some covers printed ourselves... 'cos me, Pottsy and Simon all worked in the same screen printing factory... and although we never got to use them, the design and logo were used by Riot City."

The resulting single was the four-track 'Burning Britain' EP, and, for something that was produced 'as a laugh', it remains a formidable slice of confrontational punk rock even today. With a guitar sound so jagged you could cut yourself on it (and you'd definitely need a tetanus afterwards), it was certainly rough and ready, but there's no denying the primal power of tracks like 'Victimised' (almost tribal in its repetitive simplicity) and the rabid 'Kill Your Baby'. It spent over a month in the Indie Charts upon its release in March 1982, peaking at No. 8.

"Simon wrote 'Victimised' after he got arrested for something or other," reveals the guitarist. "There was a lot of SUS (Search Under Suspicion) going on in Bristol; the police would stop you for no reason other than how you looked, it got ridiculous in the end. I remember one time I was cycling home from my girlfriend's house. My bike had a puncture so I borrowed her niece's little Chopper, and there I was riding home on this kid's bike at 2 am. Of course, I got pulled on my way home – flashing lights 'n' all – just 'cos I was a punk and they thought that I'd nicked it!

"But to be honest, back then, anyone who was different got picked on; it wasn't just the punks. We just took it in our stride."

The debut 7" was closely followed by the track 'Senseless Conflict' that appeared on the excellent Riot City compilation, 'Riotous Assembly'.

"We did a coupla gigs with Disorder in local pubs," remembers Andy. "I remember that they would always go on and be really tight... we'd just plug in and have a laugh and get bottles thrown at us! We just went for it, and all our carefully laid plans about the set-list and stuff would go out the window. We were never really into being a professional band, to be honest; punk was just about getting up and having a go, having a laugh."

Four months later Chaos UK released what many regard as their finest moment, the incredibly intense 'Loud, Political And Uncompromising' EP. Three tracks of blistering thrash; drenched in teeth-rattling feedback and with barely discernible, screamed vocals, all delivered at a punishing pace, it laid an impressive blueprint emulated by a thousand noisecore bands since.

"The first EP was recorded in one day with crap equipment, but by the time we did that second single, I'd got myself a proper amp. We'd worked on our sound quite a bit, and we did the whole thing so much better. We didn't over-produce it or anything, but that record captured us at our best, as far as I'm concerned. It's my favourite Chaos UK release by far. 'No Security' (the A-side) sounds hard. I wanted that clean, rough sound, not as much distortion as Disorder or Discharge or whoever. The studio guys hated us; we never took any notice of them. They told us that we couldn't use this £2000 valve amp they had locked away in a cupboard, so as soon as they were out the room, we broke into the cupboard and used it! They went fucking mental!"

The single was another success for both band and label, and Chaos UK soon found themselves gigging around the country with some regularity.

"And we were very excited at all the good reviews the EP got, and it sold really well. That got on Disorder's nerves... that we always got more advance sales than they did! We drove Simon mad banging on his door, asking him when the singles would be back from the plant. We were a real pain in the ass for him, but he's a brilliant bloke and took it all in his stride."

Simon Edwards himself seems to feel a similar reluctant affection for Chaos UK, having written the following for the liner notes of the band's 'Flogging The Corpse' CD:

"Of all the bands that approached Riot City in those heady days of the early Eighties, perhaps Chaos UK were the best... or the worst, depending on your level of importance given to normality. Never had I been subject to so much abuse, violence and just downright bloody-mindedness by a completely uncooperative and generally nasty, rude bunch of bastards. Permanently drunk or suffering from other abuses, recording, gigging, mastering and any other business chores were made virtually impossible by these loud-mouthed horrors! This collection of early shit is yet another example of the bollocks I was subjected to; I had no choice, they threatened my very existence if it wasn't released. What could I do? Alarmingly, the perpetrators of this still exist; I live in fear... and even worse, I love 'em!"

For various reasons – including general laziness and disorganisation – it would be almost a year before the band released their self-titled debut album, and when it arrived, it wasn't really worth the wait, not living up to the high expectations generated by the two singles at all. Despite opening with the furious 'Selfish Few', and with Andy's trademark broken-glass guitar sound in full effect, there are too many obvious filler tracks, such as 'Victimised (Part 2)', a piss-take 'dub' version. The cover packaging was also appallingly bland and slap-dash.

The record-buying public didn't seem to care though, and it spent six weeks in the Indies upon its release in April 1984, reaching a very respectable No. 16.

"That was done in such a rush, it was crazy," sighs Andy. "Simon Edwards originally talked about getting Captain Sensible to produce it for us, but he was way too expensive! So we did it ourselves… jammed for a few days, chucked down these basic tracks and did all the lyrics afterwards. Simon Greenham actually left the band just before the recording of the album, mainly due to that old cliché musical differences', so Chaos ended up doing all the vocals.

"There's really only a few strong tracks on the record; there's way too many fillers," he agrees. "We just didn't work hard enough at it; the progression we had been making up until then just stopped. In fact, I think there are only four songs on there that are credible!

"We didn't do many overdubs; our recordings just caught us how we were on the day. If we were good, we were good, but if we were crap, we were really crap. I just wish that we'd spent more time on the album… but we felt under pressure to get it out. It's one of those things though, you live and learn. It could've been so much better. We even thought about remixing and remastering it, to make it better than it was, but we couldn't locate the master tapes.

"Simon had just left and none of us knew what was happening; we were in a state of constant flux. The band had always been evolving, and still is. We weren't really focused on it the way we should have been; we were just drifting along, and before we knew it, the record was in the shops…!"

The album did however spawn one of the band's best-loved tracks, albeit a tongue-in-cheek novelty song, the hilarious 'Farmyard Boogie', that sent up the band's West Country yokel accents to a tee.

"Oh God, that was just a joke jam session to start off with. Pottsy had fucked off to the pub, and anyone who knows Pottsy knows that, when he does that, you don't have any idea when you'll see him again. So, we were just fucking about and Chaos was on a roll, and he just came up with all that stuff on the spot, improvised the lot. It turned out brilliant, so we kept it, and it became one of the audience's favourite songs whenever we played it live."

Also, it's worth noting that although the bass on the album is credited to 'Nige', Nige didn't actually play on the record, and was just a mate who roadied for the band and stood in on bass a few times. And Simon Greenham wasn't the only line-up casualty suffered by the band around the time of their first album either – Andy Farrier himself also left soon after.

"I left in the end during the summer of '83," he explains. "We should really have sat down and discussed the direction and future of the band. It was becoming quite established, but we'd spend two weeks rehearsing exactly how we were going to play our set and then two songs into every gig it'd all go fucking haywire. It got stupid in the end, and I got pissed off with it all.

"It was after a show in Birmingham, or Nottingham, I think? And it just got to me. Every time we played live, it all went out the window, and I ended up wondering just what I was actually doing there. There was literally too much chaos in the end! Our intros would go on for five minutes 'cos Chaos had forgotten to plug his guitar in! Stuff like that. I can laugh at it now, but it was very frustrating at the time.

"We played Bridgewater Arts Centre - it was the first gig we did after recording the album – and caused a riot. The manager got onstage and tried to turn us off; he was threatening to call the police, it was like something from 'Spinal Tap'. Pottsy hit one drum beat and fell off the stage; his stool just collapsed. We played all the new songs even though we hadn't rehearsed any of them.

"It got to the point where we were playing our set, literally all our songs, in less than twenty minutes! We were playing everything that fast! But when kids pay to get in, they want a bit more for their money than that, don't they?"

Before he departed though, Andy did manage to get his face, albeit briefly, on the 'UK/DK' video.

"You see me for less than five seconds in that video!" he laughs. "It was filmed at a gig where The Abrasive Wheels didn't turn up when they found out we were playing, but it was still a good night. And it helped the band's profile; we had letters from all over the world, twenty or thirty letters a day sometimes. And I was the only one who bothered to answer them all – it was just getting too much for me. I think you have to deal with those things correctly, but we all had different approaches; we were all pulling in different directions."

Perhaps sensing the dwindling momentum, Riot City re-released the first two singles as one 12", imaginatively entitled 'The Singles', in November '84. Sure enough it sold better than the 'proper' album that preceded it, but it was to be the last collaboration between the band and label.

By 1986, and with a virtually brand-new new line-up of Mower – vocals, Gabba – guitar, Chaos – bass and Chuck – drums, and following the demise of Riot City, Chaos UK had moved to new Bristol label, Children Of The Revolution (aka C.O.R.), for the fast and furious 'Short Sharp Shock' album. A convincingly brutal collection of ripping thrash tunes (check out the uncompromising distortion of the Discharge-esque 'Living In Fear'), that gave a definite nod to the more intense hardcore sounds that were filtering into England from overseas, it was a massive progression from the disappointing first full length. It seemed the band had rediscovered the focus lost after 'Loud, Political And Uncompromising', and, although their popularity seemed to have peaked and stalled somewhat in the UK, they were going from strength to strength abroad.

C.O.R. later became Manic Ears, and the first release for the 'new' label was the 'Ear Slaughter' split album between Chaos UK and the Ipswich-based thrashers, Extreme Noise Terror – a nightmare pairing for music-lovers everywhere but another resounding success for the band. It was produced by Vice Squad's Sooty at SAM Studios, and from the breakneck speed of 'Red Sky At Night' ('Every cloud has a nuclear lining!' roars an enraged Mower) to the stomping, tom-driven dirge of 'Depression', it saw the band making significant musical progress.

The last release for this incarnation of the band was 'The Chipping Sodbury Bonfire Tapes' album, on their own label, Slap Up Records. Although thinly produced, it remains one of their strongest efforts, as fast and tight as ever, but sounding slightly more hardcore in arrangement. It featured yet another riff on the 'Farmyard Boogie' theme (the 'Short, Sharp Shock' album had already included an 'extended disco-mix hyperdub version'), the rather irritating (which was probably the intention!) 'Farmyard (Cider House Mix)'.

Mower departed after 'The Chipping Sodbury Bonfire Tapes', and Chaos took over the mike, with Beki joining on bass.

They've continued to release a barrage of punky noise, most noticeably for Discipline/Vinyl Japan, and tour with great success all over the world ever since, although the majority of their recorded output falls outside the official time span of this book. Their 1992 'Making A Killing' split with Ipswich-based thrashers Raw Noise even features a storming cover of 'Police Story' by The Partisans!

Beki left after the '100% Two Fingers In The Air Punk Rock' album, due to 'ill health', and was replaced by Welsh nutter Marvin, who has since joined The Varukers. That album featured 'Happy Spastic', a scathing yet articulate attack on the drug/dance culture that castrated many a once-political punk activist. 'As far as I can see, ecstasy killed the anarchy,' rants Chaos with great feeling.

Still, as long as there is Chaos UK, there will always be a little bit of anarchy left in the world.

"I'd like us to be remembered as not giving a fuck and having a good laugh," reckons Andy, in closing. "It was never about politics, or about money, or about being better than all the other bands… it was about getting onstage and having a party and having a bloody good laugh.

"We did a big squat gig in Bristol once, with Disorder, Lunatic Fringe, Amebix, and loads of other local bands. None of us had anywhere else to play, so we took over a building. Punks came from everywhere, and it was full of bikers and hippies as well. I remember two hippies sat in the corner drinking tea and making everyone sandwiches! The press and the police came down, but couldn't stop it, and it went on for two days… basically until everyone was so knackered that they went home! That was what it was all about really – one big, friendly, constantly evolving scene sticking together and having some fun."

SELECT DISCOGRAPHY:

7"s:
'Burning Britain' (Riot City, 1982)
'Loud, Political And Uncompromising' (Riot City, 1982)
'Head On A Pole' (Desperate Attempt)
'King For A Day' (Discipline/Vinyl Japan)
'Secret Men' (Slap Up)

12"s:
'The Singles' (Riot City, 1984)
'Just Mere Slaves' (Selfish) – Japan only
'King For A Day' (Discipline/Vinyl Japan)
'Making Half A Killing' (Discipline/Vinyl Japan)

LPs:
'Chaos UK' (Riot City, 1983)
'Short Sharp Shock' (Children Of The Revolution, 1986)
'Earslaughter' (Manic Ears) – split with Extreme Noise Terror
'The Chipping Sodbury Bonfire Tapes' (Slap Up)
'Enough To Make You Sick'(Slap Up)
'Making A Killing' (Discipline/Vinyl Japan, 1992) – split with Raw Noise
'100% Two Fingers In The Air Punk Rock' (Slap Up)
'Heard It, Seen It, Done It' (Discipline/Vinyl Japan)

AT A GLANCE:
Chaos UK have enjoyed many CD reissues over the years, mainly through Anagram. Especially recommended is 'Total Chaos: The Singles Collection', which is part of the label's excellent Punk Collectors Series, as is the twenty-five track compilation 'The Best Of Chaos UK' which spans most of the band's 'career'.

CHAOS UK (GUITARIST GABBA)

So, where, when and why did you get into punk rock?
I was born in Nottingham in 1966. My mother was a teddy girl and my dad a rude boy, but he was always in and out of prison so I never saw him. He ran away and I never heard of him again. My mother had a nervous breakdown and got put on valium, and spent most of her time monging out, drawing abstract art, so I was left on my own with their rock'n'roll and ska records to play with . . . Prince Buster and Chuck Berry were my favourites, and I would play them full blast and jump about 'til I was dizzy.

Then, in the early Seventies, my mam bought T Rex's 'Bolan Boogie' which got played a lot. I loved that over-driven fuzz sound. I remember going down the Goose Fair one time and staying 'til late, listening to all the music that was being played on the waltzers and speedway rides, and when the ride had stopped I used to run up to the booth and ask who was the band and the name of song. But when I got home I had forgotten all of the bands except for Slade and The Sweet, and the next day I begged my grandma and grandad to give me advanced pocket money to buy records. I searched newsagent shops and Rediffusion TV rental shops, as they used to sell ex-jukebox 7"s for 2p and 5p. The first records I bought were Slade's 'My Friend Stan' and

'Mama Weer All Crazee Now', and The Sweet's 'Hell Raiser'.

By 1976–77, I was out skateboarding every day. My mam used to listen to the John Peel show and would write down the names of the bands she thought were good, and then tell me to find these records by the Lurkers, Damned, Ramones and Buzzcocks. At first she didn't like the idea of me dressing punk-style as there was a prostitute that used to stand at the top of our street, and I think she thought I was going to hang around with her! I started to rebel against the Catholic school I was at – mainly because I was not a Catholic and they did not like that I started to custom- ise my school uniform punk-style, had pierced my nose and started a glue-sniffing craze off. They gave me detention every day until I walked out and never went back; I didn't get to do any exams. I used to go and hang around down the town square with all the older punks, and sit on the council house steps all day, drinking cider. A lot of them were on the dole and used to sell their records for drinking money. I used to get there early so I could buy them as I was hungry for music. They showed me the record shops that were buying second-hand, and I would go and

Gabba, Chaos UK

swap my dad's ska records for new punk ones. I started to make my own clothes (grandma did the sewing) and swore to myself that I would be punk for life . . . as you do when you're young!

What was your local scene like?

The local scene was great. There were hundreds of punks that would come into Nottingham centre every weekend from surrounding small towns like Ilkeston, Grantham and Mansfield, to hang around drinking cider or go on the rampage looking for mods to fight. The police always had a hard time trying to control us. And there were always lots of gigs as the Midlands got every touring band stopping off to play.

Some Chicken was the local raw punk band in the Seventies, but it was the bands that came along in the Eighties like The Tribe, Solvent Abuse, Entry Visa, Vermin and the Skives that had a heavy hardcore sound. Hendrix Dead Boy was the local nut case; he was going to all the proto-punk gigs in the early Seventies and was very into Alice Cooper and Iggy Pop. He just went around screaming obscenities all the time and drinking bottles of vodka.

What inspired you to pick up a guitar in the first place?

I used to twang along on an egg slicer (you know the one I mean, with wire strips to cut hard- boiled eggs) and my grandma, who was great at playing any musical instrument, noticed and got me an old Spanish guitar from a jumble sale. But the E, D and B strings were broke so I only used to twang on the one string . . . with my grandad playing the spoons!

Then in 1980 I went to see Killing Joke at the Boat Club, but I couldn't get in because I was underage. I had previously got into this club before, to see Dead Kennedys, Bow Wow Wow etc., but they had caught me stealing beer and taken a disliking to me. So I was waiting outside to climb up the balcony and get in when the manager from Killing Joke came along and asked why I wasn't going in. I told him why, and he persuaded the people on the door to let me in. They said

Chaos UK Newcastle Riverside 87 by Andrew Medcalf

'Yes', but only if I stayed in the dressing room and watched from the side of the stage. Anyway, the band took a liking to me and gave me lots of merch. I asked Geordie for a guitar pick, and Youth gave me a set of used bass strings, which I took home and forced on my Spanish guitar. From there I taught myself to play. A few weeks later, my mam and grandparents gave me £40 to buy a Satellite guitar and 25-watt combo amp, and that really did annoy the neighbours when I turned it up, haha!

What was your first band?

The first band was Xtreme Bondage, but we only did one rehearsal and split up. Then I started a band with Hendrix Dead Boy called the Seats Of Piss. It was like an out of control, ultra-fast version of 'Rocky Horror' and GG Allin, with burning pigs' heads on stage, going crazy with base-ball bats and chainsaws etc. Hendrix's father had recently died and he used to play in Screaming Lord Sutch's rock'n'roll band, and left Hendrix lots of amps, cabs, guitars, fuzz pedal effects, and – most importantly – a drum machine. So we started writing songs and doing gigs, just the two of us: vocals (screaming down a traffic cone), fuzz guitar, and the drum machine turned up as fast as it would go. We started putting on Saturday afternoon gigs at a pub called the Foresters. It was free to get in and it became very popular, with bands like the Skum Dribblurzzz and the Steamroller Gloves giving regular support. These meetings started a scene that a few years later spawned bands like Concrete Sox and Heresy, and labels like Earache.

Seats Of Piss were featured on a four-track compilation tape with Deformed and Mass Of Black, but never had anything else out until 2000, when we re-recorded our first set of songs and released a picture disc on Tardis Records from Bristol.

Seats Of Piss changed into the Sic Boy Federation, with members from Solvent Abuse and the Tribe, and have had a steady flow of people from Riot Squad, UK Subs and GBH in and out of the band. They still play today but I'm not sure who is in them now.

Where was your first ever gig?

It was the Ruts at the Sandpiper in Nottingham Lace Market. It was an under-eighteens matinee and every week I saw some great bands there like The Dickies, UK Subs, Slaughter And The Dogs and Eater. All the gigs were loud, hot, fast and furious, with lots of gobbing. It felt like a fight was going to break out every minute. I remember asking Malcom Owen how you play punk music and all he said to me was, 'Give it a go!'

What other bands were you in prior to Chaos UK?

I played bass, and then switched to guitar, in the Lurkers for a few years, which was great fun – playing all the songs I had been jumping around my bedroom too . . . I also played bass in Screamer, a great band from Bristol that was a cross between Slaughter

Chaos UK, Gabba (left) and Chaos (right)

And The Dogs and Motörhead, and had a strange singer that smashed pint glasses on his head every gig! Devilman [also of Chaos UK infamy] was on drums and Martin Manners from Sons Of Bad Breath was on guitar, but after a few lineup changes the band disbanded and Martin formed the follow-on band called ANUS. That was more of a rock'n'roll party band, with horrible, insulting lyrics. I played bass, Jason from Blaggers ITA was on drums, and Cliff Vicious, who was the last singer in Screamer, was on vocals.

Around the late Nineties, some of Chaos UK started up The Wazzuks, which was an Adge Cutler and the Wurzels tribute band, playing uptempo folk/umpah/sea shanty music, with lots of songs about drinking cider. The band got very popular and our last gig at the Ashton Court festival had thousands going crazy to us.

I also played bass for Discharge on one of their West Coast American tours.

How did you end up in Chaos UK? Were you a big fan prior to joining them?

Most punks in Nottingham started getting jobs. I became bored of the town and started hitchhiking around the country, going to a gig every night. I ended up in the van being a roadie for the Bad Brains' first UK tour, and met

Chaos UK, New York Wetlands, 1991

Chaos at some of the gigs. He told me that he had heard I was a fast guitar player and that Chaos UK might need a guitarist. I already had their two 7"s and loved their sound, as back then there were no bands that sounded like that apart from Disorder and Discharge. I gave him my address but never heard anything back from him.

Then I was on the Crucifix tour the next year, and Chaos came to the London gig and confirmed that I could play in the band. I moved to Bristol and instantly started putting together a new LP.

Can you remember where and when your first gig with them was?
Yes, it was at the Trinity Hall in Bristol, on April 26th, 1984, with Disorder, Wretched [Italy], and the Mau Maus.

What are your favourite Chaos UK records you played on? And why?
'Short Sharp Shock' was great as it was recorded at Cave Studios, and the sound was so powerful and chaotic. I later found out that the recording desk was made for The Who to record 'Quadrophenia' on and they'd had it juiced up to be as powerful as possible.

'Radioactive' was a great time too, recording with Sooty. He had recorded and played with Vice Squad and Chaotic Discord, so he knew how we were, with loud volumes, screaming and feedback.

'100% . . . Punk Rock' was the best progression/regression. We did it at Paranoid Visions' studio in Dublin and turned up hung-over with flu and no energy. The sound engineer turned up late and told us that his baby had died that morning in a cot death, but he still wanted to record us as it would take his mind off it. We all felt uneasy, but just set up and recorded as many songs as we could. The situation gave us lots of energy and focus, and that can be heard throughout the recording.

There are some legendary tales of debauchery attached to the band. Tell us a few of your favourites! And maybe debunk a few myths along the way . . .
They fucked up! They trusted us!

You toured all over the world with the band. What were your favourite countries to visit?
We toured Japan in '85. It was a great experience, and that is still the best place to play by far. Everybody is so nice and respectful and their humour is the same as us Brits.

Greece is another great place, especially for kebabs and ouzo, and it's always a riot! We played on the university steps and didn't realise it was a meeting for a riot, and a few thousand people turned up. We played a very aggressive set that night. The people went crazy and had lots of fun, and then after we finished they all had a massive fight with the police and burnt the town down . . . Finland is very memorable for me too. The punks were really into Chaos UK and had been waiting twelve years to see us in Helsinki. We found this wheelchair backstage and got Chaos to come on in it, pretending he was a cripple. The punks looked horrified and some started crying . . . until he jumped out of it and started singing, and then lots of punks started taking their clothes off and dancing around him! Strange, but fucking funny.

When and why did you part ways with the band?
We stopped playing in 2001 at CBGBs. We had been on a three-month non-stop tour, and Chaos had just had enough of not getting paid – sleeping on floors and sofas had taken its toll on our aching bodies and the alcohol stopped working. I asked Chaos if he cared about the band and he said he didn't, so we stopped. A year later, due to demand, I got a new version of Chaos UK together, with Mower back on vocals. We played for a few years, toured Japan and did a few gigs

Chaos UK, USA tour, 1994

in California, but Mower started to get fed up with gigging as it was messing up his work and stopped, so I took the new songs and started FUK. We got Cliff Vicious from ANUS on vocals and put out a split CDEP with Chaos UK, but only released it in Japan. Since then FUK have recorded three LPs and a few singles. We tour Japan regularly and did a two-week American tour in 2009, ending up at the Chaos In Texas festival. We continue to play today.

Have you done anything else since Chaos UK?

Another project is Scumputer, which is my solo art, music and film stuff. First I released a track on a 12" that came free with Destroy magazine, then a CD called 'Dance 2 D-Beat' on Less Than TV. I also made a 30-minute animation film which I would show at gigs in Japan and DJ my songs to it, and a Scumputer films tour DVD with Warhead from Japan that also came out on Less Than TV.

How would you like Chaos UK to be remembered in the grand scheme of things?

As one of the first pioneers of British hardcore punk, who flew the flag through the Eighties and Nineties, when 99% of punks either got married, gave up, got drugged up or didn't support British punk bands because they were too busy following the commercial American pop punk trend. Mower's version of Chaos UK will return in 2014.

CHAOS UK (BASSIST BECKIE)

What was it that drew you to the punk rock scene in the first instance?

When I was eight, my best friend's mum had a copy of [Blondie LP] 'Parallel Lines' on tape, and we played it non-stop for months until the tape stretched and eventually broke. I loved every-thing about Blondie, especially Debbie Harry, and not long after I got into Madness and Two

Tone, as well as the usual early Eighties pop stuff. At secondary school, my circle of friends was the metal, punk, goth and alternative crowd. We stuck together because there were so few of us! I was a goth for a bit, but it was too miserable and boring after a while; punk was much more fun. I loved the energy, the rebelliousness of it. I thought punks looked cool and the music just did something to me. I was quite a quiet kid and I think it unleashed something inside me. Also harking back to the love of Debbie Harry, I especially loved any punk bands with women in them: Penetration, Siouxsie, The Adverts, The Avengers, Violators, X-Ray Spex, Slits . . .

How did you hook up with Chaos UK? Were you familiar with the band before you joined?
My younger brothers played guitar and drums and had started a band, so I thought I'd have a go at the bass . . . I thought it'd be the easiest thing to learn! I'd known the Chaos UK lot for years – the Bristol punk scene was pretty close knit – so when Mower left the band, and they found out that I played the bass, they asked if I wanted to go to Japan with them, all expenses paid! How can you say no to that when you're 21?

Where and when was your live debut with the band?
In the summer of 1991, we did a tiny little gig in Ipswich, but I can't remember for the life of me who it was with . . . maybe ENT? I don't think it was earth-shattering anyway! It was a dusty pub car park in the afternoon, with about 20 people there. Then my first real gig was in July 1991, headlining the main stage at Ashton Court festival, which at the time was Europe's biggest free festival. It was pretty nerve-racking, but after five minutes I really enjoyed it. We weren't allowed to play again after that, of course – not family friendly enough – but it was a great gig, and the sun shone! I can't remember who else played – it was a weekender and all sorts of local bands were on – but we were the only 'punk' band that day though.

Chaos UK had something of a reputation for being a bit rowdy, to say the least. How did you find it fitting in with such a bunch of renegades?
I was already used to the reputation that went with Chaos UK, and I knew they weren't loved by everyone – especially if they stayed at your house – but when I was 21 I was pretty laid back. I grew up around bands, and going to gigs and festivals. My dad was lighting designer and stage/production manager for bands like Deep Purple, The Who, Rolling Stones and Iron Maiden, so I met some pretty interesting people, and wasn't fazed by rowdy behaviour. To be honest, I quite liked the stupidity of it all at the time, although five weeks in a van on tour could test my patience sometimes.

For the record, what Chaos UK records did you play on?
I'm on '100% Two Fingers In The Air Punk Rock', the split with Raw Noise ['Making A Killing'), and 'Enough To Make You Sick'. And I think that's it? I like 'Enough To Make You Sick' the most. I had more fun recording it, and I think the album's more diverse and interesting. The songs are catchier and sound fresher. When we recorded '100% . . . Punk Rock', I think I was tired and didn't really enjoy recording it as much. So maybe nostalgia has influenced my answer.

What significant touring did you undertake with the band? Which were the most memorable trips?
We toured Japan in 1991 with Alien Sex Fiend – that was brilliant! We were supposed to support them, and the venues were huge, with all the crowds so into it, but after the first night it was clear to the promoters that it'd be better if we headlined – nearly everyone was there to see us – so we did for the rest of the week. Mr Fiend was a great bloke . . . but Mrs Fiend definitely didn't find us amusing!

Chaos UK, recording '100%...' LP in Dublin, 1993

I loved Japan. We were treated so well and had so much fun. After our five big shows with Alien Sex Fiend, we did a small gig organised by some kids from the local hardcore scene, in a little basement. It was the best gig (for me) of the whole tour. If I remember rightly, we played with Gauze and some kids from Lipcream who formed a band that night called Butterfly! I loved GISM, Gauze, Outo etc. then, so it was brilliant to meet them all and play with some of them.

After the [Berlin] wall came down, we wanted to play some gigs in Eastern Europe, so we did five weeks in October 1991, with Rectify from Wales. Rectify had a fight in the van before we even got on the ferry! They were my sanctuary though – I was able to swap vans and sit with them for some of the journey if Chaos and Gabba started getting on my nerves, haha! My best friend came with us too, which was great for me. Eastern Germany, Poland and Czechoslovakia (as it was then) were really hungry for gigs. You could really see the difference between east and west at that time – the west really wasn't that bothered about us, but the east lapped it up.

As a girl in a predominantly male-oriented scene, how were you treated, by both the band and the audience? Is our scene as open-minded and liberal as we like to think it is?
I was younger than the rest of the band, and most of the other bands we played with, so I feel in some respects I was treated more as a little sister than anything else. For example, I'd get the bed if there was only one, and everyone else would sleep on the floor. I guess you could say I wasn't being treated as equal in that respect, but I wasn't complaining either!

I was never made to feel I couldn't do what the others did and I certainly didn't have people running around trying to carry my gear for me. I was given equal say in what went on, and can't remember experiencing anything negative.

As far as the audience was concerned, it was generally positive. I was pretty insecure about my looks at the time and every now and then I'd get blokes trying to chat me up. I found it confusing and annoying. I really didn't get why just because I played in a band it made me more of a target. But I guess that's part and parcel of being in a band anyway, whether you're male or female. I think in general the scene was/is open-minded and liberal, but there were/are of course a few idiots around.

When and why did you decide to leave the band? Any regrets as to that decision since?

After three years I was starting to get tired of all the touring. I was getting homesick, but more than that, I was getting more and more ill (I had Crohn's disease) and my body just couldn't take the late nights, travelling, erratically bad food and boozing anymore. By the time we'd toured and recorded for two weeks in Ireland in 1993, I was getting pretty ill and was on steroids and strong painkillers. An American tour was coming up and I thought, 'I can't handle being away from home for three months,' and took the decision to leave before they went. Luckily they found Marv pretty quick. I don't have any regrets. They got stuck in a truck stop in the middle of nowhere for five days in the States! And I felt like I'd seen and done so much in those three years, it was time to move on.

What did you go on to do, both musically and otherwise after Chaos UK? Are you still in touch with any of the other guys?

I took a bit of a break, then joined Spite for a couple of years before I got so ill for so long that I stopped playing in bands altogether. And by the time I was well again I didn't really feel like being in a band anymore. I'd started working for a record company in Bristol, then London, and did that for eight years before moving to Berlin (I met and married a German).

I still have a chat with the lads when I see them, and we have a good laugh about the old times, but we don't hang out. My life is different to theirs (I've got a daughter now, and work in a school in Birmingham), so our paths don't cross that often. It's always nice to see them at gigs or whatever though. I'm not really sure what Chaos, Chuck or Pat are up to, but Gabba's doing his band FUK now. I saw them in Birmingham last year and they were really great.

I 'sang' a track on the last Hardskin album in the summer ('Why Do Birds Suddenly Appear?'). That was a right laugh!

What is your single most enduring memory of being in Chaos UK?

Going to Japan and all round (Eastern) Europe when I was 21 and meeting some amazing people. Loving doing gigs, hating rehearsing and recording, hating waiting for food before a gig, loving stupid in-jokes in the tour van – that stupid sense of humour you get when you're stuck with the same eight people for weeks on end, for hours a day, sleep deprived . . . you can't beat that. There are a couple of in-jokes that still have me laughing even now.

That's not a single memory though, is it? Sorry!

COURT MARTIAL

C ourt Martial were one of the youngest of the Bristol punk bands, formed in 1980 by vocalist Alex McPherson and guitarist Simon Burrough whilst they were still at school. They were originally called The Zeds, and their line-up was rounded out by Richard Braybrook on bass and John Zalokoski on drums, but John was soon replaced by Simon's thirteen year old brother, Ian, and they settled on the name Court Martial.

"Me and Alex mainly started talking about forming a punk band during some very dull geography lessons at school," remembers Simon. "The first punk single I'd bought was 'Pretty Vacant', but we were a bit young to have been fully involved right from the start, and got more involved around the start of bands like SLF, The UK Subs and The Ruts. I soon became more of a fan of such bands as Discharge, Exploited and GBH rather than all the bands on the bigger labels. We weren't anarchists or anything, we were just a bunch of kids from a working class background who formed a band for the love of music."

Despite their tender years and lack of decent gear, Court Martial were surprisingly good, and soon built up a small but loyal following in their area. Their first experience of playing live was at their St. George's School Social Club, albeit in front of a load of their mates, and their first 'proper' gig was in a local pub with a new wave band called Mind Tunnel. Although they enjoyed themselves, they never received their promised cut of the door takings because the toilets got trashed by some of their followers!

"Our age probably held both advantages and disadvantages," reckons Simon. "Being only sixteen meant that we weren't part of the main social scene so getting certain gigs often proved very difficult. And Ian was only fourteen, so technically he wasn't even allowed in some of the venues we wanted to play at! However, his tender age and the fact he was fairly small surprised so many people when they got to actually hear him play. I remember he sat in during Chelsea's soundcheck for their drummer when we supported them and Chron Gen at the Bristol Granary, and the whole band was blown away! They all proceeded to take the piss out of their drummer for the rest of the gig, saying that our Ian was far better than him!"

Although their first demo was rejected by Riot City, their next effort, a six-song affair recorded at SAM Studios, met with label boss Simon Edwards' approval. He used three songs as the band's debut EP, 'Gotta Get Out', and the Pistols-esque 'Your War' – complete with Lydon-style tonsil warbling – was included on the 'Riotous Assembly' compilation album.

That first EP, sloppily produced and jerkily played though it was, perfectly captured the band's gravelly energy, and spent a respectable five weeks in the Indie Charts, peaking at No. 15.

"The success of 'Gotta Get Out' was a total surprise," admits Simon. "We were basically just school kids doing it for a laugh. So to get other kids writing to you, many of them from overseas, saying how much they liked your stuff, was a great buzz. And we used to reply to every letter we received, cramming in loads of free stuff, like lyric sheets, badges, and stickers. We weren't into making money, we were just enjoying ourselves."

However, instead of following up the success of the single with a full national tour – something that would have been difficult given the ages of certain band members – Court

Martial only played a few sporadic gigs to promote it, opting instead to get back in the studio and record a follow-up.

"We only really played a few gigs away from Bristol, the main one being a 'Riot City gig', with us, Chaos UK and The Undead playing in Preston. It wasn't hugely attended either, as Crass were playing in Leeds the same night. Great planning!

Court Martial
L–R: Ian, Rich, Alex, Simon
(Pic: Sue. C.)

"We all went up in two Transit vans, with one getting lost on the way back and somehow ending up in Milton Keynes. They didn't get back to Bristol until 11 o'clock the following morning!"

The 'No Solution' EP was Court Martial's second – and final – vinyl outing, and built nicely upon the firm foundations laid with 'Gotta Get Out'. The raw intensity was still in full effect, but this time tempered with impressively mature songmanship and far smoother arrangements.

Surprisingly though, it sold less than their first single, and soon after its release, the band disintegrated, even though plans were already afoot for a third EP.

"Rich got it into his head that he wanted Mike Stone, who had produced Discharge and GBH, to do our next single but this never happened. Simon from Riot City warned us his fee would come out of any royalties!

"Also, Ian had begun to lose interest; only being about fifteen, he was more into BMX and the like. And we had already started looking at auditioning other singers anyway, as we were becoming disillusioned with Alex, but none of that resulted in anything. So the band disbanded rather than being dropped from Riot City.

"Rich formed another band called The Gift featuring a girl singer. He switched to lead guitar, got a mate in on bass and recorded two demos using a drum machine. I tagged along for a bit but wasn't too keen on pursuing it.

"My only real regret is that we never got to record an album. We were mates with The Undead and sat in on the recording of some of their LP, and it was frustrating that they hadn't sold as many singles as we had… but they got to record an LP and we didn't! It was our own fault though, because if we had stayed together it probably would have happened."

SELECT DISCOGRAPHY:
7"s:
'Gotta Get Out' (Riot City, 1982)
'No Solution' (Riot City, 1982)

AT A GLANCE:
Easier said than done, unfortunately, because Court Martial tracks are few and far between on CD. However, if you can track them down, the band were featured on both Volumes One and Two of the 'Riot City Punk Singles' collections on Anagram.

LUNATIC FRINGE

O ne of the lesser known but nonetheless entertaining bands from Bristol would have to be Lunatic Fringe. Formed in 1978 by like-minded school friends from the remnants of another local act, Company B., the band originally consisted of John Finch on guitar, Nick Horn on bass, and Adrian Blackmore on drums. The first singer for the band was a guy called Birdshit, but the equally unlikely-named Bear Hackenbush soon replaced him after an impromptu mass audition.

"Birdshit had some potential and a good singing voice, but ultimately proved unreliable," explains John. "Some argued that a better nickname for him would have been Bullshit. He failed to turn up in time to play our first gig (of sorts) at some point in the summer of 1980. Our set was still mainly comprised of covers at this stage, so we just played anyway and invited various members of the audience to sing along to different songs, which they did, in a kind of early punk karaoke! The most promising frontman, local scenester Bear (who went on to do the superb 'Skate Muties' and 'Bugs And Drugs' fanzines), was subsequently asked to join the band, and decided to accept.

"The band name was appropriated by myself from a head teacher, who, following the end of term exams had announced that he now expected 'the lunatic fringe element' to be leaving school; preparing for 6th form attendance, I considered that the rogue elements he had referred to were still going to maintain a significant presence and therefore suggested that we celebrate by adopting his phrase as a band name."

The band's first real gig was at Pill Community Centre, just outside Bristol, in December 1980 with Chaos UK, and of course it deteriorated into mayhem, with the bands involved in a ruck before the night's end. Little wonder then that many venues in the Bristol area were developing anti-punk booking policies, so, along with their peers in bands such as Disorder, Lunatic Fringe started organising their own shows, adopting the DIY stance out of virtual necessity. They were responsible for the sold-out Trinity Hall Punk Festival in September 1981 where sixteen bands performed, many of them with impromptu sets.

The one and only 'Jumping' Bear Hackenbush, vocalist with Lunatic Fringe

"Those early days were the best for me," reckons Nick. "Learning to play sitting in bedrooms, saving for amps, the first practises and first gigs, the crap van we all saved up for! The scene was vibrant and healthy then. Though the first phases of punk had passed us by, it had yet to turn into the crap, idiotic and mundane thrash that it became in the end (and seems to be now)… with all those thousands of Discharge impersonators and all that anarcho, hippie, political shit!"

The band's first vinyl release was the excellent 'British Man' track they contributed to Riot City's 1982 compilation, 'Riotous Assembly'. Lifted from the their first three-track demo, that had been recorded in September '81, it was a brooding and surprisingly tuneful attack on the complacency of the average patriotic Brit.

It was quickly followed by the band's first full 7" on Resurrection Records, 'Who's In Control?' Produced by Shane and Dave from Vice Squad, and recorded at Bristol's SAM Studios, the EP showed a punk band with a great deal of both musical and lyrical potential. Slightly more restrained than the output of many of their peers, the title track was still relentlessly powerful, its chorus driven by a simple but massive chord progression. And one of the B-side tracks, 'Omnibus (Bristol Buses)', with its amusing spoof intro, introduced the record-buying public to the band's anarchic sense of fun.

"Yes, it's fair to say that there was a pronounced streak of absurd humour running through the band," agrees John. "Which either helped to provide some balanced relief from the heavier themes, or was totally incongruous with our political stance, depending on your viewpoint. We were all no doubt heavily influenced by the anti-establishment Spike Milligan and Monty Python style of comedy, and sometimes, it has to be said, this was for no other function than to contradict expectations."

Such humour no doubt influenced the band when deciding to manufacture Lunatic Fringe underpants instead of the more usual, and generally preferred, T-shirts. Likewise when they occasionally played shows as Cardinal Wolsey And The Eggcups with Boobs from Disorder standing in on bass whenever Nick failed to show up. A stoical approach and this willingness to see the funny side of almost any situation helped the band keep in perspective all the various setbacks that meant it would be three years before their next single. Not least of all there was an eventful trip to France in May 1984, with their old sparring partners Chaos UK and Disorder, by which time Karl Burrows had replaced Ade on drums.

"For starters, Nick simply vanished just before we were about to arrive," recounts John incredulously. "The ferry had to be held up whilst we, and the crew, searched high and low for him, to no avail. We even checked all the lifeboats as well as the captain's cabin. To this day he doesn't remember anything about the incident, but he woke up back in England. We then proceeded to get severely hassled by the French customs officers. This ultimately resulted in us being fined; we had all our singles broken into pieces, missed our train connection and were squirted with CS gas!

"On our eventual arrival at the venue a day prior to the gig, the organiser was unhappy to say the least to discover that we had no bassist. After we had shell-shocked ourselves by constantly letting off French bangers all day, and as hangovers set in, a blanket of fear began to descend. Members of Chaos UK had already apparently had guns pointed at them by a chess-playing serial-killer fanatic; also we were told that two punks had been stabbed to death at a recent gig in Paris, and furthermore, some French skinheads were allegedly due to attend this gig with a view to killing the promoter over some dispute.

Bear of 'the Fringe', live at The Stonehouse, Bristol, 1981
(Pic: Ben Searle)

"On the night of the gig, this particular disagreement was peacefully resolved, though there was a constant threat of extreme violence hanging in the air, and some of the skinheads were apparently armed with guns. On the subject of hanging, one particularly nasty group of individuals did try to hang someone in the dressing room for a joke, but didn't succeed in their mission. When it came time for Lunatic Fringe to play, Boobs once again had to deputise for us. This proved to be difficult, as he only knew the bass lines to six of our songs, and the very scary bouncers wouldn't let us off the stage until we had played what they considered to be a sufficiently lengthy set. We were never so glad to get out of somewhere as we were that night. Once outside the venue, Bear and I literally grovelled around on a muddy bank, dreading the approaching sound of any French voices, as the streets were now being patrolled by French football fans looking for English people to perpetrate harm to. We were eventually rescued by the others, who had gone to get a car.

"Other 'highlights' of the remaining day prior to departure included a guided tour of a Gestapo torture chamber deep in the Paris catacombs, and finding my sleeping bag and hat filled with spaghetti and marmalade. Bear locked himself in an old cell to avoid a similar fate, but the spaghetti had been all we had left to eat between us, so after that we had nothing bar a stolen tin of artichoke hearts. I think that was the last time I visited France…"

Avoiding major international incidents aside, the band floundered through various lengthy periods of inactivity until February 1985 and the release on Bristol-based Children Of The Revolution Records of the hilarious 'Cringe With The Fringe' 4-track EP. The main thrust of the EP was the brilliant 'Curse Of The Bog People', but the single was rounded out with three re-recorded old songs ('Whose War?', 'Conformity' and 'Flesh And Blood'), originally written in 1980/81 that were starting to sound a little derivative four years later.

Plans for a full-length album never came to fruition, although the band did two cassette-only releases on Manic Ears, 'Lush And Live In '85' and 'Be Bad, Be Glad'. Karl was replaced with Matt Chanell, and Nick left, to be superseded by Simon Duvalier.

"The Fringe was a great thing, but a bit late, and we fell into stagnant musical times," says Nick. "I left because I had just lost interest and direction. I liked what other bands such as Joy Division, Public Image and The (early!) Cure had created with the punk sound, and I realised that I had no talent and was not going to be able to do a similar thing with The Fringe or any other musicians I knew. I became disenchanted with music and with myself really, and got heavily into drink and drugs too much. And I just got lost for four or five years after that.

"Between prison, addiction and death, there were a lot casualties back then, and that has taken the edge off the fun that we had at the beginning. I feel really lucky to have survived it all, and it would be really good if this book could remember Gill, Kevin, Hazel, and the others who sadly never came out the other side. I have a picture of them on my office wall and still think about them all."

The band itself eventually split in July '86 after a depressingly average show at the Bath Longacre Hall.

"It's a shame that we let something that was original, creative and meaningful, and which had shown such potential, fall apart in the messy way that it did," ponders John. "I do have the satisfaction though of knowing that just for a while we were good, really good, and nothing can take that away from me. It would have been nice to have recorded and released 'The Morally Good Song' and 'Several Limpets', and to have seen them rise to become the punk classics that they undoubtedly were, sitting comfortably alongside 'God Save The Queen' and 'Blitzkrieg Bop'. Oh well, at least I've still got a pair of Lunatic Fringe underpants…"

SELECT DISCOGRAPHY:
7"s:
'Who's In Control?' (Resurrection, 1982)
'Cringe With The Fringe' (Children Of The Revolution, 1985)

AT A GLANCE:
No such thing as a convenient discography of Lunatic Fringe unfortunately, although the 'Riotous Assembly' compilation they first appeared on enjoyed a CD release by Step-1 in 1994.

THE UNDEAD

T he Undead were yet another Bristol band who first appeared on Riot City's 1982 'Riotous Assembly' compilation, with the impressive low-end rumble of 'Sanctuary'. They actually formed in mid-1981, and comprised Al Scarlett – vocals, Phil 'Sick' Hamm – lead guitar, David 'Sid' Simmons – rhythm guitar, Richard Denning – bass, and Martin Hamm – drums. Popular legend has it that the band lived 'just down the road' from Beki Bondage, who passed their primitive first demo (recorded December 1981 at SAM Studios) onto Riot City boss, Simon Edwards. He then invited them to record not only 'Sanctuary' for 'Riotous Assembly', but also the double A-side single, 'It's Corruption'/'Undead', which managed a very respectable No. 18

in the Indie Charts upon release during April 1982. Some high profile local gigs were undertaken with the likes of Chron Gen and The Subhumans, although out-of-town shows were a little harder to come by, which may explain why the second single failed to chart.

That ill-fated sophomore effort was the thoroughly compelling 'Violent Visions' single, released in July '82 that again featured two tracks, 'This Place Is Burning' and 'Dead Revolutions', and saw the band maturing into something quite unique and powerful. In direct contrast to many of the other Bristol bands, The Undead seemed to favour a relentless mid-tempo groove that slowly

The Undead, L-R: Martin, Al Scarlett, Phil Sick, Sid, Dick

battered the listener into submission – as opposed to knocking them flat with a sudden burst of pure speed.

Before their split, attributed to the inevitable musical differences and apathy within their ranks, The Undead went on to become one of the few bands who released an album on Riot City, a label that primarily specialised in singles. Recorded by Steve Street at SAM in September 1983, 'The Killing Of Reality' saw the light of day early in 1984. Songs like opener 'Listen To The Wallbeat' and 'Acid Punk' seemed to pick up where the two singles left off, with their solemn riffs and pounding tribal toms, but elsewhere, tracks such as 'Let Me Go' and 'Heard It Before' were more upbeat and even added some effective melody to proceedings. The legend embossed on its back cover, 'Guaranteed: No Fuzz Boxes', was also not in keeping with that classic Bristol punk sound.

SELECT DISCOGRAPHY:
7"s:
'It's Corruption' (Riot City, 1982)
'Violent Visions' (Riot City, 1982)
LPs:
'The Killing Of Reality' (Riot City, 1983)

AT A GLANCE:
Nowadays, The Undead remain shrouded in mystery and the excellent album is sadly an obscure rarity, but the four cuts from the two singles appeared on Anagram's two 'Riot City: The Punk Singles' CDs in 1993 and '95.

Bristol went on to spawn many weird and wonderful varieties of punk bands. From death/thrash metal band, Onslaught (who began life as Discharge-style punkers in 1983 and had their first album, 'Power From Hell', released by Children Of The Revolution in 1985, but eventually ended up on major label London for 1989's 'In Search Of Sanity' before vanishing without trace) to Herbgarden (alternative post-hardcore rockers who also courted a major, East West, again with disastrous results for all concerned), no one can ever say that the musical legacy of the city has been anything but thrilling. Most recently there has been hardcore punk metallers A-KO and rampant ska fiends Five Knuckle, both destined for greatness, the former even beginning their careers on Trash City Records, Simon Edwards of Riot City infamy's new label.

DEMOB

F
ifty miles north of Bristol, Gloucester's Demob only released two 7" singles during their initial short, turbulent time together, but the power and vitality of those EPs has been so enduring over the last two decades, the band are back together by popular demand, even penning new songs that manage to be the equal of their seminal early Eighties material.

"I was eighteen and obviously spurred on by The Sex Pistols," recollects founding member, guitarist Terry Elcock. "There was a lot of unrest at the time; people were feeling depressed, there were no jobs for anyone, and we'd just left school, right in the middle of the Thatcher years... and then I saw The Pistols on the TV, and they were just outrageous. I thought to myself, 'If they can get away with this, what can we do?' I could already play three or four chords (I'd been in a church band... for my sins!) and The Pistols made me realise that anyone could get up and have a go."

So, in 1978, Terry formed Demob with school friend and near-neighbour, Johnny Melfah. The original line-up – Mike Howes singing, Chris Rush playing rhythm guitar alongside Terry, with Tony Wakefield on bass and John on drums – began rehearsing in Terry's bedroom, much to the dismay of his neighbours. It wasn't long before Mike introduced the band to his ex-army skinhead friend, Andy Kanonik, who soon became one half of the band's original two-vocal attack. The early days of Demob were wild, with the band quickly garnering an unwelcome reputation thanks to their unruly, uncontrollable following.

"There was a huge network of punks around Gloucester, a massive scene," recalls Terry. "We had such a wide circle of friends, a huge local following, and everyone wanted to be outrageous... so we formed the old posse, the Demob Riot Squad! And unfortunately, it usually all ended in violence."

"We used to just turn up and say, 'We're playing tonight!'" reveals Andy, of the band's unorthodox way of getting shows. "The guy would usually say, 'No, you're not!', and we'd say, 'Yes, we are, we'll play for nothing!' We'd just turn up with guitars; we'd have some right arguments over it, but nine times out of ten we always got on, with the likes of The (UK) Subs and The Damned... sometimes we'd only get to do five numbers, but it was a start."

"I didn't really know what was going on at the time," laughs Terry. "I'd just be told 'We've got a gig', and I'd think it was a bona fide show, and I couldn't understand why the doors were locked and we couldn't get into the venue!"

One thing that set the band apart immediately was their multi-racial line-up, a welcome and refreshing rarity in a scene that was basically dominated by white teenage males.

"It was always a close-knit scene here," reckons Andy, of the environment that spawned them. "We were all close anyway, us and all the black lads; we all grew up together, listening to punk, skinhead music, reggae, ska... it's pretty much a multi-racial city, and Demob were just living proof of that."

"To be honest, I go through my life without ever thinking about the colour of my skin, and it obviously isn't an issue with

A rare picture of the original 1979 version of Demob L–R: John Melfah, Mike Howes, Terry Elcock, Tony Wakefield, Chris Rush, Andy Kanonik.

any of my friends, so I'm kind of oblivious to all that," ponders Terry. "But I'll never forget once, we played with The Angelic Upstarts in Birmingham, and we got on great with those guys, joking with Mensi in the soundcheck and everything... but when they started letting the punters in, John and I started getting really edgy, 'cos there were all these skinheads coming in, some of them covered with swastikas! So we went backstage, for our own safety... And when we played, it really showed, 'cos no one could dance to us... and we'd taken up two coach loads from Gloucester. So a few idiots spoiled what would otherwise have been a good night, and we consequently played quite a few concerts for the Anti-Nazi League..."

Gloucester's Demob, 1980 lineup
L–R: Barry Evans, Terry Elcock, Mark 'Miff' Smith (sitting), Johnny Melfah

And at one such benefit show, playing on the back of a float at Gloucester's 1979 carnival, an unfortunate incident sparked off a virtual riot. Thanks to some knee-jerk coverage by the local media, it appeared to the casual observer that Demob's Riot Squad had struck again, when in reality it was the punks themselves who were the victims this time around.

"It was a load of bikers who started that off; they stoned us off the top of this bridge," says Andy. "The police were powerless to stop it, there were only a couple planted here and there. By the time we got as far as Gloucester Park, there were bricks and bottles flying at us... one of our mates got hit in the face..."

"I jumped off the float swinging my guitar, and I've never done that before in my life," laughs Terry, the passage of time lending the event a darkly comic edge. "But it was so frightening; all these bikers had surrounded the float, and most people had dispersed, but we had to stay there 'cos of our kit. They kept coming at us, and I jumped off the back of the truck swinging my guitar like a mad axeman!"

"It really was a case of them or us. But the truth never came out, and the punks got blamed," sighs Andy, before recounting another example of local prejudices. "All the Gloucester punks, eighty or ninety of us, used to hang around Bell Walk, the shopping centre, and the council didn't like it 'cos the shopkeepers were all complaining, which looking back was understandable, but we had nowhere else to go. So I got onto the council and said, 'Look, you find us somewhere to go on a Saturday afternoon, and we'll go', so they opened up a place called Tracy's... it's called Crackers now. And we all used to pile down there, the place was heaving... and we got 'the menace' off the streets!"

Amidst all the chaos surrounding the band, changes were afoot within Demob's ranks as well. Mike was kicked out, and Andy was forced to leave when he was sent down for three months (inspiring the song 'Three Months D.C.'), leaving the band without a vocalist. Mark 'Miff' Smith, who had just replaced Chris Rush on second guitar, took over the role of lead singer, and, at about the same time, Paul 'Fatty' Price replaced Tony Wakefield on bass. This line-up entered Tudor Studios in Swindon to record the 'Anti Police' single for Monmouth label, Round Ear, who got in touch with the band as a direct result of the deluge of press following the carnival riot.

The resulting two-track 7" (the title track being backed by the excellent 'Teenage Adolescence') was a fiery, provocative slice of soulful punk, its inherent power rising phoenix-like above a less-than-perfect sound job.

The single was a surprise success for all concerned, spending over two months in the Indie Charts during the spring of 1981, and peaking at a respectable No. 34, no doubt greatly aided by some rave reviews from the likes of Garry Bushell and John Peel.

The band followed up with a second single later the same year, 'No Room For You', which remains to this day their crowning glory, a true (but sadly largely unsung) punk classic. It's a wonderfully evocative anthem to the disillusionment of unfulfilled youth, Miff's vocals brimming with a raw pathos that can still prickle the hair on the back of necks even today, twenty years after it was committed to tape. The two speedier songs on the B-side, 'Think Straight' and 'New Breed', were similarly accomplished, both displaying a musical maturity far beyond the band's tender years.

'No Room For You' also appeared on the highly successful 1982 Anagram compilation album, 'Punk And Disorderly', which saw the band rubbing shoulders with many of the scene's biggest names. More gigs were undertaken to promote the singles, including shows with Discharge, The Beat… and even U2!

"We played with U2 in Stroud, and they'd just released their first single," Terry picks up the tale. "So they were just coming up. We were supporting them, and we did our set, and we had a huge following there; they were all booing U2 off, wanting us to go back on! And we had to go onstage and calm the audience down, so they could finish their set, saying, 'Look, lads, they've travelled a long way, let's let 'em play…!'"

Despite the band being at their musical and creative peak after that visionary second single, Demob split up soon after, apathy and musical differences rearing their insistent ugly heads. They played their 'last' show at Skunks in Islington in 1983.

"Punk had been going a while, had hit its peak, Sid had died and all that…" says Terry. "And there were all these new styles of music coming out, and you felt you had to move with the times. It was mutinous, people were going off to be New Romantics and stuff…

"And John our drummer – who wasn't that happy in the band anyway, he hated the bassist that much – was heavily into boxing, and he wanted to pursue that as a career. There was no big meeting, no big argument; it just sort of fizzled out, rehearsals got less and less… until they stopped altogether."

And by rights, that would have been the last anyone heard of Demob if an American label, Grand Theft Audio, hadn't contacted Terry a few years back, interested in releasing all the band's recordings on CD at last, and making him realise the depth of interest there still was in their music. John Melfah had gone on to open his own boxing gym in Gloucester, Miff had started another band called Garrison Damn, whilst Terry had been playing with several bands during the Nineties, including Kiss The Blade. Andy meanwhile had had very little to do with punk music for a very long time.

"I just drifted away really, lost interest completely for twenty-three years," he admits. "I got married twice… one of my mates from work had got me back interested in music… and then one night, I got in and my missus says to me, 'Terry's here!' and I was like, 'Terry who?' And she said 'Terry from Demob'…!"

The duo quickly recruited Rich Baldwin on bass and Tim 'Tillo' Howkins on drums. Rich had previously played in a band called Jellybomb, whilst Tillo had been in both Clockwork Scream and Curse, a band that also featured EMF guitarist, Ian Dench. New songs were written and recorded, and an offer to play the Holidays In The Sun festival was soon on the table. Before they knew it, plans were afoot to tour the USA, they played the H.I.T.S. show in Japan, and were drawing decent crowds whenever they headlined in their own right.

"We only ever planned to play the one show at Blackpool and get a proper album out at last, just to close that chapter really," reveals Terry. "It was originally going to be called 'Unfinished Business', because that was what it felt like to us, but then we started to realise how much the band meant to certain people."

Although the proposed album deal with Grand Theft Audio turned sour, 'Unfinished Business' emerged newly titled as, appropriately enough, 'Better Late Than Never' through Amber Records in 2002. The album saw the emergence on CD at last of all the classic tracks from the two early singles alongside a clutch of impressive new songs. It seems there's plenty of life in these old dogs yet.

"People are always asking me why we do it," Terry says in closing. "And basically, I don't wanna just fucking die and leave only a headstone. I said that to John from Round Ear once, and he said he thought we'd already achieved that anyway, which was really nice. We only released five songs back in the Eighties, and it's amazing how far those five songs have travelled and how influential they've been. I still can't believe that my poor attempts at guitar playing have brought all this pleasure to all these people around the world!"

SELECT DISCOGRAPHY:
7"s:
'Anti Police' (Round Ear, 1981)
'No Room For You' (Round Ear, 1981)

CDs:
'Better Late Than Never' (Amber, 2002)

AT A GLANCE:
The excellent 'Better Late Than Never' CD features a dozen tracks, including all the band's classic early Eighties output, and comes complete with liner notes, lyrics and lots of rare photos.

SCREAMING DEAD

Hailing from the nearby spa town Cheltenham (that has most recently belched forth the excellent 4 Ft Fingers) and all too often unfairly dismissed as some sort of gothic band on the merit of their latter releases, Screaming Dead were a fine example of early Eighties horror punk. Originally signed to Malvern-based Oi label, No Future, and finding themselves supporting such street punk acts as The Exploited and Criminal Class, their flamboyant approach wasn't really in keeping with the scene they found themselves thrown into, but their energetic, in-your-face music was more than capable of holding its own, regardless of the bill they were playing.

"I got into punk rock in 1976, when all my other mates were into crap like Thin Lizzy, and all these older bands that I had no affinity with," recalls vocalist Sam Bignall, of his formative teenage years. "My sister was in London at St. Martin's Art College, and she came home one day and told

Sam Bignall, vocalist with Cheltenham-based horror punks, Screaming Dead

me about this amazing band that had played at her college called The Sex Pistols! Not long after, they started breaking big, and although everyone I knew were saying that they were disgusting and stuff, I was really drawn to it. It seemed like something I had been waiting to happen all my life; it was fresh, it was exciting, the music was dynamic…

"My sister was quite prominent in the early punk scene, going to the 100 Club and places like that. Her boyfriend was in a band called The Suspects who appeared on the 'Live At The Vortex' album. I was going down there and hanging around the Kings Road, when it was still really Bohemian and being a punk was a dangerous thing, 'cos everyone hated you. I cut all my hair off and had it spiky, wore straight-leg jeans and a blazer, put safety pins in it, nicked my dad's little round RAF glasses and put two fingers up at authority - the whole ten yards. As well as The Pistols, I loved The Stranglers, The Adverts, The Clash, Generation X, and I just wanted to be in my own band straight away."

Beginning his musical 'career' with The Waste ("We were absolutely diabolical, but the spirit was there!"), he was soon approached by guitarist Tony McKormack to join his recently formed band, Screaming Dead.

Arriving at a solid line-up that also comprised Mal Page on bass and Mark Ogilvie on drums, they set about building a strong local following. And after a very positive feature in No. 5 of Gez Lowry's Rising Free fanzine, requests for the band's early 'Western Front' demo began pouring in from around the country. It was followed by the 'Children Of The Boneyard Stones' cassette, that was released by Bristol label, Recreational Tapes, and included, as well as a badge, a free copy of the band's fanzine, Warcry.

"We did the tape somewhere in Cheltenham, can't remember where, and it was pretty poor to be honest," admits Sam. "But everyone loved the look of the group, and we sold loads of 'em. So then, in 1982, we financed our own single, 'Valley Of The Dead' on our own label, Skull Records, basically 'cos we couldn't be bothered to wait for a record label to do it… and it was the punk thing to do, really, wasn't it?"

The first pressing of 1000 sold out within a week, bringing them to the attention of Cherry Red and ultimately No Future, who reissued the single in a standard sleeve rather than its original fold-around. An explosive assault on the senses, it also featured two strong cuts on its B-side.

"I still rate 'Schoolgirl Junkie' as my favourite Dead recording. It was quite Pistols-esque really; it had the best chord changes. And I loved 'Lilith', 'cos that was what The Dead were all about – fast, melodic punk. I always thought 'Valley…' was a bit too fast though, a bit manic… it could have done with just a bit more melody. But everyone seemed to like that one, and it did well for us. It caused quite a stir when it came out."

However, the biggest stir was caused by the ensuing 12" single, 'Night Creatures'. An instant Indie hit when it was released in September 1983, it saw the band taking a darker, more atmospheric approach, but there was still more than enough gusto in the delivery, especially when the band tore it up live, to satisfy even the most thrill-hungry punk.

"Screaming Dead were a punk rock band, there's no doubt about that!" exclaims Sam proudly. "Gothic rock hadn't even started when we were playing out looking the way we did. What we did wanna do though was bring back some of that original punk rock vibe, where all the bands looked different to each other, you know? The Pistols looked different to The Clash, and they both looked different to The Damned… it was very individual. We all had a bit of an interest in the horror theme, and that was how we decided to present ourselves. It had nothing to do with any desire to be gothic… whenever I hear that term, I think of bands like Bauhaus… and we were nothing to do with all that… or Sex Gang Children. We played with them once, and absolutely wiped the floor with them – what a load of pretentious wankers. We always used to pull punks to the gigs anyway. It was only when we reformed years later, and Tony started to market us as something we weren't, that we got tagged as Goths.

"What we really wanted to get away from was that look that was typically punk – everyone stood in front of a brick wall in their Docs and rolled-up jeans. It was all so generic, and we wanted to be different. We would wear studded leathers, but we'd wear tuxedos as well. We wanted to bring a bit of the Glam Rock feel back to it. And we'd go on with our faces painted all white, and anyone who hadn't seen us before would be thinking, 'Who the hell are these poofters?' Then we'd hit them with some of the dirtiest rock'n'roll they'd ever heard, and they'd be totally into it."

The lines were further blurred by their choice of cover for the next single, a rousing run-through of the Rolling Stones' chestnut, 'Paint It Black'. Backed by the brilliant 'Warriors', a minor punk classic if there ever was one, it spent a month in the Indie Top Forty during early 1984.

"Brian Jones, who formed The Rolling Stones and died at twenty-seven, is buried in Cheltenham, so it was a little bit of a tribute," reveals Sam. "He was more of a punk rocker than that tosser, Mick Jagger – he was a real rebel, he wasn't just a little rich boy playing at being one. One of the early Screaming Dead publicity photos was actually of us stood around Brian's grave… and then unfortunately one of our fans later went and pissed on it… oops! But it was just a great song anyway; it had those really punk chord changes, and it had a hint of the dark side about it that we obviously liked. It always used to go down a storm.

"We sometimes used to do 'New Rose' and 'Love Song' (by The Damned) as well. When I was about seventeen, I used to lock myself in the bedroom, put on 'New Rose' and jump around with my brother's guitar, and one of my ambitions was always to play that song live. So I think that was part of the reason we eventually did."

In 1984, ever keen to diversify musically, the band recruited Nick Upton on saxophone and keyboards, and signed to Nine Mile Music, who released the final Screaming Dead records on their Angel imprint.

"That was the beginning of the end for us really," sighs Sam. "I'd always wanted to try out a saxophonist 'cos I was a huge X-Ray Spex fan, and think the sax sounds brilliant when it's played aggressively, really powerful. And when he first came in that was just how he played it… but then we started to overproduce all our records and lost all our following. There were some musical differences, and we lost our direction.

"I wanted us to stay true to our punk roots. I remember we had a massive argument at the Solitaire Club in Swindon, after (Worcester punks) The Samples had supported us. We were just slow and lifeless… more melodic admittedly, but that wasn't necessarily what it was all about. I watched The Samples, and they were really fast and energetic, and I said to the other guys, 'Look, that's how we used to be!"

After two further 12"s – '84's plaintive but effective 'Danse Macabre Collection' and '85's 'A Dream Of Yesterday' – the band split up…

"For the same reason everyone else split up, I suppose. All the venues were closing, the yuppie era was dawning, and no one seemed interested in punk rock. It was a dreadful time for everybody, and we knew it was over. The spirit had gone from the whole punk scene, it basically died on its feet."

Tony went on to form Inkubus Sukkubus, and found great success in the Goth scene, but in 1997, he briefly regrouped the Screaming Dead without Nick or Mark the latter, who then lived in London, was consequently replaced by a drum machine. Two short German tours were undertaken and a new album recorded for Resurrection Records, 'Death Rides Out'. A synth-heavy exercise in atmospherics, and featuring many old Dead songs reworked as moody orchestra pieces, it lacked all the intensity that made the band such a creative force to begin with.

"Yeah, it was only Screaming Dead in name, not in spirit. We were starting to get a good following again though, to be honest, and we didn't disappoint anyone who turned up to see us live. With a proper drummer and the right publicity, we could have done something really good, but it wasn't to be. The last gig we ever played was in Whitby, a huge Gothic festival, in front of about 3000 people. The good thing was, loads of German punk rockers turned up, and went crazy down the front when we played, and scared the shit out of all those Gothic tossers, haha!

"A lot of people who came and saw us said that we reminded them of an original punk band," he adds, on the subject of the band's legacy. "Some people would say that we were similar to The Damned, but it was all about the spirit of '77 – we definitely had a bit of that about us. We were quite talented so we were always going to try and do something a bit different; we were never going to be happy just thrashing out the same three chords… but then again, that wasn't punk rock, was it? It was about music, for sure, but it was also about fashion, about politics, about rebellion – it was everything, it really was a way of life. We were lucky to be touched by something special, and hopefully we carried a little bit of that over for the people who were too young to be there in '76 or '77."

SELECT DISCOGRAPHY:
7"s:
'Valley Of The Dead' (Skull, 1982) – licensed to No Future after first pressing
'Paint It Black' (No Future, 1984)

12"s:
'Night Creatures' (No Future, 1983)
'The Danse Macabre Collection' (Angel, 1984)
'A Dream Of Yesterday' (Angel, 1985)

LPs:
'Death Rides Out' (Resurrection, 1997)

AT A GLANCE:
Angel Records' highly recommended nineteen-track 'Bring Out Yer Dead' CD compiles all the band's best work.

CHAPTER TWO

THE MIDLANDS

GBH

A longside The Exploited and Discharge, Birmingham's GBH were one of the true titans of that second wave of UK punk, and by far the Midlands' biggest punk export, releasing many – consistently good – records over the years, some of which even troubled the National Charts quite substantially. And the band are still together today; not only have they survived over two decades with three-quarters of their original line-up intact, but they are still writing strong material and pulling in enthusiastic punters the world over.

"Before punk came along I didn't have any real interest in music at all," remembers vocalist Colin Abrahall. "I was at school at the time and all these rumours would filter through the playground, stuff that was from The Sun newspaper, really silly things like, 'Punks spit down their girlfriends' throats when they kiss,' and so on! I remember hearing 'Sheena Is A Punk Rocker' on the radio and thought 'Wow, this is great'… then I heard The Sex Pistols and The Clash. I suppose I was the right age at the time 'cos it was all so rebellious and the stuff your parents would hate, and it just felt so right to me.

"My first gig was at the Top Rank in Birmingham (now the Academy). It was December 1977, The Ramones, The Rezillos and Sore Throat. I went with some people from school; I loved it but after the gig I had to get the bus home on my own, and got chased by a load of (Aston) Villa (football) fans. I am in fact a Villa fan myself but didn't think this would have made any difference to them. I got on the bus just in time but they stood outside banging on the windows… thankfully the driver didn't let them on!"

Inspired by the punk ethos that anyone and everyone could be in a band if they wanted to, Colin was soon playing his own part in the creation of obnoxious noises, and it was but a short step from there to the first incarnation of GBH.

"We used to drink in The Crown, Brum's only punk pub at the time, and if you believed anybody in there, everyone was in a band or about to form one…! I'd done stuff with a mate of mine, Johnny Chambers (who was the spit of Johnny Rotten); we used to record stuff on this battered old tape recorder. We called ourselves Assyd and had a song called 'Alarm'… which consisted of Johnny turning my alarm clock on and off and me kind of singing/talking about how shit work was!

"I bought a bass guitar for £18 off an old school friend then got an amp; I didn't realise that you needed a speaker to actually hear anything! So eventually I wired it up to my stereo… it lasted about thirty seconds before it blew up, but those thirty seconds sounded great!

"I moved into a house owned by a friend; I was seventeen and there were five of us living there. It was just like 'The Young Ones'! Mouldy stuff in the fridge, no one ever cleaned anything etc., and with 'Wilf' (Andy Williams) and a guy called Sean McCarthy we started to 'practice'. 'Jock' (Colin Blyth) had just got out of D.C. (detention centre) and the legend was he used to

The 'classic' early Eighties GBH lineup
L–R: Jock, Wilf, Ross, Colin
(Pic: Mike Stone)

play 'God Save The Queen' in the music class there, so we invited him to a practice and he could really play.

"So, we had a guitarist; Wilf wanted to be the drummer and used to bang on an old electric fire, Sean played my bass and I sang. Everything went through this old amp of mine and somehow we'd got a proper speaker. Then Jock came in one day and said he'd got us a gig; I think we were all a bit shocked!

"Sean lasted for two gigs before, in a fit of temper, as he couldn't play this one tune, he smashed up my beloved bass and said, 'I quit'. We got Ross Lomas in less than twenty-four hours later. He was from Sheldon, a part of Brum, the same as me, and I didn't realise until that first practice that we used to play football in the same team when we were eleven!

"The Crown was part pub, part drop-in centre," says Colin of the social heart of the Birmingham punk scene. "Most of us were not old enough to drink, but Tom, the gaffer, was great. On Friday and Saturday nights there was a disco upstairs. I think it was 50p to get in, and the music was brilliant, just punk and reggae. There was a nightclub called Barbarella's and after The Crown shut, we would all go there, a mob walking through the centre of town. Sometimes we'd get into fights with 'straights' on the way, but looking back now it didn't really seem all that violent; it was just high spirits… or bravado… or both. I saw some totally amazing gigs there - Iggy Pop, The Damned, 999, Generation X, The Lurkers, and many others. When it closed down, we started the band to entertain ourselves as much as anything else."

GBH played their first real show at Digbeth Civic Hall on September 12th, 1980… a benefit gig for prostitutes' rights.

"Well, we had kind of played on New Years Eve 1979 in Boring John's bedroom in that house I was living in, but I think we only had two songs, so we don't count that. We were supporting Poison Girls at the Civic, and a band called Bunker played too, who were from Holland. We were first on and at that time there were only about thirty people in the room.

"We played about ten songs, all our own. I remember being so scared... when you are on stage, it's like being totally naked. I don't think I moved around a lot; I was holding on to that mike stand so tight my knuckles were white. It was a big relief when we finished and a few people said nice things to us. Vi (Subversa) from Poison Girls said she liked a particular song; that impressed me... but I don't think she really meant it. Someone else said they thought we were 'decadent', so I went home and looked it up in a dictionary!"

Inspired by their success at several other shows in and around Birmingham, the band decided it was time to record their first demo, and some of the songs from that very first session are still mainstays in GBH's live set today.

"Our first demo was done in Leamington Spa. We were sort of being managed by this guy called Colin; he was a schoolteacher and lived in a block of flats opposite The Crown. He had this friend who owned a studio in his basement, so we saved up a bit of money between us, although Colin paid most of it, jumped on a train and went to Leamington. We didn't know what to expect but this guy explained everything to us, we had a few beers and just got on with it. We recorded four songs: 'Wall Of Sound', 'Lycanthropy', 'She's A Killer' and 'Generals'."

The band's big break came when they fortuitously hooked up with Discharge. Within months, they were on tour supporting them, and were soon even label-mates, signing to Clay in 1981.

"I just think we were in the right place at the right time," admits Colin. "I used to listen to John Peel and one night I remember he played Discharge's 'Realities Of War'. I loved it and thought, 'Hey, this isn't a million miles away from what we're doing.' A couple of months later we supported them at The Cedar Club in Brum; it had taken over from Barbarella's as a punk venue. It was a great night; we got on with Discharge really well, and after the gig we exchanged phone numbers. A few weeks later Cal called and asked if we would like to support them at a few more gigs.

"The last date of this Discharge tour was in their home town of Stoke-on-Trent, at Victoria Hall, a venue that was exactly the same as Digbeth Civic. Ross was still working as a milkman at the time, and had to bunk the train up there as we'd all gone up in a van earlier. He still hadn't arrived and we were due on at any minute, so we debated whether to do it or not, but as the band motto has always been 'The show must go on,' we decided to play without a bassist. Ross arrived just in time for the last song. And as we sat in the dressing room afterwards, wondering if it had been any good or not, this bloke resembling a six-foot stick insect with an afro poked his head around the door and said, 'Good show, lads.'

"It was Mike Stone, head of Clay Records... in fact he was Clay Records, full stop, and ran it out of a little record shop in Hanley. A couple of days later, he rang me up and offered us a deal. He had heard the legendary 'Leamington Spa Demo' as Cal had given him a copy. We all went up a few days later to sign the contract, and the advance was our coach fare back to Brum! He impressed us with his enthusiasm and his stories of signing The Lurkers and Gary Numan when he worked for Beggars Banquet."

Mike Stone quickly had GBH in the studio to record their debut for Clay, the classic 'Leather, Bristles, Studs And Acne' 12".

"We went up to Mike's shop, then all piled into his very old but none-the-less classy BMW and drove up to Rochdale. I think we did it all in one day; it was very natural... lots of drinking and messing around, and during one song a local taxi dispatcher started coming through Jock's amp! It kind of fitted with the song so we left it in.

"We got the title 'Leather, Bristles, Studs and Acne' like most of our titles – from a moment of spontaneity. We were 'dossing' about in town and went into one of those photo-booths. We all crammed in and when the photos came out, all you could see was leather, bristles, studs, etc. The photo on the back was taken on the train when we went to Leamington Spa for that demo... shit, I've got to stop mentioning Leamington Spa!"

The results were astounding, eight cuts (nine if you count 'Alcohol', the piss-about hidden bonus track) of immensely powerful, hard-hitting punk rock that took the unsuspecting scene by storm. Released in September 1981, it spent over three months in the Indie Charts, peaking at No. 8, a great showing for a debut offering by anyone's standards. As well as the social commentary expected of punk bands at the time, the EP – in particular, songs such as 'Necrophilia' and 'Lycanthropy' - also showcased GBH's fairly unique (for a UK band, at least) line in morbid horror imagery, albeit delivered with tongues firmly in cheeks.

"Yeah, I suppose we did want to write more interesting stuff than the usual 'I'm on the dole and I'm so bored'-type lyrics," reckons Colin. "I was really into horror films, and during those days there always seemed to be 'Hammer Horror' on TV late at night; we used to watch them all, and laugh at the cheesy special effects. We were also listening to The Damned's 'Black Album', which was a bit horror influenced.

"I moved into a bedsit on my own as the 'Young Ones' house' had been re-possessed in the end. I remember one time, I had no money and hadn't eaten for about three days. I was re-using tea bags from the bin with no milk or sugar! Anyway, I remembered one of the guys who lived there had some sweets in a chest of drawers so I started searching for them; I found them and also his old bus-pass, and tucked in the back was a £5 note. I ran to the corner shop and bought some instant mashed potato and a tin of beans; it was one of best meals I've ever had! After stuffing myself I jumped on the bus to town, met up with Jock and bought a ticket to see The Clash and the next day The Damned played the Odeon! You see? £5 used to go a long way back then!"

In late 1981, as part of the drive to promote the EP, the band appeared at the Xmas On Earth punk festival in Leeds.

"Xmas On Earth was brilliant," enthuses Colin. "And, as always, it was an adventure for us. We'd played Manchester the night before and stayed at a friend's house. He had a dog and Jock is asthmatic... so when he woke up his eyes were all swollen and he couldn't breathe properly, and we had to take him to hospital. I did wonder if we would make it in time to play, but after a good go on the oxygen mask he was pinching the nurse's arse and giggling! We got interviewed by Sounds after we'd played and this led to our photo being in the review. I said something about Garry Bushell not being there, and that got put in as well, so it was good for us. It snowed on the way home, and when we stopped at some services it was full of punks, and it all descended into a mass midnight snowball fight!"

And if the record-buying public thought that first 12" was as extreme as the band could get, they were about to have their delusions violently shattered, and then some. Early in '82, GBH unleashed the 'No Survivors' 7", a hell-for-leather thrasher that saw them introducing some vague metallic overtones into their sound, the rhythm section pummelling away in a fashion not dissimilar to Motörhead at their most ferocious. Unbelievably, for such an uncompromising sonic assault, it cracked the National Charts, reaching No. 63... helped on its way no doubt by Garry Bushell awarding it Single Of The Week in Sounds.

"I am not into heavy metal at all," laughs Colin. "To say I hate it is perhaps a bit strong, but I have no interest in it. Wilf was into Motörhead big time, and I like their stuff, but I wouldn't call them Heavy Metal. To split hairs I'd say they are heavy rock. Jock said in one interview we did, 'Playing fast covers up the mistakes', and it's true 'cos there is actually less time to make a mistake!"

The band's warped sense of black humour also figured strongly on their second single, 'Sick Boy', which was another Indie hit, spending four months in the chart during the summer of 1982.

Not as fast as 'No Survivors', nor blessed with the best of productions, it nonetheless remains one of the band's best-loved songs, with the hugely-successful thrash metal band Slayer even covering it for their 'Undisputed Attitude' punk covers album in 1996.

"One thing that has always kept us going is our sense of humour; even when we were in trouble at a customs post, something funny would happen or someone would say something and we'd all crack up laughing. So I suppose humour has always been part of the band make-up.

"A lot of bands did take themselves too seriously back then… anarchist ones usually. It was some quest to them, fighting the system by not drinking bitter 'cos it contained fish! And not wearing leather jackets… they didn't seem to notice that their Doc Martens were made of leather too.

"Me and Jock are both vegetarians, but we don't want to convert the whole world; it's up to the individual. Ross is a staunch carnivore and you should see his face when we play these veggie youth centres in Europe!"

A mere two months after the 'Sick Boy' 7", GBH dropped their debut album, 'City Baby Attacked By Rats', which spent a staggering seven months in the Indies, peaking at No. 2 (kept off the top spot by Yazoo's 'Upstairs At Eric's'), and even reached No. 17 in the National Charts. Garry Bushell gave it another rave full-marks review in Sounds, and not without reason. The album took all the promise of the previous recordings and refined it into a near-perfect punk album; equal parts aggressive power and fantastic tunes. From the opening salvo of 'Time Bomb' to the end of the obligatory joke track that closes the record ('Bellend Bop'), this is hard, heavy punk with every ounce of excess fat trimmed off it. Lean and mean, but maintaining a great sense of melody despite its enthusiastic acknowledgement of the scene's thrashier tendencies.

GBH's Colin Abrahall, live at the Fulham Greyhound, December 1983 (Pic: Paul May)

"Recording 'City Baby...' took three days, a marathon for us back then. Mike Stone had found this studio in Birmingham; it was called F.S.R., which stood for Frank Scarth Recording and this Frank Scarth was a good bloke. He had all these revolutionary – for us, anyway – techniques. To get a really 'live' drum track he miked up the drums as usual, but also opened a door to this long corridor and right at the end put another mike... when he mixed the two sounds together they gave a great, ambient sound.

"And as we were finishing the final mixing late one night, it was announced on TV that Lady Di had given birth to Prince William. This was in the days of vinyl, and you could scratch messages in the master, so we had 'Royal baby attacked by corgis' put round the middle of the record. If you have a first pressing of it you will see it. I think it's a record that has stood the test of time pretty well and it's probably our biggest seller too. To be honest, I wouldn't change a single thing about it, even if I could.

"At this time we used to rehearse at a place in Birmingham called Diamond Sound (grand name, shit place) and we were leaving there one evening and walking to a pub, when we passed the little kiosk that sells our local paper, the Birmingham Evening Mail. And as usual they used to have a poster with the day's headline written in magic marker behind a metal grille. As we walked past, it said 'City baby attacked by rats'... Jock remarked 'What a great song title', and I stole the poster. I still have it somewhere in my loft; it should make me a few quid when Sotheby's have their next rock memorabilia auction!"

To capitalise on the success of the album, and help push the band in Europe where some of their earlier releases had gone relatively unnoticed, Clay reissued the 'Leather, Bristles...' 12" and the first two 7"s as the 'Leather, Bristles, No Survivors And Sick Boys' album. Predictably enough, it was another big-seller, and provided GBH with a stopgap release whilst they hit the road for some serious touring.

"We took to touring like a nun to a candle factory!" laughs Colin. "It just seemed very easy and enjoyable to us, and very natural; we'd struggled to get gigs in the early days and now we had agencies booking us tours of places I'd only read about or seen on TV.

"The first tour of America totally blew our minds. I made the mistake of watching 'Warriors' on TV the day before we left and had nightmares about all these gangs chasing me through the streets of New York! I shouldn't have worried... as we walked through the customs at the airport, this old black guy was sweeping the floor; he took one look at our leather, bristles, studs and acne, stood up straight and said, 'Holy shit!'

"There was a chauffeur waiting for us with a sign that said 'GBH'; we told him it was us and he lead us out to a big, black stretch limo! It was a little treat that the booking agents had sent for us. When we got to the hotel some guy from the agency gave us advice on staying in New York... it was all 'Don't go up this or that street after dark, don't buy drugs on the street' etc., etc.

"Our tour manager had just done a tour with the Anti-Nowhere League, so we all hung out for a few days together. The League, being a bit older than us, offered us tips about surviving in the USA. It ended with Winston, their bass player, having a birthday party the day we played New York; Joey Ramone came and only said one word to anyone – 'Hi'!

"We just seemed to get on with everybody we met; it seemed that America loved us and we loved America. It sounds like a cliché but to travel across the US seeing places you've only heard about in songs was magic, and we got treated better than we had ever done in England or Europe.

"People's enthusiasm was contagious. We had a rule: no-one could go to bed 'til the bottle of Jack Daniel's – then a mysterious novelty – was empty... I can't look at the stuff now! We were getting used to all these strange customs by the time we reached San Francisco. We checked into our hotel and went for a wander up the street; we found a bar and slipped inside for a drink. We'd got used to complimentary bar snacks – little bowls of peanuts and pretzels and the like – and on the bar was a plate of chicken drumsticks, so Jock helped himself to one as he ordered. The barman looked quite shocked and said, 'What do you think you're doing?' 'Having a drumstick,' said Jock, quite innocently, 'Why?' The guy's face went purple… 'That's my fuckin' lunch,' he shouted, and chased us up the street!

"We were playing to some of the biggest crowds we'd seen… I think LA was the biggest, about 3000 people… and we were headlining! We stayed at the legendary Tropicana Hotel; it was steeped in rock'n'roll history… Jim Morrison used to live there, and Nina Hagen was staying when we did. We met up with some people who ran the Flipside fanzine; they interviewed us while sitting round the pool and ordered us a pizza the size of a dustbin lid!

"We ended the tour back in New York, then flew back home. A few months later we did another tour over there. As we drove through New York again (this time in a van), we all got this strange feeling like we had never left."

Somehow, amidst all this touring, GBH managed to remain fiercely prolific, releasing the blistering 'Give Me Fire' single in October '82, which reached No. 2 in the Indie Charts and No. 69 in the Nationals. It was closely followed by the 'Catch 23' single in early '83, and then their second 'proper' album, 'City Baby's Revenge – 101 Ways to Kill A Rat', in December of that year. Whilst not as immediate as their debut full-length, it actually contains some of the band's best work, such as the high-speed melodic opener 'Diplomatic Immunity' or the bruising title track. And just like the album before it, it contained a cover version, this time of The Stooges' 'I Feel Alright'.

"We were feeling more confident with our playing by then, so decided to try doing a few cover versions. I think the golden rule of doing covers is, if you can't do it better than the original, change it a bit and make it your own song! The Damned had covered Iggy Pop's '1969' and re-named it 'I Feel Alright'; we did it and tried to merge both versions into one song. It's great to play; it's a simple riff and ends in total chaos, and no two versions are ever the same! We even copied the 'Hey Keith!' shout at the beginning. I have since found out that The Damned got it off Johnny Thunders; when they did the Anarchy tour, Thunders was all messed up on drugs and couldn't cope without his faithful roadie Keith. And in between songs he used to shout 'Hey Keith!' whenever he'd dropped his plectrum or broken a string!

"Same with Slaughter And The Dogs' 'Boston Babies' (covered on 'City Baby Attacked By Rats')… it was a song from their first album and we loved it. It also gave Jock an excuse to do a mad guitar solo near the end. Around this time Ross's girlfriend had just had their first daughter; she was in hospital and Ross wanted to tape the practice and let his girlfriend listen to it, so I changed the lyrics to 'Ross's Baby'! I think he still has that tape somewhere… another one for Sotheby's!"

GBH released one more record, 1984's infectious 'Do What You Do', for Clay ("They were in some financial difficulty," says Colin diplomatically), before moving onto Rough Justice, a subsidiary of the metal label Music For Nations, and also then home to The Exploited. The 'Midnight Madness And Beyond' album was the first fruit of this new relationship, and it proved that GBH had lost none of their fire or fanbase when it emerged in August 1986. Hot on its heels came the 'Oh No, It's GBH Again' 12" and yet more touring, although the relentless roadwork was about to take its toll on the until-then solid as a rock line-up.

"Wilf left because he got married and moved to Texas to be a bellboy in a hotel," explains Colin. "We were in LA and had a day off. Our American tour manager at the time suggested we went to the legendary Rainbow club for a drink; we lasted about ten minutes in there. It was horrible, full of 'hair farmers' (longhaired heavy metal types). As we were walking out of the front door, these two girls were walking in, and one of them said, 'Hey GBH… big women!' To cut a long story short, we went back to their house and partied. Less than two weeks later, Jock married the one called Lia, in Las Vegas… even though he was engaged to a girl in Brum! But that's another story…

"Wilf had got off with the other one called Dee Dee. To be honest, we couldn't stand her; she was everything an annoying Yank chick could be, loud, obnoxious, and overweight; the total opposite of Lia, who was quiet, and kept herself to herself. After the tour finished, this Dee Dee came over to England and got married to Wilf; it was a strange affair, in a church. Her parents came over; her dad was a midget, and in the army or some other form of national service… he turned up in uniform with a shit load of medals pinned to him. They were from Texas so I'm sure you get the picture… a real gung-ho, go-get-'em-cowboy sort… we thought he was a prat!

"We had a rehearsal planned, and Wilf called to say he couldn't make it as he had to go and pick up the video of his wedding! We were not too pleased, but then he sacked himself, saying he didn't really want to be in the band anymore. Less than twenty-four hours later, we had called Kai Reder, who was from Hamburg, Germany, and he was in. We first met Kai when he was drumming for a band called Napalm; they had supported us on our first European tour, and, as with all our support bands, we got on like a house on fire.

"We next bumped into him while on tour in the US in San Francisco; he and his singer had gone to America to avoid national service in Germany. But they had run out of money; I think his mate had gone home and Kai wanted a lift to New York. We signed him on as an extra roadie.

"When Wilf left, he became the obvious choice as a replacement. He was a good drummer, he knew all our set and we were friends. The fact that at this time his English wasn't too good didn't really matter; he soon picked it up. I remember he told me that he had started to dream in English! To avoid the army in Germany we paid this girl in Brum £200 to marry him; it worked and soon the army gave up on him. He was with us for about four years 'til he fell in love with a girl from, of all places, Hamburg. He left to marry her…

"So we did the same thing as when Wilf had left. Joe ('The Fish') Montanaro had been the drummer for Agnostic Front, when they had supported us on a US tour in 1986. When Kai went, we called him and he joined."

1987's 'No Need To Panic' album was the first to feature Kai's lightning-speed bass drum assault, and that, possibly combined with the subliminal influence of the many hardcore bands they were touring with in the US at the time, resulted in a speedier, more metallic sound.

"Don't start with that heavy metal thing again, But I kind of agree with you. It was other elements we were seeing, and, as in most things, you try to stretch yourself. With all the playing we were doing, it was a kind of challenge, to play harder, more complicated songs. Also Kai's drumming was different to Wilf's… Wilf was a plodder whereas Kai was a bit flashier. When you change a drummer it's like putting a new engine in a car; it takes time to run it in…"

And Kai was certainly well run in by the time they did the 'Wot A Bargain' 12" in spring 1988, as it featured one of the band's strongest, most strident songs to date, the awesome 'Checkin' Out'. A LA show from the US tour of that year was both recorded and filmed, and later released as 'Live In LA, 1988' by Anagram.

GBH went on to release three more albums for Rough Justice (1989's 'A Fridge Too Far', 1990's 'From Here To Reality' and 1992's 'Church Of The Truly Warped'), with Scott Preece from Bomb Disneyland replacing Joe (who had been deported back to Holland due to lack of work papers) just as they started writing 'Church…'

In 1996, they signed briefly to German label We Bite for the 'Punk Junkies' album, but the band now currently reside with Go Kart who issued their most recent album, 'Ha Ha', in 2002. These records fall far outside the time period of this particular book, but they are all as consistently strong as we've come to expect from these Brummie punkers, although Colin has slightly mixed feelings about that period of their career.

"Maybe some of the stuff we did in the early Nineties was a bit rushed. We had a manager then, a real dodgy wide-boy. He used to put pressure on us to come up with the goods, to keep him in the style he was accustomed to!"

Nevertheless, the band soldiered on, producing great records and live shows whilst all around them so many critics were proclaiming punk to be a spent force. The latest record in particular is a great return to form, harking back to the more melodic early punk where the band have their roots without losing that distinctive GBH feel.

"We just kept going 'cos it was the only thing we knew how to do!" reckons Colin. "Bands were splitting up left and right and I think we didn't want to end up like them. We'd see people we knew at gigs and they were wearing hip hop type clothes, saying 'Yeah, The Beastie Boys… that's where it's at!' Now, to us, punk was never a fashion; we weren't doing it 'til the next big thing came along – we were in it for life. Also the touring helped keep us going. We were always going to new places, so I suppose it always seemed fresh."

GBH recently celebrated their 25th anniversary, as only they know how – by playing a low-key show in their hometown of Birmingham (of course) . And they show no signs of slowing down just yet either.

"Well, we're constantly asked this, and the honest answer is, I don't know," says Colin, when asked how much longer the band will continue. "As long as it's still fun is a glib reply, but it's true, and we still have fun doing it; I can't ever imagine it not being fun.

"We just did another US tour last summer, as well as various festivals in Europe, and some guy even e-mailed me about doing Australia… but we never really believe it until we get off the plane, if you know what I mean? A simple phone call can change everything and anything.

"I got a call once, 'Please come and play two shows in Tel Aviv'. 'Is this some kind of joke?' I said. The guy got quite angry with me, especially when I asked, 'Is it safe?'

"A few months later we went and did two shows at The Penguin Club in Tel Aviv, and it was great. We made loads of new friends, drank loads of alcohol, Jock got a new tattoo… I saw the most guns I've ever seen in my life, and learnt how to swear in Hebrew! People are people all over the world; some are bad people, but the vast, vast majority are good, and I feel lucky that I have travelled to some of these exotic ports of call, met some nice, honest people, and basically had a very good time doing it…"

SELECT DISCOGRAPHY:
7"s:
'No Survivors' (Clay, 1982)
'Sick Boy' (Clay, 1982)
'Give Me Fire' (Clay, 1982)
'Catch 23' (Clay, 1983)
'Do What You Do' (Clay, 1984)

12"s:
'Leather, Bristles, Studs And Acne' (Clay, 1981)
'Do What You Do' (Clay, 1984)
'Oh No, It's GBH Again' (Rough Justice, 1986)
'Wot A Bargain' (Rough Justice, 1988)

LPs:
'City Baby Attacked By Rats' (Clay, 1982)
'Leather, Bristles, No Survivors And Sick Boys' (Clay, 1983)
'City Baby's Revenge' (Clay, 1983)
'Midnight Madness And Beyond' (Rough Justice, 1986)
'No Need To Panic' (Rough Justice, 1987)

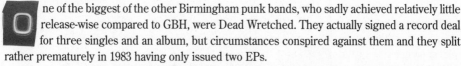

'A Fridge Too Far' (Rough Justice, 1989)
'From Here To Reality' (Rough Justice, 1990)
'Church Of The Truly Warped' (Rough Justice, 1992)
'Punk Junkies' (We Bite, 1996)
'Ha Ha' (Go Kart, 2002)

AT A GLANCE:

The excellent 2002 Captain Oi! CD reissues of the first four albums come complete with all the original artwork and lyrics, as well as detailed liner notes and bonus tracks taken off the various singles from the relevant periods. The latest studio album 'Ha Ha' demonstrates that the band have lost none of their instinctive flair for strong songwriting.

DEAD WRETCHED

One of the biggest of the other Birmingham punk bands, who sadly achieved relatively little release-wise compared to GBH, were Dead Wretched. They actually signed a record deal for three singles and an album, but circumstances conspired against them and they split rather prematurely in 1983 having only issued two EPs.

The nucleus of the band coalesced in 1979 under the unlikely moniker of Taff Nasty And The Stomach Aches. Comprising Paul 'Baz' Harding on guitar, Stephen 'Ricey' Rice on vocals, John 'Herman' Hoffman on bass, and 'New Rose Des' (aka 'Dirty' Des) Phillips on drums, they played a few shows in and around Birmingham.

They only really began to garner a serious local following, though, when they became The Wretched, replaced Ricey with Billy Idiot, and recorded a demo at F.S.R. Studios.

"They auditioned Billy over the phone," reveals Mick Coyle, who himself replaced Herman on bass soon afterwards. "He sang a Generation X song down the phone to them, and they gave him the job! His real name is Stephen Carroll, but 'Billy Idiot' came from his love of Generation X and Billy Idol. As legend goes, he was looking for a cool sorta stage name, and they were going to put a load of suggestions in a hat, and he was going to use whatever he chose at random. Thing is, they just wrote 'Idiot' on all the pieces of paper, so he was stuck with it whichever he picked!

"Then I was asked to join by mutual friends on the day of the Royal Wedding, July 29th 1981. Before Wretched (who added the 'Dead' to their name after Mick joined), I was in a band called CID, which was half Sid Vicious/half UK Subs, I suppose, but most people reckon it stood for Cunts In Disguise! It was exciting to even be asked, quite an honour really, 'cos Wretched were a pretty happening band in Brum at the time. I'd never seen 'em before I joined, but I'd seen Bill in his old band a few years previously. They were called The Burglars, but eventually became The Stale Farts – who achieved notoriety in and around Sutton Coldfield with songs like 'Has Anyone Seen My Camel?'

"My first gig with the band was at The Opposite Lock, in Birmingham, just off Broad Street, which is now called Bobby Brown's, I think It was with The Varukers; they went on first and were shit hot, and we were all wondering how the hell we were meant to follow that! But we managed somehow, and it was a classic gig. There was a big riot though, the place got smashed up, and a couple of cars got turned over outside…! We wrote 'Time To Die' after that, 'cos we heard that the bouncers from the club were all going to break our legs!"

A live rehearsal demo ("Recorded on a little cassette player at Dexy's Midnight Runners' old practise room, back of Bristol Street") was given to Inferno, who were operating out of Tempest Records in the city centre and had just signed The Varukers. Aware of Dead Wretched's growing reputation, Inferno snatched them up, and the 'No Hope For The Wretched' EP was the result. Released in March 1982, it was a roaring success for both band and label, spending two-and-a-half months in the Indie Charts and reaching No. 10.

Although 'Recession' sounds horribly throwaway now, the other three cuts have aged rather well. The aforementioned 'Time To Die' was a short, sharp thrasher, whilst 'No Justice' had a whiff of the Crass Records approach in its painful hanging guitar chords and repetitive militaristic drumming. The title track however was a raucous street anthem that wouldn't have sounded out of place on an album by someone like The Business.

"But we never saw ourselves as an Oi band," reckons Mick. "As far as we were concerned we were just a punk band... but we did have a big skinhead following too. 'No Hope...' just had a good catchy singalong chorus. As Garry Bushell said in his review, it was partly lifted from an (Angelic) Upstarts song, but we didn't worry about things like that at the time, we just banged it out." It was actually one of the band's oldest songs, one of the very first they wrote.

Dead Wretched, one of Birmingham's best kept secrets...
L-R: Baz, Billy, Mick (seated), Des

"Yeah, it was almost impossible not to be influenced by them in some way," he adds, on the subject of local punk giants GBH. "I knew (their guitarist) Jock from about 1977, from when I used to walk to school. He was one of the first hardcore punks I ever saw really. There I was in my Jam tie and my Jam badges and stuff, and when I saw Jock this one morning... well, he was quite a scary sight, to be fair! You know, I stopped in my tracks and hung back, But I went home that night, hacked away at my hair, rolled my jeans up and got my big Docs on, and that was it."

Unfortunately, although they managed several well-received London shows, including two gigs at Skunx (one of them with Soldiers Of Destruction), the band seemed to have problems securing gigs outside of the Midlands, which may account for their second single not doing anywhere near as well as the first.

Released in late October '82, the 'Convicted'/'Infiltrator' double A-side only spent three weeks in the Indies, and didn't quite make the Top Thirty. It was a powerful offering though, that thoroughly eclipsed the debut in both production values and composition, 'Infiltrator' being an intense high-speed blowout, and 'Convicted' a pounding, almost tribal chugger.

"Well, again, 'Convicted' was quite an old song as well. There was no purposeful change in direction or anything. In a way, all that stuff was like a precursor to death metal; some of the riffs just had that certain style. Baz was getting into a lot of heavy metal about then too – UFO, Judas Priest... stuff like that. But the stuff I was writing was more obviously punk rock. So maybe subliminally we were heading in that direction, taking some of the death overtones without even realising it."

It was about this time that the band appeared on national TV, as part of a current affairs documentary about Black Country youth called 'Setting Out'. It was purely by chance that they were asked to appear, when a friend of theirs who worked at the telephone exchange got talking one day to the channel's programme scheduler.

"We were filmed playing in an old derelict metal forge, amongst all these slag heaps," recalls Mick. "They paid for us to go in the studio and record two songs, 'You're No Exception' which appeared on the programme, and a song called 'Blaze', which was a tirade against Inferno Records, who we thought were ripping us off at the time. Then they blasted that recording out of these hidden speakers, concealed around the set, camouflaged by various crap placed strategically here and there, and we mimed to 'You're No Exception'.

"It was great fun. I was stoned out of my head and was sick as a dog behind my amp just before we started, which was well punk, I suppose! Baz was a bit pissed off though, because he'd spent about four hours on his hair, spiking it all up just right, and then it pissed down on us… so he wasn't too happy about that, but it was a good laugh. It was just great to be on TV really – if you couldn't get on 'Top Of The Pops' like The Exploited did, it was the next best thing really."

However, just as the band's public profile was on the rise, Dead Wretched's label Inferno hit financial problems and folded, a setback that proved too much for Baz.

"Soon after that, he just decided that he'd had enough. The last gig we did was on July 4th 1983, at the All-American Punk Independent Barn Dance in the Golden Eagle, just off the top of New Street. The pub's been knocked down since and turned into a car park. That was with GBH, Generator, and maybe Drongos (For Europe)? But the sound was awful, and at the end of it, Baz said he was packing it in… and that was the end of that basically."

Baz and Mick later turned up together, albeit briefly, in The Burning ("Which was more melodic punk really, a bit like Generation X or something"), and more recently Mick has been – by his own admission – a 'bass whore', standing in as a touring bassist for both (Birmingham death metal band) Benediction and Sensa Yuma, as well as playing for his own, now defunct, Sister Automatic.

"I don't think we were anything that special," he concludes modestly when asked about Dead Wretched's fine musical legacy. "There were loads of bands out there like us, but we did do two great singles and wrote some good songs. To be honest, it's very strange, and quite gratifying really, that there's still some interest in the band twenty years later. Who would've thought it?"

SELECT DISCOGRAPHY:
7"s:
'No Hope For The Wretched' (Inferno, 1982)
'Convicted' (Inferno, 1982)

AT A GLANCE:
Surprisingly there has yet to be any retrospective Dead Wretched CD, although US label Grand Theft Audio have just such a thing slated for release in the near future.

DRONGOS FOR EUROPE

The aforementioned Drongos For Europe were a relatively obscure punk band from the black heart of Birmingham, who did their first show on November 3rd 1979, and are still gigging actively today, seemingly getting better and better with each passing year. For that first show though, the band was made up of Tommy Farrell on vocals, Steve Devlin on guitar, Nigel 'Swainey' Swain on bass and Karl 'Gebs' Gebhard on drums, and Tommy sums that live debut up rather succinctly as, "We were so bad, it really was a night to remember!"

The Drongos were initially inspired to make their own music by the energy of early performances from bands such as The Adverts, Generation X and 999, and of course, as was so often the case with second wave punks, the banality of their own oppressive surroundings.

"Birmingham suffered a lot in the late Seventies and early Eighties," recalls Tommy. "Being an industrial city, obviously the recession bit hard, and unemployment was very high. 1979 equalled the Tories...equalled years of shite! And we are still paying the price now! New Labour? Spot the difference! I know I'm struggling to.

"I'm not sure whether living so far out of London made any difference to us," he ponders, on the question of why the band were never a big name outside of the Midlands. "We were so laid back about things, we never really wanted to push it that bit further. We were actually accused by one local journalist as being devoid of ambition... but we didn't really understand big words like that!

"What I'm trying to say is that we were too busy enjoying ourselves to make a proper go at obtaining any measure of success."

The band helped release their own debut EP in 1981, the 4-song 'Adverse Chorus' 7", which came out on Kite Records. They scrounged cheap studio time, borrowed some money off a local tattoo artist, Tony Lynx, and even glued all the sleeves together themselves. Although extremely rough and ready in both its execution and presentation, the band's distinctly raw style was already very evident, and the record – limited to one thousand copies – secured them a deal with local Indie label, Inferno, who also gave us early releases by The Varukers, Criminal Class from Coventry, and, of course, Dead Wretched.

The first fruit of this relationship was the excellent – and criminally underrated – 'Death's A Career' EP. By the time of its release in 1982, Swainey had been replaced on bass by Errol 'Ezz' Ullah, and the band were really coming into their own. All three cuts, from the bombastic title track to the infectiously anthemic 'Russian Delight', were a unique mixture of the sneer and swagger of punk's first wave ignited by the more aggressive, direct approach of its Second Coming. Some subtle (they were rather low in the mix) female vocals were provided by a friend of the band, Marie (aka 'Nightmare'!), who also wrote some of the lyrics for 'Split Breed'.

"She was a good friend at the time," explains Tommy. "I can't actually remember if she ever performed live

Live in Leeds, 1984
(Pic: Paul May)

with us. We eventually had a disagreement about unpaid royalties... so it goes! I think she is now living in Portugal."

A second EP, 'Eternity', soon followed, once again on Tempest, that saw the band rightfully gaining a strong local following. Not quite as memorable as the preceding release, it nevertheless featured three more solid tracks that really showcased Tommy's great gravelly voice. Further gigs were undertaken, and not all of them without incident.

Drongos For Europe, 1981
L-R: Tommy Farrell, Nigel Swain, Karl Gebhard, Steve Devlin
(Pic: Lozz Baker)

"We played in Burton in early '83," chuckles Tommy. "About fifty Brummie punks came along with us, and it was a great gig. Everyone enjoyed it so much that we all missed the bus home! So we set up camp in a derelict house right in the middle of the town centre, and made a huge bonfire – as you do! – that attracted the attention of the local constabulary, who decided it would be safer if they put us up for the night. They escorted us through town to the local nick; the girls were put up in the cells and the lads spent the night in the yard. Despite our surroundings, we had a great party, and we were all released from captivity early the next morning.

"A character called Lumberjack asked for some tea which they made for us in this giant tin teapot. Everyone had their fill, but Lumber could not get over the size of this pot and stamped on it until it was flat. It was such a naughty thing to do to the oh-so-kind policemen; I have never laughed so much in my life! He was still jumping up and down on it when the sergeant come to retrieve it, and Lumber, in typical style, tried to blame everyone else. Unforgettable."

Soon after 'Eternity', Ezz left, "To start a family" according to Tommy, and was replaced by Derek 'Dek' Baker.

"All the records were getting decent reviews in the music press at the time. Mr. Bushell actually said we were a cross between Crass and Anti Pasti... but I can't say that anyone else really agreed with that! When Dek joined he gave us a good kick up the arse, and we even ventured out of Brum for the occasional gig. I can remember playing the 100 Club and Skunx a couple of times, but with limited finance it was not easy... plus being out of it most of the time didn't help!"

Unfortunately, rather than push home their advantage with a full-length album, The Drongos fizzled away soon after, and didn't release anything else until 1990's 'This Town' 7" on Renegade, by which time Geb had been replaced by 'Big' Nigel Kerwan. A much poppier affair than their earlier Tempest singles, this EP is probably the most immediate Drongos record, with its insistent guitar hook and big singalong chorus. However it was to be many more years before there was further activity in the band's camp.

Tommy maintains that the band never actually split up during these long hiatuses; merely that they were doing other things. The vocalist himself spent some time living in Germany, whilst the other guys did time in various local bands, such as Slaughterhouse 5, The Burning and The Chocolate Starfish. And now it would appear that the Drongo star is waxing once again, as the band have been out treading the boards and winning over new audiences at various high-profile festivals.

"Dek met up with Jock from GBH and they ended up getting quite drunk together," Tommy explains the catalyst for their latest surge of activity. "Jock basically convinced him that it would be a good idea to get DFE back together again. We had all kept in touch anyway, so we gave it a go.

"Our official 'comeback' gig was with GBH and the UK Subs, so a big thank you to them both. I don't think any of us realised what The Drongos meant to some of our older fans, and their support and kind words have convinced me that this was the right thing to do. But we don't want it to be purely nostalgic, so it is vitally important for us that we take the band onwards by writing new material... though obviously we can't ignore our back catalogue either."

And with the release of 2003's excellent 'Barcode Generation' CD on Dislocate, and another brand new album in the making, it's very apparent that the best is still to come from this unassuming band. They've matured enough so as to stay relevant, but have kept sight of that all-important edge to their sound that always made them so exciting in the first place.

"The Drongos For Europe are a punk band, that's it!" says Tommy in closing. "That's all they have ever been and that's all they ever can be! If you like it, great; if you don't, we don't care!"

SELECT DISCOGRAPHY:
7"s:
'Adverse Chorus' EP (1981, Kite)
'Death's A Career' EP (1982, Tempest)
'Eternity' EP (1982, Tempest)
'This Town' (1990, Renegade)
'Wasted' (Intimidation, 2001)

AT A GLANCE:
US label Grand Theft Audio have plans to release all the band's old material on one retrospective CD, but for now the singles collection CD on Data, 'Return Of The Punk Monster', is an excellent place to start.

CADAVEROUS CLAN

Even more obscure than the Drongos was the short-lived Cadaverous Clan. Comprising Stewart Goldie on vocals, Damien Thompson on guitar, David Wright on bass and Mark Harrison on drums, the band only did one proper demo and a handful of gigs around Birmingham. They did however enter the 'official' annals of punkdom when they secured themselves a place on Volume Two of No Future's successful 'A Country Fit For Heroes' compilations.

"I got into punk in 1978, when I was about sixteen years old," begins Mark. "This might sound a bit weird, but I was really into Star Wars and stuff, and I used to love dressing up. One of my mates was a punk, and I used to like how he looked. And I saw Sid Vicious in all the papers, and I loved the fact that he was such an anti-hero, so I went out and bought 'Never Mind The Bollocks'... and I haven't looked back since!"

Mark was originally in a young punk band called Wild Youth, but then he and Damien, who was living in Lichfield at the time, formed Wrong Attitude.

"Damien was on bass, Wayne 'Freeby' Freeman was the singer, and we had a guy called Anarchy Joe (aka Barry Chesterfield) on guitar," laughs Mark. "We used to practise in Damien's bedroom. We only did a couple of gigs around Lichfield, in pubs like the Bridge Tavern, and then we split up."

The duo then recruited school friend David Wright, and Stewart Goldie, whom they had met at punk gigs in the city, and took the rather unusual name of Cadaverous Clan.

"We went up to that Xmas On Earth gig in Leeds," explains Mark. "And I saw a huge Scottish punk there, with this massive mohican, and he had 'The Cult Clan' painted on the back of his leather. I liked the word 'Clan', and we decided to use it in our name. I picked the word 'Cadaverous', basically because we thought it sounded cool, and I was really into all those old Hammer Horror films... I had quite morbid interests really."

The band entered Rich Bitch Studios in Birmingham on October 16th 1982 and recorded a rather fine seven-song demo, that incorporated some thrash and metal influences into the traditional punk formula to decent effect. Although admittedly generic, it was well executed, with great gusto, and gives more than a passing nod to local heroes GBH, Stewart's vocals especially reminiscent in places of Colin Abrahall.

"Damien really loved Discharge and all those thrash bands, whilst I was more into slower, powerful stuff. Like I said, I loved The Pistols, but I was also really into Motörhead; I loved Phil Taylor's drumming. Actually, I almost tried out for Discharge when Tez left! I met some of them at one of their gigs, and they told me they needed a drummer, and asked if I wanted to try out, but we never got as far as actually arranging an audition!"

As mentioned earlier, the demo earned them a place on 'A Country Fit For Heroes, Volume Two', with the speedy crossover track, 'Snow Blindness'. Unfortunately they split soon after the album's release, despite the favourable response to their contribution.

Damien went on to form the awesome Sacrilege, a grinding metal-punk band who, in 1985, released the classic 'Behind The Realms Of Madness' 12" on Children Of The Revolution Records. They then signed to Under One Flag, a subsidiary of metal giants Music For Nations, for whom they did two powerful albums, 'Within The Prophecy' (1987) and 'Turn Back Trilobite' (1989).

Mark meanwhile did a stint behind the kit with Drongos For Europe, bizarrely changing his surname to Baskerville in the process!

"Well, I was never happy being called Harrison," he reckons. "My dad was quite a famous singer, in a band called the Karl Denver Trio, who did the original version of that song, 'Wimoweh'. His real name was Angus Mackenzie, which is the surname I use nowadays, but back then I was working in a graveyard, and I changed my name to Baskerville... just for a laugh really! It only cost 15p at the time, and I mainly did it just to see the look on my mum's face! I remember they all used to howl at me in the dole office when my name was called out!"

AT A GLANCE:

Both volumes of 'A Country Fit For Heroes' were compiled onto one CD by Captain Oi in 1994, but the only way to hear the Cadaverous Clan demo in its entirety would be to write directly to Mark c/o 120 Booths Farm Rd., Great Barr, Birmingham, B42 2NS, England, enclosing sufficient postage for a guaranteed reply.

SENSA YUMA

A lthough they never released anything officially during the Eighties, Sensa Yuma were an important part of the Midlands punk scene, garnering themselves a large local following, with members going on to play in some very influential bands. They split up in 1988, only to reform in 1995, since when they have released several highly enjoyable singles and albums.

The original line-up got together in 1979, but the first solid incarnation of Sensa Yuma coalesced around 1981, with founding member Agz on vocals, Trog and Adey Davies (formerly in The Collaborators with Stu) on guitars, 'Minty' Nige Everal (formerly with Disabled) on bass, and Stu 'Pid' Jones (who would later front the band in the Nineties) on drums.

"The name came from a house in a little place called Brockton!" explains Stu. "This house was actually called Sensa Yuma, and one day, Agz knocked on the door and asked where this cool nameplate came from. It was carved out of wood and came from overseas, and apparently the boat it came over on sank, and the plane it ended up on had difficulties as well, so it was kind of a doomed name from the start. We were little kids at the time, but we fell in love with it, and that's what we called our band. You've got to have a Sensa Yuma, haven't you?"

Despite being widely regarded as a Birmingham band, with most of the members being born and eventually relocating back there, Sensa Yuma did in fact start life in Stafford, which at the time boasted a more than healthy punk scene for such a small market town. The crux of activity was the local punk club, the Riverside, which is where the various band members all initially met. They wasted little time in getting started.

"We used to practise in an art room in the local youth club, which was fantastic. I bought my first drum kit for something like £50, which seemed a helluva lot of money at the time, a battered old thing with half ruined cymbals. I raised the money for it by peeling potatoes in the local chip shop after school! All our gear was very basic, but we just used to turn it up a bit and bash away. The first Sensa Yuma gigs were hysterically bad! One of the first was with The Filth at the Dawley Town Hall in Telford. If I remember rightly, we'd been sniffing glue all night, and when it came time for us to play, I was sat behind my kit, collapsed over the drums, one cheek pressed against the snare drum… which happened a lot back then and is something I'm very embarrassed about now. It was an absolute shambles, to be honest, but people picked up on our songs very quickly. Stuff like 'Every Day's Your Last Day'; we still play them now, and people still love them. The first time people hear those songs today, they pick up on them exactly the same way people did back then – only difference is we can play them a bit better now!

"I remember being very nervous before our first gig, and the girl who owned the chip shop where I worked gave me a valium. Thing is, she didn't tell me what it did, and I had a few pints of snakebite before we played, so then I lost the plot halfway through, but I didn't give a shit by then anyway!

"We were fuelled by speed and alcohol a lot of the time. And glue, of course. I'm not ashamed of that, everybody was doing it. It was a cheap drug really… we'd just left school, so where were we going to get £10 for a gram of speed? A tube of glue was only 60p! It was a shit drug as well, but it kept us entertained.

"But everybody really enjoyed the band anyway. It was basic, but it was honest. Even today, when you get past a certain stage where you release a record and people come to see you because they like your music, it isn't as personal as those early gigs when people just turned up 'cos they were your mates. And even if you

Sensa Yuma, Stafford, 1980
L–R: Minty Nige, Agz, Stu Pid, Adey Davies

were a pile of shit, which I'm sure we were, because of the camaraderie and stuff, and because of how funny it all was, people couldn't help but be attracted to it. That's very personal, street-level punk rock, which is where we still are now, basically playing gigs to see all our mates and party hard!"

The band only recorded one demo during their Eighties period, which Stu didn't even play on because it was recorded when the band had kicked him out in favour of a more heavy metal drummer. However, the band's hardcore punk following weren't impressed with the flashy new rhythm section, and Stu was soon back behind the kit, and many more gigs were undertaken around the Midlands.

"Most of our gigs were eventful for one reason or another," he laughs. "We played a CND benefit in Cannock, and there was a jazz band on after us. The place was packed with Sensa Yuma fans, and the jazz band actually cut us off about halfway through our ninth song, to a hail of glasses and abuse. And these skinheads turned up, and battered the promoter – of a CND festival, which obviously wasn't the right thing to do – and terrorised the whole audience. The jazz band played a lot quicker than normal, just so they could hurry up and get off, and we were outside after, loading the gear into my mate Simon's furniture removal van. There were about forty of us piled in the back, and there were about twenty glue-sniffing skinheads 'monging out' with us too, dribbling and threatening everybody who was trapped in there 'cos there was no way out; it had one of those roller shutter doors! All good fun.

"Later on, we ended up at a squat party, and one of the skins stabbed someone, which wasn't so funny. So the police came, and Agz our lead singer was shagging some girl upstairs; he jumped out the top window, with his trousers at half-mast, down into the garden to escape the police running up the stairs, and left this rather embarrassed girl spread-eagled on the bed!"

Unfortunately punk's often blasé attitude towards drugs led to many a tragedy, and it was one such regrettable incident that ultimately led to the demise of the original Sensa Yuma.

"We were living in a squat, about eighteen of us, and probably the darkest day for all of us was when we woke up and found one of our friends, Dwayne Darwood, dead from heroin, and were then arrested for – allegedly – killing him, which obviously didn't stick. For most of us, that heralded the end; he was the closest person to us, almost a fifth member. A lot of things changed that day. We played his funeral, and did another gig soon after that was wrecked by skinheads, and we just got disillusioned with it all. The music was changing, the scene was changing; Adey Davies started getting into metal, Iron Maiden and stuff like that, which was completely the opposite direction to what we were doing! And we all knew it was the end, so we spilt in '88."

Stu moved on to join Contempt in 1993 and form the superbly dark and heavy Police Bastard before joining The English Dogs for several years in the mid-Nineties. Then in 1995, he reformed Sensa Yuma for a one-off show (a benefit for the MacMillan Fund, after one of his friends died of cancer) with members of GBH and Police Bastard. And, in various guises, supplemented by members of bands such as Doom, Dead Wretched, Drongos For Europe, In The Shit and POA, they've been together ever since.

The belated debut album, 'Every Day's Your Last Day', was finally recorded in 1997 by the core line-up of Stu, Agz and Minty Nige, with guitar and bass being handled by Jock and Ross of GBH, and the drums by Clive from Police Bastard.

The band have recently taken on a more international flavour since Stu moved to Spain, and recruited Mad Max on drums, Manual Lopez and Rafa on guitars, Frederick Verstraete (formerly with respected Dutch punks, Funeral Dress), and Seano Porno (aka Sean McCann) from Birmingham band, Dogshit Sandwich. Still playing frequently all over Europe, and with an excellent new album, 'Up Yours', just released in 2004 on Iron Man/Mass Productions, Sensa Yuma remain a band of great integrity and dedication.

"We put 110% into every live performance, and consequently the audience have a good time, and as long as the people who pay their money have a good night out, then it makes the 1000-mile drive to the next gig or whatever worthwhile. I'm just pleased to have been a part of it, not having just sat on my arse but having really worked for the punk scene and helped create something positive and enjoyed it at the same time."

SELECT DISCOGRAPHY:
7"s:
'Every Day's Your Last Day' (Ruptured Ambitions, 1997)

CDs:
'Every Day's Your Last Day' (Retch, 1997)

AT A GLANCE:
The brilliant new 'Up Yours' album is far superior to the 1997 CD on Retch and should appeal to even the most discerning fans of hard streetwise punk.

THE STENCH

After the demise of the rather good first wave band Neon Hearts, nearby Wolverhampton, traditionally a haven for rockers and metalheads, found itself strangely devoid of recording punk bands, until a bunch of young outcasts kick-started the scene back into life. Although musically poor, The Stench were outrageous and obnoxious enough to light up the city's underground for a brief time, more on the strength of their anti-social antics than any sort of creative ability. They formed in the summer of 1981, and their original line-up was Pete O' Shea – vocals, 'Tommo' – guitar, 'Maff' – bass ("Last names didn't seem so important back then!"), and Darrell 'Daz' Davies – drums.

"The early rehearsals were diabolical," laughs Pete. "We just made a fuckin' noise for the first few sessions. They put us in a classroom, in Tommo and Maff's school, right at the back – as far away from anyone as possible, 'cos our noise was that bad. We rehearsed on Monday and Thursday nights, and it cost us the princely sum of 10p each... I had to join the school youth club to get it cheap! We were absolutely fuckin' terrible, but it was fun and something to do.

"The first song we knocked up was 'Raspberry Cripple'. Our equipment was prehistoric. We used to meet up at Daz's house (who was the only one that could store the gear in his shed), load up this big wooden trolley with his kit and various amps, and push the fucker up the hill to the school. All the local snotty-nosed kids would come out and throw things and shout abuse at these punks pushing a trolley full of gear!"

Things became a little more serious when Tommo left, to be replaced by Shane Williams, who could actually play a few chords, and the band bought a second hand PA from their music teacher. Soon after, they made their live debut – playing thirty minutes in between the DJs at the annual youth club disco.

"We did eight songs and it was terrifying!" says Pete incredulously. "You wanna try and play in front of about sixty 11-15 year old school kids! They literally ripped us apart once they got the bottle to get within gobbing distance! We retired to the local pub soaked in chocolate and pop that they spat on us continuously for twenty-five minutes. Two local beat cops came in to survey the noise and damage and actually looked sorry for us, haha! Maff left shortly after – he'd had his fifteen minutes –and was replaced by Nigel Grove, who I knew from Wednesfield."

As the only spiky-topped band out there at the time, The Stench soon found themselves with management, in the shape of Jane Plimmer and Andy Carlin ("A duo of arty punks from the rich suburbs of Finchfield, Wolverhampton..."), and a recording deal with Sticky, a local label being run by a soul DJ called Pep ("One of those entrepreneurs around the country at the time who saw punk as a way of making a few quid.")

Before they knew it, they were in Birmingham's Outlaw Studios, where the likes of Drongos For Europe and Dead Wretched had already recorded, with engineer Phil Savage. They recorded eight tracks in less than a day, including 'Nowhere', 'Monstrosity', 'Oxfam Poster', and 'Student

Squat', naively leaving Savage to do their mix for them whilst they adjourned to the nearest pub. Of course, it sounded awful, but nonetheless Sticky released 'Raspberry Cripple', 'Nonces' and 'Adoption' as the 'Moral Debauchery' 7" in early '82. Badly recorded and played, it hardly stands as a shining example of the genre, but its spiteful lyrics, and the insane live shows the band were playing to promote it, ensured it was difficult to ignore.

The Stench, live at the Exile, Wolverhampton, supporting GBH, March 1982

"I regard it as a failure," admits Pete, when discussing the single with the benefit of hindsight. "It was a very naive, basic attempt by a band who couldn't really play very well. But I blame us as a band for that and our ignorance of the music scene and how to make a record. We got ripped off by the label for £250 each... our management did the best they could under difficult circumstances, but they were too green by half and we were too wild to take the opportunity to create something good or cover our own arses."

Thanks to their now-infamous appearance on Beacon Radio, which was brought to a premature end when the band just got too rowdy in the studio ("I think someone got a slap... I can't remember who it was, but it wasn't one of us," sneers the vocalist), The Stench's notoriety was growing. And let's not forget Pete's friend, 'Sid' Nicholls, who used to accompany the band to shows and once upstaged them by drawing a syringe full of blood from his arm and spraying it over the horrified audience.

"Anarchy Sid, or Dennis Nicholls as he was christened, was a real fucking character and one of the most notorious of the Wolverhampton punks. He did everything and more that anyone's ever written or said about him. He was fucking mad and a great laugh. Daz, Shane and Nige hated him... he even had a scrap with Daz at one local gig, supporting The Partisans; it was like watching two cats fight.

"He was my mate though, so I bought him along to gigs when he wasn't inside. He even held up a building society for £800 with an element from a kettle wrapped in a plastic bag! He was soon arrested later that day, getting off the train at Euston, London, and in typical Sid fashion, he said to the cops, 'You could've at least let me spend some of it first!' He got five years for that.

"He was destined for a sad end though, and in between regular spells in prison he relocated to London for good and got into smack. He had a son with the lead singer of Decadent Few... they split up though, probably 'cos of his reckless lifestyle. He then left London, or had to go for his own safety 'cos he was in so much trouble, but was sadly found dead a few years ago in a homeless hostel in Canterbury from a heroin OD. He'll always be remembered in Wolverhampton"

After playing as far afield as Chelmsford with The UK Subs (although Pete and Nige were arrested on the way home because the vehicle they were in didn't actually belong to them!) and Bradford (the Palm Cove Club, where Pete got stabbed in the leg with a screwdriver by an offended bouncer after their set), The Stench split when their second demo turned out just as bad as their first one.

"I had some fun and adventures in The Stench," recalls Pete fondly. "We made a record that's become much sought after by young American punks, so I've not got as many regrets as you'd expect. You have to remember my time in The Stench was at the height of the early Eighties punk boom, so lots of other stuff was going on at the same time. The Stench was just a small part of those adventures. The only thing I really regret is not paying more attention to the recording sessions, but you live 'n' learn."

Pete turned up in the Nineties in a band called Torcha Shed, who recorded several demos, but whose unstable line-up prevented them releasing anything officially, and he now runs the Nihilism On The Prowl website.

"I retired from bands; they are way too much trouble, being a fucking babysitter, minder and secretary all at the same time. I prefer doin' stuff on my own, 'cos you don't have to rely on others. Fronting a punk band is for the young, loud and snotty, not anyone over thirty, in my humble opinion. I prefer to write about punk now. I'm totally independent, have no egos to contend with, and still get excited about discovering new bands."

SELECT DISCOGRAPHY:
7"s:
'Moral Debauchery' (Sticky, 1982)

AT A GLANCE:
No such thing, fortunately, although if you visit Pete's site and ask him nicely he might be persuaded to copy you some of their stuff.

A s The Stench were playing their first shows around town, a new breed of punk band was also making itself known in Wolverhampton, no doubt inspired by anarcho bands such as the Subhumans and The Sears playing there as part of their national tours. The local polytechnic was spawning a more politically aware punk scene, and three of those bands – the female-fronted Pulex Irritans, Vendetta and 7th Plague – appeared with two tracks each on the 'Aristocrap' EP, which came out on Relegated Records (the label run by Pulex Irritans' bassist, Nick Moss) in 1984. It's a decent snapshot of some articulate punk rock bands in their infancy, although it suffers with a horribly thin production.

All the bands on the EP used to practise in the cellar of a house in St. Mark's Road, in the Chapel Ash area of Wolverhampton. Vendetta guitarist, Martin, went on to form the aforementioned Contempt, who played their first show in the summer of '84, and have been around in various guises ever since. Once 7th Plague split up, their vocalist Mark 'Borstal' Shaw (who later drummed briefly in Pete's Torcha Shed) joined Contempt as well, first as singer then as drummer.

THE VARUKERS

E lsewhere, The Varukers were the original Discore band, the first and best of the hardcore punk acts to take the simple yet devastatingly effective formula laid down by Discharge and play it as fast, hard and heavy as they could. Formed in Leamington Spa in 1979 by vocalist Anthony 'Rat' Martin, the first line-up of the band also included Bruce Riddel and Tom Lowe on guitars, Garry Maloney on bass, and 'some other guy called Gary' on drums.

"Basically we formed The Varukers because I saw The Sex Pistols on 'Top Of The Pops' and wanted a piece of that!" exclaims Rat. "I think the majority of people in the punk scene tried their hand at something or other – it just seemed so exciting after hours of watching shit bands on TV like Abba, The Bay City Rollers, and Boney M.

"And back then, The Varukers was the first thing we had ever attempted musically. Before we came together as a band, everybody just sat in their bedrooms masturbating or trying to learn to play an instrument. I just had a big gob so my choice was made for me – vocalist!"

Local gigs were undertaken and the band began to steadily accumulate a following, although not without incident.

"The first proper gig we did was quite eventful. It was at a community centre in our hometown Leamington Spa, with a local band, Flack Off. A coach load of fascist skinheads came from Coventry, and they didn't seem to like us – mind you, we had a Jamaican bass player and a half-caste guitarist... oh fuck. Anyway, it ended in a riot; a full beer can hit me in the face, and about ten skins got me in the corner kicking the shit out of me. I felt an arm come around my neck, and I looked up and it was my mother – she was wading in to protect me! I was shocked but also very relieved.

"Anyway, we managed to get the gear and ourselves out of the venue. I went home and my mum went to a nightclub; she loves a bit of dancing. The next morning, her boyfriend – I can't remember his name, so let's just call him 'Tosser' – sat at the edge of my bed and told me he wanted me out of punk rock. He offered to buy me a scooter and a suit... I think he wanted me to be a Mod! I said, 'Can I think about it?' and then before he got to the door, I said, 'Nah, thanks but no thanks!"

In 1980, a four-track demo was recorded. Featuring 'Punk Ain't Dead', 'Varuker', 'No Education' and 'Government's To Blame' (which was by far the strongest track and later re-recorded for their debut album), it was much more traditional punk in feel than the high-speed thrash they would later become famous for. Soon after that session, the drummer left, which resulted in the band becoming a four-piece with Garry moving to drums, and Tom taking over on bass.

Rat of The Varukers, circa 1984

Bruce took a copy of their second demo into the Tempest Record shop in Birmingham, to ask if they knew any record companies he could send it to, only to discover that Keith Thornton and Brian Harris who ran the store were starting their own punk label, Inferno. And in March 1982, the 'Protest To Survive' EP by The Varukers became the first release. A formidable slice of noise, it spent over a month in the Indie Charts, only narrowly missing out on making the Top Thirty, and certainly captured the imaginations of punks everywhere, whose jackets were soon daubed with the band's impaled skull logo.

The Varukers' Rat and Marvin, live in Japan, 2000

Garry Maloney left after 'Protest To Survive' to join Discharge (just in time to play on their debut album and the 'Never Again' single), and was replaced by Brian 'Brains' Rowe. The next release was the 'Don't Wanna Be A Victim' single which reached No. 15 in the Indies during the summer of '82; the title track was actually a rousing mid-tempo singalong, but the two B-side cuts were suitably frantic.

After that single, Tom left ("I don't think he got on with Brains, to be honest!") to join Anti-Sect, the anarcho grind band based in nearby Daventry, and new bassist George was dropped in at the deep end as The Varukers entered the studio to record their debut album. But things were afoot behind the scenes, and they left Inferno before the album could be released.

"We were getting a little bit pissed off with them," reckons Rat. "It seemed to take forever between the first releases; it probably didn't but we were very keen and impatient. We actually recorded our debut album 'Bloodsuckers' for Inferno, but then I contacted Riot City to see if they were interested in us. They were and so they bought the album off Inferno. Riot City had better distribution and advertised their releases a lot better, so we were pleased."

That debut album was everything fans of the band hoped it would be, and more – well played and produced, it took all the youthful aggression of the first two singles and captured it perfectly without compromising clarity for ferocity, or vice versa. Released in late 1983, and no doubt benefiting from having a more experienced label behind it, the album was the band's first Indie Top Ten hit.

However, the tiresome and predictable personnel changes came as thick and fast as the releases back then, and 'Broken Bric' stepped in to fill the departing George's shoes, and he debuted with the marvellous 'Die For Your Government' single. Still regarded by many as the definitive Varukers release, it combined the band's potent speed and power with the subtlest trace of melody, and the result was one of the finest tunes of the whole second wave of UK punk rock. No surprise then that it was the band's biggest-selling release, peaking at No. 5 in the Indies.

The band's profile was helped immensely by their appearance on the punk documentary 'UK/DK', Christopher Collins and Ken Lawrence's 'Film About Punks And Skinheads', that saw them rubbing shoulders with such genre heavyweights as The Exploited, Vice Squad and Blitz. The featured song, 'Soldier Boy', has been a staple in the band's live set ever since.

"There have nearly been riots at shows where we've told the crowd we ain't doing it!" laughs Rat. "But hey, we're just messing with ya!"

Then Brains and Brian left, the former to explore musical pastures anew, the latter because he'd become a father again, but the ever-stoical Rat drafted in new drummer Andy Baker and guitarist Damien Thompson, both of whom had been with Lichfield band War Wound. The new line-up sparked off each other immediately and the primal roar of the 'Led To The Slaughter' single could soon be heard howling up the Independent Charts. It appeared in March '83, and was followed in August of that year by the staggeringly brutal 'Another Religion, Another War' 12". Eight songs of blinding thrash, it saw The Varukers moving into a class of their own in the intensity stakes.

However before the 12" was even being pressed, Bric fled for higher ground, and was replaced by Tony May. "I think the final straw came during the recording of the 'Another Religion, Another War' EP," reveals Rat. "Tony's picture is on the cover but he didn't play on it. Come to think of it, he didn't record anything with us. Anyway, we were staying in Rochdale, where we did a lot of our recordings, and one night I fancied a game of pool. I can't play that well – I'm a typical hit-and-hoper. Still, we walked around the town and I peaked through the window of this one pub and saw a pool table in there. But I didn't go in; I didn't like the vibe I was getting… and was I right, or was I right?

"We carried on walking, then out of this pub first came two lads, then four, then eight… and eventually about twenty of them came streaming out. We obviously kept walking, getting faster and faster, into a canter, then a gallop – then into full Sebastian Coe mode! The chase was on! These guys were shouting something like, 'Where are you from? Lancashire or Yorkshire?' So, Bric in his infinite wisdom tried to reason with them and told them that we were from Warwickshire! Wallop! They whacked him anyway. Bric tear-arsed it past us, and we ran into this pub… why, I don't know. It could've been the proverbial lion's den! And we were the supper – complete with delivery service!

"I ran straight up to the bar, leaned across and said, 'I think you better call the cops, there's gonna be some blood shed – mainly ours!' I looked at our drummer Andy Baker's face and for a split second saw a look there that said, 'I wish I had never joined this band!'

"Luckily the guys never came in, just stood around outside until a local from this boozer went out and reasoned with them and they all fucked off. A taxi was ordered; we were bundled into it and dropped off back at the B&B where we were staying – the driver didn't even want any money off us. On the way there he told us that during the preceding weeks there had been a lot of trouble between Lancashire and Yorkshire, and the guys from the pub thought we were from Yorkshire. So, I didn't get my game of pool and soon after that, Bric had had enough."

In early 1984, The Varukers paid their first visit to mainland Europe. Upon their return, Damien and Tony left the band (they formed the Birmingham thrash metal act Sacrilege), and were replaced by guitarist Paul Miles and bassist Graham Kerr, who quickly found themselves back in Europe on tour.

"Paul and Graham responded to an ad we put in Sounds," reveals Rat. "They were both from a small town in Wales, so they were chuffed to be in a band that was doing something. And before you ask, no, I can't remember the band they were in before us!

"The second European tour was a blast, we were playing with The Mau Maus from Sheffield; they were a great band and that's how we met Dunk from Rot Records – he was driving them around. He said then that he wanted to put something out by us."

With the untimely demise of Riot City, The Varukers took Dunk up on his offer, and the 'Massacred Millions' 12" was their Rot debut. As fast and raucous as you'd expect, the four-track EP went to No. 30 in the Indies upon its release during Christmas 1984.

Rot also issued the rather slapdash 'Live In Holland' LP. Recorded in the Dutch town of Hengelo on June 29th 1984, the record ably illustrates the relentless pace of the band, but it sounds like it was recorded in a bucket and is best avoided unless you're a Varukers completist.

1985's 'One Struggle, One Fight' was much better, a rampant thrash attack with tracks such as 'We Hint At Things Nuclear' and 'How Can Your Conscience Allow This To Go On?' not only continuing their vicious sonic assault but also their strong anti-war stance that had been a staple of the band's aesthetic since their 'Protest To Survive' debut.

By this time though, Andy Baker had left to join Damien and Tony in Sacrilege, and had been replaced first by Gilb (ex-Dirge), and then Warren, who actually played on the album. However, he left straight after, forced to return home to Rochdale to tend to some family problems there, and was replaced by Kevin Frost from Cerebral Fix. And in 1986, second guitarist, Ian 'Biff' Smith, from Northampton's Death Sentence (who now also fronts Sick On The Bus, one of the finest punk bands of modern times), was added to the line-up ("As if we hadn't been having enough trouble keeping four people together!" laughs Rat. "Gluttons for punishment or what?") for some added power.

Biff's first show with The Varukers was supporting Discharge who were touring to promote their much-maligned 'Grave New World' album.

"It was at the Klub Foot in London, and we had a blinder of a show, but it was so sad to see Discharge playing all that 'Grave New World' crap and the hatred directed at them from the audience was unbelievable."

Other shows were played around the UK with the likes of GBH, but the lethargy that infected the majority of the second wave punk bands as the Eighties drew to a close also had its teeth into The Varukers... Of course, they didn't stay 'dead' for long.

"The band split in 1987 because we just ran out of enthusiasm really," admits Rat. "And we really didn't wanna do what Discharge had done and drag the band's name through the shit.

"But when something has been a big part of your life for so long, it's hard to let go completely. We missed it and thought we still had a lot to do, and, around 1993, the support we were getting through the mail gave us the kick-start we needed to try again – so it's all your own fault, you fuckers!"

Rat, Biff and Kevin Frost were joined on bass by Brian, and their official comeback record was the aptly-titled 'Nothing's Changed' single for Nottingham-based Weird Records. The rabid response from fans world-wide led to tours of America, Scandinavia and Japan in 1994, and the band signed to German label, We Bite, who in 1995 released the 'Still Bollox But Still Here' CD. Recorded at Premier Studios in Corby, it was basically the band's favourite tracks from their gloriously noisy past re-recorded with the benefit of a better budget, better gear and better musicianship. Thankfully none of the jagged edges that made the originals so endearing were lost in the process.

We Bite also issued a brand new Varukers studio album the same year, the splendidly fast and heavy 'Murder', by which time Brian had been replaced on bass by Canadian-born Kieran Plunkett, formerly with The Restarts. Forced then to rely on stand-in musicians for touring commitments when Kieran returned home – including Les and Mark from UKHC group Concrete Sox, Kenko from Swedish Discore band Meanwhile, Todd from US punks Distraught, and Justin from Iron Monkey – The Varukers eventually conscripted Marv (ex-Chaos UK) as their permanent bassist.

The superb, metal-tinged 'How Do You Sleep? CD was released by American label, Go Kart, and saw the band not only returning to Japan, but also touring Australia, New Zealand and Brazil for the first time. The album was released in South America by Peculio Records, and the band returned to Brazil for a second string of gigs, before Kev left to be replaced by the Portuguese drummer, Ricardo Fernandez. Shaun Duggan from Hard To Swallow has recently joined the band on second guitar too, and they are currently working on brand new material and planning yet more ambitious trips to take their uncompromising punk rock to all the corners of the globe.

"I think that last album we put out is our best – great songs, great production. And I also think our current line-up is our best too – there's some great guys with me. Biff, Marv, Shaun and young Ricardo… we work well together, and we are good mates as well as playing in a band together. The chemistry is really good; anyone who has seen us recently will agree. We try to make all our shows fun, no matter how big or small. I can't really remember having a truly bad gig… we take each one as it comes, just get out there and give it some bollocks."

In 2003, as well as doing The Varukers, Rat joined a revitalised Discharge when their vocalist Cal refused to tour to promote their self-titled comeback album. As well as an East Coast US tour, he's played several large European festivals with the band, who have another new studio album scheduled for late 2004 on Stoke-based Thunk Records, the label ran by Fish, guitarist with The Skeptix. Busier than ever, Rat remains committed to the cause of punk rock.

"It feels great to be playing with them because Tez, Bones and Rainy want to get the band back some real credibility. So we're playing all the stuff with real bollocks, classics like 'Fight Back', 'Decontrol', 'Hell On Earth'… and obviously I'm trying to put my stamp on it, so things are going well on that front.

"And as long as there are people out there still playing it, and people out there who want to see it, things look good for punk rock, and we all have a purpose in life. I mean, what else are we good at? Being a punk rock vocalist is the only thing I can do well!"

SELECT DISCOGRAPHY:
7"s:
'Protest To Survive' (Inferno, 1982)
'Don't Wanna Be A Victim' (Inferno, 1982)
'Die For Your Government' (Riot City, 1983)
'Led To The Slaughter' (Riot City, 1984)
'Nothing's Changed' (Weird, 1994)

12"s:
'Another Religion, Another War' (Riot City, 1984)
'Massacred Millions' (Rot, 1984)

LPs:
'Bloodsuckers' (Riot City, 1983)
'Live In Holland' (Rot, 1984)
'One Struggle, One Fight' (Rot, 1985)
'Still Bollox But Still Here' (We Bite, 1995)
'Murder' (We Bite, 1995)
'How Do You Sleep?' (Go Kart, 2000)

AT A GLANCE:
As the title suggests, the 2004 Anagram CD, 'Varukers: The Riot City Years', compiles the best of the band's Riot City recordings and is a great overview of that period. Meanwhile, Punkcore's 'Vintage Varukers: Rare And Unreleased' CD compiles thirteen of the band's earliest and most elusive recordings, but isn't exactly indicative of how they sound now. For that it is necessary to check out their latest – and most impressive – 'How Do You Sleep?' CD.

THE SAMPLES

 oving an hour south to Worcester, The Samples were responsible for one of the very best singles on No Future, but never had the opportunity to release a full album. If they had, they may well have shot to the upper echelons of the punk pecking order, such was their instinctive grasp of strong songwriting. They paved the way for other Worcester bands, such as Exacerbator, Achtung, Alienation and The Iranian Teaspoons, none of which actually released vinyl but tapped into the punk network they helped establish.

The original band, formed in 1978, consisted of three schoolmates – bassist Pascal Smith, drummer Tony Allen and guitarist Dave Saunders – who were soon joined by Sean 'Badger' Taylor on vocals.

"The local scene was pretty poor," claims Sean. "Although there were a couple of bands from nearby Malvern, most noticeably The Vendettas and The Tights (who released the first ever single on local label, Cherry Red). Of course, there was Satan's Rats from Evesham too, but not much else – certainly not from Worcester anyway, which seemed to be a very backward city."

"The one great thing about the local scene was that Cherry Red regularly promoted punk and New Wave gigs at the Malvern Winter Gardens," chips in guitarist Dave Evans, who joined just before the band's first self-released single. "Without those there would have been nothing of any significance locally. It always seemed weird to me that this town (Malvern) which was basically where people went to retire or die – at least that's what it looked like to an average sixteen year old – had punk rock gigs in the local theatre hall… very strange but I'm so glad they did. These gigs drew their audiences from the bigger towns roundabout, like Worcester, Gloucester, Cheltenham and Hereford, so were always well attended. I just remember this surreal scene of all these punk rockers getting on the train at Worcester, arriving at Malvern and then threading their way up to the Winter Gardens… it felt like something was really happening and it was great to be part of this scene."

The first Samples gig was at Worcester's Blessed Edwards Oldcorne RC High School, an establishment that had actually been attended by three of the band, and where they played an eight-song set that included two Ramones covers.

"The most memorable thing about it was that there were two nuns selling crisps," laughs Sean. "How punk rock is that?"

Dave's first gig with the band, bolstering them to a five-piece, albeit briefly, was at the Nag's Head in Malvern, supporting The Denizens.

"I was shitting myself with nerves," he laughs. "I also remember that the reason I joined The Samples was a) they had a manager and b) they had a Transit van. This was almost like joining a real band!"

More gigs around the area, including one supporting The Fall at the aforementioned Malvern Winter Gardens, saw them accruing a good local following, and, suitably encouraged, they decided to self-release their first single, the three-track 'Vendetta' EP in 1980.

"We just wanted to put something out!" says Sean. "Basically no one else in Worcester had done this and we saw a chance to get there first, in those days, releasing a self-financed single was all the rage and easy to do. All the independent distributors around meant that it was very difficult to fail! I seem to recall that all of the main ones were more than happy to take copies and get them distributed out to small record shops, which were everywhere in those days but seem to have disappeared now."

It was recorded for a pittance in a local four-track studio, but what it lacks in technical elegance, it almost compensates for in youthful bluster.

"We did the whole thing in a day… and it sounds like it!" says Dave. "I seem to recall hiring a guitar from the local shop as I thought that my Les Paul copy wasn't up to the job. It didn't seem to make much difference, though – the sound is/was terrible. I remember that 'Vendetta' was one of the first tunes I'd written and presented to the band and, at the time, it was miles ahead of most of their old stuff. 'Computer Future' and 'Rabies' (the two B-side cuts) were older Samples songs from before I joined… 'Rabies' was always great live.

"At that time, we were all very much learning our craft; literally, as each week went by, I

The Samples from Worcester, 'responsible for one of the very best singles on No Future...' L-R: Sean Taylor, Tony Allen, Dave Evans, Pascal Smith (Pic: Chris Berry)

remember us getting better and better. By the time we eventually released the single, we had moved on and were writing much better songs. It's fair to say that it obviously represented a time in our development but if we had recorded it two weeks later it would have been a lot better – that's how quickly we were progressing in those days."

As if to ring the changes, original guitarist Dave Saunders was sacked soon after the session, because of the lack of progress he was making with his instrument, and Tony Allen was replaced behind the kit by Rick Mayhew of The Tights for similar reasons a few months later – but not before the band had gone back into the studio to record some more new songs. Until now still unreleased, the five songs in question are the missing link stylistically between 'Vendetta' and what was to follow. Even before that first single though, The Samples were managed by Chris Berry who, of course, later set up No Future Records and eventually gave the band a deserved recording deal.

"He became our manager sometime during 1979," explains Sean. "I was on talking terms with Richard Jones who had started Cherry Red Records and who also promoted at the Malvern Winter Gardens. He worked with Chris and knew that he was looking to get involved with a band, so he told him that we wanted a manager. Chris's background wasn't in the punk scene, but he seemed to be keen and helped us put out our first single.

"Right from when he started No Future, Chris more or less promised us a single release, but, for whatever reason, it took a long time before it actually happened. I think us knowing Chris somehow worked as a bit of a hindrance, and we all felt that Richard Jones never really liked us much either."

No Future did however include The Samples on their celebrated 'A Country Fit For Heroes' 12", with the belligerent 'Government Downfall', one of the compilation's highlights that generated the band a great deal of critical praise and saw the gig offers come flooding in from around the country.

As well as locally, The Samples played many well-received London dates, including several shows at the prestigious 100 Club and a No Future showcase at the Lyceum, and storming gigs in Bridgend (with label-mates The Partisans) and Presteigne, on the Welsh borders – a punk festival they headlined that turned into a mass brawl. Unfortunately such outbreaks of mass violence weren't uncommon in the early Eighties.

"I remember we played the Queen's Head in Stockwell, London," sighs Sean. "It was another one of those 'taking your life into your hands'-type gigs! It wasn't unusual back then to have complete and utter silence as the audience reaction to a song we'd just played… why is it that crowds are so much more polite to support bands nowadays? But I know the three things that went through my mind that night were: will we even get from the car to the venue without getting beaten up? Will we ever get from the venue back to the car without getting beaten up? And what are all these West Indian guys doing vanishing up the pub stairs with little suitcases?"

Thankfully the band survived several such close calls and recorded their second – and final – single, which to this day remains one of the finest, yet criminally overlooked, of all the second wave punk releases. 'Dead Hero' racked up a respectable 7500 sales and made the Indie Top Forty when it came out in July 1982, although why it sold so few copies compared to many far lesser bands on the label at the time is one of punk's great mysteries.

"Twenty odd years after its release and people still say to me, 'Have you heard 'Dead Hero' by The Samples?" says Sean Forbes of London's Rough Trade Records, a huge fan of the band. "I didn't realise it was so good immediately, but it's one of those classic pop moments where for three minutes everything's perfect. Also in this category would be Demob's 'No Room for You'. The verse of 'Dead Hero' is actually catchier than most bands' choruses; this is a phenomenal single and the golden nugget in a near perfect No Future catalogue!"

High praise indeed, but not without good reason; 'Dead Hero' is a truly memorable, raw, infectious anthem, and the two songs on the B-side are almost as good, the forceful 'Suspicion' and the vicious, high-speed 'Fire Another Round'.

"Without sounding arrogant, we weren't surprised at how well it turned out," reckons Dave. "When we first wrote it, we knew it was the best thing we'd done by a mile. When we recorded a demo of it, it sounded even better. And when we eventually got booked into Cargo Studios in Rochdale and, for the first time, got ourselves an engineer that actually knew what they were doing (Colin Richardson) to record us, we all just looked at each other and knew that we had something really great on our hands. I remember there were smiles all round – even we didn't think we were that good!

"We multi-layered the guitar, got a fantastic drum sound and Sean came up with his best gruff vocal style to date. Also I seem to recall that we got a quick visit from some of the Blitz boys during that session. It was just one of those days when we were really up for it."

However No Future encountered financial difficulties and folded before The Samples could push home their advantage and release their proposed third single, 'Nobody Cares'.

"No Future's change of musical direction with Blitz's second album was a complete wrong turn and damaged the whole scene immensely," reckons Dave.

"Garry Bushell left Sounds and just seemed to drop all his support overnight," adds Sean. "And unfortunately without him, the scene couldn't survive."

Although they soldiered on for several years more, they never regained the momentum they lost when No Future went under, and split in 1986 after a Famine Relief benefit at Worcester's Perdiswell Leisure Centre.

"It was a combination of boredom with the band and the scene in general," says Sean wistfully. "I remember playing the 100 Club with Broken Bones and thinking then that it was all over. They refused to lend our drummer their snare drum when he broke his... whatever happened to the punk spirit of camaraderie? And I suppose we were all maturing and getting into serious relationships and stuff. We just realised that the punk scene we'd been around and grown up with had finally run out of steam and clinging onto that for the sake of it seemed a little backward."

Sean went into a band with his brother Guy (who also played in local bands, The A Brigade and The Spotty Boys) called Charity's Child, who split after a few demos, whilst Dave and Pascal formed Take The Fifth, who generated some label interest and several demos but little more.

"I think 'Dead Hero' stands out amongst a lot of dross at the time and still sounds good today," reckons Dave. "And I don't think much other stuff from that era does. The music will always be there but the memories are the things we'll take with us. Johnny Rotten sang 'I wanna be me'... and really that's all you need to do. This was what the time of our lives was like – I hope that anyone else wanting the same gets it."

SELECT DISCOGRAPHY:
7"s:
'Vendetta' (Sample Records, 1980)
'Dead Hero' (No Future, 1982)

AT A GLANCE:
Captain Oi!'s 1997 Crux/Samples split CD, part of the label's Oi Collection series, features much of the band's recorded output, plus their unreleased final session from which the third single was to have been lifted (not to mention eleven songs from Crux as well). As is usual for Captain Oi!, the booklet is packed with photos and informative liner notes from both bands.

CHAPTER THREE

THE NORTHWEST

BLITZ

Blitz were the single biggest punk band from the Northwest of England. Not only did they sell many thousands of records and physically embody the dream of tribal harmony with their half-punk/half-skin line-up, but they remain as influential now as then, their records still being acknowledged as a major influence on countless bands around the world. The scary thing is, if their cards had been dealt slightly differently, Blitz could have been even bigger and maybe even still touring today, but as it is, they left behind them a trail of ground-breaking releases and exhausted happy punters.

The band formed during the spring of 1980 in New Mills, Derbyshire, from the ashes of a school band, XS Rhythm.

"Me and 'Mackie' knew each other from when we were kids," explains guitarist Nidge Miller of how he met bassist Neil McLennen. "And we met Carl (Fisher) through the punk scene, we all used to hang around together at gigs. The three of us joined a band called XS Rhythm, which was actually started by Lloyd Cole (of The Commotions fame!) Lloyd was at New Mills Comprehensive School too, but about three years below me, so I never really knew him, and he started this band called Rhythm, in 1978, who just did Ramones covers. I think they did one gig at a school function, and then Lloyd moved to Scotland. The remaining guitarist and drummer became XS Rhythm when the three of us joined, and we did one gig at New Mills Town Hall on New Year's Day 1980. They then left, and we got 'Charlie' (Chris Howe) in on drums, and began rehearsing as Blitz in May 1980. I chose the name after the Ramones song, 'Blitzkrieg Bop'.

"To be honest, I heard The Ramones and that was it!" he elaborates, on his indoctrination into punk rock. "I wasn't really into anything before then, maybe Slade or something, but I'd never heard anything quite like The Ramones, their speed, their energy, that guitar sound. They were the band that got me into punk, not The Sex Pistols; I was more into The Stranglers, really – although it doesn't show in our music."

New Mills may not sound like a Mecca for underground music, but the second wave of UK punk rock was a rallying cry for bored youths everywhere, heard and acted upon the length and breadth of the country. The sleepy Derbyshire town spawned not one but three acclaimed bands, all of whom signed to No Future Records, all of whom shared certain sonic similarities.

"Blitz, Violators and Attak all used to rehearse in the same place, a big disused building," recalls Nidge. "It was a 20' by 10' room, and we all paid a coupla quid each week to practise and leave our gear locked up there. What little gear we had! We all used to lend each other stuff… in fact, I think everyone used to use the same guitar amp and the same distortion pedal. That might explain the similarities in sound between the three of us. I remember someone asking me once whether we got any royalties for that Attak album – that was how much it sounded like us! But there was never any competition between us; we'd all go on one coach to gigs together, a big group of us from New Mills, Chapel, Buxton… it was a great scene, all the bands and their friends and fans travelling together.

Our first ever show was actually supporting Discharge in Bradford, in May 1980, which we'd only just decided on the name 'Blitz'. Discharge were only just getting their name around then, so there were only about twenty people there. None of the songs that appeared on our first EP were even written at that time; I think the only song we played that night that we kept was 'Closedown' (which appeared on the first album).

"Our second show, which I would say was the first 'real' Blitz gig, was one we organised ourselves at a parish hall. There were a few hundred people there, a local crowd, so we went down really well. We were fairly confident by then anyhow, we'd locked together fairly quickly as a band and it was starting to show."

Inspired by their live response, Blitz went into the studio and recorded a demo, featuring 'Attack', '45 Revolutions', 'Fight To Live' and the oft-imitated-but-never-equalled classic 'Someone's Gonna Die', four early songs that showcased the band's unique style. An exciting blend of ferocious, gravelly vocals, insistent barbed-wire guitars, a strong rhythm section led by a roving bass, and rousing football terrace-style backing vocals, it was apparent even from this early session just why the band would soon capture the hearts and minds of thousands of disenchanted street urchins everywhere. And despite the violence implied by menacing lyrics such as 'We fight to live, we live to fight, we don't give a shit what's wrong or what's right', Nidge maintains that their shows were almost always peaceful affairs.

Carl Fisher of Blitz
(Pic: Tony Mottram)

"Surprisingly we didn't get a lot of trouble; our crowd was always a good mix of punks and skinheads, so there was very little rivalry. The atmosphere was always electric, everyone used to go mental; songs like '4Q' were so memorable, everyone knew them straight away and would sing along even before we had any records out. That's why there was no trouble, everybody was too busy going crazy.

"Our sound just happened, I suppose; we never set out to sound like anyone else, it was just four different sets of influences coming together. We walked it like we talked it. We were real; we were skint, unemployed… just punk fans who picked up guitars. We never dressed up for photos or anything; how we looked on the records was how we looked every day."

The demo actually ended up becoming the band's first official release, 1981's 'All Out Attack' EP, which was the opening gambit for the newly-formed No Future label, based in Malvern, Worcestershire. It was a huge success for both band and label, spending almost a year in the Indie Charts and peaking at No. 3.

"They (No Future) placed an ad in Sounds, 'New record label seeks punk bands'. They didn't even have a name for their company at the time. We'd already recorded this four song demo at our own expense – it cost us about £100, I think – so we sent a copy in, and Chris Berry got straight back to us. He wanted to release it as it was, so they came up with the name No Future and scraped up enough cash to press 1000 singles… then Fast, one of their distributors, turned round and took TEN thousand off them in one go! That was when Pinnacle picked up the distribution. That was funny 'cos Pinnacle had already turned us down earlier, when one of us had sent them a demo direct; we've still got the official 'Thanks but no thanks' refusal letter off them somewhere!

"We were all surprised how well it took off. And we know we sold a lot more than the 25,000 official sales we're credited with, but I think No Future were a bit scared of losing us to a bigger label. What they should have done was manage us and take a percentage of any earnings, and then sold us onto a bigger label that could afford to push us properly. Various tours we had planned fell through, mainly 'cos we didn't have a manager chasing things up for us. Actually, until we did some dates with GBH, we didn't do any proper touring.

"It all happened very quickly, but it never went to our heads. Even when we were in the National Charts (with the release of their debut album), we were sat in the local pub as normal; we weren't interested in moving to London or being rock stars or whatever."

October 1981 saw the release of the 'Carry On Oi!' compilation album by Secret Records, the third in the highly successful Oi series, which featured two Blitz tracks, 'Nation On Fire', with its reggae-tinged intro, and the pounding anthem 'Youth'.

"We never really liked the 'Oi' label, anyway," admits Nidge. "We just thought it was a bit silly really. Plus with the explanation mark after it, it looked like we were on an album called 'Carry On Oi'! We always thought of ourselves as a punk band, end of story. We never set out to 'break down barriers' or anything either, because as far as we were concerned, there weren't any barriers in the first place… certainly not in our crowd anyway.

"I remember one particular gig in the East End of London, at the Bridge House in Canning Town, and it was like being back at home, they treated us like one of their own. There was no north/south divide, no punk/skin divisions… it was a great gig."

The second Blitz single was the hard-hitting 'Never Surrender'. Released in early 1982, and backed by the equally fierce 'Razors In The Night', it was another runaway success for the band, reaching No. 2 in the Indies and terrorising the charts for five months. It also saw a marked improvement in production values, without losing any of that trademark abrasiveness.

"Well, 'All Out Attack' was only ever meant to be a demo. When we did 'Never Surrender', we knew in advance that we were making a record. We also knew that we were making a record that thousands of people were waiting for, so it had to be good. There were high expectations, but we had more time to prepare, more time in the studio, and we didn't really feel under pressure. The songs were just there."

'Never Surrender' was followed by Blitz's show-stealing inclusion on the four-band 'Total Noise' EP. Appearing alongside The Business, The Gonads and Dead Generation, they contributed one of their strongest tracks, 'Voice Of A Generation', with its irresistible chorus chant of 'I don't wanna be poor no more'.

"That was a bit of a mistake in hindsight. We thought that we were going to be the lead-off track, that it was essentially going to be 'our' single and we were going to get a big push from it, but that never happened. It certainly wasn't something that we needed to do; it didn't do us any harm, but it also didn't do us any good in the long run either..."

Blitz's recorded highlights came thick and fast in 1982. The 'Warriors' single (backed by a re-recorded 'Youth') appeared in August of that year, showcasing a more measured and moody side to the band, and it was chased up the charts by the immense debut album, 'Voice Of A Generation'. From the boozy singalong of 'We Are The Boys' that opens up the record, to the final

Nidge of Blitz, 'the single biggest punk band from the Northwest of England...'

crashing chord of 'Closedown', the album saw the band really introducing some subtly crafted melodies into their already formidable wall of sound, even covering Lou Reed's 'Vicious' along the way. A slew of rave reviews greeted its release, including a full marks write-up in Sounds, and it stormed up not only the Indie Charts but the Nationals too, spending a month in the mainstream Top Thirty.

"We were very prolific back then. I wrote all the music, and Carl wrote a lot of lyrics, although I often helped him arrange them for the songs. As I said earlier, there was no pressure to write the songs, it was just something that I did. If we'd only sold a thousand records, we would've still written those songs. We were doing it for fun at the end of the day, there was no intent, it all just came out naturally...

"We'd already released nine tracks by that time, so No Future were wondering what we were actually going to put on the album. But I told them, 'Don't worry, we've got the songs', and they were both surprised and elated when they heard the demo we did. We just did a rough recording for No Future to convince them to put us into Strawberry Studios, a big 24-track place. We were approaching things much more professionally by that time, and all the songs were so well rehearsed, we did them all in one or two takes. We were all a bit surprised that we managed to even remember seventeen songs – fourteen of them brand new... which was a lot for an album back then.

"I still love most of the tracks, especially 'Propaganda' – I always said that should've been a single for us – but I didn't, and still don't, like the production too much. I actually preferred the version of 'Voice Of A Generation' that appeared on the 'Total Noise' EP to the one on the album. I just didn't get that Ramones guitar sound that I wanted; the guitars are far too trebly.

"Anyway, it did well for us. In the official Indie Charts, it was kept off the No. 1 spot by

Toyah's 'Warrior Rock' album, and if that isn't ironic I don't know what is! But it made No. 1 in the NME's Indie Charts, for four weeks in a row, but they still wouldn't give us a feature, they didn't wanna know us. We were just too real for them, I suppose… student wankers!"

Despite the band riding high on the success of 'Voice…', the first chinks in Blitz's seemingly impenetrable armour began to appear in early 1983 when Mackie left for pastures new.

"He just didn't want to tour, that was the real reason," explains Nidge. "We had the GBH ('Attacked By Rats') tour coming up, so Tim Harris joined, the guy who had engineered some of our earlier records. He knew all the songs already, and we'd struck up a good friendship with him in the studio. He was a guitarist first and foremost, but could play the bass really well too, a good all-round musician.

"I said earlier we never had any trouble at gigs, but that all ended with that GBH tour. When we reached Oxford, all hell broke loose. Bottles were flying everywhere when GBH came on, a safety curtain had to be lowered, and the Oxford skins just wrecked the place. They did thousands of pounds worth of damage, and that was the end of the tour – all the other promoters pulled their dates there and then. We'd played about eight or nine shows, and there were about six to go, I think? It was a shame, 'cos the next day we were due in Glasgow, and we had a huge following up there but never got to play to them."

Thankfully such shows were in the minority, although the Oxford incident wasn't the only violence Blitz encountered on the road.

"And then there was the infamous 100 Club gig, of course, where Carl got bottled whilst we were playing. It was his own fault, if I remember rightly, something he'd said, some stupid off the cuff remark. We couldn't carry on, he was taken off to hospital, and I ended up offering out the whole audience! Luckily for me, they only had a beef with Carl! That was a shame 'cos until then – it happened about two-thirds of the way through the set – it was a great gig. That was a nice venue to play, just the right size."

Tim Harris made his recording debut on February '83's exhilarating 'New Age' single that gave him plenty of scope to demonstrate his fine bass-playing skills during its searing chorus. Almost majestic in its assured simplicity, it highlighted a much more experimental side that was emerging within the band, but nonetheless had enough grit about it to satisfy their hardcore fans. Remarkably, it was a tune that Nidge knocked out in, literally, five minutes.

"Well, Channel 4 got in touch with No Future wanting to feature us, and we ended up going on their programme 'The Tube'. So, anyway, Chris Berry at No Future phoned me up, thinking it would be a good idea to do a new single to coincide with it airing, and I wrote 'New Age' within five minutes of putting the phone down to him! Five days later we'd actually recorded it, and the single was off being pressed! And it turned out to be one of my favourite ever Blitz tunes… that and 'Propaganda' off the album."

A video clip of the song was even featured in the 'UK/DK' film, and this track more than any other probably hints at the huge potential in the band to really blossom into something wondrous… potential that sadly remained untapped when the band broke in two, then inevitably split.

"After 'New Age', Carl and Tim wanted to go in a new direction. The plan was that I would carry on as Blitz, and they'd continue under a different name, so I got back together with Mackie and carried on writing. But No Future decided to back Carl and Tim, and they released that 'Telecommunication' single as Blitz, so me and Mackie had to use the Rose Of Victory name instead. It was the Musicians Union that stopped me using the name because Carl and Tim were ready to record before us, but I've since found out that we weren't required to legally and should have contested it. I mean, it was my band, I named it, and then I lost it. It made me quite bitter."

Perhaps keen to distance themselves from the nihilistic overtones of their old name, and take the label in a new direction, No Future Records set up a new sub-label for those latter-period

Blitz releases, ironically called Future. Rose Of Victory however, with their punkier sound, remained on the original label – while it lasted – for their one and only single, a cover of Bowie's 'Suffragette City' ("We were even considering doing 'Substitute' by The Who!" reveals Nidge), which, backed by the instrumental 'Overdrive', reached No. 36 in the Indies in July 1983.

"Then No Future went pear-shaped, so we only got to do the one single as Rose Of Victory, but by then I was disillusioned with it all anyway; it all fell apart in one swoop in 1983."

The aforementioned 'Telecommunication' single was a jarring departure for the band, owing more to New Romantic electronica than second wave punk rock, although it and the 'Second

Mackie (left) and Nidge
(Pic: Tony Mottram)

Empire Justice' album both still managed respectable Indie placings, no doubt thanks to the many Blitz fans that bought them out of sheer curiosity. Those fans obviously walked away disappointed however, as the next single, 'Solar', failed to register on the Indie radar and was consequently the band's last release. They split up in late 1983.

"Oh, it's terrible, not what I'm into at all, and certainly not punk of any fashion," says Nidge of the second Blitz album. "I can remember being at the No Future offices when the master tapes arrived there, and Chris Berry wanted to chuck 'em out the window… or words to that effect! They did do one good song though, 'Husk', but they hid it away on a B-side somewhere (on the 'Solar' single). It was just so annoying that they called it Blitz in the first place; because the cover was blank, and the line-up details printed so small, a lot of people thought that I was actually playing on it! I've been screaming at people for years, 'It wasn't me! It's not my fault!'"

Blitz, or a version thereof, did reappear briefly in the late Eighties, with the 1989 'Killing Dream' album for Link Records. It saw Nidge recording with a drum machine, with Gary Basnett from Attak handling vocal duties.

"Well, Mackie wasn't interested, and Carl was living in Australia at the time, but Link offered me the opportunity to do another Blitz album, and I wanted to do it. The song 'Killing Dream' was actually written in 1983 and intended as a Blitz song anyway; it would've been the follow-up to 'New Age' if things had been different.

"But it was an odd time, there was very little going on in the punk scene, and of course, we didn't have a drummer, so we had to use this horrible drum machine, which was the main drawback. But the album did pretty well for Link here, and it came out in America through Cleopatra."

Nidge even took the band out on the road for a string of European dates, with unknown drummer Paul Lilley behind the kit.

"We did one gig in Belgium with Gary, but he suffers with MS and couldn't really tour, so when we toured Germany, I got Spike in from Blitzkrieg on vocals and Gary Sumner on bass guitar. We did two weeks there with Red Alert. The tour went well, the gigs were great, but everywhere we went, everybody kept saying, 'It's good, but it isn't Blitz'... and it wasn't, I knew that, but I just wanted to get out there and play my songs. And the original guys weren't interested. Which is why I envy bands like GBH who are still out there doing it to this day; if I had my way, I'd tour and tour myself.

"We even played one show in America – at the Milwaukee Metal Festival! There was a hardcore punk stage that year, and we played with Agnostic Front and Murphy's Law. On that occasion I played guitar and sang, Gary (Sumner) played bass and Paul played drums. But once again, it was the same old story – MTV were all there with their cameras trained on us, but as soon as they realised that I was the only original member, they were all gone in seconds!"

US label Warning even released four tracks from the 'Killing Dream' album, 'All You Want', 'Those Days', 'Don't Care' and 'Walk Away', as a single, 'New Breed'.

Blitz soon split up once again, this time for good, but their influence has pervaded the punk and hardcore scenes ever since. They've been covered by everybody from the platinum-selling Rancid, who turned in a great version of 'Someone's Gonna Die', to Judge, the seminal New York hardcore band, who rampaged through 'Warriors'. They've even had a whole album of covers devoted to them, 'Voice Of A New Generation' (released by Rhythm Vicar in 1999), which was compiled by Tony Frater from renowned Sunderland Oi band, Red Alert, who themselves contributed a fine version of 'New Age'. Other highlights came courtesy of Red London ('Moscow'), Gundog ('Nations On Fire') and Running Riot ('Warriors').

"It's a great honour of course, especially that tribute album, even the versions that aren't that good, just the fact that you've influenced all these bands. It's also frustrating to hear huge bands like Rancid who hail us as a major inspiration, basically doing what we were doing twenty years ago – it makes you wonder what might've happened...

"But if people ask me to describe Blitz to them now, I just say we were real, we had no pretensions; we just played the music that we wanted to listen to ourselves. And there's no more honest reason for playing in a band than that, is there?"

SELECT DISCOGRAPHY:
7"s:
'All Out Attack' (No Future, 1981)
'Never Surrender' (No Future, 1982)
'Warriors' (No Future, 1982)
'New Age' (Future, 1983)
'Telecommunication' (Future, 1983)
'Solar' (Future, 1983)
'New Breed' (Warning, 1989)

12"s:
'New Age' (Future, 1983)
'Telecommunication' (Future, 1983)
'Solar' (Future, 1983)

LPs:
'Voice Of A Generation' (No Future, 1982)
'Second Empire Justice' (Future, 1983)
'Killing Dream' (Link, 1989)

AT A GLANCE:

Anagram's excellent double CD 'Blitz: The No Future Years' (2000) compiles the must-have debut album and all the No Future singles in a nice digipack. 'The Best Of Blitz' CD (1998), part of The Punk Collectors Series, features all the singles, various compilation tracks, and even the best tracks from the 'Killing Dream' album.

ATTAK

Taking great inspiration from the success of Blitz, Attak formed in the summer of 1980, rising from the ashes of various bedroom punk bands such as Energy, Chaos and P45. Not only were they from the same town as their mentors, New Mills, but they also lifted their name from Blitz's debut EP, 'All Out Attack', and drummer Lindsay McLennan was the sister of Blitz bassist, Mackie. Despite a relatively short career, the band achieved considerable success in the Indie Charts with their distinctive raucous mix of punk and heavy metal, and remain quietly seminal to this day.

As well as the aforementioned Lindsay behind the kit, the original line-up of Attak comprised Gary Basnett on guitar, Sean 'Chad' Chadwick on bass, and Gary's fifteen-year-old brother Saleem on vocals.

"We were all self -taught musicians," recalls Sean. "As a kid, I spent countless hours in my bedroom trying to play along to records and trying to learn scales, much to the annoyance of my family and neighbours. And then just as I thought I'd cracked it, I found out how to tune my guitar, and had to start all over again! But with a little persistence you always get there in the end!

"Our hometown environment played a big part inspiring us," he says, of the band's early days. "Or should I say the lack of it? There was never anything to do or anywhere to go; all kids could do was hang around the streets, it was just sheer boredom!

"Also the government at the time played a huge part in our outlook on life. With one of the highest unemployment rates we had ever known in the UK, most of our lyrics had a political message. Maggie Thatcher, in particular, was hated by a large section of the community, especially in the north of England where we came from."

A demo was recorded and sent – inevitably – to No Future, the Malvern-based label that had just signed Blitz. ("We were close with the other local bands, especially Blitz obviously, but I don't think that Lindsay being the sister of Mackie opened any doors for us really; Attak were taken on their own merits," insists the bassist.) No Future included the track 'Blue Patrol' on their well-received unsigned bands compilation 12", 'A Country Fit for Heroes', and the song was undoubtedly one of the highlights of the collection. The response was sufficient enough to convince the label to offer Attak a recording contract in their own right.

However, Saleem left the band soon after the demo, due to increasing pressures at school, leaving his big brother Gary to take over the role of vocalist as well as guitarist, and the band forged a slightly different direction. No Future obviously wanted to hear the new Attak in action, and another demo was recorded. A two-track affair ('Politician Man' and 'Another Riot') recorded at Hologram Studios, Stockport, by Tim Harris, who also engineered both of the band's ensuing singles, it had the desired effect, and a deal was struck for two singles and an album.

The band unleashed the blistering 'Today's Generation' EP in spring 1982, which took the scene by storm and spent two months in the Indie Charts, peaking at No. 15. The band glowered menacingly from the black-and-white front cover, in a bleak line-up shot of them all leaning dejectedly against a brick wall that perfectly encapsulated the single's title. The EP was as raw and vital as anything that No Future had unleashed upon the punk world previously, and soon saw Attak making great headway, building a strong following outside of their own area.

"I remember the early days of the band as being tough but exciting," reckons Sean. "When we were starting out, our early gigs were all done locally and were brilliant; we had tremendous support from family and friends and we were always well received. The atmosphere of those early shows was amazing too, and although we didn't do many gigs, we very quickly managed to get a large and loyal group of fans who always turned out for us; their support was tremendous."

Attak were quick to follow up the success of 'Today's Generation' with 'Murder In The Subway', their second (and final) single. Another abrasive assault on the eardrums, it did even better than its predecessor, with a Bushell-penned feature in Sounds helping the release to storm up the Indies once again. Both the title track and also the flip side, 'No Escape', had Sean's beautiful-sounding chunky bass ushering in a breakneck thrashy riff, whilst Gary's barbed wire voice lacerated the listener and Lindsay did everything in her considerable power to dispel the myth that female drummers couldn't hit as hard as the guys.

"People were always saying what a good drummer Lindsay was… and is (she still plays). I think they were surprised but I don't know why–females can play instruments too! But she didn't get much stick off anyone," he adds laughing. "Well, all I can say is, do you want to come up and try to give Lindsay some stick? She's well hard!"

In an ideal world, Attak would have toured all over the country like some of their counterparts and ended up being far bigger than they were, but their geographical location and financial circumstances conspired against them when it came to securing gigs further afield. In fact, despite all their Indie Chart success, they only actually played in London once, at Islington's Skunx club.

"Yeah, it was all down to money and time," confirms Sean. "Money was tight and we still had to work, which didn't leave much time for gigging. Local authorities and clubs were also making it difficult for us to find gigs at the time and transport was another big problem.

"I remember when we played London, the only transport we had was Gary's mini, so just imagine for a minute, the three of us plus amps, drums and guitars, all in a mini travelling down the M1. The roof rack piled so high it probably only just went under the bridges of the motorway! It must have looked like something out of a cartoon and it was a miracle we didn't get stopped by the police!"

Unperturbed, the band entered Revolution Studios in Cheadle to record their one-and-only album, 'Zombies', but not before they had auditioned for and recruited a second guitarist, Michael 'Woody' Woodacre.

"We added a second guitarist as we felt it would help with our live sound as well as the studio work. It also took the pressure off Gary a bit too and in doing this we were able to experiment a little more with our sound. Woody added a new dimension, bringing his own ideas and style and working with us to produce the sound we had been looking for. Adding Woody certainly had the desired effect."

Whether it was the addition of an extra guitarist or not, the album was certainly the band's most accomplished work, a pounding wall of noise that combined the intensity of Discharge with the power and songmanship of GBH. And the warts 'n' all metal of early Motörhead!

"I suppose our style set us apart from other bands. Lindsay will hate this, but, yes, there was a big metal influence… well, for Gary and myself anyway. Motörhead, Maiden, Tank, we liked anything that was really raucous and thunderous; balls-out music that stirred the blood, pumped the adrenaline and made your ears bleed. I suppose this had to rub off on us somewhere, even though punk was where our hearts lay. And I think that this mix of influences, plus our own individual playing styles, all went into creating the Attak sound."

As well as uncompromisingly harsh and heavy punk rock, the album had a few surprises in store, not least of all the opening two tracks – the unusually titled 'DAGA I' and 'DAGA II' – that saw the band flirting with some subtle melodies in their guitar work.

"How did I know you were going to ask me that?" laughs Sean, about to reveal the truth behind 'the DAGA mystery'. "This has long been a question that everybody asks and nobody has been able to answer. We have heard many weird and wonderful theories over the years but people were just looking too deep. The answer… is in the track!

"So, here's an exclusive for you; it's quite simply the chords of the tracks. When we wrote it, we wrote two versions and could not decide which to go with, so we thought 'What the hell!' and went with both, making one an instrumental. We had lyrics but no title and the chords were written at the top, and, ever since then, the tracks were known as 'DAGA'. There will be a lot of people kicking themselves now!"

Attak L–R: Sean, Lindsay, Gary
(Pic: Tony Mottram)

Despite the album selling well and receiving much critical acclaim ('Young And Proud' was a particularly effective and rousing street anthem), Attak were still struggling to get gigs, and by 1984 they became so frustrated, they split up. Gary later did a stint as vocalist with a reformed Blitz, singing on their 1989 album, 'The Killing Dream', before playing alongside Sean again in Snakebite. Sean also went on to play bass in The Brethren, whilst Woody played with Three Men Gone Mad for several years, before moving to Blackpool.

"Well, I still listen to punk, as do Gary and Lindsay," says Sean, of the band's whereabouts today. "I moved out of New Mills some years ago and am now living in Rhoscolyn, Anglesey, with my partner Johanna and my fifteen-year-old son, Jamie, who is also into punk. Gary and Lindsay got married in 1985 and still live in New Mills, and we are all still good friends. We have lost touch with Woody and we have tried many times to find him, but with no luck, so if anyone out there knows him or of him, please get in touch via the Attak website!"

SELECT DISCOGRAPHY:
7"s:
'Today's Generation' (1982, No Future)
'Murder In The Subway' (1982, No Future)

LPs:
'Zombies' (1983, No Future)

AT A GLANCE:
Captain Oi!'s CD reissue of the 'Zombies' album (1994) also includes both singles and the tracks that appeared on the 'A Country Fit For Heroes' and 'Oi! Oi! That's Yer Lot!' compilations. In other words, everything of note the band ever recorded on one disc, with all the original artwork and liner notes.

THE VIOLATORS

Although widely regarded as a 'New Mills band' as well, due to their close ties with Blitz and Attak, The Violators actually formed in Chapel-en-le-Frith in 1979. Like their aforementioned neighbours, they eventually signed to No Future and released several excellent singles before sadly self-destructing rather prematurely in 1983. What really set them apart however were the memorable styles employed by their two vocalists, Helen Hill and Shaun 'Cess' Stiles.

"We originated out of The Dismal Sports that me and 'Matchi' (aka John Marchington) formed in 1978," explains Shaun. "The Sex Pistols were the impetus, especially Lydon's 'Get off your arses' mantra. The band was a creative tool where we could channel our aggression positively, have a laugh, a passport out of the constipated shit holes that were our hometowns. It was a time of recession, high unemployment; everywhere was shut and there was nothing to do. You either moved, joined a band, or died of boredom."

The other Sports members decided to move to London, including amongst their ranks Paul Hinds who joined Test Department.

"John and myself decided we needed direction to escape and so looked to a new band to achieve that aim. We just recruited friends from the local punk scene. Punk was our common bond through which we became empowered and able to overcome the adverse effect that a pierced nose and green, spiky hair had on the local population."

The Violators line up became Cess and Helen on vocals, Mark Coley on guitar, Matchi on bass, and Anthony 'Ajax' Hall on drums.

"Being close to Manchester we experienced its first 'Renaissance'. We'd go to the Factory

The Violators
L-R: Helen Hill, Shaun Stiles, Mark Coley, Ajax, Matchi

and clubs like it to watch bands such as Joy Division, PIL, Magazine, The Fall, the so-called post-punk bands. To us they were punk, but they were just not permitting themselves to be typecast. We still loved the early bands too, but, apart from The Buzzcocks, the post-punk set up was what gave Manchester its unique pulse. The north had a more DIY feel to the movement than the south – the London scene seemed driven by major record labels until the hardcore punk thing occurred.

"The Eighties political landscape was paramount for our creativity. The Violators' name itself was reflective of Britain's political elite desire to make change at any social cost. Thatcher's government was planning to violate all public sector institutions, and about to wage war on the unions in order to control public spending. In so doing, many individuals would be socially and economically hurt.

"We had read a prophetic article in The Guardian, 'Urban Violation', about the effect of Thatcherism on the inner cities. Politically we believed that it didn't matter who held political power; left or right would use parliament to benefit the ruling classes. As anarchists we wanted change too; we wanted the whole fuckin' system brought down 'cos it didn't work and was immoral."

After being evicted from their first practise 'room' – an old caravan behind a local pub – the band began sharing rehearsal space in nearby New Mills with Attak and Blitz.

"In line with the DIY thing, Mackie from Blitz got a little practice studio together that was perfect for the local hardcore punk scene. The building was filthy, falling to bits gloriously, and a punk electrician called Smithy had tapped into a local art gallery next door so we could plug in our instruments. I suppose you could say we took direct funding from our local arts council!"

The Violators did their first gig with Blitz in Bradford supporting Discharge.

"Yeah, we had to pay to get into that gig," laughs Shaun. "We only had three tracks and must have been on for all of five minutes! Tell me, what contemporary band would have the nerve do that today? None! But we just didn't permit ourselves any limitations. Punk gave us that confidence, and an audience who were open-minded enough to accept our rather unconventional set.

"I remember we even had to break into The Manchester Funhouse to perform! I don't know what had gone wrong, but we'd been booked to play a well-advertised gig. Yet the place was completely locked up and there was a queue of kids outside waiting upon our arrival. So we broke in and played a free gig that was fuckin' great. Everyone went wild – the band, the audience… and eventually the big guys with 'security' written on their jackets that turned up to try and evict us. In the ensuing violence they became utterly powerless; no one was leaving and the show went ahead regardless. Someone even managed to open up the bar; it was just one big, glorious cock-up from start to finish."

After the first Blitz EP appeared, the band sent their second demo to No Future, who used two tracks from it on their 'A Country Fit For Heroes' compilation. 'Die With Dignity' perfectly showcased Helen's sensual vocals, whilst the rabid 'Government Stinks', featuring an intense turn from Shaun, emphasised the band's harder, faster side. Both tracks elicited a very positive response, leading to No Future's signing of the band soon after.

The debut single, 'Gangland', recorded at Hologram Studios in Stockport by Tim Harris, came out in April 1982, and promptly went Top Ten in the Indie Charts. The A-side was a mini-epic that is especially memorable for a clean-cut yet powerful, melodic vocal delivery from Shaun.

"It wasn't the most musical (that honour probably goes to 'Die With Dignity'), but 'Gangland' is possibly my favourite release 'cos of what it stands for really. We thought punk was becoming a rigid formula that had to be challenged. Bands were merely trying to imitate their heroes. Some idiots were even fascistic enough to slag off bands that didn't fit into their stereotypical view of punk. Talk about missing the point–punk wasn't supposed to have any rules.

"So, with the release of 'Gangland', we tried to turn the punk formula on its head. When we read a review that described us as sounding 'like a street level Joy Division', we knew we had achieved it… but how much more street level than Joy Division can you can get? Conceptually, we liked to think of it as a video nasty put to music, influenced by all the banned films that we incessantly watched – from (John) Walters' 'Pink Flamingos', to (Stanley) Kubrick's 'A Clockwork Orange'. We admired the bollocks shown by those types of filmmakers. Being rejected by mainstream Hollywood had freed them to create what the fuck they wanted, and occasionally they produced some original, honest works of art, warts and all."

Even though the image was an ephemeral experiment, the striking cover of 'Gangland', which depicted the band sat on rail tracks dressed in Clockwork Orange attire, was the one that introduced them to the majority of their audience and saw them forever labelled Clockwork punks.

"We were never a 'Clockwork Orange band', although that's how most people remember us 'cos of the initial buzz it caused. We dropped the image almost straight after and slipped into something more comfortable… after all, bowler hats and jockstraps weren't conducive to the punk lifestyle, were they? And oh, my brothers, your faithful narrator only ever played one show dressed in the height of droogy fashion, and it was long before I knew of bands like The Adicts or Major Accident.

"Again, we just seemed to stumble upon things by accident. We thought the droogy look perfect to highlight the uniformity of the hardcore punk scene. The excitement created by those initial photographs (taken by an old mate called Hambo) inspired Kevin Cummins, whose work we all respected, to pay us a visit. He thought the image was powerful, promised to get some great shots and didn't let us down. They are realistic yet surreal at the same time, and a 'mirror image' shot of Ant and myself conveyed everything in one perfect frame. Ironically, the whole point we were trying to make with the image was never explained as we were not a high profile band. Actually, we never had chance to explain ourselves properly, full stop."

In December the band released the superb 'Summer Of '81' single. Recorded at Strawberry Studios in Stockport by Tim Harris and The Violators, it managed to be even more successful, spending almost four months in the Indies and peaking at No. 6. Unfolding from a simple descending bass lick, the song explodes into a gloriously tribal commentary of the fierce rioting seen on the streets of many British cities during the summer of the previous year, a reaction to callous government policies of the time. Helen's commanding vocals manage to be both ethereal and desperately angry as she spits with utter conviction a vehement attack on the police and their strong-arm tactics, 'There's blood on the streets and the smell is so sweet, as another blue bastard has just gone down.'

"We were playing and attending gigs in some very deprived areas so we weren't sheltered from the problems of the inner cities. I suppose we became social commentators. We just wrote about what we experienced, and our experiences made us vehemently anti-establishment, of which the police were an integral part. I still support anti-establishment issues even today, and was arrested during the 2000 Anti-Capitalism Demonstrations in London... for defending myself against three police officers in full riot gear. I was charged with 'Acting in Such a Way as Would Place Someone in Fear of their Safety' and ordered to pay a £600 fine."

If the band had played a few more choice shows to capitalise on their chart success, such was the strength and vision of their material, they could quite possibly have been as big as their local rivals Blitz. However, complacency conspired against them and they were destined to vanish almost as quickly as they arrived, but not before they had made a small but indelible mark on the UK punk scene.

"Our life as a band was curtailed quite prematurely. I don't really know the truth behind the split, but what I do know is that we left behind us some real gems that speak for themselves. We had a lot of very ambitious stuff planned ahead of us. Yeah, if we had continued as we intended, I feel we could've become very influential. We had this lazy side, which actually added to our mystic, but was detrimental to a lengthy career. I think more people actually got to see us perform by coming to our rehearsals than got to see us play live."

The band's increasing inactivity led to Helen and Coley leaving to form the brief-lived Taboo, who, despite promising responses in the press to their live performances, never actually issued any official vinyl.

"While I've never had or even needed an explanation for their actions, I believe we all began to lose sight of ourselves as individuals. If you listen to 'Summer Of '81' and 'Live Fast, Die Young', you can hear us playing as a band with total confidence in each other's ability and faith in each other's focus. Those two tracks are the reflection of us understanding each other as musicians. It's like existentialism gone crazy in that when we found each other as musicians, we lost sight of each other as individuals. We hadn't practiced prior to the split for about eight months or so, but 'cos we lived locally, John, Ant and myself still kept in touch socially, and perhaps Coley and Helen, who lived in other towns by then, began to see themselves as marginalised? But there were no ill feelings between us in the end. We merely walked away from it all 'cos we had no desire to be rock stars; it just didn't mean that much to us."

About this time, No Future compiled both their singles, along with the two tracks from 'A Country Fit For Heroes', and released them as one 12", 'Die with Dignity'. 'Summer Of '81' was also included as one of the standout tracks on the third 'Punk And Disorderly' album, 'The Final Solution'. Meanwhile, Shaun and John drafted in Louise King on vocals and Andrew Hill on guitar, and released the disappointing 'Life On The Red Line' through No Future's more commercial offshoot, Future, during spring 1983. Although it clocked up respectable sales, it was too much of a departure from the band's original sound for many fans.

"We knew we were not going to sound like the old Violators, nor did we want to. That sound had come from five individuals who all put equal shares into the finished work. Removing two of those individuals would obviously alter the sound. We wanted to create a new sound for us, but nothing prepared us for what happened to the release.

"Chris Berry (No Future boss) had the single remixed behind our backs and without our permission. Until then we had produced all our own material, and if you compare our productions to those of other punk bands they're well above average. I don't even consider it a Violators' track, but the B-side, 'Crossings of Sangsara', with Lou singing could be considered the last real Violators' release. If it's not punk, it's certainly Manchester Indie.

"To be fair, we were all naive, but Chris stabbed us in the back and in my world that's a crime. He then wanted us to sign a contract to state that our lyrics wouldn't contain swearing! We knew he wanted to turn No Future into something more radio-friendly, but that concept would merely alienate us from our audience. Perhaps he had no confidence in us as a band by that time? It's true we were caught unprepared by Mark and Helen's departure, but what he wanted and what we wanted were totally out of sync. The death knell had sounded for The Violators, and we just thought, 'Fuck it, if we're going down, he's coming with us.'"

Shaun, Matchi and Lou became Ice The Falling Rain and released one final single for Future, the dance-inspired 'Life's Illusion', that saw them veering even further from their punk roots and dangerously close to dance territory.

"Yeah, it was a complete dance track," agrees Shaun. "And I still rate it as such even today. Although we were serious, we did it just to have the last laugh really. I viewed hardcore punk as the antithesis to the New Romantic movement. Both had emerged from '77 punk; the hardcore punks had read punk's ethics to the letter and taken it once again underground, whilst the New Romantics, in their bid for mainstream acceptance, lost the ethics and guitars but still liked to dress up. Anyway, although 'Life's Illusion' was a radio friendly number, it was the simplest of our tracks to create, it cost a great deal of cash and it helped bring the label down 'cos they had no idea how to sell it. Well, if you help create a monster, you have to help destroy it!

"Looking at our short career," he adds in closing. "I suppose an outsider might say that we did everything wrong, but, if you read between the lines, you'll see we did everything right! We were true to ourselves from start to finish and no one can take that away from us."

SELECT DISCOGRAPHY:
7"s:
'Gangland' (No Future, 1982)
'Summer Of '81' (No Future, 1982)
'Life On The Red Line' (Future, 1983)

12"s:
'Summer Of '81' (No Future, 1982)
'Die With Dignity' (No Future, 1983)

AT A GLANCE:
There is yet to be a comprehensive discography CD dedicated to The Violators, but six of their songs, including both sides of the first two singles, appear on the double CD, 'The History Of No Future' (Anagram, 1999).

MAYHEM

S ome bands like to play it safe, giving the people just what they want; others like to flirt with danger, and push the envelope right to the edge of the table... but the most exciting bands have no regard for their own safety and gleefully send that envelope spiralling down towards self-destruction. Southport's aptly named Mayhem fall into the latter category, with their inspired 'Gentle Murder' 7" being a particularly deranged slice of hardcore punk. But then again, what would you expect from a band that numbered one 'Dead Cat' among its ranks?

The Mayhem story begins in 1979 in singer Mick McGee's shed, where the band rehearsed. It was there, Mick being joined by the original line-up of Chris Hind (who went on to join Blitzkrieg) on bass, Mick Johnson on drums, and Gray Bentley on guitar, that the band's sound started to take form, albeit via a bewildering string of personnel changes. The original incarnation of Mayhem only managed two local shows... one of them in a church!

"The punks in town at the time had a pretty bad reputation, 'cos there was nothing laid on for us, nowhere for us to go," recalls Mick. "A poor old mate of mine ran a disco, a predominantly heavy metal disco called Volume Ten, for all the

Mick McGee of Southport's 'blisteringly intense' Mayhem

rich kids whose mums spent hours sewing AC/DC patches on the backs of their jackets. And Kev was trying desperately to get these little venues happening around town, but we'd turn up and basically all fucking hell would break loose, you know? It started off when I was dating this girl who moved in this scene, and I would turn up at one of these discos and get a load of grief from all these heavy metal kids, and so I would turn up with all my mates the following week and give them even more grief back – and poor Kev was losing venue after venue!

"One of these venues was called The United Reformed Church Hall, and it was actually becoming a bit of a punk venue, because we'd been going there so much we were actually becoming the majority. I don't know when the idea to play there came about, but we were one of the only bands frequenting the place, and so we ended up playing this church.

"That gig was where Collo first saw us. He was our second drummer; he'd been in the Dumb Blondes before that, and we idolised them – even though we'd never heard or seen them! We'd just heard so much about them, and had seen their name all over town!"

So, Mick Johnson was replaced by Mick 'Collo' Collinson, and then Gaz Sumner replaced Gray on guitar – only to elope soon after, along with Chris, to Blitzkrieg, who had just secured their recording deal with No Future. They were replaced briefly by Will Maudsley and Trev Aindow, but eventually the band arrived at their first stable (not literally speaking, you understand!) line-up of Mick McGee – vocals, Johnny Liu – guitar, Collo – drums and Dead Cat – bass. Johnny had formerly been in Paraquat with Mick Riffone who went on to front Blitzkrieg, and Dead Cat had previously served time in The Set Up.

"Because he had the reactions of one," explains the singer of their new arrival's unusual nickname. "You could set him on fire and he wouldn't notice for a month! He drank for England... and most of Europe. Most gigs would involve three half-bottles of spirit, there would be vodka before the gig, whisky during the gig, and a brandy after the gig... He was quite introverted, and when he joined the band, he didn't speak to me for a month, but he was a lovely, sweet guy, and a very talented bass player."

Mayhem recorded a demo on eight-track that captured adequately the energy of their primal scream and landed them a place on the Riot City compilation album, 'Riotous Assembly', to which they contributed the track 'Psycho'. Despite stiff competition from bigger names such as Abrasive Wheels, Vice Squad and Chaos UK, they stole the show somewhat with a blistering track that was as short as it was intense.

Things were looking good for the band, who toured with Vice Squad and played a huge show with The Dead Kennedys at Liverpool's Royal Court, but then disaster struck when their rehearsal place burnt down, and along with it most of their equipment. Luckily Mick's mother had insured the place, and eventually, when the insurers deemed to pay out, they got some new equipment.

"No, the fire wasn't an insurance scam," laughs Mick. "If it had have been, I would have tried to make more money out of it! The exact cause remains unexplained, but there are a few possibilities... one was that papers fell against a coal stove... the other was one of our neighbours who had a particular dislike for us fuelled the situation. Either way it was bad news! Blitzkrieg rehearsed there too, and they lost their drum kit. We lost all our guitar gear, and half our bass gear, and had considerable damage done to our drums too. And I personally lost hundreds of records, some disco equipment and countless other bits and pieces unknown to us.

"Until we received the payments, we were playing gigs with burnt and water-damaged equipment, but throughout all this, the band's morale remained good. Even on the night of the fire, after the fire crews had gone, Collo stood by his burnt and melted kit and said, 'Fuck me, this is the warmest it's ever been in here!'"

In May 1982, the band recorded their first EP, the jaw-droppingly volatile 'Gentle Murder', at Cargo Studios in Rochdale. Four tracks were included, each of them as urgent as the next, and the single entered the Indies in September of that year, peaking at a respectable No. 21. The lyrics to 'Blood Money' had been inspired by the effect the band's insurance pay-out had had on some of their close friends and acquaintances, but it was 'Patriots' that caused the band most grief, with its tongue-in-cheek intro chant of 'What shall we do with the Argie bastards?'...

"Yeah, there was a backlash in the New Musical Express," sighs Mick. "And they had a lot of mail going on about 'This sick punk band, blah blah blah'. I've got no disrespect for any man who wants to lay down his life for what he believes in – it's how and what he's told to believe in... I mean, the Falklands War, with no disrespect to any of the men who died or were injured, what was it actually about? Was it about liberating thirteen thousand sheep? Was it England staking its claim to untapped oil reserves in surrounding territories? Or was it Thatcher forwarding her career, by tapping into the crusade mentality? That tribal thing that is inherent in the British? I couldn't believe what was happening in the press at the time... everyone was like, 'Let's go to war'!

"The idea of 'Patriots' was telling the people of England not to be led into war blindly, and it was about public gullibility. It wasn't a pro-war song, quite the contrary. One of my main regrets with the band is that we never had the lyrics printed on our releases, and then that song would never have been taken the wrong way. Obviously with the whole punk style, and some bad engineering in the studio or whatever, the lyrics tend to get lost in the music, but I believed passionately in everything that I wrote, and it's a miscarriage of justice for me that people were unable to discover the true meaning of the songs."

In October 1983, their second single, the 'Pulling Puppets' Strings' three-track EP, was released by Riot City. A more restrained affair than its predecessor, it saw the band exploring their more melodic rock influences without losing sight of the edgy menace that earned them their reputation, and, possibly as a result of the shows undertaken with them, there were definite tinges of The Dead Kennedys about some of the lead guitars.

A UK tour was undertaken with The Varukers, but there was dissatisfaction with their label simmering in the band. They sacked their manager of the time, and, soon after, John left, to be replaced by Chris Hind, their ex-bassist who had since taken up guitar. This version of Mayhem recorded 'I Defy' for the Maximum Rock'n'Roll compilation LP 'Welcome To 1984', one of their best songs that easily held its own against a strong international line-up showcasing some of the best hardcore punk bands from around the world.

"We'd had a letter from Ruth at Maximum Rock'n'Roll saying we could go on their compilation, specifying that the song had to be no longer than two-and-a-half minutes, and no shorter than twenty-five seconds. They actually gave us a political slant which they'd like us to write it upon... to which we wrote a letter back replying, quite abusively and arrogantly, that we had enough trouble with our girlfriends fucking telling us what to do, let alone them starting to as well!"

After a brief drug-induced hiatus, Mayhem returned to release a new single 'Fresh Blood', on their own label, Vigilante Records. Featuring two tracks, 'Blood Rush' and 'Addictive Risk' (with 'I Defy' also appearing on the 12" version), that saw the band slowing down even further, it was still a powerful outing. However, disputes over distribution of label funds led to Chris Hind's departure, and the band took more time-out to contemplate its future.

In 1986, Fred Doyle took over the drum stool, and Pete Morley joined as second guitarist alongside the returning John Liu, but although they wrote new material and played several shows a proposed recording deal with Liverpool's Probe Records never came to fruition, and the band petered out for good.

"At the end of the day," says Mick, "Freddy was a superb bedroom drummer, but when you put him onstage, and the medicine and the alcohol kicked in, he was struggling to remember the structure of each song. He was destroying it. And at the last rehearsal, I was looking at the rest of the band, and they were all looking at their feet, and Freddy was blatantly murdering the songs... and I just thought it was time to end it. I'd given it everything I'd got, and just knew it had to die with dignity... before I died of fucking boredom!"

Mick now resides in London and sings with Amphetamine Missionaries, a more tuneful band than Mayhem ever were, but just as raging, and with all that furious attitude still gloriously intact, albeit refined by the experience of maturity.

"If I reformed Mayhem, we could probably tour extensively in Japan and America or whatever, but I can't sing those songs anymore," he reasons with integrity. "It did its thing, and that's it. We were trying to achieve something with our music, and I think we succeeded. We did something off our own back, and enjoyed it while it lasted. What more could we ask for?"

SELECT DISCOGRAPHY:
7"s:
'Gentle Murder' (Riot City, 1982)
'Pulling Puppets' Strings' (Riot City, 1983)
'Fresh Blood' (Vigilante, 1985)

12"s:
'Fresh Blood' (Vigilante, 1985)

AT A GLANCE:

No such thing, unfortunately. This tragically overlooked band have never enjoyed any significant CD release, although they have two tracks each included on both Volumes One (1993) and Two (1995) of Anagram's 'Riot City: The Punk Singles Collection' CDs. The 'Riotous Assembly' compilation, featuring their track 'Psycho' also made it onto CD in 1994 courtesy of Step-1 Records.

BLITZKRIEG

B litzkrieg were another Southport band with enormous potential who, for various reasons, only released a few EPs in their heyday. However the small amount of music they did commit to tape remains as potent now as back then, and one has to wonder what might have resulted if they'd actually had chance to do a full album whilst at the peak of their powers.

The band was formed in 1979, originally comprising Mick 'Riffone' Gaul (previously in Paraquat with Mayhem's Johnny Liu) – vocals, Gary Sumner – guitar, Chris Hind – bass and Phil 'Din' Gaul (Mick's brother) – drums, and they slowly made a name for themselves gigging around the North West.

"I was listening to The Drones and The Pop Group," remembers Mick. "All those Small Wonder and Rough Trade bands made me realise that you could actually take music somewhere else, could put a political slant on it. We could see the first wave of punk bands all going a bit soft, mellowing out, and showing their real colours, and we were stuck in a provincial town and wanted to do something different, create something ourselves, for ourselves. We had very few musicians to call upon, so we had to take and groom musicians from other scenes.

"I was listening to the PiL album a lot at the time, and although there was no real political message on that record, it was like ground zero; it drew a line in the sand. It was very refreshing, a new format; it was obvious that no one was going

The 1983 lineup of Blitzkrieg
L-R: Dave Ellesmere, Gary Sumner,
Chris Hind, Mick Gaul
(Pic: Phil Gaul)

to accept five minute guitar solos anymore ."

It was only a matter of time before Blitzkrieg followed the time-honoured tradition and recorded a demo in an attempt to generate some label interest. In late 1980, Malvern's No Future Records took the bait and offered them a place on their first 'A Country Fit For Heroes' 12" that appeared early the following year.

"We went to Manchester to record, because there were no studios in Southport, and we put a tape together and sent it out. I didn't have my own phone, so I was pumping 10ps into my nearest phone box, ringing all these labels! It was that basic, it really was, but I was very driven – still am – so I was basically the founder, the manager, the songwriter, the publicist... I did everything. I tried to keep it all together. I sent the tape off to No Future, 'cos we saw an ad – one of many ads we saw, asking for bands for compilation albums – and they got back to us, saying we were going to be on an album... and we thought 'Great!' And we were lucky enough to be the first track on that compilation, which is always a good position."

The track in question, 'The Future Must Be Ours', was both a powerful opener and a formidable statement of intent from the band, laden with huge raw guitars and one of the more convincing moments of the compilation. No Future were impressed enough with the response to finance a single, the classic 'Lest We Forget' EP, but not before Phil Din was replaced behind the kit by John McCallum. Four slices of incredible driving punk rock, there was a strong anti-war message running throughout the whole EP, delivered with sneering vehemence.

"I could see that the country – and the world – was in a complete mess," sighs Mick. "And you just felt like you were a very small voice in a very dark place. 'Lest We Forget' was just saying that what had happened in World War I and II, could happen again – and it has! In Cambodia, and many other places... Afghanistan and Iraq now. Where there is great intolerance of certain points of view, and you can get shot and hung for your beliefs.

"At the time, we felt like outcasts. There was nothing vaguely commercial about what we were doing. We were just writing about our frustrations and fears. There was all this anger, this cascade of pure thought coming out. But we did work really hard on the music, to get it all right. It sounds pretentious now, but we really wanted to create a big sound with a strong message and appeal to new people; we didn't just want to preach to the converted all the time."

Despite the high regard most other people have for their debut, Mick has some reservations about the sound.

"I'd still like to get it remastered and released as a 12". They crammed all four tracks onto a 7", and there's no bottom end. It sounds shit; we hated it. Perhaps I'm just looking back on the session with rose-tinted specs, but if you heard the original masters, they were amazing... the 7" just sounds so trebly; they really cracked the sound down and lost some of the power of the recording."

To promote the release, Blitzkrieg toured the UK with The Varukers and Mayhem, and they also landed themselves a slot on the prestigious Xmas On Earth show at Leeds Queen's Hall, alongside The Damned, GBH and legendary USHC band, Black Flag.

Both a change of drummer and change of label followed, John McCallum being replaced by The Insane's Dave Ellesmere and Sexual Phonograph (a division of Illuminated) taking the place of No Future, for the second single, 'Animals In Lipstick'. Although featuring several strong songs, the single definitely lacked the visceral power of its predecessor, a fact seemingly reflected by sales, with it only reaching No. 30 in the Indies. The band split up soon after, with Dave returning to The Insane, and taking Gary Sumner with him, and Chris Hind leaving to concentrate on Mayhem.

"It was a very volatile situation," explains Mick. "Both me and Chris Hind, the bass player, liked the same kind of music, and we both wanted to be the captain of the ship. And I'd formed the band, and I was the one doing all the organising, so as far as I was concerned, I was the captain of the ship! It was purely that I wanted to move on... it was kinda like, 'Been there, done that.'

"But I have no regrets about my time in Blitzkrieg! We did the best we could with what we were given. It would have been nice to have done a few more songs, maybe with a better engineer, but it seemed right at the time. I was very into the scene, into the lyrics... I was consumed by it all in a way, but I had no game plan. I didn't want a statue made of me or anything. When all you had was a local heavy metal disco once a week, you just wanted to do something. You had to do something!"

Spike, formerly with The Parasites, who fronted Blitzkrieg from 1987 onwards...

Although that was the end of the road for Mick (who now plays in Polestar, a three-piece London-based outfit "like REM on acid, only heavier"!), it wasn't however the end of Blitzkrieg. In 1986, Dave Ellesmere joined The Parasites alongside singer Spike, and in 1987, the pair reformed Blitzkrieg, with a returning Gaz Sumner on guitar and someone called Trev taking up the bass duties. This line-up recorded a track ('One Way') for the 1988 'Saw Yourself In Half' compilation on Leeds-based Raquel Records and also played around the UK with such bands as (ex-Advert) TV Smith, Anhrefn and The UK Subs.

Trev and Dave then departed for pastures new (the latter moving to Bristol and drumming for Dr. And The Crippens), but Spike and Gary recruited ex-Mayhem members, Dead Cat and Freddy Doyle, to take their place for even more touring. Blitzkrieg split up yet again, with Spike forming Paradox UK, only to reform in 1990, this time with a bassist called Mal replacing Dead Cat and ex-Paradox UK member Ales joining on second guitar.

This 'new' Blitzkrieg recorded 'The Future Must Be Ours' album, which saw the light of day via Spike's own label, Retch, in 1991. The record contained re-recorded versions of early songs off the EPs, as well as several storming new numbers, and although boasting a kick-ass guitar sound, an enthusiastic vocal performance from Spike, and a definite chugging metallic tinge to the new songs, it was let down by some sloppy drumming and didn't recapture the magic of their No Future era. To promote the LP the band undertook a full UK tour with Discharge (who were in support of their 'Massacre Divine' album) and The UK Subs.

"My favourite shows?" ponders Spike. "Probably Manchester International on that Discharge tour; it was just a great whisky-induced happy night, and a great audience, I just loved everything about it. Also when we played at the Duchess of York in Leeds was another happy one; great crowd again, everything about the evening was good. There are probably loads but they're the ones that stick out.

"And as for my least favourite... now you're talking! The single most appalling gig would be in Manchester in the venue that was opposite the Hulme estate... it's been pulled down now. I think it was called The Factory in the Seventies. We only got through three songs, and those three kept stopping every ten seconds or so. Freddy was so pissed he fell over his kit about sixteen times even during that short a set – incredible! We made arses of ourselves that night – well Fred did, anyway – and that would probably be my least favourite show. We were supporting the City Indians, and to anyone who was there that night: I apologise!"

In January 1992, Mal was replaced by 'Scouse' John and Ales by Fast Pete, and more shows were undertaken but the band finally called it a day – for good, this time – in April of that year.

"The band eventually ran out of ideas, and any material being offered up was below par," Spike admits. "And when you run out of ideas you should be honest and just give up and move on to something else. For me personally, the Blitzkrieg train pulled into the station marked Good Taste and I got off, and we all went on to do other things. Each phase of the band had its own sound and style, if you like, and every time we reformed, we always felt that we definitely had more left in the tank, but I think we more or less emptied it by '92, and when you're just running on fumes it's time to fuck off!"

Despite the many trials and tribulations encountered along the way, Spike remembers his time in the band fondly, and rightly reckons they deserve their place in the punk rock Hall Of Fame.

"Blitzkrieg is a classic example of mixing intelligent, social commentary and political insight with full-on Ramones-meets-Motörhead-via-a-few-pints-with-The-Pistols high octane hard punk rock. It was an uncompromising, honest assault, and we were never afraid to stand alone out of the crowd and say what we thought. We were also never afraid to drink to excess and completely ruin a gig…consequences be damned!

"I think we gave it everything we had while it lasted, and it was mainly extremely hard work, but when it did work it was the best. The band's gone but the fight continues… The Future Must Be Ours!"

SELECT DISCOGRAPHY:
7"s:
'Lest We Forget' (No Future, 1982)
'Animals In Lipstick' (Sexual Phonograph, 1983)

LPs:
'The Future Must Be Ours' (Retch, 1991)

AT A GLANCE:
Captain Oi!'s 'The Punk Collection' (a split CD that Blitzkrieg shares with The Insane) compiles the band's essential early recordings, as well as one or two latter-period numbers, and is the only place to find their early Eighties output on CD. There are reproductions of all the original sleeve art and some great insightful liner notes by (ex-Vice Squad drummer) Shane Baldwin.

THE INSANE

The Insane from Wigan shared several members with Blitzkrieg at various times, although during their tumultuous existence, drummer Dave Ellesmere and guitarist Simon Middlehurst also served time in Flux Of Pink Indians. That said, they produced some great music in their own right, and their 'El Salvador' single is especially well remembered as a minor classic.

They formed in 1979, and their first line-up, as well as Dave and Simon, comprised Barry Taberner on vocals, Dean Porter on bass and Tina Walsh on second guitar.

"Originally it was just Barry, with me on guitar," reveals Dave. "I would tune the guitar so I could use one finger for everything, a bit like the guy in Crass did. Together, we actually wrote the song 'Nervous Breakdown', that The System eventually used on their first single (for Spiderleg Records)!"

Simon Middlehurst had formed his first band in late 1978, called Sammy And The Skunx ("We did garage/punk versions of old rock classics but with new and stupid lyrics!"), with his older brother Clive, who later became The Insane's roadie and driver. He ended up being asked to join the band after lending them his gear for a gig at The Mount in Orrell. "For me, the hometown and political climate was a great motivation," he reckons. "Wigan 1979, sixteen years old, no job, no money, spots on your face, no girlfriend... we were angry white youth! You didn't have to sound like Led Zeppelin to get a gig; you just got up and did it! And it was all about the music – loud and fast and energetic, perfect to get out all that pent-up aggression."

"We wanted to make the sound more powerful by adding a second guitar, and she was the only one we knew that could actually play," explains Dave, of Tina, the band's short-lived extra guitarist.

"We were all hanging out at this punk club in Wigan about that time called Trucks... basically so-called because it was a truck! The stage was one end of the truck, and the DJ booth

The Insane's Simon Middlehurst

was done out to look like a truck too; it was pretty good actually. That was where I saw Discharge for the first time. It was where all the punks hung out, and Tina used to go there a lot, and she saw us playing, got talking to us, and told us she played guitar... so we gave her a try, but it didn't really work out."

"By the time Tina joined, we were out of school and at Wigan Tech," elaborates Simon. "I met Tina in the canteen, she wanted to be in a punk band, played guitar, albeit with just one finger, looked cool, had her own gear, and was a great laugh. It turned out she knew Dean too, so she was in."

For a while at least. Not long after Tina's departure, Dean Porter was also replaced by Julian Berriman, and in 1981 the band recorded the track 'Nuclear War', a driving slice of nihilism ('What's the point of living if there's going to be a nuclear war?' wails Taberner during the vitriolic chorus) that appeared on the 'Ten From The Madhouse' compilation.

"That was on a local label called No Pier Records," says Dave, "because Wigan hasn't got a pier – despite that song 'The Road To Wigan Pier'! It was basically a compilation of Northwest bands, from Bolton and Manchester and places like that."

In May 1981, Dave joined Discharge on drums for a few months, replacing original drummer Tez, and playing on the band's seminal 'Why?' 12". He also played the 'Apocalypse' tour with the band, co-headlining across the UK with The Exploited.

"It was quite funny really, because I'd just seen Discharge playing in Wigan, and I was painting this giant Discharge face on my wall – Mick Riffone, the singer from Blitzkrieg, was helping me. And my mother picked up a copy of Sounds, and saw that Discharge were looking for a new drummer, and she called up and arranged an audition for me! My mother actually made the initial call, I didn't even know that they needed a new drummer!

"Those guys were all a lot older than me," he adds, on his departure from the band. "And they'd all known each other since school, and they weren't exactly over-friendly… the whole thing was a bit overwhelming. I never really felt a proper part of it; I felt like I was just there to fill a gap for them. I was still looking up to them really; I'd just finished painting their logo on my wall! But it was a great opportunity for me, to play with one of my favourite bands, and I took it."

From Discharge, Dave went on to join Flux Of Pink Indians, but this time he took Insane guitarist, Simon Middlehurst, with him.

"Well, I was trying to get Flux to play a CND benefit gig in Wigan, and they said they'd love to do it, but they didn't have a drummer. So they asked me if I would do it – they'd heard that I'd just left Discharge, or been kicked out, or whatever – and I brought Simon with me. And that's how I got into Flux, and then that particular show never actually took place in the end anyway!

"The trouble was, me and Simon were driving all across the country to play with Flux, and we'd play to two thousand people, and we'd get £10 petrol money, which didn't even cover our expenses…

"Flux wanted to re-record The Epileptics '1970s' single, and they knew The Insane were playing the Woodstock Revisited gig at The Rainbow, so they booked the studio for the same day, to test mine and Simon's loyalties. So we went and played the show, just because we felt that they were pushing us into a corner to make a choice between the two bands… and it was a terrible show anyway! The band before us, Case, let off these insecticide bombs, and there was all this orange smoke all over the stage. It was all around the drum riser, and it really got on my lungs, and for five years after that, I was coughing up this orange crap. I couldn't run more than ten yards without being out of breath and coughing violently… it was really bad."

Dave Ellesmere, of The Insane, who also drummed briefly for Discharge, Blitzkrieg and Flux Of Pink Indians, amongst others…

Increasingly disillusioned with life as mere hired hands, Dave and Simon reformed The Insane, and soon found themselves signed to Bristol label, Riot City. In fact, their 'Politics' 7" was the next thing to appear on Riot City after the first two Vice Squad singles.

"Uh, well, at the time, I was having a fling with Beki from Vice Squad," admits Dave, when pushed as to how the label noticed them. "It was never anything that was going to last, though; we were at opposite ends of the country. Anyway, I gave her some tapes of the band and she passed them onto Simon at Riot City, who liked them. And that's all I really wanna say about it!" he adds, laughing.

'Politics' came out in December 1981, and spent over a month in the Indie Charts, reaching No. 18. It was an incredibly raw debut, with a very 'cardboard' drum sound, but despite the primitive production values, it captured the energy of the band more than adequately. The strongest song from the single, 'Last Day', also appeared on Abstract's best selling 'Punk And Disorderly' compilation early the following year, and to this day, that remains Simon's favourite Insane song.

"We just made the fuzziest guitar sounds we could in some basement studio in Manchester," he recalls wryly. "We were laughing all day and it's even on the track if you listen closely enough. Only thing was, Barry wasn't even there for the first single! He didn't turn up, so I had to sing, and on the song 'Politics' people said I sounded like Pete Shelley, when really the track should have had Barry singing and sounding more like Malcolm Owen!"

"It's rough and ready," Dave agrees of their storming debut. "It was our first real studio experience, apart from little four-track demos or whatever, but it did really well, although when it came to royalties, they weren't very forthcoming… so we moved to No Future. And then when 'El Salvador' (the next single) sold over twenty thousand copies, all we got from them was a cheque for £90 each! And Chris (Berry, who ran No Future) had even asked us if he could give away a copy of his fanzine free with every single, so we thought 'Why not? We'll do him a favour!' And then he only tried to charge us for the printing costs of his mag…!"

To coincide with 'Politics', The Insane appeared at the Xmas On Earth festival at Leeds Queens Hall, playing alongside the likes of The Damned, GBH and The Exploited in front of ten thousand enthusiastic punks. It was an inspirational climax to 1981 for all concerned.

The aforementioned 'El Salvador' 7", the band's finest moment by far, came out on their new label, No Future, in May 1982, and was deservedly a big hit for the band. It peaked at No. 6 in the Indies, but remained in the charts for over three months. By this time, 'Dr.' Dean Mitchell had replaced Barry on vocals, and Julian Berriman had given way to Steve Prescott on bass. As well as the superb title track, 'El Salvador' was backed by a re-recording of 'Nuclear War', sounding better than ever thanks to a strong thumping production, and a sterling rendition of the old Johnny Thunders' chestnut, 'Chinese Rocks', which the band did great justice to.

However, despite the success of the single

Gary Sumner, guitarist with both Blitzkrieg and The Insane
(Pic: Phil Gaul)

– or maybe because of it – cracks began to appear in the relationship between Ellesmere and Middlehurst and The Insane split in two, both halves clinging doggedly to the name and refuting the other party's right to use it.

"In fact, the real reason it happened was, we were due to play at Skunx in Islington," explains Dave. "And the day of the show, Simon started saying he didn't wanna do it, 'cos the chances we were going to get paid were slim, and he couldn't be bothered. And I didn't like that attitude, in case people came to specifically see us and we weren't there, and they went away disappointed. In hindsight he was right (laughs), but I didn't want to let people down, and it was our first London show after the No Future single, and they were expecting a really good turnout there.

"I think we both had different visions of what we wanted for the band, different musical directions... I'd just played with Discharge, doing this really brutal stuff, so when I came back to our Subs/Ruts sorta sound, I wanted to do something faster and harder. Simon liked that Subs style, and the choppy guitars. And there was just a clash of personalities at the time."

For his version of The Insane, Dave Ellesmere kept hold of vocalist Dean Mitchell, and recruited guys name of Phil and Trev on guitar and bass respectively. Simon, on the other hand, kept bassist Steve Prescott, brought back original vocalist Barry Taberner, and recruited new drummer Keith Finch. As to who was really Insane though depended upon interpretation and allegiance.

Dave's band played out a lot more, with the likes of English Dogs and The Varukers, but when Simon's troupe self-released the 'Why Die?' 7" on Insane Records, they pretty much established their right to the name. It was a modest success, scoring a No. 38 placing in the Indies when it was released in October '83.

"Well, I guess we still had the deal with No Future records, and I came up with the name in the first place, so I was convinced that WE were The Insane, and the other guys should change their name. But again it was just a case of me and Simon being stubborn really, and not wanting to back down. We had all these promises of a new release from No Future, which just didn't come through; they let us down really, they didn't want to get involved in the argument. In the meantime, Simon was getting the money together to do his own 7", so when that came out, I just said 'Okay, you win'."

Dave then joined Blitzkrieg when their drummer John McCallum left, and played on their second single, 'Animals In Lipstick', a record that he actually rates as the worst thing he has put his name to.

"I'd known those guys since day one, and I got on really well with their guitarist Gary Sumner – right up until the Disgust record we did together (in 1993). So when their drummer left, they asked me, and I did it. I was never one to stick with one thing so long that I got bored with it!" he laughs. "I mean, hats off to people like Charlie Harper – he has a lot of integrity and determination, and it's good that he's still so into it – but I couldn't just keep doing something for that long. I prefer to capture the moment and then move onto something fresh."

However, in yet another bizarre twist of fate, Dave then returned to The Insane, taking with him Gary Sumner from Blitzkrieg, effectively leaving that band in limbo.

"They had some European dates lined up and their drummer couldn't do them, so Simon asked me to do it, which was kinda funny! The whole reason we split in half the first time was ridiculous anyway, and after the break from each other, we found we got on a lot better again. Plus Barry, the first singer, was back in the band, so it was the original stable line-up again, and they had some new material which I had to learn, so that was a lot of fun."

Simon has his own theory as to the band's seeming inability to keep together a concrete line-up for any significant period of time:

"I think the real reason was that, as we got more gigs at home and abroad, the commitment was more. And as people started getting jobs, all the rehearsals, all the money we were spending etc., it all took its toll, but we just kept moving on, keeping the band going. Then again, girlfriends probably had a lot to do with it as well. All girlfriends were banned from the tours and that upset a few along the way."

Despite such distractions, The Insane then enjoyed a short period of relative stability, during which they undertook several European tours, before splitting up once and for all. Various shows from this period were recorded and later released posthumously by Retch Records as the 'Live In Europe' album.

"I think the memories of just playing all those gigs is great," says Simon. "But the best memories have to be of all the laughs we had on the way, and all the great people who helped put the gigs together in the first place and who put the band up on tour.

"I think the gig in Zurich, Switzerland was one of the wildest. We'd played there once before, but this time we played some squatted venue. Halfway through, the Swiss Army – their SAS or whatever – all came busting in. It was great, we kept playing; it was wild, like watching a film, but being a part of it! When the police and army had gone, we had a great night with all the punks too. And it made a change from Ellesmere causing all the trouble!"

The excellent track 'Berlin Wall' was also released as one side of a split 7" with The Skeptix on White Rose Records, and the band also appeared on several high-profile compilation albums. They had the track 'The Whole World's Going Insane' – most recently covered to great effect by German punk band Oxymoron on the 'Worldwide Tribute To Real Oi' album on I Scream Records (2000) – on Mortarhate's 'We Don't Need Your Fucking War' comp, and they even managed to sneak a hidden track onto Pax Records' anti-war benefit, 'Wargasm'.

"We managed to get The System a place on that Pax album," reveals Dave. "And they finished their recording really quickly. We were all in the studio anyway, because we'd been doing backing vocals for them, and we had a song called 'We Don't Want Your Fucking War' that we hadn't recorded, so we did our song after them, and they sent our track in with theirs, all as one song. So The Insane actually had a song on (the first pressing of) that compilation, straight after The System track, but we weren't credited, so no one knew we'd even done it!

"The whole scene was fragmenting, and gigs were few and far between," adds Dave, of the band's eventual split. "It just wasn't the same anymore, it didn't have the same energy, it didn't have the same meaning for me. But punk did change me, absolutely, and for the better. It gave me a lot more respect for other people, and it made me look into things a lot deeper; I don't take things on face value anymore. Punk rock stopped me accepting things blindly."

After The Insane, Dave teamed up with latter-period Blitzkrieg vocalist Spike in The Parasites. They split in 1987, and Dave and Spike resurrected Blitzkrieg with Gary Sumner and Trev who had played with Ellesmere in The Insane during the feuding with Simon Middlehurst. Dave then went on to play with Dr. And The Crippens, whilst Simon himself played in Hotalacio with Colin Latter and drummer Martin, both ex-Flux members. He was even involved in a brief Flux reformation minus bassist Derek Birkett who by that time was running One Little Indian Records.

SELECT DISCOGRAPHY:
7"s:
'Politics' (Riot City, 1981)
'El Salvador' (No Future, 1982)
'Why Die?' (Insane, 1983)
'Berlin Wall' (White Rose, 1984) – split with The Skeptix

AT A GLANCE:

Captain Oi!'s 'Blitzkrieg/The Insane: The Punk Collection' is the perfect way to check out both bands featured. All the singles, and cover artwork, and some succinct informative liner notes from ex-Vice Squad drummer Shane Baldwin shed a great deal of light on the convoluted incestuous relations between the two bands.

THE FITS

T he Fits, like so many other second wave bands, began as something reactionary and generic, yet blossomed into something quite wondrous. The difference between their first and last recordings demonstrates the acuteness of the pronounced learning curve travelled by the band during their short time together, and one can only begin to imagine where they might have ended up had circumstances not conspired against them. The band formed in October 1979, and, in keeping with the spirit of the time, played their first show four days later.

"Andy Baron (who was to be their bassist) and I had seen each other milling around at various gigs, I think, and walking around the town," recalls vocalist Mick Crudge. "One day I remember we walked past each other in a park; he looked cool in a kilt with blue hair, and I had penny-round glasses on, orange hair and a very cool – even if I say so myself – jacket that I'd made. We talked for a while and it was his idea I think to form a band. He knew Kev Halliday and also Big Bill, the first guitarist. We met at Bill's house and did our first rehearsal in the garage. It was absolutely awful, but exciting. Kev played drums on cardboard boxes, Bill had a guitar and an amp; I think Andy had a bass, and I think I just sang with a decrepit old 'mike' made of bills taped to a broomstick! We got told to shut up, but it was enough for us all though; the fuse was lit.

"Andy knew Section 25, a local band, who were doing a gig, and he'd asked them if we could play, and they must have said 'Yes'. So we went down to this community centre in a place called Bispham, just got up and did about four songs, all stuff that we'd written in Bill's garage. I think we must have been the worst band on the planet, but, my God, we meant it. I think that was the most remarkable thing of all; we, Andy and I, really, really meant it.

The Fits 1983
L–R: Tez, Steve, Mick, Gaz

"I'd seen a lot of bands; some were good, others didn't really touch me," he continues, on his inspiration to be a singer. "I think it was January 1979, and Adam And The Ants came to play the Norbreck Castle in Blackpool. I had no idea who they were really; we just went to any punk gigs that came to town. I can recall even their roadies were weird looking. The place was fairly full, even though 'Young Parisians' hadn't yet come out at the time. Man, they were so different to that record; it's still a puzzle as to why they even released that. But from the moment they came on, the place just went nuts, absolutely nuts. Blackpool was actually quite a spoiled crowd and they never would really let go; there were too many bands in town who thought they could do better, but that night was incredible.

"When I'd first heard The Pistols, I knew that that was what I wanted to be, but when I saw The Ants that was what I wanted to do. Not even halfway through the first song of a virtually unknown band and I was buried on the floor at the front of the stage. I recall looking up and seeing Adam Ant in the air; all leather and make up, with this weird, dangerous-looking band that just came at us. Matthew Ashman, the guitarist was just so amazingly cool; I always loved his playing style, although for some reason, their sound at the time never made it onto vinyl. It still gives me a buzz when I think about it now; we were lucky to have seen them in their prime."

The Fits in Hyde Park, 1984
L–R: Mick, Tez, Steve, Gaz
(Pic: Gavin Watson)

Big Bill only lasted four gigs before he was replaced by Steve Withers, and the first real version of The Fits was born, bonded by some deep primitive desire to make loud, fast music.

On June 16th 1980, eager to document their progress, the band rushed – in retrospect, probably prematurely – into a Manchester studio ("We had no idea what to expect; it was the first time that we'd had to stay in time!") to record their first single, the defiantly-titled 'You Said We'd Never Make It'. They pressed 1500 copies and glued the gatefold sleeves up themselves.

'Listen To Me' was the standout track, a spirited rant against the system, albeit horribly out-of-tune, and it was backed by 'Bad Dream' and 'Odd Bod Mod', which indulged the obligatory tribal rivalry of the time and wasn't really in keeping with the rest of the band's output.

"All I can say is OOPS! I was just a kid! It was a local favourite, there were loads of rucks and scrapes with the mods happening at the time; they would all come to Blackpool in their thousands for the weekends. We got quite a few of the records sent back to us smashed up, and death threats from various towns across the county... OOPS again! Silly fool that I was. It wasn't a bad tune really, another Andy Baron one; the dub thing could have been great with a different set of lyrics. I still get people shouting 'Odd bod mod' at me when I go back to Blackpool, and I still blush. Wasn't really The Ants there, was it? Sorry everybody!"

The Fits hooked up with Barry Lights, a local entrepreneur ("He became a legend in his own right, didn't he?"), who helped sell the single through his second-hand record shop Lightbeat.

"That was what was really good about Blackpool though," reckons Mick. "You didn't really need distribution; it was continually fed by holidaymakers, who always brought new things to town. But it also had a very tight and happening local scene. I think the penny dropped... or at least Barry thought he heard them chinking. He always was a tight bastard! He would say he was 'careful'. Do you remember the phone boxes back then would take two pence, five pence and ten pence pieces? Well, we'd call around to his for a brew and he would bring out these long lists of calls he'd made, that would add up to £3.37 or £2.29, and ask us to cough up, saying 'It all adds up'. It used to irritate me no end."

Once the initial pressing had sold out, Lights reissued 'You Said We'd Never Make It' on his Beat The System label, which got the band to No.2 in the Punk Chart in Sounds, and saw them landing decent support slots up and down the country. In November 1981, they signed to Mansfield-based Rondelet who released their next single, 'Think For Yourself', on New Years Day 1982. Adorned with a suitably grim illustration of a guy hung up by hooks through his nipples, the two tracks on offer – 'Burial' and 'Straps' – were a vast improvement on their debut, sounding infinitely more confident and aggressive. The band was coming on in leaps and bounds.

"Now I don't know if you'll think this is weird, and I don't mean it in a narcissistic way at all, but The Fits were beautiful. People came to see The Fits. The Fits were a spectacle in those days – really! We began to get professional too. No more open back trucks with all the gear strapped down and the band with a few mates getting blown about in the back on the motorway! No sir, we had to get our act together, book vans, pay drivers... or at least beg my girlfriend to drive for us, and swear to her teary-eyed family that we would look after her out there in that big bad punk world.

"I remember we supported The UK Subs at Manchester Poly; God, they were awesome. I'd never been a big fan of them before, even though Steve and Andy had always loved them. We came on and did our little well oiled but wooden set. We were actually quite good, but then along came The UK Subs, and they were like liquid! I watched from backstage. Waves of kids rolling up and off the stage, the whole band seemed airborne, Nicky Garratt jumping from the PA stacks mid-riff... magnificent. I was most certainly a fan after that night, and we realised that we had work to do!"

During three days in March '82, the band rush-recorded their rather erratic, throwaway thirteen-track album, 'You're Nothing, You're Nowhere'. There were admittedly highlights, such as the rampant title track (which Mick still despises to this very day, spitting "It's fucking awful, we should have dropped it off the North Pier!"), but there's far too many bland fillers padding out its running time. It ushered in a low-point for The Fits, with Kev leaving after a particularly bad gig in Burnley in May '82, and Andy being asked to leave a few weeks later. They were replaced respectively by Tez McDonald from One Way System and Ricky McGuire from Scottish band, Chaotic Youth ("He came to live on my settee for a while," laughs Mick). Buoyed by fresh blood, the band recorded the 'Last Laugh' EP at Spaceward Studios in Cambridge with Knox from The Vibrators producing, which spent over a month in the Indies and went to No. 44 when it was released just before Christmas of that year.

"Now we had a band! Tez was sharp and fast, I never had to look around again, and Ricky was just very cool, reliable... a great bass player. I once said in Punk Lives that he was 'effeminate and that'; I didn't mean that at all! I just meant to say he was graceful. Steve had by now got that Gibson and a Marshall 100 watt combo he'd always wanted, and he'd developed a style and look all his own. We were now well on the way to having a real sound and, more importantly, getting tight. Though I have to say I don't think I was going too far lyrically at the time; I was too busy driving it all and that was where my focus was."

Ricky McGuire, who went on to join The UK Subs and eventually The Men They Couldn't Hang, left in February 1983 and, after many auditions, was replaced by Gaz Ivin.

"We'd looked high and low, and just couldn't find the right attitude," remembers Mick. "It was all about attitude, wasn't it? Well, Gaz turned up for an audition, and he was all hair, but he knew every song on the album. He'd travelled with his girlfriend from Stockton. He was perfect, but as one last final test, Steve decided to put them through the mangler. I don't know where from, but he found this porno film. They were sat there in his front room, really sweet and shy, good people they were too, and Steve popped the video in – he always did have a wicked sense of humour. Well, they never flinched. Steve was giggling; I don't think I could stand it for too long either. We were bastards, I still can't believe we did that to them."

The band were still floundering though, with Tez constantly battling against a persistent drug problem, but a chance meeting with John Robb from The Membranes who suggested they try Corpus Christi Records led to the band contacting Penny Rimbaud from Crass, and being invited down to that band's secluded farmhouse retreat.

"I'll never forget going out to meet them. We thought that they'd be living in some paint sprayed, piss stained squat somewhere. We weren't sure how to approach it, as we were definitely not part of the 'Anarchy Brigade', as we used to call them. We got the tube out to Epping, and called a number we'd been given from the train station. A voice told us to wait. There was something clandestine going on... well, we imagined there was anyway! Then this little, beaten up, red car turned up and it was Eve Libertine driving – gulp! We got in and made small talk and were driven out into the countryside somewhere, over cattle grids, opening and closing farm gates, down, up, over and across dirt tracks and fields. Until we saw this unbelievably beautiful farm house down in a sort of hollow in the land. It had all rows of fresh crops coming up that seemed to radiate out over the furrowed and ploughed fields and hills in all directions. Trees, birds, greenery... absolutely lovely. We were very humbled and very shy.

"If I remember rightly, they made us tea, chopped sugar from a block. Steve Ignorant drank Carlsberg and smoked our Steve's fags. We had all these ideas about them, we wondered where the home brew was, but it wasn't anything of the kind. In fact they were absolutely lovely to us. There was Eve Libertine and the other famous woman singer they had, who we both instantly had a crush on. We talked about I don't know what now. Penny Rimbaud was very serious, but not in a control sort of way; if anything, he seemed to be more concerned about us. They were charming people. We stayed for a few hours, I think, and then they ran us back to the station in the little red car. I remember looking back through the window as we drove up the dirt road away from there; it was genuinely a beautiful place. I don't recall them ever saying, 'Okay, you got the deal'; it just seemed to be understood. I think!"

The result of this unlikely alliance was the 'Tears Of A Nation' EP, an epic grandiose slab of anthemic punk that utterly eclipsed what the band had achieved up until that point. Recorded at Southern Studios during two days in June 1983, and produced by Barry Sage who had previously worked with such rock legends as The Rolling Stones, 'Tears...' reached No. 15 in the Indies and remained in the chart for two months. One of those rarest of things, a genuinely perfect and passionate moment captured in the studio, it finally saw The Fits pulling together all the pieces of their complex jigsaw and ensuring their place in the annals of punkdom. Inspired by its success, Mick and Steve relocated to London, but Tez remained in Fleetwood with his family, which was to cause tremendous logistical problems that contributed to the band's imminent demise.

Barry Sage was also producing 'The Mating Sounds of South American Frogs' album for Peter And The Test Tube Babies at that time, and he played the new Fits' material to The Test Tubes and their manager, Nick McGerr, who invited the band out for some shows. After bonding well with the Brighton punks on the 'Legs Akimbo' tour, especially guitarist Derek and drummer Ogs, who sometimes stood in for them behind the kit when Tez failed to show, The Fits ended up releasing a split 12", 'Pressed For Cash', on The Test Tubes' own label, Trapper Records, donating a track that Mick still cherishes as their finest moment, the excellent, upbeat 'Peace And Quiet'. More gigs with the Test Tubes followed, which saw the band playing in front of an audience they were increasingly unsuited to.

The Fits' Ricky McGuire (bass) and Mick, live at Blackpool's Gaiety Bar, 1982

"It was about then that we really began to see the rise in violence on the punk scene. It got to the point that we hardly ever played a gig somewhere without some sort of confrontation, or some sort of riot going on. The Test Tube Babies would just surf across it though; they were way too good for all that, but they never could quite shake that Oi tag. Even though they were light years away from it, in both their music and their attitudes as people; they were genuinely funny guys.

"Me? I took it all personally, didn't I? Fool! Those tours though, with them, and on our own, were the best gigs we ever did, but after the excitement of the initial few riots and gigs had worn off, we just got really, really fed up with it all. We were never an Oi band; we sort of just happened to be amongst it all… it was quite an education."

'Action' was the band's penultimate single. Released on August 24th 1984, it was another Indie hit for The Fits, although it could well have done better if the choice of A- and B-side had been reversed, as the track on the flip, 'Achilles Heel', had a much more dynamic and effective song structure. Hype about the release was obviously helped by the ample amount of pubic hair on display by the cover model in her patent leather thigh-high boots… considering they were on Crass Records six months earlier, no one can ever accuse The Fits of playing it safe!

Come the final single, 'Fact Or Fiction' (Trapper Records later compiled it with the 'Peace And Quiet' track and the 'Tears Of A Nation' EP as the 'Fact Or Fiction' mini-album), and the cracks in the band were beginning to show. It all came to a head on the band's final tour, and The Fits called it a day in November 1985.

"I have to come clean here," sighs Mick. "I was wearing all that fucking make-up. I cringe now, but I was just reacting to all the ugliness and violence wherever we seemed to go. I really didn't want to be part of it, but I loved The Fits. It was a sort of two fingers to it all; it was meant to antagonize, but I think it just switched people off to us. Why didn't somebody tell me? I'm sure they did! Oh well, I regret it in retrospect.

"Tez had finally thrown in the towel and gone back up north for good. We got a new drummer, though he was never one of us. It was, I suppose, all too near the end. That tour was just the worst; we played toilets, it was freezing. There were ugly scenes wherever we went.

"I remember one night in Coventry, a mob waited for us outside! Anarchist types, who we'd let use all our battered gear, even the drumsticks. We had no money to pay them – it wasn't even up to us to pay them – and we had just enough to get home to London ourselves. They took massive offence at us, and we all squared up outside. Poor Nick McGerr got punched in the mouth. We did a bit of quick thinking and somehow turned them all on each other, and there was this big fight in the street. The rest of the band had been quietly packing the van, so then we all quickly jumped in, put our foot down and took off with them running after us. It's a funny story now, but wasn't funny at the time. There were many other evenings with awful endings too. We'd just had enough, I think."

Mick, Steve and Gaz went on to play in Pure Pressure for a while, before Gaz moved to L.A., Steve headed for Spain, and Mick ended up "living in a car in America" for a few years.

"We never really had a plan," he says, in closing. "Nor did we totally identify with the later branches of the punk scene. We were just a Punk Rock band, and that was it. We were really trying our best to do something of some worth… but I suppose everybody was trying to do that, weren't they? But I was in The Fits. As I said earlier, for me it has always been a search for direction, for something good. It still is. I believed 100% in it and, at the end of the day, that is what is important to me. That we really meant it, man…!"

SELECT DISCOGRAPHY:
7"s:
'You Said We'd Never Make It' (Beat The System, 1981)
'Think For Yourself' (Rondelet, 1982)
'The Last Laugh EP' (Rondelet, 1982)
'Tears Of A Nation' (Corpus Christi, 1983)
'Action' (Trapper, 1984)
'Fact Or Fiction' (Trapper, 1985)

12"s:
'Pressed For Cash' (Trapper, 1984) – split with Peter And The Test Tube Babies
'Fact Or Fiction' (Trapper, 1985)

LPs:
'You're Nothing, You're Nowhere' (Rondelet, 1982)

AT A GLANCE:
Captain Oi!'s admirably comprehensive 'The Fits Punk Collection' compiles twenty-seven of the band's best – and a few of their worse – tracks onto one disc, complete with reproduced artwork and extensive liner notes from Mick. It comes highly recommended, especially the latter half of the disc.

ONE WAY SYSTEM

F leetwood, Lancashire, spawned one of the second wave's most powerful bands, One Way System, who unleashed some genuinely stirring underground classics over the years, and are still together, as ferociously relevant as ever, today. They formed at the very tail end of the Seventies, citing boredom as the primary catalyst for their inception, and played their live debut at J.R.'s (in Blackpool) sometime in 1978. By 1980, the initial line-up had settled as Gavin White – vocals, Dave Ross – guitar, Craig Haliday – guitar, Gaz Buckley – bass and Tommy Couch – drums.

They were soon dubbed an Oi band because of their half punk/half skinhead line-up, which wasn't a bad thing as it potentially doubled their audience.

"The half punk/half skin thing was never intentional," laughs

One Way System
Clockwise from top left:
Tommy Couch, David Ross, Gaz Buckley,
Gav White (Pic: Tony Mottram)

drummer, Tommy. "I myself considered it all to be the same – punk, skin, goth, crusty, whatever… in terms of music, we were all part of one big scene. That was then cut up by the media and offered to the masses to make of it what they would. The politics between these different segments only became evident when we travelled more and learnt that it was this that was the real separating factor. Maybe I was naive, living in a small town… but the overall scene always seemed united; it was just the inter-band slagging that needed working on. By that I mean that we could have probably got on better with all the other bands in our area at the time… although it did all work itself out, in the end.

"But as I said earlier, it was definitely all about the music for us. The fact there was not much to do in Fleetwood at the time – there still isn't, in fact– meant that the band was a great social and physical tool to have. The only politics we concerned ourselves with were local events, and that's still what fuels our songs to this day."

After releasing their 'Stab The Judge' EP on Barry Lights' local Lightbeat label, such was the critical and public response to the debut, it was but a short time before the band were taken under the wing of renowned manager, 'Lord' John Bentham (who also ran Jettisoundz Video), and snapped up by Anagram.

"Ah, yes, John was a major factor in our early successes," reckons Tommy. "He was as charged about the band as we were, but he also knew where to go to get and achieve what we wanted. The 'Lord' moniker came from us all giving out nicknames during some of the early recording sessions… and if I'm not mistaken, he actually picked it himself!

"The hook-up with Anagram came after a few companies wanted to sign us... but the Lord spoke, and we ended up signing with Anagram!"

"I first came across One Way System in 1981," says John. "They were appearing in a local 'rock battle' competition at Jenks bar in Blackpool. There was a very unusual mix of bands there. I was managing another local band, The Zanti Misfitz, at the time and I guess I became known as someone who could make things happen! I'd not really taken much notice of hardcore punk stuff 'til this point and was pretty impressed with how tight they were. They approached me about managing them, and I do recall it took me a little time to agree. They very quickly became the first signing to the newly-formed Anagram records, but I still think 'Stab The Judge' is my favourite release... even though I do prefer the version we recorded circa '82!"

And it was a seemingly astute move to make, because One Way System remained with the label for all of their early Eighties releases, and enjoyed considerable Indie Chart success. The first release for Anagram was the storming 'Give Us A Future' 7" in September 1982, and it had all the hallmarks of a classic OWS single. An insistent chest-beating chorus, a strong thick production, a great performance from the band... and a decent B-side as well – something you could always count on them to deliver!

"Well, first off, we were a well-rehearsed band," ponders Tommy as to what set them apart from their peers. "It was, and still is, our life. We rehearsed two or three times every week to develop the songs and develop our own playing. The lyrics were just real life lyrics, things that you could see and feel happening. Pair these and then add our passion and love for what we were doing, and maybe that adds up to our sound!

"Musically we were inspired by The Clash, The Damned, The UK Subs, The Ramones, Killing Joke, The Ruts, The Exploited, GBH, Crass, The Test Tube Babies...the list is endless. I don't think anyone in the Northwest really inspired us... maybe Blitz, to an extent, but then again, we were rising up at the same time as these bands anyway."

In January 1983, One Way System released what many regard as their crowning glory, the superb 'Jerusalem' single (Tommy: "No fuss, just pure impact!"), which spent two months in the Indie Charts and peaked at No. 22. Not only was it as hard as nails, but it was so catchy it hooked itself into the listener's brain like a tick and wouldn't let go. The band was maturing at a frightening rate, and so was Gav White's gravelly but soulful voice. It was backed by the cautionary tale, 'Jackie Was A Junkie'.

"Yes, we did have several songs about drugs. Just from having seen what drugs had done to certain friends and even past band members, we felt that it needed addressing. It's amazing how many people we've met at gigs who said that they listened to those songs, and then they tell you their own accounts of drug abuse, and our songs are so like their own stories, as if we were writing just for them personally. Scary!"

Hard on the heels of 'Jerusalem' came the debut album, 'All Systems Go', a sterling collection of songs that also included the A-sides of the preceding two singles. Craig Haliday was asked to leave during the recording sessions because it was apparent he didn't fit in with the band's direction anymore. Any parts he had already recorded were edited out, but his role in the band had obviously become redundant, such is the power of just Dave's guitar tracks. There was something for any discerning punk or skin to get their teeth into – heads-down thrash tracks, mid-tempo bruisers, but all bristling with big singalong choruses. No wonder Tommy remembers it as his favourite OWS release ("It was something special; it really felt like we had achieved something when it came out.") And it was powerfully produced by none other than Colin Richardson, who has since become an internationally sought after metal producer, having overseen albums by the likes of Napalm Death and Machine Head.

"I can recall those sessions we did with Colin, they were so productive. He seemed to be the studio bod... you know, the guy that knew everything in there. He always had a good idea, and was very good at interpreting what the band wanted out of a recording. He was really easy to work with too.

"I remember one night, whilst celebrating in the studio, coming to the end of the recording of the first album, we just drank all night and collapsed. On waking up the next morning, all of us dying of hangover and excess, I remember seeing Colin totally pissed off and mortified – the place was total chaos; apparently we had done thousands of pounds' worth of damage to the equipment, and the owner was on his way down! I guess that was our first real studio fine; it's funny now, looking back, but at the time, we shat our pants!"

The album was hugely successful, spending two months in the Indies, reaching No. 11. As did their next release, which again just missed out on cracking the Top Ten – a cover of Slade's 'Cum On Feel The Noize'!

"The Slade cover came about really when we were messing around in the studio," explains Tommy. "The sound guy recorded it, and then Anagram got wind of it and thought it would be a great song to release. Also, the chorus really seemed to represent us at the time. Yes, we got a slagging at first, but the more we played it, the bigger the response it got, and it's still part of our live set even now!"

Extensive touring was undertaken to promote both the album and the singles that saw the hard-working band plying their wares all across the UK and Europe.

"To be honest, I couldn't pinpoint any one gig as the best," responds Tommy when asked to name a live highlight. "Maybe I'm sitting on the fence here, but there were just so many excellent gigs and tours, too many to choose from. All the early Lyceum gigs, or the Clarendon Klub Foot gigs, and all the tours and gigs with The Exploited, The Test Tube Babies and GBH. It was just a great time.

"As for the worst gigs... same again, I'm afraid. It wasn't usually so much the gigs themselves that were bad, more what was going on outside them! Especially the early gigs in Germany, with rioting outside. Hearing all the gunshots and seeing all the violence, having people pulling guns on the band, saying they wanted to shoot us for whatever cause or other. They were bad gigs!"

Despite their gruelling live schedule, One Way System managed to be incredibly prolific in the studio as well, and their second album, 'Writing On The Wall', actually appeared just eight months after the first one.

"The two albums were recorded pretty much back to back because we just had so much material and lots of people behind us pushing us forward. Even the record company were 100% behind the band wanting more and more, which is very rare nowadays I reckon."

And although it lacked some of the spark that made their debut so special, it definitely wasn't a weak 'filler' release and featured ten boisterous new songs that basically carried on where 'All Systems Go' left off. If anything it was faster and more vehement than its predecessor, as well as being better executed, but was missing one memorable chorus too many. Once again it was recorded under the guidance of Colin Richardson and the watchful eye of John Bentham, and boasted an impeccable sound. And it actually reached No. 6 in the Indie Charts, the band's highest placing.

In the spring of 1984, One Way System released their final EP of that era, the comparatively weak 'Visions Of Angels'. Featuring four quite progressive songs with a distinctly rockier feel to them, it's a decent enough release in its own right, but when compared with the band's own back catalogue it pales into relative insignificance.

"That EP is the only thing we did that I don't really like," confesses Tommy. "The reason being, it was produced by Mike Stone of Clay Records, and we had no control over that particular recording process or production. None of our ideas for that record got used in the end, and the production was shite, even if I say so myself!"

The band split soon after, but ten years later was back together again, albeit with only

Tommy and Dave Ross remaining from the original line-up.

"First off, we were stuck in some sort of contractual wasteland," says Tommy, of their initial disbanding. "We had loads of new material but no outlet, and the scene seemed to be getting very stagnant with very few gigs to be had, so we just drifted apart for a while, I guess... but we all stayed within the music industry with other projects.

"And because we were involved in those other bands, we kept finding ourselves crossing paths with the other members from time to time, and we even did the odd gig here and there as OWS. By late '93 or early '94 we were back rehearsing again, and we had some offers of gigs abroad. It was the response we got at those gigs that lit the fuse again, and we just carried on from there."

"I accompanied the band on their Japanese tour in 1997 and recorded seventeen hours of video footage," reveals John Bentham. "And it was probably my favourite tour undertaken with One Way System. In many ways, although very energetic, the Eighties were manic and often problematic. Doing this, years later, on the other side of the world, was a pretty rewarding experience and so much more relaxed. And the full film will eventually surface one day!"

"I think the drive comes from doing something that you love," adds Tommy on the subject of the band's continued existence over twenty years after its troubled birth. "Just being part of that, with three other great friends, travelling the world, meeting new people, and seeing the response at our gigs, is truly inspiring and humbling. As for longevity, that came from the friendships within the band... that's the only real reason I can come up with, but what better reason could there be for still doing this?"

SELECT DISCOGRAPHY:
7"s:
'Stab The Judge' (Lightbeat, 1982)
'Give Us A Future' (Anagram, 1982)
'Jerusalem' (Anagram, 1982)
'Cum On Feel The Noize' (Anagram, 1983)
'This Is The Age' (Anagram, 1983)
'Visions Of Angels' (Anagram, 1984)
'Live In Rennes' (Mass Productions, France, 1995)
'Search Your Soul' (Mass Productions, 1996)
'Believe Yourself' (Brick Records, Japan, 1997)
'Leave Me Alone' (Cleopatra, 1997)

LPs:
'All Systems Go' (Anagram, 1983)
'Writing On The Wall' (Anagram, 1983)
'Return In Briezh – Live' (Mass Productions, 1997)
'Waiting For Zero' (GMM Records, USA, 1999)

AT A GLANCE:
Between the 1994 CD versions of the two albums on Captain Oi! there are actually twenty bonus tracks, namely all the B-sides, EPs and demos from that era. There is little to choose between the two discs, but 'All Systems Go' still stands as their most potent release. Elsewhere, in the Anagram Punk Collectors Series, 'One Way System: Singles Collection' (2003) is quite comprehensive, and also Cherry Red's 'No Return/All Systems Go' DVD provides a great visual document of the band, from early shows in Blackpool right through to latter-period footage from Japan and America.

INSTANT AGONY

O
ne of the fastest, most hardcore bands from the Northwest was Birkenhead's Instant Agony, who released four storming singles in the early Eighties before self-destructing prematurely in that time-honoured punk fashion. They've since reformed in the mid-Nineties and have enjoyed considerable success since, taking their frantic Mersey beat as far afield as the US and even releasing the full length album that eluded them during their initial incarnation.

"There was a group of us on the Wirral who were really into the punk scene," says original bassist (he's since moved to guitar) Paul 'Tabby' Cavanagh, casting his mind back to their humble beginnings. "We regularly went to all the gigs in the area, mainly at Eric's but also at the Empire, the Royal Court and the University, so we saw nearly all the late Seventies bands. They inspired me but I never thought that I could get a band off the ground myself.

"In 1979, after the Eric's march, when hundreds of punks got together and marched all round Liverpool in a demo to keep the place open, I moved down south to a place near Bournemouth called Swanage to work. There was a big

Instant Agony, at rehearsal in Birkenhead, 1980
L-R: Stephen, Si, Tabby, Ant

punk scene there and someone gave me a bass guitar; then a mate of mine called Anthony Yeardsley, who was a guitarist, taught me to play a few lines and it wasn't too long before I was writing my own stuff, and that's when I really thought about having a go!

"So I got the band name together, and a few songs, and moved back home up north with Ant for a better chance at doing something. We got a singer, my kid brother Stephen, and a drummer called Simon Golding, who had access to a cellar and we rehearsed for a few months before we had the chance of playing our first gig."

Instant Agony's live debut was at The Hamilton's in Birkenhead, and the band had to play their six-song set twice because it was so short ("Nobody seemed to notice," laughs Tabby). They nearly never played at all, having to negotiate with the bouncers to get their singer, who had been kicked out of the venue earlier, let back in the building.

In this guise, the band gigged regularly around their area, building up a large local following.

"In the early days, when you could still walk around Birkenhead and Liverpool and see punks wandering about with coloured, spiky hair and leather jackets, really looking the part, it was still a good scene and really exciting. I can remember that the people who came to the gigs were really enthusiastic and well into the harder look and sound of the newer bands; it had a much rawer, faster sound than the punk bands of the Seventies… what you saw is what you got, no frilly edges and no overproduced sounds. We were well into it all and we still got out to see the bands, we even played with a lot of them; it was mental, something was happening all the time.

People felt as though they were a part of something. We used to go to a pub near our rehearsal place and the punks would ask if they could come and watch us rehearse, so we used to take them back to the cellar and there were loads turning up; it was like a mini gig, it was great."

About a year after the band's inception, Stephen and Si left, after a show at Mayflowers in Manchester, and were replaced by Stephen 'Hocky' Hockenhull on vocals and Barry 'Bazza' Hilton on drums. It wasn't long before they were in S.O.S., a four-track studio in Liverpool, recording their 'Think Of England' EP, which came out on new label, Half Man Half Biscuit, run by one John Weaver from his local record shop.

Very basic and very fast, and wrapped in an eye-catching 'cut and paste' sleeve portraying Prince Charles and Lady Di in bondage trousers and safety pins, the EP went to No. 39 in the Indie Charts in July 1982, officially putting Instant Agony on the map.

"One of my fondest memories is when we finally got our copies of that first single," reckons Tabby. "To finally get hold of that record and to put it in my collection with all my other bought records was fantastic, a great achievement. We only ever thought we'd get the chance to do the one so it was real special, it meant a lot to all of us to get that piece of vinyl. We felt like we'd arrived."

Gigs were obviously undertaken to promote the single, but not as many as the band would've liked.

"One of my favourite clubs had always been Eric's in Liverpool and, one day while we were in a pub, we got a call to see if we'd be into doing a gig there… albeit after it had been renamed Brady's… supporting – I think – Anti Pasti. We agreed, but we had to get straight over there, so with the help of a load of the local punks, we ran to the rehearsal room, got our gear and caught the train from Hamilton Square station over to Liverpool. There was loads of hassle getting it all together, but we were all buzzing at the fact that we would be able to play on that hallowed and famous old stage where we'd seen all our favourite bands over the years.

"Everything seemed to be going okay; we got the gear onto the stage and were checking all of our stuff when some arsehole came over and said 'No way'! He was the mixing desk fella, a nobody who didn't want to mix any bands other than those he'd sorted out earlier… maybe he didn't like the look of us, but nothing we said would change his mind so, after loads of hassle and a bit of a slanging match, we had to take our stuff back home. Punters were coming in as we were leaving… it was a big, big disappointment; it could have been one of the highlights of the band's career to that date. I think it was the last time I ever went into the place after that; from then on, we played at the Warehouse where the next batch of Eighties bands regularly appeared."

The band's follow-up arrived in early '83, again on Half Man Half Biscuit, the 'Fashion Parade' EP. Another blisteringly quick punk assault, recorded this time at Birkenhead's Corndon House Studios, it spent over two months in the Indies, even cracking the Top Twenty, confirming that the band had, indeed, 'arrived'. It also featured another one of Tabby's distinctive colourful covers…

"Those EP covers were great to work on and I really enjoyed it; I'd have a few ideas and spend hours cutting up papers and magazines, then glue it all together. I mean there was quite a lot of that sort of thing going on, but I wanted to add my own spin to our sleeve designs.

"Again, along with the songs, people really seemed to like them and, even today, I speak to people who have still kept the early singles after all these years. Even the likes of Punkcore Records in America (the band's current label) say that those early sleeves and records inspired them and had an influence on what they went on to do. But I did want a sleeve that would stand out and be noticed; as I said earlier, we thought each record might be our last, so it had to make a mark."

The band broke the mould with their next single, 'No Sign Of Life', which appeared in August 1983. Not only had they signed to Flicknife Records, but they also took their foot off the throttle a little, revealing a more relaxed and tuneful side to Instant Agony.

"Even though we were very much in the vein of the early Eighties bands, I wanted to try to bring the influences of the earlier punk bands that had also made a big impression on me into our music," explains Tabby. "Their melody, production, arrangements etc., something to bridge the gap, and also have some lighter subjects to sing about; not just be totally political and reactionary but use as many day to day experiences and observations as I could.

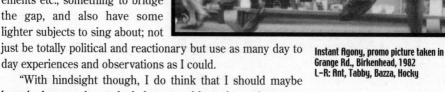

Instant Agony, promo picture taken in Grange Rd., Birkenhead, 1982
L–R: Ant, Tabby, Bazza, Hocky

"With hindsight though, I do think that I should maybe have had more of a gradual change and kept the pacier songs going, especially on the A-sides, a little longer! As for progression, myself and Bazza were musically moving a bit too quick for what we were trying to do. We got to grips with guitar and drums and pushed on a bit; the things we were doing in the early days were what we were good at so we should maybe have left well alone! I've actually gone back to the basics in the way that I am writing the songs now, and we're cranking out some really fast ones; the 100 mph stuff is great to do live again."

The band then went in to record their debut album for Flicknife, 'Nicely Does It', which unfortunately never saw the light of day, Instant Agony splitting up before its release. Two tracks were lifted from the album session as their final single, 'Nicely Does It' and 'We Don't Need You', but the rest of the recordings have been long since lost, although rumours persist that another song, 'Death Or Glory', was released in Japan at some point over the years.

"I remember one funny thing about the recording," says Tabby of the session. "We decided to leave Ant alone on one of the days to just do loads of multi-tracking of the rhythm guitar, to build up a meaty sound, so he was left in the studio for about ten hours, just him and the engineer. The rest of us went into the town and had a wander, a few drinks, some food and a look in the record shops; when we got back, we wanted to hear what had been done, but the engineer looked really frazzled and not overly impressed.

"We couldn't believe our ears! Everything was out of tune; Ant had cocked it up, the whole day had been a waste of time and it threw us well behind schedule, so the pressure was on after that. The engineer thought it was some strange punky tuning that we were into. So a lot of work done after that was a bit rushed.

"Then, to make things worse, we didn't have enough money to get home and the record company wouldn't give us any more, so I remember we were all in a phone box shouting at them that, unless we were given more money, we were going to keep the master tapes! Travel money duly arrived!"

The single itself is somewhat of a disappointment, being even more restrained than 'No Sign Of Life', the band's usual upbeat energy being subdued by a rather melancholic harmony lead guitar. Unsurprisingly it failed to chart.

"I'd have to say that's one of my least favourite songs of ours," agrees Tabby. "We had loads of trouble with it, it was badly in need of a re-mix but the people at the record company just went ahead and seemed to rush-release it.

"It had far too much lead guitar; we were just experimenting with different sounds in the studio and it was never meant to come out like that. We'd been doing the song live for ages and it always went down well; it had a much harder sound to it and should have been a decent progression from the previous single, but it wasn't. Maybe one day we will record it again and do it justice.

"I don't really know why we split up," he adds. "We had a decent record deal with another two or three albums and singles to be released, but we found it frustrating actually getting gigs away from the Northwest. We were really into doing gigs, but it was very cliquey and even though we had a name, we found it hard promoting our stuff. A lot of the agencies at that time were only dealing with certain bands and we couldn't get on any of the No Future tours… maybe our faces didn't fit? Also, there were a few tensions appearing within the band – we could really get on each other's nerves – but with hindsight we should have carried on. But hey, we were a punk band and that's what punk bands were supposed to do!"

As mentioned earlier, Instant Agony reformed in 1996, to record the 'No Pain, No Gain' 7" for Homicidal Records, with the exact same line-up that did their early Eighties singles. Since then, however, Tabby and Hocky have struggled to keep a regular bassist and drummer, but have still managed to release another single, 'Parasite', and an album, 'Death Of A Century', both for Homicidal.

Then, to celebrate Instant Agony's twentieth anniversary, Nottingham-based Weird Records released the 'Think Of England' EP, a powerfully re-recorded version of the first song the band ever released, backed by 'Everything's Alright' and 'Same Shit'. The limited edition single was a return to the Agony of old; three tracks of high speed, in-your-face punk rock, faster and harder than their output with Homicidal.

More recently, in 2002, the band played their first US shows, including a date at the legendary CBGB's club in New York.

In late summer 2003, Instant Agony then signed to well-respected US label, Punkcore, and unleashed another ripping three-track 7", 'Not My Religion' (b/w 'Misfit' and 'Ripped Off'), that ably demonstrated there's plenty of mileage left in the band, it being one of their strongest releases to date.

Instant Agony are now working on material for their long-overdue sophomore album.

"Well, we've stuck at it because we believe in what we're doing," reflects Tabby. "We enjoy it and we've got a few songs that have stood the test of time, and new ones which some people like even better. We have had to do a lot without the help that other bands have had over the years, but have kept on going regardless, and there's still so much more that we would like to do. I know that our early records are still kept in people's collections and haven't been thrown away like a lot of bands over the years, so what we did back then must have meant something to someone."

SELECT DISCOGRAPHY:
7"s:
'Think Of England' (Half Man Half Biscuit, 1982)
'Fashion Parade' (Half Man Half Biscuit, 1983)

'No Sign Of Life' (Flicknife, 1983)
'Nicely Does It' (Flicknife, 1984)
'No Pain, No Gain' (Homicidal, 1996)
'Parasite' (Homicidal, 1998)
'Think Of England' (Weird, 2001)
'Not My Religion' (Punkcore, 2003)

LPs:
'Death Of A Century' (Homicidal, 1998) – CD only

AT A GLANCE:

As the title suggests, 'Out Of The Eighties: The Singles And Rarities' is a Captain Oi! collection that features all the band's early singles, and a slew of bonus demo tracks, complete with original artwork and liner notes from Tabby. But if the recent singles are anything to go by, the forthcoming new album will hopefully be the band's defining moment.

EMERGENCY

mergency were a Manchester punk band that only released one single during their initial existence during the early Eighties… but what a great single that was! 'Points Of View' came out on the Riot City label early April 1983, and promptly shot to No. 23 in the Indies, remaining in the chart for a month. It was one of the strongest and most musically accomplished releases for the Bristol label, who tended to specialise in much harsher, noisier acts, and even Punk Lives had to admit it was a pleasant surprise, likening its 'dancing thundering beat' to The Buzzcocks. Unfortunately, circumstances conspired to make it the only single Emergency did during the heyday of punk's second wave, although they've reformed in recent years to further mine the huge vein of untapped potential hinted at by the iridescent 'Point Of View'.

Emergency, 2004
L–R: Dennis Matthews, Albert Awful, Chris Corvette, Banjo

The band strummed their first power chord in January 1982, forming from the still-smoking ashes of several Manchester punk bands. Guitarist Graham 'Aky' Atkinson and drummer Peter 'Flannel' Flanagan had previously joined bassist Chris 'Corvette' Sheridan (formerly of Random Gender) in The Hoax, a popular local band whose drummer Mike Joyce went on to join The Smiths, The Buzzcocks and PiL, and who released an EP called 'Blind Panic' in November '81. When The Hoax vocalist Andrew Farley decided he wanted to take the band in a harder, faster direction, he fired the rest of the band who were reluctant to embark on such a course, and along with influential local promoter, Dennis 'The Oi' Matthews, on vocals, they became Emergency.

Taking their band moniker from the Girlschool song of the same name – rather than the 999 song, as many of you might imagine – Emergency began to practise in nearby Riverside Studios, in the basement of a funeral directors. The first gig was a suitably inebriated affair at Dukinfield Community Centre, and a demo was soon recorded at U-Turn Studios in Ashton-under-Lyne, which brought them to the attention of Riot City.

"It was a great laugh," remembers Chris of their first real recording session. "And the breakdown in Dennis's vocals on 'Hang Onto Yourself' was caused by me and the others running into the studio stark bollock naked and doing impromptu Beach Boys-style backing vocals! We left it on the recording just as it happened.

"Dennis was totally responsible for hooking us up with Riot City, through his many contacts as a band promoter," reveals the bassist. "It's the main reason we let him join the band, actually, but don't tell him that! As for the label, well, we couldn't have asked for more. They promoted the record nationally and paid all studio expenses, including beer and takeaways, and also gave us total control of artwork. The only thing they insisted on was having 'Points Of View' for the A-side, but they let us choose the tracks for the B-side."

Emergency entered Cargo Studios with Colin Richardson to record the single, and the results were extraordinary. A confident and compelling mix of the anthemic and the melodic, as mentioned earlier, it was something refreshingly different for Riot City.

"It's certainly stood the test of time in my opinion," says Chris proudly of 'Points Of View'. "I think it was one of the best releases on Riot City, and a lot of it was down to Colin Richardson; he really knew what we wanted and he achieved it. It took us three days to record and mix, a long time by the standards of the day, but the results are there for all to hear.

" I don't know about being out on a limb," he ponders. "But we were certainly different from the herd, and thank fuck for that! The world didn't need any more identikit hardcore punk bands! We were an island in a world of noise; we looked different and sounded different. There's no need to play at breakneck speed, badly, and have a mohican to be a punk band; punk comes from within, it's an attitude, a feeling – not a fucking ripped T-shirt!"

Powerful sentiments indeed, but we can only imagine what might have happened had such a defiant attitude continued harnessed to such uplifting sounds, because, no sooner were things apparently going their way, with gig offers coming in thick and fast, than the band broke up.

"The reason the band split is a bit of a blur, to be honest, but as I remember it boiled down to Aky and Flannel not wanting to go on a UK tour we'd been offered. There was promise of a European tour to follow but they really didn't want to quit their jobs. They were also unhappy with the musical style, wanting a more Killing Joke kind of feel, whilst Dennis and me were more into The Ramones, The Clash and The Stranglers. It was always Dennis and me against Aky and Flannel... and me and Dennis usually won!"

Emergency seemed destined to be remembered as 'one hit wonders', with Chris moving to London and serving time in bands such as Hitsville UK and Sonic Sound Reaction. In late 1997, however, he teamed up with vocalist Jon 'Wah Wah' Taylor (ex-Ceed), guitarist Andrew 'Fuzz' Sutton and German drummer, Chris Martin, and decided to give Emergency another go. Fuzz unfortunately broke his hand rather badly, leaving his future as a guitarist in question, but as luck would have it, he was also an accomplished drummer, so when Chris left, he moved to the drum stool. Albert Awful from The Stains and The Only Alternative stood in on guitar. He was soon replaced by ex-Chelsea guitarist Rob Miller, and Emergency hit the gig trail again, playing several Punk Aid festivals, and even headlining their own show at the 100 Club.

In October 2001, they split once more, a decision that Chris attributes to family and work commitments, as well as more than one clash of personalities! Undeterred the bassist got original vocalist Dennis back on board, Albert Awful in on guitar, this time as a permanent member, and a Preston drummer, name of Baz, who played in a band called Slutch. Baz was quickly replaced by Banjo, from Manchester band, the Spitting Dummies, and the current version of Emergency was finally complete. They've since been busy writing material for their long-overdue debut album.

"I think punk was the best thing that ever happened to me," Chris ponders, in closing. "I've always retained that 'Fuck you, I'm gonna do it my way' ethos. In the late Seventies it was a fertile breeding ground for all the shit of society to get together under one banner and cause a bit of mayhem. The younger generation may not believe it, but it was very dangerous to be a punk in those days, but I think it has definitely shaped me into the strong-minded individual I am today, and I still dye my hair! Fucking silly old sod!"

DISCOGRAPHY:
7"s:
'Points Of View' EP (Riot City, 1983)

AT A GLANCE:
The A-side of 'Points Of View' appeared on Anagram's 1993 'Riot City: The Punk Singles Collection, Volume One', whilst 'City Fun', one of the B-side tracks appeared on 'Volume Two' in 1995. Other than that, the band themselves have released a collection of their various demos on CD entitled 'Lost And Found'.

XTRACT

tract were a comparatively obscure band from Bolton, Lancashire, who only released one single in their own right but, based on the strength of their limited output, could have been much bigger than they actually were. Formed in 1979 by bassist Mick Halliwell and drummer Eddie 'Kip' Fisher from Neon Rage, Xtract quickly recruited guitarist Karl Morris and, after trying out both John 'Greenie' Green and Steve 'Ox' Oxstaby for the role of vocalist, they were joined behind the microphone by Dave 'Harvi' Howarth from Nervous Disorder. The band made their live debut at Westhoughton Youth Centre early in 1979.

"We were all shit scared of getting onstage," laughs Karl. "I remember playing and the kids pogoing around, then we were off into the back; we were all shaking and laughing at the rush of playing in front of a crowd!"

"I remember halfway through our set, I looked up at the windows and saw people looking and watching our set from outside," adds Kip. "I looked a bit harder and realized it was my mum and next door neighbour waving at me... I was totally embarrassed!"

Sufficiently encouraged, Xtract recorded their first demo at Jamm Studios in Bolton, where they rehearsed once a week, and carried on playing as much as possible locally.

"I think the best gig we did with the original line up was at the Aquarius club," recalls Kip. "About 250 people were packed in there and the place was buzzing. We had a big crowd going nuts, people were falling all over the stage, and we were completely covered in spit... so I guess we went down really well!"

The second demo was recorded at Cargo in Rochdale, and really captured the band's abrasive but melodic style. A copy was sent to Pax Records, who used several of the tracks on their well received 'Punk's Dead? Nah, Mate, The Smell Is Jus Summink In Yer Underpants' and 'Bollox To The Gonads, Here's The Testicles' compilations (1982 and '83 respectively) before signing the band for the 'Blame It On The Youth' EP. By the time they recorded the single however, Mick had been replaced by Rod Barker from Release The Bats.

Xtract, 1981
L-R: Harvi, Kip, Karl (behind drums), Mick

"Marcus (Featherby, who ran Pax) seemed to be okay," reckons Kip. "In the beginning he came to my house to talk to the band, and he had to stay with me 'cos none of the other lads would put him up, we all lived with our parents. I remember freaking out when he sat down in our front room and took off his shoes and socks. My dad had a fit and Marcus was shocked; he said he always goes barefoot in houses!

"But after we put out the single, I felt we were being taken advantage of, and I thought Marcus was taking the piss out of all the bands he dealt with. Needless to say, we never saw a penny from any of the records."

The four-track single appeared in 1983 and was a strong release that made No. 13 in the Sounds Punk Chart. Xtract played a powerful blend of punk rock not dissimilar to the mighty External Menace from Scotland, somewhere between the infectious melody of the first wave bands and the driving intensity of the second. To promote the single, they toured with label-mates The Mau Maus, as well as notching up support slots with the likes of GBH, Broken Bones and UK Subs, including several dates at London's 100 Club.

After the EP, Karl left to join The Exploited for a few years of "Drugs, sex and lots of punk rock!" He toured extensively with the band overseas, and played on their 'Horror Epics' LP before leaving in 1985 after a successful US tour with The UK Subs, that culminated with a show at CBGB in New York City. He also played on the 'Live At The White House' album, although he had left the band by the time of its release.

"After Karl joined The Exploited, we got Pagey (aka Chris Page) in but it was never really the same," continues Kip. "He didn't have the sound Karl had and couldn't play our songs the same way, so after a few shows I got fed up with it. I quit and, as far as I knew, the band split up."

"But in early 1985, Harvi got Xtract up and running again," reveals Karl. "Kip was married by then and had given up drumming, Rod had gone back to Release The Bats, so he got in Barney (aka Phil Barnes) on guitar, Jon Kitson on bass and Dylan Jones on drums. When I quit The Exploited a few months later, I rejoined and things started kicking off a bit for us then."

However, Karl put another spanner in the works when he joined Broken Bones in 1986. Xtract split up as a result... and then Karl was kicked out of Broken Bones ten months later, after playing on their 'F.O.A.D.' LP.

"That was a strange time for me," sighs Karl. "Broken Bones were really quiet and didn't go out to party much. And Stoke was not the best place to be a punk rocker; there were way too many asshole trendies. I just didn't like the lifestyle those guys had at the time and didn't really fit in with the little scene the band had around it."

Karl went on to spend several years touring internationally with The UK Subs in the early

Nineties ("I had to learn their set from the records and did the first European tour without a single rehearsal!") before forming Billyclub, an accomplished and bombastic punk band who've released several LPs and singles to great critical acclaim over the last decade. And it even appears that the final chapter may not yet have been written on Xtract either.

"Yeah, me, Harvi, Kip and Mick have been talking about reforming Xtract," adds Karl, in closing. "We all agreed to get together and have a few rehearsals to see how it goes, and if it's good we will do some gigs... and maybe even record all the old songs for a full length album."

SELECT DISCOGRAPHY:
7"s:
'Blame It On The Youth' (Pax, 1983)

AT A GLANCE:
Anagram's 1996 'Pax Records Punk Collection' CD includes three Xtract songs, two from the EP and 'Aftermath' from the 'Punk's Dead? Nah, Mate...' compilation.

DISTORTION

T ucked away in the extreme Northwest of England, the sum total of Distortion's early Eighties releases was the – admittedly brilliant – 'Action Man' track on No Future's 'A Country Fit For Heroes' compilation. Since then though, the band have reformed in the Nineties and found some international success through concerted touring and a slew of singles.

Formed by guitarist/vocalist Nigel Ben Barton in the small Cumbrian town of Aspatria in 1981, the first line-up of the band also featured Mark Ridley on drums and Kenneth Messenger on bass. A second guitarist was found in the guise of Gordon Mattinson, and when he left to join a New Romantic band, Paul Charters took his place. It was this line-up that recorded the aforementioned 'Action Man'.

Distortion supporting The Outcasts at Preston Warehouse, 1982
L-R: Weed, Jamie Bell, Nigel Barton, Kev
(Pic: Ken Messenger)

"While Paul was in the band we even tried using two drummers for a while," reveals Nigel. "Jamie Bell being the second drummer and still a schoolboy. The problem with two drummers though was that we ended up sounding like The Glitter Band... not such a bad thing, but not such a good thing either, when you're supporting a band like Infa-Riot!"

'Action Man' was recorded at North Rock studios in Carlisle, during a session that also saw 'Factory Life', 'College Boy' and 'Out To Get You' committed to tape. An intense blast of pure youthful aggression – powered by a great-sounding bass guitar and not dissimilar to more hardcore bands such as The Mau Maus – it managed to hold its own on a strong compilation against the likes of Blitzkrieg, The Violators and Attak.

"It was a dream come true," recalls Nigel fondly of their vinyl debut. "And in Cumbria it was a really big thing with the local press having a field day. Bands from Cumbria just didn't come out on record! I can remember sending my mam into Carlisle to buy ten copies from the local record shop. A few weeks later the owner was telling my sister, a friend of his, how this sixty-year-old woman had gone into his shop and bought a load of punk rock records... 'Yes, that would be my mum,' she said!"

The buzz generated by their inclusion on 'A Country Fit For Heroes' could have potentially been a major break-through for the band – if only they weren't out on such a limb geographically. They even signed a management deal with John Bentham's Jettisoundz company (also home to One Way System), in an attempt to get shows further afield.

"The biggest problem we had was keeping the interest going in the band when we had a set but nowhere to play it," sighs Nigel. "We got round that to an extent by hiring rooms in pubs and organizing our own shows with us and a couple of other local bands, who would then return the favour. One of our most memorable was hiring a back room in a pub in Aspatria and advertising it as free entry. We then hired a couple of local doormen to extract cash from people on their way out! An absolutely shameful thing to do, I know, but it was the most money we ever got!

"The best gigs were when we played with bands like The Outcasts, Infa-Riot and The Notsensibles because we would have gone to see them anyway. The Notsensibles one was funny; it was in a church hall in the Lake District and at the end of the night we were chased out of town – I can't think why... it must have been something we said."

Unfortunately, after Gordon left, original drummer Mark followed, and that was basically the end of Distortion's first incarnation.

"I tried to keep it going but I remember the last gig we did; I looked around and I was the only original member – all my mates had left and I felt the fun had gone out of it. I wanted to be with them at weekends, out getting pissed, so I called it a day."

However, in 1993, Nigel reunited with Gordon, and reformed Distortion, who promptly blossomed into a terrific, tuneful street punk band. Although Gordon left soon after ("His heart just wasn't in it"), sixteen new studio tracks were recorded, that saw the light of day on EPs through such well-respected labels as Helen Of Oi, Knockout and Walzwerk. And with a core line-up of Cathy Parker on drums (girlfriend of Tony Van Frater from Red Alert) and the mysterious 'Pod' on bass, Nigel was able to realise his lifetime ambition and tour all over Europe during the Nineties with some of his all-time favourite punk bands.

"We were one of the many 'almost there' bands," reflects Nigel on the band's turbulent Eighties period. "Sure, we were never going to be Cock Sparrer or The Anti-Nowhere League, but without bands like us there would never have been a scene in the UK. For every band that had records out there would be a hundred or more that never did, and some were as good as the big boys. We played with bands that were brilliant, with good songs, good attitude, great stage presence... that never set foot in a recording studio. At least we left our mark, small though it is. There are very few true punk rockers from the Eighties that don't have 'A Country Fit For

Heroes' in their collection and that's nice to know. Bands like Distortion were the foundations, the big bands were the buildings... but what would a building be without its foundations?"

SELECT DISCOGRAPHY:
7"s:
'Bully Boy' (Helen Of Oi, 1994)
'Rampage' (Aggrovation, 1995)
'Fun Time' (Knock Out, 1996)
'Street Hero' (Walzwerk, 1997)
'Generation That Never Grew Up' (Relentless, 2000)
'Living For The Weekend' (Scandal, 1997) – 4-way split single with The Crack, Pobel and Gesocks

LPs:
'Demon Inside' (Relentless, 1998) – 10-track mini-album

AT A GLANCE:
Apart from the Captain Oi! reissue of 'A Country Fit For Heroes', there's no official CD release documenting the Distortion back catalogue. However, in 2001, to commemorate their '20th anniversary' (albeit not twenty continuous years), the band compiled an unofficial bootleg disc of various early demo tracks – including, of course, the storming 'Action Man' – and more recent singles. The curious reader might care to e-mail the band: nigel.barton@tiscali.co.uk

CHAPTER FOUR

THE NORTHEAST

ANGELIC UPSTARTS

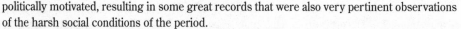

Probably the most influential band from the Northeast, The Angelic Upstarts were actually formed in South Shields in 1977 by vocalist Thomas 'Mensi' Mensforth and guitarist Raymond 'Mond' Cowie; however much of their best material was released in the early Eighties, hence their inclusion in Burning Britain. Not only were they musically superb, but they were highly politically motivated, resulting in some great records that were also very pertinent observations of the harsh social conditions of the period.

"The four original members (Mensi and Mond being joined by bassist Steve Forsten and drummer Decca Wade) were all from the same council estate that consisted of about eight streets," explains Mensi. "We somehow managed to scrape together some gear, we begged, borrowed and stole it basically. There was a really good community spirit between all the bands that were about though; we'd borrow the support band's gear, or they'd borrow ours, no problem.

"Our first gig was at the Percy Hudson Youth Club, South Shields. We used to rehearse there, and we did a gig for them. We only had six songs, but did them all three times, and it was fuckin' mega, we played in front of about a hundred kids."

The band released their debut single, 'The Murder Of Liddle Towers' (b/w 'Police Oppression') on their own label, Dead Records ("We had no choice but to put it out ourselves, 'cos no one would touch us with a barge pole," laughs the singer) in May 1978. Written about a local man who was kicked to death whilst in police custody, it didn't make them any friends in the Northumbrian Constabulary, but quickly sold out of its initial pressing of 1000 copies. It also brought them to the attention of Rough Trade, who reissued it late the following year, and John Peel, who gave them a well-received Radio One session. But by the time the session was aired on October 30th 1978, Decca had left ("It was 'cos we were having a lot of trouble with our ex-manager, nothing really to do with the band, and he later on rejoined…") and had been replaced by Keith 'Stix' Warrington.

Street punk guru Jimmy Pursey from Sham 69 loved what he heard too, and signed the Upstarts to JP Productions, planning to get them on Polydor Records alongside his own band, but things didn't quite work out as planned.

"I had a fight with a security guard at Polydor," admits Mensi. "And they didn't want us after that. So we went with Warner Bros. 'cos they had the best press department… or so Pursey told us anyway. He was a very heavy influence on me in the early days, and he had – still has, probably – a great production touch… it's just that he's a bit of a fucking nut!"

The band's first release on a major label was the classic 'I'm An Upstart' single, a storming, defiant anthem that was issued on green vinyl in March 1979 and spent two months in the National Top Fifty, narrowly missing the coveted Top Thirty by just one place.

Their Pursey-produced debut album, 'Teenage Warning', made No. 29 though, as did the album's title track when it was issued as a single that same summer (backed by their perennially enjoyable version of 'The Young Ones'). The band were invited to appear on 'Top Of The Pops' as a result.

"We actually recorded the album for free, 'cos Jimmy Pursey swiped some keys for the Polydor studios, and we did it over two or three nights, sneaking in whilst everybody was out.

"But 'Top Of The Pops' was fucking minging," he adds vehemently. "The whole thing was just fucking horrible. All I can remember is no one wanting to know us; we had a drink in the bar afterwards and no one would to talk to us, we were like fuckin' lepers."

November 1979 saw the release of the potent 'Never 'Ad Nothin'' single (b/w 'Nowhere Left To Run'), another barrage of outrage directed at the heavy-handed tactics of the police, that continued the fine Upstarts tradition of a good solid tune and powerful lyrics, continually fighting the corner for the underdog.

Two further 7"s followed in quick succession in early 1980, the super-intense 'Out Of Control' and the more laid-back 'We've Gotta Get Out Of This Place'. A damning sign of the

Angelic Upstarts
L–R: Decca Wade, Mensi, Mond, Glynn Warren

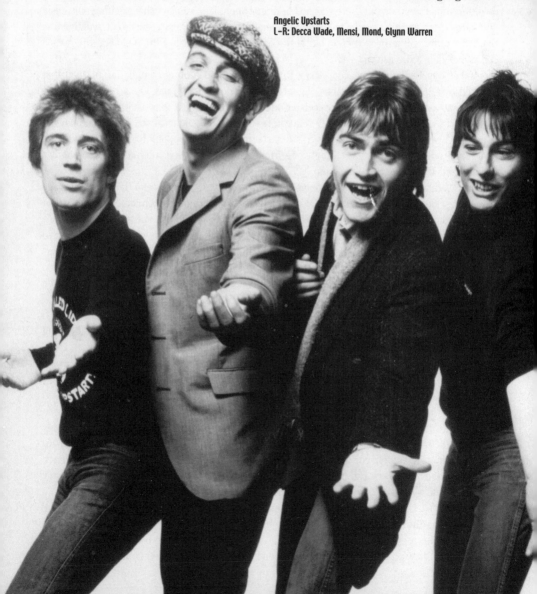

times, they both clocked up respectable sales despite their uncompromising subject matter, and the latter, originally by The Animals but imbued with new social relevance by The Upstarts, also lent its name to the band's brilliant second album.

However, by the time that sophomore album emerged in April 1980, Steve Forsten had been replaced by Glynn Warren.

"Steve left 'cos he wanted to form his own band and play a different sort of music, which was fair enough," reveals Mensi. "But the real reason was he got shit off his girlfriend for knocking about with other women! Glynn was a friend of Decca Wade's from Doncaster; he was a canny kid, and it was no problem."

Although a tremendous success for both band and label, the Upstarts parted ways with Warners soon after the album, signing next to EMI's punk imprint, Zonophone, a seemingly strange move that essentially replaced one corporation out of touch with the band's ethics with another.

"None of us understood what was going on really," reckons the singer. "You're right, one was no different to the other, but there was no big drama about it; it was just about getting our music out there. There were no fuckin' fortunes being made, they just put our records out, and that was the name of the game back then… but at the end of the day most of the people at the record companies didn't like us really."

And it was EMI that released Garry Bushell's 'Oi! The Album' compilation in 1980 that featured two Angelic Upstarts tracks, 'Last Night Another Soldier' and 'Guns For The Afghan Rebels', and saw the band forever associated with the Oi movement thereafter.

"Well, I want you to tell me the difference between Oi and punk because I know that I haven't got a clue," says Mensi. "All I know is that I started off in 1977 in a punk band and I'm still in a punk band now, so where that Oi tag came from I don't know! Is it a figment of somebody's imagination? It's not for me, thank you."

'Last Night Another Soldier' was one of the band's crowning glories and the obvious choice as their first single for EMI. It reached No. 51 in the Nationals, and was nominated Single Of The Week in Sounds, who declared it 'perfect punk'. A lofty accolade, but not far wrong, Mensi's sorry tale of a desperate youth escaping unemployment by signing up with the army only to meet a lonely death in a conflict he doesn't understand, is set to a truly uplifting and boisterous tune, complete with obligatory rousing chorus.

Stix left after the single to join the Cockney Rejects and was replaced by Paul Thompson (formerly with Roxy Music!) who debuted on November 1980's 'England' 7", one of the Upstarts' most poignant and patriotic releases, yet also one of their most misinterpreted. The Oi movement unfortunately attracted more than its fair share of right-wingers, who took the song to heart despite the band being vocally opposed to all forms of fascism.

"Yes, it's been very misunderstood," agrees Mensi regretfully. "The song was intended as a celebration of the people that fought the Nazis during the two World Wars, something I felt very strongly about because my granddad and his father both died in the First and Second World Wars and it was in memory of that.

"I don't think there is anything wrong with having pride in where you come from. The only difference with the Angelic Upstarts is that we respect people from other countries and we respect their pride as well, you know? A Frenchman has every right to be proud of being French and a Nigerian has every right to be proud that he's Nigerian, that's all. It's just been very misunderstood by some people, but we are anti-fascists and that's it."

The band's next single, 'Kids On The Street' (January 1981), reached No. 57 in the National Chart, but was the last to feature Thompson behind the kit. Former drummer Decca Wade returned for the reggae-heavy 'I Understand' 7", that also featured Jake Burns (from Stiff Little Fingers) and Terry Sharpe (from The Starjets) on backing vocals. Another controversial release, it was originally to be entitled 'White Nigger, Black Nigger', and was the tragic story of Rastafarian Richard Campbell who died behind closed doors in suspicious circumstances at Ashford Remand Centre. It was hardly any wonder that the outspoken Upstarts were being watched carefully by the police.

"Did you say 'were'?" asks the incredulous vocalist. "I still fucking get it, even now; they're like fucking elephants, they never forget! I got arrested four or five times for various reasons, I even got arrested once onstage. I was cautioned after our performance for incitement... nothing came of it, but yes, I did get lots of hassle off the police."

The band's third – and best – album was '2,000,000 Voices', a record that ably demonstrated their almost folk-like penchant for passionate protest songs, and included amongst its fourteen cuts new recordings of the previous four singles. Songs such as the irresistible 'You're Nicked' with its engaging brass section and the mournful harmony lead guitars on 'Jimmy' hinted at the rockier, more melodic direction the band would soon be taking.

In fact, 1982's 'Still From The Heart' was so poppy as to be virtually unrecognisable as an Angelic Upstarts album, and remains the band's weakest effort.

"We went too far on a couple of occasions," admits Mensi on the subject of the band's various musical evolutions over the years. "It was record company pressure, to be honest, but we should have been big enough to stand up to them and say, 'We ain't going to do it!' Unfortunately I was outvoted, but still, you can't please all of the people all of the time. And if people don't like it they should go out and do it themselves."

The irrepressible Mensi of the Angelic Upstarts telling it like it is

'Still From The Heart' wasn't popular with the fans either, and after two singles lifted from the album, 'Different Strokes' and 'Never Say Die', failed to set the world alight, the band were dropped by EMI. They found a new home at Anagram and, with Tony Feedback on bass and Paul Thompson returning on drums, enjoyed a creative renaissance in the form of the incredibly catchy 'Woman In Disguise' single. A scathing attack on Prime Minister Margaret Thatcher backed by the equally enjoyable 'Lust For Glory', it silenced any critics that doubted the band could still stir the blood with a good singalong chorus, and crashed into the Indie Top Twenty in late '82 where it remained for over two months.

The powerful acoustic track, 'Solidarity', was the next daring choice of single, and coincided with the release of the 'Reason Why?' album. A great return to form (not to mention loud guitars) after the thoroughly disappointing 'Still From The Heart', it saw the band indulging their progressive leanings without compromising their inherent thunderous roar.

Several other solid albums followed in the mid-to-late Eighties, not to mention successful touring around the world, before the band went into enforced hibernation, although Mensi refutes that they ever truly disbanded.

"That's an absolute fallacy! The Upstarts never split up... certain band members just left is all. I never called it a day, never officially, but other people in the band did, and I was just at a loss really as to recruiting new guys. Which I did eventually, but there was never an official comeback gig, 'cos as far as I'm concerned, we just found a new band and kept playing."

And Mensi has lost none of the indignant fire in his belly judging by the recent 'Sons Of Spartacus' album (Captain Oi!, 2002). Joined by Tony Van Frater and Andrew 'Lainey' Laing from Red Alert, and Gaz Stoker from Red London, he's still venting his rage at modern-day social injustices on songs like 'The Great Divide' ("Tony Blair says there isn't a great divide but in the south, a normal house would cost about £150,000, yet in the north I could take you to places where it would only cost you £10,000!") and 'Anti Nazi'.

"The main reason I continued through thick and thin was/is summed up in one word: fascism," he declares. "What was always unique about the Upstarts was that we were the first pro-active anti-fascist band. We were the first band.ever to take the fight straight to the fascists. Anti-fascist action is as important today as it was then; I still support them and always will."

SELECT DISCOGRAPHY:
7"s:
'The Murder Of Liddle Towers' (Dead, 1978) – reissued by Rough Trade (1979)
'I'm An Upstart' (Warner Bros, 1979)
'Teenage Warning' (Warner Bros, 1979)
'Never 'Ad Nothin'' (Warner Bros, 1979)
'Out Of Control' (Warner Bros, 1980)
'We've Gotta Get Out Of This Place' (Warner Bros, 1980)
'Last Night Another Soldier' (Zonophone, 1980)
'England' (Zonophone, 1980)
'Kids On The Street' (Zonophone, 1981)
'I Understand' (Zonophone, 1981)
'Different Strokes' (Zonophone, 1981)
'Never Say Die' (Zonophone, 1982)
'Woman In Disguise' (Anagram, 1982)
'Solidarity' (Anagram, 1983)
'Not Just A Name' (Anagram, 1983)

12"s:
'I'm An Upstart' (Warner Bros, 1979)
'I Understand' (Zonophone, 1981)
'Woman In Disguise' (Anagram, 1982)
'Solidarity' (Anagram, 1983)
'Not Just A Name' (Anagram, 1983)
'Machine Gun Kelly' (Picasso, 1984)
'Brighton Bomb' (Gas, 1985)

LPs:
'Teenage Warning' (Warner Bros, 1979)
'We've Gotta Get Out Of This Place' (Warner Bros, 1980)
'2,000,000 Voices' (Zonophone, 1981)
'Live' (Zonophone, 1981)
'Still From The Heart' (Zonophone, 1982)
'Reason Why?' (Anagram, 1983)
'Live In Yugoslavia' (Picasso, 1985)

'Power Of The Press' (Gas, 1986)
'Blood On The Terraces' (Link, 1987)
'Live From The Justice League' (TKO, 2001)
'Sons Of Spartacus' (Captain Oi!, 2002)

AT A GLANCE:

The Captain Oi! 2003 reissues of the first three studio albums come highly recommended, and feature the usual plethora of bonus tracks and liner notes. It has to be stressed that the brand new 'Sons Of Spartacus' CD rocks far harder than it has any right to, and won't disappoint any fans of classic Upstarts.

THE TOY DOLLS

S till one of the most unique sounding punk bands out there even today, Sunderland's The Toy Dolls exuded an irresistible manic energy that, coupled with their wacky style and flagrant disregard for the bleak aesthetics that were generally the order of the day, made them one of the more memorable early Eighties punk bands. Love them or hate them, once heard, they weren't easily forgotten, especially the virtuoso guitar playing and endearingly bizarre vocals of frontman Michael 'Olga' Algar.

"One thing was the raw sound of it all, especially the guitar sound, I loved it!" says Olga, reflecting on what drew him to the punk scene in the first place. "And also I hate ten minute self-indulgent guitar solos. Punk usually has none, or very short ones, which actually complement the songs. Another thing was the fact that the vocals didn't have to be pitch perfect; in fact, the flat and sharp out of tuneness gave it character... luckily for me!

"The anti-establishment thing was all well 'n' good too, but it was the music itself which appealed to me really. Lyrically I always preferred The Dickies, The Ramones and The Rezillos anyway. My first punk gig was The Jam at The Seaburn Hall in Sunderland in 1977; I was blown away! Two white spotlights, three guys in black suits and ties playing great songs as fast as hell, doing the Pete Townshend jumps! I loved it... even though I hate Paul Weller now."

In the earliest incarnation of The Toy Dolls, Olga just played guitar and was joined by vocalist Pete 'Zulu' Robson, bassist Philip 'Flip' Dugdale, and drummer Colin 'Mr. Scott' Scott, who were all friends of his from school. Prior to The Dolls, Olga had served an apprenticeship with local bands, Straw Dogs and The Showbiz Kids ("Once announced at a working men's club by the concert chairmen as 'The Show Biscuits'!"). He started playing at the tender age of thirteen, his earliest lessons coming courtesy of his older brother Ernie, who would later run the band's fan club and even do a short stint with them on bass.

"I never wanted to be a guitar player really!" reveals Olga rather surprisingly. "I wanted to be a bass player, after seeing Suzi Quatro play 'Can The Can' on 'Top Of The Pops'. Anyway, I saw the bass guitar I wanted and got a paper round for a year so I could buy it; I used to admire it every Saturday – it was £14.99. Then, after twelve months, I finally had enough dosh to buy it; I was as excited as hell, but when I arrived at the shop with the money it had gone up to £15.99! I was devastated, so, rather than deliver the Sunderland Echo for another month, I decided to just buy a guitar they had in the shop instead!"

The first Toy Dolls gig was during October 1979, at the Millview Social Club in Sunderland.

"Oh God, it was awful!" laughs Olga. "At working men's clubs you are expected to do two 45–minute sets... but we only had enough material for about forty minutes in total. I remember playing 'Tommy Kowey's Car' four times! The crowd, an average age of 55, hated us. We managed to persuade a local agency to give us the gig, and it was the last one we did for them.

"We used to practice at me mam's wash house on a council estate in Grangetown, Sunderland. We had no PA system and our singer sang through Flip's bass amp. We were poor, working class; we didn't know anyone whose mam owned a house... oh, apart from Flip – the posh git! These things made us the band we were/are. We wrote about local people we knew, places and situations in our hometown of Sunderland.

"I am sure if we had been born in Hampstead or some other middle class area, The Toy Dolls would have been completely different. Maybe there wouldn't have even been The Toy Dolls? Maybe there wouldn't have been that drive and ambition in us to start a band in the first place?"

After several more local gigs, it became apparent that Pete Zulu wasn't the right singer for the band (he left to form Zulu And The Heartaches, although he did rejoin The Dolls briefly, on bass, in late 1984), and eventually, after a month with local musician Paul 'Hud' Hudson behind the mike, Olga ended up taking over the role himself as well as being the guitarist.

The Toy Dolls, 1984
L-R: Pete Zulu, Olga, Little Paul

"We searched high and low for a vocalist who possessed that certain 'Toy Dollified' quality; we auditioned about twenty singers without any luck. Anyway, we had a gig coming up the following week at the Wine Loft, in Sunderland town centre, so we tossed a coin to see who would do the singin'... I lost, and have been tryin' to sing ever since!"

In 1980, The Toy Dolls released their debut single, 'Tommy Kowey's Car' (b/w 'She Goes To Fino's'), on local label GBH, named after the initials of the head of the label, George Bernhard Haswell. Although Olga regards that debut single as "A bit thin and dry" he also concedes that it will "Always be a bit special", and it certainly set out the band's stall for twitchy high-speed rock'n'roll topped off to perfection with lovably nasal and undeniably quirky vocals.

The 1981 follow-up, which Olga confirms was again for GBH even though it does say GRC on the label was the 'Toy Dolls EP', which featured four tracks, with 'I've Got Asthma' being the stand-out cut and also the most controversial. The Asthma Research Society tried to get the song banned, thinking it a cruel joke, but had they taken the time to actually talk to the band they would have discovered that nothing could've been further from the truth, with Olga himself even suffering with the infliction.

The Toy Dolls were also included on 1981's misunderstood 'Strength Thru Oi!' compilation, alongside the likes of Cock Sparrer and The 4-Skins, their two songs helping bring some much-needed levity to proceedings.

The exposure from the single and album helped land the band a deal with Zonophone, the punk imprint of EMI, which should have been the start of big things, but actually resulted in them lying low for a year whilst they regrouped and licked their wounds, before signing to fledgling local label Volume. By this time, after a rapid-fire succession of drummers (including Dean 'James' Robson, who would later become the band's bassist, Trevor 'The Frog' Brewis, and Graham 'Teddy Toy Doll' Edmundson), one Robert 'Happy Bob' Kent was providing the beats for the band's incendiary commentaries on everyday life.

"Signing to Zonophone was one of our bad moves," sighs Olga. "We thought they would re-release 'I've Got Asthma', but a director at the company went crazy when he heard it because his daughter had asthma, but y'know what? So have I, but nobody seemed to care about that! They had the option of releasing a track of their choice from our EP instead, and they chose the crap 'Everybody Jitterbug'. Then they put us in the EMI studio with their own producer. It was terrible; he tried to make me sing with a normal voice, an octave lower than my Olga voice...

"Anyway, they also had an option of another release providing they told us within a year. So we kept a low profile, hardly played at all, never called them, and they forgot about us, fortunately. We were out of the deal, thank God!

"The Volume thing only came about after being turned down by a million independent companies. I remember coming back from York on the bus having been turned down by yet another label; I was dying of the flu and depressed as hell, and I thought I'd give it one more try. Volume to the rescue! I couldn't believe it – a new company, and on our doorstep too. If that hadn't came about when it did, we were gonna call it a day... really!"

The first fruit of the new union was the band's brilliant debut album in 1983, 'Dig That Groove, Baby', and an accompanying single of the same name.

"We recorded in Durham, in a terraced house, in a little town called Pity Me... crazy name, eh? It only took three days to record and mix, so there was no time to fix mistakes. Happy Bob recorded his drum bits whilst on his lunch break from a local hospital where he worked. My favourite songs on it are 'Dougy Giro' (it's written from the heart and is completely true; we knew Dougy well), and also 'Glenda And The Test Tube Baby'. I really love the chorus; it has minor chords which I like a lot, and it's one of our best compositions. I actually think the album has aged very well, and it always sounds fresh – unlike some of the garbage we have written. It's the most special album for me anyway, because it was our first, but it's also one of the best."

The album set the madcap tone that The Toy Dolls would become well loved for, but the band were far more sophisticated than the superficial 'novelty' tag they've so often been lumbered with over the years. It made the Indie Top Ten upon its release, during early 1983, and remained in the chart for two months. It was supported by an intensive touring schedule that saw the band criss-crossing not only the UK and Europe, but also the USA (twice), no doubt gathering wry stories along the way that would later surface in their songs.

"Most of it is actually taken from next door neighbours," explains Olga of the inspiration for his often-surreal observations. "The lads down the pub, girlfriends, everyday happenings, and idle gossip. Most of the lyrics are fact, or based on fact; it's a lot easier to write fact than fiction for me... I just copy down what's in me head! And we usually use the real names of people and places too, which is a bit risky, mind you! I think the reason we decided to adopt this style is because of my voice; you are kind of restricted when your singing sounds like Orville The Duck! We are deadly serious about our songs and performance though, and yes, it does piss us off being called 'pathetique' or whatever. It's really difficult writing zany lyrics which don't cross the borderline into comedy, and most of our songs are written about depressing situations, ie 'Ernie Had A Hernia', 'I've Got Asthma', etc."

The Toy Dolls also enjoy doing unexpected cover versions of non-punk songs in their own inimitable fashion, and it was one such off-the-wall rendition of 'Nellie The Elephant' that earned them their very own fifteen minutes of fame. Originally released by Volume for Christmas 1982, it reached a modest No. 16 in the Indies, but when it was reissued two years later, it not only topped the Independents but reached No. 4 in the National Charts too.

"Yeah, just a bit!" laughs Olga, when asked whether the runaway success of 'Nellie' took him by surprise. "I did get kids in the street shouting 'Wooooo!' at me everyday, and I got a gold disc on the wall in me council flat!

"Most of the time," he adds candidly, "the covers we use are shoved in 'cos we have 'dried up' when writing. Also we put the classical instrumental covers in our live shows to give my voice a rest. It's hard work choosing which covers we should Toy Dollify; we've actually tried loads that just didn't work. Many times we just can't think of how to do them! Either that or they just sound like an uninspired copy of the original, and I don't see the point in just copying a song if you can't add your own thing."

In early 1983, Olga lost his long-standing partner in musical crime, Flip, who left in search of sanity.

"Flip left at the same time as Happy Bob, two days before a big tour supporting The Angelic Upstarts; he just couldn't face another month of sleeping and travelling in the back of the van. I searched the rehearsal rooms for two guys who could do the tour, and found Freddie 'Hot Rock' Robertson for the bass and Nick Buck for the drums (later to join The Upstarts himself); we practiced two days solid then went on tour."

Nick and Freddie left as soon as the immediate touring commitments were fulfilled, to be replaced by 'Bonny' Baz Warne and Alan 'Dirty Dicka' Dixon – who would himself leave before the year was out to join Red Alert. This line-up was responsible for the Top Ten Indie hit single, 'Cheerio Toodle Pip' in autumn '83, which was closely followed by another 7", 'Alfie From The Bronx'. By this time though, Dicka had been replaced by Dicky.

"I think there's only been one or two that got the boot!" laughs Olga when asked to account for the revolving door policy seemingly in effect for the early line-ups of the band. "Most members leave because of the intensive touring; they just get burnt out or they want to settle down and have kids. I think in this business you need a girlfriend who is completely understanding or just plain stupid!"

As a result of the buzz surrounding 'Nellie The Elephant', and much to the disgust of their more elitist fans, The Toy Dolls ended up providing the theme tune to the kid's pop/rock TV programme, 'Razzmatazz'.

"It was an okay programme!" reckons Olga. "A few silly parts, games and quizzes and stuff, but it actually had some good bands on it as well. We landed that through Volume, who were friends with the producers, and suggested that I write it. They asked me to make a demo, but I didn't have the money, so I took me acoustic round to Tyne Tees Television HQ and sang it to the producer in the office! And I got the job!"

The second Toy Dolls album, 'A Far Out Disc', continued their fine tradition of cheeky choruses (probably best of all on the sublimely ridiculous 'My Girlfriend's Dad's A Vicar'), oddball interludes (the track 'Commercial Break' was basically an advert for their first album!) and guitar-led instrumentals. It spent over a month in the Indies during the summer of 1985, peaking at No. 4, and was preceded by the 'She Goes To Fino's' single, a re-recorded version of the track that appeared on 'Strength Thru Oi!'. Backed by the hilarious 'Spiders In The Dressing Room', the 12" version also included 'Come Back Jackie'.

By this time the band personnel had settled down (at least by Toy Dolls' standards anyway), with the return of ex-drummer Dean James on bass. And with Teddy Toy Doll back behind the kit, they recorded the popular 1986 album, 'Idle Gossip', which saw them reaching new heights of accomplished silliness with songs such as 'You Won't Be Merry On A North Sea Ferry' and 'If You're In A Pop Group You'll End Up Paying A Fortune Practising At Peter Practice's Practise Place'. It was supported by tours of the USA, Scandinavia and Japan, plus the UK.

"I remember in London, in 1986, we had this stage routine where Dean ran sideways across the stage, and I went in the opposite direction to play a guitar solo. Except Dean forgot to stop and ran off the edge of the stage, over the monitor desk into the audience, and landed on his back. He managed to get back over the monitor guy's head and up onto the stage, and you know what? He didn't get a note wrong! Mind you, he only had two notes to play in that bit anyway…

"But there's been so many highs and lows on the road… gettin' me tooth knocked out by a skinhead on stage in Sao Paulo would probably feature. Can you believe that he even came backstage after, saying how much he loved the show and bragging that he was the guy who smacked me in the gob? Crazy world."

A rather poor video was shot of the whole album in a local Sunderland park ("Rough as hell and made on a shoestring!") by Jettisoundz, before Teddy was replaced by Martin 'Marti' Yule and the band signed to Nit Records. A division of respected metal label, Neat, they released 1987's 'Bare Faced Cheek', an album that was recorded at Newcastle's Impulse 24 Studios by Keith Nichol which Olga holds little love for.

"We've done a few poor records, but I would have to say that 'Bare Faced Cheek' is the worst; it's awful, even the sleeve is dire. The sound was poor; my guitar was broken at the time so I had to use the engineer's guitar with a fuzz box thing… and I hate effects pedals! There is one good track on it though, 'Yul Brynner Was A Skinhead'."

After 1989's 'Ten Years Of Toys' album, which as the title suggests was to commemorate their tenth anniversary, Dean James left to join Evil Mothers and was replaced by John 'K'Cee' Casey, whilst the band departed Nit to join Receiver Records.

With this set-up, The Toy Dolls released four brilliant albums – 'Wakey Wakey' (1989), 'Fat Bob's Feet' (1991), 'Absurd Ditties' (1993), which is Olga's personal favourite ("Great songs, great production and a great guitar sound") and 'Orcastrated' (1995). And although their profile in the UK was virtually non-existent, they were still packing them in around the world, religiously undertaking global touring commitments to promote every new record.

"K'cee was an amazing bass player," enthuses Olga. "We were on the verge of splitting when he joined. He really was an asset, and virtually had his own fan club in Japan. When he unfortunately left in the late Nineties, he actually married a Japanese lass."

The departing K'Cee was replaced by Gary 'Fun' Dunn for 1997's 'One More Megabyte', a strong entry to the band's catalogue probably best remembered for 'The Devil Went Down To Scunthorpe', a stunning punked-up re-working of The Charlie Daniels Band's 'The Devil Went Down To Georgia'. However subsequent touring revealed some cracks in the new line-up, and The Toy Dolls went into hibernation to plot their return to world domination.

During 2000, Olga and Marti came out of hiding to celebrate the band's twenty-first birthday in style with 'Anniversary Anthems' for Shakedown Records. Our diminutive guitar hero has since been spotted handling bass duties for The Dickies all across Europe, America and Japan ("I loved every minute of it, they are great guys and I reckon Leonard is the best singer in the world!"), and even standing in briefly for The Adicts. Most importantly though, he has recently finished work on a brand new Toy Dolls record, ominously entitled 'Our Last Album?', and is about to undertake a massive international touring spree to let the world know that they haven't seen the last of this most entertaining of UK punk bands.

SELECT DISCOGRAPHY:

7"s:
'Tommy Kowey's Car' (GBH, 1981)
'The Toy Dolls EP' (GBH, 1981)
'Everybody Jitterbug' (Zonophone/EMI, 1982)
'Nellie The Elephant' (Volume, 1982) – reissued in 1984
'Cheerio And Toodle Pip' (Volume, 1983)
'Alfie From The Bronx' (Volume, 1983)
'We're Mad' (Volume, 1984)
'She Goes To Fino's' (Volume, 1985)
'James Bond Lives Down Our Street' (Volume, 1985)
'Geordie's Gone To Jail' (Volume, 1986)
'Turtle Crazy' (Receiver, 1990)

12"s:
'We're Mad' (Volume, 1984)
'She Goes To Fino's' (Volume, 1985)
'James Bond Lives Down Our Street' (Volume, 1985)
'Geordie's Gone To Jail' (Volume, 1986)

LPs:
'Dig That Groove, Baby' (Volume, 1983)
'A Far Out Disc' (Volume, 1985)
'The Singles 1983 -1984' (Volume, 1986)
'Idle Gossip' (Volume, 1986)
'Bare Faced Cheek' (Nit, 1987)
'Ten Years Of Toys' (Nit, 1989)
'Wakey Wakey' (Receiver, 1989)
'Twenty Tunes From Tokyo' (Receiver, 1990)
'Fat Bob's Feet' (Receiver, 1991)
'Absurd Ditties' (Receiver, 1993)
'Orcastrated' (Receiver, 1995)
'One More Megabyte' (Receiver, 1997)
'Anniversary Anthems' (Shakedown, 2000)

AT A GLANCE:
Thanks to a caring, comprehensive reissue programme, virtually everything by The Toy Dolls is available on CD, complete with original artwork, lyrics, liner notes and bonus tracks. In 2003 Sanctuary Records reissued the first three albums in attractive card slipcases, whilst Captain Oi! did their usual sterling work with the other eight full length records, even compiling all the band's memorable cover versions onto one disc, 'Covered In Toy Dolls'.

RED ALERT

A lthough widely regarded as an Oi band, Sunderland's Red Alert were very much a punk band when they began life in 1979. They also possessed a natural flair for catchy song-writing not dissimilar to The Cockney Rejects that is still in evidence today (although the band split in 1984, they reformed in 1989). It was guitarist Tony Van Frater that formed Red Alert, recruiting 'Cast Iron' Steve Smith and Paul 'Dona' McDonough from local band, Cheapskates, on vocals and drums respectively, and school friend Gaz Stuart on bass.

"When we started out everyone was still at school apart from Steve," recalls Tony fondly. "This meant that there wasn't much money about and it wasn't easy to buy equipment. We would literally rehearse anywhere we could, bedrooms and garages included. Transport was also a problem as none of the band could drive, and most were too young anyway. We took this big trolley from the back of some carpet warehouse and for about a year we could be seen all around Sunderland pushing it about piled high with drums and amps. One night, on the way back from rehearsing somewhere, we were stopped by the police. Obviously we thought we were gonna get done for stealing the trolley but all they said was to get a light on it if we were gonna push it on the road! In fact, we actually carried all of our equipment onto a bus to get to a gig across town one night. It was all piled up down the aisle; people couldn't even get on the bus, but we knew the driver so it was cool."

Red Alert's first gig was at an annual open-air carnival organised by the local community centre; complete with second hand clothes stalls and children's games, it was hardly an appropriate event to play, but the band were too keen for their own good.

"Yeah, looking back it was a bit of a disaster," laughs Steve. "The stage was just a load of wooden blocks put together on some uneven ground inside this small marquee. The PA kept going down, the drummer turned up without the legs of his bass drum, and there was a load of the local drunks rolling out of the bar as we went on stage. So, there we were, doing our first gig, tripping all over this uneven stage with microphones going down every two minutes and someone sitting on the stage holding the bass drum in place! Then, of course, we had the drunks to contend with, all these shouts of 'Who the fuck are you? Donny Osmond?'

"Anyway, after putting up with it for as long as I could, I decided to give some back. Within minutes, the crowd of about hundred or so, in and around the marquee, began scattering all over the place as the main pole keeping the tent up started to keel over. The drunks had gone round the back and took all the ropes and stuff apart and the whole thing came down! Luckily no one was hurt and at the time we were pissed off with what had happened, but looking back now it was hilarious."

Dona left to join The Street Boys, a band featuring Steve's brother Patty Smith on vocals and Kid Stoker on guitar that later became the well-respected Red London who in 1983 released the 'Sten Guns In Sunderland' EP for Razor Records (although by that time Dona had left them anyway). Strangely enough, he was replaced in Red Alert by Gary 'Mitch' Mitchell – the drummer of The Street Boys! – who stayed with the band for about a year and played on their first EP, the ultra-rare (only 250 copies were pressed) 'Third And Final' single on their own label, Guardian Records.

As well as the title track, it featured the songs 'Border Guards', 'Sell Out' and 'District Boredom' and was recorded in 1980 at a studio in County Durham. Just like their live debut, their first time in a recording studio was an eventful one.

"The studio was alright; the only problem was the arsehole that owned the place," reckons Tony. "As soon as he told us that the drum kit once belonged to Keith Moon, we sussed him as being full of shit straight away. And knowing full well that he was charging us by the hour, he would make excuses up for having to nip out for a while and return about two hours later. He knew it was our first time in a recording studio so he thought we knew no different, but what he didn't know was that we'd talked to other bands who'd been in there and they'd warned us what to expect. We put up with it for a while before heading down the local bar and getting smashed. We went back there with a dustbin (it was all we could find) full of yet more booze. It all ended up with him in tears pleading with us not to smash the place up.

"On top of that, Mitch got arrested going back to the bar pissed on his motorbike. They took him to Durham Police Station and confiscated the motorbike. About two hours later we couldn't believe what we saw coming towards us along the road… it was Mitch with his crash helmet on, riding this old pedal bike. He'd only been released and stole a bike from outside the police station, then rode back the couple of miles to the studio!"

After quickly selling all the singles locally at gigs, Red Alert returned to Guardian to record another four songs – 'In Britain', 'Screaming At The Nation', 'SPG' and 'Whose Laws?' They didn't have time to mix the latter track, and it was subsequently lost by the studio, but the other three songs were sent to Garry Bushell at Sounds, a move that proved to be a turning point in the band's career.

"Yeah, as soon as he heard them, he contacted us and invited us down to London to record two tracks for the 'Carry On Oi!' album," says Steve gratefully. "We recorded 'SPG' and 'We've Got The Power' but for some reason only 'SPG' was used. It really helped 'put us on the map'; we got a lot of exposure from it, not just in the UK but worldwide too. As well as the recording, we got called into the Sounds offices and met Garry, who also got that legendary photographer Ross Halfin to take photos of us. We thought to ourselves, 'This is the start, we're getting there'.

"It was at this meeting with Garry Bushell that he told us to send our demos to No Future. As soon as we got home, that's what we did. And literally within two days we were signed to them. It was comical; when the call came that they wanted to sign us, we were all out in the street screaming and shouting. We thought we'd done it, what a feeling. All the hard work had paid off, and, no matter what is said or written about him, we'll always have Garry Bushell to thank for pointing us in the right direction."

The fiercely anthemic 'In Britain' EP was the first fruits of Red Alert's union with No Future in early 1982. It spent over two months in the Indie Charts, and only narrowly missed out on making the Top Ten. Featuring two songs, 'Screaming At The Nation' and 'In Britain', from the band's second demo, the third cut on the single, 'Murder Missile', was lifted from the band's third studio session. This was also the first recording to feature new drummer Les 'Nobby' Cobb (formerly with Section 2 and The Possessed).

They returned to the studio one final time during summer of '82 to record the rousing 'Take No Prisoners' 7". This release did make the Indie Top Ten – No. 7, in fact – and featured on the B-side both 'Empire Of Crime' and a re-recorded version of 'Sell Out' from the 'Third And Final' EP, a track originally penned by Kid Stoker from Red London.

"Next up was the 'City Invasion' single," says Tony, picking up the story. "This time, Chris Berry at No Future decided to put us in a different studio, Utopia in London, and we just did the two songs, 'City Invasion' and 'Negative Reaction'. Then, in 1983, we did our debut album 'We've Got The Power'. For this we went to yet another studio, Cargo, just outside of Rochdale. The band went down and stayed in this hotel for about a week, travelling to the studio each day to lay down the backing tracks. Steve, never the most patient bloke in those days, arrived at the end of the week and did all the main vocals in about an hour. The whole recording and mix went well though and we were very happy."

Indeed they should have been because 'We've Got The Power' is a thoroughly convincing album, one of the stronger debuts of the period and rammed full of rough-hewn melodies and rousing laddish singalongs. Even featuring a great re-recording of 'Third And Final' from the first single, the whole album crackles with youthful frustration, the crystal-clear production and the atmospheric arc of Tony's lead guitars lending a genuine air of class to proceedings. By rights, it should have catapulted the band to great things, but tucked away in the Northeast, with local gigs often blighted by football rivalry between Sunderland and Newcastle, they had problems finding suitable shows to promote themselves.

"I remember our first time in London though, we played at Skunx in Islington," says Steve. "They were putting all the main bands of that time on, so we were really excited about playing down there. Apart from arriving totally pissed and being threatened by the promoter to sober up or we wouldn't play London ever again, the gig was a non-event. We did manage to sober up but only about thirty or so paid in. We did our best but it was like pissing in the wind. It was thanks to Micky Fitz (of The Business) that we salvaged some pride, when he got up and sang a few songs with us. To cap it all off, we only got paid £15, barely enough to get home. And sure enough, we ran out of petrol forty miles from home and had to go to a police station and borrow a fiver for more juice!

"We did play there again a few months later and it was a great gig, packed out. Unfortunately, the banter with the crowd went too far, and we had to be locked in the place after the gig to save us from the fifty-strong lynch mob waiting outside. We'd also had our driver arrested that afternoon for being pissed and crashing into two cars outside of the venue! He was eventually released, missing the gig and having to go back down to London to appear in court at a later date. That was the night when we all took turns to drive the van back. There were lads who'd never driven before in their lives having a go! We got away with it... though we'll never know how."

Red Alert recorded one more EP for No Future, once again at Cargo, the rather light-

Red Alert's Tony Van Frater, live in Berlin

weight (and hampered by a weak production) 'There's A Guitar Burning' 12", but the band then parted company with the label, citing the inevitable musical differences as the main reason the relationship ran aground. The record itself got lost in the confusion when No Future went down soon after its release and failed to chart.

In early 1984, Nobby left to get married but Red Alert soldiered on for a few months with new drummer Matty Forster, even recording six new songs at Sunderland's Bullseye Studios which garnered an enthusiastic response from several labels, including Clay. It was too little too late though, and the band split up that summer.

"We felt as though we'd had our day and it was all downhill ahead of us," sighs Tony. "The feeling wasn't there, the buzz you get from being in a band. We'd always said that if we couldn't put 100% into it then we'd call it a day. On top of that, all the band were becoming fathers and it just seemed like the right time to end it. We had a big gig arranged with The Angelic Upstarts and Red London in Sunderland, a benefit gig for the striking miners, and we saw this as a good opportunity to bow out in style, which we did. At the time it felt like a relief; it was sad but it felt the right thing to do, to end on a high after five great years."

Matty and Tony joined Red London, whilst Gaz kept his hand in playing bass for several club bands, and it wasn't until they were jokingly challenged to reform by the promoter of a new local club, the Kazbah, that they realised most of them still had a deep belief in the music and spirit of Red Alert.

After that electrifying comeback gig at the Kazbah in February 1990, supported by Attila The Stockbroker and Red London, Gaz decided his heart wasn't in it, and the band recruited Tony's cousin, Tom Spencer, a veteran of the scene who had even been in Sunderland's very first punk band, The Rebels.

With various drummers and bassists coming and going, including Keith 'Stix' Warrington of The Angelic Upstarts and The Cockney Rejects, Red Alert stormed the Nineties, releasing several well-received albums, and touring all over the world. Their current line-up is Steve and Tony on vocals and guitar, Gaz Stoker on bass and Andrew 'Lainey' Laing, formerly with HDQ and Leatherface, on drums. Between them they have enjoyed tremendous highs and appalling lows, not least of all the tragic accidental death of their one-time drummer, Ian Syborn, to whom they've dedicated a song, 'Distant Rhythm', on their latest album, 'Excess All Areas'.

"Ian's death was the worst day in Red Alert's history," intones Steve. "He tripped and fell down the stairs where he lived, and broke his neck. There was a lot of tears shed amongst the band; we've always been a tight-knit unit, even with former members, so this was a really hard thing to deal with. We had a Spanish tour organised for two weeks after that and decided to still do it. It probably helped us get over Ian's death in a way, as it was still fresh in our minds and we sat each night talking about it, toasting his memory. A couple of months later we did a memorial gig for him here in Sunderland, and it was a great night, a fitting farewell to a great drummer and great mate; someone Red Alert will never forget, not ever."

They've even been the subject of a book, Red Alert: The Story So Far by Kid Stoker, who also wrote the Northeast punk tome Oi Stories. And in recent years, Tony Van Frater has also joined The Cockney Rejects on bass, and (alongside his band mates Lainey and Gaz) The Angelic Upstarts on guitar, although he remains as committed to Red Alert as ever.

"Obviously I'm in the position of being in three 'name' bands, which are all still active on the gig circuit and in the recording studio," states Tony. "It's not really as complicated as it sounds though, as the bands just work around each other. It's very rare that the bands play together, just the odd festival here and there. It might seem a bit of a nightmare trying to play in all three the whole year round, but who wouldn't want to be in any of these bands?"

SELECT DISCOGRAPHY:
7"s:
'Third And Final' (Guardian, 1980)
'In Britain' (No Future, 1982)
'Take No Prisoners' (No Future, 1982)
'City Invasion' (No Future, 1982)

12"s:
'There's A Guitar Burning' (No Future, 1983)

LPs:
'We've Got The Power' (No Future, 1983)
'Blood, Sweat 'N' Beers' (Nightmare, 1992)
'Beyond The Cut' (Nightmare, 1993)
'Breakin' All The Rules' (Dojo, 1996)
'Rebels In Society' (Get Back, 1997)
'Wearside' (Rhythm Vicar, 1999)

AT A GLANCE:

Captain Oi!'s 1993 CD reissue of 'We've Got The Power' includes fourteen bonus tracks, conveniently rounding up all the band's recordings for No Future, and as such is the perfect snapshot of Red Alert's early years.

TOTAL CHAOS

N ot to be confused with the Californian punk band of the same name (who didn't form until the early Nineties anyway), Total Chaos hailed from the far grimmer climes of Gateshead. They formed in 1979, with guitarist Nolic Nosnihctuh (aka Colin Hutchinson!) and drummer Gary 'Gaz' Gray founding the original line-up.

"Colin was actually the first to be in any other group before the formation of Total Chaos," remembers Gaz. "He was in a band called The Officers who practiced at the Boys' Brigade Club on Prince Concert Road in Gateshead. Towards the end of The Officers, I had a chance to meet with Colin on his way to a practice, as we had attended school together years before, and followed him to the club. The other members of the band had already left and I sat behind the kit and played with my hands. I mentioned to Col that a friend of mine, Jed (Pitt, who was to be the TC bassist), was into punk and we agreed to look at starting a new band. We looked for various singers by word of mouth, then eventually put an advert in the local paper, the Gateshead Post, to which Keeks (McGarry) replied. Keeks had also attended school with Jed as a child."

With Colin having an already established connection with the Boys' Brigade Club, it seemed obvious for Total Chaos to commence their own rehearsals there. Using what little equipment they could muster on their shoestring budget, they began in that time-honoured tradition by jamming out the usual covers of The Pistols and Clash, before tentatively penning some furious compositions of their own.

"Soon though, practising at the BBC was no longer possible, as their main office was broken into and all supplies of Kit Kats, Nutty Bars and Chewits were taken onto the streets and sold at knockdown prices, haha! However we soon found alternative space at,

Total Chaos, Keeks (vocals) and Gaz (drums), live Gateshead 1982

believe it or not, a local hotel owned by God... named St. George's Church! Actually it was their Community Hall; we heard a hippy band (sorry, language of the day) practising upstairs. A Reverend Underhill gave us the cellar and unbeknownst to us began charging people who came to listen to the band... Christian enterprise, eh?"

The band were to not only solve their problem of where to practice but to play a large part in the shaping of their local alternative scene when they teamed up with local band The Surge (who, featuring Keeks' brother, Andi McGarry, went on to become The Model Workers) and set up the area's first truly independent venue.

"A few us negotiated with a community group, Them Wifies, for the use of a disused garage on the ground floor of their premises. The Garage, as it was known and named by us, was in Bells Court just over the Tyne Bridge on the Newcastle side.

"Remarkably Them Wifies gave us carte blanche to do it up as a venue. Thus we spent lots of our time clearing it out, painting the odd circled 'A' around the place, building a stage and a disco area. The building remained suitably grotty with one toilet (which gave the Newcastle constabulary reason to close it down a year and a half later), and we had the responsibility of opening/locking up, cleaning it, running the gigs, advertising, flyposting etc.

"The Garage opened in June 1979 for the first gig with us, The Surge and The Funeral Directors playing. We kept costs to a minimum, so entrance was 25p and folks brought their own refreshments... usually 'Evo-stik Chateau '77', Woodpecker Cider or Special Brew!"

That first Total Chaos show only attracted fifteen local punks, most of them personal friends of the band, but by the time The Garage was closed down, the band were regularly attracting crowds of several hundred. Not to mention printing their own newsletters and a fanzine called No Comment.

Ironically enough, after their first venue was shut by the police, the Gateshead Gig Collective ("After hassling some local council suits") relocated to The Station, which was actually the old Gateshead Constabulary clubhouse!

Encouraged by the growing interest in their music, Total Chaos recorded a seven-song demo in a studio on the Newcastle Quayside, which they sold for 50p at shows. It sold well, and the next logical step was to release a single, so in early 1982, using money from the Gateshead Lottery Fund ("Money paid by the people for the people, so to speak!"), they set up Slam Records and entered Soundlink Studios in Shieldfield, Newcastle, to record their debut 'There Are No Russians In Afghanistan' EP.

"We were very naive and daunted at the prospect of recording something for vinyl," admits Gaz. "It is fair to say that, due to our inexperience, we went along with the engineer's advice and I think the excitement of producing a single overrode any efforts to be critical of production or sound quality. Still, I think that the record is what it is and has a raw quality. We asked a good friend Trevor Atkinson to design the cover; he was also responsible for the 'Factory Man' artwork."

'No Russians' does indeed have a 'raw quality' about it, but it's also an incredibly fresh-sounding single even today. The title track is a compelling rant against media manipulation of public sensibilities, whilst the two B-side tracks hint at the more experimental, diverse side of the band. 'Primitive Feeling' is much more subtle, a subversive melody weaving in and out of its simplistic riff with hypnotic effect, whilst 'Revolution Part 10' is a daring drums-and-vocals-only track, again succeeding largely due to its confident minimalism. It was later included on a compilation album by Italian label, Attack Punk Records.

The single quickly sold out of its initial pressing and was subsequently picked up by the then-fledgling Newcastle label, Volume, who were impressed both by the band's unique sound and their DIY work ethic. Not to mention their ever-growing following in the Northeast.

"All the Gateshead and Newcastle punks used to meet up and hang around in a record shop called Listen Ear. In 1981 it got taken over by Volume, who heard our demo and the single. So we arranged to meet in the Bridge Hotel. At this point we were very anti-capitalism to the point of not being interested and admittedly naive in the business side of distribution and marketing etc. But at eighteen years of age, when a couple of guys turn up, offer to buy you lots of booze and pay for a record to be made... well, I need say no more. I still had a copy of the original contract up until a short while ago, but lost it. We made a few hundred quid between the four of us, but not life changing amounts. They most likely made a lot of cash initially but we never gave a shit, as we were just happy to have the records out and the ability to have a say in how much they sold for."

In fact, the Volume version of 'No Russians', as well as having 'Pay no more than £1' emblazoned across the front, even has an apology from the band on the back for it being slightly more expensive than the original run on Slam Records. It was also the very first release for Volume (a label that went on to find chart success with The Toy Dolls), with its hasty follow-up, the 'Factory Man' EP being the second, which spent six weeks in the Indie Charts, peaking at No. 17 during October 1982.

The sonic diversity embraced on their debut was taken to the next level on 'Factory Man', with the passionate rebel ballad 'Brixton Prison' rubbing shoulders with the far thrashier title track, the band obviously at pains to challenge their audience intellectually as much as themselves musically.

Unfortunately, Total Chaos, who by now were being managed by their best friend, Rob Meek, never made it as far south as London to play ("Nor did we want to"), mainly confining themselves to the North.

"Probably my favourite ever gig was in the Marlborough area of Newcastle, with Parallax as support," reveals Gaz. "Just as were going on, the manager asked us all to leave. Apparently the people downstairs were shaking and spilling drinks with the noise. This was a big problem for us because our transport wasn't due back until late. So we suggested to the crowd that we continue the gig back at the Garage... every punk in the place picked up various bits of equipment and walked about half a mile to the Garage, which was opened, the gear set up and a great night had by all. And not one bit of gear was nicked en route."

The ambitious 'Fields And Bombs' 12" followed in 1983, but was sadly to be the band's final release. A shame as Total Chaos refused to conform to expectations, so who knows where their musical muse may have taken them? Whilst flawed, it was anything if not adventurous, its six tracks encapsulating everything from doom-laden dirges to ambient soundscapes... even dabbling with a folky jig on 'Where Is The Fellowship?'

"Do you know, when I asked the other guys about it, we could not remember when and why we split up! Incredible, isn't it? We do remember that we all had other commitments at around the same time. Keeks was going to college in York, Nolic had contracted a terrible bowel syndrome which meant he could not stay on stage too long, Jed went off to breed wild birds, which he still does today, and I became a daddy at eighteen. We used to take my daughter Nicola to gigs and all the punks would put all their leathers and other garments in a pile and she would sleep right through! So that obviously had some effect on how and why we stopped the train, I guess. The word 'Chaos' comes from the Greeks and means 'No regulation'; this suited us and, to be honest, I never felt we've outgrown it, not even today."

"I have absolutely no regrets," he says in closing, of his time in the band. "We were a group of young people from a very working class area, with no real prospects, deciding to be productive and creative, to be in a band for the sake of it, with no ideas of fame or fortune, just to have a whole load of fun. We met and became friends with some of the wackiest, funniest and truly loveliest people you could ever wish to call friends. People who knew what fairness, honesty and respect really meant and would live by these qualities always."

SELECT DISCOGRAPHY:
7"s:
'There Are No Russians In Afghanistan' (Slam, 1982) – reissued by Volume the same year
'Factory Man' (Volume, 1982)

12"s:
'Fields And Bombs' (Volume, 1983)

AT A GLANCE:

Unfortunately there is yet to be an official retrospective CD release for this visionary punk band, but it's well worth the effort to track their releases down on vinyl if the opportunity arises.

UPROAR

U proar were another great punk band, from Peterlee in County Durham, who never really managed to escape the clutches of the Northeast. Although they eventually gigged as far afield as Ireland and Germany, they never actually played a show in London, which may account for their unfortunate lack of profile; despite the high quality of music they released, much of it sneaked under the radar of the major press.

"I went out and bought the first Jam album, 'In The City'," explains guitarist Dave Cook of his introduction to punk rock. "And I listened to it non-stop until I'd learnt a few of the chords on an old acoustic guitar I'd had for about five years. My older brother was listening to 'Sabbath Bloody Sabbath' at the time and challenged me to learn the instrumental 'Fluff' off that album. I'd never had a guitar lesson before (still haven't actually) but I persevered until I'd learned it Les Dawson-style!"

Soon after, Dave moved to London where he got to experience the punk rock explosion first hand, and where he also discovered his all-time favourite band, The Ramones ("They became my benchmark, a real catalyst"). Uproar, L–R: Dave Cook, Barry 'Baz' Gordon, Stu Henderson, Ian 'Goic' Gordon

It was whilst on a return visit home to see his horrified parents, who hated his new image, that Dave took the plunge and formed a band.

"I met Stu (Henderson), who was also getting into the same bands as I was, so we decided to try and make some music together. After a few transients had passed through the band, we arrived at a rough line-up of myself on guitar, Stu on bass, no proper drummer as such, and Stephen 'Steppa' Thompson on vocals. Steppa rode a motorcycle, and one day left my place to go home and get some lyrics, but got hit side-on by a car pulling out in front of him, and was pronounced dead at the hospital. That day turned out to be the last we ever saw him, and in a way we decided to carry on in memory of Steppa."

Originally calling themselves The Demented, but soon changing it to Uproar, with Stu moving to vocals, the band gigged locally in youth clubs, and eventually found themselves a stable rhythm section in the shape of two brothers, Barry and Ian 'Goic' Gordon, both formerly with Fungus And The Bogeymen, on bass and drums respectively. The band had a hard-edged aggressive sound, perfect for venting the frustrations they felt with mainstream society.

"Our hometown, Peterlee, was, and still is, that fucking small-town mentality personified, full of cunts with bigoted narrow minds, who live in the same narrow streets all their sad lives," spits Dave with feeling. "I couldn't go anywhere without some knuckle-scraper wanting to have a go at me! It's the same all over; anything or anybody even slightly different is frowned upon and ostracised… but I loved it! Even though being labelled as a punk meant you were always cautious about people – you were basically treated like a leper by their plebeian society – I felt so different, so much better, than most of the people around me… is that elitist? I hope so! I felt different anyway, and I didn't want a 9-to-5 lifestyle, not ever."

"Peterlee, the place to be', was our local council's old motto," chuckles Stu wryly. "I suppose it was as good as any other new town. It was surrounded by pit villages… some still had their pits back then, but some were already well on their way to becoming ghost towns. We were never short of rehearsal places, though, and the town was small enough that we could transport our gear to practise in shopping trolleys… or even on skateboards! Yes, really."

After more gigs, mainly in and around Sunderland with local band Section 2, they recorded their first demo on a mobile eight-track studio. They sent it around to various Indie labels and secured themselves a two-single/one-album deal with Blackpool-based Beat The System Records, the label that helped launch The Fits and One Way System. They recorded their storming 1982 debut, the four-track 'Rebel Youth' EP, at Ric-Rac Studios in Leeds, and also contributed two tracks – 'Soldier Boy' and 'Boring Senseless Violence' – to Beat The System's 'Total Anarchy' compilation LP.

The release of 'Rebel Youth' saw the band building a strong fanbase in the Northeast. And as they cut their teeth, they were also earning a reputation as a formidable live band, with every show becoming an outpouring of intense energy that left audiences blissfully satiated and any other bands on the bill running for cover with their tails between their legs.

"Those early days were brilliant," reckons Stu. "We were young, with time on our hands, and in a band! Plus we had a brilliant bunch of mates; the early shows were a great place to be, you never knew what was gonna happen. We weren't the best musicians around, but we kept it raw and exciting. And we were learning all the time, each gig was an improvement on the previous, and the crowds got gradually bigger and better too, especially as people started to know the words… a lot of good memories. That's what it was all about, playing gigs and having fun, travelling around and meeting new people… what else was there to do? I loved every minute!"

"This was our way of expressing our opinions and frustrations," says Dave, "at a society that I had nightmarish thoughts about, turning me into an unthinking unfeeling robot. This is also, looking back, when I began self-harming myself, aged about eighteen. All that was on offer were crappy government schemes for £12 a week that meant joining some pecking order or other. I was once working in the stores at Easington Pit (now long gone) as part of a six-month scheme (I lasted three!) and the so-called store manager gave me a pen. He told me I was only allowed one 'cos I was new, but if I worked hard and did what he said then I might get another one in a week or two. He said all this whilst proudly pointing at the dozen or so pens he had sticking out of his own top pocket. What an asshole!"

Although thinly produced – the drums sound especially weak – Uproar's debut remains a potent exorcism of youthful anger; delivered at high speed and with terrific passion, it would be churlish to dwell on its technical failings with such genuine outrage on display.

The band's hard work and perseverance started to pay off when their next single, 'Die For Me', recorded at Park Lane Studios in Fleetwood, went into the Indie Charts at No. 21 and stayed there for nearly two months upon its release in March 1983. A vibrant five-track affair, featuring some great roving bass playing, it featured such rabble-rousing anthems as 'Better Off Dead' rubbing shoulders with frantic blasts of speed such as 'Dead Rockers'.

Spike Sommer, a northern freelance writer for Sounds magazine, reviewed several shows the band played during this period, and although he appreciated the effort and enthusiasm put into their delivery, was rather damning in his condemnation of their apparent lack of originality. One particularly eventful show in Darlington supporting The Fits even ended up with hecklers from the audience onstage rucking with the band.

"Maybe I said something I shouldn't have…" begins Stu cautiously. "But what can you do when an element are there determined to do you harm? We later found out that certain people had only attended the gig specifically to fight us, I don't know why. It was just unfortunate that that particular gig was being reviewed for Sounds! But as they say, any publicity is good publicity, and after the gig we had loads of people who wrote to us saying how much they enjoyed our set anyway, so that was good news."

Continuing on where the two singles left off, the hard 'n' heavy debut album, 'And The Lord Said…', followed in September of that year, and although it only spent a short time in the Indie Charts, it reached No. 25. The crudely drawn front cover depicted a naked woman being broken on a wheel in the depths of hell, and it indicated a growing fascination on the band's part with morbid subject matters and sexual imagery… including a scantily clad dominatrix ready to dish out some heavy discipline. The album even sported the rather bleak tagline, 'To be dead… to be really dead… that must be glorious!'

"Let's face it, death comes for us all sooner or later, so why not explore the concept?" reasons Dave. "My sense of humour has always been a bit morbid anyway, and I did experiment with LSD a lot in those early days, which sort of made me think that Heaven and Hell are what exist in the conscious and subconscious minds of individuals. I did read a lot of dodgy books on mental illness and states of mind, mainly to pull me back from where I could easily see myself going. I used to tell people that my ambitions were to be in a straitjacket and own my own methadone clinic! Things like demonic possession, schizophrenia, all things you would be burned or locked away for, are still shunned and never really talked about… people are scared to say what they really feel. I hate societies based on cultural militarism, religious dogma based on superstitious indoctrinated bullshit. The need for people to kill each other, the cruelty of people to each other and animals, dictatorships, the evilness of the mind… all just a natural fascination with the macabre. Stu's lyrics, for me at least, emphasised these thoughts, as well as the hell of being in loveless relationships, in bondage as it were. That 'To be dead' tagline on the album was all about never being able to fit in with what was on offer."

"My lyrics may have seemed sombre, but they were never meant to be," claims Stu. "I just didn't want to come across as some sort of preacher, so I wrote songs that people could interpret in different ways. I know a lot of people don't know what my lyrics meant, and some did, but it was all personal stuff, some of which people could relate to, some they couldn't.

"I know that some people thought we were sexist because of some of the images on our records and posters, but nothing could have been further from the truth. Nowt was meant by any of it; if something caught our eye, we usually used it. And hey, we were young lads with a healthy interest in sex! Still, you can't please all the people all the time, right? Whatever we did, someone, somewhere would have twisted it all out of context… shit happens."

After the album, a disillusioned Goic, sick of the music business and the band's constant lack of funds, left, and was replaced by Gav Scollen, who was previously with The Crime (best remembered for their 'Johnny Come Home' single) and The Epileptic Fits. The band, whose contract with Beat The System was up, signed to Newcastle-based label Volume for one EP, 'Nothing Can Stop You', which appeared in January 1984, and made the Indie Top Thirty, spending four weeks in the chart.

Recorded on November 1st 1983 at Impulse Studios, that third Uproar single was a superb four-tracker that amply demonstrated the band's growing confidence as songwriters. The hyper-speeds attained on their previous releases were pretty much long gone by this time, and in their place were huge infectious choruses and melodic flourishes, all realised via some nice lean arrangements.

They played some very successful shows in Germany, which brought them to the attention of German label, Wave. Wave had them return to Germany to tour with The Exploited and they recorded their second album, 'Never Forgive', at Spygel Studios, Kircheim, during October 1985.

"We were originally invited out there just to do a single," reveals Stu. "But when we got there, they wanted an album, so we were locked in the studio for 48 hours straight; we ate there, slept there and got it done. I would like to point out that we never mixed it ourselves though, so it isn't exactly how we envisioned it, but I still think it's pretty good.

"Peter, the guy who ran the label, came to my house to sort the contract out, which we all signed, and then we never saw him or heard from him again! Despite millions of phone calls and letters and all our friends in Germany trying to find him too. So, Peter, if by any chance, you're reading this… I'd like to kick your fucking head in! Nah, only joking… we must do lunch!"

A much rockier take on their original sound, 'Never Forgive' was very similar in style to the Abrasive Wheels' sophomore full length, with Stu's vocals in particular sounding like Shonna, vocalist with the well-known Leeds troupe.

By this time however, Dave had left the band, Barry had moved from bass to guitar, and a guy called Woody, who unfortunately died of meningitis in 1997, had joined on bass. With Dave gone, the essential spark was lacking from the band, and Uproar petered out soon after the release of 'Never Forgive'. Although a fine record in its own right, it wasn't fiery enough to satisfy hardcore fans of the band (despite what its garish overtly punk sleeve artwork might have suggested) and, with very little promotion or distribution outside of Germany, it sank without trace.

"I think we all have different reasons for the split of the band," reckons Dave. "The plan was to get a new bass player, and have Barry move to guitar with me, but I didn't wanna be in a band with more than four people – five was one too many as far as I was concerned. Plus I was beginning to show signs of depression and mood swings, getting pissed whenever I could, basically doing everything to excess.

"For example, and I still don't really know why it happened to this day, but after recording the (first) album, I was back home in Peterlee, in a flat I was sharing with Mick Ward ('Doyley' as he's still known), one of the old Uproar roadies, and everyone had gone to see Black Flag play a festival in Leeds. I just remember feeling very jaded on drink and LSD and I cut my wrists. I can remember watching the blood hitting the ceiling, then calmly telling a friend who was staying over to get an ambulance. It was only fifteen years later that I was told I suffer from depression and the need to self-harm, but it shocked me into never wanting to do anything like that ever again. I want to live, to achieve something. Anyway, I wished the band good luck and couldn't wait to get pissed forever."

"In the end, I basically just stopped enjoying it," adds Stu. "Plus I was a bit pissed off with the whole German thing, and thought 'Sod it!' We just seemed to come to a standstill. I don't regret leaving the band, 'cos it was the right thing to do at the time, but I do wish we hadn't been ripped off as much as we were. Not that I was in it for the money, but if there was any cash made off the band, I would have liked to have seen it put to better use than lining some bastard's pockets."

After Uproar, Dave, Gav and the aforementioned Doyley, formed The Kildares (yes, they were named after the TV doctor!), who gigged extensively around the Northeast, and even recorded a live session for Great Northern Radio. In more recent years, Dave has formed a three-piece band called Caesar Reel, who peddle a nice line in loud, guitar-driven alternative rock, but he still remembers his time in Uproar fondly.

"I loved being a part of Uproar; it was a springboard, a leap of faith, for the music that I'm writing today. My fondest memory of the time is feeling a part of something, which seemed to have no limitations in its quest to extinguish all self-doubt. Those times when you think and know that you could change your life to the way you want. For better or for worse, I wouldn't change any of it."

SELECT DISCOGRAPHY:
7"s:
'Rebel Youth' (Beat The System, 1982)
'Die For Me' (Beat The System, 1983)
'Nothing Can Stop You' (Volume, 1984)

LPs:
'And The Lord Said...' (Beat The System, 1983)
'Never Forgive' (Wave, 1984)

AT A GLANCE:
In 1996, Step-1 reissued the fast and furious 'And The Lord Said...' album on CD with ten extra tracks, namely the first two EPs and the compilation track, 'Soldier Boy'. With most of the lyrics, artwork and photos from the original layouts also included, it's the perfect place to check out this oft-overlooked band.

MAJOR ACCIDENT

ailing from the cultural desolation of nearby Darlington, Major Accident were a prolific second wave punk band that enthusiastically embraced the Clockwork Orange image and were responsible for more than a few great tunes. Formed by brothers Paul and Constantine 'Con' Larkin in late 1977, the first proper line-up of the band also included guitarist Dave Hammond and drummer Colin Stephenson.

Their first gig was at Skerne Park Youth Club, where the band unveiled some of their own compositions in amongst a set of Ramones and Clash covers, but from such humble beginnings, they never looked back. Gigging anywhere and everywhere in the Northeast, they quickly built a good local following, even being supported at one youth club show by (popular alternative comedian) Vic Reeves' band, The Eels Of Sex.

"Mmm, they weren't really my cup of tea," says Con. "But the atmosphere at those early shows was fantastic and we soaked up everything we could read about punk and squeezed it for all it was worth. We believed all the art school rubbish and took it to the council estate. We ripped off anyone who made a record, whether it was dripping paint on our clothes, sticking zips on our T-shirts... even down to our first drummer, Craig Newnham (whose brother Shaun was briefly the very first singer for the band), having a rat in his bass drum. It wasn't that punk tho', 'cos he told his mum it was a giant African mouse or she would have thrown him and it out of the house!"

By early 1980, drummer Colin had been replaced by his brother Paul 'Porky' Stephenson ("Thin as a stick and as hard as an iron bar," quips Con), and the band entered popular local studio Guardian to record the 'Terrorist Gang' single. Little did they know that the recordings wouldn't see the light of day for over sixteen years...

Major Accident, 1981
L–R: Stu Lee, Dave Hammond, Paul and Con Larkin

"We had planned to release 'Terrorist Gang' with a couple of B-side tracks, 'Self-Appointed Hero' and 'Sidelines'," explains Paul. "Our erstwhile manager at the time tried some dodgy deal that meant we didn't pay for the studio time but the engineer was one step ahead of him and wouldn't release the tapes without being paid. Needless to say the tracks from this session later appeared on the 'Clockwork Demos' CD without our knowledge."

This version of Major Accident also recorded the original version of the 'Massacred Melodies' album, which again never appeared when planned. The majority of the tapes were ruined by an engineer that applied too much Dolby and ended up with a muddy mess. However, a remix of most of these tunes appeared on the 'Clockwork Heroes' CD which was released during the band's period of retirement in the late Eighties/early Nineties.

After various local gigs, Porky was replaced by Stu Lee, and a deal was struck with Step Forward Records, who finally issued the re-recorded 'Massacred Melodies' LP in late 1982.

"One of the night clubs in Darlington was running a Battle Of The Bands contest," recalls Paul. "And as we couldn't even get past the bouncers of the club due to our attire and those smart hair cuts of the time, we thought it would be a laugh to enter the competition and see if we could get to play. Unfortunately it wasn't to be, but the title of the tape we sent them and the band's name caught the eye of one of the judges, who had contacts with Step Forward. And he telephoned us to see if he could send the tape to his buddy and, lo and behold, your humble narrators had themselves a record deal."

Opening with the memorable guitar refrain of the storming 'Schizophrenic', and, apart from tracks such as the moody 'Psycho', maintaining a frantic pace throughout, the album quickly put Major Accident on the punk map as a force to be reckoned with. The ensuing tour with Chelsea also helped establish them nationwide as an exciting live band, and introduced punters to their striking Clockwork Orange image.

"Our feel of the Clockwork theme came from the book," claims Paul. "Some of our look came from stills and clips from the film, but there were times that I dressed as in the book in the height of fashion – all in black with my head shaved on top in the style of an old man. My mother nearly had a stroke when I arrived home after the Chelsea tour!"

"He never did look quite macho enough in the ballet tights though," laughs Con. "And it took a lot of persuasion to make him drop them in favour of the old cricket trews. The look did land us in a bit of trouble as we used to wear the gear when we went out drinking and in those days, in the Northeast, people weren't as forgiving and tolerant as they are now. In fact, we were wearing the platties in our social lives long before we took them onstage."

"Yes, we did regularly get the old stop-search by the constabulary of that time who took great interest in our walking sticks and brollies looking for hidden or sharpened ends," confirms Paul. "Also, many a time we had to protect our luscious bowlers from the hands of undesirables, which quite often landed us facing the law again."

The band's strong image was further reinforced by a consistent and striking look to all of their records, whose sleeves were all designed in simplistic black/white tones by local artist, Paul Dillon.

In early 1983, the band released the brilliant 'Mr. Nobody' single (b/w 'That's You'); an effervescent perfectly-formed pop punk gem, it remains one of the unsung classics of the period. On the strength of the critical acclaim it lauded, Flicknife Records signed the band for another great single, the anthemic 'Fight To Win', which spent a month in the Indie Charts, reaching No. 24.

By this time Stu had been replaced behind the kit by Paul 'Evo' Evans, who also played on the infectious 'Leaders Of Tomorrow', the band's next single which went to No. 19 in the Indies upon its release in August '83. The 'Leaders…' 7" also saw the band expand to a five-piece with the addition of second guitarist Andy Harding. More gigs were undertaken the length and breadth of the country, some of them supported by The Blood and Dogsbody, a few of the more memorable ones happening dangerously close to home.

"We played a charity gig to help the financially failing Darlo (Darlington) football team and arranged a night at a local venue with four bands playing, two from Darlo and two from neighbouring Newton Aycliffe. The night was going well, but just as we were about to hit our first note topping the bill, a glass sailed through the air and all hell broke loose. We made the front page of the local press with the headline of something like 'Major Accident Causes Major Incident!' As the fight broke out, we tried to play on, hoping to distract people and get them interested in the music again, but the PA bloke had seen enough and ran for cover."

Evo left in late '83 (going on to play with The Blood, Angelic Upstarts and punk-metallers Warfare) and was replaced by ex-Seizure drummer Gareth 'G' Jones. This line-up recorded 1984's 'A Clockwork Legion' LP and the exceptionally melodic 'Respectable' (b/w 'Man On The Wall') single. They also made an appearance on national TV, on the BBC's 'Off The Peg' programme.

Explains Paul: "We got wind that the BBC were to record a series of local bands in the Northeast and people had mentioned Major Accident to them, so the TV scouts contacted us, flew up from London to see us and agreed to put us on the show. We said we wanted an atmospheric black 'n' white shoot in the practise room, with us in our Clockwork attire, which would look really good. But they said it was really hard to do filming in black and white (so much for modern technology), and they instead set up a gig in the Teesside Poly. Here, apparently, we could invite friends, and they would supply the PA, then after we finished filming we could play a normal gig. It took an age for them to get their sound levels right, then we did dozens of takes of the songs they wanted… and then, when they had finished, they started to wrap up. And as the PA was going through their system we couldn't play, so we had one very irate crowd."

"We also got into a load of shit after that that gig," says Con. "Someone in the audience made a racist comment to the wrong person and the next thing we know, Paul is on the front page of the Northern Echo in (and I quote) his 'Clockwork Orange suit'! And we were being slagged off by the Polytechnic. Luckily the people from the BBC stood by us, as they had got to know us quite well, and after a couple of solicitor's letters we got a full apology."

"Then, on the night it was shown on television, we'd been gigging and were returning to Darlington when we were pulled by the police who were doing a routine check on the van," chuckles Paul. "Con was led away to the waiting patrol car by one cop as the other tried to give us the friendly, 'Alright lads, had a good night? Where have you been and what have you got in the van?'

"Seeing the gear, he was quick to put two and two together. 'Oh, you're in a band,' he said. 'Did you see that crap on the TV tonight? God, they were terrible! What a load of crap, nothing but noise. What were they called? Major Accident or something? Anyway, what do you call your band?' My word, his face was a picture when I said that we were Major Accident!"

Soon after the programme, both Hammond and Harding left in quick succession, but undeterred, Major Accident recruited ex-Blind Attack guitarist, Paul 'Staps' Staples, and continued as a four-piece again. As if to ring the changes, they shortened their name to just Accident, which is how most people referred to them anyway.

Late 1984 saw the release of the live album, 'Tortured Tunes', by Syndicate Records, but it featured a show recorded the previous year with the old line-up (at the Kings Head, Ferryhill) so was hardly representative of the band at the time. It was followed by a singles collection on Flicknife, 'Pneumatic Pneurosis'.

A semi-new release came in the shape of the 'Crazy' LP for US label, Toxic Shock Records (it was later released in the UK by Link), which featured six new songs plus seven re-recorded tracks from the second album. A short US tour was undertaken in support, that saw Evo briefly back on the drums when G. pulled out of the trip because of work commitments, and had the band playing such huge venues as the Santa Monica Civic Auditorium in LA.

Upon their return, a new drummer, Mark 'Rich' Richardson, was found, who played on the track 'Sherwood Rangers' that appeared on the UK version of 'Crazy', and played an eventful French tour with the band.

"We asked where we were staying after one gig, I think it was Besancon," elaborates Con. "And we were told 'on the train'. 'Strange,' we thought, but after the gig the sleeping arrangements soon became apparent. We had to break into the yard where the trains were parked up overnight and then onto the trains for a nice kip. The train we chose had those old-fashioned cabins like 'Murder On The Orient Express', with bench seats that were actually pretty comfortable. So, we all bedded down for the night – Major Accident, Sherwood from France, and another band from Sweden, plus full entourage.

"Next thing I remember is waking up in a cabin with Craig our roadie shouting, 'We're moving!' Before we came to our senses, a guard walked in and shouted something in French. Obviously we responded with the old 'British' routine, and he then said 'Passport' – at which point, Craig hands his over. 'Are you daft, lad?' says I, and the guard makes a move to leave but is swiftly pinned against the wall by Craig and the passport retrieved.

"We go to make our exit and are greeted by the sight of a platform packed with French commuters looking on in horror as thirty or so punks and skinheads jump off the moving train and make a break for freedom! We ended up in a café having a good laugh about it all, but got our comeuppance when a SWAT team from Customs And Excise descended upon us and whisked us all away in handcuffs!"

But after the tour, the band split up, when Con, the glue binding the group together, left to get married.

"I was basically sick to death of it. The audiences were getting smaller and smaller and I was fed up of being skint. I needed to get a proper job to get married and I couldn't do that and be in the band. Remember Major Accident weren't being paid or anything as ludicrous as that."

Happily though, Major Accident reformed in 1996 with new drummer Andrew 'Laze' Lazenby and were a highlight of many a punk festival until they split – this time for good – in 2003.

"Hard to say, really, 'cos we don't know where we might have ended up without it," ponders Con in closing, on what path his life might have taken without Accident. "I was looking at a gleaming career as a quantity surveyor before I jacked it in to go on the Chelsea tour, so I would probably have been quite comfy now with my head stuck up my own arse. But I wouldn't have seen half as much of the real world, apart from those holidays on beaches and in nice hotels. Needless to say, if I had my time over, I would do it all again."

"After fronting Accident, I walk this world a wiser, more experienced wreck of a man," agrees Paul. "But it was fun and, like Con says, not only did we see parts of the world we never would have seen, but we saw them from a very different angle to that of a regular tourist, so I second Con and would do it all again."

SELECT DISCOGRAPHY:
7"s:
'Mr. Nobody' (Step Forward, 1983)
'Fight To Win' (Flicknife, 1983)
'Leaders Of Tomorrow' (Flicknife, 1983)
'Respectable' (Flicknife, 1984)
'Representation Not Reality' (Upstart Productions, 2000)

LPs:
'Massacred Melodies' (Step Forward, 1982)
'A Clockwork Legion' (Flicknife, 1984)
'Pneumatic Pneurosis' (Flicknife, 1984)
'Tortured Tunes – Live' (Syndicate, 1984)
'Crazy' (Toxic Shock, 1985)
'The Ultimate High' (We Bite, 1996)
'Cry Of The Legion' (DSS, 2002) – split LP with Foreign Legion

AT A GLANCE:
Captain Oi!'s 1994 'Clockwork Heroes: The Best Of Major Accident' CD compiles all the band's singles, plus select tracks from the studio albums, and comes complete with lyrics and a discography. Also in '94, Captain Oi! compiled the first two albums onto one CD, all bar the track 'Bad Company', which was left off due to running time restrictions but appears on the 'Clockwork Heroes' collection anyway.

ABRASIVE WHEELS

The Abrasive Wheels were by far the biggest punk band from the Leeds area, who specialised in the sort of massive rowdy choruses that could put a grin on the face of a dead man. Like so many of those intense bands of the time, their fire burnt brightly for just a relatively short time, but the shadows it cast, and the colourful musical legacy they bestowed the punk scene, were both important and influential. The band recently reformed and have been playing sporadic shows and even writing a new album.

"Me and Dave were at the same school together, in the same year," recalls vocalist Phil

'Shonna' Rzonca. "We met each other when we were eleven on a football pitch doing trials for the school team. We weren't best friends then, but we knew each other to speak to. We got into punk in 1976, both at the same time... that summer was really hot, if I remember rightly, and punk was just breaking whilst we were on our school holidays. I was about fifteen and starting to get into different music; I'd just been to see The Sensational Alex Harvey Band. But after Slade (who were my favourite band) lulled in '73 or '74, it was all just disco crap, wasn't it? And I wanted something louder and more aggressive... and along came punk! I read all about it in the tabloids, and saw the Pistols on 'TOTP', and then I started delving deeper, buying Sounds and stuff.

"When I was sixteen, I went to see The Vibrators at Leeds Poly, and I can remember being frightened to death! But the atmosphere was so electric, you could cut it with a knife. At the Alex Harvey show, everyone had been sat down... and the punk show was just so wild by comparison. From then on, I thought, 'Right, I'm a punk rocker'!

"Then I met Dave on a bus on the way to a Stranglers gig, and we started going to the F Club in Leeds, checking out new bands together, and it went from there. We were only sixteen or seventeen, and we decided to start a band ourselves."

Shonna wanted to be the bassist, but ended up as singer by default, mainly because he didn't have a bass guitar! The rest of that early line-up consisted of Dave on guitar, Dave's cousin Robert Welch on bass, and Shonna's brother Adam on drums. Thankfully it was Shonna and not Dave who had the last say when it came to choosing the band's name...

Abrasive Wheels, 1982
L–R: Harry, Shonna, Nev, Dave
'... the first 'real' lineup of the band...'

"We were looking for a name, and Dave had come up with The Perambulators!" laughs Shonna. "I said 'Fuck off, that's another name for a pushchair! Who's ever heard of a punk band named after a pram?' Anyway, I had an apprenticeship at a heavy engineering firm, and I kept seeing these signs saying 'Danger! Abrasive Wheels!' We had a lecture one day at work all about these abrasive wheels, and the guy pulls one out of his bag to show us, and it was about 7" across, and round, with a label in the middle, and I thought 'It looks just like a fuckin' record! What a great name for a band!"

The Wheels made their first public appearance in late 1977, at a house party for one of their mates, Poz, and soon after they played a Rock Against Racism show at Leeds Polytechnic, where they were pleasantly surprised by the positive response they received... to begin with.

"We did a few more RAR gigs, and then someone at the Poly suddenly thought 'Hang on a minute, this band aren't really suited for these shows, they're too aggressive', and that was the end of that. Then we got a call, at really short notice – the afternoon of the gig, in fact – to go and support The UK Subs in Bradford. We'd never heard of them at that point, but they were brilliant, an awesome live band.

"That was Adam's last gig with us; it was a shame really, 'cos he was a fuckin' brilliant drummer. I remember The UK Subs stood at the bar watching us soundcheck, and they were all staring at Adam; he was going fucking mental just in the soundcheck, never mind the actual gig!

"Anyway, The Subs had travelled up in just a Transit van, and they had nowhere to stay, so they all came back and crashed over at our houses. It was great to see a band of that calibre and hang out with them; it gave us a new inspiration."

After the Subs show, Adam left the band to become a chef, and Rob went off to college, leaving Shonna and Dave to recruit two mates who lived nearby, Mark Holmes on drums and Dave Hawkridge on bass. This incarnation of the band recorded a demo and soon set their sights on releasing a single.

"We'd been looking through all the ads in Sounds and New Musical Express, and we sent a demo to a label who came back to us and said they'd release a single by us if we gave them £300 or whatever. So we did that, and nothing happened for several months," explains Shonna.

"We were doing a few gigs at the time for a local promoter, Ray Rossi, who was the brother of Mick Rossi from Slaughter And The Dogs, and he offered us a tour with Slaughter, and we obviously said 'Fucking hell, too right'! We did thirty gigs with them, and one of the gigs was down south near this label that had ripped us off, so we turned up on their doorstep and threatened them! They gave us this sob story about their cash flow and everything, and ended up giving us a metal acetate of our single they were going to press. It looked like a record to us, so in our eagerness to hear ourselves on vinyl, we went and played it on a normal turntable and fucked it up! So that was £300 wasted; we just didn't have a fucking clue what we were doing half the time!

"The deal on the tour was that Slaughter would lend us a van to get to the gigs in, and we'd get a bit of food and petrol money. I drove us all over the country in this van, and I didn't even have a licence then! And it was a piece of shit, this van; it was knocking so badly, we thought it was a diesel, so we'd only had it for five minutes and we pulled into a garage to diesel it up… and then found out it was petrol! You can imagine what Ray Rossi said when he found out we'd fucked his van! But we had the tank drained, and off we went, and we managed to crawl around the country in this van that went faster downhill in neutral than it did on the straight, and we went down really well.

"Slaughter were a great band to tour with," he recalls. "They were very polished, with all these lead breaks everywhere. Whereas we were just raw, ferocious… pure energy… we were riding the very cusp of the second wave of punk that was about to break, and we made a lot of new fans on that tour."

Deciding they were better off putting out a record for themselves, Dave and Shonna started their own label, Abrasive Records, and scraped up the £600 they needed to release their own single.

"Dave had a motorbike which he sold, so he came up with his half of the money, but I had fuck all of any value and I had to find the same amount," says Shonna. "We'd already set up an account in the name of Abrasive Records in readiness of doing this label, so I went to the bank and said I was the managing director of Abrasive Records and managed to get a loan! I walked out of there with £300 in my hand… it was fuckin' amazing! I felt like I'd robbed the bank!"

The band went into Look Studios in Huddersfield and recorded the 'Army Song' EP (aka 'The ABW EP'), an impressive and incredibly raw debut that literally crackled with pent-up energy. The title track was an adrenaline rush of pure aggro, and the two tracks on the flip side – 'Juvenile' and 'So Slow' – didn't hang about either, both pounding punk of the highest order.

Not only did they release it themselves, but Dave designed the cover, and they delivered copies to all the local shops themselves as well. They soon had a distribution deal with Red Rhino in nearby York, and the single quickly sold out of its initial pressing of 3000 copies; it even raised enough money to buy them their own van to tour in. Cherry Red picked up the band's publishing, and they put Simon Edwards from Riot City in touch, who quickly signed the band to his label.

Abrasive Wheels' first release for Riot City was the fast 'n' furious three-track 'Vicious Circle' EP in early 1982, and, encouraged by its success (it spent three months in the Indie Charts and reached No. 12), the label re-released 'Army Song', this time on red vinyl, two months later. The band also contributed the storming 'Criminal Youth' to Riot City's showcase 1982 compilation album 'Riotous Assembly'. Thanks to the vitriolic strength of these early releases, the band started to build a large and loyal following of punks and skins the length and breadth of the country.

"The press were calling us 'Hardcore' or 'Oi' or whatever, and we were thinking 'What the fuck are they going on about?' We didn't like labels anyway, but as far as we were concerned, we were just a fuckin' punk rock band. The press wanted to pigeonhole us with all the other bands that were emerging at the time, but we were just writing what was coming out naturally, what we felt; there was nothing contrived about us at all. We were just angry young punks, all of us on the dole, all of us disillusioned with society. We had no respect for reputations or authority. As far as I'm concerned, real punk music comes from the streets; it doesn't matter whether it's fast or slow, it's the sentiment behind the music that's important. For us it was always a working class thing, and maybe that's why we got called an 'Oi' band in the press."

About this time, Dave Hawkridge and Mark Holmes were replaced by 'Harry' Harrison on bass and 'Nev' Nevison on drums, both of them previously members of another Leeds band, The Urban Zones.

"Harry and Nev joined us right before the first album; that was the first 'real' line-up for me," reckons Shonna. "Before that it was basically just me and Dave against the world. The previous guys before Harry and Nev were just stand-ins really, and when they joined, that was The Wheels' first proper line-up."

The new improved Wheels were soon in the studio recording their third (and, for many, their best) single, 'Burn 'Em Down'. Although it was still frantic, it was by far their most mature and memorable composition up to that point, and the irresistible chorus was something straight off the terraces, yet executed with more flair than most other bands could even dream of. The sound was also vastly improved thanks to the production skills of Mike Stone, whose work with GBH and Discharge the band had so admired. Backed by the more generic 'Urban Rebel' (classic chorus though), the single was another great success, and paved the way nicely for the band's debut album, 'When The Punks Go Marching In'.

Fourteen tracks of pumped-up street punk, it gripped the listener from start to finish, via the pounding 'Voice Of Youth' (complete with its infamous chant of 'Put Maggie Thatcher on the dole'!), the boozy singalong 'Just Another Punk Band' and the insistent 'Slaughterhouse', which is The Abrasive Wheels at their raucous best. The album peaked at No. 3 in the Indies in late 1982, but was to be the last release for Riot City, because Abrasive Wheels then eloped to producer Mike Stone's Clay Records, home to Discharge and GBH.

"We decided we needed help with that first album," explains Shonna, "and Mike Stone had done 'Burn 'Em Down' for us, which we were really pleased with. He brought a lot of new ideas to the production and made us sound a lot more professional. And we got on with him like a house on fire... even though all he kept saying to me in the studio was 'Diction! Diction! Diction!' 'cos he couldn't understand a word I was saying! And this is from the guy who did the Discharge album!

"We kept in touch with him after the album, and he seemed genuinely interested in us. He was almost like a big brother to the band; he was 6'3", skinny as a beanpole, looked like fuckin' Clint Eastwood with his little brown cigars... and he had a BMW! He was cool as fuck! I mean, I don't think I ever even spoke to Simon at Riot City on the phone, let alone met him, so we ended up going with Stoney and Clay."

The first single for their new label was a surprising, and thoroughly enjoyable, cover of 'Jailhouse Rock' in the summer of 1983, which had many of their hardcore punk following scratching their heads in amazement. The B-side was 'Sonic Omen', a rabble-rousing call to arms for working class kids across the country that was more traditional Wheels in its approach.

"We just didn't like being told what to do," says Shonna defiantly. "And we didn't like people thinking they knew what we were about when they didn't. My philosophy has always been, 'I'll do what I want how I want when I want if I want!' I've always been like that, and still am today, a right stubborn fucker!"

It was followed by yet another strong single, the 'Banner Of Hope'/ 'Law Of The Jungle' double A-side, which reached the giddy heights of No. 10 in the Indie Charts just before Christmas '83. After 'Burn 'Em Down', 'Banner Of Hope' remains probably the best song the band ever put their name to, a perfectly arranged and relentlessly catchy pop-rock song that suggests, given the lucky break they never received, the Wheels could have enjoyed the sort of success afforded someone like The Alarm.

'Law Of The Jungle' however was a tongue-in-cheek rompalong that again saw the band indulging their sly humour and more diverse musical tastes.

"That had a big influence borrowed from The Cramps, who I quite liked at the time," reveals Shonna. "At the end of the day, when you're making music, you're making it for yourself. You hope that others will like it, but that's really of secondary importance. You can only write from experience and be true to your influences. I liked the simplicity of rock'n'roll, and the stomping power of Slade, and the energy of skiffle... let's face it, rock'n'roll was the people's music, and so was punk. Fuck all these fretboard wizards, we were about something much purer and to the point. Punk ROCK basically."

And so the way was paved for the second album, 'Black Leather Girl', which appeared in March 1984. Recorded over the course of two months in Strawberry Studios, Stockport, and produced by Mike Stone, it saw the emergence of a much slicker-sounding Abrasive Wheels, oozing confidence and well-realised vocal harmonies. It's a great album, no doubt about it, but is just too glossy when compared to their vicious debut. Long gone were the frantic tempos and chainsaw guitars, replaced by something much more restrained. They sounded bigger and better than ever, but The Wheels had been polished until they shone, and had lost some of their early edge. The title track even featured a screaming sax underpinning the raunchy hip-jerking rhythms.

Soon after the album, another single, 'The Prisoner' (b/w 'Christianne'), was moderately successful, but didn't do as well as previous releases. It was the beginning of the end for the band who split in late 1984 following a heavy bout of international touring.

"I'm not really into touring much anyway. Harry left after the American dates, and we got Jez in on bass for some European gigs, and it just wasn't the same. It was starting to seem like work to me... we had to go and do this, we had to do a new demo, had to write some new stuff, do this gig or that gig... it was all work and no play.

"And when we did 'Black Leather Girl', Dave's writing style started to change, and we all had our own, very different, ideas about direction. The new material, I didn't like too much at all – it just wasn't me, so I said I'd had enough."

The band all went their separate ways, and interestingly enough, Shonna actually had chance to meet Margaret Thatcher, the inspiration for more than one of his scathing lyrics, several years after The Wheels disbanded.

"I went on to be a taxi driver and then I opened a few pizza parlours in Leeds... until Maggie Thatcher upped the interest rates and put me out of business. So she had the last laugh in the end, didn't she? Fuckin' slag! Anyway, I was working as a barrow boy on Leeds market, and I turned up for work one day, and all the top brass are there, all tarted up, with carnations in their buttonholes and what not. And I'm told that Maggie Thatcher is doing one of her walkabouts at the market, and she's down to visit my fuckin' stall! I thought, 'Fuckin' hell, I ain't missing this!' So I was hanging around the back of the shop when she turns up, and she saw me and asked who I was, and I got introduced to her. She shook my hand, and I felt like putting the fuckin' nut on her (laughs), but I just kept it all in check and shook her hand, as you do if you wanna keep your job. She was actually very charming – if only she knew what I really thought of her and what I'd sang about her a few years earlier..."

For many years after that, Abrasive Wheels were nothing more than a fond memory, and one of those bands that no one thought would ever consider reforming... but now they're back, as loud and brash as ever, and they've even finished recording that aforementioned new studio album. "I'd never thought about reforming The Wheels; in fact, I was probably dead against the idea for many years... until Nev said he wanted to drum in a band with me and 'Why not call it The Abrasive Wheels?' My biggest problem is I'm too headstrong for my own good, and even though it was a logical idea, I said 'Fuck off!' But the idea was ticking away in the back of my head and it seemed to make more and more sense.

"Then Harry, who's now a lecturer up in Scotland, said he wanted in if we did it, and I thought 'Well, if Harry and Nev are on board, I gotta ask Dave'. And it turned out that he'd been thinking the same thing anyway 'cos he'd been getting calls asking us to play some festivals, so he agreed. Everything seemed to just fall into place at the right time. If I'd have been asked to reform the Wheels ten years ago, I would have said 'Fuck off, been there, done that', and that would've been it, but the circumstances are different now.

"So I got Steve Popplewell in on second guitar, and he's slotted in so well, it's untrue. And me and Dave have written all the new songs. We know exactly what we want to achieve this time around. In the old days we just did it without thinking.

"Y'see, I've just turned forty, and now I want to make the album we always threatened to make but never quite delivered. I want to get it out of my system once and for all, and not be left wondering 'What if...?' for the rest of my life. Me and Dave are both 'doers', but we know that if we don't do this now, we never will."

SELECT DISCOGRAPHY:
7"s:
'The ABW EP' (Abrasive, 1981)
'Vicious Circle' (Riot City, 1982)
'Army Song' (Riot City, 1982)
'Burn 'Em Down' (Riot City, 1982)
'Jailhouse Rock' (Clay, 1983)
'Banner Of Hope' (Clay, 1983)
'The Prisoner' (Clay, 1984)

12"s:
'The Prisoner' (Clay, 1984)

LPs:
'When The Punks Go Marching In' (Riot City, 1982)
'Black Leather Girl' (Clay, 1984)

AT A GLANCE:

If you're more interested in The Wheels at their Abrasive best, the 1994 Captain Oi! CD reissue of their first album also includes all the tracks from their first four singles, and even the track contributed to the 'Riotous Assembly' compilation. If you'd prefer to check out their more melodic, rockier material, Captain Oi! also reissued the second album in 1995, the bonus tracks on this CD comprising the band's last three singles. Either CD comes highly recommended.

THE EXPELLED

T he Expelled were formed in Rothwell, just outside Leeds, during that long, tense summer of 1981. Put together by drummer Ricky Fox and bassist Craig 'Macca' McEvoy, they chose to round out their original line-up with Tim Ramsden on guitar and a young lady name of Jo Ball fronting them. Aware of the growing similarities in sound between many of

the punk bands emerging at the time, Ricky desperately wanted an original edge to his band, and seeing as he was a huge fan of Vice Squad – there was only really Beki Bondage flying the flag for aggressive female singers when The Expelled first got themselves in gear – getting a girl singer seemed the perfect solution. Ironically, they got a female vocalist to avoid those constant comparisons to all the other bands out there, but as a consequence lived out their short existence in the perpetual shadow of Vice Squad. Such is the costly price sometimes of good intentions.

"Constantly being labelled the next Vice Squad was pretty annoying at the time," recalls Ricky. "We always set out to be different from anyone else and while it seemed that loads of new punk bands were all sounding like each other, we had a similar sound to just one... but people like Garry Bushell could never mention The Expelled without saying Vice Squad in the same sentence!"

"I never really thought about the comparison between us and Vice Squad," claims Jo. "I'd actually never heard of Beki Bondage – it was our drummer Ricky who worshipped them – until we played with Vice Squad ourselves. And when I did hear them, it was fairly blatant that they were so much better than we were!

"To be honest, I wasn't really influenced by anyone, 'cos I wasn't a trained singer. In fact, I never had any aspirations to be a singer at all, it was just something that happened. Subsequently, I never took any of it too seriously; I was too young and inexperienced... even though I felt mature back then!"

Such considerations are only really relevant in hindsight though, because at the time, things moved along for the band at a frightening pace. They were spotted by a local promoter at their very first show just a few months later, and were soon treading the boards opening up for the likes of The Exploited and The Business. And then their very first demo tape secured them a deal with Riot City Records... all within six months of their first rehearsal!

To be fair, there were definite similarities between The Expelled and Vice Squad, and it wasn't just Jo's vocals either. Both bands favoured pacey tempos and abrasive guitars, and once they were on Riot City and became label-mates with Vice Squad, it was almost inevitable that they would soon be gigging together. Members of Vice Squad even ended up lending the band their experience as informal producers for some of The

The original, and most popular, incarnation of The Expelled L–R: Jo Ball, Ricky Fox (on steps), Macca, Tim

Expelled's studio sessions. And Ricky remembers some of those early gigs with his mentors very fondly.

"Probably the best gig we ever did was at the 100 Club in London with Vice Squad. It was great to play at such a well-known venue, the place was packed, and we got a tremendous reception seeing as it was our first time in London.

"And one of the craziest gigs we did with them had to be the Leeds Bierkeller. They were staying at a B&B just outside Leeds. After the sound check they wanted to go there to check in and pick up the keys, but they didn't know where it was, so I went in the van with Beki, Dave and their driver to show them the way. But after checking in, the van wouldn't start; it took us half an hour to get it going and we arrived back at the gig only to find The Expelled already on stage without me, with Vice Squad drummer Shane behind the kit! Fortunately when I arrived they were only on the second song, so I was able to take my place for the rest of the gig."

The first fruit of the Riot City deal was the 'No Life, No Future' EP, which saw the band down in Bristol's Cave Studios, re-recording the three best songs from their demo. The EP was a roaring success, with one song in particular, (the 'very girly' in Jo's own words) 'Dreaming', catching the ear of the record-buying punker. Every band has their defining moment, and the majority of fans would agree that it was with 'Dreaming' that The Expelled earned a place in the punk rock history books.

The other two songs – namely the title track and 'What Justice?' ("The thought of trying to sing that fast now invokes an asthma attack!" laughs Jo) – were both solid enough too, but lacked such a punchy memorable chorus. The overall effect though was still of a very strong debut from a promising new band. In fact, the only thing to let down the EP was the desperately unimaginative sleeve.

Never ones to hang about, they appeared on Riot City's very successful 'Riotous Assembly' compilation – with the track 'Blown Away', which had been recorded at the same time as the EP – and then raced around the live circuit to promote both releases. Mere months later, they were back in Bristol – this time at the more prestigious SAM Studio – to record the follow-up.

Actually bettering such a cracking opening gambit was never going to be easy, but The Expelled pulled it off with great aplomb. 'Government Policy' was another classic track, with Jo adopting a slightly deeper pitch that worked perfectly with the urgent choruses. The song on the flip-side, 'Make It Alone', although the weaker of the two tracks, was picked up by John Peel for frequent plays on his show, and actually resulted in the band being offered one of his coveted sessions.

Things couldn't have been going better when, as is so often the way, disaster struck, and Jo decided to leave the band to get married.

"One can only drink so much cider, eat so many chips, sleep in a Transit van with several flatulent youths and tolerate so much groping and spitting," she recalls. "We didn't have the motivation that comes hand in hand with proper promoters, managers and agents; it wasn't a professional set up at all. Everything we achieved was definitely through more luck than judgment. And we never made a bean either; to this day I can only recall receiving £90, and I only got that 18 months ago!"

"I think we were a bit naive and lacked experience," agrees Ricky, "But at the end of the day, if Jo hadn't left when she did it probably wouldn't have gone so wrong so quickly, because replacing her proved to be a major problem. Her decision to leave was due to personal circumstances; she got herself a new boyfriend who was quite a jealous character and he made her leave as he didn't want her touring around with three lads. It didn't leave a bad taste as such but sometimes I wonder what might have been…"

Things were all downhill from there. Rather than miss out on the Peel session, they took a chance and recorded it with an inferior vocalist, Jewelie, who they soon parted company with following a short UK tour. She was replaced by Penny, a girlfriend of Vice Squad guitarist, Dave Bateman, who recorded two new songs with the band, but never set foot on a stage with them. The songs did actually see the light of day on Volume One of the Rot Records compilation, 'A Kick Up The Arse', a year after the band had split up, but sound a tad immature compared to their previous singles.

As a last ditch attempt to keep the Expelled dream alive, they decided to make a go of it as a three piece, with bassist Macca handling vocal duties. Although this no doubt surprised the band's following, who had grown accustomed to a fetching female fronting the band, the excellent songs recorded for their unreleased 12", 'Waiting For Tomorrow', suggest that there could have been a new era about to dawn for The Expelled – if only they'd been given the chance. Attendances were dwindling at their gigs, Riot City called it a day before the aforementioned 12" could be released, and Macca bailed out to join The Underdogs.

"Although I say it myself those four songs we did with Macca were head and shoulders above anything else we ever recorded," recalls Ricky wistfully. "So when all that happened and they never got released, we just couldn't believe it. We did send some demos off to other labels but by 1984, record labels didn't seem interested in signing punk bands anymore; they were more interested in anyone with a synthesizer! Riot City going under was definitely the most frustrating thing that happened to us and that was basically the end of the band."

And that was all we heard of The Expelled until 1999 when the enterprising Captain Oi! label released a compilation CD, and Ricky was so shocked by the interest it generated he decided to resurrect the band.

"I genuinely couldn't believe that people would still buy Expelled stuff after all this time! Also I still went to punk gigs and would bump into a lot of old faces, some of whom would get onto me saying we should reform, so I decided to get in touch with Macca. I knew he was still on the circuit playing bass, and when I asked

Ricky (drums) and Jo of The Expelled, live at The 100 Club

him he was very apprehensive about the idea at first, but said he would give it a go. The main problem was that Jo and Tim had not done anything for years and it's not that easy just to pick up where you left off after all this time, and after a couple of rehearsals it was obvious things weren't working out as I had intended and we went our separate ways.

"For a time it seemed that was it, but deep down it had always bugged me that The Expelled had ended prematurely and I really did want one more go. Also during this period I'd joined a band called The Tricycle Thieves that contained a female singer/guitarist, Becky Laurance, so I asked Becky if she fancied fronting The Expelled. After she said 'Yes', I once again contacted Macca who agreed to give it one final go. He brought along Dougie, the lead guitarist from his other band, The Poison Hearts, and we took things from there.

"Personally I thought we sounded miles better than before," reckons Ricky wistfully. "And although I say it myself Becky was by far the best vocalist we ever had; the thing is, she didn't want to play the old songs all the time and quit the band after we played Morecambe in 2003. It's a shame 'cos it was the best gig The Expelled ever played... but at least we went out on a high."

SELECT DISCOGRAPHY:
7"s:
'No Life, No Future' EP (Riot City, 1982)
'Government Policy' (Riot City, 1982)

AT A GLANCE:
'The Expelled: A Punk Rock Collection' (Captain Oi!, 1999) compiles every single thing recorded by the band, and includes extensive liner notes by Vice Squad's Shane Baldwin. It comes highly recommended.

THE UNDERDOGS

T he second wave punk scene spawned several noteworthy one hit wonders, not least of all The Underdogs from Rothwell. Formed in January 1982 and originally known as Revolt (until they inevitably learnt of another band by that name), The Underdogs were U.G. – vocals, Colin Lawson – guitar, Martin Allchurch – bass and Bill – drums. They played their first show at Bradford's Palm Cove Club, a benefit for a local church that was falling derelict, and many other gigs were undertaken – mainly at the Palm Cove, but also at Brannigan's in Leeds – with the likes of One Way System, The Destructors, The Test Tube Babies and The Subhumans.

In 1982 they recorded a five-track demo which brought them to the attention of Riot City Records, who released their minor masterpiece, the 'East Of Dachau' single, in August 1983. Recorded at Woodlands Studios, Normanton, by Neil Ferguson, the single remains one of the more memorable releases of the time, the title track a genuine unsung classic, incredibly powerful and driving yet invigoratingly melodic at the same time, mainly

The Underdogs from Rothwell, whose 'East Of Dachau' EP remains one of the more memorable releases on Riot City...

thanks to U.G.'s superb rough-hewn vocals. The two songs on the B-side, 'Johnny Go Home' and 'Dead Soldier', maintained the high standard, refusing to pander to the throwaway thrash that was the order of the day, crackling with an almost tangible passion and urgency.

Inexplicably, it barely troubled the Indie Charts at all, just scraping into the Top Fifty for but two weeks. Macca from The Expelled joined the band soon after its release, and although several more demos were recorded, 'East Of Dachau' remains the band's only official release, apathy and disillusionment with the scene leading them to split in 1984.

SELECT DISCOGRAPHY:
7"s:
'East Of Dachau' (Riot City, 1983)

AT A GLANCE:
Although there is in fact a very limited unofficial twenty-six track bootleg CD, 'Riot In Rothwell', compiling all the band's studio recordings as well as several live tracks available, 'East Of Dachau' was also included on Anagram's 'Riot City: The Singles Collection, Volume One' CD, whilst 'Johnny Go Home' appeared on 'Volume Two'.

ULTRA VIOLENT

ebden Bridge's Ultra Violent really were one of UK82's great losses. They released an incredible 7" on Riot City, 'Crime For Revenge', one of the most intense of the period in fact, but then split soon after following a row over – that old chestnut – musical differences. Thirty years later, that single still sizzles with a tangible energy, and all we can do is imagine what might have followed if they hadn't come apart at the seams so quickly.

"My brother used to come home and play David Bowie LPs," recalls vocalist Adie Bailey, "And then he started listening to the John Peel show at night, and I could hear it too. I had heard all about the Pistols and The Clash but it seemed to be changing, and then one night I heard a record that I instantly fell in love with, and it was 'In A Rut' by The Ruts. It just sounded so different to everything else at the time. I loved his voice and that was it for me, I was hooked. This was around 1978; I was fourteen and I recorded that song on an old cassette recorder I had and used to play it to anyone that would listen. A friend called Andy Griffiths loved it as much I did."

Inspired by the DIY ethos of the second wave of punk, Adie and Griff 'formed' Delinquents, who weren't actually a band but, "more of an idea, that we would call ourselves Deliquents if and when we ever did get a band together!" But that idea actually started to gain momentum when Griff bought a guitar, and Ultra Violent eventually became a reality when Adie and Griff met two like-minded individuals – bassist Simon Duffy and his younger brother, drummer Jared Duffy – who were in a similar "concept band" (i.e. just talking about it), Dreaded Cult.

"We would play stuff by Angelic Upstarts and Sham 69, just jamming at first. Griff came up with the name Ultra Violent. He had seen it in a book and we all thought it was a great name. But we never thought anything would come of it and were just doing it as a hobby really. At the time I never thought we would even play one gig.

"We practised avidly, and when we turned up one night, Griff said he had wrote a great riff. He played it, and it was the riff that became 'Crime For Revenge'. We were all so excited that we

Grif and Adie (with microphone) of Ultra Violent, a 'frighteningly powerful and focused act...'

Ultra Violent's Adie Bailey, 2011, pic by John Bolloten

had our own song. Griff wrote the words too, and they fitted perfect. When we played it together for the first time, it just came together so well . . . we were on our way!

"For the size of the town, Hebden Bridge had a thriving punk scene between 1980 and '84," continues Adie. "But we were mates with all the punks from Halifax too. There was really only one other local band around at the time: Crash, who released a record on No Future. When they rehearsed, in this small village in the hills, there would be 20 or 30 people go and hang out there, and it would be like playing a gig most nights.

"There was a couple of small venues to play in Hebden and Halifax: the Trades Club in Hebden Bridge and the Pot o' Four pub in Halifax, where there were some seriously mad nights, but apart from those, there wasn't much else in the area."

Within six weeks of writing their first song, Ultra Violent did their first gig, at the Hebden Bridge Youth Club, in early 1981, a typically low-key but empowering affair.

"I think we played the youth club because Jared was still going there, so he managed to talk them into it," laughs Adie. "There was about 30 kids there, and all I remember was that it went okay, and how relieved I felt afterwards that we had got it over with – but after that we wanted more!"

Encouraged by the enthusiastic response to their live debut, Ultra Violent began gigging in earnest, building a strong and rampant local following ("We took a coach full of our fans when we played Rochdale Football Club, who caused complete mayhem . . . I think they are still paying for the damage now!"), before they tracked their first demo in early 1982, straight to a tape recorder in their rehearsal room. Although rougher than a camping weekend in the Pennines, it captured their live energy to a tee and featured six original songs – 'Crime For Revenge', 'Where Angels Dare Not Tread', 'Dead Generation', 'Kill The Coppers', '1982' and 'Sign Of The Times' – bringing them to the attention of Riot City Records, who had them re-record the first three of these tracks for the now-classic 'Crime For Revenge' single.

"They sent us to Cargo Studios in Rochdale, where some of our favourite bands had recorded, and it was to be Colin Richardson who would produce it for us. We were really nervous about it all, as we had never been through a proper recording process . . . We actually thought we would all have to go in one room and just basically do it live. We were very naïve about it. I remember saying, 'What, we have to do it separately? How does that work?' But Colin was great with us, and I think it turned out well. It took us about six hours to record the whole thing.

"We actually wanted to do a four-track but Riot City insisted we did only three songs. The other song from the demo we wanted to do was '1982', which we thought was a good song, but we just shrugged it off and said we would save it for the next one."

Unfortunately for all concerned, there wasn't a 'next one', despite the band's growing reputation on the live circuit.

"After the record came out, we started getting bigger gigs," confirms Adie. "We played with Abrasive Wheels a couple of times, and we supported the UK Subs at Drifters in Manchester, which was a great gig. The crowd loved us; we were loud and aggressive and quite a tight band by then. We had also acquired a live female singer too, called Wendy Peacock, and we did a very different version of 'These Boots Are Made For Walkin' . . . It was a great live number, and the crowd always loved it.

"It was amusing sometimes when we got asked to do gigs, as Jared was that young we always had to ask his dad if he could play them, especially if it was midweek as he had to go to school the next day! But his dad was always cool with it, and actually drove us to most of the gigs. At the Drifters one in Manchester, they really weren't going to let him in because of how young he looked. It was touch and go at one stage whether we would actually play, but eventually it was Charlie Harper who persuaded them to let him in.

"Anyway, we got offered another single by Riot City and had some great songs ready for it. We had two new ones written, 'The Mad Axeman' and 'Survivors', which we had played live and they went down really well. I used to actually swing an axe round amongst the crowd during 'Mad Axeman'. I really don't know how nobody got hurt, but it seemed like a great gimmick at the time, and I always got away with it."

The end when it came, as these things so often are, was unexpected, anti-climactic and mildly farcical.

"I remember we played at the Pot o' Four in Halifax," sighs Adie. "The place was packed and we were getting about a bit gig-wise, and things were looking good for us. That gig was late 1983 and it turned out to be our last gig. It wasn't meant to be, but I remember going to rehearsals a week or so after, and Griff came out with the bombshell that he wanted to put keyboards into some of our songs. I was fucking livid. My argument was that we had only just learned to play the instruments we had and only just become a decent live band . . . I have nothing against keyboards but I just didn't think it would suit our band. Griff and myself had a massive argument about it and I stormed out. There was just no way I was having that, so I told them that if they put keyboards in I was out. To be honest, the argument was between me and Griff, and Jaz and Simon kept out of it. They actually tried talking me out of it for the next couple of weeks, but there was no going back for me, so that was the end of that. And that is how the band split up; I was pissed off about it for quite a while, but then another opportunity emerged about six months later."

Opportunity did indeed come knocking when original vocalist Wakey left the well-respected English Dogs, and Adie was invited to audition for them, just as they were just crossing over into their more metallic phase.

"I sort of knew they were going into the crossover stuff, which I was also into by then, so I was happy about that," reckons Adie. "I got the job but realised I had a big pair of boots to fill replacing Wakey. They already had gigs booked around the country and I only had a couple of weeks to learn all the stuff. It was a very much more professional approach. My first gig with them was at Oddy's in Oldham though, which was great as it wasn't far from where I lived so I had a lot of mates come along, and after that I felt comfortable with it and was very well received.

"I have some great memories of that period, but the US tour in '86 is the best of all. We went there for nearly a month and only played nine gigs, so it seemed more like a holiday, but it was a great tour and the gigs were the best ever."

Adie eventually left the English Dogs in 1989 ("Because it had ran its course"), and had nothing to do with music ("Apart from going to the occasional gig") for twenty years – until he was asked by Gizz Butt to join the reformed 'metal version' of the English Dogs (as opposed to the 'punk version' fronted by Wakey) in 2009. A successful US tour was undertaken in 2012, with support from The Casualties, Toxik Holocaust and Havok, and a new (Andy Sneap produced) album (entitled 'The Thing With Two Heads') is in the works for 2014. Unfortunately Adie can't shed any light on what the other members of UV went on to do, as he lost touch with them once the band fell apart.

"I used to love being in Ultra Violent," he adds, by means of conclusion. "I think that single was just going to be the start of it, and we had songs in the bag that were a lot better than that, but unfortunately it became the end of us. I am just so glad that people got so much enjoyment from that record and are still doing so today. It did really well – sold out of the first pressing really quickly and got into the Top Ten in the Independent Charts at the time – so we were getting national coverage in the music papers. It felt strange going to my local record shop and seeing our record there. We really never thought it would ever come to that, but I regard it as a classic slice of punk rock and am very proud of what four teenagers from a very small town in Yorkshire managed to produce. I can still listen to that record with a huge grin on my face even today."

SELECT DISCOGRAPHY:
7"S:
'Crime For Revenge' (Riot City, 1983)

AT A GLANCE:
Sadly no such thing as a dedicated Ultra Violent reissue, although at the time of writing it looks as if Californian label Video Disease will re-release the 7" in 2014.

CRIMINAL JUSTICE

Huddersfield's Criminal Justice may well have only released one single, but they made a significant impact on the scene, not least of all as the subject of TV documentary 'First Tuesday', presented by Jonathan Dimbleby. Founding members Andy 'Brooky' Brook (drums) and Paul 'Nobby' Ibbotson (guitars) were originally, with Mark 'Newey' Newbould and Kev 'Raggy' Riley, in The Infected, a band who split up after just one gig with (another influential Huddersfield band) The Xpozez in Hull.

By the summer of 1982, they had recruited bassist Kev 'Kitty' Kitson and vocalist Lee 'Chaz' Netherwood and become Criminal Justice, taking much of their early inspiration from

The Sex Pistols, who actually played their last ever UK show in Huddersfield. The town had a vibrant punk community that quickly got behind the band.

Excepting an invite-only public debut in Chaz's front room, that saw so many Huddersfield punks turn up to witness it, most of them had to stand in the garden and watch through the window, Criminal Justice did their first proper show at the Fraternity Hall in Huddersfield in September 1982. They were supporting The Macc Lads and played just the four songs they would later record for their first demo, namely 'Lebanese Lifestyle', 'Victim Of Religion', 'Frenzy' and 'The Race Is On (For NATO)'.

"We weren't nervous but were quite excited about it," says Brooky of their first studio experience. "We'd done some rehearsal tapes and were keen to hear something proper. We all chipped in with the finances and booked a day at Woodlands Studio in Castleford. We liked the sound the engineer had gotten on the Xpozez stuff and we asked Tez (aka Andy Turner, who went on to front the hugely popular Instigators) and Trimble (aka Andrew Turnbull, who also ended up in The Instigators) of The Xpozez to come in with us and help produce it, which they did."

Brooky actually joined The Xpozez as drummer soon after (immediately following their '10,000 Marching Feet' EP for Red Rhino in fact). He recorded a further four singles and undertook a six-week European tour with them, whilst also playing in Criminal Justice, although staying loyal to both bands without compromising one or the other was sometimes a struggle.

"On one occasion both bands had gigs on the same night – different venues, different towns! Somehow I managed to play them both; one was in Huddersfield with Criminal Justice and the other in Bradford, about twenty miles away. As soon as the Justice set was finished, I got a lift to Bradford and arrived just as The Xpozez were about to get onstage!"

Another demo followed in December 1983, again recorded at Woodlands, with two frantic tracks from the session – 'Machines And Systems' and 'Middle East Mayhem' – appearing on the eighteen-track Sane Records compilation, 'On The Street' (1984), before a deal was struck with Oxford-based Endangered Music. Criminal Justice's impressive 'Hierarchy Of Hell' EP was only the second release for the fledgling label that was actually ran by Steve Beatty, who was later to start up the very successful Plastic Head Distribution, and it quickly sold out of its pressing of 1000 copies. It also saw the band, rather unusually for a punk act, flirting with satanic imagery and lyrics, most obviously on the Exploited-esque 'Son Of Lucifer'.

"The satanic stuff was a tongue-in-cheek thing really," reckons Brooky. "We were very anti-religion at the time. We didn't like all the hypocrisy that went with it and all the wars that were caused by different religions. Chaz wrote 'Son Of Lucifer' and also did the sleeve artwork; it was basically two fingers up at organised religion."

Lee 'Chaz' Netherwood of Criminal Justice

Inevitably the touring undertaken in support of these releases was sporadic and produced mixed results.

"Probably our worst gig ever was at Fleetwood in Lancashire, which also turned out to be our last gig before we split. The venue was crap, a football club, and during the soundcheck the club steward kept pulling the plug and telling us to turn down the volume. Then Chaz head-butted the singer of the support band for smashing his new microphone. In the end we didn't even play… not surprising really!

"There were one or two humorous moments, to tell the truth, and probably a few more which we've forgotten due to the drink! We played at the Bunker in Sunderland and before the gig we sneaked upstairs and found a room all set out for a jumble sale. We got dressed up in all sorts of clothes that we found, duffle coats, corduroy trousers, flat caps, old-fashioned glasses, and did our set dressed like that. That was a laugh. I also remember Chaz giving Kitty a haircut as we walked down the street visiting various pubs before a gig. It was a very wonky mohican due to him stepping off kerbs and not walking straight! We also did a short UK tour in an old sixties bread van which had Chaz's mum's settee in the back. Luxury indeed!"

As mentioned earlier, the band's big break came in 1985 when they appeared on the ITV current affairs programme, 'First Tuesday', even though things didn't go quite according to plan.

"Chaz was placed on a government training programme, one of those 'Get back to work' things. He had to do some painting and decorating at the National Children's Centre building in Huddersfield for a couple of weeks. The Centre's boss, Hazel Whitmore, noticed him, 'cos of his appearance no doubt, and they got chatting. He said he was in a band and she told him of her friend Ruth Pitt at Yorkshire TV who might want to speak to him about a documentary she was going to do about punks in Huddersfield, and, to cut a long story short, that's how we were eventually approached to take part in the programme.

"The film crew followed us around for about a week. They bought Chaz cider early in the morning and he played right into their hands! All they seemed to want to do was to portray us all as drunken yobs and for the most part they succeeded! We said a lot of positive things about the scene in general but it was all edited out. Still, it was a pleasing experience to get on TV and play some of our stuff and in the end the programme did us no harm."

However, any opportunity to capitalise on this mainstream national exposure was trounced when musical differences reared their ugly heads, and Criminal Justice changed their name and their musical direction, and somehow lost their focus in the shuffle. They disintegrated in early 1986.

"We were getting into the thrash metal thing and we were starting to evolve musically. We changed the band name to Damage Inc., still with the same line-up, and recorded the 'Damage Inc.' demo, intending it to be a fresh start and a move away from Criminal Justice. It was at this time that Chaz was playing most of the guitar tracks; Nobby wasn't improving and, realizing this after struggling on most of the demo tracks, he soon left the band.

"Me, Chaz, and Kitty went on to form a new three-piece band called Diekreist. We did record one two-track demo but disbanded for good not too long afterwards because of other commitments.

"Kitty is no longer involved in music. Nobby went on to become a salesman and was last heard of living in Ireland. I joined a punk-pop outfit called All Over The Carpet but am no longer playing in bands. Chaz went on to play guitar in various metal bands including Karrion and Solstice and is currently working on an album with his new band, Fireblade.

"Looking back I think I'd like us to be remembered just for getting out of the rut that others were in at the time," he concludes. "We didn't end up in factories or mills like most kids we grew up with; we went out and did our own thing, said what we thought and left our mark!"

SELECT DISCOGRAPHY:
7"s:
'Hierarchy Of Hell' (Endangered, 1984)

AT A GLANCE:

Unfortunately, despite their TV appearance and several highly recommended demos, Criminal Justice remain too obscure for an official retrospective CD, although it may be worth contacting Brooky (enclosing sufficient return postage) directly c/o 35 Coupland Rd., Beeston, Leeds, LS11 6AL, England.

MAU MAUS

ormed in Sheffield in late 1979, The Mau Maus began life as a second-rate covers band, but soon developed into one of the harsher sounding acts of the genre – due no doubt in part to their depressing local environment, but also as a direct result of the band's affinity with the faster US hardcore bands of the early Eighties. The core of the band – Chris Taylor on vocals, Kevin 'Bunny' Warren on bass, Andrew 'Lev' Levick on guitar, and Paul 'Podge' Barker on drums – had all been best mates at school, and upon leaving, Lev and Podge set to work down the nearest coal pit, whilst Chris and Bunny went on the dole.

"It was a time of Thatcher's government that seemed intent on rubbing working class people's noses in the grind, so for four working class lads just leaving school, the future looked bleak," recalls Lev. "We decided to form the band under the precept that all four of us felt exactly the same way – bored shitless, and wanting to do something that we all actually enjoyed. The name Mau Maus came about from an American band of the same name that disbanded in 1980… we all liked it, and at the time, it was a toss-up between that and a name that Chris's mum had come up with – The Foursomes! Need I say more?

"We started by doing mainly cover versions, playing local youth clubs and pubs. It was about this time that we first heard Discharge, and the way they wrote about what they really believed in, and the simple but effective way that they put forward their songs, really appealed to us. From then on we started writing more of our own material."

A local promoter, Marcus Featherby, soon took notice of the band, and offered them their first high profile show, supporting The Angelic Upstarts at Sheffield's Marples Club. It was to mark the beginning of a long – often 'love/hate' – relationship with Featherby, who also ran Pax Records, the label the band would soon sign to.

"Marcus saw us at rehearsal prior to the gig, and remarked that if he'd heard us earlier, before he'd put us on the bill, he would never have booked us!" laughs Lev. "This really pissed us off, and straight away we ditched all our cover versions, and were determined to write all our own songs, mainly to prove Featherby wrong. Our determination and friendship were too strong to let an outsider put us down.

"We played that gig with The Upstarts with a whole set of new songs, a new determination and a real feeling of knowing which direction we wanted to go in. At the end of the day we were four really good friends playing the kind of music we loved listening to. Soon as we came off stage, Featherby offered to pay for us to record our new songs, and we jumped at the chance."

Generous to a fault, Marcus booked them into Kayley Studios near Rotherham, with a budget of £50… which brought them all of five hours recording time. Undeterred, and no doubt overjoyed at such a chance to prove themselves, The Mau Maus managed to batter out eight raw, aggressive songs that saw the light of day in August '82 as their 'Society's Rejects' EP. Despite an admittedly basic production, the songs pulse with the sort of vitality only attainable by naive

Chris Taylor, vocalist of Mau Maus, 'one of the harsher sounding acts of the genre...'

youths with their backs to the wall and their eyes on the clock. Although not to everyone's tastes, Chris's guttural vocals also helped set the band apart, and the EP spent a very respectable ten weeks in the Indie Charts. One of the songs, 'The Kill', also appeared on Pax's very successful anti-war compilation album, 'Wargasm', alongside the likes of Captain Sensible, The Dead Kennedys and Flux Of Pink Indians.

On the back of the EP, the band, who had already built a strong local following, started to play further afield, and even managed to land a support slot to The Upstarts at London's 100 Club, an experience which Lev remembers as, "An anticlimax! We were much happier playing smaller venues, with bands that were on the same wavelength as us."

The band's next release, the three track 'No Concern' 7", was produced by Lee Wilson, vocalist with North London Oi band, Infa-Riot, who had previously shared vinyl space with the Mau Maus on the 'Wargasm' record. It sounded considerably better than their primitive debut, but thankfully didn't loose sight of the blue-collar grit that was the backbone of the band's sound. A fourth track, 'Give Us A Future', was recorded during the same session, and appeared on yet another Pax compilation album, 'Punk's Dead? Nah, Mate, The Smell's Jus' Summink In Yer Underpants', which, despite the appalling title, reached No. 2 in the Indies.

However it was the band's third EP which was to be both their defining moment and their crowning glory. The 'Facts Of War' EP materialised in the summer of '83, and shot up both the Indie Charts and the Punk Chart in Sounds. It featured the five best songs the band had written up until that point, and a strong, thick production that finally did their hard-edged thrashy approach some real justice. Tracks such as 'Just Another Day' even had Chris wringing some stubborn melody from his barbed wire tonsils, but it was the breakneck title-track that had the front rows of their shows whipped into an apoplectic frenzy.

"I believe our lyrics were what set us apart," reckons Podge. "Marcus once described us as 'Very socially aware'. We sang about problems that were happening both in Britain and throughout the world, both political and social issues.

"The 'Facts of War' EP is my favourite of all our releases," he adds. "It was recorded on twenty-four tracks at Revolution in Manchester and cost ten times what our first EP did! The production and sound quality was far superior and the songs were better too."

"It was definitely our finest moment," agrees Lev. "We regard that EP as being the closest you would have got to hearing us live without actually being there; we got the sound just right for once.

Sheffield's Mau Maus

Marcus Featherby supplied us with the idea for the cover – a picture of the Earth with a gas mask on, and in each eye the flag of Russia and America, which he got from some magazine."

The press rewarded the band's efforts with their most positive reviews to date, and tours with both Infa-Riot and The Exploited were undertaken to promote the release. However, things took a tragic turn for the worse on the very last night of The Exploited tour, when bassist Bunny announced that he had cancer. The news shook the morale of the band to its very foundations.

"To us the band was a little family," recalls Lev. "We were totally devoted to what we were doing, and to have to come to terms with this terrible news was unreal. About a week after hearing about Bunny's illness, we were offered a ten-day tour of Germany with GBH; this would have been a dream come true, but, to be honest, without Bunny it just wasn't the same.

"Eventually though, after talking with Bunny, we decided to recruit an old mate of ours, Alf, who stood in for Bunny and we did the tour. It so happened that GBH pulled out about three weeks prior to us going to Germany, and they were replaced by The Varukers, whom we became good friends with. The tour went down brilliantly and was a whole new experience for us."

To add to the difficulties facing The Mau Maus during this period, the Miners' Strike also meant that now all of the band were without work and struggling to make ends meet, and the lack of any financial support from Pax was starting to sour somewhat their relationship with Marcus Featherby.

Following in the footsteps of another UK punk band who were at their best in the live environment – Peter And The Test Tube Babies – The Mau Maus decided to make their debut album a live one. A rough and ready document of their undeniable stage prowess. When 'Live At The Marples' was released in February 1984, it spent two months in the Indie Charts, reaching the giddy heights of No. 3.

"We always did prefer to play live in front of an audience anyway," explains Podge, before admitting, "But the real reason for releasing a live album was the fact that things had happened so quickly for us, we didn't actually have any more material written!"

Pax then rush-released 'Running With The Pack', a Mau Maus compilation primarily intended for export, to cash in on the success the band were enjoying at that time, but it was to be the last thing Featherby put out for them. Yearning to be more in control of their own output, the band bravely set up their own label, Rebellion Records.

"At the time, we were getting disillusioned with Marcus, because of the lack of money and progress we were making," explains Chris. "We had some contacts at Red Rhino, and they said that they would put the money up for our own label, so we took the plunge! A local promoter who became our advisor, called Tony Perin, also helped us out in a big way studio-wise and with press releases. But it was harder than we thought… you see, we didn't have as many top-notch contacts as Marcus did. It was nice to be in control, but we just didn't have the experience to do it justice!"

Their first release on the fledgling label was the 'Tear Down The Walls' EP, which, although lacking the furious conviction of the preceding 'Facts Of War', saw a definite maturity emerging in the band's more confident arrangements. Chris also took a slightly less abrasive approach with his vocals, resulting in something more akin to the hardcore sounds reaching the UK from across the Atlantic. Recorded and produced by Simon Hinkler (who later enjoyed chart success himself as guitarist with The Mission) at Fairview Studios in Hull, it was a strong release with which to launch the new label, but frustratingly for the band, it sold poorly by their own standards, and marked the beginning of the end for The Mau Maus.

Their debut studio album proper, 'Fear No Evil', was also a commercial disappointment, despite UK tours with The English Dogs and The Varukers, and the final nail in the coffin was the 'Nowhere To Run' 12", released in early '85, that saw the addition of a second guitarist, Richard Hall. It also saw the return of a recovering Bunny on bass, who had been conspicuous by his absence on the other two Rebellion releases, but even he couldn't save the band from leaving as their unsatisfactory epitaph their least essential release by far. 'Nowhere To Run' is indeed a decent slab of poppy punk in its own right, but following as it did such a legacy of incendiary politico-thrash, it's no real wonder that the hardcore fans of the band lost interest; it's hardly recognisable as a true Mau Maus record.

Chris concedes that, "The sound was nowhere near heavy enough", before also admitting that it was he himself who unwittingly instigated the eventual split of the band in late 1985.

"Musically we were always trying to progress, trying to get more melodic, and I was finding it harder and harder to do justice to the new songs that Lev was writing. Plus I had just started a new job, and getting time off to do gigs was almost impossible. So, I had a long hard think about the situation, and decided it would be best all round if I quit the band. I left on good terms with all the other band members, but they didn't really do anything else after that point."

It's pleasing to know that the members of The Mau Maus didn't allow the demise of the band to affect what had drawn them together in the first place – their friendship – and they remain as close today as they were back then.

"Looking back we played with some excellent bands," reminisces Lev fondly. "And we all agree that it was the best part of our lives, and, even if we could, we wouldn't change a thing. There were a lot of ups, and a lot of downs, but to this day, our ideals remain the same and we are all still good mates."

"We would like to be remembered first and foremost as a thrash punk band; we liked to play fast and loud!" says Chris, in closing. "We would like our music to be remembered for its energy and honesty. We weren't the best musicians in the world by a long shot, but we always gave 100% at every gig… and enthusiasm can get you a long way!"

SELECT DISCOGRAPHY:
7"s:
'Society's Rejects' (Pax, 1982)
'No Concern' (Pax, 1983)
'Facts Of War' (Pax, 1983)
'Tear Down The Walls' (Rebellion, 1985)

12"s:
'Nowhere To Run' (Rebellion, 1985)

LPs:
'Live At The Marples' (Pax, 1983)
'Running With The Pack' (Pax, 1984)
'Fear No Evil' (Rebellion, 1985)

AT A GLANCE:
The excellent 'Mau Maus: The Punk Singles Collection' on Captain Oi! (1996) is as good a place as any to start your investigations, compiling as it does all the band's EPs, along with original artwork and detailed liner notes from Stuart Newman, the editor of Control! fanzine.

RED LONDON

ed London were a Sunderland punk band that started in 1981, with close ties to Red Alert, and roots stemming back to 1977 and The Rebels, who were the area's first real punk band.

"I was the guitarist and main songwriter in The Rebels," begins Gaz Stoker, the bassist on every Red London recording, explaining the Red London family tree in more detail. "At that time I was sixteen years old and still at school. We lasted a couple of years, got quite well known locally, and were a big influence on a lot of bands who followed, including Red Alert, Red London and Leatherface.

"In fact, Red Alert actually took their name from a Rebels song of the same name and that song was also recorded by Red London on our first album. It was my brother, Kid Stoker, who formed Red London and I went to a few of their early gigs, and after the Rebels split up I was asked if I wanted to play bass for them. Their original bass player pulled out of a gig they really wanted to play and they didn't want to cancel it, so they asked me to stand in for him. I'd never played bass before but I learnt the songs and did the gig, and they must have been impressed because they asked me to stay! This was in late 1981, and the year after we signed to Razor Records."

As well as Gaz on bass and Kid on guitar, the original lineup also comprised vocalist Patty Smith (brother of Red Alert's Steve Smith) and drummer Raish Carter.

Taking a name like Red London, the band clearly made their political affiliations known from the outset, aligning themselves with other left-wing punk bands such as York's Redskins, and by association the Socialist Workers Party, and playing many benefit gigs in support of the striking miners etc.

"Actually, when Red London started I was still in the Rebels and they asked me to suggest a name for the band," reveals Gaz. "I knew 'Red London' was the B-side of a Sham 69 song [their '77 debut, 'I Don't Wanna'] and I thought it sounded like a good name for a band. That's what I suggested and they took that name, so originally the 'Red' in the title wasn't really significant.

Red London

Red London live

But we've always been working class and obviously left wing, so this came across more and more in the music.

"As for politics in music . . . ? I think it's okay as long as it's not extreme and you're not shoving your views down people's throats. There's nothing wrong with a bit of social comment. A lot of bands that really mean something to people sing about real life, social injustice etc., and that can be a good thing. It becomes more than just a song and gets people thinking and can unite common causes.

"But this is nothing new; it goes back a long time, long before punk. I admire people like Bob Dylan who stood up for what he believed in during the Sixties and I admire similar people or bands who have stood up for what they believed in since. We never played with the Redskins ourselves, but I met them at a gig in Sunderland and they invited me to a television show they were recording in Newcastle the next day. The show was called 'The Tube' and I went along on their guest list. They were a really talented band.

"Yes, we played a lot of miners benefit gigs in the Eighties. At that time there was only two main sources of employment in Sunderland, one was the shipyards (years ago, when Sunderland was a town it was the biggest shipbuilding town in the world) and the other was the coal mines. When the miners went on strike it lasted for nearly a year and broke up whole communities. A lot of our friends were miners, so we were happy to play as many benefit gigs as we could to support them."

Taking their influence from the more tuneful punk bands like The Clash, The Ruts and The Jam, Red London were always going to be more melodic than many of their thrashier peers of the early Eighties, and they soon came to the attention of Razor Records, who had one of the more like-minded rosters of the period and offered them a deal for a single. So, in 1983, the band went into Wapping's Elephant Studios with Nick Robbins to record three songs for the wonderfully sombre 'Sten Guns In Sunderland' EP, which sold well enough for Razor to agree to also issue the band's 1984 LP, 'This Is England'. Unfortunately Raish had been imprisoned for assault and robbery, so the band were forced to recruit new drummer Max Muir, although their

Red London's Gaz Stoker, 2011, picture by John Bolloten

deftly melodic approach to songwriting was thankfully unaffected by the personnel change, the album being one of the more memorable and anthemic releases of 1984, earning itself a 5 out of 5 review in Sounds from John Opposition (aka Attila The Stockbroker).

"All the bands that influenced us were really melodic, so that's the way we thought punk should be played – and still do," confirms Gaz. "By the time we got to release records though, the punk scene and punk sound had started to change, and not for the better. The so-called second and third waves of punk had come along. Some of it was good but some of it turned into a totally unmelodic mess, where songs got faster and faster and the vocals were just shouting. That's not what original punk was about. And how can you get a message across when no one can understand you? So we stuck with what we believed in, and all the original punk bands were still releasing great tuneful records so we were in good company.

"The song 'Guitars And Crime' on the first album was about Raish," he continues. "We didn't tell the record company we didn't have a drummer, for obvious reasons, so we needed a drummer fast, and Max Muir used to play drums in the next room to us where we used to rehearse. He wasn't in a band, but just set up a drum kit and rehearsed on his own. He was a student who wasn't from Sunderland, and was totally different to us, but seemed like an obvious choice for us as we needed a drummer to learn the songs straight away.

"He did the album and a few gigs, but then graduated and moved to a different part of the country to take up some job. And we never heard from him again! As I said, he was totally different to us and someone who we didn't even regard as a friend, so it was no great loss."

Matty Forster from Red Alert took over the drum stool full-time, and 1985 saw them heading out to Europe for the first of many continental tours, making enough of an impression on French label Gougnaf Mouvement to offer them a 7". However Patty Smith left the band and was replaced on vocals by a returning Raish.

"Patty's then-girlfriend was not happy with him being in a band and going on tour etc. Basically she didn't trust him and was always trying to get him to leave the band, and he finally gave in (this was to be a recurring theme over a number of years). Anyway, Raish was released from prison and wanted to re-join the band on drums, but we were happy with Matty (who stayed with us for the next fourteen years!), who was a much better drummer than Raish. So we gave Raish a chance on vocals instead. He sounded all right, but looking back he just tried to copy Patty's vocals. He did the EP with us and it sounded okay, then, believe it or not, he got jailed again not long after, so we decided that was the end of Raish being in Red London."

Raish was replaced by Marty Clark on vocals (and second guitar) in time for the band to hook up with another French label, Negative, for 1989's 'Outlaws' LP and a single entitled 'The Day They Tore The Old School Down'.

Red London live

"The first school me and Kid ever went to was Stansfield Street School," recalls Gaz ruefully. "Some years later the school closed and then reopened as a sort of college. This stayed open for a few years and then it closed again, but the building still stood for a long time, just boarded up. Then one day, without warning, the bulldozers moved in and demolished the whole building. It was sort of an end of an era, and Kid wrote the song, not only about the school but about change, and I think he really captured what we felt like at the time. The lyrics are really good and really sad in a way."

Red London continued throughout the Nineties, releasing some sterling punk rock along the way (1997's Frankie Stubbs-produced 'Days Like These' an especially powerful highlight) and never once compromising their commitment to a good hook or the independent underground. They eventually hung up their boots in 2002 but will be fondly remembered by all that were touched by their music over the years.

"By the time we did our final European tour in 2002, we had Steve 'Cast Iron' Smith [of Red Alert] on vocals as Patty had left and returned and left again on too many occasions. The last gig of the tour was in Paris and that seemed like a good place to call it a day as France was the first country we played outside the UK back in 1985. The gig was great and it just seemed the right time to bow out. Someone did video the gig and I've got our whole set on DVD, and I'm over the moon I've got a copy of Red London's last-ever gig.

"I still played with Red Alert for a while – I was in that band for 12 years. I went on to play in the Angelic Upstarts as well (strangely enough, I've been in the Upstarts 12 years too) and I still play with them. I also played bass in The Dipsomaniacs, an amazing band who never got the recognition they deserved but I'd put them up against anybody.

"I thought Red London were a great band," he says proudly in conclusion. "We were a bit different to a lot of other punk bands, but we had the tunes and we had the songs. The most important part of any band is the songs and I'm still proud of those songs and the lads that made them possible. I'd also like to thank Attila The Stockbroker. He believed in us right from the first time he saw us live in 1983. He became a lifelong friend and in my eyes will always be a punk legend."

SELECT DISCOGRAPHY:
7"S:
'Sten Guns In Sunderland' (Razor, 1983)

'Pride And Passion' (Gougnaf Mouvement, 1987)

'The Day They Tore The Old School Down' (Negative, 1989)

'Downtown Riot' (Combat Rock, 1997)

LPS:
'This Is England' (Razor, 1984)

'Outlaws' (Negative, 1989)

'Tumbling Dice' (Released Emotions, 1990)

'Last Orders Please' (Knock Out, 1994)

'A Look Back In Anger (Live Sessions)' (Step-1, 1996)

'Days Like These' (Knock Out, 1997)

'Once Upon A Generation' (Knock Out, 1999)

'Live In Leipzig' (Step-1, 2001)

'The Soundtrack Of Our Lives' (Trash 2001/Knock Out, 2002)

AT A GLANCE:
Probably best to check out Knock Out's 'Street Life: The Best Of Red London' CD (2000), which contains 21 tracks culled from most of the band's releases.

CHAPTER FIVE

THE NORTH AND EAST MIDLANDS

DISCHARGE

W hilst not the most consistent or long-lasting of the early Eighties punk bands, Stoke-on-Trent's Discharge are probably the most influential. They inspired literally hundreds of copycat bands, eventually spawning a sub-genre all of their own (usually referred to as 'Discore' or 'D-beat') and they not only helped shape the face of punk rock but also that of extreme metal, with the likes of Metallica, Slayer and Anthrax all citing them as a major influence. They're even back together since 2000 with 75% of the original recording line-up intact, a new studio album in the racks, and sounding better than ever.

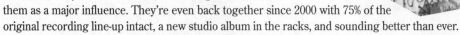

Terry 'Tez' Roberts and Roy 'Rainy' Wainwright started the band in 1977, singing and playing guitar respectively, and they wasted little time recruiting Tez's younger brother, Tony 'Bones' Roberts on lead guitar, Nigel Bamford on bass and Tony 'Acko' Atkinson on drums.

"I was trying to learn guitar at school when Tez asked me to join the band, but they wouldn't give me music lessons, saying I was 'too advanced' for the classes!" laughs Bones. "I only knew one song at the time and that was 'The House Of The Rising Sun'! The band didn't really sound like the Discharge you can hear on the records back then though; it was much slower, more like the Sex Pistols or something. And the lyrics were quite bizarre as well, all about dead babies and stuff!

"We were pulling six or seven hundred people at local gigs even before we recorded anything, but I think everyone was into it back then anyway. There was a huge punk scene in Stoke; everyone used to play there. All the big bands would play the Victoria Hall in Hanley – we supported The Clash and The Damned there. There were loads of little bands around too; the whole place was buzzing."

"Really early Discharge sounded more like the bands that we grew up with," adds Tez. "All the bands that were around then – The Pistols, Cock Sparrer, Chelsea… all those '77 punk bands… but there were a lot of kids into us even back then."

"When Acko got fed up and left, we just had a reshuffle," explains Bones. "Cal (aka Kelvin Morris) joined on vocals, Rainy moved to bass, and Tez to the drums. Cal was just one of our roadies who had a go at singing at one of our rehearsals."

"He was one of my closest friends at the time, and he wanted in, so we put him on vocals," elaborates Tez. "And I wanted to play an instrument rather than sing, and the drums were available, so I went for it."

This new version of Discharge underwent a startling musical metamorphosis, taking their earlier interpretation of traditional punk rock, speeding it up and mangling it into something uniquely ferocious. It wasn't an immediate transformation though; neither was it one that the band were particularly aware of.

"It just happened really, nothing was planned," reckons Bones. "We were all still at school then, and we didn't really sound like anybody. We just got faster and harder bit by bit; it wasn't an overnight thing, but once we wrote 'Realities Of War', and found our own style as it were – 'cos no one was really doing anything like it before then – the songs started pouring out. And there was no stopping us!"

Discharge did their first gig with the new improved line-up at Northwood Parish Hall, a sold–out show in a local church hall. In the audience that night was one Mike Stone, who owned a local record store but who had also just started up a brand new punk label, Clay.

"One of Discharge actually bought me a tape into my shop," reveals Mike. "But it was with the old line-up, and it really did sound a lot like The Sex Pistols, and my first reaction was, 'What's the point of having another band that sounds like The Pistols?' But they told me that they had a new line-up that was a lot different, and that they were playing that night at the Northwood, so I went along, out of curiosity more than anything else…

Discharge, probably the most ferocious and influential of the early Eighties punk bands L–R: Cal (vocals), Rainy (bass), Bones (guitar)

"The first thing I can remember happening when I walked into the venue were some cow's innards flying across the room, from the direction of the stage, and splashing on the floor in front of me! Something from a butcher's shop anyway. I hadn't seen anything like it before, and was quite taken aback really."

"That first gig was crazy," chuckles Tez. "Everything was crazy, you could get away with anything back then. Everybody was behind us though, 'cos we were so different. We just used to mess about, throwing bits of meat and entrails around the gigs; we were only eighteen or nineteen, and we'd pick up shit we found in the bins outside the fuckin' slaughterhouse! You just wouldn't get away with that nowadays, but back then, no one knew what to expect!"

"So, I spoke to the lads after the gig, and asked if they wanted to put a record out with me," continues Mike. "We had very limited conversations to start with; they basically communicated with me through a series of grunts, but I suppose they didn't really know me or trust me fully then. And when I offered them a proper contract, they were quite surprised, but I wanted to do everything right."

Mike had already signed another local band, The Plastic Idols, to Clay prior to that fateful night at the Northwood, but Discharge excited him so much, their debut single, 'Realities Of War', ended up being the very first release on his label. Recorded and mixed in just three hours at Market Drayton's Redball Studios on February 12th 1980, under Mike's supervision, the four–track EP was a searing attack on the senses that gave the then-flagging punk scene a much–needed shot of attitude and testosterone. It spent an incredible forty–four weeks in the Independent Charts, peaking at No. 5.

"We had done a few demos with Tez singing, and just gave 'em away really to all our mates," says Bones. "But 'Realities' was the first recording we ever did with Cal. We did it all in one day; it was sent off to the plant the same day we recorded it, and it was out a few weeks later! We used to bang it out, to keep the essence of what we were writing."

"We kept it really simple," says Mike, of the startling cover image that launched a thousand studded leather jackets. "I still think it's the best cover I ever released, it's so striking. I can remember going round in my car with boxes of this single, up and down the country, selling them to distributors by hand, but then John Peel played it, and it went ballistic. I was decorating my house at the time, and when that blasted out the radio at me, I nearly fell off the ladder!"

Bones: "And the picture on the back of 'Realities' was taken in our rehearsal room, a tiny little office in a nearby factory. We'd be in there until 3 o'clock in the morning some nights; no one there but us and the guard dog, a big Alsatian that used to scare the shit out of us. We'd open the door and he'd be outside barking!"

The band pushed home their advantage with the five–track 'Fight Back' EP, which was even faster and harder than their debut, and was another huge seller. It spent almost a year in the Indies, this time reaching No. 4.

Tez: "I think 'Fight Back' is my favourite of all our early releases, 'cos that was what we were doing! That's why we started the band – to fight back! And that's still true, even more so, now."

Suddenly distorted guitars and enraged vocals were big business, and literally hundreds of bands sprang up in Discharge's considerable wake, hotly pursued by tens of new labels eager to help them unleash their righteous anger on the youth… and make a few quid in the process. Magazines who had previously declared that punk was dead were now clamouring for an exclusive with the band that helped reanimate the genre, albeit in an even more snarling, anti–social guise, but Discharge weren't keen to play ball.

"Well, we did a Sounds interview," spits Bones. "I can't remember who did it, but everything we said, they turned it around and twisted it to make us look stupid, so we didn't do many interviews after that. Whenever anyone asked me about the band, I would just answer 'Yes' or 'No' anyway – at least I couldn't be misquoted that way."

"We've never really been a band that felt a need to explain ourselves," growls Tez. "We always preferred to let the music do the talking. But when all's said and done, any press is good press, y'know? The thing is, the only person they ever asked anything of was Cal, and he was way too shy, and considered every interview a confrontation."

The almost frightening intensity of the 'Decontrol' single followed in late 1980, this time making No. 2 in the Indies. Backed by 'No TV Sketch' and 'Tomorrow Belongs To Us', but benefiting immensely from a far bigger bottom end to the sound than the two 7"s that preceded it, 'Decontrol' saw Discharge honing their ferocity to a new level of breathtaking power, and remains for many their crowning glory.

"Yes, that's always been my favourite Discharge record, too," confirms Mike Stone. "I remember that song was recorded on the second take. Rainy was actually squatting on the floor, leaning against a pillar, when he played that. It was just a perfect moment out of time.

"We did most of those records in just one or two takes though; the band just played live… and fast. We wanted to capture the spirit and energy of the performance, and that's why those early records have stood the test of time so well. I don't really consider myself a producer in the traditional sense of the word anyway. I was always enthusiastic and had a good set of ears, but I'm not an arranger. Most studio engineers back then had very little time for punk bands; they didn't know how to handle them, so I was like a go-between for the band and the engineer, helping them work together properly."

However, despite the momentum the band were gaining with each release, they suffered their first casualty after 'Decontrol' when founding member Tez left for pastures new. "We created our own sound," he says, on his reasons for leaving just as the band were hitting their stride. "We stumbled upon it, and built on it, but we weren't refining it fast enough for my liking, and that was one of the reasons I left. I still really wish that I'd been a part of (fifth single) 'State Violence State Control' though; that turned out just how I always wanted the band to sound, but

I had other plans... I wanted to play with as many bands as I possibly could.

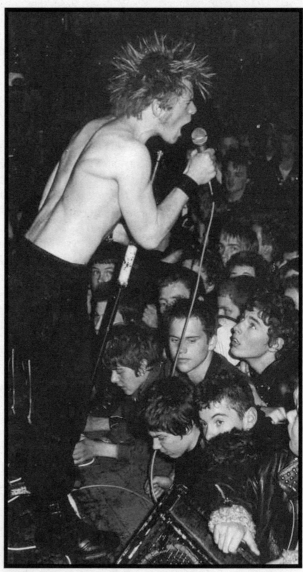

"I joined The UK Subs, and I did The Urban Dogs thing for a bit with Charlie and Knox... I got left behind in Canada. I was on tour with The UK Subs and The Exploited, and I hit the tour manager with a bag of shit, but I forgot that he had my passport and he put it in a mailbox, so I couldn't get it. So I was stuck in Canada for a while, and that was the end of my American tour with The UK Subs! Those guys still talk about that even now...

"I came back home and got back into Broken Bones, first of all playing guitar, but I sang on their US tour in '88, in front of some huge crowds, and we did some Discharge songs, and the kids went fuckin' crazy.

"That summer I decided to stay in the States, in Chicago. I was playing with Naked Raygun t, then I got the Ministry job, then I jammed with Pegboy... same guys, different name! Then I got back with The Subs, and it was during that tour in '96 that I decided that I was gonna play with Battalion of Saints, who were supporting us. Then it was Murphy's Law – I did a stint for them with Agnostic Front – then Billy Club, The Business and Discipline!

A typically intense live shot of Cal from Discharge

"I love doing it, so why not? What's to stop me? I love a

challenge too, and drumming for Discharge again now is quite a challenge, I can tell you, 'cos I hadn't played drums for twenty years prior to this."

After adverts in Sounds resulted in several auditions, Discharge found a new drummer, albeit for a short time, in the shape of young Dave 'Bambi' Ellesmere, previously with Wigan's The Insane. He wasn't with the band for long, but he still played on the now–legendary 'Why?' 12" – surely one of the gnarliest punk records ever committed to plastic – and the Apocalypse tour that the band undertook to promote it, sharing stages the length and breadth of the UK with The Exploited, Anti Pasti and Chron Gen.

"We were stuck in this tiny room – about ten metres square – for two weeks, writing and rehearsing the songs for it," recalls Dave proudly, if not exactly fondly, of the 'Why?' record. "It was actually recorded in the studio of Gavin Sutherland who was one of the people who wrote Rod Stewart's 'Sailing'! We went in and set up, did the backing tracks in one take, then Bones did his overdubs in one take, and Cal did his vocals in another... we were in the recording studio less than three hours! The whole reason you can still listen to it now, and it still sounds so intense, is because it wasn't overproduced. The songs were only two weeks old when they were recorded, so they were all fresh, and it was really 'Wham bam'!

"It was the first thing of its kind, since The Pistols toured with The Clash anyway," he adds on the subject of the Apocalypse dates. "And it was really a showcase for all the upcoming punk bands of the time. It was a riot. All the bands went down really well, and the audiences really appreciated that they were able to see all these bands in one place at the same time. The crowds weren't as huge as some people think though... the biggest was probably just over 1500 at the Lyceum."

Not only was the 12" loaded with devastating tracks such as 'Ain't No Feeble Bastard' and 'A Look At Tomorrow', but it came in a truly harrowing cover that graphically depicted the atrocities of war. It remains to this day one of the most potent anti–war records ever made, and it gave Discharge their only Indie No. 1 when it was released in May 1981.

"It was Cal who had all the ideas about the artwork and stuff," reveals Tez. "He was the one who was really anti–war. The rest of us didn't really give a shit about it personally; we just wanted to go out there and make a fuckin' noise and piss some people off! And we're still pissing people off now, twenty years later, it's great."

Ellesmere soon decided that he wasn't fitting into the tight–knit band as well as he had hoped he would, so he left to rejoin The Insane and was replaced by Garry Maloney, formerly of The Varukers. Garry's recording debut was the brutal 'Never Again' single, another defining moment in hardcore thrash that really saw Bone's fluid lead work coming to the fore. The single even made No. 64 in the National Charts in October 1981, and it paved the way for the debut album, 'Hear Nothing, See Nothing, Say Nothing', surely one of the greatest punk albums of all time.

A cascade of drum rolls ushers in the apocalyptic title track, and from that moment on there is no let–up. Each song is a blood–curdling blast of outrage, the band locked so tight, they sound like one of their despised war machines bearing down on you, the whole thing rumbling along on Rainy's immense gurgling over–driven bass. Even the slower songs, such as the measured, chugging 'Protest And Survive', leave you reeling with their effortless power.

Discharge truly came into their own with the album and seemed untouchable. Bones, of course, is the first to play down any historical significance hysterical journalists might place on the record.

"The early singles set the tone for what we were going to do. We didn't change that much; we couldn't actually play that well, so we progressed as best we could. I would spend six or seven hours a day practising on my own; we all wanted to sound as good as we possibly could really. We started off with these crappy guitars and stuff, that had cost us about £100 from a catalogue, and we only really got any decent gear just before we did the album. It was still cheap and nasty by today's standards, but it did the job.

"The studio was basic too, so the sound on the album is unreal when you think about it. I only did two guitar tracks, which Mike panned in stereo, but it sounds like two hundred! But as far as we were concerned, we were just knocking out another Discharge record, we were totally unaware of the impact it would have. Even then though, some of those songs sent tingles down my spine – and they still do today, there's just something about some of them. Some of the brand new songs do as well though, so that's a good sign.

"I used to just make the riffs up on the spot at practice. We wrote the whole of the first album in a week, then recorded it in a couple of days. Everything in one take, more or less, just banged it out live. I think I went back and added a few guitar bits here and there about a week later, but the whole thing was done really quickly. You know what Stoney's like… 'Time is money, boys!' He hurried us along."

Fourteen tracks of undiluted primal anger delivered with an ominous focused power, the album not only made No. 2 in the Indie Charts, but also No. 40 in the Nationals. It was another resounding success for Discharge and saw the band travelling the world to promote it.

"We toured all over really, and everywhere went mental," says Bones. "It was weird how fast the word spread. The first time we toured the US, we played small clubs that held about two hundred people… the next time we went back we were playing fucking arenas, that sometimes held ten thousand people, and they were sold-out, everyone going crazy. We were there thinking, 'What the fuckin' hell's going on?' No one had even heard of Stoke, but everyone knows where Stoke is now. We put Stoke-on-Trent on the punk map!

"That first US tour was meant to go to Canada and then America, and we were trying to cross over at Buffalo, but they wouldn't have us. Both countries wanted us deported! One customs official pulled a gun on us and said, 'We don't want you in our country, you're a bunch of animals!' Just 'cos we had leather jackets and spiky hair… mind you, we all had criminal records as well! We were given twenty–four hours to go back into Canada and clear all the relevant paperwork. We came back with proper permits, all signed and counter-signed, and they had to bite their lips and let us through. We played with everybody… The Circle Jerks, Black Flag… everyone who was anyone played with Discharge on that tour."

But, inevitably, the end of an era was approaching for Discharge, and following another classic single, 'State Violence State Control' in late 1982, Bones left the band and started up Broken Bones with his brother Tez.

"The 'State Violence' single is still my favourite old Discharge song," says the guitarist. "Not only was it something a bit different for the band, but it was the last one I played on, my parting shot. We just weren't getting along by that time, it was all getting too big. Cal and Gary were letting it go to heir heads, and I was never into all that shit anyway. Rainy just plodded along and hung in there, he wasn't bothered either way."

He was replaced by Peter 'Pooch' Pyrtle, but it was never the same again; the gap that Bones left was subtle yet significant.

"After I left the whole band didn't sound right really," agrees Bones. "Rainy couldn't play the same without me; he never really gelled with their subsequent guitarists, and there seemed to be someone different on every fucking record after that!"

Although Pooch's vinyl debut was the totally acceptable 'Warning: Her Majesty's Government Can Seriously Damage Your Health' 12" in late '83, it marked the end for Discharge as a credible hardcore punk band. Well produced and forcefully delivered, it saw the band begin their descent into the realms of heavy metal, and, most worrying for die-hard fans, Cal began to trade in his throat–shredding bark for a painful high–pitched yelp. Sales and gig attendances began a steady decline as word of mouth slowly but surely damned the new style the band was forging for themselves.

"That metal stuff they did was horrible," exclaims Bones. "I could hardly stand to listen to one song, let alone go out and play them every night. I saw a video of them in Japan once, and it was terrible; they sounded like a covers band with Cal singing. They were playing all the old songs in that metal style, and it just wasn't working at all. They got bottled off stages in the US when they wouldn't play the old stuff properly!"

"Yes, it's true, it was a miracle that they got back alive," confirms Mike. "Promoters were ringing me every day and telling me that the crowds were going mental 'cos Cal refused to play any old songs. They were having ashtrays – even dustbins – thrown at them; it was a disaster."

Two more singles followed in winter '83 and summer '84, 'The Price Of Silence' and 'The More I See', but by the time the latter appeared in the racks, both Pooch and Garry had deserted the sinking ship, leaving just Cal and Rainy to regroup the band. Meanwhile, 'The More I See', a better–than–average metal record admittedly but sadly lacking any of the bite of the original band, made the Indie Top Three.

To buy the band some time, Clay issued the 'Never Again' album in August 1984, basically a 'Best Of' collection, albeit featuring a number of new mixes of classic tracks. It served as a stopgap whilst Cal and Rainy recruited ex–Demon guitarist Les 'The Mole' Hunt and one Haymaker on drums and recorded the 'Ignorance' single. Backed by the plodding 'No Compromise', it did little to reassure old school Discharge fans upon its release during the summer of 1985. Another guitarist was found in the shape of ex–Skeptix man, Steve 'Fish' Brookes, who played on the 1986 album, 'Grave New World'.

The real nail in the coffin for Discharge, it saw their gradual metamorphosis from groundbreaking punk band to pedestrian hard rock band finally complete. It still managed the Indie Top Ten though, showing just how much the fans wanted

Bones (guitar) and Tez at an early Discharge rehearsal

to believe that the band still had what it took, but it vanished from the chart as quickly as it appeared, a poor showing when compared to the band's scene–dominating glory days.

Rainy left before the album was even released, and one Nick Bushell played bass for the ensuing touring duties. Both Steve and Nick later departed to join Demon, Nick playing on one of their albums ('Taking The World By Storm'), Steve on five!

"I was never really happy with Discharge when they went in that metal direction," sighs Mike Stone. "The 'Grave New World' album is very good musically, but I never liked the vocals. Cal was listening to a lot of Black Sabbath and Led Zeppelin, and I'm sure it was that Robert Plant style he was going for, except he couldn't pull it off properly. He was too monotonous; he was best when he was shouting his head off. I was actually really pleased with the production, but those vocals just weren't right. I didn't like the cover either; we nearly fell out over that as well, to be honest!"

In the face of rising adversity, Discharge split in 1987, only for Cal to reform the band in 1991 following Clay's 1990 release of 'Live At City Garden, New Jersey'. Re–recruiting Garry Maloney on drums, the pair were joined by Andy Green on guitar and Anthony 'Jake' Morgan on bass for 1991's 'Massacre Divine' and '93's 'Shootin' Up The World'. Both records were fine post–thrash metal workouts, but did little to woo back the band's fanbase.

And that, by rights, should have been the last that anyone heard of Discharge outside of the occasional dewy–eyed reminiscing, but in recent years, the original line–up that recorded the first three singles reunited, after meeting, ironically enough, at a party of Nigel Bamford, the very first Discharge bassist. In 2001 they recorded a brand new studio album. Simply entitled 'Discharge', it appeared through Sanctuary in 2002 and both surprised and excited fans by being a genuine return to form.

"The truth is, that awful metal thing Discharge turned into was a big reason for coming back," says Tez of the unexpected reformation. "We just had to do another record, we couldn't let Discharge go down like that. It was me and Rainy that got everyone together in the first place, and we couldn't leave it the way it was.

"Well, you know, I'd never been an innovator before," he adds candidly. "And don't think I ever will be again, so I'm hanging onto it. It was a special time for us in the early Eighties; we were creators of something, and not everyone gets a chance to do that. The crazy thing is, we had no idea what we were doing at the time. Although we thought we were a good live band, we never really planned to record anything."

It would have been a huge loss for the underground music scene had they not, and the latest album is a welcome addition to their catalogue, especially as it exceeds all expectations. Songs like 'Hell Is War', 'Hype Overload' and 'Almost Alive' are so fast and frantic, they could almost have been lifted from one of the early EPs.

"I've never bought a record since I started playing guitar," says Bones, trying to explain how it is that he can so effortlessly turn the clock back twenty years with one sweep of his plectrum. "I don't listen to music at home, 'cos I don't wanna sound like anyone else, I wanna do my own thing. Really, the only record I've bought in the last twenty years was some movie soundtrack album… and I'm not really sure why I bought that! You know what it's like though; no matter how hard you try not to, you can't help but be influenced by something you hear if you like it.

"I have two separate writing heads, one for Discharge and one for Broken Bones (who are still a big priority for the guitarist), and I swap between the two. It's weird, but it's easier than it sounds; I just know whether a riff I've written will be for one band or the other.

"As for the solos, I just knock 'em off the top of my head. If the note doesn't fit, bend it! Every time I play a solo it might be different, but I like to keep it interesting. That's probably why these old songs still sound as fresh to me now as the day I wrote them… it's like I never left the band! Me and Rainy have a great chemistry; we each know what the other is going to do before they do it, and being back with Tez behind the kit... well, it's fuckin' brilliant."

Sadly Cal wouldn't commit to touring to promote the album, so despite plans for it to be the original band in its entirety, Discharge replaced him with Rat from The Varukers, and an inspired choice it is proving to be. He's brought a terrific urgency to the band's live show, and sounds the spitting image of Cal when he performs the old songs.

"I just wanted to do a proper Discharge record really, to put it all right for the fans of the band that felt cheated by the metal stuff they did," reiterates Bones, in closing. "I'd been stockpiling Discharge riffs for years anyway, whilst I was in Broken Bones, so there was no shortage of material. We wanna do this properly though; we're not some punk karaoke band, just back together for the money; we're all still into it, always have been, always will be."

"We don't just wanna play to all the old faces either," adds Tez. "It'd be great to get some new kids into the Discharge thing, those kids are the future of the band right there. But I just wanna be remembered for coming up with that fuckin' D–beat in the first place! And inspiring all those fuckin' great Discore bands around the world!"

SELECT DISCOGRAPHY:
7"s:
'Realities Of War' (Clay, 1980)
'Fight Back' (Clay, 1980)
'Decontrol' (Clay, 1980)
'Never Again' (Clay, 1981)
'State Violence State Control' (Clay, 1982)
'The Price Of Silence' (Clay, 1983)
'The More I See' (Clay, 1984)
'Ignorance' (Clay, 1985)

12"s:
'Why?' (Clay, 1981)
'Warning: Her Majesty's Government Can Seriously Damage Your Health' (Clay, 1983)
'The More I See' (Clay, 1984)
'Ignorance' (Clay, 1985)

LPs:
'Hear Nothing, See Nothing, Say Nothing' (Clay, 1982)
'Never Again' (Clay, 1984)
'Grave New World' (Clay, 1986)
'Live At City Garden, New Jersey' (Clay, 1990)
'Massacre Divine' (Clay, 1991)
'Shootin' Up The World' (Clay, 1993)
'Discharge' (Sanctuary, 2002)

AT A GLANCE:

In 2003, Sanctuary released the definitive trilogy of Discharge reissue CDs. 'Why?', 'Hear Nothing, See Nothing, Say Nothing' and 'Never Again' all enjoyed a long-overdue revamp, this time boosted with twenty-five bonus tracks between them, basically compiling all the essential Discharge material. Packaged with original artwork, photos and lyrics, plus liner notes by Captain Oi!'s Mark Brennan, and topped off with attractive card slip cases, these three CDs really are a must-have for any fan of the band, new or old.

BROKEN BONES

A s mentioned earlier, Broken Bones were formed by guitarist Bones when he left Discharge in 1983, and were one of the first, not to mention best, UK bands to successfully merge punk with metal. Taking the expertise of execution – and a lot of guitar solos – from the metal scene, and the speed, lyrics and attitude from their punk rock roots, the band were an aggressive blur of lightening tempos and jackhammer drums. A heady hybrid of styles that certainly highlighted the flaws in the pedestrian direction Discharge took following Bones' departure.

"Originally though, and not many people know this, " adds Paul 'Oddy' Hoddy, who soon joined the band on bass after their first single was released. "Broken Bones started off playing rhythm 'n' blues for a few months, but thankfully they scrapped that idea – even though they were quite good at it! – and went back to doing what they know best... good old punk rock!"

Prior to Oddy joining however, the band consisted of Bones and his brother Tez, who had originally been in Discharge with him. Plus a well-known local punk 'Nobby' (aka Nick Dobson) on vocals and Darren 'Baz' Burgess on drums, who had previously played in a band called Asylum... that went on to become Political Asylum, not to be confused with the Scottish anarcho band. Their first show was a CND benefit at the Staffordshire Polytechnic.

Broken Bones circa 1984
L–R: Baz, Nobby, Bones, Oddy

Unwilling to enter a studio prematurely ("We were still in the writing stage and not ready to record," explains Bones), the band quickly built up a name for itself on the live circuit, making their performing debut at London's prestigious 100 Club.

"I can't remember who was on with us, I got too pissed afterwards," laughs Bones. "But it was a fucking great gig, I can't recollect anything more about it! To be honest, I don't think we ever did a bad gig as such, every show felt fuckin' brilliant."

He is quick to deny that the Discharge connection opened any doors for the band either. "No, we got there on our own merit. Discharge didn't influence me, and I think that showed in later releases of theirs. I wanted to prove that I could still be an influence in my own right in whatever band I was in."

Broken Bones signed to Fall Out Records soon after that first storming London show, and the 'Decapitated' single was released in February 1984. Recorded in Waterloo's Alaska Studios by then-UK Subs guitarist Captain Scarlet, it was a truly awesome debut and was an immediate Indie hit, staying in the chart for almost three months and peaking at No. 10. The title track was a cautionary tale of what could happen to young women who walked home alone, and was armed to the teeth with a ripping riff and alight with searing solos, whilst the two B-side tracks, 'Problem' and 'Liquidated Brains', provided more of the same. For many a frustrated punk fan, it was the ideal antidote to the self-indulgent heavy metal that Discharge were veering dangerously close to at the time.

Interestingly enough, the cover art was courtesy of one Stuart Duthie, who had actually played harmonica for Broken Bones during their short-lived flirtation with the blues. Trivia fans may also be interested to know that The Meat Man, who, according to those early record sleeves, took care of the band's correspondence, was in fact a fictitious creation, and all letters went to Bones' mother who passed them onto the band members!

The band's next single 'Crucifix' was released in spring 1984, and consisted of three tracks recorded during the same session as the 'Decapitated' single. As well as the anti-religious rant of the title track, the virulent 'IOU' on the B-side remains one of the band's finest moments, and the excellent release was rounded out with 'Fight The Good Fight'. It was another resounding success, reaching No. 12 in the Indies, but before it was even released Broken Bones underwent their first line-up change. Bassist Tez was replaced by the band's roadie, Oddy, who was by then in a band called D-Fekt, but had previously played with Baz in Political Asylum.

"It was after a gig at the 100 Club," recalls Oddy. "Tez was approached and asked to join The UK Subs, and after discussing it with the rest of the band he decided to join them. I was a roadie for the band at that time, and I was also sharing a house with Bones, so they asked me the next day if I wanted to join and I jumped at the chance. Tez even helped me with some of the songs to settle me in!"

In April 1984, Broken Bones entered Cargo Studios in Rochdale with Mike Stone at the helm for the recording of their debut album, 'Dem Bones', which spent almost three months in the Indie Charts during the summer of 1984, reaching No. 5. Apart from the throwaway novelty title track, it was a savage and accomplished punk metal album, one punishing sonic assault after another, with songs like the devastating 'Annihilation No. 3' frantically tearing along as if there was no tomorrow. If the lyrics were to be believed, there wouldn't be. Incredibly, it was all recorded, mixed and mastered in just three days.

"Listening back to it now, it sounds a little too polished and maybe a bit empty," reckons Oddy. "I would have liked to have filled the sound out more. Mike Stone brought the best out of Bones with his guitar sound though."

"It was great to work with Mike again after the Discharge stuff," agrees Bones. "And we had a good laugh in the studio. I still think it stands up well, even today."

Surprisingly enough, these early incarnations of the band never played any European shows, although there was tremendous interest from punks on the continent to see Broken Bones live. German label Aggressive Rock even licensed the first two singles, releasing them, along with a track off the album, as the 'IOU Nothing' 12". But, as well as the usual round of UK shows to promote the release, the band did undertake a highly successful coast-to-coast US tour, that saw them play fifteen shows during the month of January 1985.

"That was an amazing tour," recalls Oddy. "We started at the Rock Hotel in New York on New Years Eve, where the club capacity was 850, and there was 1,000 people in there, and more outside that couldn't get in! With The Circle Jerks and Murphy's Law supporting us! Then we went across the States, stayed in Washington, and went to see The Minutemen at the 9:30 Club. We nearly crashed the tour bus in Denver, 'cos it was snowing so heavily, spun around on the road a few times then stopped suddenly. We played Phoenix, San Diego, Long Beach... where we got kicked out of Disneyland because the security said that the tourists would be taking pictures of us and not Mickey Mouse 'cos we all had spiky green hair! San Francisco and Berkley were great because that is where I met my good friend Andy Anderson from Attitude Adjustment and the guys from Exodus. Then we played the Olympic Auditorium in Los Angeles with Steve Jones from The Pistols playing in the support band Kraut, in front of 5,000 people... and when you are nineteen years old and see that many bodies in front of you, it's pretty amazing!"

But the best was yet to come, as Oddy reveals.

"After the tour finished in Long Beach, we were in a hotel in Hollywood, when we got a message from the tour manager, Captain Scarlet, that the promoter in New York, Leona Faber, had said that the tour didn't make enough money to fly us back to the East Coast. So she flew one of her guys out to Los Angeles to drive us back instead! It was a 3000-mile journey; the fuel alone must have cost as much as a flight would, and this guy fell asleep at the wheel a few times too, so Scarlet helped him drive. It was non-stop to New York, day and night, only stopping for the toilet and food.

"Once back in New York, a gig had been arranged at CBGB, which helped take our mind off going to kill the promoter for doing that to us. Getting to the gig we caught two cabs, one with Bones and Nobby in, and one with me and Baz in. We arrived after them, and opening the door there was this tall blonde guy with a little guy, and the tall one said, 'Hey, it's The Bones', to which I replied 'Hello!' I didn't have a clue who he was!

"After the soundcheck, these same guys came up to us and introduced themselves. 'Hi, I'm James Hetfield from Metallica and this is Scott Ian from Anthrax, we are big fans of your band!' So, after much banter, we found out that Metallica were playing at L'Amours in Brooklyn that night and, seeing as we were doing an all-ages gig at 5pm, they gave us backstage passes to their show.

"Anyway, we were just into the first song 'Death Is Imminent', I jumped to the front of the stage and this bald guy tried to get up and whack! His head hit the jack-plug on my bass and snapped it. I didn't have a spare, but guess who pops up with one? Billy Milano of SOD, albeit a shitty little medium scale thing but the only one there so I had to make do. As I was swapping over guitars, Bones started to play 'Jump In The Fire' by Metallica, much to James's amazement. The one thing that will always stay etched in my mind is James on Scott Ian's shoulders, headbanging to Broken Bones!

"After the CBGB gig, we got a lift off the drummer from Agnostic Front to the Metallica show, and Billy Milano was trying to make me pay for loaning his shitty bass! So I gave him $15. At the gig we went right to the front of the queue and got our passes. After watching WASP, Metallica hit the stage, and seeing Cliff Burton playing made my day – they even dedicated 'Fade To Black', my all-time favourite song, to Broken Bones!"

Unfortunately, despite – or possibly because of – the rollercoaster highs and lows of the US tour, another line-up change was imminent upon their return.

"Yeah, Nobby left the band after we got home from the States. We were due to play another gig at the 100 Club; he knew about the gig, but never got in touch with us as to when he was coming back from the States. He stayed out there when the rest of us flew home, and consequently we cancelled it, as we hadn't heard anything from him. On the day of the gig, he phones from London asking where we were! After explaining to him the situation, he was told that it didn't matter anyway as he was no longer in the band."

Broken Bones were one of the first UK punk bands to successfully merge punk and metal L–R: Bones, Nobby, Baz, Oddy

"He got married to some American woman and thought America was better than here," elaborates Bones. "Who knows what goes on in some people's minds?"

After Nobby's impromptu departure, Oddy took over on vocals as well as bass for what remains one of the band's finest releases, '85's excellent 'Seeing Through My Eyes' EP. The single was actually produced by Colin Jerwood, the singer with outspoken anarcho punk band Conflict, who Oddy would later join as bassist, and appeared as not only a regular 7" but also as a picture disc and a 10" as well.

"We had a new song waiting for the new single so we went to rehearsal as just the three of us. I started singing the songs, just to fill in really, and it happened to sound okay, so we went from there...

"Mike Stone as producer was a one-off deal for the album, probably because he might have wanted a percentage of the royalties for doing it! As for Jerby (Colin Jerwood) doing it? I was starting to listen to Conflict a lot and liked the sound of their 'Increase The Pressure' album, and as we both had a connection with Jungle Records, we met up and asked him to produce the single. Him and Bones even ended up sharing the backing vocals together!"

In a strange twist of fate, Oddy ended up leaving soon after, with Nobby and Tez rejoining the band, restoring Broken Bones to their original line-up once again – albeit for a short time – but not before he'd recorded the in-your-face five-track 'Bonecrusher' 12" at FSR Studios in Birmingham.

"I think that was actually packaged as an album in America by Combat Core," says Oddy. "Because it had the 'Seeing Through My Eyes' 12" on as well, making ten tracks in all. The front cover was a picture that we ripped out of a book in a local library, put some brown card over and burnt to give that.'old photo' look. Also, the Indians dancing sound effect at the beginning of the title track was from the 'A Man Called Horse' film. We even thanked James Hetfield on the back cover, 'for the backstage passes', and there's also 'a big F.O.A.D.' to Leona Faber, who promoted that first US tour.

"Anyway, I left after it was recorded; Tez had rejoined the band on rhythm guitar, and he was angling to get back on the bass and to get Nobby back singing, and the only way to do that was to get me out. Luckily, after Colin (Jerwood) had seen me playing bass during the recording of 'Seeing Through My Eyes', he wanted me to play for Conflict. So it worked out fine for everybody in the end. I think it was just one of those things; it was always pretty unstable, with band members flying in and out all the time."

"We only did 'Bonecrusher' to fulfil a contractual obligation," adds Bones. "And we didn't think with Nobby coming back it would be good for the band if it was released here, hence the US-only release. Oddy left after 'Bonecrusher' basically because he and Tez didn't see eye to eye... and, well, blood's thicker than water. After that it was all up in the air for a while, to be honest."

After the appearance of the unofficial bootleg album, 'Live At The 100 Club', in 1985, and the 'Decapitated' album, that was basically a compilation of the band's first three singles, the 'Never Say Die' 12" was released by Fall Out in early 1986. Broken Bones then entered Strawberry Studios in Stockport during June of that year to record seven new songs for the studio side of their 1987 Fall Out album, 'F.O.A.D.' The live side of that album was recorded soon after, at the Fulham Greyhound that August. Produced by Richard Scott, and resplendent in an eye-catching cover of skeletal warriors by Andrew Screed, the riotous album ably proved the band had lost none of their initial spark.

It was followed in July 1987 by the blinding seven-track 'Trader In Death' 12", which not only came out on Rab Fae Beith from The Wall and The UK Subs' label, RFB, but was also produced by him as well. And what a great job he did too; the 12" sounds superb, with 'Money, Pleasure And Pain' tearing out of the jokey prelude during which Rab admonishes the band for attempting to open the record with an acoustic intro. It made No. 21 in the Indies and stayed in the chart for over two months.

However, the band split up soon after its release, until the following year when Bones put together a whole new band comprising Craig 'Quiv' Allen on vocals (who sounded very similar to Nobby anyway, with a nod to GBH's Colin in his style as well), Darren 'Daz' Harris on bass and Cliff Moran on drums. Daz had previously played guitar and sang for Exit Condition, who shared the same rehearsal space as Broken Bones, and who have recently had an impressive discography CD released by Bedfordshire label Boss Tuneage. This line-up undertook an extensive US tour in 1988.

"That was probably my favourite tour to date," enthuses Bones. "It was with The UK Subs, and we were doing massive venues, including playing to 20,000 people in Los Angeles... what a fucking brill gig that was!"

The new-look Broken Bones made their recording debut with 1989's 'Losing Control' album for Wolverhampton-based Heavy Metal Records. The new label name suited the music too, because 'Losing Control' was a very polished affair that saw the band really stretching – and indulging – themselves musically, with Bones' playing, especially his very accomplished leads, really coming to the fore. It sounded more like an American thrash metal band than anything to hail from the UK punk scene.

Although they were no longer with his label, the band retained the services of Rab for the recording, which took place at Wolverhampton's Madhat Studios, and the record came in yet another colourful horror cartoon cover, this time a gatefold sleeve by Gary Underhill.

"I met the other guys in a pub and we all thought it would be good to give it another go," laughs the guitarist about the band's rebirth, before adding on the subject of the slight change in direction, "That was all my fault. I went through that whole 'I'm a great guitarist' thing, you know, showing off a bit. I think all musicians go through it at some time or other, before going back to what they are best at."

Another strong 12" was released by Heavy Metal, 1990's 'Religion Is Responsible', which saw the band posing on the front in an abandoned church. They then signed to Rough Justice, a division of metal giants Music for Nations and home to such metallic UK punk bands as GBH and The English Dogs, for the 'Stitched Up' and 'Brain Dead' albums, released in '91 and '92 respectively. Despite being well received by die-hard fans, it was apparent the band's popularity was waning along with people's general interest in UK punk bands, and Broken Bones disbanded once more in late 1992.

"I'm not really sure just why we split that second time," admits Bones. "I think it was more a case of everyone wanting to go off and do their own stuff. The whole punk/metal thing had a lot to do with the diminishing popularity of punk as well, but I just weathered the storm really. Once a guitarist, always a guitarist!"

Apparently so, because, since 1998, Bones has been playing again in Broken Bones, alongside Oddy, Quiv and new drummer Dave Bridgwood. Successful European shows have taken place, and a convincing comeback album released, 2001's 'Without Conscience', that heralded a return to a more aggressive hardcore sound. 2002 saw the release of the 'Fuck The World' CD by Berlin-based Superhero Records, a four-way split that Broken Bones shared with Past Glories and Cutdown from Finland and One Million Thoughts from Germany. It received great reviews, Broken Bones being unanimously heralded as the best band appearing.

"Well, the band was originally called Choke Hold when Bones joined," explains Oddy. "He wasn't doing anything when we were looking for a new guitarist, so I asked him to join. After trying to do gigs and doing various demos and getting a 'Thanks but no thanks' from all the record labels bar one, Rhythm Vicar (a sub-label of Plastic Head Distribution) told us that if we changed our name to Broken Bones, they would sign us. So, after much deliberation, and believe you me, it nearly didn't happen, we thought, 'Why not?' We have two original members in me and Bones, Quiv sang on the later albums, and Dave had been signed to Clay Records with his other band Rebel Christening... a loose connection I know! But if we are doing it for the 'punk cash-in', as some people have intimated, we are still waiting for the cash...

"I think that we are a lot wiser now, musically, and far progressed in our ability to play, so the chemistry is a lot better and much more relaxed. Plus there is no pressure from anyone to do this and do that, so we're all a lot happier."

Newly signed to Californian label, Dr. Strange, and with a new album and a US tour slated for release in 2004, the future once again looks bright for Broken Bones.

"Loud and uncompromising," laughs the bassist when asked how he'd like the band to be remembered. "Our past music was hardcore for the time, but the music we're making now is taking hardcore punk to a different, higher level!"

Bones however is a little more succinct in his defiant summary. "Just listen to the fucking music and make your own mind up!"

SELECT DISCOGRAPHY:

7"s:
'Decapitated' (Fall Out, 1983)
'Crucifix' (Fall Out, 1984)
'Seeing Through My Eyes' (Fall Out, 1985)

12"s:
'IOU Nothing' (Aggressive Rock, 1984)
'Never Say Die' (Fall Out, 1986)
'Trader In Death' (RFB, 1987)
'Religion Is Responsible' (Heavy Metal, 1990)

LPs:
'Dem Bones' (Fall Out, 1984)
'F.O.A.D.' (Fall Out, 1987)
'Losing Control' (Heavy Metal, 1989)
'Stitched Up' (Rough Justice, 1991)
'Brain Dead' (Rough Justice, 1992)
'Without Conscience' (Rhythm Vicar, 2001)

AT A GLANCE:

Fall Out's 1990 CD release of 'Dem Bones' also includes the 'Decapitated' 'singles album', making for twenty-five tracks in total of the band's earliest and best material. In 2000, Fall Out also doubled up the 'F.O.A.D.' album with the 'Bonecrusher' 12" on one rather raging CD. That said, the recent 'Without Conscience' release was a great return to form, and bodes very well for the future.

THE SKEPTIX

One of the bands from the Potteries seemingly damned to always live in the long shadow cast by Discharge were The Skeptix. Guitarist Steve 'Fish' Brookes and drummer Ian 'Chig' Chadwick first got together in Longton as The Vermin in 1978, and by 1980 they had been joined by vocalist Paul 'Snotty' Burton and bassist Trevor 'Ush' Usher and had changed their name to Chaos.

"I'd wanted to be in a band from an early age, and started playing the guitar as soon as I got into punk, when I was about thirteen years old," remembers Fish. "I just wanted to play in a punk band, and it was great – anybody could do it! At that age, I wasn't really geared up so much on the politics… ignorant twat, you might think, but I was more into that whole raw energy that punk had.

"Those early days were really good, everyone was just out to be different; the crazier you looked, the better. I always felt a bit jealous of the older guys… at fourteen, I wasn't allowed to get my nose pierced or hair dyed… not for a short time anyway!

"The atmosphere was great, all the early gigs were packed out. The first band or proper gig I went to was The Ramones, with support from The Rezillos at the Victoria Hall in Hanley, and I was blown away. Then I was just as blown away by about every punk band I saw there… The Damned, The Clash… all the first wave bands… well, except for Siouxsie And The Banshees. I hated them; they did nothing for me at all. It's funny, 'cos they were one of Snotty's favourite bands… hmmm, I wonder if that's why I hated them so much? I remember the guys from Discharge at the front of the stage heckling them and causing havoc…"

The Skeptix, live
L–R: Chig (drums), Snotty, Fish (guitar)

Soon after, the band changed their name one last time to The Skeptix, and swiftly began building a substantial local following through some concerted gigging. Two demos were recorded at The Clock House in nearby Keele University, and were actually produced by one of the band's old music teachers. Fish recalls those formative recordings as "Absolute crap... the sound was abysmal", but they brought the band to the attention of Dave Salmon from Neon Records in Stafford, who had them back in the studio to record their first single for his punk imprint, Zenon.

The result was 'Routine Machine', which came out in 1982 and was an impressively confident debut. Fast and abrasive, it was hard enough to win the hearts and ears of hardcore punks up and down the country. In fact, Snotty still cites it as his favourite Skeptix track, "Because it was the first song we ever recorded, and the lyrics summed up the feelings of thousands of people without jobs... plus the crowds usually go mental for it!"

Buoyed by the positive response to the single, The Skeptix played out nationally, with all the major bands of the era. They were soon signed by German label Rock-O-Rama, who released their one and only Eighties album, 'So The Youth', and they even ended up headlining a German punk festival at The Stollwerk in Cologne in August 1983 to help promote it. It was a memorable gig for more than one reason.

"It was in a disused factory in Cologne," recalls Snotty, "where punks and skinheads from different German cities fought running battles outside the venue before the doors opened. Also at this gig, Chig was feeling ill, so he wanted to come off as soon as he could, but someone kept chucking water over him, so he kept on playing. After the gig we found out that this person throwing the water had knifed and killed someone at a football match that same day!"

"Snotty had had too many beers and fell through a window just before we went on," continues Fish. "And my guitar ended up thrown across the stage narrowly missing him... I can't really remember why. There are two conflicting stories. I seem to think that the strap nut had pulled out of the wood on the guitar, and I threw it across the stage. But Kalle, an eyewitness from Germany, says that we tried to start the same song three times and on the third attempt I threw it at Snotty…!"

Also on the bill at that fateful show was another English band, The Insane, who The Skeptix later released a split 7" with, on White Rose, the following year. The Skeptix contributed 'Vendetta', whilst The Insane offered up 'Berlin Wall'. This was unfortunately the band's only entry into the Indie Charts, spending two months there in early 1984 and peaking modestly at No. 26.

Rock-O-Rama also released 'The Kids Are United' split 7" for them, pairing The Skeptix with yet another band from that Stollwerk show, O.H.L.

Although 'So The Youth' is an intense affair, executed with tremendous speed and precision, it isn't regarded with much fondness by the band themselves, mainly because of the thin trebly sound which removed most of the power from the material.

"It's my least favourite of all our records," confirms Snotty, "Because of the poor production. Everything was just so rushed; we were literally learning the tracks in the studio as it was being recorded."

Much of this problem was caused by the band recording in Germany, instead of their usual haunt, Cargo in Rochdale.

"Herbert Egolt from Rock-O-Rama fixed it all up," explains Fish. "We got an all expenses paid trip to Cologne's Studio Am Dom, where Fashion recorded one of their albums… I bet they never went back though, especially if they were as unhappy with their production as we were! Anyway, the guy in Germany wasn't into punk – or us! He was just a miserable sod and a crap engineer. There was no language barrier as such, 'cos he hardly ever spoke to us. I do remember him saying one thing: 'I have not come to here to see Snotty rehearse'. What a twonk, eh?"

Upon their return to the UK, a second single was released, 'Peace Force', which as well as their customary thrash attack also featured the chugging 'Born To Lose', which highlighted a more metallic side to the band.

The band's third and final single, 'Return To Hell', came out in '83, and, as well as being their finest moment, saw them further eroding the barriers in their sound that barely existed between punk and heavy metal. In fact, the main riff of 'War Drum' wouldn't have sounded out of place on a Motörhead album.

"We never intended to sound like a metal band. We just wrote tunes that sounded good to us, and occasionally some of them sounded that way. We weren't an all-out metal band, though," reckons Fish, before admitting, "But we did listen to Motörhead a lot!"

Unfortunately Zenon Records went bankrupt soon after its release, and Snotty left – due to the inevitable 'musical differences' – only to be replaced briefly by Colin from local punk band D-Fekt. This new line-up was short-lived though, as the band split up soon after.

"It was all my fault, you see," sighs Fish, on the demise of The Skeptix. "I wanted to make a career out of music and the other guys wanted to too, but they all had taxing, regular jobs that tied them down. I was in contact with Mike Stone at Clay Records about signing The Skeptix; in fact I drove him mad always hassling him to sign us! In the end he said that he didn't want to… but Discharge needed a new guitarist for their new album and tours of Europe, America and Japan… so what was I to do? Work around the other guys' jobs or be a total sod and leave them to it? Well, I couldn't ever see The Skeptix touring like that, so I took the position with Discharge.

"I did regret it a few times. The Skeptix were all mates from school, but I made my bed and lay in it. Why don't you ask them why they didn't just get a new guitarist?"

And for many years, that really was the last anyone heard of The Skeptix. Until recently, when the guys got back together, and issued a brand new album, 'Hate And Fear', on their own

Thunk Records ('Thunk' was actually the name of one of the musical projects Fish undertook after he left Discharge).

Although slightly more restrained than their youthful thrashings, 'Hate And Fear' will not disappoint any Skeptix fans. It proudly bears all their trademarks of old, only this time executed with the benefits of greatly improved musicianship and a much thicker production – something which, by their own admission, was often sadly lacking from their earlier recordings. Snotty's voice has lost none of its abrasive edge, and the metallic guitars and racy tempos are still in full effect.

"We reformed because Ush found an old demo tape, which he thought still sounded very good," explains Snotty. "Then upon searching the internet we found that there was still a lot of people interested in the band; there were even Skeptix T-shirts and vinyl for sale in the USA! So we began to practise again, and found that the old spark and aggression was still there. So we then decided to record and release the songs from the demo tape Ush had found."

"Apparently, The Casualties from New York cited us as a big influence upon them in all their interviews which created a bit of interest in us," continues Fish. "Then we were contacted by Captain Oi to do all our releases on one CD, which we went ahead with. It was about then that we started talking about recording the tracks that never got recorded first time around... but it took another three years before we got it together. We didn't even know that we had a fan base in the States until our web site went up, and then we got bombarded with e-mails; that's when we thought, 'Wow, what's all this about?'"

SELECT DISCOGRAPHY:
7"s:
'Routine Machine' (1982, Zenon)
'Peace Force' (1983, Zenon)
'Return To Hell' (1983, Zenon)
'The Kids Are United' (1983, Rock-O-Rama) – split with O.H.L.
'Vendetta' (1984, White Rose) – split with The Insane

LPs:
'So The Youth' (1983, Rock-O-Rama)
'Hate And Fear' (2003, Thunk)

AT A GLANCE:
Captain Oi!'s 'Pure Punk Rock' CD (1998) compiles every Skeptix track worth hearing from the Eighties (basically all their original recorded works, bar the crappy demos) onto one CD, complete with liner notes and lyrics. The brand new album, 'Hate And Fear', is pretty damn good as well.

ANTI PASTI

I f The Exploited, Discharge and GBH were the 'Big Three' of the early Eighties UK punk scene, Anti Pasti, alongside the likes of Vice Squad, Blitz and the Anti-Nowhere League, were definitely one of the young bands snapping at their heels. They sold huge amounts of records, topping the Indie Charts on several occasions, and were even the first of the second wave UK punk bands to tour North America.

Formed in Derby in 1979 by vocalist Martin Roper and guitarist Dugi Bell, Anti Pasti's first line-up was completed by bassist Stu Winfield and drummer Stan Smith, and they quickly made a name for themselves on the local gig circuit, including a prestigious slot opening for The Clash when their London Calling tour hit the Derby Assembly Rooms in 1979.

After releasing the ultra-raw 'Four Sore Points' EP on their own label, Dose, in early 1980, Martin and Dugi ousted Stu and Stan in favour of bassist Will Hoon and drummer Kevin Nixon, both of whom were previously with The Egyptian Kings.

"I was with them pretty much from the beginning," explains Kev. "I used to be their roadie and sold their records and stuff. We were all just part of the Derby punk rock scene, all mates together really. We'd all end up going to see the same bands together, hitchhiking off to places, then trying to find somewhere to stay... a sort of gang, I suppose. You had to have that mentality, you had to keep on your toes and one step ahead of all the straight people who might wanna punch your lights out!

"It felt a bit more scary and intimidating being a punk rocker in those days, but that might've been 'cos I was only sixteen or seventeen, and a lot more timid than I am now. Having said that, if I hadn't been sure of myself, I wouldn't have been marching around in the kit I was in, hitchhiking off all over the country to see The Clash...!

"I used to look at those bands up onstage, and think, 'I wanna do that!' The whole punk ethos encouraged you to have a go, and punk music lends itself to people who are just learning their instruments anyway. Before punk, people who wanted to learn guitar would try to learn 'Stairway To Heaven' or whatever, but we were trying to learn 'Sheena Is A Punk Rocker' or 'Blitzkrieg Bop'! And if you put those songs next to 'Stairway To Heaven' even now, I still know which I'd rather play!"

Kev and Will's first show with the band was in Huddersfield; the second was at Derby's Ajanta Club, where they were snapped up by Mansfield-based Rondelet Records, who promptly reissued the 'Four Sore Points' EP on clear vinyl in late 1980. As well as the supremely thunderous 'No Government', it included amongst its four tracks 'Two Years Too Late', an excellent mid-tempo punk song that was actually written by The Epileptics (who went on to become Flux Of Pink Indians) a year earlier!

"Yeah, there was a piece in the NME or Sounds, asking about 'Two Years Too Late'," laughs Kev. "They reckoned that we'd nicked it off The Epileptics too, and I wrote a letter in explaining what had happened. Basically, we'd played with them, and either Martin or Dugi had said to their manager that they liked this song, 'Two Years Too Late', and he turned around and said, 'Okay, have it then! You can use it if you want.' It's a better song by Anti Pasti anyway!"

Ironically enough, Kev's first recorded output with the band was the 'Let Them Free' single, issued on red vinyl in January 1981, which featured 'Another Dead Soldier', a song he willingly admits bears more than a passing resemblance to 'Teenage Kicks' by The Undertones! Recorded at Cargo in Rochdale, it crashed into the Indie Top Ten and earned the band a place on the bill of the Apocalypse tour, alongside Discharge, The Exploited and Chron Gen.

"I can't remember a lot about it, to be honest, we drank that much. You have to remember, we were all teenagers, and every night our dressing room was full of crates of free beer. We used to go onstage half pissed! I remember one time we played a matinee show at the Mayfair in Manchester, and I knew I'd had too much to drink before we even went on; they had to come and wake me up, I was lay down behind the mixing desk! I found I physically couldn't play the drums properly; they had to get some young lad out of the audience to play a few songs whilst I got myself together! Wonder where he is now?"

The split EP with The Exploited, 'Don't Let Them Grind You Down', which appeared on Superville following the Apocalypse dates and went to No. 1 in the Indies in December 1981, seemed to be a cementing of their new-found friendship with the Scots, but apparently it was merely a cash-in on the growing popularity of both bands.

"That had absolutely nothing to do with us! Those two songs ('Ain't Got Me' and 'Another Dead Soldier') were just taken from a demo session Anti Pasti did before me and Will had even joined, and somehow it ended up on that EP. It was a bit of an embarrassment for me and Will, and there was still this element of bitterness from Stan and Stu, who suddenly thought that we owed them some money! They might not have been in the band anymore but we were still walking the same streets, after all."

Anti Pasti, L-R: Will, Dugi, Martin (on the gate), Kev

On September 5th 1981, to coincide with the late August release of their debut album, 'The Last Call', Anti Pasti even found themselves gracing the front cover of Sounds magazine, getting higher 'billing' than regular pop stars such as ABC and Pat Benatar.

"I couldn't believe it. I'd only been in the band less than a year, and already I'd recorded an album, and now I was on the front cover of a music paper I'd been buying for years! It was surreal, but because we were so young, we just took it in our stride, and went with the flow. We didn't give a shit, as long as something was happening! It's when it all stops happening that it becomes a problem, when you're left wondering, 'Why aren't we gigging tonight?'

"Smash Hits (a mainstream magazine aimed at teenage girls) even had a full page of our lyrics and a photo of us in it! Punk was verging on becoming a teenage trend… which was good in a way 'cos that made it far more accessible to a lot of new kids. After all, The Clash changed their musical style and covered many genres, and that enabled them to get their message across a lot more effectively. So, were we to become like them, or end up like Crass, for example, ranting and raving but never reaching anyone outside hippy communes? You tell me which is better!"

With all the exposure the band were getting, it was no surprise when 'The Last Call' was a huge hit, not only topping the Indies, but even reaching No. 31 in the National Charts. Its success wasn't just down to hype though; it was an incredibly strong debut that still sounds fiercely relevant today, compelling in its simplicity, invigorating in its anthemic power. What it lacked in speed and aggression, it more than compensated for with brooding presence on songs like 'Freedom Row' or 'Truth And Justice'.

"I nicked the drum intro for that from 'Ubangi Stomp' by The Stray Cats!" admits Kev. "It wasn't like we were ripping all these bands off, though, just tipping our hats to 'em for influencing us."

Another Indie No. 1 followed in November '81 in the guise of the 'Six Guns' EP. Riding the crest of a wave, Anti Pasti headed off to the States, the first UK punk band to tour there since The Damned in 1978. Travelling in a modest three-axle Transit, they played twenty shows over the course of a month, starting in New York and ending in LA, where they headlined two nights and were interviewed for the LA Times. En route they played Milwaukee on Christmas Day, a cowboy bar in Minneapolis, and supported The Dead Kennedys in San Francisco in front of 7000 kids.

"It was mad, we landed and straight away we were doing a press conference in the Peppermint Lounge, where the bloody Twist was invented! We were like, 'What do you mean? A press conference?' We'd only ever done a few interviews with fanzines up until that point!

"That night we played a gig there, and a guy from one of the fanzines came running into our dressing room and told me that Topper Headon (The Clash drummer) was in the audience, so I asked to be taken out to meet him. So this guy took me to the bar of the Peppermint Lounge, and there was Topper. I tapped him on the shoulder, and said, 'Hi', and he said, 'I know who you are, I've seen your pictures, how are you doing?' I was stunned! He might have just been saying that, who knows? But fair play to him for being humble anyway. I wanted to buy him a beer and get him backstage to meet the other lads, but he wasn't really interested… I think he was in the grip of Mr. Brown, if you know what I mean?"

Many other memorable gigs were also undertaken in the UK upon their return.

"One of my favourite shows ever was at the Zig Zag Club in London. It was the day of a tube strike, so there wasn't a very big turnout, but we were performing our old set and some of the new album, and I absolutely loved it! There was a damning review in Melody Maker the following week, which slagged everybody off but me! They said Dugi thought he was one of The Rolling Stones, 'cos he'd stuck his cigarette on the machine heads of his guitar, said Martin looked like a headless chicken, and that Will thought he should be in a James Dean movie! They really hammered everybody, then said that the drummer ought to get himself in a better band with a bigger swimming pool! The other guys never mentioned that gig to me again...

"We even headlined that Woodstock Revisited festival at the Rainbow. It was completely beyond me; there were ten bands on before us, and there were bands like The Angelic Upstarts and Chelsea below us on the bill. It was difficult to take at that age, 'cos those bands did some of the first punk records I ever bought, so I was sat there thinking, 'What the hell are we doing here, headlining?' I'm not being humble for the sake of it, but I just couldn't understand why we were the band that people were picking up on."

Unfortunately, the bubble was about to burst. Keen to capitalise on the success of 'The Last Call', Rondelet rushed the band back into London's Greenway Studio to record the slightly disappointing 'East To West' single (complete with surf-tinged guitars) and the ambitiously diverse 'Caution To The Wind' album. Both the single and the album made the Indie Top Ten upon their release in May and July 1982 respectively, but they marked a significant departure musically for the band, who were veering in a much more subdued rock direction. They were the first Anti Pasti records to feature new rhythm guitarist Olly Hoon, who was Will's brother and had previously been a guitar roadie for the band.

The title track of the album was also released as a single in November 1982, but it barely registered on the charts, clearly indicating the waning interest of the fans.

"For 'Caution...', we'd been given a proper producer, and, for better or worse, he encouraged us to use some extra percussion and even some keyboards, to help thicken the sound," explains Kev. "But we alienated our audience, without ever finding a new one to take their place. We could have probably got even more popular if we'd just released another album exactly like 'The Last Call', but we would have been short-changing ourselves if we'd done that.

"We had musical ambitions, we loved to write music. To start with, we were playing gigs, and watching the support bands play us under the table in the soundchecks, but eventually we got quite capable as musicians, and we really wanted to express ourselves through the band, really wanted to push ourselves.

"A lot of that second album was rushed, we were writing some of the songs whilst we were in the studio. With hindsight, some of it sounds clumsy, and the production's shoddy, but we thought we could get away with it. We thought we could do whatever we wanted and the fans would stick with us."

The final blow for the band's popularity was when Martin was asked to leave in early 1983; he was disillusioned with the new direction, whilst the rest of the band were fed up with his lack of creative input.

"Martin's main contributions were his vocals, his personality, and his knowing everybody and stuff; he was a big draw, a great performer. He was also a fantastic artist, and did some great work on logos and sleeves, but he had no creative input on the musical side of things. Maybe we made him the scapegoat, but, in the end, he was pushed. If I could do it all over again, I think we made a mistake, but we couldn't get past the fact that he wasn't contributing anything to the writing.

"I remember seeing him in the street, and shouting his name, and going over to see him, and he got quite agitated with me, quite upset. The other guys had told him he was sacked but hadn't told me that they'd told him! It was very unfortunate.

"But the animosity didn't last long, 'cos Martin had the last laugh really; after he went, the band was over. And I don't think he was happy with how some of the newer songs were going anyway... but that was partly his own fault 'cos he never contributed anything to help guide the material's direction."

Kev actually took over vocal duties for the band's next demo, but essentially that was the end for Anti Pasti, who split in early 1984.

"I'd done vocals in the studio before," says Kev. "Half the vocals on the second album, I did first and Martin copied; I laid down vocal patterns and stuff that suited the lyrics, so I got quite comfortable with that. After Martin went, we recorded four songs with me doing vocals, including an old song called 'Gaoler Bring Me Water'…

"I never sang for the band live though, only in the studio. We did do a tour of Holland, where Dugi sang, and that went down really well. But eventually we realised that we weren't the same thing without Martin. Even though as a group we were better – the four of us all finally getting to grips with our instruments and pulling in the same direction – we were without our figurehead, our public talisman, and we went our separate ways. Olly and Will formed another band called The Link Men, who signed to Kitchenware Records for a bit, the same label as Prefab Sprout."

In 1996, Anti Pasti reformed briefly, with the full 'Caution In The Wind' line-up, for some select dates in the UK and Europe, including the Fuck Reading festival at the London Astoria.

Martin Roper (vocals) and Dugi Bell (guitar) of Anti Pasti, live 1981

"It was just a short-lived thing, we knew it wouldn't be anything permanent; we just wanted to get it out of our systems. We did a few UK dates, then toured Belgium, Holland and Germany, and it was great fun to play the songs again and see a lot of old friends.

"I think we stayed true to our roots," he reckons in closing. "We resisted the urge to just play what everyone else was doing, all that 1000 mph thrash stuff. I think we stood out from all those bands 'cos we wrote good, strong songs; they weren't fast or anything, but they were good songs all the same."

SELECT DISCOGRAPHY:

7"s:

'Four Sore Points' EP (Dose, 1980)

'Let Them Free' (Rondelet, 1981)

'Six Guns' (Rondelet, 1981)

'Don't Let Them Grind You Down' (Superville, 1981) – split EP with The Exploited

'East To The West' (Rondelet, 1982)

'Caution In The Wind' (Rondelet, 1982)

LPs:

'The Last Call' (Rondelet, 1981)

'Caution In The Wind' (Rondelet, 1982)

AT A GLANCE:

Anagram's 1995 CD release of the brilliant 'The Last Call' album, featuring seven bonus tracks from the early singles and liner notes from Mark Brennan and Kev Nixon, comes highly recommended, as does Anagram's 1998 'The Singles Collection', which obviously compiles all of the band's EPs and 7"s.

THE ENEMY

L ike so many punk bands from the second wave, The Enemy from Derby never really got the kudos they deserved; quite probably their obvious aspirations to pen some damn good tunes actually worked against them with the average hardcore punk in the street. Even listening to their material today, one is struck by the band's ear for subtle melody and the maturity of their efficient commanding arrangements. Yes, they let their quality control slip occasionally (who didn't?), but overall the musical legacy they left behind is one they can be justifiably proud of.

Formed in early 1980 ("For all the usual reasons, really, mainly boredom") in and around their local youth club, it wasn't until summer 1981 that they arrived at the stable line-up of Mark Woodhouse – vocals, Steve 'Mez' Mellors – guitar, Steve O' Donnell – bass and Mark Herrington – drums.

"I started listening to punk when I was at school and fancied being in a band but not as a musician, too much like hard work," laughs Mark. "Then one night at a youth club I heard Steve, Mez and Mark playing... well, sort of... without a vocalist. So I just asked if I could join in, and the rest is, as they say, history!"

"There were lots of local clubs like the Havana, which was previously a reggae venue, or the Rainbow and the Cosmo, which were both old cinemas," says Kevin Lamb, who replaced Mellors on guitar after the release of their third single. "The Ajanta was another old cinema; the first gig there was Stiff Little Fingers, and that made the headline of the local evening newspaper – 'Punks Wreck Local Cinema'! Which basically meant that the first few rows of seats collapsed after people were standing on them. The Ajanta used to have bands on every week; U2 even played there as a support band many years ago. Some great gigs – and some great fights – took place at the Ajanta..." Mark also has fond memories of the venue. "Great atmosphere... blood, sweat, weed, piss... and that stuff all the rockers wore... petunia oil, wasn't it? Mmm, lovely!"

The Enemy played their own first show at Woodlands Youth Centre, before landing themselves a support slot to Anti Pasti in Huddersfield. Encouraged by their success they entered Old Cottage Studios in Derby and recorded their first single, '50,000 Dead' (backed by 'Society's Fools' and 'Neutral Ground'), which they released on their own label, Tin Tin.

"Me and Mez were the only ones working, so we paid for the pressing and recording," explains Steve. "We all thought at the time that it was the only way forward, and also the only way to get signed and get publicity. We called the label Tin Tin because Mez looked like him… although he also looked a bit like a pigeon as well!"

'50,000 Dead' did remarkably well for a self-released effort, and Fresh Records, who distributed it on behalf of the band put The Enemy in touch with Fall Out, a brand new label started by one Steve Brown. They became the first band he signed to the label, and catalogue number Fall 001 was nothing less than their 'Fallen Hero' single. With a B-side comprising 'Tomorrow's Warning' and 'Prisoner Of War', it was released in May 1982, and spent three weeks in the Indie Charts, reaching No.44. With a compelling chorus perfectly complementing the passionate anti-war lyric, the title track became the band's best-known track, especially after it appeared on the hugely successful 'Punk And Disorderly Volume 2: Further Charges' compilation, which was a Top Ten Indie hit.

The second single for Fall Out, the three-track 'Punk's Alive' EP, was probably rushed out to capitalise on the success of 'Fallen Hero', and was consequently their weakest release ("Crap lyrics and very cliché," snorts Mark derisively). Even the cover was generic, a cartoon of a brick wall with the title spray-painted across it.

The Enemy realised they needed to ring some changes within the band, and, as mentioned earlier, soon after 'Punk's Alive' failed to trouble the Indie Charts, Steve Mellor was replaced by Kevin Lamb from local punk band Total Loss. He brought a much-needed energy to the band's live performances.

"The first gig I did with The Enemy was at The Vines in Hanley, Stoke-on-Trent, in the middle of winter," recalls Kev. "It was snowing from what I remember, and we took a coach load of people from Derby, which included quite a few Total Loss fans.

"I remember being very nervous but couldn't wait to give it everything I'd got. The Enemy had never struck me as a very lively band on stage so I was there to change that. It felt fantastic and the crowd reaction was great."

In late 1982, the band released the excellent 'Last Rites' 7", backed by the uptempo 'Why Not?', that featured a strong vocal

Steve O' Donnell (bass) and Mark Woodhouse of The Enemy, live

performance from Mark uncannily similar to Anti Pasti's Martin Roper. It was followed in early 1983 by their debut album, 'Gateway To Hell'. A fine collection of tuneful gritty punk rock that transcends its murky production and stands the test of time rather well, the album received much critical acclaim, and sold accordingly.

"I was very pleased and proud of the first album," reckons the guitarist. "Although, in hindsight, I should have bought the 2" multi-track master tape when I was offered it for £65, then it could have been remixed today; it would've been interesting to hear what it sounded like. Steve Brown from Fallout Records was great; he didn't rush or hassle us at all, but would come down to the studio each day to check on progress."

"Yes, but not totally," adds Steve, when asked whether he's still pleased with 'Gateway'. "The music and songs were good, but it never received enough publicity, or enough backing all round really, because our record company were from London and we were from Derby."

However, before 'Gateway To Hell' was even in the racks, The Enemy underwent another line-up change, with Dave Hill replacing Mark Herrington on drums.

"I can still remember the name The Enemy carved into desks when I was at school," says Dave of his recruitment. "The name seemed to be everywhere, even on my local bus stop. As I remember, I got a call from Kev Lamb, who was a friend of a friend, and he got me a so-called audition. I then found myself having to learn the whole of 'Gateway To Hell', plus all the singles, and then playing my first gig with them a few days later. I was shitting myself! I had never done what I thought then were 'proper' gigs, so it was quite a shock to suddenly be playing the 100 Club and places like that. What I do remember is being amazed at how many venues around the country had punk nights… usually on Tuesdays and Thursdays, for some reason. I remember playing in London somewhere when the record label guy bought the new pressing of the 'Gateway To Hell' album down. Mark had done a great drawing depicting a set of gates to a spooky graveyard with the band standing silhouetted against a blood red sky… except the printing caused the sky to look pink. Not very punk, but very funny at the time!"

"My favourite gig was probably at the Lincoln's Inn in Liverpool," reminisces Kev. "The place was only small, and we had no PA and had to borrow one from an all-girl punk band called Iconoclast. The club didn't open until about 10pm and when we arrived there was no sign of life at all, but the crowd turned out to be absolutely brilliant, the best crowd I've ever played in front of. I still have one of the posters somewhere, which says, 'At last, coming to Liverpool – The Enemy'!

"The stage area (if you could call it that) was so small; the ceiling was very low with condensation dripping off it, and the atmosphere was electric. Compared to playing, say, the Xmas On Earth festival at Leeds Queens Hall in front of about 5000 people, the 200 we had that night at the Lincoln's Inn won hands down for me."

"But that was what we were all about – live music," adds Steve. "Not all the gigs were great though. The worst was Feltham Football Club with Dead Mans Shadow; there was no crowd reaction and too much violence. Everyone just stood round the edges of the hall when we played; they hated us 'cos we were from the north… fuck 'em."

Despite the success of the 'Gateway…' album, Fall Out chose not to take up the option for further Enemy records, and in 1984, the band signed to local label Rot Records, which was run by Riot Squad vocalist Dunk. The single 'Last But Not Least' was the result, and it acted as a suitable teaser for an album of the same name. With one side recorded live at the Leeds Bierkeller on March 28th 1984 and the other recorded in Rochdale's Cargo Studios two days later, the album title turned out to be most appropriate, as it transpired to be the band's final release. In a constant state of musical evolution, The Enemy's lofty ambitions to achieve as much as they possibly could as musicians eventually tore the band asunder. It remains a fitting epitaph for the band though, being by far their most accomplished and powerful work.

Not many second wave punk bands managed to develop convincingly without losing sight of that raw edge that made them so exciting in the first place, but with (the studio side anyway) 'Last But Not Least' pulls it off with aplomb, rocking out righteously without compromising itself in the aggression or integrity stakes.

"One or two people called us thrash but we always argued against that and still would," reckons Kev. "It was difficult for us when new bands were getting so much exposure and we weren't, but we felt our type of music definitely had a place alongside the thrash element. As we started to write for the second album our musical styles developed and grew; the studio side saw us maturing musically, and really starting to produce listenable, powerful music. The live side also saw more effort going into how we sounded but, due to financial restrictions from Rot, we didn't have anything to do with the production. That's one of the biggest regrets I have about the band, because I think it sounds terrible.

"The second album also saw the introduction of a fifth member, Russell Maw, on lead guitar, who had been playing guitar for years and was well established in the Derby music scene, playing for Aftermath and The Egyptian Kings…it seemed like a natural progression for us to ask him to join for the album. So he played on both the live and studio side."

"Why not?" reasons Steve, when asked why they did a half-live/half-studio record instead of a proper full album. "We had thought about a live album for a while, so when we signed to Rot we just thought it was the right time… even though the live recording was shite. Anyway, what the fuck do you mean by 'proper'? It was proper! To be honest, it was my favourite Enemy record; I thought it was great, almost ahead of its time, with a great sound… just a shame about the lack of publicity financial backing!"

Predictably enough, given the absence of any real promotion and with the band seemingly at odds with the very scene they were confined to, the album failed to sell in any significant numbers and The Enemy called it a day.

The Enemy circa 'Last But Not Least'
L-R: Steve, Mark, Dave Hill, Kevin Lamb, Russell Maw

"I wanted to do a cross between U2, Simple Minds and Big Country and Mark didn't, so we split," explains Steve.

"As I remember it," adds Dave, "we were trying to sound more like some of the bands that were in the charts at the time. More musical in a rocky way and less rough and manic, but this caused some problems from a playing perspective."

"Personally I didn't want to branch off into anything else," confirms Mark. "I liked what we achieved but it had just reached its expiry date."

"I'm proud of what we did," says Steve. "We were energetic, melodic, powerful, aggressive, easy to listen to… and ahead of our time – unfortunately!"

Steve now resides in Spain, and although the other members of the band still nurture that defiant punk attitude (Mark: "Born a rocker, die a rocker, as they say!"), only Dave is still active as a working musician.

"I am still playing the drums and have done for all sorts of bands and most kinds of music.

Over the last few years, I have played with metal band Apes Pigs & Spacemen, Crowded House singer/songwriter Neil Finn, Smiths guitarist Johnny Marr and, most recently and regularly, with ex-Creation signing Arnold whom I record and tour with as a band member. I still like the punk sound and the rough, raw edge of playing that style."

SELECT DISCOGRAPHY:
7"s:
'50, 000 Dead' (Tin Tin, 1981)
'Fallen Hero' (Fall Out, 1982)
'Punk's Alive' (Fall Out, 1982)
'Last Rites' (Fall Out, 1982)
'Last But Not Least' (Rot, 1984)

LPs:
'Gateway To Hell' (Fall Out, 1983)
'Last But Not Least' (Rot, 1984)

AT A GLANCE:
The Captain Oi! 'Gateway To Hell' CD includes as bonus tracks all the band's singles for Fall Out, and their self-released debut on Tin Tin, plus original cover art and some informative liner notes from Mark Brennan. A good place to start, and a good little album. However, The Enemy's finest moment was definitely 'Last But Not Least', and although it's officially unavailable, Kevin Lamb is more than willing to copy it for anyone keen to hear it if they cover his costs. Contact: kevin@lambfamily99.freeserve.co.uk

RESISTANCE 77

Resistance 77 are an unpretentious raucous punk band from South Normanton, Derbyshire. They recently released a great album, 'Retaliate First' on Captain Oi!, but life for the band started as The Anti Heroes back in December 1979, practising in the bedroom of drummer Gary Naylor.

"We all knew each other from going to school together, even though we were in different years due to our age differences," recalls bassist Kieron Egan of their humble beginnings. "We kept in touch and in late 1979, the original band members, brothers Guy and Gaz Naylor, started playing guitar and drums respectively. Another lad, Mick Clarke, had a bass, and, along with Oddy (Ian Hodson) and myself, we used to make a noise in Gaz's bedroom, playing various Pistols, Clash and SLF songs. At this time I was just singing along with Oddy. We started getting people standing on the street outside the house on our practice nights listening to what we were doing!"

The Anti Heroes played their first gig in November 1980, at the (long since demolished) South Normanton Miners Welfare Club, a benefit show for a local footballer who had broken his leg. The song 'Banned From The Welfare', that later appeared on their debut album, was inspired by the fact that they were forbidden ever to return to the venue!

"The committee complained that the ceiling was shaking downstairs," laughs Oddy, before continuing. "I remember, Gaz used his holiday money to buy his first set of drums so we fucked off to Spain without him! And we used to rehearse in his bedroom, poor fucker; the coppers came more than once to tell us to turn it down due to complaints from the neighbours!"

After the gig, Mick Clarke left and Kieron took up his position as bassist, and early in 1981, they changed their name to Resistance 77.

The original lineup of Nottingham's
Resistance 77, 1981
L–R: Gaz Naylor, Kieron, Guy Naylor, Oddy

"There were just too many bands with 'Anti' in their name," explains Kieron. "Mind you, there are too many with '77' in their name now! Also, we were playing a style of music more associated with '77 than with the stuff at the time which was a lot more thrashy.

"To be honest we never really were part of the punk scene as such," he reckons. "We just played together but carried on life as normal, playing and going to watch football, drinking and going to see loads of bands. We never got noticed in the early days, mainly as we were out in the sticks and the only gigs we got were ones that we put on ourselves. We never came across any other bands that were local to us; the nearest ones were Anti Pasti from Derby and Riot Squad from Mansfield, whose singer Dunk ran Rot Records who eventually did our first album.

"We played a few gigs here and there, in youth clubs and schools, etc., but our more legendary ones were at the Black Horse Pub in Somercotes, near Alfreton. The room was only fire-licensed for ninety people and at one of our gigs there we had 230 paying customers! Plus, of course, those who blagged in for nowt, not willing to splash out the 50p admission! There wasn't really a scene as such though, and we never got going as far as getting regular gigs because there just weren't many venues putting bands on."

"All our early gigs were self-promoted," adds Oddy. "We used to have to bullshit clubs to put us on. Once we said we were a blues band to play in Nottingham… and obviously had a falling out with the landlord when we played! At Ripley, the bogs got trashed and, as we had to foot the bill, no-one left without putting into a collection, which raised more than the gig did! To be honest, we used to get wrecked before the gigs back then, but now I try to save that 'til after. Every gig has its memory; even the shittiest ones were good, I'd do it all again."

A demo was duly recorded, which found its way into the hands of Simon Edwards who ran Riot City Records. He liked what he heard and included the song 'Bricks In Brixton' on his 'Riotous Assembly' compilation. A chugging mid-tempo number, its catchy chorus powered by some pummelling toms, the song (complete with its quite endearing Oohs and Aahs!) was one of the highlights of the album and the response to it positive enough for Riot City to offer the band a deal for a single.

The 'Nowhere To Play' EP came out in late November 1982 and sold about 3000 copies, reaching No. 5 in the Sounds Punk Chart. A strong debut, the EP opened with the forceful 'Nottingham Problem', its commanding hook built on some militaristic snare drum (think 'Tommy Gun', only ten times faster!). The 'problem' in question was that bands such as themselves had nowhere to play, hence the EP title. The other three songs were just as 'in your face', but still pleasingly tuneful – albeit in a raw primitive way.

"We have always tried to make our songs listenable, with a good tune," claims the bassist, attempting to define just what may have set Resistance 77 apart from the rest of the pack. "And the older and more experienced we get, we try that little bit more each time. We just can't do the fast thrash or aggressive type of punk, and it has never been our style. I think that maybe because we don't have any one particular sort of following, we just try and please everyone…

"Our songs were mainly observations and views; in fact I think that probably contributed to us getting nowhere, as we didn't protest, provoke or try and be controversial. As we were all normal lads with normal homes, and we weren't on the dole or anything, it would have been hypocritical to take the stance of angry punks against authority, the monarchy, and the police… 'cos we weren't!"

Many gigs were undertaken to promote the EP, including dates with The Exploited, The Four Skins and Flux Of Pink Indians, but in 1983, Guy left the band and was replaced by Marc 'Luggy' Ludlam. The band also parted company with Riot City.

"I don't think we fitted in with the style of music that they were looking to produce. I think that our image problem played a big part, too… basically we didn't have one!"

The following year, Resistance 77 signed to Mansfield-based Rot Records and contributed two tracks – 'Send In The SAS' and 'Communist Cunt' (demonstrating a Cold War paranoia that was to be continued with 'Russia' on their next EP as well) – to the 'Wet Dreams' compilation album, that also featured, amongst others, Riot Squad, External Menace and Dead Man's Shadow.

It was followed soon after by the five-track 'Vive Le Resistance' EP which made a brief appearance in the lower echelons of the Indie Charts. Once again it was a fast (but never overly so), furious affair, with the emphasis on good bouncy singalongs as opposed to all-out thrash, cementing the band's reputation as a consistently enjoyable old school punk band.

Rot were obviously pleased as they advanced the band the grand sum of £150 to record their debut album with! This bought them less than three days' studio time, but they still managed to bash out the dozen tracks that comprise 1984's 'Thoroughbred Men', in a frantic session that captured the urgency of the band by virtue of necessity!

"Yes, the recording was an experience," laughs Kieron. "We used a country musician's studio and his son did the engineering. We were very inexperienced with recording and a lot of ideas came whilst we were actually in the studio. We knew we couldn't piss about but as the studio was cheap we managed to crack through the songs quickly live, only adding an extra guitar track afterwards. If we had a bit more time and money I think it could have been better, but we were all pleased with it anyway. And it was still good enough to get a 4-star review in Sounds off Spike Sommer!"

Barring an ill-advised cover of Clive Dunn's No. 1 hit song, 'Grandad' (which is just as horrible as it sounds), 'Thoroughbred Men' is a cracking album, full of memorable songs and, despite the less than perfect sound, throbbing with its own natural power. It got some great reviews – as well as the aforementioned rave write-up in Sounds – and is regarded as something of an unsung classic even today.

Unfortunately the band seemed unable or unwilling to capitalise on its success, and they actually gigged less and less rather than more and more – something they blame on "Work, marriages, families and other distractions!"

During a long quiet period for the band, Oddy left the fold, but Resistance 77 continued as a three-piece with Kieron taking over vocal duties as well as bass. After several gigs in this guise, Gaz also became disillusioned and quit, but in 1988, Oddy rejoined, and with him a new drummer, Paul 'Mushy' Marshall.

This line-up of the band got through to the final of the National Battle of the Bands in Bradford, and in April 1990, as a result of footballer Stuart Pearce being a punk at heart and a fan of the band, they also released 'You Reds'. A football single to celebrate Kieron's beloved Nottingham Forest getting to the final of the Littlewoods Cup, it was backed by 'Young And Wrong' and came out on the band's own Resistance Records.

Gigs were still hard to come by, though, and, frustrated at the lack of progress finding a new label, Luggy left the band. He was replaced with not one but two new guitarists, Rob and Spike, but Oddy had yet more problems with motivation. "I just got sick of the same shit over and over again," he sighs. "We couldn't get gigs and ended up just playing our old songs in rehearsal. I think we lost a lot of inspiration from that lack of gigs. We didn't have a city base, which meant we missed out a lot; interest was there from people, but we couldn't get the support slots we needed and deserved. Plus I had a real bitch of a wife back then – she's still a bitch now but at least she's my ex-wife these days – who got me into shit. With hindsight, we should never have packed up; that's one of my biggest regrets, 'cos now we're doin' good, getting great crowds… who knows what we might have done if we'd kept going?"

And by rights, that should be the end of the R77 story, but in 1994 Captain Oi! reissued the 'Thoroughbred Men' album on CD, and the ensuing surge of interest in the band spurred Kieron into action once again. He recruited a brand new guitarist, Tom 'Angus' Young (since replaced by Ellis Waring), and some high-profile shows were undertaken, including several of the Holidays In The Sun festivals, both in the UK and America. Then, in May 2001, almost twenty years after the first one, Resistance 77 finally unveiled their second studio album, the rather good 'Retaliate First'.

"The 'new' Resistance 77 is obviously more experienced and, as we have played more gigs in the past four years than during the previous nineteen, it is more enjoyable and we are more enthusiastic," enthuses Kieron. "It is also nice that we now feel more accepted by 'name' bands as we were previously on the outside looking in.

"We would say just have a listen," he continues, when asked what he thinks they've contributed to the punk scene over the years. "No one can force anyone to like music, it just happens. But I think we would like to be remembered as a good set of blokes who got on with everyone, didn't offend anyone on purpose, and didn't try to change the world… but had a good time trying to play decent tunes.

"My biggest single regret really is that we didn't achieve what we could have earlier. As you get older and kids come into the equation, it makes things so much more difficult. However, when you still act like seventeen-year-olds all the time anyway, like we do, it doesn't really make much difference!"

SELECT DISCOGRAPHY:
7"s:
'Nowhere To Play' (Riot City, 1982)
'Vive Le Resistance' (Rot, 1984)
'You Reds' (Resistance, 1990)

LPs:
'Thoroughbred Men' (Rot, 1984)

CDs:
'Retaliate First' (Captain Oi!, 2001)
'Long Time Dead' (Captain Oi!, 2004)

AT A GLANCE:

The 1994 Captain Oi CD reissue of 'Thoroughbred Men' contains not only the whole of this excellent album, with lyrics, original artwork and liner notes, but both the band's first two 7"s and various compilation cuts – twelve bonus tracks in all. Mention should also be made of the band's latest effort, 'Long Time Dead', which brings their melodic, powerful sound convincingly up-to-date.

RIOT SQUAD

ansfield-based Riot Squad formed in 1981 and made quite an impact on the scene, not least of all with their vehement 'Fuck The Tories' single. As mentioned previously, original singer Duncan 'Dunk' Mason went on to form Rot Records, who released some brilliant music not only by The Enemy and Resistance 77 but also by the likes of The Varukers and English Dogs.

The earliest incarnation of the band was Dunk singing, Nigel 'Nello' Nelson on guitar and Paul 'Pommi' Palmer on drums.

"I met Pommi through his brother who I was good friends with, and Pommi knew Nello," explains Dunk. "When we first started up there was just the three of us; Pommi had never played drums, I had never sang or written a song, but thankfully Nello was an accomplished guitarist. I loaned Pommi the money to buy a drum kit and we all went round to his mum's house when she was out one evening and bashed out twelve songs to go with the lyrics I had already written.

"We had the inspiration to start our own band, talent or no talent, during the time of the first wave of punk that both Pommi and I were heavily into. We saw a documentary John Peel did that featured, amongst others, The Desperate Bicycles, and how they started a band, and basically we thought, 'What the hell! Anyone can do it and get their records pressed themselves!' That's what we felt punk was all about."

There weren't a lot of conventional punk gigs to be had in the area at the time though, so Riot Squad desperately took what they could when they could.

"We played our first gig at the King Of Diamonds pub, Langwith Junction, which is in a small village near Mansfield... to a very bewildered and unsuspecting crowd of local miners and friends! We went down very well considering the audience was mainly made up of Northern Soul fans and the fact that we were only a three-piece with no bass guitar! This was all just two weeks after we had decided to form the band and we just got up and did it.

"A few weeks later, we did a gig at a local working men's club," he continues. "We had to play two sets and stop halfway through so they could play bingo! Needless to say, there were not many people left to watch the second half! However Wayne (Butler) came to see us that night and offered to become our bass guitarist. He also found us some decent venues to play, so we could actually get some much-needed practice and we suddenly became a much tighter outfit altogether."

Having a half skinhead/half punk line-up, a similar aesthetic to bands like Blitz and The Business, meant that the band quickly attracted followers from both subcultures, and also meant that their gigs were often rowdy affairs.

"Mansfield didn't really have a punk scene at the time," reckons Dunk. "There were punks but to have a good night out we all travelled to Sheffield, Derby or Nottingham to see bands play live. There was however a reggae band called Rankin' Steady and a New Romantic band called B-Movie. There was also a '77 type band called Alleyway Arts who were the most punk, I suppose. We didn't have any live venues as such, but you could persuade some places to let you play occasionally, like the Mason's Arms who had an upstairs room. We focused more on playing away from Mansfield anyway, and as a band we soon decided we wanted to tour as much as possible. I think we only ever played in Mansfield three times during the whole time we were originally together."

Dunk borrowed £45 from his dad, and Riot Squad entered a basement studio in Mansfield for an afternoon to record their first three-track demo, 'Religion Doesn't Mean A Thing'. Dunk set up Rot Records, which began life as just a tape label, to help recoup the costs, and sold copies of the demo at shows and by mail order. An ad placed in Sounds helped generate interest, and the band eventually sold 1500 copies, one of which found its way into the hands of Mike Commaford who signed them to his label, Rondelet, then home to Anti Pasti and Special Duties.

He put the band into FSR Studios in Birmingham, and the resulting 'Fuck The Tories' single spent almost three months in the Indie Charts, reaching No. 23 upon its release in August 1982. A very rough and ready affair, it highlighted the inexperience of the band yet also captured their raw power and energy. And both the striking picture sleeve and not-so-subtle title ensured that even those keen to dismiss it as generic surely couldn't ignore it.

"That was my favourite release," recalls Dunk fondly. "It was really apt at the time and I felt it said exactly what a lot of people felt about the Thatcher years and how bad they were. It gained us some worldwide recognition and did quite well in the Indies; it even made the Top 100 in the main charts. Not bad at all seeing as I actually wrote the track whilst sat on the toilet!"

After Nello had been replaced on guitar by 'Staz' ("He had to learn all the songs at one practise, 'cos we had a gig the next day!"), Rondelet then released the band's 'Religion…' demo as an EP, but sloppy production values hindered what would otherwise have been a raucously enjoyable single. Staz lasted just one tour with the band and, when he left, Wayne moved to guitar and 'Chedd' was recruited on bass.

With the demise of Rondelet, Dunk then decided to make Rot Records a proper label by releasing vinyl, and his first three releases were, naturally enough, all by Riot Squad. However, he stepped down as the band's vocalist after the 'Religion…' 7", deciding to concentrate on Rot full-time ("I'd had enough, basically, simple as that!"), and was replaced by one of the band's roadies, Wayne's brother, Lee.

Recorded at the ever-reliable Cargo Studios in Rochdale (as were all their subsequent releases), the band's first single for Rot was 1983's 'Don't Be Denied' EP. Featuring 'Lost Cause', 'Suspicion', 'Unite And Fight' and 'Police Power', it saw some marked improvements in playing; the drumming especially was far more convincing than on the first two singles. And Lee's voice was very reminiscent of Wattie from The Exploited, to whom the band were likened more and more by the music press. The EP was another Top Forty Indie hit for Riot Squad, and was

quickly followed by the 'I'm Okay, Fuck You' single, a solid three-track EP (standout cut being the pounding mid-tempo 'In The Future') that narrowly missed the Indie Top Ten.

Duncan 'Dunk' Mason, original vocalist of Riot Squad, who also ran Rot Records

By the time of their early '84 'There Ain't No Solution' 7" (b/w 'Government Schemes'), the band were coming apart at the seams with the onset of frustration and the inevitable musical differences, and it was to be their last release. However, Dunk compiled the posthumous 'No Potential Threat' album, that comprised all the Rot singles and several unreleased new tracks, and even after the band had split up, it still managed a No. 13 placing in the Indies.

"I am not sure as we sort of lost touch," admits Dunk, when asked what happened to the ex-members after the band's demise. "I obviously went on to do Rot until our distributors, Red

Rhino, folded; then I went and sold cars of all things! Pommi was – still is – a postman; as for the others, I have no idea.

"Riot Squad however have recently reformed and are now gigging again, playing some old and some new songs; I think they're even planning to go into a studio to record some of the new tracks. Although I don't have anything to do with it anymore, I look forward to hearing the results and wish them all the best for the future."

SELECT DISCOGRAPHY:
7"s:
'Fuck The Tories' (Rondelet, 1982)
'Religion Doesn't Mean A Thing' (Rondelet, 1983)
'Don't Be Denied' (Rot, 1983)
'I'm Okay, Fuck You' (Rot, 1983)
'There Ain't No Solution' (Rot, 1984)

LPs:
'No Potential Threat' (Rot, 1984)

AT A GLANCE:
Anagram's 1995 CD, 'Riot Squad: The Complete Punk Collection', features twenty-one tracks, basically everything the band recorded of note, and reproductions of all the original covers, making it an ideal overview of the band.

SEPTIC PSYCHOS

The Septic Psychos formed in Chesterfield in 1979, while all the band members were still at school, but did little else other than rehearse until 1981, when they played their first shows in local pubs. "The first gig was at the Buck in Chesterfield," recalls Mick. "Me, my twin brother Chiz (vocals) and Hawkey (Neil Hawkes – drums) were all seventeen, and we had a guitarist called Phil Goodwin, a rocker/hippy-looking fella who was a bit older than us. I was going out with his sister at the time, but that was his only gig; we were the only band on. I remember the pub was full, but we set up in another room that was empty. When we switched on our gear and started to tune up, I had my back to the door, but when I turned around there was a wall of bodies and faces. I froze and shit myself, and I don't think that anything but my fingers moved all the way through the set!"

With the hurried departure of Phil, the band were left in need of another guitarist who arrived in the shape of Paul Riley, found hanging around outside one of their rehearsals listening to them play.

"We asked him to come in for a proper listen, but then we found out he could play guitar himself so we let him have a go – and he was great! But he had no equipment or money of his own, so we had to beg or borrow everything for him. The thing is, he was in care, because he was a 'difficult' child; I don't think he and his dad saw eye to eye at all. He was a bit hyper, always excitable, and hardly needed any sleep; he said he could manage on one or two hours a night. Whenever we crashed out anywhere with him, he never seemed to sleep at all!

"Anyway, we used to have to 'break him out' of the care home whenever we played a gig because of their curfew, but it was fairly low security, so we'd just park Chiz's car outside and wait for him to climb out of a window. Then we'd speed off, but his social workers knew he was in the band and kept a check on the local gig scene so they knew where to send the police! We would tell all the audience to watch out for them, and, as you can imagine, they were only too

keen to help. They always sent uniforms so we just had to hide him until they'd gone, and we always used to play 'Kill The Bill' when they showed up!

Septic Psychos
L–R: Paul Riley, Neil Hawkes, Chiz and Mick Shakespeare

"I remember one gig when they came in unexpectedly, walked up to us with a picture of Paul in their hands, and asked if we'd seen him anywhere, producing a photo of a lad in school uniform with bushy, curly hair. We all pissed ourselves and said 'No'! They then showed the leather-jacketed, mohicaned punk rocker Paul Riley a picture of himself and asked him too! So, as you can see, they weren't too hard to outsmart..."

One particularly memorable show was in 1981 at the Whitworth Institute in Darley Dale with Society's Victims and The Corpse.

"It was thick snow and we had a right job getting there," Chiz picks up the story. "There was no bar on, and the other two pubs in town shut for the night when they heard about the punk gig, but a few lads broke into one of the pubs, turned the pumps on and started serving themselves! Obviously the cops were called, so they ran back to the gig, and when the police turned up, we all pelted them with snowballs. John Hall, of Society's Victims, was grabbed and thrown in the back of a cop car, and when the copper went to use his radio, John reached over and ripped it out. He got a smack in the mouth for that. Vans soon arrived with dogs and chased us all over the place, and we kept chucking snowballs at them. About half of us were taken to the police station, and it made the front page of the Matlock Mercury: 'Punk Rockers Run Riot'!"

The band eventually went into Hologram Studios in Stockport, which was also frequented by the likes of Blitz and The Violators, and recorded four songs – 'Not Wanted', 'Get That Band Off The Stage', 'Kill The Bill', and 'The Thatcher'. There were, of course, a thousand and one anti-Margaret Thatcher songs being written by punk bands in the early Eighties, but the Septic Psychos' track 'The Thatcher' stands out by merit of its tongue-in-cheek slant, portraying the then-Prime Minister as a B-movie monster stalking the land feeding on the poor. 'We all know why the doggy howls, the doggy knows The Thatcher prowls,' yells Chiz in the chorus. Although undeniably generic musically and sparsely produced, the band's energy and enthusiasm are very apparent from these recordings, even today.

The band set up their own cassette label, Brain Splat Records, and managed to sell over 500 copies of their self-titled demo at shows and through local record shops. Marcus Featherby who ran Pax Records picked up a copy at Rat Records in Sheffield, and put two of the tracks – 'The Thatcher' and 'Not Wanted' – on his well-received 1982 compilation album, 'Punk's Dead? Nah, Mate, The Smell's Jus Summink In Yer Underpants', alongside the likes of Mau Maus, Xtract and Mania.

The band soon fell out with Marcus over non-payment of studio costs and, despite the album garnering them significant interest, they split without releasing anything else, apparently because Paul Riley was becoming increasingly unreliable.

In 1985, Chiz and Mick ended up in No Dead Meat with the aforementioned John Hall from Societies Victims and Jeremy 'Jez' Bateman from another local band, The Corpse. Setting up their own promotion agency, Noize Ain't Dead, they booked shows for, and played with, many bands such as Disorder, English Dogs, UK Subs, and Peter And The Test Tube Babies. They also recorded a rather good fourteen-track demo which basically picked up the baton where their previous bands had left off, albeit faster and harder, but failed to get them signed.

"John Hall was the main man in No Dead Meat," reckons Chiz. "He made up most of the songs, but, as with most punk musicians, he couldn't read or write music. He would phone me up at all hours and play me his newest tune down the phone… so I could try and remember it in case he forgot it himself once he went to bed! You could write a whole book on the antics of John Hall alone, but unfortunately in December 2001; he drank himself to death on his 39th birthday."

In the face of ever-increasing apathy in the scene ("No records, no gigs, no nothing," sighs Mick), No Dead Meat eventually split and all the members went their separate ways, but Mick remains philosophical about their contribution to punk rock.

"We were just a ripple, a drop in the ocean. A feeling, the anger of youth put to music. We didn't take ourselves too seriously; our main objective was just to have fun, which we did. We made no money, had no fame… but we had a go! Punk's not about any particular band; it's a movement of like-minded people, and we were a part of it."

AT A GLANCE:
Neither The Septic Psychos or No Dead Meat have yet been immortalised on any official CD release, but if you ask Mick nicely and cover his costs he might be persuaded to copy you all their recorded output: mick@mshakespeare.fsbusiness.co.uk

CHAPTER SIX

THE EAST AND SOUTHEAST

THE DESTRUCTORS

A n often-overlooked band from Peterborough, The Destructors probably failed to make a profound mark on the music world because they never really captured the power of their live sound in the studio. They released many records and garnered quite a following for themselves thanks to some concerted gigging on their part, not least of all a slot on GBH's infamous 'Attacked By Rats' tour, but, along with so many other of the genre's 'second division' bands, vanished pretty much without trace during the mid-Eighties. Their origins were tightly entwined with another Peterborough band, The Blanks, who self-released their own single, 'Northern Ripper', an early version of a song that appeared on the first Destructors album.

"I suppose we started our first band, The Blanks, soon after leaving school in the summer of '77, because of what we had read in all the music papers," says vocalist, Neil Singleton. "We were all sixteen and thought punk was great – anti-social and different, and most important of all, easy to play! The Blanks were basically three schoolfriends from Market Deeping, a small town six miles north of Peterborough. I sang, there was Andrew Jackson on guitar, Andrew Butler on drums... and we had a friend of Jackson's from Peterborough on bass, but I forget his name!

"Anyway, Jackson and Butler were also in a Peterborough band called The Destructors, and when they split up, the singer, Alan Adams, joined The Blanks as bassist. We played a few local gigs and recorded the 'Northern Ripper' single in a storeroom round the back of Jackson's father's pub. It was an old Destructors song that Alan wrote. We did it with a reel-to-reel tape player and two mikes, so it's basically just a live recording. Shortly after that, Jackson and Butler left, so me and Alan recruited more members and reverted to The Destructors."

Those new members were Dave Ithermee on guitar and Andy McDonald on drums, although it wasn't long before The Destructors would recruit a talented, young guitarist, name of Graham 'Gizz' Butt, from another local band, The System (not to be confused with the anarcho punk band who released two EPs on Flux Of Pink Indians' Spiderleg label). He soon became a major factor in the band's creative drive, writing about half of their music (Alan wrote all the lyrics), including 'Neutron Bomb', the only Destructors song to ever be played on John Peel's radio show.

"I began playing the guitar by learning a few chords and listening to punk rock records, just trying to figure out the chord sequences," explains Gizz. "The family moved from Manchester to Peterborough and immediately I was on the case looking for other musicians. There were too many dicks around everywhere. It was lonely as an eleven year old kid at a new school, and being in a band was a positive alternative to being in a gang.

The Destructors
L–R: Alan Adams, Neil Singleton, Gizz Butt

"The first bands I played in were The Exits, Berserk, and then The Maniacs, but my first real gigging band was The System. It was around 1980, and we used to hire out local community centres and put on our own shows. We pulled an army of punks from the region and supported The Destructors in one of their earliest lineups a couple of times.

"And it was at a legendary local gig where The System played a venue called the Gladstone Arms that members of The Destructors were in the audience and approached me then to join the band. It was very exciting, being a fourteen-year-old kid in a band of fully-grown punk men. The first jam was revealing, I couldn't believe how shit they were musically! I was showing them how to play their own stuff!

"The big difference came when we played live. Neil Singleton, the lead singer, was able to govern much respect from the crowd and the first gig I played with them was packed with punks going simply mental! It was at Colsterworth village hall, near Stamford."

In early 1982, the band signed to Carnage Records and released two EPs in quick succession, 'Senseless Violence' and 'Religion', both recorded at Stix Studios in Peterborough by Dave Colton. The four-track 'Religion' was especially powerful, in sentiment if not in music; Alan's profound anti-war lyrics ('Maggots feast on once proud men, in dead minds lie letters unpenned') towering above the rather feeble production values of a song like 'Corpse Gas'.

They then signed to Illuminated for their debut album, 'Exorcise The Demons Of Youth' and the 'Jailbait' single. The album was a rather ripping affair, despite a thin, weak production, opening with a reworked version of 'Northern Ripper', complete with Gizz's accomplished lead guitar work running rampant all over it. It was a modest success, spending three weeks in the Indie Charts, peaking at No. 12.

"Musically I have to say that the band tried to utilise a heavy rock guitar approach which was more Motörhead and Thin Lizzy than bands like, say, Varukers who were really Discharge-sounding… and Discharge were kinda speeded-up Black Sabbath anyway," reckons Gizz. "Don't get me wrong, I don't want to sound dismissive or anything, 'cos I love Discharge. It was their guitarist Bones himself who, in 1983, told me he was a huge Black Sabbath fan.

"The Destructors' drummer was really hopeless, though, and could only play a fast straight 4/4 beat, which made every song sound almost like 'Shout!' There were times when we sounded like The Stooges with a country and western drummer; the guy was dismally weak! Neil's vocal style was pretty laid back too, and was definitely his own. He did have a kind of Iggy Pop thing about him… minus the schlong!

"That helped, 'cos we didn't really sound like anyone else. Dave the rhythm guitarist was into totally different stuff to us, like Bauhaus and The Banshees. That helped set us apart as well. Alan wrote nearly all the lyrics and, man, that guy is well read! It was political stuff."

"I think that was the one main thing that set us apart from a lot of other bands," agrees Neil, of the band's lyrical content. "Alan wrote all the songs, and they could be very complicated and a right bastard to remember. He also seemed to have a fixation with serial killers!

"When we were in our prime we were influenced by a lot of American bands; most of us were into that sort of music, but whenever we met and talked with other English bands they didn't seem to know anything about it. We even used to do covers of The Dead Boys and The Germs."

Despite being a clumsy, unremarkable tune, the title track of the 'Jailbait' single, a delicate ode to the temptations of young female flesh, became the band's best-known track when it appeared on Anagram's best-selling 'Punk And Disorderly' compilation.

"I think that's one of our weakest songs, which is a shame," agrees Neil. "None of us had any idea that that was the compilation that everyone would rush out and buy. I was introduced to the singer of Poison Idea a few years ago, and that was all he kept singing to me, 'Underage, underage, underage sex'!

"In fact, I can honestly say that I don't think we ever made a really good record! They never ever lived up to our live shows; we were so much better on stage. I suppose, therefore, that our best record was the live one, with 'Forces Of Law' being the best single. Even when the band was going I never really listened to our own records – by the time we'd spent all night recording, I was sick of them! I only have one album and two singles left, the rest I've given away."

Gizz agrees that the live album, 'Armageddon In Action', which appeared on Radical Change in September 1983 and actually made the Indie Top Ten during its five-week chart run, is a decent representation of the band at the time.

"The tracks were recorded at a gig where we supported The Sisters Of Mercy; it was only their second ever gig. They let us use all their gear which sounded great; the guitars are mega-loud and the drums are compressed all to hell, so the sound is really powerful."

Like most bands that pride themselves on their live performances, The Destructors played out as much as possible, garnering themselves a significant following despite a general lack of serious coverage in the music papers of the day.

"We did a tour with The Abrasive Wheels, GBH and Blitz," says Neil, of the aforementioned 'Attacked By Rats' shows. "I remember that was really good. It was the first time we'd been on tour instead of playing one-off gigs, and we improved a lot because of it.

"We also did a few very good gigs at the 100 Club. The last one there, we filled the place, but when it came time to be paid the promoter said the place was half empty and knocked us on the money!"

"We supported Flux Of Pink Indians at the Stevenage Bowes Lyon House," recalls Gizz. "When we played the whole hall exploded into life. The bands came out and danced to us too. That was a moment when the hairs went up on the back of my neck. Flux were really cooking and the whole night was magical.

"The worst gig ever was at the Brixton Ace supporting The Exploited. I tell you, there were over a thousand Nazi skinheads in that crowd. They dogged Broken Bones, who played before us, and they walked off after four songs. We went on and they invaded the stage; they circled all of us, stole the microphone off Neil and started 'sieg heiling' through the PA. There was a line of them standing like soldiers at the front, and a girl had her throat slit; it was a sad night, kind of signalling what Britain had come to, really."

After the live record, The Destructors signed to Reading-based Criminal Damage for their heaviest release, the 'Cry Havoc And Unleash The Dogs Of War' 12", that sported a front cover illustration by renowned American artist Pushead (aka Brian Schroeder), who has since gone on to fame and fortune painting for Metallica. Actually recorded in 1982, once again at Stix by Dave Colton, but not remixed and released until late '83, it captures the band at their most cohesive and convincing, with Neil sounding uncannily like Casey Royer from Californian hardcore punks DI. Lurching from a melodramatic spoken word intro, opener 'Nerve Gas' jerks and twitches, aptly mimicking musically the death throes of a choking victim, whilst elsewhere, the band pull off a magnificently moody run-through of The Stooges' 'I Wanna Be Your Dog'.

Next followed the 'Merry Xmas And Fuck Off' LP, and then finally 'Bomb Hanoi, Bomb Saigon, Bomb Disneyland', through Carnage once again. Having come full circle, and back on the label they started from, the band split.

"Neil couldn't get on with Alan," reckons Gizz, "and me and Dave didn't want Andy on drums anymore. We weren't happy with Alan organising everything and neglecting his bass-playing role; also, he worked at Huntingdon research centre and, when news got out, it caused a lot of trouble for us!

"There was never any money and my gear was crap; we were quite popular but Neil wanted to move from the area and our relationships were fraught, even though Alan was once my best mate. I enjoyed being with the band and I gave it my all, but it was never going to be ideal because musically it was so weak!"

"I left because I was just bored and wanted to live somewhere else," Neil (who later fronted Trench Fever) remembers it slightly differently. "I think the band had basically run its course by then anyway. I remember a meeting we all had with the owner of our record label, Illuminated, before we played a gig at the 100 Club. This bloke was wearing a suit jacket and had a ponytail... and was telling us that punk was finished, and that we should change to being a rock band. Certain members of the band were nodding in agreement, and right then I thought, 'That's it, I'm out of here!'

"But it was basically a great time for me, and let's leave it there. I've got no regrets and I won't slag anyone off; it's not my style. If I've got a problem, I prefer to sort it out face to face. Although I was reading a book the other day at a friend's house, all about punk bands, and The Destructors were in it with a comprehensive list of all the people who'd ever been in the band... except me! I would like to get to the bottom of that one..."

Gizz Butt (guitar) and Neil Singleton of The Destructors

One final release came in the shape of the free 'Electronic Church' 7" given away with the relatively local Kings Lynne-based fanzine, Trees And Flowers, that both Gizz and Neil agree was the best thing they ever recorded.

Alan resurrected the band with himself as singer, and some of his mates playing backing, as Destructors V for 1984's four-track 'TV Eye' single on Criminal Damage, and the band played a few European dates to promote it, but it was a short-lived reunion.

Gizz went on to form The Desecrators (which actually featured Neil on vocals for a few rehearsals before he moved to Cornwall) and, more recently, Janus Stark. Along the way he joined the Grantham-based punk band, English Dogs, when they 'went metal', but he really hit the jackpot when he joined hugely successful cutting edge dance band, The Prodigy, on guitar.

Despite having negative feelings about his time in the mainstream limelight ("I still get nightmares now, nearly every fucking night!"), Gizz has nothing but affection for how he remembers his role in The Destructors.

"We were a great live band that made politics fun and interesting; a really important East Anglian punk band, with a great devoted following. There were lots of leather jackets with our logo on, mate, fucking loads! Everybody get in touch with Alan and get him to make our unreleased demo available, so someone can release it... but don't listen to the fucking drumming; it's the pits!"

SELECT DISCOGRAPHY:
7"s:
'Senseless Violence' EP (Carnage, 1982)
'Religion' EP (Carnage/Benelux, 1982)
'Jailbait' EP (Illuminated, 1982)
'Forces Of Law' EP (Illuminated, 1983)
'Electronic Church' – free 7" given away with Trees And Flowers fanzine

12"s:
'Wild Thing' 12" (Illuminated, 1983)
'Cry Havoc' EP (Criminal Damage, 1983)

LPs:
'Exorcise The Demons of Youth' (Illuminated, 1982)
'Armageddon In Action' (Radical Change, 1983)
'Merry Xmas And Fuck Off' (Death, 1983)
'Bomb Hanoi, Bomb Saigon, Bomb Disneyland' (Carnage, 1984)

AT A GLANCE:
Tragically, nothing has been reissued officially on CD by The Destructors, although their 'Jailbait' track appears on the CD version of Anagram's 'Punk And Disorderly' compilation.

DESTRUCTORS (BASSIST/VOCALIST ALLEN ADAMS):
What year did you get into punk?
That would have been 1975. I was a big fan of the Flamin' Groovies, and I went to their gig in London, and there was a brilliant support band ... called the Ramones! So I got into the Ramones from that, and I was always into the Velvet Underground and New York Dolls and Patti Smith. I was an avid reader of Sounds and NME, and you'd get glimmers of things in columns from Lester Bangs ... and you'd run out and buy these marvellous vinyl records with bits cut out of the corner!

Basically we then went to see Eddie And The Hot Rods play at the Marquee and there was this bloody awful support band who just did a load of covers and a couple of their own songs before they broke one of the PA speakers – and they turned out to be the Sex Pistols! Then, over the next couple of months, we saw them at two other colleges . . . we'd gone to see the main band, 'cos we liked the whole pub rock scene, Dr. Feelgood and all that, and they were on the bill, and then the Pistols broke and that's how I got into it. I would have been eighteen or nineteen?

Was it the energy that drew you to it all?

Well, yes, it was. Picture the scene at Eddie And The Hot Rods . . . all denim and long hair – and then the Pistols came on, haha! And I just met these other like-minded people wandering around Peterborough . . . and that was The Now. There were only thirteen original punks in Peterborough . . . I think Gizz and his lot were second generation. It was certainly a few years after The Now when I walked up to Gizz and a load of his friends and gave them a Blanks single. That would have been 1979? But there were successive generations every few years. All I know is that there's a famous photo of the thirteen of us all up against this wall. It's pretty funny though, because one's now a producer, one works for Channel Four, Steve's a computer security expert, Mike teaches criminology at university!

It's also interesting because one of his mates, Simon Hallsworth (who also teaches and lectures in criminology), has a book out called 'Gangs', and it says in it, 'In Peterborough there was a band called The Destructors who professed to kill music . . . and they did!'

When did you decide to take up a microphone in a band yourself?

Well, that was really bizarre, because I'm legendary as 'Allen Adams, 21, manager of The Now' – I was 21 for at least three years running! But basically one day, there was this bloke called Fat Pete on the market, this big hippy with a giant wart on his forehead. We always used to claim it controlled him! That his body was controlled by this giant wart! Anyway, he'd met this other band from out in the sticks somewhere, called Six Six Sick, who wanted a singer. They subsequently became The Gestapo and then The Destructors.

And that was the original Destructors that went from late '76 through to '79. We did about thirteen gigs – the one I remember the most was the Key Theatre, one of these Sunday lunchtime gigs, and people were throwing pints of beer over me. One bloke got a whole bottle of lime cordial and tipped it down my neck, and there was this small kid there – people kept filling up his glass just so he could throw it over me! They tried to turn us off, so Dip the bassist at the time kicked the manager of the Key in the nuts . . . surprisingly enough, we were barred for a few years.

So you formed The Destructors in the late Seventies?

Yes. There's a seven-track demo tape that was done back then, that's never been released. Dave Colton, who plays for the band now, produced it, and the joke is that he's been in every band from Peterborough ever because he had the three things that enable him to be in any band: a van, a rehearsal space and a PA! And that's why Dave Colton's been in so many bands, because he ticks all the boxes (we love him, really)!

There have been many versions of The Destructors since that time. Both Dave and Steve from the current lineup have drummed for The Destructors in past incarnations, even before the 'classic' lineup was put together. Anyway, we recorded these seven tracks with him that have never been released – 'Dachau', 'Writing On The Wall', 'Tits', 'Thalidomide', 'Police State' . . . and I can't remember what the other two were!

Were you writing the lyrics for the band back then?

I was, yeah. I can always remember the first ever lyric I wrote: 'Sewage Worker'. I just write stuff all the time. I've now got over 8,500 lyrics, and it's all on computer, so if I come up with a subject, I just type it in, gather all the lyrics together and see what's worth using or not. We've always got loads and loads of lyrics!

You had a bit of a fascination with serial killers, didn't you? Especially on that first LP!

There will be a whole 'Serial Killer EP' one day! I have written some new serial killer songs – and 'Psycho Killer' would have to be one of the covers. A lot of that fascination came from the band whose sticker you can see on my bass guitar – 'TG' [Throbbing Gristle]. I was a good mate of

[vocalist] Genesis [P-Orridge] . . . I can remember going to the first ever gig they did at the Centro Iberico in London.

A lot of people think that the Blanks predated the Destructors, or that they were running in parallel, but it wasn't quite like that, was it?
No, not at all. The Destructors broke up, and the Blanks lost their bassist, and because we'd played together at gigs, they knew I had a bass guitar and an amp – even though I wasn't a bassist. So I got called up one day, and I learnt all the songs in one afternoon – the guitarist taught me how to play them – and that same night we supported The Only Ones at the Sandpiper in Nottingham.

The last gig the Blanks ever did was supporting Discharge at Cottesmore Village Hall. They were horrible! They were throwing bits of cows into the audience. They wrecked the hall and scared our guitarist so much he left the band that night. They also stole his H&H amplifier!

The lads all came round one day and said, we'll take your old Destructors songs, and we'll take these Blanks ones, like 'Breakdown' and 'Overdose' and stuff, so we had a set ready, and we became the new Destructors. We had a weird postman drummer for a while, who is still a postman in Peterborough, and then we got Andy McDonald. Now, everybody slags Andy off, but our current drummer can't play a lot of the stuff that Andy did! It's amazing really. Andy only had two basic drum patterns, but he was really good at them . . . but then Crass only had two drum patterns, and no one slags them off.

What was the punk scene like in Peterborough?
Well, it sort of grew! You had the early Seventies punks, and there were thirteen of us. We used to go to gigs at local places like the Grenadiers in March to see bands like Eater and 999 (fair play to these as these were tough places to visit). Then we hired a transit and squeezed about 20 people in it to go to The Roxy and The Vortex etc. After The Now there were a few skinhead hangers-on, like Mitch from Black Marias, who we got on really well with . . . and then there was

Squiggy! How to describe him . . . ? Can you imagine a Ted with no neck? It just went from there really, picking up strays as we went along.

We had the famous one-day punk/ted war in Peterborough. I didn't actually see any of it. I was just sat in town, and some of the others were getting chased around. But anyway, I was sitting there, and Squiggy came over, and I said, 'I hear you lot have got a problem with us punks? And I don't know why because I like rockabilly!' And he got talking to us, then said, 'This is stupid, give us five minutes . . .' Then he came back, saying 'War's over!'

Also, which was really bizarre, we had a big gay following as well. 'Cos when I first moved to Peterborough, the only people who used to talk to me were these five gay blokes, so I'd sit with them and chat and be highly amused by who was going out with who because they were quite promiscuous, very flamboyant. Anyway, after about six months, I went over and started chatting to this girl, and she was like, 'Why are you chatting to me?' 'Cos I fancy you!' 'But you're gay!' 'No I'm not!' But all their friends used to come to all our gigs.

We had a very mixed group of people come to our gigs, and there was very little violence. We had a bit of trouble with soul boys, but that didn't amount to much. Later on, we had a pretty good scene, and we used to hire a coach to take to gigs, and we'd charge everyone £2, and put the PA on the back of the bus and have a collection for the driver. It all worked very well until the Rutland Angler gig.

And what happened then?
Well, there was the skins and the punks, and one of them was being ill, so he was sick in a bag, and I said, 'Next stop, chuck it out the window . . .' But one of the punks grabbed the bag and threw it at one of the skinheads, so they threw it back, and someone got a bit of dribble down their trousers – and the bloke got so annoyed, he kicked it – and it exploded! I was sat there, trying to impress this girl, and whoosh, I got it right in the back of the head. Needless to say, she wasn't impressed and never came again!

So what brought about the final schism in the band?
I was totally unaware of it, but we were on the way to do a gig with Conflict in Cambridge that we were headlining, totally sold out. The coach turned up to pick me up, and they said, 'Oh, you and Andy aren't playing . . . !' And I said, 'Rubbish! It's my gig, I've organised it, I'll phone up and cancel it right now . . .' So we came to a compromise – the original band would do a set, and then their new band would do a set, and that's what we did. We did the gig, and I got quite pissed, and you can imagine what the atmosphere was like on the coach on the way back.

Anyway, that was the last time they called themselves Destructors, because later I handed them a solicitor's letter, telling them to cease and desist – I owned the name, I'd registered it with Companies House – so they had to change it to the Desecrators. Subsequently Dave only lasted a couple of weeks, and Neil only lasted six or seven weeks before he left to go to Cornwall.

So it all ended acrimoniously?
Well yes, very acrimoniously. It's taken me thirty years to get over it! But I get on with Gizz now a lot better than I used to. He's even written two songs for this pirate project thing that I'm doing that are really good.

So after the Destructors, you did Destructors V?
We put a set together in no time at all, and then we went to Europe, and then we became the Angels Of Malice, one of the early British thrash metal bands, with our track 'Fast Forward To Hell'. It's bizarre, because at the time we got slagged off for being the worse track on the [Metalworks compilation] album [also titled 'Fast Forward To Hell'], but just recently, with

hindsight, we're the "lost band of British thrash . . . !" And there's a whole album of material we'd written that never got recorded, and if we'd got round to doing that, we would have probably done all right as a thrash metal band!

And after that I sort of gave up, I just lost interest. I became a huge science fiction and Dr Who fan and went to lots of conventions and stuff. I co-wrote the Babylon 5 Security Manual with Jim Mortimer . . . well, Jim didn't write much of it. I did all the research and my mate who was in the Birmingham Dr Who club whipped all my notes into shape.

Then basically Steve [Rolls] contacted me asking after some photos of The Now (as they had been approached by Last Year's Youth Records to re-release their original singles 'Development Corporations' / 'Why' and 'Into The Eighties' / '9 o' Clock'), because I took a lot of photos at their gigs and have a massive archive, and that got me thinking about getting the band together again. It took me a year from that point to get it together, and we went in to record a one-off split single with The Ruined – it was never meant to be anything more than that, it should all have ended there, but I sketched out an idea to do a few more split singles with younger bands from Peterborough, although it didn't quite work as intended until we started doing it with older bands. And they all get great reviews now.

How many releases have you done since?
The 44th one came out in November [2013]! We've written 169 new songs . . . recorded 80 covers . . . and we've re-recorded about 40 of the old Destructors songs! I worked it out the other day, and we've spent almost quarter a million quid on this project – but it's just the original £8,000 we invested that keeps going round. We've got a great mailing list that buys everything we do, and we have this record club.

Think we're only up to fourteen gigs though. We normally play at the Met Lounge where I work, which is weird, because people come in to see the band, and the person who's taking their coat and their money is suddenly up onstage.

We'd like to do more gigs, but I find it somewhat depressing really. When The Ruined were going, I used to go to some of their gigs, and it would remind me of when we played Bradford to five men and a dog – and the dog left when we started playing! But because we gave it everything when we played to those five people, when we came back the next time, the venue was full. Always been a great believer that it doesn't matter if the people are there or not, you have to give it everything.

What about you working at Huntingdon Life Sciences (one of the reasons sometimes cited for the band wanting to part ways with Allen)?
The band knew about it all along. The only time I ever had any hassle at all was when we did an ALF benefit (for their Whales & Dolphins section), and there was a couple of lads that were apparently going to come onstage and throw me off.

The real reason they wanted me out of the band was Andy McDonald's drumming. They wanted a better drummer in the band, and I said no, he'd been with us the whole time – and that's why the schism happened! 'Cos I stuck up for Andy.

And then I subsequently ditched Andy for a better drummer in my next band anyway, haha!

How would you like Destructors to be remembered in the grand scheme of things?
We killed music – and we still do! I admit I can't sing – but I have lots of ideas all the time, thinking about stuff . . . I read somewhere once that this is a vanity project, but it isn't. People like what we're doing, and more importantly *we* like what we're doing – it's the best band I've ever been in, even though we hardly ever socialise with each other.

What people forget about the punk scene at the time was, you had the Exploited type of punks, who were all 'Oi!' and chaos and girls, and then you had this other lot, going 'Life's all depressing, we're against everything.' And of course, where did the Destructors sit? Right in the middle on the fence, we could write songs like either of them.

But the new Destructors are far superior to the original band, a huge leap forward. There is still the spirit of the original Destructors and as long as we enjoy doing it we will continue. We have picked up a load of ideas over the years and fused them into a new blend of punk/scuzz/garage sounds. As Blue Mink said, we're in a great big melting pot!

Any regrets?
There's two big regrets I've got with Destructors. 'Wild Thing' would have gone really far if Illuminated hadn't had a cash flow problem and could have pressed up more copies at the right time. And, if we'd released [new album] 'The Sublime, The Perverse, The Ridiculous' back in 1984, we'd have been right up there with Broken Bones and GBH . . . but of course, I didn't realise that some of the band were plotting behind my back.

The only money we ever saw from Destructors was £500 we got from Illuminated for the album. It sold really well, so we got a bit of money off them. We were also owed six grand by a German label that put it out over there, but they said, sorry, they could only give it to Illuminated. At which point, Illuminated had broken up and the guy's wife took all the money and ran off to Nigeria! Oh well!

ENGLISH DOGS

The aforementioned English Dogs were one of those pioneering punk bands who dared cross unashamedly over into metal territory. In one interview, when asked why they were 'jumping on the punk/metal bandwagon', they responded that they weren't jumping on any bandwagon, they were driving it! Such self-confidence could be interpreted as arrogance, but the band weren't making idle threats, and more than had the musical firepower to back up their claim. However, they certainly weren't a technical speed metal band when they started up in Grantham in 1982, as Gizz Butt, their lead guitarist from 1984 onwards, explains.

English Dogs L-R: Wakey, Wattie, Jon, Pinch (Pic: Mike Stone)

"The original line up was Pinch (Andrew Pinching) on drums, Jon Murray on his battered old 'Flying V' guitar, Wakey (Peter Wakefield) on vocals and a second guitarist called Greg... I don't know too much about him, but I did meet him in Derby once, and I think he may now be dead! They didn't have a bassist to start with.

"Pinch formed the band. He was younger than all the others and went to Grantham Boys Grammar school. He was a good boxer and won a shitload of awards. His parents split and left him in Grantham with Wakey as his legal guardian. They lived in a punk rock, ducks-in-the-bath, shit-on-the-carpet, twenty-four-hour party house! It was there that the band was born, amongst knives blackened from hot knifing sessions and plastic bags stuck together with Evo-stik glue."

They were soon joined on bass by Mark 'Wattie' Watson, and quickly set about building a huge following both locally and nationally. A task made all the easier when they landed themselves tours with the likes of GBH and One Way System – and let's not forget they had the irrepressible Wakey fronting the band.

"He was a bit like Wattie from The Exploited," reckons Gizz. "Larger than life, a bit fatter than your average speed freak; tough, fuelled and influential with his humorous stage approach... which often consisted of ripping the stage apart or throwing shit around. And I literally mean shit!"

Gizz first noticed The English Dogs – and vice versa – when they played a show with his former band, The Destructors. "The English Dogs played their second ever gig supporting us in Barrowby. It was a great gig; they were real fast and hungry. Their songs reminded me of

Discharge mixed with Black Flag, and I was a fan of both bands. I used Jon's amp at the gig, an unreliable old Marshall combo that had to be thumped every two minutes to make it work. I swapped addresses with him at the end of the night. In those days it was rare for punk band members to have a phone.

"The Destructors took a coach load of Peterborough, Market Deeping and Stamford punks to the gig and they must have got on with The Dogs' Grantham following because it was a rare occasion when they didn't fight. The Destructors 'Death Squad' had some real fuckin' hard cases amongst them; The English Dogs gloriously won a good number of them over that night, though.

"They actually played with The Destructors a few times and even came to some of our gigs. At Retford Porterhouse, a punk rocker ran out of the gig with my Ibanez guitar. Alan (Adams, Destructors' bassist) spotted the guy and grabbed the guitar from him. This punk was then throttled by the bouncers and marched to the police station. I went down there and got them not to press charges, because it was Jon, The English Dogs' guitarist, high on glue!"

After being recommended to label boss Mike Stone by GBH, The English Dogs signed to Clay Records, and their storming debut was the 'Mad Punks And English Dogs' 12", six devastatingly powerful punk songs that saw the band crash into the Independent Top Twenty in October 1983.

It was followed the very next summer by the superb 'Invasion Of The Porky Men' album. Recorded at Strawberry Studios in March '84, and produced by Mike Stone and Chris 'Iceman' Nagle, it spent over three months in the Indies, peaking at No. 3. Like the 12" that preceded it, the album was incredibly well played and produced for the time, and the band's material was forceful, catchy and minimalist all at once.

Unfortunately, just as the band were gaining some serious momentum, Wakey left after several German tours were marred by senseless violence. A new vocalist was found in Troy McDonald (who would later front Rabid), and a second guitarist, Tracy Abbott, recruited, but this lineup only lasted long enough to record a disappointing demo. It was then that Wattie approached Gizz with the idea of joining The English Dogs as lead guitarist.

"The Destructors had split and I had my new band, The Desecrators, by then," says Gizz. "We fused our punk with plenty of metal riffing and soloing and a strong US hardcore influence. I actually thought we were much better than The Dogs. We had a great demo and were starting to build a cool following, but our singer had just left so I thought I'd give them a try.

"The first rehearsal was my audition, I guess. What struck me more than anything was how great a drummer Pinch was but I sensed that he didn't like me much. They smoked a lot of hash at the rehearsal which was in a freezing back room above a pub in Harlesden. There was no singer there and my Peavey Classic was drowned out by Jon's Marshall stack. Wattie was one of the best bass players I'd played with and definitely had the best sound, a bit like Lemmy or Ross from GBH. They used an electronic tuner and insisted on a certain amount of tightness... I only say 'a certain amount' because you'd never tell, listening to some of the records. At the end of the night they told me I was their lead guitarist. though Pinch didn't exactly look 100% sure!"

Gizz joined The English Dogs just as the band were moving in a much more thrash-metal direction, and his fluid lead playing was the missing piece of the jigsaw. His first show with the band was with The Abrasive Wheels at the Lyceum, and his first Dogs recording was the amazing 'To The Ends Of The Earth' 12", a four-track EP of slavering high-speed crossover. It appeared through Rot Records, the Mansfield-based label ran by Dunk from Riot Squad, after the band had a contractual falling-out with Clay, and reached No. 4 in the Indies during December 1984. It was also the recording debut of new vocalist Adrian 'Adie' Bailey, formerly with Ultra Violent (that released the excellent 'Crime For Revenge' single on Riot City), who had a higher-pitched, more rasping voice than Wakey and was more suited to the new style.

"We recorded it at Cargo studios in Rochdale with the engineer and producer, Ian McNay, who was great; that recording experience was one of my favourite ever. I recorded everything in pretty much one take. It felt great; none of it was perfect but the spirit was there. After a solo I'd look up to the control room and see them all applauding. Everyone really wanted the full-on metal solo thing."

As soon as they'd finished the 12", the band began work writing a full album of ever more metallic hardcore punk, and the wonderful 'Forward Into Battle' was the result. Beautifully packaged with an overblown sword 'n' sorcery sleeve, the music was almost as epic as the artwork. Opening with the obligatory – for metal albums of the era, at least – instrumental intro, it careened headlong into some serious riffing, ably underpinned by pummelling double bass drums.

"I think that album contains some of the best punk/metal songs ever written," says Gizz proudly. "But they're not played that well and produced really badly. I think Metallica should cover the whole album! We wrote them shortly after 'To The Ends Of The Earth' was recorded, starting with 'Final Conquest' and 'Ultimate Sacrifice'."

It was another great success for The English Dogs, once again reaching No. 4 in the Indies, where it remained for over two months during August 1985.

The band were by now making the desired ripples on the metal scene, as well as the punk one where the more open-minded fans still appreciated their musical progression, and it was only a matter of time before they registered on the radar of a bigger label. In early 1986, they signed to Under One Flag, a subsidiary of Music For Nations, and it seemed they were destined for ever bigger and better things. However, after the convincing three-track 'Metalmorphosis' 12", which featured a great ghoulish cover from horror artist, Les Edwards, they fumbled the ball big time with the overly ambitious, Tolkien-esque concept album, 'Where Legend Began'.

"The way the punk/metal thing developed seemed really natural at the time," reckons Gizz. "Before punk came along I had checked out Black Sabbath, Lynyrd Skynyrd, Deep Purple, Thin Lizzy and, of course, Hendrix. Punk came about, but the metal stuff was still always gonna be there to an extent. Then Motörhead played 'Top Of The Pops' and we all thought they were great. And so it went Pistols and The Clash… to UK Subs and Motörhead… to Discharge and GBH… to English Dogs and Broken Bones… and so on. I think Discharge reached a peak when they made 'Hear Nothing, See Nothing, Say Nothing'; it was like pre-punk/metal. And when The English Dogs released 'Metalmorphosis', we peaked with what we were trying to create. Punk/thrash metal; a bit more progressive than Discharge, more complex but still intense."

Despite some virtuoso musicianship, 'Where Legend Began' had very little intensity about it and the band's constant twisting and turning was so convoluted that even the most die-hard fan was left disappointed and confused. Matters weren't helped by the thinnest guitar production in the history of rock music, and a horrible muddy bass drum sound that lacked any punch whatsoever.

"We weren't ready to do what we had taken on and so a lack of maturity and control were the blaming factors," sighs Gizz. "We tried to move along too fast and there was little of the feeling we'd had on the previous three releases. The guy who produced it lost the hardcore edge. He was using cocaine and up late every night, fucking around with some girl. He drove his Porsche 911 in late every day and had about as much knowledge of thrash metal as he had taste in clothing… and he dressed like Robert Palmer! He was a wanker, better suited to tape op for Gary Glitter. I won't forget the shit that came out of his mouth every day. And this was our producer – we were fucked from the beginning."

Jon actually left just before the band recorded the ill-fated album, leaving Gizz to play all the guitar tracks, and soon after the record's release Pinch walked away as well. The English Dogs were falling apart and, although they drafted in Jamie Martin on rhythm guitar and Spikey Smith from Alternative Attack on drums, the final straw came when Adie left after a gig at the Birmingham Mermaid during the summer of 1987. Despite the acrimonious way it all ended, Gizz still has many fond memories of The Dogs' metal period, especially of their US shows and all his musical mentors he met along the way.

"When we were in the USA the second show was in Fenders Ballroom. The night before, we'd played in front of 8,000 people at the Olympic Auditorium. This night the place was jammed full too; you couldn't get any more people in anywhere. DI (the seminal SoCal punk band who supported that night} were good guys and lent us their gear. We'd had a few drinks and a few smokes, and the Pigs raided the dressing room trying to cause shit. We went out to an ecstatic crowd and the temperatures rocketed. Halfway through, Pinch vomited on his snare drum and had to vacate the venue for a few minutes to catch his breath. For a crack I got on the kit and we banged through 'Free To Kill'... what a fucking great moment! Pinch came back on and we finished the best gig we ever played.

"A few nights later, we played San Francisco and met (Metallica guitarist) Kirk Hammett's brother. He told us that Metallica were fans of our stuff! And then, when we were recording 'Where Legend Began', we got a phone call from our A&R man Mark Palmer who told us Metallica were in town and wanted to visit us. We went round the corner to a pub and up they came, James (Hetfield), Kirk and Cliff Burton. We shared a few stories and beers and went back to their hotel room for a smoke and to listen to some music. I don't know if you've heard of a stupid old trick where you get a group of about five people and one sits on the floor with his back against someone's legs? All the others place their hands flat one on top of the other on top of the sitting guy's head. They all push hard down hard for exactly one minute whilst he keeps himself bolted upright, with a firm-as-hell neck. After that minute everyone immediately places the first finger of both hands under the now laying body of the sitting guy and picks them up, raising them to the ceiling. We did it to Cliff Burton and what a great sport he was. He looked like his neck was gonna snap and then he went up so fast that he banged his head on the ceiling! We were all amazed! Shortly after, we were all thrown out, and a week later Cliff Burton died (in a bus accident in Sweden) – RIP.

"If only we'd had a manager and consistent production," he ponders how things might have worked out better. "If I'd had guitar lessons and got some better equipment... if Adie had stuck to his great performance on 'To The Ends Of The Earth' and not tried to sound like Paul Baloff from Exodus... if only we'd chilled out on the LSD, mushrooms, speed and smoke just a bit. If we'd wised up and got our arses more in the USA where they didn't care so much for the Wakey line up, then we might have lived for a whole lot longer. The main regret above all though is that when we were

English Dogs, live during their 'metal' period, Jon Murray (guitar) and Adrian Bailey (vocals)

good we didn't stick to the formula; we had to go over the top with 'Where Legend Began'. Maybe then the five of us would have stayed together, because, by the end of the USA tour, we were fucking roasting."

At the same time The Dogs split, The Desecrators also folded ("I remember my girlfriend left me at the same time; I was doing well!"), so Gizz formed the rather good, but sadly short-lived, Wardance before putting together Sundance and then reuniting with Pinch in the uninspired hard rock band, Monkey Jungle. Back together with his old Dogs sparring partner, it was only a matter of time before – acting on the advice of close friend (and former Soldiers Of Destruction vocalist turned writer for mainstream metal mag Kerrang!) Mörat – Gizz was reforming The English Dogs.

The potentially great lineup of Wakey, Pinch, Jon, Wattie and Gizz played five shows together, before personal tensions had the band coming apart at the seams again. Jon and Wattie left, but by then they'd already landed themselves a deal with German label, Impact, so new bassist Stuart West was recruited from Peterborough punk band The Uprising. This lineup toured the UK and recorded the 'Bow To None' album during early 1994 at Outrider Studios in Northampton. A thoroughly enjoyable disc, featuring some great high-octane tracks such as 'Face Pollution' and 'Nipper Tripper', and even new versions of old classics such as 'Fall Of Max' and 'Psycho Killer', it was somewhat tarnished with one too many throwaway filler songs.

Wakey and Stuart both left after a well-received six-week German tour, and were replaced respectively by Stu Pid (of Police Bastard and Sensa Yuma) and Swapan 'Shop' Nandi, who had roadied for the band around Germany. This version of the band recorded the superb five-track 'What A Wonderful Feeling… To Be Fucked By Everyone' CD for Retch. A genuine return to form, it even included a fantastic cover of Stiff Little Fingers' 'Wasted Life'.

After a tour of Scandinavia with Chaos UK, Pid left to concentrate on Police Bastard, and Gizz took over the vocals as well as guitar, resulting in the slick, assured 'All The World's A Rage' album (Impact, 1995). Featuring a mammoth seventeen tracks, every one of them a vibrant fusion of raw punk energy and accomplished metal musicianship, it is an overlooked modern punk gem, and stands as a fitting epitaph to the band, who basically split for good when Gizz joined techno giants The Prodigy.

However, the last chapter of the turbulent English Dogs soap opera still hadn't been written. The 'All The World's A Rage' lineup reunited to play a great set at Holidays In The Sun 1996, before Gizz put together Janus Stark, who signed to well-respected Nottingham label Earache and released the often overlooked album, 'Great Adventure Cigar' ("Still a massive high point for me," he reckons). He has since put together a harder, thrashier act, The More I See.

Pinch, Wakey, Jon and Stuart West reformed the Dogs yet again – without Gizz – to play another H.I.T.S. festival, and even toured the USA in 2003… but not before Gizz had been out there under the moniker ATWAR (i.e. 'All The World's A Rage'). Alongside old friends Shop, Spikey, and Gavin King, he put together a strong set of Dogs tracks culled from 'Forward Into Battle', 'To The Ends Of The Earth' and, of course, 'All The World's A Rage'. Unfortunately most of the promoters decided to bill the band as 'English Dogs' to pull the punters in, which annoyed Gizz immensely, but not as much as it annoyed the official English Dogs who were due over there to play a few months later.

"We took so much acid that we could see a world where punk and metal came together gloriously," reflects the guitarist on the Dogs' troubled history. "It was possible for punks to get wasted and to blow their horn as loud as they wanted at the same time. We broke the rules in a scene that was all about breaking rules anyway. You could be fiercely anti-racist and play like Van Halen or John Bonham. Race relationships didn't mean a great deal to the heavy metal world but it meant a lot to us, and that came through in our approach.

"I want nothing more than people to have a good time to what I've done and to share my contempt of the class system. Get happy, get aggressive, get laid. Bang your head, raise your fist, release whatever it is you've got in there. If anyone remembers us when we've all gone, that'd be cool and if anyone's life has improved at all from anything I've ever done then that's a bonus… actually it's a dream come true."

SELECT DISCOGRAPHY:
12"s:
'Mad Punx And English Dogs' (Clay, 1983)
'To The Ends Of The Earth' (Rot, 1984)
'Metalmorphosis' (Under One Flag, 1986)

LPs:
'Invasion Of The Porky Men' (Clay, 1984)
'Forward Into Battle' (Rot, 1985)
'Where Legend Began' (Under One Flag, 1986)
'Bow To None' (Impact, 1994)
'All The World's A Rage' (Impact, 1995)

CDs:
'What A Wonderful Feeling...' (Retch, 1995)

AT A GLANCE:

Captain Oi!'s 1995 CD version of 'Invasion Of The Porky Men' also features the 'Mad Punx...' 12"
and is hence the ideal place to check out the powerful early Dogs material. The highlights of the
ensuing metal period can be found on the 1995 Step-1 CD that compiled the 'Forward Into Battle'
LP and the 'To The Ends Of The Earth' 12" onto one disc.

ENGLISH DOGS (VOCALIST WAKEY)

So when did you get into punk?

Having been born in 1961, punk happened at exactly the right time for me. When you look at
the music scene pre-punk, there was so much dirge, it was terrible. I was brought up on The
Beatles and The Kinks, and The Who were a cool band, and The Stooges, so it seemed okay as a
child, but once I became a teenager, between me and my brother, we got all three music papers –
Sounds, NME and Melody Maker – every fucking week without fail. Thursday was an important
day, when these papers arrived, and even a thirteen- or fourteen-year-old, I would be scouring
them for anything about Alice Cooper or Doctor Feelgood or the Sensational Alex Harvey Band.
Funnily enough, early Status Quo, when there was nothing else about. My first tattoo was Status
Quo – I did it myself with Indian ink, having watched them on the Old Grey Whistle Test, and –
fucking half-wit that I am – I spelt it wrong! But I was still the first kid at my school with a tattoo,
so I was pretty chuffed about that!

Then everything changed in '76. Punk was stirring everyone up, and 'punk' became a swear
word. People were saying, 'You fucking punk rocker!' 'Punk' was the new word for 'cunt'! And I
thought, 'Whoa, I like this!' And me and Nigel Hatter were the first two punks in Grantham. It
changed the whole structure of my life – it gave me something to fight for, something to believe
in . . . It was one up to society, to the authorities, the police, the magistrates, the bullies at school.
I've always been a believer in the underclass, the underdog, and still am. I loved every second
of it, and to be honest, I thought it would only last a few years, and it did decline after the initial
rush of the original bands – until 1980, and it went fucking mental again.

It changed my life. I'm 53 now, and I'm still the same. I live in a bus. And I've lived in a bus, or
a caravan, or an ambulance, or a bender, or a tent, for 24 years, and for me it's the purest form of
anarchy you can get. I don't pay no rent, don't pay no rates, and I live out in the beautiful countryside. My daughter's in a punk band . . . my grandson's christian name is Lydon . . .

What was your first punk gig?

That was The Clash and The Slits at Leicester De Montfort Hall in January 1978. I'm a bit pissed off that I never went to a gig in '76 or '77, but in '76 I was still at school, and in '77 there was hardly any gigs – there was so few punks in Grantham, no bands came anywhere near the East Midlands. I was quite preoccupied with football – I followed Newcastle United . . . for no other reason than they had a hard following! I was quite excited by football violence – going to games and trying not to get my fucking head kicked in. Then I dropped the football thing and got properly into the music instead. And that Clash gig was fucking amazing. We were completely enthralled by Ari Up's bush! I was down the front, up against the stage, looking up her skirt at her bush. She had a great bush, all bursting out the sides there . . . and the music was okay as well.

And the De Montfort, and Leicester University, was one of our early haunts. Thing is, we weren't very good punks coming from Grantham – there were no shops selling punk clothes or crazy-coloured hair, so you had to do it all yourself. One gig, about five of us, we put food colouring in our hair, and the Leicester punks all mocked us and thought we were wankers, especially by the end of the gig when the food colouring had all sweated into our faces. We all had either green or blue or orange faces. So that never happened again, but I've never forgotten what cunts we must have looked.

What prompted you to form your own band?

I'd never had any thoughts of being in a band at all. I don't like Pinching, and I don't mind it going in the book that I don't like him – we haven't spoken properly for seven years – but I will give him credit where due. As a fourteen-year-old spotty urchin, he came and banged on my door when I nearly twenty, and said, 'As the main punk in Grantham, would you want to join my band? I need a face to sing for us.' I'd never ever considered singing before, but once the offer came along, it immediately appealed to me. It felt a bit weird being in a band with a couple of kids, so I also got hold of another older punk, Jon Murray, who had been in The Brick Wall Band, Grantham's only other punk band, to play guitar as well. But it was Pinching who had the vision and ambition to get it started. And very quickly it gelled; the songs and ideas came together very quickly.

It only dawned on me years later that actually we were never mates. We were punks, in the same small town that wanted to be in a band, and we all had a bit of talent. But no one ever kept in touch with each other outside of the band, it was a shambles, we were only together out of necessity. I find that incredibly sad really.

But there was a great chemistry in the band – hence you getting picked up by a label like Clay and doing such a great first record.

Absolutely, we wrote thirty or forty songs in the first few years. And they were good songs, but we *were* lucky it sounded so good. It just clicked in the studio with Chris Nagel, the producer. I don't quite know why it came out so well, but that incredible production helped set us apart and was one of the reasons we took off so quickly. We were lucky – we'd played no more than three or four local gigs before GBH and the UK Subs started picking us up for bigger support slots.

Where was the first English Dogs gig then?

It was upstairs at the Earlsfield pub in Grantham, January 14th 1981. There was 50 or 60 people there, and I think we did a cover of 'So What?' We did a few other local gigs and then it wasn't long before we did our first big support, at the Norwich Gala with the UK Subs. And once we'd sent a copy of the first demo to Colin from GBH, we got a load of supports with them, and became firm friends with them. And we still are now. But we were lucky, no doubt about it. We worked hard, but we had a bit of luck too.

English Dogs live, 2013,
pic by John Bolloten

English Dogs 2013,
pic by John Bolloten

I've always regretted the name though. I came up with that name and logo – which came straight out of a Letraset book, which is where we all got our logos back then! But the 'English' in the name caused us a lot of grief, especially back in the Eighties when you had a lot of skinheads ruining gigs. But even now, when I'm asked what the name of the band is, I'll say 'English Dogs . . . but we're not racist! We're just Dogs . . . from England!' A lot of people like the name, and so do I really, but I really wish I'd come up with something else. But I loved Slaughter And The Dogs, and just thought 'Dogs from England . . .'! And over the years, of all the 27 members that have been in the band, I've not heard any of them utter a single racist comment. I wouldn't put up with it – I'd knock them out, or throw them out at the very least.

How did Clay come to pick you up?

I know Mike Stone was looking for another punk band for Clay, and I'm pretty sure it was GBH who put a word in for us, because we got on so well with them. We even went and played Germany with them. This was still 1981, and GBH were one of the first of the Eighties punk bands from the UK to go to Germany, and they invited us along. We just turned up and played unannounced! In all these fucked-up squats across Germany. But yeah, Mike needed another punk band, he came and saw us play a few times, and we just seemed right for the label at the time.

Was 'Left For Dead' based on a true story?

Yes, definitely! Most of our songs are based on true stories in fact. But yeah, back in the day, Wattie our bassist fucked this girl who was the missus of this right hard cunt from Grantham, and when this guy got out of jail, he beat the fuck out of him! He scraped his face all along this Artex wall . . . But you know, if you're going to fuck another man's wife, be prepared to get your face garnished with Artex!

What can you remember about the writing of the first LP?

It was just a continuation of 'Mad Punks . . .' really. We had fifteen or twenty songs to choose from when we recorded 'Mad Punks . . .', and after the success of that, Mike Stone was very keen to get 'Porky Men' out. But we only really had to write two or three more songs, and do the cover of 'Cranked Up Really High' to have the album ready. Mike Stone was quite the visionary – I remember when I first heard 'Fight Back' by Discharge, I thought, 'What a fucking horrible row!' but then a month later I was painting them on the back of my leather jacket – and he'd just had the Abrasive Wheels in to do 'Black Leather Girl'. He told them that punk was on the decline, and that they should tone it down and make it more rock than punk. They were in just two weeks before us, and he told us exactly the same thing, so we actually drastically slowed down at least a third of the songs on Mike's advice. But it was a good call for us, because it turned out great, and it sold a fucking load, it went through the roof. It got to No. 3 in the Independent Charts. We used to rush out and buy Sounds every week to see where we'd got to. At the end of 1984, we were in the Top 30 best-selling independent albums of the year in Sounds – we made No. 19, above Elvis Costello and The Smiths! We were the only punk album in there, I think, I was so proud of that.

'Mad Punks' went in the Independent Charts at about No. 18, and it even got into the National Charts at 187 – just for one week! We felt like the new Seekers!

But sure enough, as always, greed shines through, and Clay ripped us off, and we had to take them to court twice, and then Clay sold up to Trojan, who then sold it to someone else . . . and we've never seen any money since! I certainly can't be arsed to chase it up again, I find my happiness elsewhere.

Did you do much touring on the back of that LP?

We did the 'Never Again' tour with Discharge. Antisect were originally booked to do it, I think, but pulled out, so Mike Stone got us on it, which did us a huge amount of good. Calv from Discharge rang me up and asked how much we'd play for every night, and I was so pleased we were doing the tour, I said we'd play for a fiver a night. It was costing us £15 a night to hire a van off this terrible Grantham metal band called Marz! We had to get the Grantham punks to come with us to chip in for the petrol, and we were siphoning petrol whenever we could as well. We went all over Britain with Discharge, slept in the van every night, and he kept to his word and only gave us £5 a night. I didn't complain at the time, but they were on £600 or £800 a night, and we got a fiver. I don't blame the rest of the band at all, but Calvin . . . what a cunt. He wasn't a man of the people at all. He ripped us off right royally. But we worked hard, we'd play anywhere, we built up a good following.

What brought about your departure from the band?

The main thing was that the other guys were beginning to back-comb their hair into flamboyant bouffants and were listening to Slayer and Ozzy Ozbourne and Anthrax. And Pinch got rid of his Doc Martens and bought some boxing boots, and double bass drums. And I was going, 'But we're a punk band . . . !' And all they said was, 'But this is the way it's going . . .'

It was the first time I looked around at the guys I was with and thinking, 'I ain't sure I like you that much . . .' I realised they were into rock'n'roll stardom, climbing the ladder and making money, and I was the only one who seemed to have any punk rock principles. To see the people who had been my closest friends for all these years, the people I'd first sniffed glue with, the people I'd first taken acid with, travelled abroad with, to see them turn into this . . . this . . . bull-shit, it was so poor. I had no interest in it anymore, and it was a hard decision, I was very sad about it, but I couldn't be with those people anymore. But Sal also fell pregnant with our first girl about that time, which was another very good reason to leave.

I suggested they try Adie Bailey, because I loved Ultra Violent. That single they did is magnificent, and he's a good guy with a good gravelly voice. And they did do some good stuff after I left, like 'To The Ends Of The Earth' 12", but they took it too far. Fair play, they were the first crossover band in the world, but they thought they could do anything and they just vanished up their own arses. Music For Nations sacked them off, and that was that, they were a spent force. And I laughed.

What prompted the 'Bow To None' reunion then?
I came down from Scotland for that, because they wrote and asked me if I wanted to try it again. With hindsight they probably only wanted my name on the album. I'm proud of a few songs on there like 'The Hanging Wanker', that's a good song, but it was basically a sham, a horrible album, and without a doubt the worse thing I've ever done. I've left English Dogs four times over the years, four times I've walked away because I've not been happy with the other guys in the band.

But you've got a settled lineup again now, right?
Yes, we have, and we've got a new album out, called 'We Did, We Do, We Always Fucking Will'. Nunny Dave, a lovely guy, upped £1,000 for us, and we put it into the same studio we always use in Nuneaton, and we've been recording this over the last year – rather than go in and record it all in one go. Which is how it's usually done, but we've been going in every six to eight weeks, writing a few more songs and recording them . . . and all the while listening to the songs we already recorded so you can keep tweaking them. And this is the best stuff we've ever done. I know everybody says that about their new stuff, but I'm so excited about this. The fact the 'metal Dogs' have a new album coming out too has really brought the best out in us! It has to be the best we can do to put these wankers to bed!

What's the story with the 'Punk Rock Power' tattoo you've got on your neck?
Sally was very poorly a few years ago. She's always had like a barrel tummy. She's not greedy, she doesn't over-eat or anything, so we just thought it was one of those things. Eventually she got poorly with irritable bowel syndrome, and she went into hospital for an x-ray and they said, 'Forget about the irritable bowel, you've got a tumour the size of a rugby ball in your tummy, and it could well have been growing in you since you were a little girl.' They tested it, and it was non-cancerous, thank fuck for that, but if it kept growing, it would start to push on her internal organs, so she had to get rid of it. About two years ago, January 2012, she went into hospital, and it took them over eight hours to remove it, after they'd said it would only be four, because the tumour had attached itself to the aorta artery. They said that if there hadn't been a vein specialist in the hospital, she could easily have died, which was a shock in itself. Anyway, the consultant we'd been seeing had to fuck off for a few days, and this new consultant came in, and took me, and Josh, my son-in-law, to one side, and told us that Sally was dying. All the tests had apparently been wrong, and she was riddled with cancer, and she only had a few weeks left to live. And we've been married over thirty years, she's my soul-mate in everything I do, my best friend, and I was distraught. I said, 'Is there a Plan B?' And he said, 'No, she's dying.' So I started ringing up family and friends, to tell them this terrible news, and the most amazing thing happened . . . over the next week or so, the whole punk scene turned up in Bristol . . . people came from all over, Scotland, London, Cornwall . . . people flew in from abroad . . . Sal was lay there, full of tubes . . .

I was in bits, I was drunk and high . . . Staff and Gabba and Danny, those three guys came in to look after me every day . . . but there was somewhere in the region of 70–100 punks came down to see us that week, to say goodbye to Sal and look after me, to show their love and support for both of us . . . They had to open a whole new room up for everyone! And it showed what a great community there is in punk rock – you won't find it in any other music scene. We look after our own.

Anyway, when our proper consultant got back, he said we'd been misinformed, he was so sorry, and he rushed her into dialysis, and she survived! They lied to us, and we could probably sue them, but we don't want to – how can you take money out of the NHS? But what a wonderful story! How the punk rock family rallied around us . . .

So the future is bright for the current band and new album?

After twenty-seven members in the English Dogs, after all the disappointments, after searching and searching, to finally be with the lineup I'm with, and to be doing the music we're doing at the moment, is utterly fantastic. It's taken thirty years to get here, but we're finally a band of brothers: Grizz on drums, Tat on bass and Nick, my closest friend, on guitar. They're the nicest, kindest people you'll ever meet, genuinely beautiful blokes . . . So anyone out there in Book Land, frustrated that they can't find that magic lineup, don't stop trying – it is out there, just believe in yourself and keep going and one day you'll find it . . . unless you're a cunt, then you won't – and I have no sympathy for you.

ABH

A.B.H. formed in early 1981 in Lowestoft, Suffolk. They originally went under the name Stretcher Case, and had a set made up of punk covers, by all the obvious bands like the Pistols and The Damned, but once they'd cut their teeth with a few well-received shows, they soon realised it was easier to write their own material, and a brand new punk band was formed.

The original line-up was Nigel Boulton on bass, Tony Cullingford behind the kit, Pete Chilvers providing vocals and Chris Brinton on guitar, although he was soon replaced by Steven Curtis, who brought the harder-edged skinhead influence to the band's sound that helped define A.B.H.'s subsequent musical output. They renewed their efforts on the live front, slowly building a local following, and even managed to secure their first London support slot, opening up for Chelsea at the Oxford Street club Gossips.

"We saw ourselves as a new breed of bands from our region and wanted to demonstrate this by breaking away from the usual round of parochial gigs," remembers bassist Nigel, acknowledging at the same time the problems they faced trying to get themselves noticed whilst out in a relative backwater. "We made strenuous efforts to play in London which, as ever, was the heartland of music in all its forms. This involved a lot of effort because of the costs of hiring a van, the time involved in travelling; the midweek bookings were especially difficult for those who had jobs. We weren't able to be available for last-minute gigs, nor were we there when it mattered to capitalise on rumour and gossip, to establish useful contacts and generally become known on the circuit of venues, promoters and bands. The possibility of moving to London was never discussed and I think that it was our separation from a centre of influence that, in part at least, was responsible for our lack of real success and our eventual demise. I say this knowing full well that because we were so channelled and blinkered, any success we might have had would be very transient. Of course, with the energy and enthusiasm of un-jaded youth a flash of success was all we wanted; I think our sights were always set fairly low!"

A.B.H. in rehearsal, 1982
L–R: Nigel Boulton, Pete Chilvers, Tony Cullingford, Steven Curtis

Further shows were undertaken whenever possible, with the likes of Broken Bones, The Exploited and their near-neighbours The Adicts, and a strong friendship was cemented with Peter And The Test Tube Babies following a triumphant show in Great Yarmouth. In July 1982, the band felt confident enough in itself to enter Hillside Studios in Ipswich to record their first demo tape. "More by luck than judgement", according to Nigel, the band emerged with a terrific debut recording as the result of their labours, and two of these songs, 'Country Boy Rocker' and 'Wanna Riot', eventually ended up appearing on No Future's 'A Country Fit For Heroes, Volume 2' compilation album.

Sadly, these were the only songs to actually get an official release during the band's all-too-short existence.

More great gigs followed, opening for, amongst others, The Partisans and The Varukers, and the band even clawed their way to victory at the Halesworth Battle of the Bands! One of the gigs Nigel would rather forget though was at the Regis Rooms in Kings Lynn in late 1983.

"Most of the bands playing that night were from London," he recalls. "I think we were the only 'local' band there, and it was a hundred mile round trip even for us. The atmosphere was tense from the outset – perhaps the other bands had had some trouble on the way – and there was soon a police presence at the venue. This was unusual as, despite our own misplaced belief in how radical, important and dangerous A.B.H. were, we hadn't had any problems with the police at previous gigs.

"I suspect though that there had been some unfriendly interaction between the locals and 'the interlopers up from the Smoke'. The result of it all was that halfway through the set of the first band (us!), the police demanded that we finish and that was it for the night. By this time it seemed that things were likely to get nasty. Fortunately, we had got there under our own steam so didn't have to stooge around; we packed up our gear and left with as much dignity as we could!"

A.B.H.'s second demo, recorded once again at Hillside, in 1983, saw them building upon the solid foundations established with their first effort, and included the song 'Don't Mess With The SAS'. In 1984, long after the band's demise, the song actually appeared on Syndicate's 'The Oi Of Sex' compilation, but before then, they also used the song in their own video, one of the few punk promo clips shot in that period. Shot by a friend that was at Lowestoft College of Further Education, it's a wonderful little time capsule, with the band in full flight, wild-eyed and sneering and obviously more than a little uncomfortable with the presence of a camera in their rehearsal room.

Despite such encouraging signs, the band disintegrated before the year was out, citing the obligatory 'musical differences' as one of the main reasons for their split. Nigel and Pete went on to do a stint with The Silly Vicars, and Nigel still plays in bands even today.

"In the circumstances we did the best we could in the way we thought was best. Of course, times then were very different from now and with the benefit of hindsight and experience there are many things that we should have done differently, or not at all, as well as things we missed out on.

"I would have liked to have been less derivative in terms of our sound; to have had more time to experiment; to have had more money, equipment, and opportunities to do more and better recordings and gigs. All these would have been useful but in the end those things aren't really regrets, only observations on how it might have been different, not necessarily better."

AT A GLANCE:
Captain Oi!'s 'The Oi Collection: ABH/Subculture' CD (1998) compiles the whole of both A.B.H. demos onto one disc, alongside ten tracks from Cambridge's Subculture, and includes extensive liner notes by Nigel.

THE ADICTS

T he Adicts began life as The Pinz, in their hometown of Ipswich back in 1976. They scored many Indie Chart hits in the Eighties, and are still together making great music with the same line-up – Keith 'Monkey' Warren, vocals, Mel Ellis, bass, Pete Davison, guitar, and his brother, Michael 'Kid' Davison, drums – to this day. "I think we all started for different reasons," recalls Monkey, of their distant origins. "Pete and Kid were already playing on their own, using pillows for drums in the front room. Mel had just failed the audition for Nik Kershaw's band (too tall, apparently) and I was a punk without a cause. Exactly what year that was may vary depending on who you talk to. Some say '76, some say '77. I think I have a flyer from March '77, but before that we had played our first show in a scout hut in Aldeburgh, Suffolk – not exactly top of the list for all time top punk venues! We strung a rope across the room to keep the 'crowd' back and had a motor bike for a lighting rig. As far as our musical education goes, I think Pete took music at school, and Kid just liked to hit things. I don't know where Mel got his 'talent' from but it seems to run in the family. I still can't play anything."

They soon changed their name to The Adicts, and became known for their distinctive Clockwork Orange 'Droog' image, which, along with their urgent, uptempo music and light-hearted lyrics, helped set them very much apart from the rest of the genre.

"We became The Adicts because The Pinz was such a shit name," deadpans Kid. "At the early gigs we just used to wear punk clothes, but never anything bought, like those posers who went down to Kings Road. After a while though, black came in and it all became boring, so we started to dress in white to be different, and 'Clockwork Orange' had been a major influence on us, though not for the violence, more the teenage angst…"

"The 'Clockie' thing didn't really evolve until about 1979," reckons Monkey. "And the image is an amalgam of many things. It may have been a conscious effort to set ourselves against the somewhat unimaginative appearance of early Eighties punk bands or just a perception that looking a certain way might be interesting and entertaining. We got some stick from some of the self-appointed 'real' punk bands for not being punk enough, or whatever, but I don't remember anyone really making an issue of the image… other than saying I must be a poof!"

The band spent the next few years gigging and building up a strong local following. They even managed, after their very first London show, at the Brecknock, to secure a basic deal with Dining Out Records, who released the 'Lunch With The Adicts' EP in 1980. It was a scintillating, cock-sure debut, surprisingly well executed for an opening gambit, and featured four songs, two of which remain constants in the band's live set even today: the pounding mid-tempo 'Easy Way Out' and the irresistible 'Straight Jacket'.

"We wrote songs about unemployment, disillusionment, and all that happy stuff, but that was really a conformity with the non-conformists," remembers Monkey, of their early searchings for that little something a bit different. "We just did what punk bands did until we developed our own style and voice. It was, and is, all about the band as a concept, not just the music, but the look, the attitude, the essence of The Adicts that is not found anywhere else.

"I remember the early days as a time of discovery, adventure, and intellectual and artistic awakening. Punk rock encouraged people from small towns all over the UK to think differently and to take a different path. My mum wasn't too pleased when I quit my job and came home with purple hair, but it was a personal revolution. I may have been a fashion victim, but I was also a liberated mind ready for anything. The gigs were also a strange mix of freedom and fear. Punks from different towns united at shows and vented while the band was on. But as soon as you went your separate ways, you had to watch your back for lads looking for a weirdo to kick in."

"I was a rather violent youth and spent half the time scrapping with the neighbours or at a football match," admits Pete. "The gigs were a mixture of curiosity, fun and hate for most of the punters; ducking ashtrays or pint glasses was a new skill we soon learned. I once played whilst having darts thrown at me; one stuck in my guitar and another in my leg! Now, that's not nice, is it?"

The Adicts, L–R (foreground): Monkey (behind hands!), Kid, Mel, Pete (Roadies Laurence and Tim in the background) (Pic: Tony Mottram)

Within a year, The Adicts unveiled their first long-player, 'Songs Of Praise', through Dwed Wecords, their 'own label' but essentially a division of Fall Out. It took all the unique ingredients that had made the 'Lunch With...' EP so memorable, and refined and developed them, producing several of the band's greatest moments. Quite contrary to the relentless thrash that was becoming so popular at the time, The Adicts dared to incorporate cheeky melodies and overtly pop overtones into their sound. 'Tango' even sounds like early Ants...

"There might be a bit of the Antz in there. In fact I have recently been sectioned under the mental health act," laughs Monkey, before commenting on other possible influences, "I don't think there were any other bands around Ipswich that were inspirational, except perhaps the shitty pop covers bands that we definitely didn't want to be like. Once we got into the band I didn't listen to that much other music; what we were doing was enough for me. It wasn't until several years later that I caught up and realized that Pete and Kid had nicked bits off everyone from Lou Reed to Lulu...!

"'Songs Of Praise' is my favourite release, not just for the music but for the way that we did it all ourselves. I can still remember being in the back of the van just after we had picked up the first pressing and the LP sleeves. I think we were all getting off on the fumes from the glue. I took the first record and put it in the first sleeve and we all cheered as I held it up. I wish I knew what happened to that one!"

Arguably the best song on the album, and certainly the most anthemic, 'Viva La Revolution', was chosen as a single. Ably backed by 'Numbers' and a non-LP track – the superbly-titled '(My Baby Got Run Over By A) Steamroller' – it spent over three months in the Indie Charts, cementing The Adicts' rapidly-growing reputation as one of the most innovative and popular bands of punk's new wave.

November 1982 saw the release of their sophomore album, 'The Sound Of Music', for Razor Records. It was preceded by two weeks with a single, the ludicrously infectious 'Chinese Takeaway'. Both releases were classic Adicts, bubbling over with their own unique wacky energy, and it was hardly surprising when they took the charts by storm. 'Chinese Takeaway', backed by the brilliant 'Too Young' and a cover of 'You'll Never Walk Alone', spent four months in the Indies, peaking at No. 7, whilst the album managed No. 2, only being kept from the coveted top spot by Toyah's 'Warrior Rock'. It even dented the Top 100 of the National Charts, no mean feat right before Christmas!

More chart success followed when the anthemic 'Bad Boy' single was released in May 1983, so it was hardly surprising when the major labels started sniffing around the band, and that summer The Adicts signed to the Warner Bros. offshoot, Sire. It was the start of troubled times for the band, as both they and their label struggled to find a commercial compromise somewhere between easy listening radio hits and deviously daring punk rock.

Incredibly, they appeared on the kids' TV show, 'Cheggers Plays Pop', albeit as The Fun Adicts, so as not to blatantly offend any parents who were tuning in. Less than a year later they were known as ADX, for the disappointing 'Tokyo' single, produced by the ex-Vapors frontman Dave Fenton. By their own admission, it is the band's least favourite of their own releases ("It was a much better song than the production made it out to be," quips Monkey). Thankfully it was backed by (as well as the rather bizarre, but fun, 'ADX Medley') 'The Odd Couple', a speedy track that reassured their diehard punk fans that the band still had some fire in their bellies.

Kid plays down the reasons for the name changes as, "Because we couldn't spell! And one was for TV; they thought The Adicts sounded too naughty! But ADX was just because we couldn't spell!" Monkey and Pete however, despite having nothing but good things to say about Keith Chegwin ("Our mums loved it! Our one and only UK TV appearance!"), have a slightly more cautionary tale to tell.

Monkey: "That was bit of a dodgy period for us. There was some perception that 'Adicts' had negative connotations for radio and TV. We had signed to Sire who were going to make us big, and we were taken in by it. They did nothing for us and we were left to pick up the pieces..."

"We were controlled at this time by record labels and we were too slow to pick up on it," sighs Pete. "And we were so out of our heads back then it's all such a blur. I remember some dictator from Sire wanted us to sack Monkey 'cos he couldn't sing... but of course we instead gave them shit for being a bunch of cunts. We kept the Monkey at the cost of fame and fortune!"

Pete of The Adicts, during soundcheck
(Pic: Tony Mottram)

Another lame single followed in May '85, the horribly dull 'Falling In Love Again', and when that failed to rake in sufficient coinage Sire promptly – not to mention, predictably – lost interest in the band and went searching elsewhere for the next big thing. Reverting to their intended moniker, and back on Razor once more, The Adicts bounced back spectacularly with the excellent 'Smart Alex' album.

As well as their hit single, 'Bad Boy', and a remixed (but still rubbish) version of 'Tokyo', the album features a whole host of styles and themes, all indelibly stamped with The Adicts' own quirky identity. From the sultry singalong of 'California', via the stomping, almost-rockabilly 'Crazy' to the lilting, Fifties-ish 'Runaway', no one could ever accuse 'Smart Alex' of being generic, and it remains one of their most endearing and adventurous albums. The punters were obviously pleased to see the band back on form, too, as it sold well and spent over a month in the Indie Charts, peaking at a very respectable No. 7.

But yet more turmoil was just around the corner. Parting ways with Razor, The Adicts expanded to a five piece, with the addition of keyboardist James Harding, who still plays with the band today on their studio recordings. They released the 'Bar Room Bop' 12" on their own Dwed Wecords (again through Fall Out), and then in 1986, they ended up recording their next album in Germany, a country where they had – and still have – great success touring. 'Fifth Overture', was initially released by German label, Gama, before being picked up for the UK by Fall Out a year later, albeit with a different sleeve, but it was a poorly promoted, relatively weak effort from the band, that indulged in far too much New Wave pomposity for its own good, and it sank virtually without trace.

"Even then, we always regarded ourselves as a punk band," insists Monkey. "I had big arguments with Geordie, our manager at the time, when he put 'New Wave' on the posters. I also had a big argument about selling out when the price to get in went up from 35p to 45p! I don't think we have ever had conscious aspirations or agendas. We get together, the songs come out. If we like it, we're happy."

"Yes, of course we were, and we still are, a punk band," agrees Pete. "The music may be interpreted through the many different styles we have, but at the end of the day, we are a punk band... aren't we?"

Arguments over genre specifics didn't stop the band from enjoying tremendous live success though, and they toured all over the world, even releasing a live album (recorded in front of their loyal German audience), 'Rockers Into Orbit', in 1988.

"During that gig someone pulled me off stage and booted me in the guts and then everyone piled in," laughs Monkey. "We had all that on tape too. I don't know why it never made the final cut.

"Kid got drunk and disappeared, or passed out, all over Asia, America, and Europe," he continues, recalling some of their other on-the-road antics. "We've got lost, robbed, ripped off, attacked and arrested... well, I got arrested at least! We've puked, pissed, slept, shagged, and shat together all over the world. We've been treated like kings and accused of being queens... well, I have!

"There are of course hundreds of stories and each member has their own version of the truth. One of my favourites, and one of the most disgusting things happened at the end of a European tour in the mid-Eighties. We had been on the road for weeks and ended up in Hamburg for the last show.

"Afterwards we were at the hotel. A party was revolving through about four rooms. After a while most of us were in one room. Soon someone had put their arse through a window and someone else had pulled the sink from the wall.

"Yet another genius decided to soak the room with the shower and there was the usual surfeit of girls, booze, and drugs. Somehow we got bored with this and the notion of a puking contest was suggested. This apparently, was an entertaining idea and a bunch of us sat around the waste paper basket. After a couple of rounds of retching and gagging (I think there were some rules but they were never written down!), all that had slopped into the bin was about an inch of bile.

"To make things more interesting it was proposed that, for a sum of money, someone should drink the colon cocktail we had regurgitated. We all dug deep in our pockets and began to throw pfennigs and marks on the table. On seeing the pile of cash, our 'Bastard Roadie Number One' took up the challenge. We all moved close to the broken sink and he lifted the bin to his lips. He put it down again.

"Several times he raised it to his lips and balked. Finally he got the rim on his bottom lip and began to tip the bin. As the slime slid towards his mouth someone – it might have been me – said, 'And you have to gargle'.

"He didn't stop; he opened up, threw back his head and gargled the stomach contents of about half a dozen punks. He didn't throw up, but he might have screamed and jumped around a lot. Victorious, he grabbed the money... which when converted back to sterling came to about two quid. It wasn't a very successful tour!"

Monkey of The Adicts, one of the more inventive and colourful bands of the Eighties (Pic: Tony Mottram)

Eventually though, the band grew tired of the road and took a break for several years to lick their wounds and nurse their creative muses back to full power. They returned, without James Harding, in 1992 with '27' ("Because numbers 5 through to 26 weren't very good!"), for US label Cleopatra.

A much harder and more satisfying album than 'Fifth Overture', it was picked up for Europe a year later by Anagram, who allowed the band to incorporate an interactive Adicts board game into the sleeve art, which had participants doing everything the band themselves enjoyed doing whilst on tour, from rolling spliffs to eating vindaloo.

Whilst not as inspired as any of the first three albums, '27' was a good return to form. The speedy opener 'Angel' reassures you immediately that you're back in classic Adicts territory, and the rousing singalong 'Fuck It Up' just proves that you don't have to play fast to sound anarchic. The album even features a belated sequel to '(My Baby Got Run Over By A) Steamroller' in the shape of '7:27', which sees a train to Liverpool Street taking the place of the original automaton!

It was to be another ten long years before The Adicts deemed the time right to enter another recording studio. They went into Earles Studio in Ventura, California during 2002, where they wrote, rehearsed and recorded all nineteen cuts of their most recent album, 'Rise And Shine', there and then. Basically relying upon the unique chemistry they've developed over their long, eventful history to help shape some of their strongest and most diverse songs to date. They licensed the album from their own Dee Dee Records to Captain Oi! as part of an extensive plan to reissue the majority of the band's back catalogue.

"We've never been afraid to experiment or to play just what we feel," reckons Kid of the new album. "The new stuff is still fast, fun and furious, but there are a few songs that will completely blow your head off because they're so different! And we've got Pete in the studio who is a genius. Overall we are still a good team…"

Meanwhile Monkey tries to shed some light on where they vanished to during that decade following '27'. "We did a few tours here and there, but basically we all went off and did normal things to see if we liked it. Some of us liked it better than others. Kid had kids, Mel had letters to deliver, Pete had other bands to produce… and I sat forlornly in my room, putting on my make-up and waiting for the phone to ring!

"Our message, such as it is, has always been, have fun," he continues, attempting to define the secret of their longevity. "That's timeless and appeals to everyone. If your songs are about the political state of the country, or a victim of police brutality in the Eighties, then the agenda that you established for yourself becomes obsolete. You become an anachronism…

"To be honest, I never thought our music would be remembered in years to come. I used to be happy if someone remembered a song straight after we played it. Actually I used to be even happier if we remembered the song while we played it!

"The only thing I would have done differently," he says, in typical deadpan Adicts fashion, "is to have been in a different band, with different people and with different songs. Oh, and no make-up. Other than that it's been perfect!

"In 2002, we added Mel's brother, 'Scruff', on rhythm guitar, which has worked out very nicely… two sets of brothers and a monkey! Have a banana!"

SELECT DISCOGRAPHY:
7"s:
'Lunch With The Adicts' (Dining Out, 1980)
'Viva La Revolution' (Fall Out, 1982)
'Chinese Takeaway' (Razor, 1982)
'Bad Boy' (Razor, 1983)

'Tokyo' (Sire, 1984)
'Falling In Love Again' (Sire, 1984)
'Bar Room Bop' (Fall Out, 1985)
'Angel' (Cleopatra, 1992)

LPs:
'Songs Of Praise' (Dwed Wecords, 1981)
'Sound Of Music' (Razor, 1982)
'This Is Your Life' (Fall Out, 1985)
'Smart Alex' (Razor, 1985)
'Fifth Overture' (Gama, 1986)
'Rockers Into Orbit' (Fall Out, 1988)
'27' (Cleopatra, 1992)

CDs:
'Rise And Shine' (Captain Oi!, 2002)

AT A GLANCE:
Most of the band's back catalogue is now easily available again, complete with bonus tracks and additional artwork, thanks to a comprehensive CD reissue programme by Captain Oi!, who also issued the band's latest studio album. 'The Complete Adicts Singles Collection' (1994), part of Anagram's excellent Punk Collectors series, is also a great place to start, featuring, as you might expect, all of the band's brilliant 7"s in chronological order.

SPECIAL DUTIES

One of the more controversial acts of the time, Colchester's Special Duties' strong divisive stance against certain factions of the punk scene, as well as helping promote the band, eventually led to their undoing. Their biggest selling release, the 'Bullshit Crass' single, was ironically also the one that got them blacklisted by not only many of their peers and potential listeners, but also several influential distributors. They nonetheless turned out some fine obnoxious punk rock in their time, and have even reformed in recent years, meeting with considerable success.

"I was fifteen in 1977, which was when I first heard The Ramones and The Pistols, and I just loved the energy," begins vocalist Steve 'Arrogant' Green. "I'd always liked music... before punk I liked glam rock. Stuff like Slade and T Rex. In fact, I always thought that glam and punk were never that far apart, and punk was a natural progression of glam's loud guitars and drums.

"I think at fifteen, most kids wanna be a popstar... except 'pop' to us was punk rock! But for the first time you were being told by your idols that you didn't have to be able to play a guitar or have a trained voice – you could just give it a go! And because we had role models like The Ramones and The Lurkers, you could actually sit down and learn that stuff quite quickly. You didn't have to be ultra-talented... well, to actually write the songs you did, but to sit down and copy them was quite easy.

"So by the time we'd managed to buy some amps, and hassled our parents for money for guitars, and things like that, you suddenly found that you could get together in the garage and blast out songs like 'Shadow' and 'Blitzkrieg Bop' quite easily! And once you had those three chords sorted, it wasn't that hard to change them around and make your own tunes... it all started from there..."

The very first line-up of Special Duties coalesced in October 1977; Steve on vocals, bassist Steve 'Duty' Norris, guitarist Nigel Baker, accompanied by a seemingly 'revolving door' parade of various early drummers. The band was originally to be called X-pelled, but changed its name – rather opportunistically – to Special Duties when some badges fell conveniently from the back of a lorry!

Special Duties, 1998
L–R: Steve Duty, Stuart Bray, Steve Arrogant, Bart Povah

"We were going to get some badges done, but someone we knew had stolen a load of prefect's badges from a school in Colchester," laughs Steve. "And prefects in those schools were called Special Duties because they would stand in the doors, and they were head boys and that sort of thing. Anyway, they were quite nifty badges, and a box of about two hundred came into our possession, so we figured we could save ourselves some money if we just changed our name to Special Duties!"

The band was soon gigging regularly at local venues such as the Rock Club in Chelmsford, but their debut public performance was a little less orthodox. It took place on a Sunday afternoon in 1979... in a Marks & Spencers' loading bay!

"One day we decided we were going to put a gig on underneath the new precinct in Colchester town centre one Sunday lunchtime. We spread the word through the underground punk grapevine, and hundreds of punks turned up, and we set up and played in this precinct... we only actually knew one song, 'There'll Be No Tomorrow', so we played a fifteen-minute version! And considering that song is only two chords, and the verse is virtually the same as the chorus, it was a good job the police turned up and pulled the power on us and dispersed the crowd before everyone got bored and lynched us! Even for us it was getting monotonous..."

In 1980, Bart Povah ("The first member who could actually play properly") joined from local band Day Release. The band recorded their first demo soon after, at Colchester's Albert Street Studios, with a guy called Mick playing drums and Nigel actually moving to bass, because Steve Duty had temporarily left the band at the time. The demo sold well at shows, and even earned the band a glowing review in Sounds. It also secured them their first basic recording deal.

"We'd sent it to John Peel," reveals Steve. "And he sent a nice letter back, saying that it was interesting, but we needed to get a bit tighter if we were to stand a chance of getting a recording contract. We also sent it to Charnel House Records, who'd already put out the Anti-Establishment single '1980', and they rang us back, saying they'd actually release a single straight off the demo. But we thought, rather than put two demo tracks on there, we'd go in to re-record 'Violent Society', and also 'Colchester Council' which we'd written in the meantime."

In quite a remarkable coup for the time, Steve managed to secure the services of Lurkers' vocalist, Howard Wall, to produce their first ever vinyl offering.

"I used to go the Fulham Greyhound and watch bands down there, and The Lurkers used to play there a helluva lot. I got to know Howard Wall quite well, and he was stuck for a lift home after a gig one night, so I said tongue-in-cheek, 'I'll give you a lift if you record our single for us!' He gave me his number, and so, three weeks later, I rang him up, told him that I'd booked the studio and, we needed him to be producer... and he was true to his word! It was really good. To spend a whole day in the studio with Howard Wall for us at the time was really 'making it', 'cos he was one of the people who got us into being in a band in the first place!"

By the time of the recording, the returning Steve Duty had replaced Nigel, and Mick had given way to Mark Gregory behind the drum kit. The resulting single was raw and primitive, but blessed with infectious, brash rhythms and hooks, and it did much to cement their reputation as a rapidly growing band. However, Special Duties themselves didn't feel that they were growing fast enough in relation to the scene around them, and they soon moved to Rondelet Records and let go drummer Mark Gregory (now playing with Condemned 84) whose tender age was hindering them when getting shows at many venues. He was replaced by Stuart Bray, late of the Waxwork Dummies.

"We started the band as a result of '77 punk, but before we knew what had happened, with all the lineup changes and the demos and the Charnel House thing, it was 1980, and we were starting to get left behind," explains Steve. "The second wave of punk had started, and all these bands like The Partisans and Blitz were signed to No Future and releasing records... Anti Pasti were on Rondelet... so we sent a demo and a copy of the Charnel House single to both of those labels. No Future said they liked it but they already had too many bands on the label, but Rondelet wrote back and said they'd be interested in re-releasing the 'Violent Society' single...

"We'd already recorded that song for the first demo, then re-recorded it for Charnel House – although we weren't too happy with how it came out – and we weren't too keen to do it yet again! But they offered us a three single/one album deal, if we would agree to record those two songs for them. We were really chuffed, because Anti Pasti were one of our favourite bands at the time... although the old adage about not getting to know your heroes in case you're disappointed became reality for us, because Anti Pasti really didn't like us at all; they resented us being on the label, and even tried to pull their songs off the Rondelet compilation album 'The Only Alternative' if we were going to be on it! They didn't like our lyrics, apparently!"

So, the first Special Duties single for Rondelet was basically a reworking of the Charnel House 'Violent Society' 7", with a stronger production, new (not necessarily improved) artwork and an extra track in the shape of 'It Ain't Our Fault'. The single did modestly well, but it was with their follow-up release that the band started to finally come into their own. The 'Police State' EP featured four songs that were not only faster and shorter, but more aggressive and delivered with a fierce, focused intensity, topped off to great effect by Steve's distinctive tonsil-shredding bark. It came out in May '82, and broke the Indie Top Thirty, remaining in the chart for two months.

"We've always been a very lazy band," admits the vocalist, "And we've always spent most of our time drinking, so whenever anyone booked a studio, we'd get it done as quickly as possible so we could get down the pub. We never wanted to spend much time with the actual production side of things, so that got left to the guy in the studio, who probably had very little allegiance to punk. So we always had a bad sound, but I think a lot of bands back then often did.

"By the time we came to do 'Police State', we knew that we were not as powerful as the bands like Discharge who we were trying to compete with, and we knew that if we were to stand any chance of lasting any period of time, we had to get better songs and a proper production. So we went up to Rochdale to record that EP, and Mackie from Blitz and Helen from Violators came in on the day we recorded it. They offered us loads of advice and encouragement, and Mackie was almost coaching us, saying, 'Oh, you need to go and do that bit again' and stuff. So they were almost like the secret producers in a way, and to this day I think that's quite a strong EP."

The band and label decided to capitalise on the EP's success by rushing out the debut Special Duties album, '77 In '82', soon after. A little too soon in fact for the band, who went into FSR Studios, Birmingham, with Mike Stone at the desk, not as prepared as maybe they ought to have been.

"We were never happy with the production on the first two singles, so we recorded those three songs yet again, and then we did another three or four songs… and one of those was our cover of 'First Time'. And then Mike Stone said, 'What's next?' and we all looked at each other, 'cos we didn't have anything else finished! Our live set at the time was just made up of the singles and some cover versions. He started ranting about it being an eight minute album, and stormed out, saying 'I'll see you tomorrow morning, make sure you've got some more songs!' It was all Rondelet's fault, 'cos they booked the studio for us to go and do an album, but they never asked us whether or not we had enough songs!

"And we literally stayed in the studio all night, writing songs, and stuff like 'Delayed Reaction', 'Distorted Truth', 'CND' and 'Britain In '81' were all written that day! If we tried to do something like that now, it'd be taking the piss out of people, but we lived and breathed punk rock, and to sit and write a punk rock album wasn't a chore to us really… it was a bit of a luxury, in fact. We were getting paid to do something we loved. And I was angry and young and had something to say, so I didn't have any problems writing all the lyrics that quickly."

The results belie the conditions under which the record was made, and the album is a damn fine collection of belligerent punk rock. However, both the title and the choice of cover they included (the aforementioned Boys' song) were an indication of the band's growing disenchantment with the scene they were a part of. It seemed that Special Duties were nostalgic for the excitement of their teens at the age of twenty-one!

"By the time it got to 1982, almost all the melodies and tunes had gone out of the window! Bands like Disorder and Chaotic Dischord seemed to have taken all the catchy choruses out of the scene. You went from the two-minute singalong songs by bands like The Ramones and The Buzzcocks, and all of a sudden it was five minutes of someone shouting over what sounded like a chainsaw! And to be honest, I could see us getting sucked into all that speed-freak hardcore stuff, because that's what people wanted to hear, but we still tried to cling to a bit of melody as well.

"But this glue-sniffing intimidating atmosphere that you started to get at gigs in the early Eighties was nothing like what it was in '77. Back then you could go and see a gig, and although the audience was wild and rebellious, there was a bit more intelligence attached to it. It was just starting to get me down, driving hundreds of miles to play somewhere and half the people who came to see us had their heads stuck in glue bags! It was disappointing to see that happening to punk rock."

As a result of this rising indignation, the band began rallying against things they perceived as destroying the traditional punk scene. As mentioned earlier, the resulting 'Bullshit Crass' 7" was both the band's best-selling release yet ultimately the one that spelled their untimely demise. It came complete with a Crass-style cover and a chanted intro of 'Fight Crass, not punk' that parodied one of that anarcho band's best-known songs.

"It was the fact they said 'Punk was dead', and they played this really tuneless music," spits Steve, when asked about his distaste for the band. "Also, none of the punk bands I was into ever preached at their audience. I mean, The Clash were political, and had some very intelligent lyrics about the state of society, but they never really preached. Crass were just so extreme, I saw them as almost a religious cult, and I didn't think they were doing these young kids who were getting into them any good in the long run. We live in one of the best countries in the world, but they were convincing everyone that it was one of the worse.

"Everything I said about them at the time, I meant, and I still feel as strongly about it now as I did back then. It wasn't a publicity stunt or anything… if it was, it wasn't a very good one, to tell everybody that we hated their favourite band! We alienated almost everybody! It sold quite well, but that may have been because it looked a bit like a Crass record, and their fans were so stupid they thought it was one!"

The resulting storm of controversy in the music papers of the time actually led to Rough Trade and Small Wonder refusing to stock the record, and had such influential bands as the Dead Kennedys keen to publicly distance themselves from the Duties.

Not long after the single, Rondelet Records split in two, and Special Duties were the first band signed to Expulsion, a new label set up in its wake. Their 1983 'Punk Rocker' single was their last gasp of defiance before calling it a day.

"I kinda knew that was going to be the last record. The Crass thing sort of opened up a whole new arm of punk rock, which was much more doom and gloom, everybody wearing black... everything that I loved had been sucked out of the scene. They turned the whole outlook of punk from this colourful, happy community to this downtrodden nihilistic movement. I just didn't want to be associated with it all anymore."

The years passed, and although Steve kept in touch with the punk scene, he was unaware of the impact his band had made around the world until Captain Oi! reissued the '77 In '82' album on CD in 1995. Encouraged by the response to the release, the band reformed in 1996, with their comeback single 'Mutt' coming out through One Stop Music that same year. Split singles with Red Flag 77 (for German label, Knock Out) and Japanese punks The Creed (for Bricks Records, The Creed's own label) soon followed, and in 1997, Captain Oi! released Special Duties' belated second album, '77 In '97'. Another split single with the aptly–named US band, Violent Society for GMM Records never materialised, although the songs eventually saw the light of day two years later as a 7" on Data Records. The band even recorded a football single, 'Wembley! Wembley!', to celebrate Steve's beloved Colchester United reaching the 1997 Auto Windscreens Cup Final!

"Yeah, that's my proudest moment! The rest of the band probably don't think the same, but that made it all worthwhile for me. I managed to combine my two greatest loves of punk rock and football, and the actual team came in the studio and did the backing vocals. In fact, they still run out to that song!"

Another dream came true in July the following year when The Duties flew to the States and played CBGB's in New York, one of punk rock's truly legendary clubs. They couldn't resist releasing their set as a limited live CD, called quite simply 'Live At CBGB's 1998', on their own self-titled label.

Special Duties have come a long way from torturing two chords under a shopping precinct and even today make live appearances at the occasional festival. Ironically though, given the original intention, whenever their name is mentioned, the word 'Crass' is never far away in the conversation... their nemesis to the bitter end?

SELECT DISCOGRAPHY:
7"s:
'Violent Society' (Charnel House, 1980) – re–released by Rondelet in 1982
'Police State' (Rondelet, 1982)
'Bullshit Crass' (Rondelet, 1982)
'Punk Rocker' (Expulsion, 1983)
'Mutt' (One Stop Music, 1996)
'Wembley! Wembley!' (Captain Colchester, 1997) – CD only
'I Wish It Could Be '77' (Data, 1999) – also released by Soap 'N' Spikes (2000)

LPs:
'77 in '82' (Rondelet, 1982)
'77 in '97' (Captain Oi!, 1997) – CD and vinyl

AT A GLANCE:

Captain Oi!'s 1995 reissue of the debut album also features all of the band's Rondelet singles, as well as the early versions that appeared on the Charnel House 7", making it an essential purchase for anyone interested in the band's fiery early years. The 'Punk Singles Collection' (Captain Oi!, 1999) also features the latter-period 7"s, as well as bonus covers of The Exploited, The Killjoys and The Clash that appeared on various American tribute compilations in recent times.

NEWTOWN NEUROTICS

One listen to the first single, 'Hypocrite', by the Newtown Neurotics should be enough to convince anyone that they were never your average punk rock band. The title track is an honest, intelligent attack on the scene's poseurs, whilst the B-side, 'You Said No', as well as being an unashamed love song, is based around the heavy bass and choppy rhythm of traditional reggae. Even from their earliest recordings, they were a band who set their moral sights higher than most, and set about their task with a disarmingly honest passion.

Formed in Harlow during the heady days of late 1977 by guitarist/vocalist, Steve Drewett, they more than merit inclusion in this book about the second wave of punk because the majority of their works were released after 1980.

"I got into punk after seeing The Sex Pistols on the Bill Grundy show," admits Steve of his band's humble conception. "I'd already had an attempt to learn to play guitar before then, but had reluctantly given up as my girlfriend at the time wasn't interested in my musical side and was more concerned with us settling down together... and I wasn't really ready for that. The other thing that stopped me playing was the mindset of the time, that if you couldn't play the intro to Led Zeppelin's 'Stairway To Heaven' note perfectly, you weren't entitled to call yourself a musician and play in a band. The Pistols changed all that of course! Also, I had been so fed up with rock music as it was back then that I had started to get into reggae and was really pleased to find that it played such an important role in the punk scene.

"I started off as a consumer of punk, going to lots of live gigs but, taking the punk idea to the full, I had given up on going to stadium gigs or even large venue gigs. I wouldn't even go to see the current punk stars, I took the whole homegrown approach to live music and supported our own local punk scene and tried to create something in Harlow. I followed the first Harlow punk band, The Sods, and in doing so they started encouraging their audience and myself to start creating something for ourselves. They said, 'Look, here's three chords, go and form a group', and I took them seriously. I dusted off the guitar under my bed and realised I had already learnt the necessary three chords, so I was pretty much ready to go; all I needed was someone to play with. Once I had expressed the desire to form a band, The Sods had started offering me support gigs so the race was on; I needed a name, a bass player and a drummer and I'd be away."

The final piece of inspiration came when Steve attended a Ramones show at the Rainbow, on New Years Eve, with his friend Colin Dredd. As 1977 drew to a close, the Newtown Neurotics were born.

"This gig was eventually released by the Ramones as the 'It's Alive' album," recalls Steve proudly. "The inside cover of the album shows me with long fair hair down the front on one of the small photos! After the gig I asked Colin if he would play bass in a band with me, and he said 'Yes'... despite having never held a bass guitar in his life! I had a really cheap bass at home I'd been playing with to see if I wanted to be a bass player, and I said he could have that. I also had an old hi-fi amp he could plug it into, so all we needed were some speakers... and a drummer of course."

The band started writing and rehearsing as a two-piece, and actually did their first gig with a stand-in drummer.

"The first show was in the summer of 1978 at Standon Village Hall in Hertfordshire. I remember the stand-in drummer was called Martin, who was also playing in a Buntingford-based fun band called The Teenbeats. The name was especially funny because they had all left their teenage years behind long ago!"

Thankfully that gig had actually been organised by Tig Barber, who himself was a drummer, and when asked to join the band, he agreed.

The Newtown Neurotics were truly products of their environment, and chose their moniker as a direct result of the dreary town they had been brought up in, and the seeds of discontent that shaped them into the politically aware act they were to become were sown very early on.

"I think Harlow had entered a period of decline at the time the band had formed," explains the guitarist. "When it was originally built, it supplied people with a good clean environment and homes to live in and standard healthy entertainment like swimming and other sports activities. Harlow was once known as Pram Town because of the high proportion of babies to be found there... well, eventually those babies became teenagers, and they all soon found that, unless you were into sports, there was nothing to do. Youth music and culture were absent from the town and all that was available were boring youth centres that the County Council struggled to fill.

The politically-charged Newtown Neurotics, 1982 L-R: Simon Lomond, Steve Drewett, Colin Dredd (Pic: Tony Mottram)

"Actually, the real Newtown Neurotics were the parents of these teenagers who moved out of close knit communities in the East End with the promise of open spaces and new housing. What happened then was, all these new parents found they no longer had the benefit of that close community support network in this open plan new town, and isolation and frustration started to creep in, which was reflected in the children they brought up. This was not always a big problem, but it is the accumulation of groups of small problems that ultimately make us a product of our environment. The difference with us as a band was, we were not going to leave it there, we were going to sing about it!"

The aforementioned 'Hypocrite' single was released on the band's own No Wonder label, so named after they were rejected by Small Wonder Records. And, after an eventful mini-tour of Belgium, they quickly followed it up in 1980 with the wonderful 'When The Oil Runs Out' 7". Grimly prophetic lyrically, yet blessed with sublimely uplifting melodies, it has lost none of its provocative power even today.

"It's one of my most durable and topical lyrics," reckons Steve. "The song was inspired by a film I have managed to misname in print every time I've mentioned it, so let me put the record straight now; it's 'Three Days Of The Condor' which starred Robert Redford. The film is about war games the Americans played for invasion of the Middle East should the oil supplies of the western world ever be in jeopardy. In real life now, Saudi Arabia is seen by the Americans to be unstable and could fall into the hands of Islamic militants in the near future (remember Osama Bin Laden was originally a Saudi citizen). The invasion of Iraq was an attempt by the Americans to take control, and influence, of the oil supplies of the region and then they would be nearby if they should need to move into Saudi Arabia."

The band's ensuing output was no less intelligent. In 1982, after replacing drummer Tig with Simon Lomond, they signed to the short-lived CNT label, and released the anthemic 'Kick Out The Tories', probably the song they are best remembered for, even though the B-side, 'Mindless Violence', is the stronger of the two compositions. The single was also the first Neurotics release to trouble the Top Fifty of the Indie Charts, albeit for just a week, and 'Kick Out The Tories' was also included on the well-received 'Punk And Disorderly III: The Final Solution' compilation, where in many reviews it was singled out as one of the standout songs.

"We began singing about personal politics right at the start of our careers, when I was basically non-political but with a liberal hippy stance. That changed because the formation of the band coincided with Margaret Thatcher coming to power; the country then started to change and us with it. At the height of the British Empire, when Britain was at its most powerful, the working class was at its poorest. Thatcher's infatuation with Victorian values rang alarm bells for me, and I thought, 'What does a good punk band need?' Something to fight against', and so I became a lot more political."

1983 saw the release of 'Licensing Hours', yet another strong 7", before they moved to the larger, better-distributed Razor for their debut album, 'Beggars Can Be Choosers'. An accomplished diverse work, both lyrically and musically, it touched on subjects until then ignored by most punk bands, and unveiled the band's new-found confidence with daring melodies. As well as songs about apathy ('Wake Up') and sexual double standards ('No Respect'), the album even demonstrated a sly, self-effacing humour, not

Steve Drewett of Harlow's Newtown Neurotics (Pic: Tony Mottram)

least of all on 'Does Anyone Know Where The March Is?'

As an appetiser for the album, two months before it hit the racks, Razor released the band's 'Blitzkrieg Bop' single, their highly enjoyable Ramones cover, complete with new, more political lyrics. It was backed by a new version of 'Hypocrite', the first song the band had ever written and now sounding better than ever with a thicker production and more fire in the delivery. An additional Ramones cover (this time lyrically intact), 'I Remember You', appeared as a second B-side track.

"Well, The Ramones were a sort of template that I wanted to build on," enthuses Steve, when asked to explain his love of the seminal New Yorkers. "It was a simple equation: energy plus melody plus good song structure equals great rock'n'roll! I wanted to add passion and good lyrics to this mix and call it mine!"

Both the single and the album did well, with the latter spending six weeks in the Indies, and peaking at a very respectable No. 6. The Ramones influences continued unabated, with Steve guesting on Action Pact's cover of 'Rockaway Beach' for their 'Yet Another Dole Queue Song' EP. And the next Neurotics' single was 1984's 'Suzi Is A Heartbreaker', the title seemingly a nod to classic Ramones songs such as 'Sheena Is A Punk Rocker' and 'Suzy Is A Headbanger'. The lyrical content was nowhere near as 'dumbed down' though, with the A-side tackling media allegations that the riots were being co-ordinated by members of the (at the time) prolific CB radio network, and on the B-side 'Fools' was an inspired attack on fascist attitudes.

The single saw the band back on their own No Wonder label, and although it was a good seller, things were afoot in the Neurotics' camp. They dropped the 'Newtown' from their name, and signed to Jungle for their next single (a live version of 'Living With Unemployment' from their 'Beggars...' album) and three further albums, the remainder of their existence.

These latter releases have all the subtle power and rough-hewn harmonies of the earlier Newtown Neurotics material, as well as a daring diversity that saw the band utilising not only a piano but also a brass section for certain songs, lending a tremendous depth to their already profound sound.

"Most people just referred to us as The Neurotics in the end, anyway," explains Steve of the shortened moniker. "The name change also reflected the fact that the band had matured and changed; people who heard our early material on compilations and came to see the band live were expecting to see that band and we were no longer it. We also got sick to death of people who would call out for 'Kick Out The Tories' throughout our set because it was the only number they knew of ours whilst our main fans wanted to hear newer material.

"We eventually split because we were exhausted and Colin was ill. We had been playing together for ten years and Colin decided to call it a day. His health wasn't so good (he had pleurisy) and the sex, drugs and rock'n'roll (also read: travelling for hours in the back of a freezing/sweltering, smoke-filled van, boring soundchecks, bad food and no sleep!) lifestyle wasn't helping much. I didn't want to continue the band without Colin and the material I was beginning to write was so far removed from my first songs, I thought I could do with another band to play them. At this point I toyed with playing guitar for The Clash as they were going through some lineup changes at the time... but they didn't know this, and I decided against it in the end!"

SELECT DISCOGRAPHY:
7"s:
'Hypocrite' (No Wonder, 1979)
'When The Oil Runs Out' (No Wonder, 1980)
'Kick Out The Tories' (CNT, 1982)

'Licensing Hours' (CNT, 1983)
'Blitzkrieg Bop' (Razor, 1983)
'Suzi' (No Wonder, 1984)
'Living With Unemployment' (Jungle, 1986) – as The Neurotics

12"s:
'Living With Unemployment' (Jungle, 1986) – as The Neurotics
'Never Thought' (Jungle, 1988) – as The Neurotics

LPs:
'Beggars Can Be Choosers' (Razor, 1983)
'Repercussions' (Jungle, 1985) – as The Neurotics
'Kickstarting A Backfiring Nation' (Jungle, 1986) – as The Neurotics (live)
'Is Your Washroom Breeding Bolsheviks?' (Jungle, 1988) – as The Neurotics

AT A GLANCE:

The 'Punk Collection' on Captain Oi! (2001) rounds up all the band's No Wonder, CNT and Razor recordings, and also includes the 'Beggars...' album (arguably their finest moment) whilst Anagram's 'Punk Singles Collection' includes the latter-period EPs recorded as The Neurotics, but at the expense of any album tracks. And the 2003 Jungle reissue of the two Neurotics studio albums on one CD demonstrates just how the band lost none of their musical bite or political savvy as they matured.

ANTI ESTABLISHMENT

Formed in 1978 as Cardiac Arrest, but forced to change their name soon after when they learned of another band with the same name, Anti-Establishment were an underrated punk band from Epping who sadly split after three rather good singles. The band was put together by vocalist Gavin Gritton and guitarist Haggis, but they soon recruited drummer Nick Freeston, who hooked them up with rehearsal space at his local youth club, the Haunt in Ongar. He also found them a stand-in bassist, Matt Johnson, who afterwards went on to enjoy some major label chart success as The The. He was soon replaced by Colin Little, who remained with the band until after the release of their first single.

"It was always about the music for us," recalls Gavin. "Me and Haggis started going to the Marquee in Wardour Street in 1978, watching bands like The Saints, Penetration, Gloria Mundi and Chelsea, amongst others, and we just wanted to form a band of our own. It wasn't about politics, more just being a teenager in the late Seventies, trying to earn a living working in the factories. Our name was mainly my influence, being a fan of The Rolling Stones, who were widely regarded as being 'anti-establishment'."

The band debuted live in November, 1979, at Ingatestone Youth Club, and soon found themselves recording their first single for Charnel House, a small independent label whose only other release, as detailed earlier, was the 'Violent Society' EP by Special Duties. Somehow they managed to procure the services of one Rat Scabies, then the drummer of first wave punk legends The Damned, on the production stool.

"I met Rat whilst with Haggis, some time around 1979, at the Electric Ballroom in Camden Town," reveals Gavin. "He was at the bar with Lemmy of Motörhead. Haggis noticed him and had the idea to ask him to produce this single of ours as we had heard that he was producing bands. We nervously introduced ourselves and bought them both a drink; surprisingly one of them had a gin and tonic! Rat agreed to do it, and we exchanged phone numbers. At that time, meeting Rat Scabies was the most exciting thing to ever happen to us in our whole lives! To us, he was – and still is – a punk rock god!"

The result was '1980', a rather raw introduction to the band, that's described by Gavin now as 'A bit one dimensional'. Nonetheless, it possessed a certain rough charm and spent over a month in the Indie Charts, peaking at No. 13. It also raised their profile sufficiently to land them gigs with the likes of Vice Squad and Infa-Riot, the latter being the infamous Acklam Hall show on March 4th, 1981, that led to the departure of Colin Little from the band's ranks.

The only lineup shot of Anti-Establishment in existence, so excuse the quality...!

"The only real trouble we had had before then was at the Manor in Ipswich," says Gavin, "where Colin had been constantly spat at throughout the gig... which resulted in him hitting the young offender over the head with his bass! This brought the concert to an abrupt end!

"We did Acklam Hall because we knew the promoter, Gary Butterfield, and we had also been promised by Garry Bushell that if we got a couple of live reviews in Sounds, he would do a feature on us in the magazine – even though we weren't quite what he was into really, as we weren't skinheads. To be honest, we only did those gigs because that was all we could get at the time.

"I can't remember an awful lot about it, to be honest, but we played our set and it was pretty quiet as we were the first band on. Infa-Riot then played and I'm not sure whether they finished or not, because a gang of local youths came in and started a fight, and it turned into a Wild West-style free-for-all!

"This was the worst violence I'd ever seen in my life, even worse than at football, and people were throwing bricks at each other, using chairs as shields. We were not involved as we were upstairs backstage, where we saw a young boy brought back whose head was pumping blood, who was getting some medical help from the police who had just arrived.

"I can remember that Phil, our friend who had supplied the lights for the gig (as a favour!) had only one light left by the end – the rest had been used as missiles! And Colin's girlfriend, who had fainted at the sight of all the violence, and who I think had been hit, was being given a brandy to calm her down. This was the deciding factor that made Colin leave... and who could blame him?"

After some hasty auditions, Kevin 'Gluey' Read, 'A milkman from Leytonstone', filled Colin's shoes, and two demos were recorded at 8 Track Studio in Bishop Stortford, with the aim being to land a new record deal. Glass Records signed them in early 1982, and released their second 7", 'Future Girl', which saw the band making significant headway musically. Ushered in by a decidedly 'nice' acoustic intro, the song explodes into a rousing punk romp, very reminiscent of the early Damned material... which was no great surprise as Rat Scabies was once again at the desk during recording.

Rat also helped land the band a support slot with The Exploited, whose drummer was a friend of his, on their UK tour, but soon after, guitarist and co-founder Haggis announced his decision to concentrate on his career as a mechanic. He was replaced by Gary Dawson, who played on the band's third and final single, 'Anti Men'.

Once again produced by Rat Scabies, it was to be their crowning glory; he elicited a very 'Damned' performance from Gavin, and the feisty guitar solo ignites the mid-section perfectly. And on the flip side, 'Misunderstood', was even better, a strong vocal melody daringly given ample space in the sparse arrangement, making for a very dynamic, passionate song, suggesting that Anti-Establishment were a deep well of potential that was to unfortunately go untapped. They split soon after the single's release.

"We basically split because we never really got over Haggis leaving," reckons Gavin. "His heavy punk riffs were a major part of our sound, and it never felt the same after that. After all, he was one of our best friends and a main part of the band's formation in the first place. Looking back now, instead of trying to replace him, we should maybe have just started again.

"We were a grass-roots punk band that totally believed in our music and thoroughly enjoyed every minute of it all. We just wanted to make punk music as we thought it should be played, nothing more, nothing less. I suppose we would like to be remembered as normal lads who wanted to do it for themselves, which is what it was all about, and still should be really. No bullshit!"

DISCOGRAPHY:
7"s:
'1980' (Charnel House, 1980)
'Future Girl' (Glass, 1982)
'Anti Men' (Glass, 1983)

AT A GLANCE:
Captain Oi!'s 'Anti-Establishment: The Oi Collection' (1997) compiles everything the band ever recorded, including all their previously unreleased demos… some of which are actually as good as the material that found its way onto vinyl. In the absence of any full-length album, this is the definitive Anti-Establishment release.

CHRON GEN

One of the very best of the early Eighties bands, Chron Gen mixed subtle melodies, intelligent lyrics and uptempo catchy tunes to create cerebral punk music that sounds as fresh now as the day it was committed to tape. The three founding members of the band – vocalist/guitarist Glynn 'Baxter' Barber, drummer John 'JJ' Johnson, and Adam Warwicker on bass – all got into punk in 1977, and within a year were taking their first tremulous steps towards making their own music.

"JJ and I were both into music and playing instruments long before punk came along," recalls Glynn. "We took drum lessons during school hours, and it was a natural progression to want to play in a band. I started out playing drums with a Status Quo type band called Barracuda Rock and then in a free form experimental band called Friction. I also played drums in the school dance band under the direction of the mighty George Cropley (RIP).

"In late '77, we found some other guys at school who played guitar and we formed our first punk band called The Condemned. There is a version of 'Pretty Vacant' by this line up on 'Puppets of War – The Collection' (Rhythm Vicar Records, 2002) which was recorded in my mum's living room in February 1978… check out the budgies at the end!

"At that time, we all lived on the Jackmans Estate in Letchworth and transported our equipment around on a couple

Glynn of Chron Gen (left) with Wattie of The Exploited (centre) and Animal of The Anti-Nowhere League

of skateboards. And just out of interest, the '99' bus route was from Jackmans Estate to Luton via Hitchin... as described in 'Living Next Door To Alice'!"

Adam came up with the name Chron Gen, although he was soon replaced after their first demo when Glynn and JJ hooked up with guitarist Jon Thurlow and bassist Pete Dimmock from another local band, Optional Xtras. In 1981, encouraged by the response they were getting at shows, Chron Gen recorded the 'Puppets Of War' EP at the Crypt in Stevenage ("So called because it was under an old disused church") and released it on their own label, Gargoyle. Despite a spartan production, it was a scintillating debut, loaded with simple, effective melodies, and the title track had a brooding atmosphere of impending doom that managed to transcend its weedy guitar sound. The single was a runaway success, spending nearly ten months in the Indie Charts and peaking at No. 4.

"Our manager up to and including the Apocalypse tour, Gez Lowry, was a good organiser and made all the bits and pieces come together," explains Glynn. "I think the studio session only cost about £70, which was cheap even in 1981, but we were pleased with the result, it captured the moment.

"The first Gargoyle pressing of 1000, with a blue label, sold very quickly. The next 5000 on Gargoyle, with a white label, also went quickly; we were selling these on our first tour. Fresh Records picked up the pressing and distribution from then on, and 'Puppets Of War' became resident in the Sounds Indie Chart. I recall it being named as the longest serving member of the Indie Charts in 1981, according to the end of year charts review. So, yes, we were pleased with the response!"

On the back of their heightened profile, the band landed themselves a slot on the aforementioned Apocalypse tour that ravaged the UK during May 1981, and saw the band rubbing shoulders with scene heavyweights The Exploited, Discharge, and Anti Pasti, with the Anti-Nowhere League also appearing on the London bill at the Lyceum.

"That tour was a big experience for us, and was certainly highly prestigious. We slept in the van, which we also shared with our backline, the second pressing of 'Puppets Of War' (all 5000 copies!) and a few mates. It was a great party from start to finish. The van eventually died and we crawled back from Cardiff to Hitchin at an average speed of 15mph.

"And the tour gave us a lot of good opportunities, although with hindsight, we should have made more of them. To be honest, we made some regrettable decisions regarding our choice of management and record companies in the period after the Apocalypse tour. And those decisions set our destiny."

The next single, 'Reality', this time for Step Forward, clawed even higher up the Indies, and was only kept from the coveted No. 1 slot by Depeche Mode's 'Just Can't Get Enough'. Ushered in by a characteristically insistent chugging guitar riff, 'Reality' is one of Chron Gen's finest moments, driven by Barber's urgent vocal delivery and a roaming inquisitive bass line. It was backed by the heavier, more ominous 'Subway Sadist', a cautionary tale of the dangers lurking beneath the surface of urban bustle.

Inevitably, the larger labels came sniffing at the scent of such strong sales, and a deal was inked with Secret, who were also, of course, home to The Exploited. The first release for their new label was the 'Jet Boy Jet Girl' single, backed by live renditions of 'Subway Sadist' and 'Abortions'.

"As a big fan of The Damned, I followed each of the bands that formed after their original split," says Glynn, of their choice of cover version. "Captain Sensible's band, King, did 'Jet Boy Jet Girl' on a Peel session (July 20th, 1978) and I loved it. We copied it and it became a flagship song for us in the early days along with 'Living Next Door to Alice'."

Their high-octane rendition was enjoyable enough, and the single acted as a tasty aperitif for their debut album, which followed hot on its heels during spring 1982. And although Glynn has reservations about the sound quality ("Our budget was inadequate and we were inexperienced in the studio"), 'Chronic Generation' was an impressive offering, with its gritty observations of youth's trials and tribulations set to some of the most enduring and exuberant punk rock of its time.

"Many of the early songs (and bear in mind that these were written by spotty fifteen year olds!) were based on the type of spirit behind the first Damned album cover... be shocking and silly for the sake of it! Songs like 'You Make Me Spew', 'Ripper' and 'LSD' were more tongue-in-cheek than anything designed to influence a revolution. Most of the effort was put into the melody, and little attention given to the lyrics... something we paid for in blood when the first album was released. Things did improve on the lyrical front eventually, and I wrote many songs which I am still proud of, though the limelight had faded by then, of course!"

It wasn't all juvenile shock tactics though, as 'You'll Never Change Me' demonstrates, with its defiant punchline set to one of the more insidious hooks on the album, all draped in swathes of shimmering guitar. Elsewhere 'Rockabill' was a sorry story of the inevitable consequences of inter-tribal rivalries.

"I went through a phase of getting some right royal kickings," laughs Glynn. "And 'Rockabill' is an almost verbatim account of one such pasting! About ten or twelve late-teen rockabills, escorted by another four or five twenty-something big blokes, decided that it would be a fair fight to pick on me and two other skinny punks one Saturday afternoon in Letchworth town centre. I reckon they must have still been a bit scared of us though, because they needed to be tooled up. I took a crowbar in the forehead, but somehow got away with a few stitches!"

The first ten thousand copies of the album even came with a free live 7", featuring 'Puppets Of War', 'Ripper' and 'Living Next Door To Alice', as a bonus for fans who purchased the record promptly.

"Incidentally," adds Glynn, "The guy on the original album cover's nickname was Gem. He was Toyah's boyfriend and worked at Secret Records. We were never any good at contributing to ideas for record cover artwork, so we just left it to the record companies. And the re-released CD had a different bloke on it... but I have no idea who he was!"

1982 also saw the inclusion of 'Clouded Eyes' on the 'Britannia Waives The Rules' 12" (which, as well as Chron Gen, featured an exclusive track each from The Exploited and Infa-Riot) and the release of surely the band's crowning glory, the superb 'Outlaw' EP. This underrated masterpiece saw the band finally realising their true potential; a great chorus, an intelligent lyric, and Baxter really flexing his vocal muscles for the first time, power and melody in perfect unison. And not only was the A-side a genuine classic ("It was inspired by the reaction I got from a number of the crowd at an Iron Maiden concert I went to," reveals Glynn), but the B-side featured two more excellent cuts in a similar vein. Surprisingly the EP didn't do as well sales-wise as the preceding singles, possibly a result of the increasingly blinkered punk scene objecting to its unashamed musicianship.

"Some bands progress and want to extend themselves and their abilities," Glynn reckons, on reflection. "Some take the attitude that 'If it ain't broke, don't fix it', and end up plodding out the same old material year in, year out. Chron Gen always wanted to extend its abilities. Our music was always different to most second wave punk bands anyway, as was widely commented in the music press, and I make no apologies for this. We never really appealed to the hardcore punk fraternity."

To promote the album and single, the band took to the road in earnest in 1982, hooking up with the Anti-Nowhere League again for their 'So What?' tour, before heading off to the States for their own headline stint over there. Jon Thurlow was replaced by Mark 'Floyd' Alison right before the 'So What?' dates, and made his recording debut on the 'Britannia Waives The Rules' 12".

"Stewart Copeland, the drummer with The Police, actually filmed the 'So What?' Tour in '82 (although I haven't seen it on official release). He liked us a lot and if I were to pick one highlight, it would be the soundcheck in Birmingham where he took to the ANL drum kit and joined in with us playing 'Jet Boy Jet Girl'… fantastic!

"We had a great time," he continues, on the subject of their American dates. "Although there were obviously some low points. Most of the tour, we were on our own, often playing in regular music clubs and bars. They enjoyed us anyway.

"In contrast, Detroit was not good. It was a hardcore skinhead gig and we got the distinct feeling that we were not very welcome. I recall that JJ made some derogatory comment from behind the drums (as he often did), then I got hit by a flying, full size dustbin. We had a shotgun escort to the van that night!

"We were privileged to play with the Gang Of Four in Minneapolis. I remember JJ and me going back to the Best Western Hotel in Minneapolis with them for a post-gig party, only to find that Chron Gen were booked into the Best Western Motel, which was on the other side of the city. We had no money and had to make the long walk back at 3:00am!

"We also played with a number of now-legendary US punk bands at an open air gig in Berkeley, California such as Hüsker Dü, Jodie Foster's Army, and Wasted Youth. And we played great gigs at the Whiskey-A-Go-Go and the LA Olympic Auditorium, too."

The touring began to take its toll, and Pete was replaced by Roy Horner in 1983. The next release was 1984's 'Nowhere To Run' mini-album, for Picasso Records, and although Roy's picture appeared on the sleeve, the bass had actually already been recorded by session musician Nigel Ross-Scott. The record may have taken some of the band's diehard punk fans by surprise, but when considered alongside the 'Outlaw' single that preceded it, it seems like a logical progression… albeit in a much softer, more rock-orientated direction. There's even a whiff of Seventies glam rock about some of the rhythms and synthesised hand claps, but the guitars and vocals are pure Chron Gen and there are some real gems lurking, still undiscovered by many, amongst its grooves. It was also blessed with the band's best production to date.

"'Nowhere To Run' went a long way to putting the record straight," agrees Glynn, "But again, we had to contend with a silly budget. Two sets of quality producers quit once they were told the budget they had to work with. We were booked into a semi-functional studio, on the cheap, which we had to abandon after laying down the drum tracks. As a result we could only really use

six of the twelve tracks that we originally recorded, which is how it ended up as a mini-LP. Some of the ditched songs were later re-recorded and some appear as demos on the 'Puppets Of War – The Collection' CD."

Predictably enough, the adventurous 'Nowhere To Run' barely dented the Indie Charts, and the band were soon on the

Chron Gen, early 1984
L–R: BB Floyd, Roy Horner, Glynn Barber, John Johnson
(Pic: Tony Mottram)

rocks without a label, ultimately splitting, says the frontman, "On the weekend of the Brighton bombing of the Tory Party Conference, when JJ failed to show for a recording session. He was working in Brighton at the time, and decided to stay down there for some Saturday overtime instead of turning up for the studio. As you can imagine, I wasn't very happy."

And apart from several live albums, assorted collections, and the occasional well-received reunion show ("For the crack"), that was the last anyone heard of Chron Gen. Floyd went on to play with The Occasional Tables, but sadly died in late 1999. Simon 'Si-X' Harvey played lead guitar with the band at the aforementioned reformations.

"We tried to stretch the musical boundaries of our punk roots," says Glynn in summation of their colourful musical legacy. "There was nothing sinister or revolutionary about us; we just wanted to generate some high-powered melodic sounds that made people smile."

They succeeded.

SELECT DISCOGRAPHY:
7"s:
'Puppets Of War' EP (Fresh, 1981)
'Reality' (Step Forward, 1981)
'Jet Boy Jet Girl' (Secret, 1982)
'Outlaw' (Secret, 1982)

LPs:
'Chronic Generation' (Secret, 1982)
'Nowhere To Run' (Picasso, 1984)
'Apocalypse Live Tour' (Chaos, 1984)
'Live At The Waldorf' (Picasso, 1985)

AT A GLANCE:
Captain Oi!'s 1994 'The Best Of Chron Gen' is an excellent collection of the band's best material, complete with original artwork and a discography, but 'Puppets Of War – The Collection' (Rhythm Vicar Records, 2002), a double CD featuring well over two hours of music, is also highly recommended. It numbers many rare and unreleased demo cuts amongst its thirty-seven tracks, but is let down somewhat by its uninspired packaging.

UK DECAY

The second wave of UK punk is generally a scene held in high regard for its gritty realism and street-wise social politics, so it was inevitable that any band singing about the supernatural rather than urban high-rise grimness, preferring theatrical atmospherics over thrashing teenage angst, would stand out like a black sheep. Or in the case of UK Decay, a black cat! One of the more enigmatic of the early Eighties punk bands, they helped open the floodgates of the goth scene, and are still held in great regard today, despite never having been reissued officially on CD for the younger generation's consumption.

Formed in Luton in 1978, UK Decay were originally known as The Resistors. Steven 'Abbo' Abbot played guitar, Paul Wilson sang, Steve Harle was on drums and Martin 'Segovia' Smith the bass. During the summer of 1979, they changed their name and self-released the 'Split Single' 7" with local band Pneumania, on their own Plastic label. It featured two tracks apiece from each band (UK Decay contributed 'UK Decay' and 'Car Crash', Pneumania 'Exhibition' and 'Coming Attack') and sold extremely well, mainly thanks to a damning review in the N.M.E. where they were described as one of the worst punk bands of all time! And not only did the band start their own label but also their own monthly fanzine, The Suss, to promote future releases.

However, just before the recording, Paul Wilson left the band, leaving Abbo to sing as well as play guitar, something he didn't really take to very well, so he remained as the vocalist and roped in Steve Spon from Pneumania on guitar. It was an inspired move as the new lineup clicked instantly and the chemistry within the band came dramatically to life.

"With the new line up and name, it wasn't long – a matter of weeks, in fact – before we played our first live show," remembers Steve Spon. "It was at Luton Town Hall. All I can remember is Steve Harle's pounding tribal drums and Martin's enraged bass lines pulling my – at first nervous – guitar along,

Martin 'Segovia' Smith of UK Decay live at The Moonlight, 1980 (Pic: Mick Mercer)

with Abbo taunting the packed crowd. By the end of the show we had whipped them up into an electric, frenzied mayhem! And in the midst there stood Abbo, in this 35-degree sweatbox, fully dressed in a long heavy Macintosh coat shouting 'Necrophilia'! There was definitely a vibrant rapport between us… even though the show ended in a massive riot, which was quite common for us in those days!"

The second release for Plastic was the band's 'Black Cat EP', which came out in early 1980, and registered in the Indie Chart for three weeks, managing a No. 42 placing. It brought them to the attention of Alex Howe from Fresh Records, who not only offered to license the first two singles off them, but signed UK Decay to the label for several new 7"s and an album. The band celebrated with their first out of town show, with Bauhaus at the Northampton Racecourse Pavilion.

"We felt they (Bauhaus) were the nearest act locally that were saying and doing the right things," reflects Steve. "They used light shows creatively and theatre dramatically! But I felt we were more down to earth. We did our best to support other local bands and would always talk to our audience (when we could!); the buzz of that inspired us! But we all had differing influences; Abbo was into early Banshees and Ants as well as obscure German writers! He had a good ear for new things.

"And it wasn't only music that influenced the rest of us either; at that time I had discovered the wonders of H.P. Lovecraft and Steve was reading Edgar Allan Poe. I (secretly!) admired Pink Floyd and Hawkwind and was knocked out by the original Siouxsie And The Banshees line up. We were all very interested in many aspects of the supernatural too! I think it would be wrong to suggest that we were obsessed with 'the dark side' all of the time; in fact, even though songs like 'Necrophilia', 'Rising From The Dead' and 'The Black Cat' did indulge in what later became known as goth, it wasn't to be taken too literally. We saw every gig that we did as being a celebration, a kind of warped-out last night of the proms with our ever-growing set of anthems.

"Not far from Luton, there was an abandoned church which was decided would be an excellent backdrop for our 'Black Cat EP' cover; this was the sight of the last recorded occurrence of necromancy in the UK, so we piled up there with a photographer. It was late at night and spooky, we all fled after a few photos! Driving back down the lane, we rounded a bend and right in front of us an apparition of a white horse beheld us; moments later, it vanished! We, as a band, were profoundly affected by this experience and our gigs took on a new light thereafter."

The first official release for Fresh was September 1980's 'For My Country' single, which became a huge Indie hit, spending eight months in the chart and reaching (appropriately enough) No. 13. Its delicate meandering guitar line exploding into a tumultuous crashing chorus, it was a deceivingly powerful, passionate and articulate plea for peace.

"That's my favourite early release," reveals Steve. "My mother once said to me when I was much younger, the best things in life are the simple things, and in retrospect 'For My Country' is a very simple, structured song, with a cynical, sarcastic anti-war message, brutal in its pomp, lethal as an encore! Whilst on the B-side, 'Unwind' was like a coil of tension becoming more and more compressed, finally unleashing a tumult of energy, before slowly unwinding to a graceful end."

The single was promoted by a UK tour with raging political US punk band The Dead Kennedys.

"That tour was really responsible for bringing us into the spotlight. I enjoyed every moment; The Kennedys were really brilliant but often they would have to work really hard to follow us. We had some wild parties, including our after show party in Luton that ended up with ourselves and The DKs running amok in the town centre car parks in the middle of the night!"

'For My Country' also appeared on the hugely successful 'Punk And Disorderly' compilation album, that saw the band rubbing shoulders with many of their noisier, more generic peers; its subtle intricacies in stark contrast to much of the fuzzed-out thrashings elsewhere on the collection.

"We didn't see any problem with appearing on it; I think Fresh Records sorted it out. They thought it would be a good idea to do it, good value for money, and I guess it added to our fan base. You know we always maintained respect for our audience. They were quite adequate at thinking for themselves and they would often let us know if they didn't like something, but mostly, they respected our right to hit them with something different! There was little or no problem once they had been to a few of our shows. Most understood us and saw that we were bringing something new into the equation. It was only a matter of time before a large number of them were forming their own bands, so we would try to give as many as possible a 'leg up' with a support slot or a co-organised show. Nothing mattered more to us than our audience; whatever the critics would say, negative or positive, didn't have any effect on our relationship with our fans, apart from the fact that the numbers kept growing. And yes, I think at the time we felt we were being innovative, but what was more important for us was to create our music the way we wanted to and not to be compromised."

The 1981 singles, 'Unexpected Guest' and 'Sexual', also sold well, both effervescent waltzes of dark intent, the former actually achieving the band's highest Indie Chart placing of No. 4, and paving the way for UK Decay's splendid debut album, 'For Madmen Only', released by Fresh in December of that year.

Powered by a lilting hypnotic bass, that fuses with dissonant guitars and schizoid rhythms to create a ritualistic conjuring of sublime magnitude, the album remains to this day a moody masterpiece, a slow-turning carousel of dread, that draws the listener inexorably into its velvet caress before it strikes for the heart.

The band had actually started work on the album a whole year previous, but had to delay recording it several times for various reasons; not least of all, numerous line-up changes and a US tour with The Dead Kennedys!

"Before The Kennedys left for home, Jello (Biafra, singer) suggested that we do a tour of the West Coast of the USA the following spring but in the meantime Segovia, our bass player, left the band, so we put any notions of touring the US out of our heads whilst we set about finding a replacement. Then one Wednesday afternoon we were rehearsing and got a phone call, saying that the tour was still on and the first gig was that Friday night in San Francisco! 48 hours away! And, 'Don't worry, there is a guy out here that knows all your songs and will play bass for you!'

"It was a logistical nightmare over the next couple of days but somehow we got there. Our anxieties about the bass player (Creetin Chaos from Social Unrest) turned out to be unfounded; he was cool! We did a number of gigs with The Kennedys and set about a tour of the West Coast in two gigantic station wagons with Social Unrest as support; we went from Los Angeles to Vancouver and everywhere in-between!

"At that time surf punk such as Black Flag was the thing over there, slick fast music that everyone was into and the punks would throw themselves headfirst off the stage into the crowd; it was manic! The musicians were, to our ears at least, too good, too polished, with very expensive gear; it was surreal compared to what we were used to. We were over there playing our brand of comparatively slower, darker music and it was a real challenge without our usual audience, but we seemed to attract an enormous amount of interest everywhere we went. One gig I recall had a line of heavily armed security police one-third of the way back in the audience; at another someone left us a severed dog's head outside our dressing room door! We also played an international punk festival in Seattle that ended in a massive street riot and we had to be bailed out by the local Feds. The US was a very strange place!"

After Segovia left, Lorraine 'Lol' Turvey from The Statics stood in for some UK dates and a European tour in late 1980, but after the US shows, the band invited Creetin (aka Jason!) back to the UK for their first headlining tour with The Dark and Play Dead supporting. Following that stint he returned home and Eddie 'Dutch' Branch (aka 'Twiggy') from Northampton joined on bass, just in time to play on the album.

"During the recording of the album we were beginning to get more adventurous," says Steve. "On the Kennedys tour we had established a relationship with a sound engineer, 'Grizz' from Scan, who wasn't afraid to experiment. He let my guitar harmonics soar through his Roland Space Echo and made Steve's drums thunder; I guess it all added up to what was becoming 'our sound', and we regarded Grizz as our fifth element right up to the very last gig!

"It became important to us to get some of this live feel onto our album. In 'Battle Of The Elements', the thunder and lightning was achieved by bashing my Space Echo sending the 'spring reverb' roaring and then bending some dripping harmonics to create those 'storm cloud' sounds, then Abbo would dramatise the atmosphere with his chanting, a Michael Angeline-like 'master of ceremonies'. Doing it live was one thing but trying to record it was another kettle of fish! But with the guidance of John Loder at Southern Studios, we made slow at first but purposeful progress.

"Our gigs in Berlin had profoundly affected us (this was a decade before The Wall came down), so this came out in the music that went on the album too. Abbo was into German literature and a lot of that went into the lyrics; we were moving into deeper territories. I listened to the album again after September 11th and particularly to the title track 'For Madmen Only', and I shuddered at those terrible images of collapsing towers. 'I met murder on the way, he wore a mask like today'... for me it has an unnerving feeling of prophecy!"

Unfortunately Fresh went bankrupt soon after the album's release, and the band were caught up in the ensuing management buy-out by what would become Jungle Records. With the help of John Loder and Southern Studios though, they managed to buy up the rights to their back catalogue and set up their own UK Decay Records. Loder also introduced them to Penny Rimbaud from Crass, which resulted in the 'Rising From The Dead' 12" coming out on Crass's Corpus Christi label in August 1982.

It was yet another suitably desperate incantation, with Abbo's sibilant tones dancing up and down the listener's spine like icy fingers.

Abbo (vocals) and Spon (guitar) live at the Moonlight, 1980 (Pic: Mick Mercer)

However, despite encouraging sales, an "Extremely fatigued" UK Decay split up in late 1982, and a posthumous live album, 'A Night For Celebration', was released during the summer of 1983.

"I think the truth of the matter was that we had lived life so intensely in the few years the band had been going, that we just blew ourselves apart," reflects Steve. "At the time, musical and personal differences were rumoured, but there was also a sense the band had just run its course. On a personal level, it seemed a devastating loss; it was terrible for me to come to terms with hearing the end of the band being announced on stage at the (as it happened, penultimate) gig, at Klub Foot in the Hammersmith Clarendon Hotel. It was on December 22nd 1982; that was the first I knew about it!"

Abbo went on to form Furyo with the other members of UK Decay minus Steve.

"Yes, it seems in retrospect, everybody else knew about it for a few weeks beforehand except me. I felt this was a coup de grace on Abbo's behalf; we had always previously made all our

decisions by consensus and whilst we admittedly didn't always see eye to eye with each other, usually we got on reasonably well. I don't know why else they didn't keep the name going, there were offers coming in left, right and centre; they only had to replace me! But I think Abbo needed to make the new band more accountable to his imagination, and this I think is why both myself and the name UK Decay were sacrificed.

"However, I will never in my whole life forget that last gig of UK Decay, it was purely emotional! We played a pair of shows at Klub Foot, and Abbo announced at the first of the two shows that the following gig was to be the last, so that set the stage for the end. The gig was like some kind of celebratory wake with tears from nearly everyone that was there. It really was the ultimate 'night of celebration', with Abbo screaming, 'It's not the end, it's a new beginning!

"Looking back to those few short years we were together, I would say we were like a marriage of four trying to get it on in a Transit van! It was a time in our lives when nothing seemed more important than the band; we were 365/24/7, constantly touring and recording. My memories are a total blur and in some way I'm still in denial even today! This interview has opened up a Pandora's box of cascading remembered thoughts; the first time since the band split up that I had to do such a thing."

Steve Spon still works with underground music even today, both as a producer at the Luton Marsh Farm Academy of Performing Arts, and as a solo artist, under the name Nostramus. Tragically Steve Harle passed away in 1995; he died back-packing in India, aged just thirty-four.

"We had become close friends again a few years after the band split and occasionally would spar our reminiscences of the old days," sighs Spon. "Steve had a unique style of drumming, a tribal powerhouse with thoughtful execution. I am convinced to this day that we had a musical telepathy together; we would jam and we would just know what was coming next! In the early Nineties we even started working together again although we both had other obligations. One thing we did start to take onboard together in, I think, about '93, was to re-release UK Decay on CD, so we visited Southern Studios (now S.R.D.) and listened to what we had got. We were discussing the format the CD would take, but there were several things that needed tracking down before we could start. It all seemed to drag on, and eventually, Steve became disillusioned with it all; he was having problems getting his head round the past.

"One day he said to me, 'Sod it, I'm going to India, do you fancy coming?' I was halfway through recording my Nostramus album and was obliged to complete it by the end of the year, so I turned him down. The CD project was to go on hold 'til his return, but unfortunately, this was not to be; instead, sadly, his wake was to be the last reunion to this day of UK Decay.

"His passing was a huge blow not only for me but a large community of punks and musicians still living in Luton; indeed for weeks there were people showing up from all over to pay their respects! I was devastated; I had lost my musical soulmate and the effect it had on me was profound. I stopped writing music, which was my life, and to this day have not completely recovered. It was the end of all possibilities of future collaborative projects and the planned CD reissue has, to this day, not happened."

SELECT DISCOGRAPHY:
7"s:
'Split Single' (Plastic, 1979) – split with Pneumania
'The Black Cat EP' (Plastic, 1980)
'For My Country' (Fresh, 1980)
'Unexpected Guest' (Fresh, 1981)
'Sexual' (Fresh, 1981)

12"s:
'Rising From The Dead' (Corpus Christi, 1982)

LPs:
'For Madmen Only' (Fresh, 1981)
'A Night For Celebration' (UK Decay, 1983)

AT A GLANCE:

Unfortunately, nothing comprehensive has yet appeared by UK Decay on CD, although a previously unavailable version of 'For My Country' recently (2003) appeared on the 'Post Punk Volume 01' double-disc compilation on Rough Trade. Hopefully a full, thorough and long overdue CD reissue of the band will take place one day soon.

SUBCULTURE

S ubculture were a bunch of Cambridge herberts that seemed poised for great things in the early Eighties, releasing the 'Loud And Clear' EP and opening most of the Oi! shows in and around London. As with so many of those bands though, the constant violence at gigs led to a frustrated early retirement and a tantalizing question mark over what they could have achieved given half a chance. But now they're back playing together again and able to ponder philosophically what might have been.

Formed in 1980 by guitarist Dean Tyrell and bassist Phil Parker, the original singer was Tom Hipkin, but by the time of the aforementioned 'Loud And Clear' EP, Tom had been replaced by Pete Matthews. Matt Johnson rounded out the lineup on drums.

"Well, as with a lot of early punk, it was very middle class," begins Pete, on the subject of the Cambridge punk scene. "But then things changed! Sham emerged, then the Upstarts and the Rejects . . . and I was off, I loved it oh so much. At the time there was a pub, The Great Northern; that was a punk pub, and next door was the Sound Cellar, a brilliant place where you could see all sorts of bands – and I mean *all sorts*, from Crux to Big Country and Mary Wilson! All before they made their mark . . .

"After that was the Sea Cadet Hall and everyone but everyone played there too. We used to get the call to play there every week it seemed – playing with Vice Squad, the Adicts, GBH and so on and so on. We eventually got banned for me taking a glass on stage though (ooh, shock horror!), but we were then playing London a lot so thought, 'Fuck it!' But it wasn't long before a band didn't turn up and we got the call to come play again – as long as we were good boys and didn't wind up the audience!"

Before Pete joined the band though, Subculture recorded a demo at the now-legendary Spaceward Studios, which so impressed Garry Bushell and Lol Pryor, they were invited to contribute the track 'Stick Together' to Secret's 1982 Oi! compilation, 'Oi! Oi! That's Yer Lot!' Their Cockney Rejects influences were really to the fore on that one – possibly because Micky Geggus produced and sang backing vocals.

"He was a bloody nice chap, and one of our heroes," recalls Pete fondly, before explaining why Subculture had a one-off vocalist for that song, and elaborating on some of their other early influences.

"The bloke singing on the 'Oi!' LP is actually a chap called Carl Colum who used to follow the band back then. For some reason they had a row with Tom and ended up with Carl doing 'Stick Together', which, in hindsight, was a silly choice!

"Our main influences were the Pistols, The Jam, The Clash, The Ruts, The Who, Eddie Cochran and SLF . . . amongst many others, of course. We listened to punk, skinhead . . . all of it.

Why do we have to have all these boxes? None of us ever had a mohican or wore 'the uniform' – we wore what we could afford: plimsolls, Harrington's, flying jackets, Fred Perry's, punk T-shirts, Air Wears . . . To be fair, there was a lot of pretentious tossers around, and we had to deal with them."

With some influential movers and shakers behind them, Subculture began playing London on a regular basis, hewing a strong following from the tough 100 Club and Skunx audiences in readiness for a debut release in their own right.

Subculture, Pete, 100 Club

"The 100 Club was always great fun," smiles Pete. "We did a great night supporting The Exploited. It was very weird for me; a few months earlier, I had seen The Exploited on Top Of The Pops, and then there I was doing a sound check, with Wattie nodding along to 'Rogue Trooper' in front of me! Nice chap too . . . although I did have to listen very carefully to what he was saying – his accent was amazing!

"Cock Sparrer's return gig at the 100 Club was also, shall we say, lively. We had a coach load of our supporters with us, and it was very busy; the place was rammed. It was during the Falklands war, and Sparrer came on stage with 'Argy Bargy'! Followed by 'England Belongs To Me' . . . I think some of the nastier side of the audience read this as they always will and started waving their arms about, and shouting about 'sea gulls' or something [i.e. Nazi boneheads sieg-heiling] . . . this in turn got them a prompt kicking! Sparrer's record label was less than impressed with the audience participation!"

After turning down an offer from Secret Records, which Pete now admits was a "Big mistake!" ("We could maybe have been up there with the Business and Test Tubes if we had . . . bloody twats, eh?"), Subculture hooked up with Alan McGee's Essential Records for their one and only EP of the Eighties, the timeless slice of tuneful street punk, 'Loud And Clear', which made it to No. 16 in the Independent Charts.

"There was a small advert in the Melody Maker, asking for 'politically aware bands with recorded material' to send a good old cassette to some PO box or other. Phil sent off our tape and got a call back from Alan who liked a couple of the tracks, especially, I believe, 'Rogue Trooper'.

"The EP was recorded at Rock City studios in Shepperton. I was impressed. It was owned by one Mr Gary Numan . . . who turned up and gave us loads of flight cases and leads and stuff, bless him! We were in the 'cheap' 16-track studio whilst Shakatak were in the 32-track studio next door. When Dean recorded his solo, Shakatak left the studio and went up the pub . . . and although I haven't listened I'm sure you can hear the lead break of 'Loud And Clear' in there on one of Shakatak's plinky plonky bits!

"Anyway, the EP did better than we were told, and sold a hell of a lot more than the 3,000 we were told were pressed."

Sadly, despite the success of the single, Subculture struggled to stay positive in the face of often overwhelming negativity at their gigs – a negativity nurtured in mindless violence – and split soon after its release.

"Unfortunately violence had become a fashion in '82 and '83," sighs Pete. "I understand the whole territorial bullshit of it, but as a band, with the figurehead being football violence and general despondency to what you could expect from life, we were fucked! It definitely wasn't the romantic notion that some people have of UK82.

"The last proper gig for Subculture back then was at the Fisher Hall in Cambridge city centre, and to be honest it was a shameful fight all the way through . . . it was a pity it ended the way it did. And a few weeks before that, we had started a tour with Cock Sparrer – only for the first gig at the 100 Club to turn into . . . well, let's just say it wasn't a picnic! I was furious after that 'cos we took the blame. I won't say any more, but it was *not* our fault at all!"

The band went their separate ways, all of them a million miles from their life in Subculture: Pete starting up his own refrigeration repair business, Phil becoming a caretaker at Cambridge university, Matt a plumber and Dean a teacher. They also kept their hands in musically though, with Dean a successful DJ, Phil setting up his own home studio, and Matt drumming with many local bands. It was almost inevitable that Subculture would get together again at some point to lay some unfulfilled demons to rest.

"There was *always* unfinished business with Subculture," agrees Pete, "So it was decided to put together a remixed album, of bits and pieces we'd recorded, which became the album 'Herbert Street To The 100 Club' [on Phil Parker's own Council House Records]. We had been offered lots of gigs, including Rebellion etc. before, but always turned them down . . . God knows why from my personal point of view!

"Anyway, as soon it came out, the gig offers came flooding in again, and there was much discussion about whether to or not, and we played a few gigs keeping away from out and out Oi! gigs (we were still bothered about what happened in the 'glory' days, we really were . . .) Then we got a support with my heroes SLF, and it was all systems go. What a great gig, it was fantastic . . . The bug, for me at least, was back!"

Council House also released the 'Just Play The Music . . .' EP in 2012, which was followed in quick succession by the 'Voice Of The Young From The Good Old Days' 7" (Clockwork Firm Records) and the 'Blood And Dust' 7" for German label, Contra, with Phil Parker then being replaced by Steve Gungle.

"We didn't realise we had gained a sort of cult status with the young 'uns! Oh dear!" laughs Pete, before concluding with how he would personally like Subculture to be remembered.

"Probably for being the band that got there late, that got picked up by the biggest genius in the music business at the time – then disappearing with so much unfinished business. The voice of the young . . . the real ones – who didn't wanna kill everyone, I mean. And remember, kick it 'til it breaks!

"And there's plenty more where this lot came from – even if I am fifty!"

SELECT DISCOGRAPHY:
7"S:
'Loud And Clear' (Essential, 1983)
'Just Play The Music . . .' (Council House, 2012)
'Voice Of The Young From The Good Old Days' (Clockwork Firm, 2012)
'Blood And Dust' (Contra, 2013)

LPS:
'Herbert Street To The 100 Club' (Council House Records, 2011)

AT A GLANCE:
Captain Oi's 1998 'The Oi Collection' CD features the band's Oi! LP appearance, first EP and demo tracks (and is a split release alongside Ipswich's A.B.H.)

CHAPTER

SEVEN

London

UK SUBS

T he UK Subs are one of the few examples of a first
wave punk band that not only both influenced
and survived the second wave, but outlived
it as well. A London group that formed in 1977,
they are still active today, still touring extensively,
and still raising the roofs off venues all around the
world. And they more than merit inclusion in this
book as they released some of their finest material
within the time frame it focuses on.

Obviously, inevitably, there have been many line-up
changes over the years, but vocalist Charlie Harper (aka
David Charles Perez) has remained an immovable constant, becoming in the process a bona fide
punk rock icon, albeit an approachable likeable one. Now aged sixty (yes, he was born in 1944),
he still dedicates the band's song 'Teenage' to himself, and can still run rings around performers
less than half his age.

"I grew up in Leicestershire, England," explains original guitarist Nicky Garratt of his
inception into punk rock, "and in the summer of 1976, became aware of a monolithic movement
forming under the shifting sands of pub rock mediocrity. A flash fire scorched the land and only
the deepest-rooted artist survived. Careers were burnt to a cinder. I moved to London on
January 1st, 1977, and joined The UK Subs that very summer.

"I guess I was inspired by The Herd, The Beatles, The Kinks and such like in the Sixties,
then by 1970 I was inspired to play by Black Sabbath, Deep Purple, Family and Curved Air. I got
into jazz to some extent through Pharaoh Sanders and by 1973 became a fan of Magma, the
French band led by Christian Vander. I was not into T Rex, David Bowie, MC5 or The Stooges
like many early punks claim. I was in a string of bands around Leicester from 1970 onwards...
firstly playing blues (with Honey Boy Hickling and Big Al Taylor), then hard rock and, by 1973,
jazz, soul, and funk. In 1976 I played in a band with JB, who later became the sax player in Dexy's
Midnight Runners. On electric guitar I was mostly self-taught but I did study classical guitar
under Cathleen Warner for a few years."

Nicky bought this unique blend of influences to The UK Subs, who were essentially vocalist
Charlie Harper's previous band, The Marauders, under a new name. They were originally known
as just The Subs (and always will be by the majority of their fans), but the 'UK' prefix was soon
added to differentiate themselves from a Scottish band with the same name.

The first Subs' line-up consisted of Charlie and Nicky, along with Steve Slack on bass, who
was soon replaced by his brother Paul, and drummer Steve Jones, himself soon replaced by
Rory Lyons. After contributing two live tracks to the 'Farewell To The Roxy' compilation album,
Rory was replaced by Pete Davies in April of 1978, and a session was recorded for John Peel's
Radio One show. The excellent debut single 'C.I.D.', appeared in August 1978 on City Records,
on several different coloured vinyls (setting a band precedent for ensuing releases in various
garish colours), and its success spurred GEM Records into signing the band. In May 1978 they
released the hugely enjoyable 'Stranglehold' single, which went to No. 26 in the National Charts,
and saw the band appearing on 'Top Of The Pops'.

"The first time on 'Top Of The Pops' was a stiff affair, I guess we were a bit nervous," reveals Nicky. "As I recall, Charlie sang live, but the backing track was recorded. Surreal images still come to mind as we set up to play on one stage while some mainstream crooner or novelty performer was finishing on the other. Then, later on, there was the infamous Top Of The Pops where somehow our hardcore fans got through security, I think that was for the 'Party In Paris' single. It ended up in a stage invasion. Now to me that would have been compelling TV, but unfortunately they didn't air it. Perhaps they were afraid of starting a trend that would result in equipment damage. Perhaps it simply wasn't that interesting, we'll never know.

Alvin Gibbs (bass) and Charlie Harper (vocals) of The UK Subs, New York City, 1982

"Anyway, I didn't get too much attention from being on TV," he laughs. "As for being 'famous', I used to change my hair colour a lot and was quite hard to recognize. Even my grandmother thought I was Paul Slack! Charlie was recognized everywhere though…"

Several UK tours were followed by the band's seminal debut album, September 1978's 'Another Kind Of Blues', which was recorded at London's Kingsway Studio by Ian Gillan (of Deep Purple fame)'s bassist John McCoy. It remains to this day a near flawless collection of short, memorable, raucous punk rock tunes, and began a tradition of each official UK Subs' album taking its title from consecutive letters of the alphabet. It reached No. 21 in the National Charts and the track 'Tomorrow's Girl' was chosen as the next single, which promptly went Top Thirty too.

"Ian Gillan put 'Tomorrow's Girls' in his Top Ten list printed in one of the big music papers. I'm sure it was mostly to do with it being recorded at his studio, but for me the validation from one of my early heroes was fantastic."

Two more Top Thirty singles followed: 'She's Not There', a Zombies cover, with lead vocals courtesy of bassist Paul Slack ("Because it was in a difficult key for Charlie") in November 1979, and, in March 1980, the classic – in every sense of the word – 'Warhead'. Powered by an insistent bass line (apparently something Paul just used to jam out during soundcheck) and some mournful back-up vocals, it is possibly the Subs' best-loved track and still an indispensable staple in their live set today.

The second studio album, 'Brand New Age', appeared in April 1980 on clear vinyl, and saw the band honing their sound to be that much harder and more aggressive. 'Emotional Blackmail' was especially explosive, with its dynamic, threatening intro bursting into a fierce chugging riff. Possibly to ring the changes, Nicky and Charlie even decided to produce the record themselves.

"Well, 'Another Kind Of Blues' was a document of what we had been playing live over the previous couple of years," explains Nicky of the differences between their debut and its follow-up. "There was still a lot of blues influence in some of the songs, but 'Brand New Age' was a collection of new stuff, with the exception of 'Teenage' which was actually written before the first album. I produced 'BNA' with Charlie because we felt that unless we were going to get a particular sound from a producer we may as well do it ourselves. I was very involved in the details of the recording of the first singles and album and had gained some experience through that. I still like a few songs on 'Brand New Age'. 'Rat Race' (oddly enough modelled after the Syd Barrett song, 'No Man's Land'), 'Emotional Blackmail' and, of course, 'Warhead'. 'Rat Race' and 'Emotional Blackmail' were structurally the furthest from 'Blues', which I'm not crazy about. 'Warhead' is an atmospheric song and a nice change of pace."

The simplistic yet unforgettable anthem 'Teenage' was chosen as the logical single from the album, and shot to No. 32 in the Nationals, making five Top Forty placings within one year, a feat virtually unheard of for a real punk band in the early Eighties. They were soon headed off to the States for their first US tour, which included several shows with The Police.

"The show in Philadelphia with them was probably the best of that tour if my memory serves me correctly," reckons Nicky. "However the NYC show was pretty funny… although not so at the time. Charlie had left the building and couldn't get back in as his real name was on his ID. Anyway, there were a few thousand fans waiting for The Police whose 'Walking On The Moon' had just gone to No. 1. The promoter gave us an ultimatum, 'Play now or not at all'. We were just about to walk on stage and have Paul sing 'She's Not There', then maybe go into an unrehearsed instrumental, when Charlie finally showed up!"

The Subs were well on their way to becoming a household name, and it was only a matter of time before they were bootlegged. The 'unofficial' – not to mention, three years too late (it was recorded at The Roxy on New Years Eve, 1977) – 'Live Kicks' was released whilst the band were on tour in Europe supporting The Ramones.

Perhaps in response to that substandard bootleg, perhaps because they were rapidly garnering a reputation as the best live punk band out there at the time, The UK Subs decided to release an official live album, and the result was September 1980's 'Crash Course'. Recorded at the Rainbow Theatre in London on 30th May 1980 and mixed by Nicky Garratt and engineer Nick Bedford at Matrix Studios soon after, the twenty-song set perfectly captured The Subs' patented ultra-tight, fluid, urgent take on punk rock, and it scored an incredible No. 8 slot in the Nationals, earning the band a gold disc for their troubles! Initial pressings of the album came with a free 12", 'For Export Only', which featured a further four live tracks not on 'Crash Course', recorded at the Lyceum in July '79.

"I can't actually remember why we did a live album," admits Nicky. "I do think we were better live, but the action wasn't always in the sound. The gold disc was nice; I think stuff like that validates you once the dust has settled. The line up with Pete and Paul was very different from the following one with Alvin and Steve. Pete and Paul had replaced Rory and Steve (Paul's brother) in January 1978. Paul's brother was a very natural musician and Paul took over as a novice. Over the next couple of years he grew into a very solid bass player and took particular care about his sound. Pete was a rock-steady drummer and you could always count on the snare beat being there. We organized the set well, I think, the dynamics were all in the right places.

"When Steve took over there was a wall of sound behind you which even enabled both Alvin and I to perform instead of just playing. Charlie had some interesting thoughts on live performance. One of which was that each person was responsible for making his part of the stage exciting. That may have been our biggest triumph…"

Anyone in need of proof of the primal potency of The UK Subs as a live act should be referred to the 1980 tongue-in-cheek punk documentary 'Punk Can Take It' which contains plenty of vintage concert footage. Mainly shot during the UK tour to promote the 'Stranglehold' 7", it sees the band in fine form, with Nicky in particular hitting all sorts of unfeasibly painful rockstar shapes.

"Our label at the time, GEM, also ran GTO films, and they had the ability to get our little film on as an opener, first for 'Scum' and later for 'Quadrophenia'. They also had all the necessary contacts to make it happen. You'll notice that some of the stuff, including a few of the actors, is left over from 'The Great Rock'n'Roll Swindle' which Julien Temple had just finished."

Seemingly at the peak of their powers, it was only a matter of time before fate intervened and threw a well-aimed spanner in the proverbial works, and after 'Crash Course', the band lost their whole rhythm section when, in late 1980, after an appearance on a Dutch TV show, Paul Slack and Pete Davies left to form The Allies. As mentioned earlier by Nicky, they were replaced, respectively, by Alvin Gibbs (previously with The Users) and Steve Roberts, who had formerly drummed for Cyanide, a band that had opened for The Subs on several occasions.

"I think the pressure within the band was quite high at that time," says the guitarist of the split. "Pete and Paul seemed to be unhappy and as I recall complained a lot. We were doing an awful lot of shows. Charlie and I felt that The Subs were our baby, I suppose. We were working on stuff all the time and a natural crack formed between us. Alvin got the job at auditions, he had the right pedigree and fitted immediately. It was a different band in some ways. Steve was a much more dynamic drummer and wanted to show everyone. Alvin was a strong songwriter and that was a big change as until then Charlie and I had written most of the stuff."

Pete and Paul turned up again briefly, alongside Chelsea guitarist James Stevenson, on Charlie's 1980 solo single, 'Barmy London Army'. Meanwhile, the 'new' UK Subs wasted no time in cutting the brilliant and fun 'Party In Paris' single, complete with accompanying promo video, and hitting the road in support of it, a UK tour that culminated euphorically with four sold-out nights at the Marquee. The album 'Diminished Responsibility' hit the streets in early 1981, and although the requisite choruses and guitar licks were present and correct, the record sounds almost too slick for its own good when compared to other early entries in the band's catalogue.

"The unfortunate thing about that album was the production," agrees Nicky. "It was done, or should I say not done, by Mike Leander who did Gary Glitter. He barely showed up and managed to get a kind of hollow sound throughout the whole thing. I re-mixed as best I could, but for the most part the damage was done. For myself I wanted to expand our sound to simply make better and more lasting recordings. Of course, the other major difference is that Alvin co-wrote a number of songs on the album."

A new single was recorded straight after the album, April '81's 'Keep On Running ('Til You Burn)', a great track based around an effective guitar hook, and the cover photo even saw the band tarted up as New Romantics.

"We thought we could tap into Duran Duran's pool of groupies," jokes Nicky. "Actually the label gave us money and told us to go and get 'Kings Road' clothes. So we did. I didn't really care, it made a change in a way, but I guess we overshot a bit, right? But you know what? I don't remember anyone really caring about it. Maybe they did, but I think we had such a store of credibility that it didn't matter and to be frank it was nice to see Charlie wearing something other than the 'flasher' raincoat he'd been wearing for the previous six months!"

Maybe it was the extravagant clothes budget that did it (!), but GEM went bankrupt soon after the single was released, and the UK Subs moved to independent label, NEMS, for late '81's ponderously heavy 'Countdown' single. It paved the way for the marvellous 'Endangered Species' album that was unleashed on March 19th 1982 and spent two months in the Indie Charts, peaking at No. 11. Their fifth, and possibly their strongest, album, it not only captured the Subs at their most uncompromisingly powerful and hard-hitting, but also, paradoxically, at their most restrained and reflective. On one hand you have the viciously metallic title track, or the scything, sneering 'Living Dead' (with a great lead vocal from Alvin, who also wrote the track), but on the other there is the tasteful pop sensibilities of 'Sensitive Boys', and the dark, moody atmospherics of 'Ice Age' with its gnarly, gurgling bass and swirling guitar harmonics. Add into that already potent mix the irresistible and quirky 'I Robot', and 'Down On The Farm', an understated but great rock song that was later covered by platinum-selling US act Guns N' Roses on their 'Spaghetti Incident' record, and you have quite an album.

The eclectic nature of the album even prompted Alvin Gibbs to later comment that 'Endangered Species' was a record 'of two halves'.

"It's our most listenable record. The production is big, the performances are sharp and the songs a little more fleshed out without being over-baked. I think the simple guitar solo on 'Countdown' is among my best ever, and it features some of Charlie's most introspective and interesting lyrics, for example 'Divide By Eight, Multiply By Five'."

Soon after the album's release, drummer Steve Roberts was replaced by ex-Chelsea sticksman Sol Mintz (aka Mal Asling) and the band headed out for yet another US tour, this time with The Anti-Nowhere League.

"That was a great tour," recalls Nicky fondly. "Real rock'n'roll Babylon stuff... we even managed to get thrown off a commuter plane! By the end of the tour we all looked like walking zombies. Some nights we had no sleep at all and simply flew to the next show right from stage. 4.30 a.m. wake-up calls were very common even after we'd only got offstage at 1 or 2 a.m.! And that went on for six weeks! The shows were all packed though and there was a real feeling of some sort of historic significance at some of them. Members of The Bad Brains, Minor Threat, Henry Rollins and countless others were up front in the tangled mass of the audience."

However the line-up changes weren't over, and after the release of the storming 'Shake Up The City' EP for Abstract in November 1982, which itself introduced a new drummer, Kim Wylie (aka John Towe), formerly with The Adverts, the unthinkable (at the time, anyway) happened. Not only did Alvin Gibbs leave the band, but Nicky Garratt, Charlie's partner in musical crime for the previous five years, followed suit.

"We felt a bit trapped in a cycle of endless shows," explains Nicky. "And I really wanted some time to come up with a strong follow-up album to 'Endangered Species'. That just wasn't going to happen, so Alvin and I formed a band with Ken Scott of Wasted Youth after leaving The Subs. We felt that it was a low point with no management to speak of, no label and only the prospect of endless touring. But we'd just played our biggest ever headline show, to 22,000 people in Warsaw, Poland, so we ended on a high point.

"The new band fell apart after half a year or so. I needed a change and was a bit down, so I moved to New York…" Where he set up the New Red Archives label…

"I started NRA to release the 'AWOL Sessions' by UK Subs. I felt I needed to take control of my own career, as the industry was proving obstinate in the extreme as regards accounting to us. It quickly snowballed into a real label when (seminal NYC hardcore punk band) Kraut asked me to reissue their 'An Adjustment To Society' album. Other triumphs abound… Samiam, Anti-Flag, No Use For A Name, Swingin' Utters, Reagan Youth… and I would have to say that the failures are all related to shortfalls in my own personality. Never one to lavish money on the media, I instead promoted from inside the scene with my 73 minute/33 band/$1 comp CD 'At War With Society'. Although highly successful, one could argue that I haven't promoted the bands enough, and I think that's a fair assessment. My personality dictates that if you don't like the stuff I put out, don't buy it. I'm not going to twist arms or beg. But, after sixteen years, the label's still solvent… if somewhat dormant. For the future, when I hear something I like, I'll put it out, but I don't feel inclined to simply 'feed the machine'."

Alvin went on to play with Charlie in his Urban Dogs side project (that also featured Knox from The Vibrators), but as detailed earlier, the new band he did with Nicky was a short-lived affair.

"Drugs ensured an early demise to that project," sighs Nicky. "Something that Alvin and I were ill-equipped and unwilling to deal with. After moving to New York, I formed the Rebekka Frame. That fell apart after one mini album, and a few shows, including CBGBs. I went onto Los Angeles where I formed a band, Ten Bright Spikes, with Jason Honea of Social Unrest who resided in San Francisco. We did a couple of 10" EPs before I moved up to the Bay Area to work more closely on the project. The band also included violin player Lovely (daughter of André) Previn, bass player Jacek Ostoya (who later turned up on The Subs' split 7" with the Swingin' Utters, 'Postcard From LA') and Mario Petriga, the drummer from (well-respected old school German punk band) Upright Citizens. We ended up doing two albums to great critical acclaim and fanfare, 'Astro Stukas' and 'Blueland', before we took a hiatus. Last year we did actually get back together and recorded a new album for Substandard Records. It's a strange mix of Brian Wilson meets Magma, of Pharaoh Sanders and Brit-Pop. Ahead of our time or delusional? Only time will tell. When I'm in San Francisco, I also play in a six piece Burt Bacharach covers band doing soft jazz treatments called Something Big. But I have been living for the last few years in Hannover, Germany."

So, within six months of releasing one of the best albums of his career, UK Subs vocalist Charlie Harper found himself with no label and virtually no band. It's a tribute to his intestinal fortitude that he didn't just roll over quietly there and then, but instead he picked up the pieces and forged on ahead regardless. He quickly re-recruited his old bassist Steve Slack and talented newcomer Dave 'Captain Scarlet' Lloyd on guitar, and signed to Fall Out.

This version of the band debuted with September '83's 'Another Typical City' EP, which reached No. 11 in the Indies, and was followed in November of that year by the 'Flood Of Lies' album. Resplendent in striking cover art - a cartoon rendering of Margaret Thatcher as a repulsive diseased leper – it was another strong entry to the Subs canon, albeit sounding a little obvious and generic after the visionary 'Endangered Species'. That said, the title track remains one of the band's finest moments, and many of the other tracks translated well to the concert environment, as was evidenced by 1985's 'Gross Out USA' live album. By the time of that release though, Slack and Jones had been replaced by Terry 'Tez' Roberts, of Discharge and Broken Bones fame, and returning ex-drummer Pete Davies, but not before they contributed to 1984's rather disappointing four-track 'Magic' EP.

1986's 'Huntington Beach' album saw Charlie endure yet another complete change of guard. Joining him this time were bassist Plonker Magoo (aka Ricky McGuire, previously with The

Fits), guitarist Jim Moncur from Combat 84, and drummer Rab Fae Beith, who had formerly served time with The Pack and The Wall. In fact, the album appeared on Rab's own RFB label, which also put out the red vinyl 7" 'Live In Holland' the same year. The line-up remained the same for 'In Action', a live album commemorating the band's tenth anniversary.

However, before the band's next studio album, 'Japan Today' (1988), it was all change yet again. Ricky departed to join The Men They Couldn't Hang, Jim left to become a full-time guitar tech, and Rab left to concentrate instead on running his label. Undeterred, Charlie recruited bassist Dave 'Flea' Farrelly, guitarists Alan Lee and Darrell Bath (who left halfway through recording to join Dogs D'Amour, before rejoining for '91's 'Mad Cow Fever' album), and a returning Steve Roberts on drums. The album was preceded by the frankly ludicrous 'Hey Santa' 12", the title track being a punked-up cover version of the novelty song by Australian comedian Kevin 'Bloody' Wilson, that saw Charlie hamming it up admirably with lines such as 'Hey Santa Claus, you cunt, where's my fucking bike?'

The 'Killing Time' album followed, which saw Nicky and Alvin back in the ranks, albeit for a record that Nicky still rates as his least favourite Subs offering.

"It was a partially aborted attempt to do a reunion, but with neither the time nor the money to do it properly. A couple of songs are okay, but many were just songs I wrote for The Rebekka Frame. Charlie had to leave before we were finished, so Alvin sang a couple of numbers... but the worst aspect of the album is that I even sang a couple as well... and no one should have to listen to that!"

A full US tour was undertaken, with Lee and Flea, supported by the Broken Bones, after which Steve Roberts left the band, to be replaced by Matt McCoy (son of Gillan bassist John McCoy who produced 'Another Kind Of Blues') just in time to record the 'Motivator' 12" for Released Emotions Records... a record that saw a rousing version of 'Auld Lang Syne' rubbing shoulders with manic instrumental 'Cycle Sluts From Hell'!

Released Emotions also released the 'Live In Paris' album, before the band returned to Fall Out for the 'Mad Cow Fever', 'Normal Service Resumed', 'Occupied' and 'Peel Sessions' albums. Then, to celebrate twenty years of the UK Subs, Charlie got together with Nicky and Alvin, and drummer Dave Ayer (of Samiam fame) to record two albums back-to-back, 'Quintessentials' and 'Riot', both of which were issued by Nicky's New Red Archives label in late 1996. They saw a superb return to form for the band after several shaky mid-period albums that had contained more than their fair share of filler material, capturing once again that raw magic energy that made the band's debut so utterly indispensable. Indeed several of the tracks on offer are a match for some of the vintage classics of the late Seventies/early Eighties.

"Charlie and I recorded a Subs single together in the mid-Nineties which was quite well received, particularly the B-side 'Nobody Move'. We talked in vague terms about the possibility of an album, and with Alvin participating it seemed feasible to actually do two albums at the same time. Our approach was to keep the songs very simple and write very quickly as we did back in '77. Clearly these were not master works of composition! However, working within such limits presents opportunities for invention. How to make these miniature punk explosions endure?

"Having Dave Ayer from Samiam on drums was a big plus, a weight off our minds, and logistically a time saver. We wrote, rehearsed, recorded and mixed both albums in around three weeks. I like the energy on those albums. Without a doubt the chemistry was instantly rekindled and I feel on many of those recordings lies some of my best lead guitar work. Of course we could have spent five weeks in a top flight studio and got the big 'rock' sound like we did on 'Endangered Species', but the spontaneous feel of four guys really having a great time is perhaps just as appealing. To judge by the reviews, people overwhelmingly agreed. My only caveat in hindsight is that if a sufficient number of people were paying attention, which they weren't, then those two records could have been distilled into one extremely strong album."

In 2000, The UK Subs were part of the gruelling Social Chaos tour that saw more than a dozen punk bands criss-crossing the US, and the following year they toured South America. Alvin and Nicky also participated in 2001's 'Time Warp: Greatest Hits' album for US label, Cleopatra, a rather pointless, but great fun all the same, collection that saw them, as the title suggests, re-recording all their hits from over the years.

Then the most recent studio album came in the shape of 2003's 'Universal' for Captain Oi!, a surprisingly fresh-sounding record, with Charlie being joined by Alan Campbell on guitar, Simon Rankin on bass, and Jason 'Dulldrums' behind the kit.

Songs such as 'Spoils Of War' and 'Third World England' ably demonstrate that the evergreen frontman has lost none of his zeal for the scene, nor any of his lyrical invective.

It was even preceded by an amusing, limited novelty single, a Subs-style reworking of the traditional '(What Shall We Do With A) Drunken Sailor?' And, of course, the touring machine rolls ever onwards, with the band seeming to never tire of travelling the world in small vans and meeting face-to-face their legions of die-hard fans.

"I have maintained, perhaps, a somewhat 'silent partner' status since the first reunion," admits Nicky. "But I will be touring again with the band this year (2004). I could easily walk away from playing, but fortunately I don't have to be in an 'all or nothing' situation.

Charlie Harper and Nicky Garratt (guitar) of The UK Subs, 1977

"In fact I have even been toying with the idea of taking a year off and just travelling around the US playing table tennis, one of my other passions – but if I did, I would most likely just pick up the guitar again afterwards anyway.

"Possibly the greatest gift The Subs has given me is the absolute assurance of an alternative to the mundane, and, through my association with Charlie, a positive 'can do' attitude. Charlie is the most positive person I've ever met. I think what I'm trying to say is that I was converted from a dreamer to a doer. I don't think I have ever been 'young at heart' – that phrase may be more fitting for Charlie – but music certainly helps keep one focused.

"I think I would like my work in The Subs to be remembered for its intensity live by those who were there. Our biggest influence was surely to bring movement to the stage, something that was picked up on by the hardcore bands in particular. After The Subs, punk bands couldn't just stand there anymore."

SELECT DISCOGRAPHY:
7"s:
'C.I.D.' (City, 1978)
'Stranglehold' (GEM, 1978)
'Tomorrow's Girls' (GEM, 1979)
'She's Not There' (GEM, 1979)
'Warhead' (GEM, 1980)
'Teenage' (GEM, 1980)
'Party In Paris' (GEM, 1980)
'Keep On Running' (GEM, 1981)
'Countdown' (NEMS, 1981)
'Shake Up The City' EP (Abstract, 1982)
'Another Typical City' (Fall Out, 1983)
'This Gun Says' (Fall Out, 1986)
'Live In Holland' EP (RFB, 1986)
'The Road Is Long, The Road Is Hard' (Fall Out, 1993)
'Postcard From LA' (New Red Archives, 1994) – split with Swingin' Utters
'Betrayal' (NRA, 1994)
'War On The Pentagon' (NRA, 1997)
'Day Of The Dead' (NRA, 1997)
'Cyberjunk' (NRA, 1997)
'Riot '98' EP (Fall Out, 1998)
'Drunken Sailor' (Captain Oi, 2002)

12"s:
'Magic' EP (Fall Out, 1984)
'Hey Santa' (Fall Out, 1988)
'The Motivator' (Released Emotions, 1988)
'Sabre Dance' (NRA, 1988)

LPs:
'Another Kind Of Blues' (GEM, 1978)
'Brand New Age' (GEM, 1980)
'Crash Course' (GEM, 1980)
'Diminished Responsibility' (GEM, 1981)
'Endangered Species' (NEMS, 1982)
'Flood Of Lies' (Fall Out, 1983)
'Gross Out USA' (Fall Out, 1985)
'Huntington Beach' (RFB, 1986)
'In Action' (RFB, 1986)
'Japan Today' (Fallout, 1988)

'Killing Time' (Fallout, 1989)
'Live In Paris' (Released Emotions, 1990)
'Mad Cow Fever' (Fall Out, 1991)
'Normal Service Resumed' (Fall Out, 1994)
'Occupied' (Fall Out, 1996)
'Peel Sessions' (Fall Out, 1996)
'Quintessentials' (NRA, 1996)
'Riot' (NRA, 1996)
'Time Warp: Greatest Hits' (Anagram, 2001)
'Universal' (Captain Oi!, 2002)

AT A GLANCE:

Impossible to narrow it down to a single CD with such a lustrous back catalogue to choose from, but the recent Captain Oi! CD reissues of the first five albums come highly recommended as they are generously bolstered with additional bonus tracks and liner notes by Nicky Garratt. The last studio album, 'Universal', has plenty of fire in its belly too, suggesting that Charlie Harper and his merry men still have much to offer that is relevant to the underground music scene.

THE WALL

Although formed in Wallsend, Sunderland, in early 1978, The Wall are generally remembered as a 'London band', two of their key members – guitarist/vocalist Ian Lowery and bassist/vocalist Andy 'Andzy' Griffiths – having relocated there after the unexpected success of their debut single. No doubt helped by regular airplay on John Peel's Radio 1 show, the quirky and excellent 'New Way' EP for Small Wonder Records sold in excess of 10,000 copies. For that release, The Wall also comprised additional guitarist John Hammond and drummer Bruce Archibald, alongside Lowery and Griffiths, but once that core duo relocated to the capital, they were replaced by Nick Ward on second guitar and Rab Fae Beith behind the kit, the latter having relocated to London himself from Scotland.

"When I first came to London in late '76, I was hanging out down the Albert Embankment," recalls Rab of his introduction to punk rock. "I had my first taste when I saw a group of punks coming along the road who had just left the Roxy. I was amazed at the movement in 1976, nothing came close for shock value; it looked brilliant, it really stood out. We got chatting and after that I started checking it out in more detail."

It wasn't long before, in true punk fashion, Rab decided he wasn't content being just a passive observer of the scene and wanted to be directly involved.

"After meeting the punks, I started hanging out in the so-called 'right places', down the Kings Road etc., and meeting people," he explains. "It was then I decided to buy a drum kit, and, after bashing around for two weeks and picking it up really fast, I bought Sounds and started applying for drum jobs. I went to two auditions and hated both bands, but the third one seemed something special. I went to the Heathrow area and met Kirk Brandon for the first time; we rehearsed for a week and it clicked. Originally it was me on drums, Kirk on bass with two guitar players, and we were called The Pack Of Lies, but we only did one show, in Torquay, before the two guitarists left. A few weeks and several auditions later, we found a guitarist and bassist, with Kirk now handling just vocals, and we changed the name to The Pack which would later become Theatre Of Hate."

Rab played on two singles by The Pack – the self-released 1979 debut, 'Brave New Soldiers', and 'Long Live The Past' for Cyclops Records – before falling out with Brandon.

"In time his ego just got the better of me so I started auditioning for other bands," reveals Rab. "My first audition was for Patrik Fitzgerald who had a deal with Polydor; I got the job and at last

The Wall, live at the Rainbow Theatre, 1981
L-R: Andzy (with microphone), Heed (guitar)
and Claire Bidwell (bass)
(Pic: Tony Mottram)

I was earning money from drumming, landing a three-month contract for gigs and recording.

"My first tour with Patrik was a 37-day UK tour with support from The Teardrop Explodes and an up and coming Small Wonder band, The Wall, who were out promoting their 'New Way' EP. At the end of the tour, Ian Lowery didn't hold back in showing how much he hated his drummer, telling me he was getting sacked straight after the tour, and would I like to join? I had one month of my contract left with Patrik, so I said, 'Yes, when I've finished my recording commitments' (1979's 'Improve Myself' single). It was while recording with Patrik that I got to know Pete Wilson, who had also produced Sham (69), The Jam and The Upstarts, and who would later feature a lot in my own recording career. After my month was up, I went to meet The Wall at the last gig with their old drummer, and it was there in the audience that we met Paul Cook and Steve Jones. They approached the band after the gig and said they'd like to work with us."

The fruit of this unholy union was the strident 'Exchange' single, which spent a month in the Indie Chart during early 1980, peaking at No. 26. Backed by 'Kiss The Mirror', it was harder, heavier and subtly darker than the band's debut offering.

"I joined The Wall, and then two weeks later I was in a studio with Cook and Jones!" remembers Rab, incredulously. "It was like a dream come true back then to be working with The Pistols, and, contrary to whatever anyone else says, The Wall were the first band ever to be produced by a Sex Pistol! It wasn't Joan Jett as some magazines claim. Also in the studio at the same time was Andy Allan who we found out over the next three days was actually the bass player on the 'Never Mind The Bollocks' album... sorry, Sid fans, sad but true! Anyway, the single 'Exchange' was released six weeks later, but it was to be the last Wall recording for Small Wonder as Pete was calling it a day with his label."

Undeterred, Rab, who by this time had taken over not only as drummer but also as the band's manager, wasted no time in landing The Wall a deal with Fresh, who released the excellent 'Ghetto' single in August 1980. An incredibly visceral tune, dripping with haunting echo and driven by an aggressive military rhythm, it was a huge success for the band, spending fourteen weeks in the Indies, even cracking the Top Twenty, albeit briefly. The single was supposedly produced by Sham 69's Jimmy Pursey, although Rab remembers it a little differently to the history books.

"It was really Pete Wilson who produced The Wall but Pursey took all the credit; he actually spent most of the time out in the bogs with Honey Bane! After Pursey's bullshit we decided not to work with him again, so he decided not to bill us for his work.

"We originally recorded 'Ghetto' with Lowery on vocals, but this is when things took a nasty twist," explains Rab of the complications that ensued and led to them replacing their singer. "I was in a bar in Clapham and met a guy I had seen with Lowery... and he told me that Lowery had auditioned him and he would be with The Wall on guitar for the up and coming Angelic Upstarts tour! I told the rest of the band and we decided between us to get Ivan Kelly from (Belfast punk band) Ruefrex in on vocals.

"At the start of the tour we were to meet Lowery outside the Astoria in London en route to the first gig in Trowbridge. When we arrived Lowery was there with his new friend and informed us that Nick was sacked and that this was his replacement. Of course we had other ideas and told him 'No, you're sacked and this is your replacement!', and drove off to Wiltshire to start the 'Teenage Warning' tour. We never saw Lowery again, and after three weeks on the road we went back and replaced Lowery's vocals with Kelly's. We then went into the studio to record the 'Personal Troubles And Public Issues' album."

Ian Lowery went on to form Agent Orange and Ski Patrol, the latter of whom released several singles through Malicious Damage. He also recorded a solo album, 'King Blank', for Beggars Banquet, but sadly died in 2002.

'Personal Troubles And Public Issues' meanwhile was a fine album, a twelve-song collection that saw the band tastefully juggling power and passion, understated melody and controlled distortion. Released in two different sleeves, both designed by bassist Andzy who had an art degree, the album was another Indie hit for the band during Christmas 1980.

"After recording the album we were at a stage where we sold a lot of records but were shit at pulling a crowd for gigs," reckons Rab. "Nick Ward decided to leave as he was a big fan of gigging and shows were few and far between. We had been playing a few gigs with The Straps about that time so we decided to nick their guitar player! Enter Andy 'Heed' Forbes.

"It was also around this time that I managed to get us a deal with Polydor as a friend there, Dennis Munday, offered us a contract. I'm sure it was more of a favour than A&R as Dennis was such a nice guy. A few weeks after signing we went to Polydor's recording studio to record our second album, 'Dirges And Anthems'.

"On the way to the studios one day, we were all walking from Bond Street tube station over to Polydor. Ivan Kelly was pissed up, and, as we crossed Oxford Street, an old man in his sixties looked over at Ivan. Ivan flipped, shouting 'Who the fuck are you looking at?' and proceeded to give him a right kicking! We were all shocked and disgusted, so he was sacked there and then, and we never did find out what made him snap. Andzy decided to take over vocals as we thought it would be quicker to find a bassist than a singer. We were then offered the Stiff Little Fingers 'Go For It' tour later that same day, so had to act quickly as it was in just five weeks time."

The Wall recorded the three-track 'Remembrance' EP to coincide with the dates, which saw Andzy both playing bass and singing in the studio, whilst a stand-in bassist was recruited for the actual tour, which Rab remembers fondly as one of the live highlights of the band's short career. Claire Bidwell from The Passions joined the band on bass upon their return, allowing Andzy to fully concentrate on his vocals.

"Then halfway through recording 'Dirges…', Heed left to be a lawyer and Claire's friend Bazz finished the album with us. At the same time as we went to Polydor, Fresh Records were pissed off that we had left them so soon, and, seeing as they had been so good to us, we gave them the outtakes from the 'Remembrance' EP for free. They were later released as the 'Hobby For a Day' EP which was our last release on Fresh."

'Dirges…' appeared in early 1982, complete with a free three-track 7", and saw the band experimenting with the more commercial facets of their sound, even introducing a saxophone and acoustic guitar on some tracks. Polydor insisted that the band lift the radio-friendly 'Epitaph' track as a single. Unsurprisingly the Indie release for Fresh – the brooding, ominous 'Hobby for A Day' single – sold far better than the major label stuff, resulting in The Wall being dropped by Polydor soon after its release, a cheque for £10,000 in their back pocket, as a leaving present.

As a result of all the label turmoil, Rab and Andzy soon found themselves keeping The Wall afloat as a duo, signing to No Future, and recording the 'Daytripper' EP, which saw Rab not only playing guitar, bass and drums, but also producing the session too! Appearing as both a nine-track 12" and a four-track single, it was to be the band's final release, but one of their strongest, a well-rounded pop punk outing that had the band bowing out with a defiant bang. The title cut was a Beatles cover (apparently chosen by Rab because he had played it previously with The Pack and could still remember how it went), but the stand-out track was the perfectly-formed, iridescent 'When I'm Dancing'. The EP reached No. 21 in the Indies, but even its relative commercial success couldn't undo the rot that had already set into the band.

"As No Future were a skinhead/Oi label, we didn't want to be tarred with the same brush, so we got them to change their 'OI' prefix catalogue number for our record. That's why The Wall were the only band on No Future that didn't have an 'OI' number, it was 'O2' instead. By then, me and Andzy had decided to do one more gig (at The Blue Boy, London), as a three-piece with 'Keghead' (aka Al from Four Minds Crack) on guitar, but we weren't that interested anymore and so we split soon after, whilst we could still be friends.

"Funny thing was, two punks came all the way from Leicester to see that last gig. They got talking to me and I found out that one of them was a drummer, so I told him to come up onstage if there was an encore and I'd let him play my drums. Of course, he thought I was taking the piss, but we got an encore and I called out for him. So, 'Uniforms' and 'Suckers' were then played by a fan... some guy from Leicester was the last live drummer for The Wall, whilst I stood beside Andzy doing backing vocals. I bet it made his journey worthwhile..."

Rab briefly played with Goth-rockers And Also The Trees before joining The UK Subs in 1984, playing on their 'Huntington Beach' and 'In Action' albums, which actually appeared on his very own RFB label.

"RFB was a one-man operation. RFB stood for Rab Fae Beith, of course, but if anyone asked I'd say it stood for 'Rab's a Fat Bastid', haha! Same thing, I suppose. 'If it sounds shit, it ain't on RFB' and 'If you hate shit music, you'll love RFB' were my slogans at the time. I set up the label when I was with the Subs and was sick of seeing no money from Jungle. Steve Brown (from Jungle) once said to me 'If you don't like it, then release them yourself'... so I did! I had just recorded 'This Gun Says' with The Subs and got Charlie (Harper, The Subs' main man) to sign with me, also Broken Bones and Condemned 84. Thanks Jungle!"

Nowadays Rab is a motorcycle mechanic, having recently signed over RFB's back catalogue to Captain Oi! Records for future reissue, but he has no regrets.

"I'd recommend joining a band to anyone! I had a great laugh and time, but, having said that, I don't miss it; it's more fun looking back than doing it now, as my new love is motorcycles. I'm getting as much fun with bikes now as I ever did with music then... maybe it's just my body's way of telling me that I'm a sad old bastid?"

SELECT DISCOGRAPHY:
7"s:
'New Way' (Small Wonder, 1979)
'Exchange' (Small Wonder, 1980)
'Ghetto' (Fresh, 1980)
'Hobby For A Day' (Fresh, 1981)
'Remembrance' (Polydor, 1981)
'Epitaph' (Polydor, 1981)
'Daytripper' (No Future, 1982)

12"s:
'Daytripper' (No Future, 1982)

LPs:
'Personal Troubles And Public Issues' (Fresh, 1980)
'Dirges And Anthems' (Polydor, 1982)

AT A GLANCE:
'The Wall: The Punk Collection', a 1998 CD from Captain Oi!, compiles the band's best tracks from their Small Wonder, Fresh and No Future releases, along with artwork, liner notes and a discography. There's nothing included from their short stint with Polydor (blame the accountants), but their Indie material was by far their strongest anyway.

THE DARK

A musically innovative band from Islington, The Dark are possibly best remembered for their thunderous cover version of the 'Hawaii Five 0' theme tune that they issued as a single in late 1980. But it was 1982's 'The Masque' that really hinted at the band's vast potential, perversely wasted when they split soon after its release.

"Phil Langham and I formed The Dark in 1978," reveals original vocalist John Flannagan. "We were both doing our A-levels at Kingsway College, London… for the second time, by the way! Both of us loved music, and punk seemed an easy way in, as neither of us could play a note. We were all Bowie casualties anyway. Phil bought a bass and learned to play on one string; he also cut his long shaggy David Coverdale mane into a vaguely punky crop.

"It was an exciting time, when things seemed very wide open and changing every minute. And even as we formed, the whole punk rock scene – the first wave anyway – was nearly over. I got a friend Billy O'Neill down from Witney, Oxford, to play guitar, and Jamie Kane in on drums, and there we had the group. Great for us… a disaster for the music industry!

"Phil and I had never played before in any bands, but as I was going to sing, that didn't matter. Billy was already an outstanding musician by the time he was fifteen or sixteen, and, although his heart lay with Rush, Zeppelin and Genesis, he decided to give his all to the punk cause."

The band even played their first show at Kingsway College, supporting The Gentry, who would soon after change their name to Spandau Ballet and find fame and fortune as a major New Romantic pop act. "We were both Islington bands and there was a bit of rivalry," remembers John. "It was very nerve-racking for us, even though it all passed by in a flash. Afterwards everyone thought we'd blown them away… 'everyone' being all our best friends, of course!"

In early 1979, The Dark were joined by guitarist Andy Riff, an ex-Menace roadie, who not only expanded the band's sound but, through his many contacts, helped secure them their recording deal.

"I was already in a local band called The Rotten Klitz, but we found it easier to get gigs as The Rotten Naughty Partz!" laughs Andy. "Eventually that became The – far less terrifying – Suspects. We did eight gigs, supporting UK Subs, Eater and Menace.

"The first proper gig of the recording Dark line-up was at the Pegasus on March 1st 1979, even though I only came on for the encore and played two songs. But Billy, who was the unofficial band leader by virtue of actually being able to play, felt that I improved the sound massively, and that was that, I was in.

"I knew Noel Martin, the old drummer with Menace, who became our manager; he was friendly with the owner of Fresh Records, and they were looking to sign new bands at the time. I'd only been with the band two weeks when we did a live audition for them, playing our entire ten-song set.

"They decided to pick three songs for the first single, and chose 'My Friends' as the A-side, narrowing it down to a choice between 'John Wayne' and 'French Toys' for the B-side. All five of us were then asked to vote, and eventually, after much wrangling, we chose 'John Wayne', a song I'd brought from The Suspects."

The infectious and bubbly single, produced by Menace guitarist Steve Tannett, actually appeared as a double A-side during summer 1979, but John and Billy left after memorable shows with The Ruts and The Vibrators to promote it.

"Phil was driving me mad at the time," sighs John. "I had written the lyrics to 'My Friends' with him, and he'd gone behind my back to take my name off the credits on the single. All very petty, I know, but we were only young. Another reason was, I'd got into drama school and wouldn't be able to tour or rehearse very often. It was a nutty time, and I loved it, but I knew it was time to leave.

"Billy O'Neill left for several reasons, mainly to hone his Rush guitar solos (he went on to play with Blast Furnace And The Heatwaves), but also because, believe it or not, he decided to become a priest, which was going to take him seven years to study for."

Billy was replaced on guitar by Den Perdicou, whilst it was decided after auditioning many unsuitable singers that Phil Langham should handle the vocal duties as well as bass.

"I was in a few bands before joining The Dark," says Den. "Most notably The Limit, with my friend Mario Rocca. I was self-taught, I started playing when I was about twelve years old, but I was drawn to punk rock because it gave young people everywhere a chance to get involved with the music industry even if they weren't expert musicians."

The revamped Dark made their public debut at The Bridge House in Canning Town on February 12th 1980, with the first vinyl following in the shape of the aforementioned 'Hawaii Five 0' single, which made No. 42 in the Indies in September 1980. The delightfully eccentric 'Einstein's Brain' (b/w 'Muzak') appeared as the next single, which was Den's last recording with the band.

"We were at a private party for Fresh Records in the Starlight Rooms on West Hampstead, and I had an argument with Phil over something stupid and I just walked out. Being nineteen, stubborn and half-drunk didn't help matters!

"I have some great memories of my time with The Dark though. Most punk bands were perceived as just noise, but we were so much more than that. I always thought of us as a high-energy rock band really. We worked well together; never tried to upstage each other and always acted professionally onstage."

Den (who now teaches guitar when he isn't driving London taxis) was replaced by Jim Bryson, previously with Demon Preacher, who joined the band just in time for their

The Dark, 1980
L-R: Jim, Den, Phil, Riff

UK tour with UK Decay and Play Dead and the frantic 'On The Wire' 7". However it was the band's one and only album, 'Chemical Warfare', and 'The Masque' single lifted from it, which saw The Dark scaling new musical heights.

Opening in fine style with the Damned-esque 'Disintegrate', 'Chemical Warfare' was a vibrantly tuneful and uptempo punk rock album that included reworked versions of 'John Wayne' and 'On The Wires'. Guitarist Jim Bryson even played keyboards and sang on the moody 'Pleasure Is Pain', a real departure for the band that, given the right push, could well have garnered some serious airplay. The album was justifiably The Dark's best selling release, spending a month in the Indies and reaching No. 16 upon its release during April 1982.

"We recorded it in Carnaby Street," says Andy. "It took two and a half weeks to do, and was obviously an incredibly magical, memorable time for all of us. So many stories, so many arguments over whom should sing most of the songs. Jim certainly wanted to sing more than one, but Phil's giant ego, and equally big stomach, won out in the end, and he sang them all but one. I spent a lot of time at loggerheads with Phil over the sound of the guitars; I knew a lot more about it than he did, and the producers racked their brains for a way to get him out of the studio."

The album was preceded by the forebodingly atmospheric 'The Masque' single in March '82. Led by a deliciously dark and seductive melody, it has deservedly attained the status of a goth-punk classic, and in September of that year it was also included on the 'Punk And Disorderly: Further Charges' compilation.

"It was the way I think we could've gone," reckons Andy. "The first time that I felt we really had our own sound. That said, there's nothing that we recorded that I'm ashamed of. Every record was different and had its own sound. 'Masque', for example, was very different to 'Hawaii Five 0', and if you put them back to back, you wouldn't think it was the same band. We'd only really just begun to explore our potential.

"We weren't some silly little punk band; I felt that we had a lot more to offer than that… on a comedy level if nothing else! Basically there were two sides to the band, which made for some hilarious creative tension. When we started, John was hoping we would turn into Fleetwood Mac or something, and I was going to miraculously morph into Lindsey Buckingham. Come to think of it, maybe he thought he was Stevie Nicks? Billy was into complicated metal solos and worshipped at the church of Alex Lifeson (Rush), whilst the rest of the band were full-on punks. Really into take no prisoners, 1000 mph punk rock. Every time John would beg us to slow down, Jamie – who otherwise said very little – would bound onto his drum stool and shout out what was to become his mantra, 'Ignorance!' Kind of said it all really."

Despite their obvious promise, The Dark began to come apart at the seams just as they were poised on the brink of real success, with Jim Bryson being fired and Jamie Kane leaving to join The Satellites. He was replaced by Nicholas 'Razzle' Dingley, another ex-member of Demon Preacher, and Charlie Casey, formerly with Menace, joined on bass to allow Phil to focus on his role as vocalist. This version of the band played the final ever Dark show at London's 100 Club on June 29th 1982, before, unable to agree on their future direction, splitting up. Some of their set from that night was released posthumously as 'The Living End' LP by Fall Out Records.

Andy Riff went on to form The V2s and the short-lived Danse Macabre, whilst Phil became a respected producer and set up Anagram Records, who signed, amongst others, One Way System and the Angelic Upstarts. Sadly he died a drug-related death several years later, aged 27. Razzle meanwhile became the drummer for Hanoi Rocks, although tragically he too died, in a car accident in the USA during December 1984.

"We obviously left our mark on the fans that followed us and liked our music," concludes Andy. "But I think even if I was a young punk fan today, I would've enjoyed seeing us play, and I wish I could have stood in the crowd and watched us in our prime, as it was extremely energetic and powerful. I'd love to go back and enjoy it all over again. I do wish we'd never got caught up in petty arguments though; I never even signed a contract, no five-year deal with no cunt. All Phil's bollocks, playing about with credits, was a waste of time and energy; we were all equal in my eyes."

"It was a great time in my life," adds Jamie Kane. "I think about it a lot, and I will bore my kids stupid with Dark stories when they are old enough to understand them! I just hope that we made some small contribution for those young kids who went on to start their own punk bands."

SELECT DISCOGRAPHY:
7"s:
'My Friends' (Fresh, 1979)
'Hawaii Five 0' (Fresh, 1980)
'Einstein's Brain' (Fresh, 1981)
'On The Wires' (Fresh, 1981)
'The Masque' (Fresh, 1982)

LPs:
'The Living End' (Fall Out, 1982)
'Chemical Warfare' (Fresh, 1982)

AT A GLANCE:
Captain Oi!'s 1995 'The Best Of The Dark' CD collects all the band's Fresh Records output, and comes complete with comprehensive liner notes, previously unseen photos and reproductions of relevant covers.

ACTION PACT

One of the more unique punk bands to emerge from the Southeast in the early Eighties would have to be Action Pact. They were blessed with not only an ear for a great tune, but also a keen sense of social conscience, and one of the most distinct and powerful female vocalists to have ever graced the punk scene. However when the band was originally assembled in 1980 by founding members Des 'Wild Planet' Stanley and Kim 'Dr. Phibes' Igoe, it wasn't always on the cards that they should be fronted by a young lady.

"After getting caught up in the first explosion of punk," remembers Des, "We decided that instead of just standing back and admiring all these groups, perhaps it would be a good idea to have a go at it ourselves.

As regards who was going to play which instrument, we both had a go on an old electric guitar I had, and we decided that I was perhaps the slightly more proficient, so I would play guitar and Kim would play bass!

"Joe 'Fungus' Fulinger was roped in on drums after he was heard practising in his garage, and Kim's brother John Igoe helped us out on vocals and guitar for two or three rehearsals. When John went to dedicate all his time to his main band, Dead Man's Shadow, we were a bit stuck for a singer, until someone informed us that there was a certain girl at school who really wanted to sing in a band. So we said, 'Tell her to come and have a go'. Alison 'George Cheex' Charles turned up one day, absolutely terrified, and proceeded to shout out our songs with great enthusiasm. The band was now complete!"

Thankfully Des and Kim decided against using their original choice of name – Bad Samaritans! – and Action Pact was born. They were soon making noises anywhere and everywhere they could.

"The earliest gigs we did were marvellously loud, chaotic affairs in our local pub," says Des. "I recall a lot of damage being done by over-enthusiastic pogoers, and on one occasion the whole mosh pit landed up on the stage, trashing all our drums and breaking poor Joe's arm! The atmosphere though was always one of general geniality and encouragement. We thought to ourselves, 'This is fun, let's have some more of it!'

"It was about this time we decided to document our progress by making a record, just in case we didn't get any further. So 'London Bouncers' and 'All Purpose Action Footwear' were recorded and committed to vinyl as a split single."

Recorded in late '81, and released by Subversive in early '82, when half the band were still at school, the 'Heathrow Touchdown' split EP was so-called because the band lived within a stone's throw of Heathrow Airport's Terminal Four. It troubled the lower end of the Indie Charts for only one week, but served as the perfect introduction to Action Pact's intoxicating musical cocktail.

Driven by an insistent riff and George's deliciously mischievous shriek, 'London Bouncers' in particular (the other song they contributed was 'All Purpose Action Footwear', a sensitive ode to Doctor Marten boots!) ably demonstrated that here was a band with something exciting to offer. Their tender years didn't seem to put anyone off booking them either.

George 'Cheex' and Des 'Wild Planet' of Action Pact

"We never really had a problem with people not taking us seriously because, although Joe and Alison were only fifteen or sixteen, Kim and myself were actually in our twenties. So half of the band was school age... but the other half comprised two hairy-arsed concrete navvies! And we didn't really have to go hunting for gigs anyway, as they just seemed to find us. We seemed to be in demand, because, having a female chanteuse, we were a bit different to all the gruff-voiced bands around at that time."

The single inevitably came to the attention of John Peel, who invited the band to do a session for his show, which was produced by Dale Griffin, ex-drummer and founder member of Mott The Hoople, and broadcast on February 22nd, 1982. Fall Out were quick to pick up on the buzz, with label-boss Alan Hauser (who went on to become the band's manager) snatching them from the clutches of Rondelet at the last minute, and releasing the 'Suicide Bag' 7" that summer. It promptly spent three months in the Indies, peaking at No. 6, and its positive anti-glue sniffing message was a welcome ray of sunlight in an otherwise often dark, nihilistic scene. Despite a fraught recording session with Neil Brockbank at Hallmark Studios, it remains a vibrant compelling listen.

"I was very disappointed with the 'Suicide Bag' single," sighs Kim. "We turned up at the studio with what we felt were our strongest songs at the time, only to be met by a producer who completely misunderstood us. Neil spent twelve hours trying to make us sound like Haircut 100! We left the studio feeling deflated and disillusioned. In the end we put it out with layers of guitar overdubs to try and salvage the operation, but, to my ears at least, it only just camouflages the mess beneath."

The ever-supportive John Peel gave them another session, which was broadcast during August '82, and more gigs were undertaken, with the likes of The Outcasts and The Urban Dogs, but then Fungus left the fold.

"We were all disappointed to lose Joe, as we all agreed he was a very talented drummer for such a young geezer," recalls Des. "Dale Griffin offered to stand in for Joe if we were stuck for a sticksman, but someone was already scribbling us a letter from Tunbridge Wells as soon as he heard Joe had left."

Late 1982, and enter Chris 'Grimly Fiendish' Lee, previously with little-known biker-punk acts, Sheer Filth and Vermin, who counted amongst their fans members of the Anti-Nowhere League and boasted songs such as 'I'm A Fucking Maniac'! He impressed everyone in Action Pact by being so familiar with their material he could play their set by the end of his first rehearsal with the band, and, needless to say, he was in.

"I remember Chris and Nick from The League used to drop in on Sheer Filth rehearsals to check on our progress and have a few tins," says Chris of his pre-Action Pact days. "Once, we had arranged a free gig at Matfield Village Hall, and during our set Chris and Nick turned up, with Winston from The League and Captain Sensible in tow; they had just blagged their first tour with The Damned. After we'd finished, I stayed on drums, and was joined by my mate Thistles (who would soon become a member of Action Pact as well) on bass, the Captain on guitar, and Nick on vocals, and we did a medley of Ramones songs, finishing with 'Suzy Is A Headbanger' and 'Let's Dance' off 'It's Alive'! The four of us had never played together before, yet we knew that particular album so well, it was completely natural to us! Just goes to show the influence of The Ramones...

"Anyway, we then retired to a local pub, where the locals took exception and started a ruck. I remember one of them got a right pasting, with knuckle-dusters... ouch! We were all thrown out, and as we were leaving Captain said to Winston, 'It's no wonder you guys can't get anywhere to play!'"

The new-look Action Pact was soon back in Alaska Studios, recording their sophomore EP for Fall Out – 'People', another three tracks of urgent melodic punk, illuminated once again by George's cheeky vocals. For Kim, this is the Action Pact recording he is most proud of.

"Apart from being a strong, enthusiastically played tune, it was, in retrospect, very prophetic," he reckons. "The whole yuppie 'me' generation of greed, born of Thatcherism, is encapsulated in that song. Even when I listen to it now, I feel it is still valid."

In early 1983, the debut album 'Mercury Theatre – On The Air' was recorded over two long weekends at Pineapple Studios in Southall with Phil Langham of The Dark occupying the producer's chair. A fine collection of songs, albeit slightly over-produced and perhaps lacking some of the energy of the earlier EPs, the album was a great success and featured a particularly intense vocal performance from George, especially on the ranting 'Things That Need'. The opening track, '(Drowning Out The) Big Jets', made reference to how loud the band had to constantly turn their amps up, seeing as they practised right beneath one of Heathrow's busiest flight paths.

Immediately after the album's release however, Kim Igoe got fed up with it all and left, to be replaced by the band's producer, Phil

Alison 'George' Charles of Action Pact, 'one of the most distinct and powerful female vocalists to have ever graced the punk scene...' (Pic: Tony Mottram)

Langham. Phil only lasted for a few gigs, plus a Kid Jensen radio session and the recording of the 'London Bouncers (Bully Boy Version)' 12". He was ousted because he was considered unreliable, but to show there were no hard feelings he was retained as producer for the next single.

"I'd begun to feel disillusioned about the scene, and recent gigs had left me feeling quite cold," explains Kim. "I remember one day being approached by a stereotypical punk, complete with coloured mohican etc., who complained about the 'ordinary shirt' I was wearing. Having accused me of looking 'like a mod', I began to question whether people like him were getting the point of Action Pact.

"This wasn't the sole reason for stepping down, of course, but I saw it as a symbolic, eye-opening moment. It was, I must stress, an amicable parting with the rest of the group, and I was actually quite flattered when asked to continue writing the lyrics."

"At the time I joined, the band were gaining rapidly in popularity," adds Chris, "but Kim never really enjoyed the 'being in a band' part of being in a band! He just wanted to write lyrics, I think, so he decided to step down after 'Mercury Theatre' had been recorded. It seemed obvious to get our producer, Phil, to step in because he knew the material and was such a great bassist.

"I loved Phil like a brother, and had been a huge fan of The Dark, but he could go a bit over the top at times, and he and Des never really inhabited the same world. So during summer 1983 we replaced Phil with my best buddy Neil, who'd been hanging around with us for quite a while beforehand, and this, for me, was the definitive line-up of Action Pact. The onstage nuttiness developed from here, and the songwriting matured because we all got on so well. There were no personal tensions, so we all relaxed and enjoyed ourselves a lot more."

In keeping with the band's love of bizarre pseudonyms Neil Craddock was dubbed 'Thistles' after a donkey from a TV advert that ate thistles, and soon after made his live debut, a mere week before being plunged into the studio to record the 'Question Of Choice' EP.

"My first gigs with the band were two in a row one weekend," he reveals. "The first night was in Cambridge, which was a bit of a strange affair. I remember one bloke standing in front of the stage for the whole of our set doing Nazi salutes… a bit disturbing for my first show! The next night was the Futurama festival in Leeds, which was a whole different thing. Killing Joke were headlining, with The Smiths… what a gig! We rocked."

Despite a decent mix, 'Question Of Choice' remains the band's weakest release, sounding a bit scrappy and lacking the infectious hooks of their stronger songs.

"Given that we recorded all the individual drums separately, it could've been a lot worse, but there's no fluidity to the rhythm section," agrees Chris. "I remember Thistles and I went round to Winston from the Anti-Nowhere League's house to borrow a guitar cab for Des, and we played him it. He especially liked the drum sound, but I'll never forget the drive back from the lock-up to Winston's place. The cabinet took up all the room in the back, and Thistles was driving, so I had to sit on Winston's lap! Not many people can say that… well, not many blokes anyway! As for Winston's reaction? 'Blimey, what if New Musical Express or Sounds get a picture of this? 'ANWL up Action Pact!' Two careers finished for the price of one!"

1984 saw the band gigging frequently with the likes of Red London from Sunderland, their new-found friends the Newtown Neurotics, and even one Porky The Poet… who went on to find fame as comedian Phill Jupitus!

The next single, 'Yet Another Dole Queue Song' was backed by a cover of The Ramones' 'Rockaway Beach', which saw George doing a vocal duet with The Neurotics' Steve Drewett. Although the A-side is a bouncy slice of vitriol, the cover song on the flip literally bubbles with enthusiasm and steals the thunder from the song it was meant to play a supporting role to. The 12" version contained two extra songs, the comparatively disappointing '1974' and another fun cover, of Gary Glitter's 'Rock And Roll Part 2'.

"The Ramones will always be one of the all-time great punk rock bands," acknowledges Neil. "That song meant a great deal to each member of the band for different reasons. And Steve was the obvious choice for the duet with George; we were growing very close as bands and Steve was a Ramones expert!"

To celebrate their alliance, the two bands undertook a short European tour together, and upon their return, Action Pact entered Greenhouse Studios with Phil Vinall to record their second album, 'Survival Of The Fattest'. It featured some of their finest compositions, seamlessly blending their early edgy aggression with a confident maturity, and included the superbly atmospheric 'Up On The Heath'. Although it garnered significant critical acclaim, it failed to chart.

'Cocktail Credibility' was lifted from the album as a single, and also failed to set the world alight. It turned out to be the band's last release, as they split up in 1986. Painfully aware of dwindling interest, Chris decided to leave in late '85, soon after plans to tour and record in the USA fell through, and his departure was the last straw for Des.

"I just couldn't be bothered going through auditions and rehearsing again," he admits. "Lethargy set in. Looking back, George and me should have really kept something going, but hindsight is a wonderful gift, and we didn't!

"But I thoroughly enjoyed my time in Action Pact, especially meeting all the different people around the country. Alan Hauser, our manager and label boss back then, should get an extra special mention for being such a great bloke and sticking with us through thick and thin.

"At the end of the day, we were just four people who were out for a bit of fun, and who cared passionately for the underdog, the planet and fair play for all. We also played very loud! I just hope we will be remembered as caring people."

"You may recall a pathetic song by The Exploited called 'Fuck The Mods'?" adds Kim (who went on to spend some time in The Mancubs in the late Eighties alongside ex-Dead Man's Shadow members, Matt Brown and Ian Fisher). "This was the type of shallow, self-defeating nonsense that we were aimed against. There seemed to follow endless records that tended to advocate violence. When questioned about it all, bands like Blitz would say, 'Well, it happens'. But to us, that wasn't good enough. We were determined not to sit on the fence and treat our listeners like morons.

"We also believed that if you did have something worthwhile to say, then it should be accompanied by a good tune. What's the point in constantly preaching to a few converted punks, when a strong song can reach a far wider audience?"

SELECT DISCOGRAPHY:
7"s:
'Heathrow Touchdown' (Subversive, 1981) – split release with Dead Man's Shadow
'Suicide Bag' EP (Fall Out, 1982)
'People' EP (Fall Out, 1983)
'Question Of Choice' (Fall Out, 1983)
'Yet Another Dole Queue Song' (Fall Out, 1984)
'Cocktail Credibility' (Fall Out, 1984)

12"s:
'London Bouncers (Bully Boy Version)' (Fall Out, 1983)
'Yet Another Dole Queue Song' (Fall Out, 1984)

LPs:
'Mercury Theatre – On The Air' (Fall Out, 1983)
'Survival Of The Fattest' (Fall Out, 1984)

AT A GLANCE:
In 1995, Captain Oi! released the excellent 'Action Pact: The Punk Singles' CD, which compiles all of the band's 7" and 12" tracks, and comes complete with liner notes and original cover art. The following year, the label also conveniently doubled both Action Pact albums up onto one CD, a release that included reproductions of all the cover art and lyrics.

DEAD MANS SHADOW

s mentioned earlier, a band who had close links with Action Pact, and another of the more challenging acts of the early Eighties, both musically and lyrically, was Dead Mans Shadow. During their formative periods, the two bands not only shared stages, vinyl space and even musicians, but also a similar healthy disregard for punk convention.

"I was attracted to the energy and rebellion of it all," says guitarist John Igoe, when prompted as to why he got into punk rock in the first place. "And a great time it was too! I was listening to bands and thinking, 'Fuck me, I can do this!' It wasn't something you considered as out of reach. People were buying cheap guitars from their mums' catalogues and actually having a go!

"I remember buying one of those 'Teach yourself guitar' books from the local music shop and off I went. My first stab at it was singing in an outfit called The Bad Samaritans, who would later become Action Pact. Meanwhile, Matt (Dagnut – bass/vocals) and Fish (Ian Fisher – drums) started off in a band called Vomit! Naturally that silly name had to go, and when I became involved, I suggested the name Dead Mans Shadow."

Armed with a clutch of early songs, the trio entered local studio Pet Sounds ("Nothing to do

Dead Mans Shadow
L-R: Ian Fisher, Matt Dagnut, John Igoe
(Pic: Mick Mercer)

with the Beach Boys, of course, but a quaint facility beneath a pet shop," laughs John) in 1980 to record their first demo. John borrowed £300 from his brother, Kim, then still bassist with Action Pact (who also drew the cover), and they released the four song 'Neighbours' EP on their own Hog Records. As well as the title track, it featured the cuts 'Poxy Politics', 'War Ploys' and 'Morons', and although crude compared to their latter recordings, it quickly sold out of its pressing of 1000 copies and definitely helped kick-start the band's career.

"John Peel picked up on the EP, and that generated some interest from several small independent labels. One of these was Fresh Records, a punk outlet that had groups like The Dark on their books. They took over the distribution of 'Neighbours', and when it began to sell out, they offered to record us, thinking we might make them some money.

"Because my brother Kim had helped us financially, we gave over one side of the next recording to his band, Action Pact. Cutting two tracks each, we put it out on our own Subversive label (distributed by Fresh) and this became known as 'The Heathrow Touchdown' EP, at Kim's suggestion."

In early 1982, Dead Mans Shadow signed to Rondelet, and released the three-track 'Bomb Scare' EP, which spent a month in the Indies and reached No. 34. The title track is particularly stirring, possessing a menacing power not dissimilar to Killing Joke in their prime, and driven by an insistent choppy guitar riff.

Their second single, 'Flower In The Gun', was another quantum leap forward in terms of mature songwriting that probably took many hardcore fans by surprise with its measured tempos and strident melodic chorus. Like the single before it, it was produced by Phil Langham of The Dark, and had more in common with The Ruts and SLF than The Exploited or Discharge.

"Our first loves came in the shape of people like The Clash and The Jam," reckons John. "Here you had great tunes paired with earnest lyrics, something we wanted to emulate. But I have no problems at all being likened to bands like The Ruts and Killing Joke; they all helped prove that you could play with power and aggression without descending into cacophony. And while it's true that these groups had fired our imaginations, we were never going to be content just being sound-alikes. D.M.S. were always out to surprise people, even if we upset the purists.

"At the end of the day, it comes down to tunes. Take a group like Discharge, for instance. I thought their hearts were in the right place, but they were churning out the same old tired clichés over the top of a lot of tuneless thrash. Rather than browbeat the listener with our views, we felt that we could get them across in a more positive way. Like I've said many times before, it is possible to be creative without sacrificing that power…"

Unfortunately the band's grand vision was only witnessed by a small percentage of the record-buying public who might well have appreciated it. Thanks to under-promotion and poor distribution, 'Flower In The Gun' didn't even register at the lower end of the Indie Charts. Dead Mans Shadow jumped ship to Expulsion soon after.

"Although keen to get records out, we, and many other groups like us, were often hampered by shoddy labels. We'd become disillusioned with Rondelet, and when one of their number said

he was starting a new label based in London, we took up his offer to join. Expulsion had big ideas and promises… yet like so many others before them, eventually folded themselves."

The band's debut album, 'The 4 Ps', appeared in May 1983, a great collection of songs recorded at Alaska Studios the preceding December, that became the band's best-selling release, actually making the Indie Top Twenty during its brief three-week chart run. Incidentally the four 'P's referred to in the title are pride, pacifism, passion and perseverance, all adjectives that could be readily applied to the sound, lyrics and approach of Dead Mans Shadow themselves.

"Looking back on that first album, I'd say my fave tracks are 'Needles', 'We Can Do It Together' and 'Greed'. I really like the end part of 'Greed', and I think perhaps we should have done more stuff like that. 'The 4 Ps' sold very well, and unfortunately people remember it more than 'To Mohammad A Mountain' (the second D.M.S. album), though I think we could have done it better. I don't really like to criticise any of our recordings because they all hold a special place in our hearts, but it's not like anyone ever stuck us into Abbey Road, is it?"

Dead Mans Shadow guitarist, John Igoe (Pic: Mick Mercer)

In May '83, Dead Mans Shadow recorded the tragically underrated 'Toleration Street' 7" at Wickham Studios in Croydon with Kevin Nixon at the desk. Two new songs that showcased their rapid evolution as an incredibly innovative outfit, not to mention Matt's newfound confidence as a vocalist, it inexplicably failed to chart. It was their last release for Expulsion, although Criminal Damage was waiting in the wings, contract at the ready.

"My personal preference is for that Criminal Damage material," reveals John. "We'd really matured by the time we signed to them and we were ready to do something different. I think we achieved that aim with our second album, 'To Mohammad A Mountain'. I think the label wanted 'The 4 Ps Part 2', but in no way were they going to get it!

"It was a great time making that record, and I have fond memories of it. There was this farm in Wales, miles from anywhere, that had a studio inside a barn. We had two weeks in the wilderness to make that album, were totally relaxed and focused, and I think that shows in the end result. "Sadly this is the record I think people have heard the least. It's a shame really because there's some great melodies and variation going down on that album. Likewise with our last single, 'Another Year' (backed by 'One Man's Crusade'); it was catchy, punchy and contained some nice guitar lines."

Ironically, the band's best material received their worse distribution, and, frustrated at the lack of support from both label and scene, Dead Man's Shadow called it a day soon after.

"That would be early 1984, not long after 'Mohammad' appeared. We felt that the scene had run its course, and that we were just banging our heads on a brick wall. I'd started listening to groups like The Smiths, and saw something much more appealing in that than a movement that had gone stale.

"I'd just like to say that as a band we had some great times together, full of memories to cherish, and laced with adventure," John says, focusing on his positive memories of the time. "Of course, we never changed the world, but at the time we believed we could, and we had fun trying. That was the great thing about punk; it gave you the chance to express yourself, and knocked down barriers. It was never seen as a route to riches by us, but rather an escape from our mundane lives.

"It was also a platform for us to be creative, and I think I can say we were. I'm glad to have been involved in that whole crazy scene, and I'm sure we made our mark with somebody. We had some great times on the road and met some fine people along the way... as well as a lot of right wankers! But looking back I'd certainly say the positives of being in the band far outweighed the negatives..."

Since D.M.S., John Igoe has remained active in music, and, although his musical tastes have diversified ever more over the years, he still feels a strong affinity with the punk ideals he discovered in the late Seventies and early Eighties.

"In 1985, I cut a track, 'Serious', as The Mancubs for a compilation album called 'Gunfire And Pianos'. Released on a subsidiary of Beggars Banquet called Situation Two, it received quite a bit of airplay from John Peel."

And, as detailed previously, once he had discarded the name The Mancubs, it was adopted briefly by his brother Kim who was jamming at that time with John's ex-band mates, Matt Dagnut and Ian Fisher.

"In 1992," continues John, "I made a dance track called 'House Trap' under the name of Dove-Active, which became a much sought-after 12" by rave DJs... I kid you not! I really related to that whole 'House' thing; the DIY aspect really reminded me of punk. The only drawback is that it's a lot more expensive to get started equipment-wise and out of reach for many working class kids, and I don't like that.

"Recently I made a limited edition CD, 'The Interocker' EP, under the guise of Feeler No. 1. This is a guitar-based project and is available on my own label, Sasi Pie.

"Nowadays I'm just doing what people my age are supposed to do, holding down a job, enjoying fatherhood etc., but my heart is right in there with the music. I never get staid; my ear is always on the ground listening out for great new things. I must confess though that I often return to my old punk collection to blast the cobwebs away; it never fails!

"Punk music definitely gave me the belief that I wasn't destined for the shop floor. Anyone involved in punk will reiterate these sentiments because it was a liberating experience for us all. Without punk we'd all be sat around just accepting whatever the music industry served up without question. Punk cried out 'Have a go!' and it's a feeling that's reverberated ever since. How many of those clubbers leaping around to my dance track in Ibiza are aware that it was an indirect result of punk?"

SELECT DISCOGRAPHY:
7"s:
'Neighbours' (Hog, 1980)
'Heathrow Touchdown' (Subversive, 1981) – split with Action Pact
'Bomb Scare' (Rondelet, 1982)
'Flower In The Gun' (Rondelet, 1982)
'Toleration Street' (Expulsion, 1983)
'Another Year' (Criminal Damage, 1983)

LPs:
'The 4 Ps' (Expulsion, 1983)
'To Mohammad A Mountain' (Criminal Damage, 1984)

AT A GLANCE:
In 1997, Italian label Get Back released a CD version of 'The 4 Ps' album that also included the two Rondelet singles and the 'Toleration Street' 7". Although it's unfortunately difficult to track down, and doesn't include the Criminal Damage period of the band's recording career, it's by far the most definitive CD release of Dead Mans Shadow, and well worth the effort if you can locate a copy.

ERAZERHEAD

E ast London's Erazerhead always had more in common with the happy-go-lucky sounds of The Ramones and The Dickies than the uptight thrashings of their UK contemporaries, but their relentless enthusiasm and manic vibrant energy ensured their place in the annals of UK punk. Although they formed in 1980, their frontman Lee Drury was of the old school, and his passion for rock'n'roll would help colour Erazerhead's musical outpourings.

"I left school in 1976, wishing I had a time machine to take me back to 1956," begins Lee, wistfully. "Then bang, it happened. In early '78, I formed a band called The Corvettes with some local lads. We did about fifty gigs in the East London area, many at the legendary Bridge House in Canning Town, which was sadly knocked down last year, but we never made it up the West End. In 1979 our bass player, Paul Spicer, was killed in a hit and run and that was that, so to speak."

The Corvettes' guitarist Steve Pear joined The 4-Skins ("Even though he had a giant quiff!"), whilst Jeff Wilmott went on to drum for In Camera who recorded for 4AD Records.

"I started squatting at Kings Cross and going down all the wrong roads," continues Lee. "This was where I met Frenchie Gloder, our future manager and Flicknife Records boss. I even got thrown out of my apprenticeship with the gas board, no mean feat. I sang the 'Rock'n'Roll Swindle' live with Cook and Jones (of Sex Pistols infamy) at the Moonlight in West Hampstead.

We were backed by Tenpole Tudor. I was friends with all of them and, with a little string pulling I managed to front the band for this one song. It was great... I wish videos were invented then!

"Then I met Yvonne, my future wife, and calmed down a little bit. This was when Jim Berlin approached me in the Bridge House and asked me if I would be the singer in a band that he was starting. I wasn't really interested as Jim wasn't one of the 'in crowd', if you know what I mean. He kept on pestering me though and, after a few weeks, I agreed to go to a rehearsal on the strength of a promise that we

Erazerhead, pictured at Beckton Gasworks, 1982
L-R: Jim Berlin, Gary Spanner, Lee Drury, Billy Trigger
(Pic: Jeff Wilmott)

would sound like The Ramones. That was all I needed. The line up included Bernie Cairns on bass, who only used the D- and G-strings, but never made a mistake, and Billy Trigger was on drums; he'd only been playing for a few months and wasn't finding it easy! He kept losing the beat, then coming in backwards, snare where bass should be and vice versa. I began to wonder what I was doing there. Jim put on his guitar and did a perfect medley of Ramones songs. That sounded okay so we began to practise playing songs from their first album. I was used to writing as a band, but Jim was prolific and the songs began to pour out. The more he wrote, the better they got. He would rarely finish one – he was too busy with the next – so that job went to me. I would write the odd verse here and there, work out a few endings, a few intros, and so we carried on."

Lifting their name from the surreal David Lynch horror movie – but spelling it differently to avoid any legal hassles – Erazerhead rapidly established themselves with some frantic gigging around the capital.

"Me and Billy were part of the London club scene, so we knew everyone and getting gigs wasn't a problem. We supported nearly every punk band that played at the Bridge. That was easy as I was best mates with the landlord's son! The cleaners would find me in the mornings, rolled up in the pool table covers! I don't know who was the most startled, me or the poor cow that tried to re-cover the table.

"Then Bernie moved to Harlow and we never saw him again. We put an ad in the music press and had two replies. One was the bass player with an old punk band that I used to go and see called The Low Numbers. I loved 'em, but he didn't want to do stuff like that anymore. The other bloke came to an audition but he was unlucky 'cos Gary Spanner turned up too. Gary had a live Erazerhead tape and had learned it all; there was no contest, and he got the job. Plus he used the E- and A-strings so all of a sudden we sounded right!"

In 1981, the band raised just short of £300 ("A lot of money back then!") to record their debut single, 'Apeman', which saw the light of day through Terry Razor's Test Pressings label. Backed by 'Wipeout' and 'Rock'n'Roll Zombie', 'Apeman' remains a tuneful punk gem, what the drums lack in power compensated for by buzzing guitars and a wonderfully raw but melodic turn from Lee.

It sneaked into the lower echelons of the Indie Charts for a month upon its release in September 1981, and, in conjunction with yet more high-profile shows at the 100 Club with the likes of Theatre Of Hate, landed them their deal with Flicknife Records.

The 'Rumble Of The East' album was recorded in Brixton and unleashed in November 1982, reaching No. 21 in the Indies, and was preceded that summer by the thoroughly enjoyable 'Shellshock' and 'Teenager In Love' singles, that both rattled along at an effervescent pace.

"I hated nearly everything that we recorded with Flicknife. It all sounded tin pot and 'Mickey Mouse'. It's really frustrating when you give it your all and it doesn't sound right. Only the first single and the live EP (1983's 'Live At Klub Foot') came close to capturing our sound. I hated the single 'Teenager In Love' so much that I refused to sing on the track. When we did it live, people went nuts and it lasted ninety seconds, but this was a dirge. We had a massive row in the studio, and they recorded the backing track when I was at work. I was outvoted and had to do it or leave! I agreed, but only if 'All For Me' was on the B-side. This was a 'golden oldie' of ours that the others wanted to bury. Needless to say it bombed and I'm still embarrassed by it."

Indeed the band were at their best whilst onstage, and many adventures were undertaken to prove the point.

"We were banned from Canterbury Art College because our roadie, Mongo Tom, drank our after-show beer and wine, got on stage and people thought he was the support act. He stripped naked to the background music, put Billy's drum sticks up his arse, and began to gyrate while balancing our last bottle of wine on his head. You should have seen the faces of the punters as they walked in. After this hilarity, he disappeared. He got in the back of his van, passed out and shat himself! Very runny it was too; he rolled around in it for a few hours until we had finished our set. All was going well until I went to find him. When I opened the van doors, the smell was bad; he staggered out crying, 'Help me, Lee!' I ran a mile.

"As we were packing up the gear he went back in – no one would go near him – and removed all the fag machines from the walls! These were hidden in his van. Then he turned up at the after-show party at one of the student union houses. He got in every bed to clean himself up, stole all of the girls' underwear and generally made an arse of himself. That was the only gig that he did with us. He eventually ended up in nick for drug smuggling!

"The best gigs were probably with the (Cockney) Rejects up the Bridge House. A bit like Oasis at Main Road, if you know what I mean? They tried to get us on EMI with them, and we did a showcase gig at EMI House in Manchester Square. We saw Hank Marvin and Paul Weller there and thought that we had arrived. This was the pre-'Apeman' days and we were very nervous, plus I had only just knocked one of my front teeth out at the Music Machine and was finding it hard to sing without making strange fluffing noises. They told us to get a new guitarist and try again! Jim couldn't do lead breaks, to which we replied, 'Neither can Johnny Ramone!' They didn't see it that way though, so we walked."

On June 14th, 1982, the band recorded a well-received session for John Peel's Radio One show. Featuring 'I Hate You', 'Teenager In Love', 'Martian Girl' and 'No One Sees Me Now', the session actually saw Lee handling bass as well as vocal duties for the first time.

"Gary Spanner was on holiday so I stepped in and played bass. I always loved Dee Dee Ramone and Sid Vicious so, to be like them, I had taught myself how to play. This would come in handy later when Gary left the band over a fight about royalties. He realised that Jim got it all, didn't agree and left. I stepped in and we became a three-piece, but it was nearly the end.

"We recorded our second album (1984's 'Take Me To Your Leader') but Frenchie didn't pay the studio fees so they wiped all the tapes, and we had to do it all over again! That album was a direction change for us. Everybody always banged on about us being 'Ramones soundalikes', so we thought, 'We'll show 'em!' It got a five-star review in the press but Frenchie refused to promote it, so obviously it bombed."

A further two fine singles, 'Werewolf' and the rather mellow 'Summertime Now', beat the album into the racks, in May '83 and early '84 respectively, but, frustrated and disillusioned with the industry, not to mention some of their own band members, Erazerhead decided to quit while they were ahead and called it a day soon after.

"With the first album, we wanted to blow everyone's ears out with minimal, but tuneful, slices of noise. By the time we did the second one, I guess we had grown quite a bit musically, and we were listening to more Bowie, Bolan, Iggy and Roxy stuff. None of us liked the hardcore scene and I think we began to look back to the stuff that we listened to in our early teens for inspiration.

"Jim had moved to Brighton by then and only turned up for gigs, leaving us to lug all the gear about – including his own! Then after the gig he would disappear again. He had a new circle of friends down there who were not like us; they were filling his head with all sorts of stuff and it began to show in the songs that he was writing. When we got in the studio all we had were some tapes that Jim had made at home, and we finalised the songs as we learned them, which wasn't such a good idea as most songs change quite a bit from when you write them to when you record them.

"Consequently the first album was full of old, well-worked songs, but the second was recorded without ever being played live so we didn't really know what was going to work, and what wasn't. Then, when the album was in the can, Jim introduced us to a friend of his from Brighton called Steve, who he wanted to be our second guitarist. He seemed okay so we agreed to give it a go. We had a gig at the 100 Club to showcase the new material, and when Jim and Steve showed up, they were in makeup, headbands, leather sombreros and lace gloves! We all thought, 'What the fuck?' The new look and sound didn't go down too well; I think we did two more gigs after that, the last one minus Jim, whose dad was very ill. Strangely enough, we went back to the old material with me on bass and Steve on guitar and went down a storm. Deep down I knew it was all over though, and put everything into that last gig. I'm glad the last one was a good 'un!"

Billy Trigger went on to play in The Tall Boys with former bassist for The Meteors, Nigel Lewis, before touring the world with PiL as their drum roadie. Upon his return, he went on to tour-manage Primal Scream and even Oasis during the glory days of Brit Pop.

Lee played one show – a Greenpeace benefit – with the aptly named Stand Ins, a band he formed with Jeff Wilmott of The Corvettes on guitar and Big Sid of Rubella Ballet on drums. He then joined The October Revolution, a band begun by guitarist Mick Atkins who had previously been with Wasted Youth. They played seven shows in and around London, one of them supporting The Tall Boys at The 100 Club.

"Jim has asked me a couple of times recently about reforming," reckons Lee in closing. "He thinks there is money to be made, but I think it's wrong. I know everyone and their dog is doing it, but to me it was always about being young, skinny and angry. Not fat, bald and forty! I ain't fat or bald, but you know what I mean. I have got up and sang with a couple of bands on the spur of the moment, and loved every minute of it, but I think it's best left alone. In 1977 we used to go down the King's Road to fight the Teds and some of them were in their forties, and we thought they were a joke. Now the tables have turned and punk is in danger of becoming some kind of Showaddywaddy cabaret act. Best left to the young kids of today to listen and learn from; that's how I see it, at least."

SELECT DISCOGRAPHY:
7"s:
'Apeman' (Test Pressing, 1981)
'Shellshock' (Flicknife, 1982)
'Teenager In Love' (Flicknife, 1982)
'Live At Klub Foot' (Flicknife, 1983)
'Werewolf' (Flicknife, 1983)
'Summertime Now' (Flicknife, 1984)

LPs:
'The Rumble Of The East' (Flicknife, 1982)
'Take Me To Your Leader' (Flicknife, 1984)
'Shellshocked: The Singles' (Flicknife, 1985)

AT A GLANCE:
The excellent 'Shellshocked: The Best Of' CD (Captain Oi!, 1994) collects all of Erazerhead's singles, plus selected highlights from the first album, providing a comprehensive overview of the band, and also features in-depth liner notes by Flicknife boss, Frenchie Gloder.

THE STRAPS

lthough originally formed in 1977, The Straps qualify for inclusion here because none of their recorded output appeared until the early Eighties. Also, as well as having much in common musically with the first wave punk bands, their records crackled with all the aggressive intensity associated with the second.

Guitarist Steve Macintosh formed the band in Battersea, South London (although The Straps later relocated to Brixton, where they squatted for a while), and he was soon joined by guitarist, Dave Reeves. After a brief stint with Howard Jackson on vocals, Brad on drums, and Green on bass, who sadly died of a drug overdose, John 'Jock' Grant became the permanent vocalist, whilst Andy 'Heed' Forbes took over as second guitarist. After a short spell with Andi from Sex Gang Children filling the position, Stan Stammers became the new bassist, and Luke Rendell took up occupation of the drum stool.

"But before we got Luke in, we had a drummer called Cliff 'The Glue Bag' for a while," laughs Dave. "We bought him some new cymbals for £450... which he then sold a week later, and bought 45 tins of glue with the money! Needless to say, he didn't last long in the band.

"Andy was named 'Heed' by Rab Fae Beith, who he went on to play in The Wall with, because of his big head! Stan and Jock used to work in (ultra-hip King's Road clothes emporium) BOY, and we used to play in their shop window before we went to rehearsals! Our manager was actually Charlie Dunnett who managed the shop.

"Our first gig was with The UK Subs at a pub called The Park Tavern, near Streatham, in South London. Their singer, Charlie, was a hairdresser in Tooting at the time and used to cut my hair. The gig was brilliant and I remember Charlie saying to the crowd after their set that he thought we would go far as a band! We went on to do quite a few more gigs with The Subs, and also The Pack, if I remember rightly."

Indeed, Stan and Luke left to join Theatre Of Hate, the band formed by The Pack vocalist, Kirk Brandon, whom they eventually went on to be in Spear Of Destiny with. They were replaced, respectively, by John Werner and the jazz-trained Jim Walker, and, with Heed departing for The Wall, John's brother, Simon, stepped in as lead guitarist, to create the definitive Straps line-up. All three new members were Canadian born; Simon and John had formerly played with The Pack, while Jim had previously drummed with (ex-Sex Pistol) John Lydon's Public

Image Ltd, playing on both their self-titled single and debut album in 1978.

"We started to get quite a following in London and would headline some decent size venues, often pulling over five hundred people a show," recalls Dave. "We used to have a residency at the Music Machine in Camden where we could draw anything up to 1500 people on a Tuesday night! We then had a residency at the 100 Club in

The Straps
L–R: Simon, Jock, Pete Davies (of The UK Subs, drums), John, Dave
Taken at Klub Foot, Clarendon, June 1980 (Pic: Lynn Werner)

Oxford Street although I remember us being dropped one night because some band called the Rolling Stones were playing a secret gig there... what a bloody cheek!

"We also played the Hammersmith Odeon with Stiff Little Fingers. We knew Jim Reilly from SLF, who used to hang out at the Music Machine with us. Jim once phoned me at home at 3:00 am to tell me he was going to leave SLF and join us... but he never did; it must have been the beer talking! We also played the Marquee with Brian James from The Damned."

In fact, The Straps undertook a successful, if a little costly, UK tour with The Damned in 1980.

"I was living near Croydon at the time, and used to hang out with (Damned guitarist) Captain Sensible in all the local pubs, and that's how we got on their 'Blackout' tour. It cost us £2000 to buy on it though... Jim Walker paid... and we did about twenty dates. It was brilliant 'cos I was only eighteen and living a dream come true! My ambition when I started playing guitar at thirteen had always been to play Hammersmith Odeon and I ended up playing there twice, once with SLF and once with The Damned!"

The band's first single was the almost-Rockabilly in feel, 'Just Can't Take Anymore', which they recorded at Rollerball, a London studio that was actually owned by one of The Glitter Band. Released in early 1981 on drummer Jim's own Donut Records, it managed No. 49 in the Indie Charts, despite being a rather unusual choice of song for their vinyl debut.

"That's my least favourite of our releases," says Dave. "It wasn't really our type of music in the first place... good song though. I was just messing about when I wrote it with Stan. We should have released our version of 'The House Of The Rising Sun' as the first single, I think that would have done really well.

"I recently saw Tim from The Polecats who said that they actually wanted to release 'Just Can't Take Anymore' as their second single, but their record company wouldn't let them 'cos they thought it was too punky. Which is a shame 'cos I might have made some money!

"I remember playing the Marquee, supported by The Stiffs from Blackburn," he adds, reminiscing about the shows undertaken to promote the single. "There were about 800 people in and the club only officially held 450; it was rammed. A lot of famous faces turned up like The Stray Cats, SLF, UK Subs, Gene October from Chelsea, Boy George before he was famous... even Liz Hurley! Captain Sensible got up and we did 'New Rose' for an encore and the place went mad. The stage was invaded and the PA ended up in the crowd – fucking brilliant!"

The band's blistering second single 'Brixton' (backed by the moody semi-instrumental, 'No Liquor') was recorded at Hillside Studios in Tulse Hill, London, and remains their finest moment. A wildly energetic release, again on Donut, it made No. 43 in the Indies during July 1982.

The band's self-titled album followed soon after, this time on Simon's own label, Cyclops (who also issued The Pack's 'Long Live The Past' EP when Simon was playing with them), but due to financial restraints it was a rather rushed affair.

"We recorded it all in six hours, 'cos we didn't have any money! So we had to just do it live, as though we were playing a gig, with no overdubs or anything."

Pete Davies from The UK Subs stood in on drums for the recently departed Jim Walker (hence the change of label), with Captain Scarlet (aka Dave Lloyd, one of The UK Subs' many guitarists) and Andi Sex Gang providing backing vocals. All things considered, the album sounds amazing, with some high-octane speedier tracks sitting quite comfortably alongside darker, more melodic material reminiscent of classic-period Ruts.

A third single was recorded, but unfortunately, disillusioned and without management, The Straps split before it could be released. Jock and Simon went on to work briefly with Jah Wobble (aka John Wardle, the former PiL bassist).

However, in August 1993, Dave and Jock reformed a version of the band for a one-off appearance at the Fuck Reading festival. Held at the Brixton Academy, it was headlined by the likes of Sham 69, UK Subs, The Vibrators and Chelsea.

"How would I like The Straps to be remembered?" ponders Dave. "Well, just to be remembered at all would be great! But also I think we were a band who proved the punk belief that you didn't have to be great musicians or songwriters to get somewhere in life. I had my fifteen minutes of fame and I loved every minute of it!"

DISCOGRAPHY:
7"s:
'Just Can't Take Anymore' (Donut, 1981)
'Brixton' (Donut, 1982)

LPs:
'The Straps' (Cyclops, 1982)

AT A GLANCE:
A long overdue discography CD of The Straps is at last scheduled for release by Captain Oi! for late 2004.

THE GONADS

O ne of the more mischievous bands of the early Eighties, The Gonads were of great significance as the brainchild of one Garry Bushell, the Sounds journalist who has since became a successful TV personality and tabloid writer. Although their musical influence has also been far-reaching, even inspiring the actual formation of some US bands such as The Press and The GoMads. Bushell is also widely credited with the popularising of the second wave of UK punk in his writings for Sounds, in particular the 'street' branch of the movement, which he dubbed 'Oi!' and, love him or hate him, there's no denying the impact he had on the scene. For many punks, his column in the magazine was the only regular source of information on upcoming new bands and they clung to it fiercely like a lifeline. A review from him could almost make or break a band, depending upon its bias, such was the weight many punk fans gave his words at the time.

Having been a musician long before becoming a professional scribe, it seemed inevitable that he would create his own punk music as well as just writing about that of others, and so The

Gonads were born, basically various mates of Garry's getting together, having a few too many beers and a right old knees up. However, The Gonads weren't always such a nebulous concept…

"The Gonads guard our own history with an almost occult secrecy and have constructed our own mythology. But seeing as it's you…" laughs Garry, when prompted about the origins of the band. "We originally formed in late '76 out of the remnants of Pink Tent, a band we started when we were teenagers and into (Monty) Python. We got together at school in Lee (SE12), the same school that Mickey Fitz (from The Business) went to, though he was younger than us. We wrote comedy sketches and started jamming round mates' houses. There was me, Al Strawn on bass, Pete Lunn on drums, Mark Gladding on guitar (and mandolin!) and Zoe Bailey, who we were all in love with, was our pin-up. Chris Culmer played cowbells. We weren't normal kids; we were working class dissidents at a grammar school.

"There was another guitarist in the Pink Tent days whose name was John Mitchell. He was a Communist, but he was the most right wing out of all of us, because we were all playground Trots and Maoists! We organised a cell of the Schools Action Union at our school and distributed the Little Red School Book! We were the rebels of our year; we called ourselves Groucho-Marxists long before that was an old joke. We were into stunts, so, for example, when we had a French teacher called Herring I filled his desk with rancid fish."

Clyde Ward joined the band on guitar, and in 1977 The Gonads self-released the 'Stroke My Beachcomber Baby' single ("Recorded in someone's shed in Blackheath") on their own label, Scrotum, which had two hairy testicles tastefully adorning the centre label. They split up soon after, in 1978, at which point Garry joined the staff at Sounds, a natural follow-on to the work done on his own fanzine, Napalm, which he started in 1977, and where he interviewed, amongst others, Jimmy Pursey and Poly Styrene.

In 1981, Garry put together his first joke version of The Gonads to record the track, 'Tucker's Ruckers Ain't No Suckers', for Secret's 'Carry On Oi', the third of the popular Oi compilations. It was only a matter of time before he contributed a track of his own, seeing as it was he who'd been compiling the series anyway; in fact, he'd almost been single-handedly championing the Oi scene since its inception in the pages of Sounds. It was also the best of the Oi albums, with its picture postcard artwork indicative of an album trying to capture the humour in a scene until then mainly, and unfortunately, renowned for its aggression. And of course, it was doubly appropriate because The Gonads themselves had as much, if not more, in common with Sid James as Sid Vicious. Their song itself was a decent slice of yobbish street punk, and did well to hold its own on a collection that featured many rising stars such as Blitz and The Partisans at the peak of their powers.

"What do you mean, 'joke band'? We'll see you in court; that's an outrage," chuckles Garry. "Seriously, though, we always did songs we found funny, although we had serious songs as well, like 'Dying For A Pint', about nightclub bouncer brutality, and 'Jobs Not Jails'.

"The Gonads became 'a joke band' because the original band split up, largely through work commitments and people moving away, and I reinvented us as a piss-take concept using musicians from other bands. The Business initially. We didn't actually become a 'real' band again until 1997, although the joke-Gonads were a very popular in-joke. The (Cockney) Rejects played with me on one track ('TNT', contributed to the 'Total Noise' compilation EP), The Blood with me on others. Even bands like Iron Maiden, UFO and Def Leppard wanted to record as the Gonads. Ozzy Osbourne too, but we never got it together. It never got past the 'late night hotel bar' stage!"

The Gonads next contributed a horrendous version of 'White Christmas' to the Secret compilation EP 'Bollocks To Christmas', before Secret let them loose with an EP all their own, 1982's 'Pure Punk For Row People'. Five simplistic, cheeky punk party anthems, it spawned what was probably the band's best-loved track, 'I Lost My Love To A UK Sub', a hilarious ode to Subs' frontman Charlie Harper's over-zealous libido. Cue several UK Subs song titles doubling as sexual innuendoes in the lyrics – 'He got her in a Stranglehold', 'He showed her his Warhead', etc.!

The single was a great success and actually spent over two months in the Indie Charts, reaching a very respectable No. 6. It was closely followed by the 'Peace Artists' EP, that the band released as The Magnificent Gonads, which Garry has little enthusiasm for ("I hate the production; it sounds like shit on a stick!") The best track, 'Punk City Rockers', really saw Garry's pre-punk rhythm 'n' blues and boogie-woogie influences coming to the fore, making for an interesting combination of styles.

Another single followed in '83, this time as The Brothers Gonad, a collaboration with Max Splodge from Splodgenessabounds, called 'Delilah', for Razor Records. A suitably boozy butchering of the Tom Jones chestnut, it troubled the Indies for but a week, only just scraping inside the Top Fifty, and it became apparent the novelty factor of the band had diminished considerably with the record-buying punters. Although the band blamed Razor's poor distribution and lack of promotion, the fact they never played live outside of London's SE7 borough didn't exactly help sales either. In fact, the only 'tour' they managed was of local curry houses!

"Well, 'tour' may be stronging it a bit," admits Garry. "Basically we turned up with acoustic guitars, bongos and a banjo and asked to play in exchange for food. We went down well in Charlton village because we kept the bar afloat but in Lewisham the chef chased us out with a chopping knife!"

With the band appearing on several other Oi collections (contributing 'Getting Pissed' to 'Oi! Oi! That's Yer Lot'; 'Jobs Not Jails' and 'Lager Top Blues' to 'Son Of Oi'; and their reworked version of 'Pleasant Valley Sunday', 'SE7 Dole Day', to the 'The Oi Of Sex'), it seemed their forte was singles and compilations. Garry also appeared on the 'Son Of Oi' and 'The Oi Of Sex' comps under the guise of Prole, alongside Steve Kent from The Business, with whom he later went on to 'form' Orgasm Guerillas.

Indeed the only full-length appearance of The Gonads in the early Eighties was a bootleg double live album, 'Live And Loud', which appeared through Syndicate in 1983. Although it failed to chart, Garry rates this as the most representative release by the band, especially 'The Beer Drinkers Medley', "Because that was what we were all about."

With Garry becoming increasingly disillusioned with the punk scene, and vice versa ("The second wave was so promising because it was more real than the first, but it failed gloriously"), not to mention his spiralling commitments as a journalist and manager of manic Charlton metal punk band, The Blood (he also managed The Cockney Rejects for a short time), The Gonads faded away like a long-lingering beer belch. Garry became a TV critic for The Sun, had his own late night show, 'Bushell On The Box', and even organised the smash hit Ferry Aid single.

"When the Zeebrugge ferry sank I organised a Band Aid-style record, 'Let It Be'," he explains proudly. "It raised £1 million for the families of the victims and the survivors. Peter Waterman produced it, and we had Gary Moore, Boy George, Mark Knopfler, Mel and Kim, loads of people on it. Even Mickey Fitz was on the video. It was No. 1 for a month! (Paul) McCartney filmed a clip for the video... Michael Jackson gave us clearance to use the song, which he owned. It was awesome at the time."

In 1989, Link released the posthumous 'The Revenge Of The Gonads' collection, and as a result there were sporadic sightings of The Gonads during the early and mid-Nineties. 1997 actually saw an official comeback single, 'Oi! Nutter', released on 1234 Records in the UK and Pub City Royal in the US, followed by an eventful US tour in '98, with Casanova Kev on bass, Rockin' Dave on guitar, and The Romulan on drums.

Captain Oi! Records, whose owner Mark Brennan was a regular Gonads collaborator in the early Eighties, signed the band in 1998, and since then they've released three albums, including the rather rocking 'Schiz-Oi!-phrenia'. Although rumours constantly abound of a final decisive split, Garry is keen to point out that morale in the band is at an all-time high right now.

"The problem was, Clyde was playing guitar for Right Said Fred, Steve Bishop has his own studio on the coast, and Dan, our drummer, has his own band, his own age, called Spyx. It was making it hard to get together, which is why we were talking about knocking it all on the head.

"But then André Schlesinger joined the band; he is based in New York, and was in The Press, a left-wing NYC band who formed after being inspired by 'Tucker's Ruckers'. We are currently co-writing songs over the internet, and it looks like he's going to make the band much rawer once again. The last track we wrote before André joined was 'Unky-Bunk' anyway, and that was our heaviest song since 'Eat The Rich'. We will play again in 2004; I don't ever want to stop."

With the arrival of Schlesinger in the band, he might not have to. And Schlesinger himself is as fired up about the rejuvenated Gonads as Garry:

"About a year ago, my current band, Maninblack, had just recorded the song 'New York, New York, USA', and I had put together a website as our official on-line press kit," he explains of his unexpected recruitment. "I sent an e-mail announcement promoting the song and the site to anybody and everybody associated with Oi, and out of all of them Gal was the only one who replied.

Garry Bushell of The Gonads, who played a large part in popularising the Oi scene (Pic: Tony Mottram)

Seriously! And I really considered it quite an honour to have him review what I was doing. After that I related some ideas I had about producing a new Oi compilation, and we began talking about collaborating on some music, for what I thought was going be Gal's new solo project, The Garry Bushell Experience, and even my idea for a Gonads tribute album.

"Anyway, I got an e-mail from Gal saying, 'We put some information up on The Gonads' web site about you and you need to review it to make sure it's correct', and I'm, like, 'Oh great, Bushell's probably made me the official correspondent for his fan club or something'... but when I go to The Gonads website news section, I see the announcement that I've been recruited for the next album!

"The first and foremost thing I plan on doing when I arrive in England is to buy a round," he adds, laughing. "If only so in the event that I have a falling out with the band, Gal can't accuse me of never having done so! I plan on documenting this event on video with plenty of witnesses!"

Garry and Schlesinger are even compiling a brand new, global Oi album together.

"When I think 'Oi', I immediately think The Gonads," elaborates André. "Their unique combination of what I felt was a very flat but rhythmic guitar sound coupled with a simple, hurried one-two-one-two beat and Gal's abrasive vocals. The sound probably had much to do with The Gonads' musical ability, or lack there of, minimal equipment, and recording on the cheap, but it had a particular effect. To me this sound was not unlike hearing music through an old time tube radio or phonograph.

"Also, Oi shares many similarities with folk music, besides its often simple musical structure; quaint in some respects and crude in others, not to mention often brutally honest, it usually tells a story based in truth. It means to relate on a peer to peer level. I think that these are qualities that The Gonads helped establish and something that I tried to emulate with The Press and Maninblack."

For many years, The Press, who split up in 1994, were the only genuine committed Oi band from New York, and they even recorded for Roddy Moreno from The Oppressed's Oi Records label.

"Well, Oi pretty much got me blacklisted by polite society," reckons Garry philosophically. "I've spent the last twenty-two years being called a fascist by liberals and a commie by the ultra-right screw-jobs! But I still stand by Oi and have no regrets other than I wish we'd set up our own label back in 1981 and done our own thing instead of getting Secret involved.

"I think I helped create a climate that allowed working class bands to flourish. I get accused of 'creating' Oi, which is a lot like saying Columbus created the USA. I was deeply involved, there's no denying that; I managed the Rejects, got them their EMI deal with Jimmy Pursey, I compiled the Oi albums, and I got the 4-Skins signed up. That was my past and I won't deny it.

"And as for punk, it changed my life. I would not have become a journalist without The Clash. I wouldn't be on TV now if it wasn't for Sounds. Joe Strummer has a lot to answer for! Punk made me realise that most of the barriers in life are there to be torn down. I still love that DIY ethic; big corporations are the curse of modern life.

"We are possibly the greatest punk band of them all!" says Garry of The Gonads. "What did we bring to the underground music scene? Tunes! Music Hall! Cockney culture... and, of course, the legend that is Sandra Bigg!"

SELECT DISCOGRAPHY:
7"s:
'Stroke My Beachcomber Baby' (Scrotum, 1977)
'Ripper's Delight' (Scrotum, 1980)
'Pure Punk For Row People' EP (Secret, 1982)
'Peace Artists' (Secret, 1982)
'Delilah' (Razor, 1983)
'Oi! Nutter' (1234 Records, 1997)

LPs:
'Live And Loud' (Syndicate, 1983)
'The Revenge Of The Gonads' (Link, 1989)
'Punk Rock Will Never Die' (Captain Oi!, 1998)
'Oi! Back And Barking' (Captain Oi!, 1999)
'Schiz-Oi!-phrenia' (Captain Oi!, 2001)

AT A GLANCE:

The most recent album for Captain Oi, 'Schiz-Oi!-phrenia', is probably the band's most accessible and enjoyable release to date, but Link's late Eighties collection, 'The Revenge Of The Gonads', is the best place to check out the band's early tracks... if you can hunt a copy down. The Captain Oi! CD reissue of the 'Carry On Oi' compilation is well worth a purchase too; wrapped in an attractive card sleeve with a collectable postcard of the cover art, it also features some enlightening liner notes from Garry.

COCKNEY REJECTS

I f ever there was a band that truly captured the yobbo spirit of teenage tearaways on vinyl, it was the Cockney Rejects. Formed in the East End of London in 1979 by brothers Mickey Geggus (guitar) and Jeff 'Stinky' Turner (vocals), the band combined powerful punchy riffs with massive singalong choruses that were straight off the football terraces and a 'take no shit' attitude that has oft been imitated but never equalled.

"Me and Jeff formed 'a band' called The Shitters," reveals Mickey. "It was basically me on guitar and Jeff on vocals, and we played in anybody's front room that we could... until we were thrown out!"

Recruiting Chris Murrel on bass and Paul Harvey on drums, they wisely changed their name, to the Cockney Rejects, and quickly began building a local following, not to mention a formidable reputation.

The East End of London's Cockney Rejects, 'a band that truly captured the yobbo spirit of teenage tearaways...'

"The early days were manic," recalls the guitarist fondly. "Like most bands we didn't have a pot to piss in, so we obviously had to resort to certain measures... like waiting outside venues until the opportunity arose to nick as much backline and stuff as possible; we'd keep some and fence the other half up the road!

"Rehearsals were usually in an old school, where we used to bung the caretaker a few quid to let us have the odd hour here and there. The first gig wasn't a problem; the band were all faces on the old Bridge House scene, so when we thought we were ready, we told the guv'nor, our old mate Terry Murphy, and he let us support The Damned! It was spot on! It was all our crowd anyway, so they went bonkers. The Damned seemed a bit gobsmacked, but we thought that they were good sports and a terrific band, and still do.

"Those early gigs were great. We broke all attendance records for The Bridge House and ended up having to play under assumed names and stuff. People ended up hanging from the old rafters in the ceiling. I remember it being the hottest place I can remember... even in the winter."

It was only a matter of time before the Rejects would come to the attention of the music industry, but ever ambitious to the extreme, the band weren't prepared to wait for a label to come to them.

"We recorded a demo in a small eight-track studio of three songs, 'Flares And Slippers', 'I Wanna Be A Star', and 'The Fight Song'. I took them to Small Wonder up the road in Walthamstow, and asked to see the owner Pete Stenett. Pete came down, this little hippy bloke, and told me to put my tape in the basket of other demo tapes on the counter, saying 'Call me at the end of the week and I'll let you know'. I said, 'Bollocks, mate, you play it now and call me tonight!' And he did!"

Signing to Small Wonder for one single, the Rejects roped in Sham 69 vocalist Jimmy Pursey to produce it, and, in early 1979, the 'Flares And Slippers' EP grabbed the unsuspecting music scene by the scruff of its scrawny neck. Backed by the brilliant 'Police Car' (introduced with the passionate rallying cry of 'Freedom? There ain't no fuckin' freedom!') and the slightly more sedate 'I Wanna Be A Star', the single spent over four months in the Indie Charts, reaching No. 24, and brought them to the attention of EMI Records.

"After doing the recordings of (their second single) 'I'm Not A Fool'/'East End' at Polydor Studios, we hawked the product around for a few days. Three companies put in what were huge offers at the time – Polydor, Warner Bros, and EMI. We were all Queen fans and fancied seeing our debut album on the same label as them, simple as that! Of course, the public schoolboys who ran EMI hated us and the fact that we would stroll into their Manchester Square HQ unannounced and nick just about everything in sight... and there was nothing they could do about it!"

Stinky Turner of The Cockney Rejects (right), with Mensi of The Angelic Upstarts (Pic: Ross Halfin)

It was also about this time that the band arrived at what many consider their classic line-up.

"Vince (Riordan) played guitar with Darren Murphy's Dead Flowers, who used to play at The Bridge House a lot. We were all members of the same scene, so after a five-a-side football tournament in Kent, I asked Riordan if he wanted to join the Rejects on bass. He thought for about a second and said, 'Yeah, and I'll bring Andy Scott (of the other Bridge House band, The Tickets) with me on drums.' Life was never the same again…!"

'I'm Not A Fool' became their EMI debut and it made No. 65 in the National Charts upon its release in October 1979, as did its follow-up, 'Bad Man', early the following year. One of the band's finest moments, 'Bad Man', with its melodic lead guitar, belligerent vocal delivery and gang back-up chants, helped set new standards for what was to become known as street punk; not to mention a solid blueprint for the imminent Oi movement.

"Oh, that was great," says Mickey of their unexpected chart success. "I just think that most of the kids at the time knew that we were just like them – plus I always knew how to write a great chorus!"

Their 1980 debut album 'Greatest Hits Vol. 1' (modestly rated by Mickey as "Right up there with the best three punk albums of all time!") actually made No. 22 in the National Charts, but was their last collaboration with Pursey. A cracking collection of tough street-wise anthems, it even featured a 'cover' of 'Get Yourself Killed' by Scott's previous band The Tickets, a track which originally appeared on the 'Farewell To The Roxy' album, now reworked as The Rejects' theme tune, 'Join The Rejects'.

"Jim had a good heart, but because his background was so totally different from ours (we were a lot more world-wise and cynical, despite being younger), we got a bit tired of his antics in the end and began to take the piss. We got bored quickly and almost trashed Polydor's main studio during the recording of that first album; they threw us out and we had to finish it at Shepperton!"

Sean from London's Rough Trade Records certainly shares Mickey's enthusiasm for that monumental full-length debut:

"No one since has got anywhere near sounding this thuggish and great at the same time. It's a one-trick pony but I love that one trick. It's all about building up the song until a mob chorus comes in and sweeps the song to another level. The Rejects themselves never got anywhere near repeating the greatness of this record and they lost the plot totally when they turned into a metal band. 'Greatest Hits Volume One' mixed football and punk… what more could you need?"

Another album apparently, because the Rejects followed 'Greatest Hits Vol. 1' with, of course, 'Vol. 2', fourteen more songs of blistering uncompromising punk rock. Mickey believes it to have more filler material than Volume One, but there's no doubting the quality of the standout tracks. Most bands couldn't write one good album in two years, but The Rejects managed two good albums in one… and effortlessly at that. They even found time to replace Andy Scott with Nigel Woolf during the interim.

"Songwriting thankfully came easily to us, and what we then called 'The Ramones Format' – three-block chord structures, middle eight, and huge choruses – were quickly and easily put together. It was always about finding the hook; that's what most bands these days just don't understand… you have to get 'em singing along! Plus it always helped that we enjoyed the studio environment; we worked hard… and played even fuckin' harder."

Aided and abetted by several 'Top Of The Pops' appearances to promote the two singles that preceded it – 'Greatest Cockney Rip-Off' and 'We Can Do Anything' – the album made it to No. 23 in the Nationals.

"Total chaos!" laughs Mickey, when asked for his recollections of those TV appearances. "Fights, fun and wobblers. Oh, and shaking hands with Sammy Hagar on the way out… then having to bunk the tube home 'cos we were skint!"

Whilst performing 'The Greatest Cockney Rip-Off' for the BBC, the band had proudly worn West Ham United shirts; indeed, with songs such as 'I'm Forever Blowing Bubbles', they had always been vociferous regarding their support of the East London football club. Unfortunately it began to attract a violent element to their shows which made booking proper tours increasingly difficult.

"It's hard to remember specific shows from this period because the workload was pretty intense and one gig seems to blend into another. The big London shows at the Electric Ballroom were wild, but the football problem arose almost straight after that.

"We thought – naively, as it turned out – that everybody up and down the country would just regard our West Ham schtick as a harmless bit of fun... after all, Iron Maiden had also been proclaiming their West Ham support on their album covers. Well, we were wrong, but we weren't about to be abused or threatened by anybody over our support for a football team. Granted, the vast majority of our fans couldn't give a shit about our football leanings – they were purely into the music and the message – but those who came looking for trouble more often than not found it... and came off worse too!"

It was about this time that The Cockney Rejects became widely regarded as the premiere band of the aforementioned Oi movement, with their track 'Oi! Oi! Oi!' opening up 'Oi! The Album' (EMI, 1980), the first of the series, that also had Stinky appearing as the 3-D cover model. Garry Bushell even managed the band for a short time, and they returned the favour by backing him as The Gonads on the 1982 'Total Noise' compilation EP with – possibly the best Gonads song of all – 'TNT'. The Rejects also appeared on the EP themselves, albeit under the assumed name of Dead Generation, with the rather forgettable 'Francine'.

"The Rejects were awesome in the beginning," says Bushell. "The music had a punch like Tyson, but they were utterly unmanageable. They needed a Frank Warren figure... they got Tony Gordon who also managed Boy George. When I managed them it was chaos; they wanted to fight everyone all the time..."

After the second album, Nigel Woolf was replaced by Keith 'Stix' Warrington from the Angelic Upstarts. "Nigel just didn't seem to fit in with the three of us," reckons Mickey. "And Stix was a more complete drummer anyway."

After the 1981 'Greatest Hits Vol. 3: Live And Loud' album ("The cunt that tacked on the phony 'applause' afterwards should have been shot," spits Mickey), The Rejects began a musical transformation that wasn't to everybody's tastes, taking their basic formula of rousing singalongs and big, dirty guitar riffs and arc-welding it onto some solid hard rock rhythms.

Recorded at the huge Rockfield Studios in South Wales, 1981's 'Power And Glory' was way more polished and melodic than previous albums, with a more subdued moody vocal delivery from Stinky.

"But I was – and still am – very proud of 'Power And The Glory'. Wherever we play around the world, it's always the album that people say influenced them the most."

It was however a halfway house between the abrasive early Rejects and the gleaming heavy metal version that rose defiantly to its feet with 1982's 'The Wild Ones' LP. With the band coming across like a beefed-up AC/DC, Mickey Geggus really came into his own as a lead guitarist on this more mainstream material, but they inevitably parted ways with some of their more punk-orientated fans.

"Myself, Jeff and Vince had all been brought up on a steady diet of Queen, Black Sabbath and Zeppelin etc., long before the punk explosion began," he explains. "And as much as we loved well-structured punk, we still loved the heavy bands, and as our understanding of our instruments grew, we wanted to make the fullest use of them possible, rather than just keep rehashing the same old stuff. We had done what we had done, and we weren't going back on it for anyone or anything... because that would really have been a rip-off!"

Produced by ex-UFO bassist, Pete Way, 'The Wild Ones' was The Rejects' first album for AKA Records, the band having parted company with EMI over arguments about their musical direction after 'The Power And The Glory'. It was followed in 1984 by the bluesy 'Quiet Storm' for Heavy Metal Records and ultimately by the ten-track 1990 effort, 'Lethal', for Neat.

"After many years, tours and albums, we just decided that it was time to go. Unlike some of our friends in the business, we all had a strong work ethic and basically didn't like the limelight much anyway, so we just said, 'Fuck it!' and went back to our day jobs."

But the lure of the stage is just too strong for some people, and The Cockney Rejects returned with a vengeance just in time for the millennium.

"In 1999, our friend Stuart Black received a call from a company asking us to do a covers album of our old songs," explains Mickey. "We hadn't seen Vince or Stix for years, so I phoned my old friend Tony Van Frater of Sunderland's Red Alert and asked him to play bass and provide a drummer (Andrew Laing, who was replaced by Les Cobb after the record), and thankfully he said 'Yes!' The resulting album (on Rhythm Vicar), 'Greatest Hits, Volume 4' was recorded surprisingly easily and it made me and Jeff think...

"We hadn't even considered playing live, but an old friend persuaded us to reform for a comeback gig in our old stomping ground of Northern Spain. The nerves were terrible and we didn't know what to expect, but as we walked onstage 3000 people erupted and we felt like we'd never been away... and we've been playing ever since."

In 2002, Captain Oi! released a brand new Cockney Rejects studio album, the stirring 'Out Of The Gutter', which proved beyond all shadow of doubt that Mickey and Jeff can still write a bloody good punk rock tune, and – to paraphrase one of the lads' new songs – it still means something. With a book by Jeff Turner devoted to the Rejects set to appear in late 2004, it would seem that the final chapter has yet to be written on this classic band.

"Now there are no drugs, and no drinking... at least not before the show!" reckons Mickey, on how the new band compares to the dangerous days of old. "And there's none of that stupid football rivalry. It really is much more fun now... seeing the young Rancid and Limp Bizkit fans – and their parents! – enjoying every minute of our shows gives us immense pleasure. The atmosphere is always brilliant and we strive hard never to let ourselves or the audience down.

"I'll tell you this though; there has never, ever been a band as totally honest as The Cockney Rejects, and I don't think that any have rocked so hard and given so much to finally bring the old ship home."

SELECT DISCOGRAPHY:
7"s:
'Flares And Slippers' (Small Wonder, 1979)
'I'm Not A Fool' (EMI, 1979)
'Bad Man' (EMI, 1980)
'The Greatest Cockney Rip–Off' (Zonophone/EMI, 1980)
'I'm Forever Blowing Bubbles' (Zonophone, 1980)
'We Can Do Anything' (Zonophone, 1980)
'We Are The Firm' (Zonophone, 1980)
'Easy Life' (Zonophone, 1981)
'On The Streets Again' (Zonophone, 1981)
'Til The End Of The Day' (AKA, 1982)

LPs:
'Greatest Hits, Vol. 1' (Zonophone, 1980)
'Greatest Hits, Vol. 2' (Zonophone, 1980)
'Greatest Hits, Vol. 3 (Live And Loud)' (Zonophone, 1981)
'The Power And The Glory' (Zonophone, 1981)
'The Wild Ones' (AKA, 1982)
'Quiet Storm' (Heavy Metal, 1984)
'Lethal' (Neat, 1990)
'Greatest Hits, Vol. 4' (Rhythm Vicar, 2000)
'Out Of The Gutter' (Captain Oi!, 2002)

AT A GLANCE:
Anagram's 1997 'Cockney Rejects: The Punk Singles Collection' CD is a compilation of (you guessed) all the band's singles, whilst the 1999 CD 'The Very Best Of Cockney Rejects' ignores a few B-sides in favour of several standout album cuts. Both CDs have twenty-two tracks apiece, and are loaded with bona fide pugilistic classics, not to mention original artwork and photos.

THE BUSINESS

Formed in 1979 in South London by guitarist Steve Kent, The Business were a hugely influential Oi band, who are still touring the world, and still as popular, today. In fact, some of their more recent albums have been the equal of anything they produced during the early Eighties, suggesting that the band are far from outliving their welcome.

"We were all school friends really," explains singer Micky Fitz of the band's humble origins. "Steve was a self-taught guitarist, he'd always played, and we were all in the Northbrook, this pub where we knocked about, and kept talking about doing a band. He conned Nick (Cunningham) into buying a drum kit, and had an old bass that he gave to Martin (Smith), and then I walked in the pub one day, and he said, 'Here's our singer!' And I was like, 'You what?' We started rehearsing just for fun really.

"Our first gig was a party (in February 1980); no paying punters, just close friends, and all my best mates were stood there laughing their heads off! But after three or four songs, I became aware that they were getting into it, nodding their heads, tapping their feet. And afterwards, quite a few of 'em said that they'd come and see us again. We only played for twenty minutes, mainly doing covers, 'All Right Now' by Free, 'Rosalie' by Thin Lizzy... but we punked 'em up, made 'em faster."

One of Micky's mates, Lol Pryor ("I'd known him for years, we were both West Ham fans"), offered to manage the band, and they began gigging whenever and wherever they could, quickly building a small but devoted – not to mention rowdy – following. Encouraged by the reaction at live shows, they entered Goldcrest Studios in Sidcup, Kent, where they demoed their first four songs: 'Strangers', 'Out In The Cold', 'Unevenly Pretty' and '19'.

Lol then got the band onto VU's 'A Sudden Surge Of Sound' compilation album, with a re-recorded version of 'Out In The Cold'.

"It was shit," laughs Micky honestly. "But I was so proud to be on it 'cos The UK Subs were too. When it came out, it was my first ever recording... and The Subs were on it! Charlie has always been a god, anyway, but they were huge back then.

"I'll never forget being in the studio singing that track. It was only a little place, but it was the first time any of them had heard my voice without music, so I'm stood there with the cans on, and they were pissing themselves laughing. I gave 'em hell afterwards.

we still play 'Out In The Cold', even today, and loads of people always ask for it, usually young punk or skinhead girls who've had something go wrong in their lives. But there's always light at the end of the tunnel, that's what I tell 'em, and none of us should forget how important music is to people… even our music in some instances."

In May 1981 The Business played their first Oi gig supporting The 4-Skins at the Dueragan Arms in the East London borough of Hackney. The gig was reviewed favourably in Sounds by Garry Bushell who had just overseen the very first Oi compilation album, and the band would be closely linked to the fledgling movement from that moment on.

"Garry and Lol were mates, and the Oi scene was just kicking off. I was a skinhead and it all came together without any planning really. It was slow taking off, though; we were all working… we wanted to do more shows but couldn't. I'd left home when I was nineteen and had rent and bills to pay. It didn't hit me really though, 'cos by the time The Business were part of 'the scene' I was part of the scene myself already, so it was all very natural. We were just there and it happened. It never occurred to us that there was a movement forming; we were just in bands like all our other friends were.

"Anything we said or did was basically us being us, it wasn't planned. I was the only skinhead in the band, but I would never write or sing anything that I didn't agree with. None of it was contrived, there was no guidance from labels or managers; it was honest and from the heart."

Unfortunately, although most of the people involved in Oi were there for the music, there was a small minority with a political agenda, and as a consequence outsiders were quick to dismiss the phenomenon as right wing, despite many of the bands lending their support to Rock Against Racism gigs and the like. The short-sighted choice of Nicky Crane, a notorious Nazi skinhead, as the choice of cover model for the 'Strength Thru Oi' compilation merely added fuel to the fire, but the controversy that caused was just a storm in a teacup compared to what went down at the Hambrough Tavern in Southall in July 1981.

Mickey Fitz, vocalist of The Business, live at the Blackpool H.I.T.S. festival, 1996

It was part of a series of Oi festivals around the country, and The Business were supporting The 4-Skins and Last Resort. Southall was already a tinder box of racial tension, following serious rioting sparked by National Front meetings two years earlier that resulted in the death of schoolteacher Blair Peach, allegedly at the hands of the SPG, so the gig couldn't have been booked in a more volatile area. Possibly as a pre-emptive strike against what they thought would be a violent invasion, local Asian youths laid waste to the pub and complete chaos ensued. Although the bands played their sets, they were lucky to escape unharmed.

"If there's one word I hate in life, that would have to be 'Southall'!" Micky can laugh philosophically about it now, but at the time it was a serious situation. "People drag it up a lot even today, and we've worked bloody hard to get over it. It wasn't any fault of ours; we were just in the wrong place at the wrong time. You had to be there to believe it really, it was terrifying. Look at the main picture of the Hambrough Tavern from the papers at the time and that burnt-out Transit van is ours! We got out of it literally five seconds before the petrol bomb went through the windscreen!

"I was working in the Northbrook at the time, and I phoned the guv'nor up the next day and told him I wasn't coming in, and he said, 'Why not?' I asked him which paper he was reading, but I knew him well enough to know the answer. 'All of them, you prat, I always get 'em all!' So I said, 'What's on the front of all of 'em then?' 'Oh, something about a riot in Southall...' 'Well,' I said. 'You see that van? It's ours!' And he was like, 'Fuck off, you're having a laugh! You better take the day off then...'

"We used to hire some vans from some right dodgy companies too. So, that day we put the keys back through the van hire place's door with a little note saying, 'Dear sirs! Here's the van keys – it's parked outside the Hambrough Tavern... we hope you are insured like you said!'"

The next few months were awkward ones for The Business, with dates being cancelled left, right and centre as a result of the frenzied media circus in the wake of the riot. In October 1981, they contributed the infectious 'Product' to 'Carry On Oi!', and the following month saw the release of their thoroughly enjoyable debut single, 'Harry May', for Secret, surely one of the most memorable yobbo punk songs of all time. Backed by the furious 'Employer's Blacklist', it spent over three months in the Indie Charts, peaking at No. 13, receiving rave reviews in N.M.E., Melody Maker and, of course, from Garry Bushell in Sounds.

"The Business had some very solid anthems," reckons Garry. "I was blown away by 'Harry May', which probably would have gone Top Twenty today on the sales it generated. Only the Southall backlash stopped them taking off, and though they could do the terrace/singalong stuff they also wrote songs as different and intriguing as 'Out In The Cold' and 'Suburban Rebels', one of my favourite ever Oi songs. They've worked hard, never stopped touring and deserve their success."

After contributing the track 'Bollocks To Xmas' to the 'Bollocks To Christmas' compilation EP and undertaking a stint around the UK co-headlining with Infa-Riot, The Business fell to pieces around Micky's ears with Steve, Nick and Martin deciding to leave and form Q-Bow, who soon changed their name to Smack, recorded two demos and split. Steve Kent them teamed up with Nick Austin from Chelsea in Bandits At 4 O'Clock.

"Steve didn't really wanna play that sort of music, and he hated playing live as well," explains Micky. "Martin got bored really quickly and wanted to concentrate on his building, and Nick fucked off to get married, but there was no animosity. We're all still mates to this day. They could see the band taking off and pulled out at the right time."

Micky and Lol asked Graham Ball to join on guitar, and he brought Mark Brennan from upcoming London band The Blackout along to audition as bassist. Playing with Mark in The Blackout was a talented young guitarist, Steve Whale, who also joined The Business, and the new-look band was rounded out with John Fisher, a mate of Lol's, on drums. They made their

live debut in January 1982 at the Mayflower in Manchester
supporting Blitz and The Test Tube Babies, after which it was
agreed that Graham and John (the latter would play in both
Combat 84 and The Warriors) weren't really right for the band.

The Business, circa early 1982
L–R: Mark Brennan, Mickey Fitz, Steve
Whale, Kev Boyce

They reverted to a four-piece, with Mark and Steve bringing in the old Blackout drummer
Kev Boyce.

This version of The Business was unveiled at the Bridge House in East London in February
1982, supporting The Rejects, and their first vinyl appearance came the following month with the
incendiary 'Smash The Discos' EP. With its insistent, aggressive chorus, it made No. 3 in the
Indies, and even troubled the lower ends of the National Charts.

"Yeah, it was very inflammatory, but it was the attitude of that whole scene that bugged me,"
says Mark Brennan. "Even to this day, you can go down to any club, or disco or whatever,
anywhere that plays the kind of music that attracts that muppet mentality, and I can guarantee
you now, come 1 o'clock, kicking out time, there'll be a big fuckin' tear-up at the kebab van, or
there'll be an argument over some old Doris. Every fuckin' week without fail, there's people
kicked to death, stabbings, God knows what else…

"But you have one punk gig where there's a bit of graffiti or whatever, and in comes the
heavy mob to shut it all down. And it's that mentality that I can't get to grips with. I've no interest
in that scene at all, especially since all that bloody rave cobblers… you've gotta be on drugs to
listen to the bloody rubbish."

1982 was a hectic year for The Business. After a short spring tour, they recorded their debut
LP, to be entitled 'Loud, Proud And Punk', the title track of which also appeared on the 'Total
Noise' compilation EP. However before it could be released, the album tapes vanished after
disagreements between the band's label and the studio. Having also parted ways with their
manager, Lol Pryor, they had to raise the money themselves to re-record the LP at Jacobs
Studios in Farnham, Surrey, but this time they enlisted Mickey Geggus of The Cockney Rejects
to produce it. As a consequence, the original album was restructured considerably and renamed

BURNING BRITAIN

'Suburban Rebels' by the time of its release in May 1983, almost a year later than intended. It had also been remixed by Secret without the band's permission "Because the guitars were too loud."

Despite the trials and tribulations behind it all, it was a great album by anybody's standards, featuring such storming tracks as 'Blind Justice' (an old Blackout song reworked for The Business, that also appeared on the 'UK/DK' documentary) and 'Real Enemy' (which was included on the fourth Oi album, 'Oi! Oi! That's Yer Lot'). Surprisingly though, it was crucified by Bushell in Sounds, where the band were dubbed 'Rebels Without A Clue', and it received little or no push from Secret who were facing financial difficulties at the time. Frustrated at the total lack of support, the band split up, with Micky and Steve forming Chapter (with Tony Fitzgerald and Dave Strickson) and Mark recruiting Steve Kent, Simon Hart and Steve Brewer for Sabre Dance. Both bands recorded demos but neither played any shows.

A year later, following the success of a retrospective demos and live compilation, 'The Business 1980-81', for his new label, Syndicate, Lol Pryor persuaded the band to reform and record a 'live' album, in the studio with crowd noise dubbed on afterwards, 'Loud, Proud And Punk'. The LP turned out well, with the band obviously enjoying themselves, even turning their hand to covers of 'Pretty Vacant' by the Sex Pistols and 'Do They Owe Us A Living?' by Crass, and successful dates were undertaken to promote it, including their first on the continent.

Kev Boyce was replaced by Micky Fairbairn from Skinflix, and the 12" EP 'Get Out Of My House' (the title track originally by an obscure Seventies band, Hustler), was released by Lol, who was by then calling his label Wonderful World. It was about this time that The Business became aware of two other bands with the same name. One of them had as their singer Lady Theresa Manners, daughter of the Duke Of Rutland, and had a residency at Stringfellows nightclub. The real Business soon hit the news again when one of their entourage took matters into his own hands.

"That was quite funny actually," chuckles Mark. "It was a mate of ours, Chopper, who was running around getting quite lively with 'em all, ringing the press up and everything. He was really serious... you know, 'I'll do you in a car park, mate, I know who you are!' and all that! The police got involved and everything. It was just a wind-up, but we got so much press out of it. He even rang up Stringfellow and said, 'Listen, String bean, I'll have you'...!"

The other 'bogus' Business were a band from Scotland, Big George And The Business, and unfortunately for Big George, he billed himself as just 'The Business' one night and about fifty disappointed skinheads turned up to have a look.

In late 1985, Wonderful World reissued four Business albums as two double-LP collections, 'Back to Back' Volumes 1 and 2, as well as a brand new studio album, 'Saturday's Heroes' and a single lifted from the LP, 'Drinking And Driving'. A tour of the same name was undertaken to promote the slew of releases that once again saw the band hit the front pages. Explains Mark:

"I remember this journalist rang me up about it, and he said, 'You know that four out of ten road accidents are caused by drunken drivers?' To which I replied, 'So, who caused the other six then? It must be people who aren't drunk! Are you saying it's safer to drink and drive then?' Of course, as soon as I said that, they went through the roof, and had a field day with us... but it was tongue in cheek! That song is pure Chas and Dave, innit? We were just winding people up, but fuck 'em if they can't take a joke!"

August 1986 saw the band headlining the second night of the Isle Of Wight Scooter Rally, a huge show that unfortunately ended in predictable chaos.

"Yeah, when it went, it usually went big time," sighs Mark. "It was a big do, 10,000 people or thereabouts, and we got up to do our thing, and someone threw a bottle and hit Mickey on the head, and down he went. I hadn't seen the bottle hit him, and just assumed he was drunk and fell over, but fair play to him, he got on with the set anyway, and we did a great show. These big lights got turned on the crowd in the middle of 'Harry May', when we take it all down and there's this quiet bass bit, and I was walking across the stage doing the Chuck Berry thing and all you could see were thousands and thousands of hands clapping along. That's probably one of my proudest moments.

"But after that it went off again. They raided and set fire to the beer tent, which might not have been such a bad thing except there was a caravan in there full of gas canisters, and they went up. The Old Bill turned up and the fire brigade, everyone was fighting, it was a nightmare."

In late 1986, Mark Brennan and Lol Pryor started Link Records, and the first release for the new label was another Oi compilation, 'Oi! The Resurrection', which of course featured a track by The Business. The 'Do A Runner' 12" followed in 1987, and – after the turbulent 'Main Event' show that saw the London Astoria getting CS-gassed! – the rather rocking 'Welcome To The Real World' LP in '88. Revealing a surprisingly atmospheric side to the band, the LP still had all the classic Business ingredients in full effect, but for the first time they were tempered with a confident maturity and slick production that saw the band revelling in their latent musicality rather than battling with it.

"Steve Kent was back in the band, and he's a brilliant guitarist," says Mark, on what was to be his last record with the band. "It was the first time I'd written with him, and we were both into stuff like Thin Lizzy; we never meant to go 'rock' or anything, it was just a natural progression. The lyrics were still the same, and the whole vibe still felt as aggressive to us. But we had to move forward – we couldn't keep churning out the same two-minute punk songs, but we didn't wanna go heavy metal."

After the LP, things went quiet on the gig front again, and The Business eventually fizzled out as Mark became ever busier with running the label. He did put together a band called The Guv'nors with Steve Kent, Mark Brabbs (the drummer from Tank) and Steve from The Crack, but despite a promising demo ("It was really good, an extension of 'Welcome To The Real World'"), the band never played live and soon split up. Meanwhile Steve Whale went on the road with Max Splodge before forming the Heavy Metal Outlaws, with Roy Pearce of The 4-Skins and Last Resort (who issued two singles, 'Swallow My Love' and 'Can't Stand The Sixties').

The Business went into hibernation until 1992 when Micky Fitz performed several impromptu Business songs with The Elite (a band put together by the band's old roadie, Mark Hannan) when they supported The Adicts and Cock Sparrer at the London Astoria. He reformed The Business, with Lol Proctor from The Elite on bass (Mark Brennan declining to rejoin the band because of commitments elsewhere), to play a benefit gig for Bobby Moore, the famous West Ham captain who had just died of cancer, at the Stick Of Rock in February 1993.

And realising that The Business still had a lot to offer the music scene, Micky and Steve have steered the reformed band through thick and thin ever since – deals with German punks Walzwerk, metal giants Century Media and respected hardcore label Taang, too many line-up changes to mention and some incredibly successful gigs all around the world.

"Yeah, me and Steve had both been made redundant at about the same time, so we decided to give it a go," says Micky. "I've got fuck-all to show for it, of course, except a spare room full of strange CDs and hundreds of good friends and memories, but I prefer it now… maybe 'cos I'm not so green? I'm enjoying it more. I loved the scene back then, don't get me wrong, but I feel like I'm helping people a lot more now. I'm still banging my head against the same brick walls as I've always been, but no-one takes the piss nowadays."

And that love is very much apparent on such latter-period Business albums as 1997's triumphant 'The Truth, The Whole Truth, And Nothing But The Truth', which is a proud match for anything the band produced in the Eighties. Produced by Lars Fredericksen from Rancid and released by Taang in 1997, the album is a near-perfect street punk album, every single song a modern Oi classic in the making, the title track in particular built around a massive chorus.

"I'd just like to be remembered for the silly little things," reflects Micky when asked what kind of mark he has made on underground music. "Like in Richmond, Virginia, where it wasn't an all-ages show, but we got the security to open the back doors and let the young fans who couldn't get in, watch from outside. I worked with the security so they could see the show. Little things like that matter a lot to people.

"And it's very flattering when people walk up to you on the other side of the world and tell you that your music has changed their life! It's wonderful! I go bright red every time, haha! And I really can't envision a time when there won't be a Business. Whenever I need a little inspiration, I only have to look at Charlie Harper, and if he's still out there doing it, why can't we be?"

SELECT DISCOGRAPHY:

7"s:
'Harry May' (Secret, 1981)
'Smash The Discos' (Secret, 1982)
'Drinking And Driving' (Diamond, 1985)
'Anywhere But Here' (Walzwerk, 1994)

12"s:
'Get Out Of My House' (Wonderful World, 1985)
'Drinking And Driving' (Diamond, 1985)
'Do A Runner' (Link, 1988)

LPs:
'Suburban Rebels' (Secret, 1983)
'The Business, 1980-81' (Syndicate, 1983)
'Loud, Proud And Punk – Live' (Syndicate, 1984)
'Back To Back, Volume One' (Wonderful World, 1985)
'Back To Back, Volume Two' (Wonderful World, 1985)
'Saturday's Heroes' (Harry May, 1985)
'Welcome To The Real World' (Link, 1988)
'Live And Loud' (Link, 1989)
'Keep The Faith' (Century Media, 1994)
'Death II Dance' (Century Media, 1996) – 5-track CD
'The Truth, The Whole Truth, And Nothing But The Truth' (Taang, 1997)
'No Mercy For You' (Burning Heart, 2001)
'Under The Influence' (Rhythm Vicar, 2003)

AT A GLANCE:
Those interested in checking out early Business material are recommended to pick up the excellent digipack CD versions of the band's first three studio albums, complete with attractive posters and bonus tracks, released by Captain Oi! in 2002. It should be stressed, however, that, never ones to rest on their laurels, the band's superb new material is more than worthy of investigation as well.

H aving appeared on all the early Oi compilations, The 4-Skins are widely regarded as the quintessential band of the genre; they were also one of the best, penning some classic tunes right from their very inception. Formed in the Bridge House one drunken evening in 1979, the original line-up consisted of 'Hoxton' Tom McCourt on guitar, Gary Hodges on vocals, Steve 'H' Harner on bass and Gary Hitchcock on drums.

"We all met at the Wellington pub midweek and booked an hour at Alaska Studios around the corner," says Tom. "No instruments, just a few beers, but, if I remember rightly, Hodges wrote the lyrics to 'Chaos' and 'ACAB'. The name was obvious, as we were all, or had been skins, since '77 or '78. I was actually only asked to join as a temporary measure!"

Tom was in fact one of the first skinheads in London, and before that he was one of the original punks.

"I got into punk in 1976. Although I lived in Hoxton, I went to school in Camden and one of my mates asked me to go to a gig with him. I went… and that was that, my trendy hair and my clothes went DIY overnight. It was an exciting time; you went out and saw The Clash, the Pistols, The Damned, and the Buzzcocks in small pubs and clubs all over the place. It was dangerous as well; you seemed to be fair game for anyone.

"I remember one day going home and deciding that I'd dye my hair… and my mum said she'd do it for me. The very next day it was gold! People thought that we were lunatics but my mum was brilliant about it all, even when I was sewing zips into plain black T-shirts and putting chains on my blazer.

"There was always an edge with punk, but it was the King's Road fights against the Teds that really started it for me. If you look on the cover of 'Clash City Rockers', those were the main organisers of the punk side; I'm there in the middle photo with an ear across most of my face, but you can recognise the eyebrows, and my old mate John O'Connor is next to me. And that was what punk looked like to me; every Saturday from the Roebuck we'd go up and down the King's Road looking for them, the sense of camaraderie was brilliant.

"How I became a skinhead is a different story," he continues. "In about late 1977, I bumped into a bloke in full skin regalia –

Sta-Prest, Ben Sherman, Crombie and Loafers – which was a bit of a shock to the system. The last proper skins I remembered, at the age of ten or eleven, were my uncles and cousins in '69 or '70. I was already into The Jam, and Sham 69 and Menace filled the gap in live music terms. The decision was simple, move away from something I'd enjoyed to being different and sharper.

"At first being a skin was class; everyone who got into it went looking for the right gear, visiting every old tailor and

Hodges of The 4-Skins, live at the Bridge House for 'Garry Bushell's birthday bash…'

army surplus store hoping to get Ben Shermans in the 'wooden boxes'. It didn't matter where you were from if you were a skin; away from the grounds, football and politics were unimportant. We'd meet down Brick Lane on Sundays and go off for a beer.

But the politics started to move in and, as the first lot of revival skins were a fairly hard bunch, more and more of the plastic skins started arriving to latch onto it.

"It sounds elitist, I know, but as it became more popular, it started to go downhill for many of us. Just as mohicans and begging did for punk (no one had a mohican in 1976), the glue sniffers and idiots did for the skin scene. Some of us started growing our hair and thought of ourselves as 'suedeheads', others were already into the emerging mod scene. The end of '78 and '79, it seemed to pick up again, with new bands and the same 'community atmosphere'. What was funny though was that the glue skins now seemed to think anyone in a suit was a mod and ready for a battering; something they soon found out wasn't true. At a Rejects' Electric Ballroom show, some of 'em were digging me for wearing a mohair suit, which ended with them getting a battering from The Rejects. And, later that night, feeling brave and thinking we'd all left, they started playing football around the floor with a young kid in a parka, which led to The Rejects clearing the place out. They were hard times, there were rows at most gigs..."

The 4-Skins actually made their live debut supporting The Rejects and The Damned at the Bridge House during the summer of 1980. Although Gary Hitchcock couldn't make the gig, the band played three songs ("All we had at the time!") with Mickey Geggus of The Rejects on drums. Garry Bushell was in the audience, and, despite the band regarding themselves as little more than a laugh, The 4-Skins turned in a good enough performance to convince him to invite them to appear on 'Oi! The Album'. They contributed 'Wonderful World' and 'Chaos', two instant streetcore classics that were ably produced by Mickey Geggus, who also played lead guitar on the latter.

"The music was punk but it was faster," reckons Tom accurately. "A lot heavier and more basic, like Sabbath meets The Ramones, with terrace chants."

"The 4-Skins had even better songs than The Rejects," says Garry Bushell enthusiastically. "I know Mick played on 'Chaos', but The 4-Skins wrote it. Here was a band that just throbbed with menace; Hodges had a great gruff roar of a voice, he meant every word. Johnny Rotten may have said he wanted to destroy passers-by, but The 4-Skins sounded like they just might do it. They were 'Clockwork Orange' made flesh."

Things were looking good for the band – they were even offered a major deal with Decca, as long as they changed their name to 'Skins 4' ("After we'd stopped laughing, we said goodbye!") – when H. decided to leave to roadie full-time for The Rejects. Tom moved to bass ("Easier to play when drunk!" he laughs) and Steve 'Rockabilly' Pear joined on guitar; Gary Hitchcock also left, to concentrate on managing the band, and was replaced behind the kit by John Jacobs. This new line-up appeared on the 'Strength Thru Oi' LP with '1984' and 'Sorry', and recorded the brilliant 'One Law For Them' single. However disaster struck the very night before they entered the studio to record the EP, in the unfortunate shape of the aforementioned Southall riot.

"We had agreed, with The Last Resort and The Business, to play some gigs together outside of East London, and then possibly across the country," explains Tom. "We all arranged one show each. We booked the Hambrough Tavern in Southall, as we had a large following of punks and rockabillies from Ealing, and this seemed like a logical place. So, what happened? We got down there at lunchtime, set up for an early sound check, had a game of pool and some beers. Then some of us went out for a curry and got back to the pub at about 6.00pm.

"Stories started surfacing that there had been an incident in a nearby chip shop and that the Southall Youth Movement were reacting to it; bear in mind that, by this time, we had already played in Hackney and Manchester with no trouble whatsoever. The Last Resort coaches turned up and they all came straight into the pub (and there were no Union Jacks on any of them as far as I could see). At about 7.30 or 8.00 pm, the police said that there was basically a picket across the road and that trouble was brewing. We offered to meet them, to try and sort things out, and this was rebuffed, but we agreed to make sure that everyone was kept in the pub and the gig went ahead. It sounds melodramatic but as we were finishing our set, the windows came in and then it all went off! What is never commented on though, is that the police were actually in the pub at the time. When we got outside, the pub hadn't yet been firebombed and people started leaving, to the west. There were fights but it also went on into the next day, and even, I think, the next night. Just after the gig, Rockabilly Steve, a committed socialist by the way, got caught on his own on his way back to his car, chased across some gardens and hit with a frying pan....

"Afterwards came all sorts of stories, most of them inaccurate or downright lies – like the perfect right wing leaflets 'found' in the burnt out pub...? At the time, the audience did include right wingers as well as left, although I'd already been involved (with the ICF) in giving the BM Leader Guard a pasting at Barking, and we weren't thought of highly by them because of this.

"Also because we always stuck to our guns to be apolitical. Out of all the reports, only The Guardian gave a balanced account. The N.M.E. were amongst the worse, dragging out a previous interview which was a load of bollocks. Their journalist was crapping himself when we met in the Horn Of Plenty at Mile End, but we bought him a few drinks and had a good laugh and then he stitched us up in print! When I spoke to him afterwards, he was all apologies, but then again we should have expected it."

The 4-Skins L–R: Gary Hodges (bottom), Steve Pear, John Jacobs, Hoxton Tom (top)

The ensuing 'One Law For Them' 7", on their own Clockwork Fun label (distributed by Secret), remains the band's crowning glory; it was nominated as Single Of The Week in Sounds, but many shops and distributors refused to stock it in the aftermath of Southall. It still managed No. 4 in the Independent Charts though, and on the back of it, Secret signed the band for one album and two singles.

Frustrated at the unfair publicity and attempting to 'clear their name', The 4-Skins and The Business played under false names – The Skans and The Bollguns respectively – at the Mottingham Prince Of Wales, a show that was reported on by the BBC's Nationwide programme, but again the band felt misrepresented.

"We thought that we could clear some things up, but I watched it again only yesterday... and fair and balanced it ain't!" spits Tom disgustedly.

Gary Hodges and Rockabilly Steve left soon after the programme aired, and in the resulting restructure, the band's roadie, Tony 'Panther' Cummins took over the mike, with John Jacobs moving from drums to guitar, and Pete Abbott filling the vacant stool behind the kit. This line-up debuted with a cracking, tongue in cheek cover of Slade's 'Merry Xmas Everybody' for Secret's 'Bollocks To Christmas' EP in December 1981, before releasing the 'Yesterday's Heroes' single the following February and the album, 'The Good, The Bad, And The 4-Skins', that spring. Despite a weak production compared to previous efforts, the album especially was a great success. Opening with the infectious, ska-heavy 'Plastic Gangster' that featured ex-drummer/manager Gary Hitchcock on vocals and almost ended up being issued as a single under The Plastic Gangsters moniker in an attempt to generate some airplay, the album topped the Indies, and even made the Top Fifty of the National Charts.

Following October '82's Mickey Geggus-produced 'Low Life' single (b/w 'Bread Or Blood'), and a UK tour with Combat 84, John and Pete were fired, and Panther left to become a DJ, leaving Hoxton Tom to lick his wounds and regroup.

"Gary (Hitchcock) and I left it for a few months," he says. "We even thought about a new band but it always came back to sticking with what we started and not re-inventing ourselves. We were never gonna be millionaires, but we enjoyed the gigs and recording. We got Paul (Swain) and Ian (Bramson) from an advert we placed. They were good blokes; Paul was the best guitarist we ever had and Ian was just as good as John on the drums. We started rehearsing again and things seemed to come out harder and tighter; it sounded like we were getting back to our best form again, just like the early days."

Joined by Roi Pearce from the recently disbanded Last Resort, the new 4-Skins released the excellent 'A Fistful Of 4-Skins' LP in late 1983, followed by the live album for Syndicate, 'From Chaos To 1984'. They also contributed 'On The Streets' to the 'Son Of Oi!' compilation, but, unable to fully revive their former glories, they split up for good in '84, after a short UK tour with One Way System.

"Getting Roi in gave the whole thing a good buzz again, but what was gutting was that that was the line-up we needed when Hodges left. 'A Fistful of 4-Skins' was a good, solid punk album, no frills, no mess, and we did some great gigs all over the country, but it got harder and harder and in the end we just called it a day. The last line up was a good laugh, but we should have split a bit earlier, to be honest; it was definitely getting a bit stale."

Admirably refusing to reform in the Nineties ("I didn't want us to end up like the old Teddy Boys we used to hate so much when we were younger!"), Tom still regards his time with The 4-Skins fondly.

"On a general point, other than a row with the bouncers in Edinburgh, where they were beating up young kids, and in Scarborough, where a load of herberts tried to take on the Cockneys, we never had trouble at gigs all across England and Scotland, and we met loads of decent people and thoroughly enjoyed ourselves. But I just hope that we're remembered as an honest, working class punk band... that maybe even helped pave the way for the recent punk revival a la Green Day and Rancid."

SELECT DISCOGRAPHY:
7"s:
'One Law For Them' (Clockwork Fun, 1981)
'Yesterday's Heroes' (Secret Records, 1982)
'Low Life' (Secret Records, 1982)

LPs:

'The Good, The Bad And The 4-Skins' (Secret Records, 1982)
'A Fistful Of 4-Skins' (Syndicate Records, 1983)
'From Chaos To 1984 (Live)' (Syndicate Records, 1984)

AT A GLANCE:

Captain Oi!'s 1999 CD, '4-Skins: Singles And Rarities', features twenty-three tracks from all periods of the band's existence, as well as an informative booklet crammed with original cover art and liner notes. The attractive 2003 digipack reissue of 'The Good, The Bad And The 4-Skins' is also recommended, and comes complete with bonus tracks and poster.

A rare picture of (pre-Ejected) Dawn Patrol in action
L-R: Gary Sandbrook, Dawn Payne, Jim Brooks

THE EJECTED

Punk shows in the early Eighties were nowhere near as corporate as what often passes for punk two decades later, but even today you sometimes find a scruffy mohawk hanging around outside the venue, trying to scrounge enough money to get inside and buy himself a beer. The plaintive plea of 'Ere, mate, have you got 10p?' – and, of course, the inevitable exasperated reply, 'Nah, mate, not me!' – can still be heard occasionally as you queue for a show, but twenty years ago, it was a deafening chorus outside any gig, similar in volume and frenzy to a flock of hungry gulls bothering a rubbish tip!

Which may account for the success of The Ejected, a street punk band from Dagenham in Essex, who got lumped in with the Oi movement by merit of their inclusion on the 'Carry On Oi' compilation, but who leapt to prominence with their 1982 EP for Riot City, 'Have You Got 10p?' On the surface a simplistic humorous rant, but driven by a wonderfully raw guitar and fleshed out with an annoyingly catchy chorus, it embedded itself in the ear of anyone who heard it like a persistent leech. Unfortunately, its novelty factor typecast The Ejected for the rest of their short career as some sort of goofy joke band, when in reality, the people involved had far greater aspirations.

"Firstly, I always wanted to be in a band!" recalls guitarist/vocalist Jim Brooks, having no qualms about revealing the real motives he had for learning his first power chord. "From a very early age I romanticised about the idea of being famous, writing songs and travelling the world. From our album sleeve notes you can see that (bassist) Gary (Sandbrook) and me were always into music, and influenced by virtually everything. Alice Cooper, Patti Smith, Lou Reed, The Stranglers, Bowie, Ultravox… the list was endless. I grew up with Seventies glam bands like Sweet, Suzi Quatro and Mud; it was an exciting time for British pop. Later it was Dr Feelgood, Kiss, AC/DC and hard rock bands like Led Zeppelin.

"But then along came punk and blew it all wide open. Anything went. Most importantly, no previous experience or musical knowledge was necessary; it was like applying for a job without having to show your CV!"

And in such a fertile climate even bands like The Ejected could find their proverbial fifteen minutes. Although the group that released that wacky debut single sounded quite different to how Jim originally envisaged his music would turn out. Figuring that having a girl in the band might give them an edge securing radio play and coverage in magazines such as N.M.E. and Sounds, Jim and Gary began by auditioning many female vocalists, most of whom were promptly scared away by the crude advances of the guitarist!

"I was a horny bastard and kept trying to get off with them all," laughs Jim. "And they'd be frightened off 'cos I had absolutely no finesse… if they looked sexy and could sing a bit, they were in! And if they rejected my sexual advances, they were out again! It makes me cringe now to think about it… and how Gary put up with me, I'll never know! I was acting like a love-sick tosser."

Despite his overactive libido conspiring to thwart his musical career, Jim eventually secured the right girl for the job, Dawn Payne, who even lent her name to their chosen moniker, Dawn Patrol, and with the long-overdue addition of a decent drummer ("We'd had loads, but they were all crap!"), things were finally going according to plan for the two East End lads.

"Dawn was very punky and quite an inventive lyricist. We soon had some great songs, and I've still got a couple of good noisy demo tapes from that period. When we eventually split from Dawn, she carried on with a new line-up and released a 12" EP, which was pretty good. One track in particular, 'The Prisoner', was excellent. If anyone knows what Dawn is up to these days, I'd love to get in contact with her again! Get in touch with me via the publishers of this book.

"Anyway, I remember after a rehearsal one day, us all stepping out into the street in our leathers, studs, bullet belts, boots, leopard skins and dyed hair, and seeing our reflection in shop windows across the street. Gary turned to me and said, 'I don't believe this, we actually look and sound like a really good punk band!' And I agreed; it seemed like we were on the verge of something momentous. But then I went and fucked it all up…"

In a 'Spinal Tap'-like turn of events, Jim found out that Dawn, who he was dating at the time, was seeing the new drummer, and quit the band out of pure jealousy. He took Gary with him, and the two of them vowed to have nothing more to do with female singers or dreams of fame and fortune. And so The Ejected were born.

"We put Dagenham on the map music-wise," claims Jim. "We were hugely influenced by The UK Subs, Cockney Rejects, Angelic Upstarts and The Clash. I decided that raw guitar, throbbing bass and powerhouse drums were what turned us on. We always had catchy singalong choruses too. Lyrically we were a bit tongue-in-cheek, but we sang about everyday stuff – football, sex, gangs, police, drinking, gigs… that sort of thing. We were keeping it down to earth."

Even keeping it down to earth though, the band's – seemingly inoffensive – lyrics managed to land them in a few scrapes, mainly thanks to the undercurrent of tension that sometimes manifested itself at gigs in the shape of mindless violence. Take, for example, one of the songs they contributed to the 'Carry On Oi' album, 'East End Kids'.

"We were playing Feltham Football Club, headlining over The Partisans. They had brought a load of their fans with them, and they went down a storm. They even did two encores, and we thought, 'Oh shit, we're gonna be a big anti-climax as the headlining band!'

"As we took the stage, only about twenty people stood before us, but we launched into 'East End Kids' unperturbed. Of course, it being in West London, all the skins and herberts took great exception to this, and started shouting at us, so I quickly changed the words to 'West End Kids', and everyone piled through from the other bar. They were all onstage, nicking the microphones and stuff, but at least we went down well!"

Even the comic banter of their first EP was – quite literally – thrown back in their faces…

"Oh yeah, when we supported The 4-Skins at the 100 Club in Oxford Street, we were pelted with 10p coins all the way through our set! We played everything ultra-fast and got off quick!"

Following the success of 'Have You Got 10p?', both band and label wanted to be on the ball with a follow-up, and although 'Noise For The Boys', released in December '82, was just as strong musically as their debut, it lacked that quirky humour that had set their opening gambit apart. It consequently only spent half as long in the Indie Charts, and only managed to reach No. 28, twenty places below where 'Have You Got 10p?' had peaked. It also saw the band enlist a new drummer, Paul Griffiths, who replaced Mick 'Sticks' Robinson.

"The 'Have You Got 10p?' thing did typecast us as a sort of cartoon band, I suppose," sighs Jim. "We couldn't follow it up with anything funnier or more original. The press had lots of great stuff to say about the first single – but after that, they were disappointed with 'Noise For The Boys'. It was like they just wanted us to continue in exactly the same vein, but we wanted to be taken seriously. Once you're pigeonholed though, that's it! Even Garry Bushell, who'd given us a lot of encouragement and interviewed us for Sounds, turned on our first album…"

That being the competent, but flawed, 'A Touch Of Class', which emerged in early '83. With a cover that had the band lined up against a graffiti covered wall, opposite three punkettes dressed in leather mini-skirts and high heels, the sixteen-track album is about as subtle as a kick in the testicles, but great fun from start to finish nevertheless.

"We hoped having three birds on the cover of our first album would make us look like real womanisers! And we thought it might help shift a few copies to some of the horny young herberts – like me! – of the time. Incidentally, the girls are Anita, my ex-wife, who is sadly no longer with us (she provided the female voice that featured in the middle section of 'Have You Got 10p?'); Paula, who was Gary's bird back then, who used to play guitar in The Gymslips (she became a lesbian after being with Gary! It's true!); and Debbie, a sexy young punkette drafted in at the last minute by Paul Griffiths. His girlfriend Mandy dumped him the night before the photo shoot, so he got his sexy cousin to deputise. Paul is now married with two boys."

Although harshly described as 'Completely empty of any real substance' by Punk Lives, 'A Touch Of Class' contains some enjoyable songs and still notched up decent sales, but it was apparent the band's popularity was already waning. Jim has his own theory as to their inability to build a fiercely loyal following.

"Our biggest problem really was how bad we were live. We were awful! We never really planned our sets, and never thought about the impact of a good running order. We weren't any good at between-song banter either. We more interested in getting pissed, pogoing to the support bands and talking to any music celebs who might have turned up…"

In an attempt to bolster flagging interest, Riot City roped in The UK Subs' Nicky Garratt, to produce the band's second album, 'Spirit of Rebellion', which came out just six months after their first. He brought a much more polished finesse to their sound and contributed a song, 'The Enemy Awaits' ("I can't even listen to it now, it's a dirge"), which he later re-recorded with The UK Subs.

"I'll always remember our van pulling up outside Dagenham East tube station to pick Nicky up for one of our rehearsals, and catching sight of him with his beard; we were shocked! I was so nervous, because he was a real hero of mine, but we got on really well with him. He was great with us, even lent us his amps and guitars. He liked our rawness and our melodies, but the real reason he wanted to produce us was because our new songs weren't yet complete, so there was lots of room for his own ideas. When you listen to 'Spirit Of Rebellion', his ideas, mainly harmonies, backing vocals and some guitar bits, are everywhere. He turned some average songs into absolute gems.

"I remember he once said that 'The Ejected are a democratic band run by a fascist dictator!' Meaning me! We loved that!"

The band also added a second guitarist, 'Dynamo' Kev Pallett, who thickened their sound somewhat, although he departed soon after the album's release – along with Gary, who "Wanted to play different stuff". Jim doggedly recruited Paul Quain (ex-D.I.R.T.) on bass, and released the 'Press The Button' EP, to yet more diminishing sales. It was to be their last release, as their next recordings, for an EP to be entitled 'Public Animals', never reached the pressing plants because of Riot City folding.

And that spelt the end for The Ejected. With no label to back them, and the Oi movement seemingly floundering, the lads lost interest. Jim joined Gary in a pop/reggae band called Jo Jo Republic, who also featured three girl singers, a saxophonist and keyboards. They played a few shows but split before they could land themselves a deal on the back of their sole demo tape. Jim has no regrets, though.

"My son, Adam, is twenty now and a big grunge, metal and punk fan. He loves all those old Ejected songs, and his own band did a version of 'I'm Gonna Get A Gun', which flattered me. I think our music will be remembered as throwaway Oi, but I still meet people who have our records and loved them, and I still have people asking me for 10p in the street, so I don't think we'll ever be completely forgotten!

"I'm very proud of what The Ejected achieved, even though it wasn't much really. We had a great laugh and produced some classic little anthems. To be honest, I think our songs were a lot better than most of the other punk and Oi bands around at the same time as us, and if a big label had picked up on us, we could've gone onto bigger things. I've got no regrets, though. We made mistakes; we were stupid and naive, but at least we did it; we lived our dream, if only for three short years. It was great, and we treasure the memories, both good and bad."

SELECT DISCOGRAPHY:
7"s:
'Have You Got 10p?' (Riot City, 1982)
'Noise For The Boys' (Riot City, 1982)
'Press The Button' (Riot City, 1983)

LPs:
'A Touch Of Class' (Riot City, 1983)
'Spirit Of Rebellion' (Riot City, 1983)

AT A GLANCE:
Definitely 'The Best of The Ejected' (Captain Oi!, 1999), which features choice cuts from all the above releases. It also unveils for the first time the unreleased 'Public Animals' EP and the band's one-off comeback session of 1997, plus all the original cover art and some informative liner notes.

E lsewhere the thriving London scene included such big hitters as Infa-Riot (their debut LP for Secret, 'Still Out Of Order', is widely regarded as a genre classic and went Top Fifty in the Nationals) and Charlton maniacs, The Blood, whose 'False Gestures For a Devious Public' LP (Noise, 1983) was an exhilarating collision of punk and heavy metal.

The spirit of '82 is proudly continued to this day by the likes of The Foamers, The Filaments, 17 Stitches and, of course, Deadline, whose excellent second album, 'Back For More', came out in 2003 on Captain Oi!.

Infa-Riot, who later became The Infas
L-R: Lee Wilson, Mark Reynolds, Barry
D'Amery, Floyd Wilson (Pic: Tony Mottram)

INFR-RIOT

O f all the many street punk bands that emerged from the UK in the early Eighties, Infa-Riot surely epitomised the zeitgeist of the period better than most – their name itself was an abbreviation of 'In For A Riot', but more importantly they were genuinely street kids, working class through and through, who were penning simplistic knockabout songs for a disenfranchised youth straight from the heart. No pretentious posturing, just ballsy, tuneful punk rock. Unfortunately all their early promise fizzled out with an ill-advised name change and a disappointing second album, although the band reformed in 2010 and have done much to make amends since.

"We were all punk fans!" begins vocalist Lee Wilson, of how he ended up fronting an explosive act like Infa-Riot in the first place. "I especially loved going to gigs. I never did go to discos or clubs – and still don't – so it was a natural route for us to follow. I loved Sham 69. I could really relate to their songs, so I started writing about what I saw and experienced on the council estate in London where we all grew up.

"It was the whole punk scene I loved, not just North London, but around us were lots of other bands all having a try. It was a great 'can do' atmosphere and a great time to grow up . . . Our father was an original teddy boy, so he got the rebellious side of punk/Oi! straight away; in fact, all our parents loved it . . . and why not? We had nothing in the first place, and so we had nothing to lose!"

The band formed in late 1980, seventeen-year-old Lee being joined by his fifteen-year-old brother Floyd on bass, and (also only fifteen back then) guitarist Barry D'Amery. They predictably went through a few drummers before they eventually arrived at a steady lineup with Mark Reynolds, but their first drummer was Gary McInerney, who played on their first demos before losing interest.

"My brother went to school with Barry," recalls Lee, "and when he got a bass guitar we went round to Barry's house to learn from what he knew . . . By the end of the evening we had the beginnings of a band. We certainly didn't have any deluded ambitions or anything, but we did have a stroke of luck when the Angelic Upstarts moved to our area; we got to know them and had our first gig with them, just four months after forming. We did a half-hour set, of all our own songs. I still feel proud of that."

Said first gig was at the Lordship Pub in Woodgreen, North London, during April 1981 ("We went down quite well and even got a mention in the NME . . . as 'Infra-Riot'!" laughs Lee, "And from what I remember I knew that instant it was something I had to do . . ."), with Mensi, the much-respected vocalist of the headlining Upstarts, becoming an outspoken fan of the young band. Indeed, after demoing the songs 'Riot Riot' and 'Five Minute Fashions' in "a student's front room studio", Infa-Riot toured with the Upstarts and were taken to heart by the burgeoning Oi! scene of the time, contributing two songs ('We Outnumber You' and a re-recorded 'Riot Riot') to the second Oi! LP, 'Strength Thru Oi'.

"That whole Oi! thing was invented by Garry Bushell, and he realised this bunch of young bands were not the arty types like all the other bands around at that time. Originally it was known as 'the new breed', but eventually became known as Oi! We all started as punk-type bands and Oi! was created around us. We owe a lot to Garry, and he remains a friend to this day . . .

"Those songs were done in a studio down the Old Kent Road," continues Lee, before admitting, "When I hear them now I think they're awful. We had a producer and I don't think he understood what punk was all about, but we were so young we assumed he knew best."

Lee might well regard the tracks as awful, but they were certainly highlights of the collection, imbued with an almost tangible youthful urgency, and they brought the band to the attention of Secret Records, who issued the debut Infa-Riot single, 'Kids Of The '80s', in October 1981. Produced by Max Splodge (from Splodgenessabounds, of course), and boasting an iconic

Infa-Riot, courtesy of Mark Brennan

cover image of a skull with a mohawk, it was a high-speed, chaotic offering and crashed into the Independent Charts at No. 8, and the band promoted it with UK tours in support of both The Business and The Exploited.

"We did have an offer from another record company and we nearly signed for them," reveals Lee, "But Secret called me literally in the nick of time and said they had just signed The Exploited and that we should join them on the label. It was run by Martin Hooker, who used to work for EMI and was the man behind The Knack. He always promised us the earth, and said many times that the cheque was in the post – which it rarely was, haha!

"The name and the logo was my idea. I had this vision of a skull with a mohawk, and the cousin of our current drummer Alex was a bit of an artist. He said he could do us something and he came back a few days later with the logo that we still use and love today.

"As for Max Splodge, he was a mate from the pub. He said he used to work in a studio, so he offered his help and we took it. Maybe, in hindsight, the production's a bit too fussy, with too many guitar overdubs, but that's how it goes, I suppose?"

The Exploited were touring on the back of their hugely successful 'Dead Cities' single, so the gigs were packed ("And Wattie remains a good friend – he's a total one-off, I love him!"), and alongside a track ('Each Dawn I Die') on the 'Carry On Oi!' compilation, it was a good way to close out a great year for the band. And 1982 was just as busy, with the band making the most of their newfound momentum.

After playing at the opening of London's infamous Skunx Club in February, Infa-Riot were included on the Pax Records compilation, 'Wargasm' (their track 'Power' neatly subverting a football terrace chorus with a strong anti-war message), before issuing their second single, 'The

Infa-Riot live, pic courtesy of Mark Brennan

Winner', which sneaked into the Indie Top Ten that May, cementing the band's position as one of the leading lights of the emerging Oi! scene.

"That was the first song we produced ourselves," says Lee proudly, "I wrote it about an ex-girlfriend, but I guess it's one of those songs people can relate their own personal stuff to, which is what I always want when writing."

'The Winner' was lifted from the band's first LP, the storming 'Still Out Of Order', which garnered a 5/5 review in Sounds, a rave review more than justified by rousing cuts such as the superb cover of Girlschool's 'Emergency' (a surprise opener, but totally suited to the band's thumping style) and the ultra-cynical anti-poseur anthem, 'Five Minute Fashions'. Enough copies changed hands to briefly trouble the National Top Forty chart, and the future did indeed look bright.

"They were just the songs we wrote as we evolved," says Lee. "We produced it ourselves, and Secret said, 'There's the studio, go and get on with it', so we did! I remember it going down really well, and I'm still proud of those songs. They seem to be part of people's youth, and when we play them live the whole audience sing along, wherever we are playing. It's a great feeling!"

September '82 saw the release of the 'Britannia Waives The Rules' 12" from Secret Records, featuring their three biggest sellers, namely The Exploited, Chron Gen and Infa-Riot, the latter contributing the brooding 'Feel The Rage' to the garishly packaged EP (phallic lighthouses, anyone?)

Unfortunately, despite their enthusiastic desire to unite the subcultures under one working class banner against Thatcher, like many frustrated Oi! bands of the period, Infa-Riot found their gigs increasingly becoming a battleground for warring factions, which resulted in venues shutting their doors on them, punters shying away from the constant aggro and eventually the band changing their name in an attempt to throw their more rowdy followers off the scent. Abbreviated to The Infas (apparently the nickname bestowed upon them by Mensi himself), their sophomore album was the somewhat neutered (despite the promising title) 'Sound And Fury'. Issued by Panache in early 1984, with the title track also appearing as a 7" single too, it failed to capture the band's old fire and subsequently their old fans.

"The hardest thing for a band to do is staying and building on what you have," says Lee ruefully. "We failed to do that; we were young and inexperienced. Also at that time Secret had financial issues, and Panache were a publisher who had financially backed Secret. It was an office of older men who thought we should make a pretentious second album . . . and didn't we just do that! Looking back now, I'm not sure who we had in mind as the audience for The Infas? Saying that, I think there's a few good songs on it though . . .

"We hated the trouble at gigs that used to happen back then! We've played through semi-riots, with punch ups going on all over the place, but thinking back nobody got killed, and maybe the chaos added to the flavour of it all? But we changed the name because we were getting so much trouble at our gigs. With hindsight, it was a very wrong move, and the change of musical direction was never in our hearts. I do regret that, but ain't we all clever with hindsight?

"And then we never played as The Infas anyway. I can't remember where the last gig was, but we didn't decide to split – it just fizzled out, and that was that."

Not for long though, as there was an ill-advised attempt at a comeback in late 1985, which lasted all of one drunken gig, at Adam And Eve's in Leeds, before Infa-Riot was laid to rest for the best part of two decades.

"What a nightmare that was," agrees Lee. "We decided to make this comeback in the mid-Eighties, so my brother found a drummer and we started rehearsing. It was sounding great, so we organised a gig in Leeds . . . where our new drummer got smashed out of his head on beer and whiskey and didn't play a single note that we had rehearsed. I could have lived with it and moved on with someone else [on drums], but none of us knew it was being recorded and later released as a live album. [It came out through Link Records as part of their 'Live And Loud' series.] To this day I have never listened to it, and never will."

With Lee becoming an antiques dealer, as well as moving to Spain for ten years where he plied a trade as a locksmith, and Barry working hard as a builder, the possibility of another Infa-Riot reformation looked decidedly unlikely, yet against all the odds the band have indeed regrouped and have recently been touring the world, much to the happy dismay of many an international Infa-Riot fan who had long ago given up hope of ever seeing them perform live again.

"Well, when I came back from Spain in 2010, I wanted a new challenge," explains Lee. "Then an old friend said we were owed royalties by a record company, and in turn told me we should reform. I hadn't spoken to Barry or Alex for 25 years, but I tracked them down and we agreed to give it a go, and we're loving it.

"I've only ever been in Infa-Riot, and that will forever be the only band for me, but Barry is a natural musician and has done the odd side project in the past, and Alex the drummer has played for the Angelic Upstarts, Bad Manners and various other bands, but now we are all focused on Infa-Riot and only Infa-Riot.

"And we're enjoying it a lot more now," he adds in closing, pondering on why the appeal of their music has managed to transcend three decades. "The punk/Oi! scene is alive and well all over the world, and we all feel very lucky, because not many people have a second crack at something they love doing.

"I would like to think that if anyone saw us live now, they could still see our energy, passion and love for this music, and that's important to us. We were one of those bands that had no education, that came from a poor, working class background, but we could always knock out a decent song now and again."

SELECT DISCOGRAPHY:
7"S:
'Kids Of The 80s' (Secret, 1981)
'The Winner' (Secret, 1982)
'Sound And Fury' (Panache, 1984)

12"S:
'Britannia Waives The Rules' (Secret, 1982) – *split with The Exploited and Chron Gen*

LPS:
'Still Out Of Order' (Secret, 1982)
'Sound And Fury' (Panache, 1983)
'Live And Loud' (Link, 1988)

AT A GLANCE:
Has to be the Captain Oi! CD issue of 'Still Out Of Order', which includes the first two singles and
'Feel The Rage' from the 'Britannia . . .' 12" as bonus tracks.

THE BLOOD

"The truth is that I got into punk rock because I have always had a predisposition to tell
people to fuck off in an amplified ambience," claims The Blood vocalist, Colin 'The Cardinal
Jesus Hate' Smith – and it's a most apt beginning to one of the most irreverent chapters of
UK punk rock. But what did you expect from a band that began life known as Coming Blood?

"I had been in two bands before I met Jamie [Cantwell, aka guitarist J.J. Bedsore]," reveals
Colin, "And we did two shows, one in Woolwich and the other in Welling, as The Tripe Hounds.
At this point Jamie was an avid fan of Motörhead; however, we decided after plenty of arguing,
and a few vats of vodka, to form another band and play more harmonic melodies infused with
irony whilst keeping the metal thrash. I played guitar at first in Coming Blood, but very soon
decided that I just wanted to be the vocalist or the frontman in the new band. I think Kenny Day
and Garry Granger initially came from Tripe Hounds into Coming Blood, but they did not like
the punk direction the band was taking as they were perhaps more metal musicians.

"As well as Motörhead and metal, Jamie also adored The Damned, as did I myself, and it was
on this common ground that The Blood began to musically correlate its anthems. Lyrically, at
the time, both Jamie and myself were hedonistic, anarchistic and nihilistic individuals, who spent
our whole time in a narcotic oblivion watching 'Derek And Clive', 'Laurel And Hardy', 'Top Cat',
'Bilko', 'Foghorn Leghorn' and 'It's A Mad, Mad, Mad, Mad World'. The creation of the songs
came about through an alcoholic miasma whilst we avidly watched our favourite films and sat
with our guitars on our laps in Jamie's parents' house."

The band's first manager, Gary Billingham, came up with the short-lived name Coming
Blood, and it was the Cardinal that insisted they shorten it to The Blood, in time for their first
gig at the Marquee.

"Gary also wrote the lyrics to [album tracks] 'Mesrine' and 'Rule 43' when he was doing
time!" laughs Colin. "The 'when' and the 'why' we shortened the name are probably not relevant,
in the sense that it's just what bands do as they evolve, but I did like the fact that saying 'The
Blood' out loud seemed to jar in an oblique sense if that can be counted as a why?

"As for that first gig, I remember it only because it was our first live review, and it said
something like, 'The Blood are undisciplined, unorganized and unprecedented – but why are

they playing here on Monday the 9th instead of at the end of the week on Friday The 13th?' Jamie and I liked this lucid critique very, very much!"

Whilst still known as Coming Blood though, the band contributed the anarchically infectious 'Such Fun' to the fourth Oi! LP, 'Oi! Oi! That's Yer Lot!' With the ultimate singalong yobbo chorus ("Chin up, my son, we're having such fun."), it was primarily an attack on the excesses of the Catholic Church, and in particular the Papacy – a theme that would be carried on with their next release, the timeless 'Megalomania' 7" for No Future, which saw the band fully realising their promise to fuse together the best of both Motörhead and The Damned.

"No Future had The Blood's first demo, and then Lol Pryor and Dave Long made No Future an offer they could not refuse," chuckles Colin mischievously, before adding, on the subject of Stinky Turner from the Cockney Rejects being the one that apparently 'discovered' the band in the

The Blood, courtesy of Mark Brennan

first place (it was Stinky's brother, Micky Geggus, that produced 'Such Fun' for the Oi! LP):

"I think there is *some* dimension of truth to it! I met Jeff Geggus [aka 'Stinky' Turner] in the White Swan Pub in Charlton. He was going out with a girl who lived along the same road as the pub itself, and I ended up going out with her sister. Anyway, Jeff *did* introduce me to Garry Bushell. I think the flip side to what is true or not is that, The Blood were probably discovered by not just Stinky, but also Garry Bushell, No Future Records, Lol Pryor, and Dave Long."

Not only was the A-side of the 'Megalomania' single a runaway train wreck of gloriously unhinged vocal hooks and searing hot guitar abuse, but both of the flipside cuts were equally as rowdy and compelling as well, and it remains one of the strongest EPs issued by No Future. Bizarrely the label only chose to release the one record by The Blood (turn to the interview elsewhere with No Future main man Chris Berry, and you'll perhaps start to understand why), which meant the band relocating to Noise Records for their 'False Gestures For A Devious Public' LP and second single, 'Stark Raving Normal'. By which time original drummer Dr Wildthing had been replaced behind the kit by Evo, from Major Accident and proto-thrash metal band Tank.

"Lol Pryor just decided The Blood needed another drummer!" explains Colin, before expounding upon the virtues of the band's truly irrepressible sonic assault. "'Megalomania' will possibly become one of the most important songs in the history of punk, just as will 'Stark Raving Normal' and 'False Gestures For A Devious Public', which, arguably, is probably the best punk album ever made. I am being polite – what the fuck! 'False Gestures . . .' is what punk is all about!

"Musically, lyrically, and ironically, The Blood's anthems are as real as it gets. JJ and I lived each and every moment of the creation of those songs. You might say those songs have a life of their own now, but were literally IV-dripped right out of our intoxicated veins and imaginations.

The Blood, pic courtesy of Mark Brennan

The Blood songs are the life blood of JJ Bedsore and The Cardinal!"

The Cardinal's boasts are not without substance either, the album being a deliriously heady rampage from the start of incendiary opener, 'Done Some Brain Cells Last Nite', to the fading ring-out of debauched blues dirge, 'Throttle Ya Blue'. It reached No. 5 in the Indie Charts (and No. 1 in the Punk Charts!), scoring a 5/5 review from Sounds and even landing the band a feature in Kerrang!, the popular mainstream metal weekly – The Blood apparently being the first UK punk band they deemed worthy enough to feature. Touring for the LP was no doubt eventful, but unfortunately Colin can't recall many details.

"Back in the day, and on tour, I was too drunk and drugged out of my brains to know what the fuck was going on – sorry!"

Just as well, I suppose, if lyrics like 'Degenerate' and 'Sewer Brain' are anything to go by! Things weren't calming down much by the time of the band's six-track mini-LP, 1985's 'Se Parare Nex' for Conquest Records, although, despite being produced by none other than Cronos from metal legends Venom ("But I had never heard of Venom at the time," admits Colin), the results were nowhere near as cohesive as the anarchic glory of 'False Gestures . . .'.

"'Se Parare Nex' was our attempt to play songs in the style of Alice Cooper whilst keeping our colourful and playful lyrics," reckons Colin. "We also wanted to do a very long song like The Damned's 'Curtain Call', so we wrote 'Attic Case' . . . just as 'Such Fun' had been written as a result of JJ and I wanting to write a song like The Damned back when The Blood began. We were seriously influenced by The Damned in all aspects of what we did – avid fans both of us, and I still am. The Damned's work stands alone against all other music . . . except The Blood's!

"'Force Fed Brain Dead' [also on 'SPN'] was another pop at the phenomena of religion and those who sleep on opium as its spectre continues to ethnically cleanse our global theatre. 'I Dreamt Of Your Death Last Night' was a sonnet to splatter movies, whist 'Incubus' again articulated a further 'Kiss my tradesman's entrance!' to those who believe themselves to be holier than thou. With 'Se Parare Nex' itself, you get a sonic Sistine Chapel covered in cum . . . !"

Link Records issued 'South London 5, Hull 4 (Full Time Result)', a split album between The Blood and The Gonads, in 1988, but the seven Blood tracks were all previously released, culled from the demos and singles. Colin eventually left the band in 1994 ("Because it felt the right time to leave – and I have no regrets about anything . . ."), who continued without him for 1996's 'Smell Yourself' and 1999's 'Spillage' albums. The Nineties also saw two EPs from The Blood, 'Fabulous As Usual' and 'Boots', both for Blind Beggar. Tragically, JJ died in 2004, from alcohol-related organ failure.

"I actually did not know anything about what The Blood did after I left, until JJ went off to the undiscovered country," explains Colin. "I went to his funeral at Saint Luke's in Charlton and thought that it was a ludicrous event. Jamie was the one clear stand-out genius of the punk epoch in every way, and everything he believed in said 'Fuck off!' to ceremonial bullshit and state etiquette. His life was a machine gun vendetta against all those who are Stark Raving Normal and the bleach and repression that gets force fed down the gobs of the placid banal citizens who bow before the thrones of nation-states. JJ told me when we were composing and spewing out our

Eighties libretto satires that he would one day take a pre-emptive strike on his own life through narcotics and alcohol – and he did. Respect!

"The relationship we had was emotional, hysterical, difficult, painful, fun, creative, destructive . . . it was imagination on a stick! JJ was as funny as Peter Cook, and as gifted as Jimi Hendrix. In fact he was the funniest man I ever met, and I have met all the Eighties comedians face to face when I moved around with Garry Bushell during his time with The Sun."

In 2006, Colin reformed The Blood and released 'Kill The Pimps', commenting on the vile practise of human trafficking, and since then they have released two LPs, a DVD, and toured around the world several times over.

"The Blood's musical work is infinite and, almost every time someone hears The Blood for the first time they become a fan," Colin proudly says of the band's undeniable longevity. "The Blood has many people all over the world who genuinely love the band's songs. In America, Japan, Canada, and Spain, teenagers all knew all the words to all the songs. We've played recently in all these countries and really enjoyed the experience, and I want The Cardinal to be singing 'Megalomania' and 'Such Fun' in Rio to the new Pope when the World Cup takes place in Brazil 2014 . . . !"

And lastly, what does The Cardinal make of Ghost, the Swedish metal band who appear to have borrowed liberally from his stage persona?

"ABBA getting fucked by a poltergeist . . . ? IKEA's version of the Trojan horse . . . ? Or perchance, do I really give a shit . . . ? The Blood are invulnerable to time and space; The Blood are a work of art and will always be there!"

SELECT DISCOGRAPHY:
7"S:
'Megalomania' (No Future, 1983)
'Stark Raving Normal' (Noise, 1983)
'Fabulous As Usual' (Blind Beggar, 1996)
'Boots' (Blind Beggar, 1997)

MLPS:
'Se Parare Nex' (Conquest, 1985)

LPS:
'False Gestures For A Devious Public' (Noise, 1983)
'South London 5, Hull 4 (Full Time Result)' (Link, 1988) – *split with The Gonads*
'Smell Yourself' (Blind Beggar, 1996)
'Spillage' (RnB, 1999)

AT A GLANCE:
Captain Oi's welcome CD reissue of 'False Gestures . . .' also includes the first two singles, outtakes, compilation and demo tracks, and is, of course, an absolute must-have.

SOLDIERS OF DESTRUCTION

L ondon band Soldiers Of Destruction have always been something of a mystery, playing a clutch of high-profile gigs but guaranteeing their mystique by choosing not to record anything during their short existence. In fact, they are probably best known – outside of London – for Peter from the Test Tube Babies wearing one of their shirts on the front cover of the classic 'Pissed And Proud' LP.

"Basically I was at a Chelsea show at the Marquee in London," recalls vocalist Cameron 'Morat' Mouat of his recruitment into the Brixton band, circa 1981, "and Gene October shouted out for someone to get up and sing 'No Fun'. I vaguely remember pushing him out of the way and then diving off stage at the end. [Guitarist] Mark's then-girlfriend, Lynn, picked me up and asked me if I wanted to sing for a band . . . and fuck knows how we kept in touch, since none of us had phones!

"The funny thing was, I got down to their rehearsal space and I recognised Mark from the Christmas On Earth show because I'd bought some speed off him and halfway through the deal he'd just run off to watch Black Flag, leaving me with this huge bag of blues. It was Mark that got me into Black Flag. I'd never met [bassist] Bill or [drummer] Carlos before, but we all got on pretty well, and I think they were fairly desperate because they'd already tried a bunch of different singers. I hadn't been in London long [having relocated there from the Isle Of Wight] so I think I just fell off the right stage at the right time."

Exact lineup details are sketchy at best, due to a combination of years under the bridge and alcohol consumed then and since, but punk was never really about formalities, was it?

"The only time anyone used their real name was when we were getting stopped by the cops, and even that was only after we'd tried making something up," laughs Morat. "Bill was just Bill, or Bongo, or Beetroot Bill because of his purple hair. Carlos was Carlos, and Mark was Shark, or sometimes Dinsdale – but I believe his actual surname was Rennie.

"As far as I know, none of the others had been in bands before, but it wouldn't surprise me if they had. I'd sung for two bands before myself: The Legislators, who played one show in 1978 at a club I wasn't even old enough to get in to, and Thin Red Line, that started in 1979 and got to open for The Damned at a local show. They were both covers bands, doing stuff like The Clash and The Sex Pistols, but people seemed to like Thin Red Line, probably because we had Razzle on drums who later went on to play with Hanoi Rocks. I remember him and Rat Scabies getting on really well, and Scabies even joined us for a few songs. That was my first gig with Thin Red Line because the original singer left about a week before, but we played a few other gigs after that."

Taking their musical lead from "anything really heavy and fast" – so think Discharge, GBH and The Exploited, with some Motörhead thrown in for good measure – Soldiers Of Destruction wasted little time taking their enthusiastic sonic onslaught to the live setting, Carlos landing them a bizarre debut appearance at the pizzeria where he worked – which also garnered them a lead live review in Sounds magazine.

"I can remember that gig surprisingly well considering it was over 30 years ago," reckons Morat. "Carlos was the only one in the band that had a job – or was even remotely employable – and he worked in this pizza place in Shepherd's Bush, right near where Paul Cook got a kicking from the teddy boys. We used to rehearse in the basement after he'd finished work, take a bunch of speed and stay up all night practising. It was a terrible place to get to, especially if there was a football match on, and there's also an army base there so the squaddies would give you a kicking too, if they got the chance.

"I'd only been in the band a week or two when we played that first gig though, and it was really funny because it sort of overlapped with the place being open to regular customers. There were all these punks traipsing through the restaurant to see the punk show in the basement, while people were still eating. I'm sorry I don't have any idea of the date, but I remember it being a fun show. And I have absolutely no idea how we got such a big review in Sounds. I think they were there to review Nikki Sudden, who was somehow opening for us, and we ended up being the main feature? Fucked if I know! I remember seeing it the next week and being pissed off that they got my name wrong, but it didn't really mean much. We were playing another gig with Charlie Harper's Urban Dogs the night I saw it and I'd had to leave my girlfriend unattended. She had serious drug problems, so there was a 50/50 chance she'd be dead when I got back.

That was more pressing to me at the time. Gene October seemed to get a bit upset that we'd got such a big review for our first gig, but other than that, and a few people asking for autographs to take the piss, it really meant nothing more to me than people getting my name wrong for the next 30 years."

The band managed to land themselves a raft of prestigious support slots with many of the big names in UK punk at the time – The Adicts, English Dogs, The Lurkers and The UK Subs, to name but a few – even headlining the 100 Club in their own right, a miraculous feat to consider trying to pull off today with nothing recorded to your name.

"At a guess I'd say we played 30 or 40 gigs, but no one ever counted. We must have played the Clarendon and the 100 Club about ten times each, plus a few at Gossips on Dean Street and a few others like the Lyceum, the George Roby, the Ad Lib in Kensington, the Hope And Anchor . . . there were a handful of shows at Skunx, too, opening for Dead Wretched and The Partisans and Peter and the Test Tubes Babies, and probably a couple of others that I'm forgetting.

"Skunx was a horrible shithole in Islington that was always full of boneheads starting fights, and the only good thing about it was that the stage was the right height to kick people in the face if they started on you. We had a few bad gigs, but the one we played there on my birthday, my nineteenth, I think, was probably the worst. We were headlining and I got hammered on Bells whiskey and kept having a go at the sound man because we sounded so bad, not realising that we sounded so bad because we were fucking hammered. I felt really guilty because that was the first time I was aware of us actually having fans, and these kids had come a long way to see us play, and we were fucking awful.

"We only played two shows that fucked up and we should have learned the first time, but the other one was opening for English Dogs at the 100 Club. Let's just say we got a bit over-excited about opening for them and we were about the right amount of 'buzzed' for sound check, then we sat around drinking for three or four hours. That gig was a mess, but English Dogs were brilliant even after I gave them acid.

"Probably the best gigs we played were opening for The Exploited or GBH, and we played with the Test Tube Babies a fair bit, which was always fun."

Given their growing live popularity, an official release by the Soldiers Of Destruction would almost certainly have sold very respectably, but the band had no interest in such a thing, turning down more than a few offers from independent labels of the time. Their music was getting heavier and faster, with more and more (thrash) metal influences creeping in, and it's highly likely they could have ridden the crossover wave to even greater notoriety.

"We didn't think we were good enough to make a record," explains Morat candidly. "Not that we weren't good, but not good *enough*. It was almost unspoken that if we couldn't get Mike Stone to produce it and make something as good as 'Hear Nothing, See Nothing, Say Nothing', something as heavy as that, then it wasn't worth doing. Any fucking idiot could get signed to an independent label back then and make a horrible tinny-sounding record, but we wanted that caveman production. Not that we really knew what production was, but that's how we wanted to sound if we made a record and that opportunity never came up. We got offered about fifteen record deals and turned them all down on the spot because none of them were with Clay or Bronze Records.

"Mark and myself also liked the idea of only being able to see the band live. That's probably why Carlos quit the band. He was more about getting signed because he was the only one with a job and any sense that we should be taking that side of it seriously. We didn't even want merch and Carlos went nuts when I threw all our pin badges in the crowd. We were halfway through a gig at Gossips and all these T-shirts and badges showed up. I was like, 'What the fuck is this? We don't have merch!', and started throwing it all to the audience. Carlos stormed off stage and we got this nutter called Sniper to finish the set on drums, which made things worse since Sniper was a terrible drummer – and I think that was the last gig Carlos played with us [he was replaced

Soldiers Of Destruction, live at the Clarendon

by Rick Copcutt]. In hindsight he was right in some ways – bands can't run on fresh air, even if you're only getting the rehearsal space paid for and travel costs – but I'm glad we never made any records and there's just the badly recorded live stuff on YouTube or whatever. Funnily enough, there's been a few bands who've talked about doing covers of S.O.D. songs, and I'd be fine with that because 30 years after the fact it would probably sound heavy enough."

So, apart from playing a near-riot on the Isle Of Wight, and the band's T-shirt turning up unexpectedly on Peter Test Tube's chest on the front cover of 'Pissed And Proud', Soldiers Of Destruction's short-lived reign was confined to the London punk circuit, and the self-destructive streak that made their live performances so entertaining also ushered in their premature demise, the band falling victims to the ever-present drugs and violence.

"Well, the end of the band was pretty much when our [second] bass player Paul Thwaites was murdered trying to defend his friend's squat [in Morningside Estate, Hackney]. It was probably over before that, but that was *definitely* the end. Having said that, the downfall of S.O.D. was more to do with drugs than violence right from the start. We started off being a speed-fuelled band but then Mark got more into heroin, same with Paul. On top of that we played a great gig at Gossips one night and my then-girlfriend overdosed in the toilet and I had to spend all night in hospital with her . . . There was always some fucking drug drama, and I hate all that shit; it gives drugs a bad name! Punks should have stuck to speed and acid, haha!

"As far as the violence was concerned, that killed the scene more than it killed the band. No one wants to spend all night in casualty waiting for your friend to get stitched up, which is what punk shows had become to a large extent, so people stopped going to shows and drifted away from the scene towards metal because it was safer. We'd played shows to no one but a room full of Nazi skinheads, so it wasn't like that was going to stop us, but eventually you have no audience. We did one gig at the Old Queens Head in Stockwell where we got there to find that Brutal Attack were opening and they'd just pulled our backdrop down and spat on it, but we played anyway – even though all our fans had left – and I stood on the PA taking the piss out of them. I've taken a lot of shit for talking about this before, but fuck it, let's do it again. The main thing that killed punk, or at least seriously damaged it, was skinheads. I'm sick of all this revisionist rose-tinted history of people going, 'Oh, they weren't all like that . . .' Well, where the fuck was everybody then? All I ever saw was a bunch of sieg-heiling knuckleheads. There were a handful of non-racist skinheads, one of whom used to squat with us and go on anti-apartheid marches, but they were few and far between. At one point people actually thought our song 'You've Been Cheated' was called 'You Big Shithead' because I'd sing that at the boneheads.

"I don't mean to insult anyone who wasn't like that. I remember Infa-Riot getting a kicking for speaking out, and no one fucked with The Oppressed, but let's not pretend there were armies of left-wing skins charging to the rescue when Skrewdriver showed up at the 100 Club, or when it all kicked off at Skunx at every other show. That whole thing scared so many talented people away from punk because it wasn't fun anymore – great, now you've just got a roomful of shirtless, racist, homophobes wanting to beat the snot out of everyone. And the irony is that quite a few of them were gay and should have just fucked each other and got it out of their system, instead of inflicting all their insecurities on everyone else. It's not like we don't have our own to deal with, and no one would have given a crap if they were gay anyway! The denial, these days, that any of that ever happened is ridiculous, particularly when it comes with that whole attitude of, 'We were never violent thugs and we'll kick your ass if you say we were.' That's what killed punk rock in my opinion."

Playing their last ever gig at the Hope And Anchor on Halloween 1984, with Port Talbot's Shrapnel in support ("They were a fucking great band . . . they blew us off stage!"), Morat got more into the biker scene and became a despatch rider for several years, before carving himself out a career in music journalism and photography. Carlos and Bill are apparently both "still into music", and Rick's son, Joe Copcutt, plays bass for popular alternative metal band Axe Wound (alongside Matt Tuck from Bullet For My Valentine).

Sadly, Mark died of an "HIV-related illness", but against the odds, the band's memory has somehow endured, despite their songs only ever being captured on lo-fi live recordings.

"I'm fucking surprised we're remembered at all, to be honest," admits Morat, who now resides in Los Angeles. "It amazes me how many people are still into the band and how many new fans there are. I get letters from around the world asking when we're playing again – which is highly fucking unlikely, to say the least – and the fact that we never recorded anything seems to have added this mythical quality to the band which I think Mark would have appreciated.

"As far as what set us apart from other bands, or would have if we'd been able to record it once we'd got it nailed down . . . ? I suppose it was that, even though we were very much a British hardcore punk band, there was an American influence from bands like Dead Kennedys, Black Flag and Bad Brains. We also listened to a lot of AC/DC and Motörhead, pretty much constantly at one point, so there was that influence that none of the other punk bands seemed to have at the time. How about this for an epitaph: 'Soldiers Of Destruction: might have been quite good if they'd got their shit together'?"

AT A GLANCE:
Nothing – you'll just have to Google them up on YouTube, I'm afraid.

CHAPTER EIGHT

THE SOUTH

ANTI-NOWHERE LEAGUE

Moving south of London, The Anti-Nowhere League were, are and always will be, one of the most distinctive of the second wave punk bands. Formed in Tunbridge Wells in 1979 by vocalist Nick 'Animal' Culmer and guitarist Chris 'Magoo' Exall, the band were both musically and visually a threatening amalgam of the punk, biker and skinhead genres, with a memorable yen for offensive lyrics too.

"I was running with a biker outfit called The Chosen Few," recalls Animal. "Magoo wasn't a member, but he was a mate of mine – we'd known each other since we were ten years old – and we were both riding Harleys and listening to punk rock. We were into The Pistols and The Damned obviously, but at the time the bike scene was into The Stranglers and stuff as well.

"I slipped into punk rock quite gradually really," he adds. "When it all started in 1976, I suppose I thought it was going to be a fad or something, but it did touch a nerve with me, and it planted a seed. I actually started playing guitar in 1979; I was originally meant to be the guitarist, but after six months, I was still fucking awful. Magoo used to say to me, 'With fingers that fucking fat, you'll never play anything'… and he was right! But he was quite good on guitar, so I got a microphone and had a go at shouting, and we both agreed that it was the worse thing we'd ever fucking heard, so we decided that was what we were going to do; he would play guitar and I would 'sing'! It's pretty funny, 'cos over the years we've done a few duets at various weddings and whatever, where he's had an acoustic and I've sang along, and we're always fucking crap! But something just clicked between us, it really was just so fucking funny… and that attitude has always been the backbone of the band really, just to fucking do it and have a laugh."

The League's first line-up was completed by bassist Chris Elvey and drummer Tony 'Bones' Shaw ("The only person we knew who had access to a drum kit; he wasn't very good, but then neither were we, haha!"), and they made their public debut in a nearby village hall. Thankfully they resisted the urge to call themselves, as originally planned, the National Somewhere Party, and by the time they graduated to playing local pubs, Chris had been replaced by Clive 'Winston' Blake.

"He couldn't actually play bugger all, but he was a well-known skinhead – a right thug – from Tunbridge Wells," reveals Animal. "It was a strange scene in Tunbridge; you'd get all sorts of yobbos – skinheads, bikers, punks – all drinking in the same pubs and all being friendly, and outsiders who came into town could never suss it out!

"It's a weird place to live really; it's not a city, it's more like an oversized country village… very cliquey. It can be a bit violent, but there didn't seem to be any major factions dividing people up back then, and it was just a very natural thing for the band to have bikers and a skinhead in it. We were just mates; we'd been to school with Winston as well, but he was such a fucking yobbo. He'd been in and out of Borstal and prison, but Magoo said, 'Okay, we'll teach him how to play the bass', and we did."

The band arrived at what many consider their classic line-up with the arrival of Iranian-born drummer Djahanshah 'PJ' Aghssa, but not before Bones had played their first big London show at the Lyceum with them.

"PJ was bought in, 'cos when we started to get more shows, Bones, who was a gold bullion dealer, had to choose what he wanted to do with himself," explains Animal. "It was alright when we were knocking about the local pubs, but when things started to get serious, he had to decide whether he was in or out. So we took on this drummer, Chopper, another bike bloke who now runs a local pub in Tunbridge, a really nice guy, and PJ came on board to be his tutor. But because we had a few shows lined up, and he couldn't get Chopper ready in time, PJ ended up playing them himself, and eventually Chopper stood down and PJ took his place. But, like I said, Chopper owns a pub now, so he's having the last laugh! We don't fade away in this town, everybody just IS – it's very fucking weird, but if you go down Chopper's pub today, it's pretty much like it was twenty-five years ago, except we're all a lot older in there now!"

It wasn't long before the Anti-Nowhere League came to the attention of influential London promoter John Curd, who not only took the band under his managerial wing, but also signed them to his fledgling WXYZ label.

"I think we were causing quite a stir in Tunbridge Wells, playing up on the Common and being bloody yobbos, and we went up to meet John in London. We had a sort of manager at the time, and he introduced us to John Curd and his partner, Chris Gabrin, so we turned up at this pub in London on our bikes, and gave Chris a pint of piss! That was our introduction to our

Anti-Nowhere League, early 1982
L-R: Magoo, Winston, PJ, Animal

management – we all pissed in a beer glass, put a bit of brown ale on the top and brought it out to him outside the pub! And we made him drink it; we were a right bunch of wankers!"

Surprisingly enough, the first single for both band and label was a cover of Ralph McTell's folk hit, 'Streets Of London', albeit a turbo-charged punked-up version. It entered the Indie Charts on Boxing Day 1981, where it spent fourteen weeks and reached the coveted No. 1 spot.

"When we sat down and talked about the choice of a first single, we hadn't been writing that long together, and our set was 90% covers, and that was just one of the covers we used to do. But we also did 'Denis' by Blondie, a David Bowie song, a Monkees song... so many covers. But we used to take the chords and just do verse/chorus, verse/chorus, verse/chorus, then end. And we did that to every song; we didn't care, as long as we were making a noise for the locals!

"But 'Streets Of London' sounded so wrong the way we played it, it was always a favourite of ours, and when we started recording, we included it as part of our first demo. That was just a four-track thing, which we did at this little farm studio in East Peckham, Kent, about five miles outside Tunbridge. It was £20 a day or something, but it was enough to get our name out there a bit. We just gave it out to people... including Rat Scabies, and that got us on The Damned tour. (Captain) Sensible came in on the first day and said, 'Oh, is this the band that did that demo that sounded like a load of prepubescent choirboys?' This from the guy that recorded 'Happy Talk'!"

Of course, as good a song as the A-side was, it was the B-side of 'Streets Of London' that grabbed all the headlines and catapulted the band to instant infamy. The bombastic, obscenity-laden 'So What?' was on a par with 'Friggin' In The Riggin' by The Sex Pistols for gleefully rubbing expletives in the unsuspecting faces of the British public, but its musical merit has been validated in recent years when it was covered by platinum-selling metal band, Metallica, to great effect. Not only did it conquer the Indies, but it made No. 48 in the National Charts as well, despite – or quite probably because of – Radio One DJ Tony Blackburn dubbing it 'The worst record ever made'. However sales came to an abrupt halt when all remaining copies were seized by the Obscene Publications Squad due to the somewhat colourful lyrical content!

"It was just a simple song, about those big-headed fuckers you overhear in the pub, saying 'I've done this, I've done that... yeah, yeah, yeah, but anyway, I've been here, I've been there!' To which my reply has always been, 'So fucking what?' The song was just about the fucking stupidity of those people and their conversations, but that's the magic of songs; they can be about the simplest of things. They just pop into your head on the spur of the moment.

"But never once as we recorded it, nor even when it was actually out on the record, did I have any idea it would affect my life as much as it has! It's actually an important part of my whole existence! The guy at the publishers was even saying recently that he'd mentioned to Robbie Williams that he should cover 'So What?'! It'd be great if he does! Feel free, thank you very much!

"We were never in it for

the money, but when you're getting royalties from a band like Metallica for a song you wrote twenty years ago, it's great! Thanks guys, think I'll have another bike...! Their version is

Anti-Nowhere League in Yugoslavia
L-R: Winston, Animal, Magoo
(Pic: Goranka Matic)

very heavy metal – they did it so well, in fact, that I think they've taken something away from it.

"But it's like when Guns N' Roses did 'I Hate People', and they didn't put it on their 'Spaghetti Incident' album 'cos Axl Rose couldn't sing it properly! Now, I never rated myself as a singer, not ever, but it's funny that all these people who are meant to be top singers can't do what I could. What we did just cannot be reproduced! Like it or lump it, love it or hate it, and even though we wrote most of it in five minutes, what we did was original, and that's what has given it its longevity. And hopefully people keep covering the songs, and new people keep getting to hear them."

The first single cover also spawned the band's well-known fist, ball and chain logo that has been a staple of every release since.

"It was based on a fist of power. Me and Magoo sat down to design the logo, and he wanted something like a sheep being fucked up the arse or whatever, but I wanted something medieval. And when we used to ride with this bike club, there were a lot of these ball and chains lying around – it was, shall we say, our weapon of choice… someone had picked a load of them up in a local antiques shop or something! So I took one of them off the club wall and wrapped it round my hand, and then I drew it. It was literally drawn with my right hand whilst I held it up in my left hand! Magoo thought it was too complicated and that no one would wanna paint it anywhere 'cos it would take them hours to do it, but I stuck to my guns with it, and it's been with us ever since."

Riding high on their success, the band embarked upon the sold-out 'So What?' tour, that took them around the UK with Chron Gen, The Defects and Chelsea in tow.

"That was great, looking back, but at the time we were getting a bit tired," admits Animal. "Everything was happening a bit too fast for us, and we were burning out really quick. Too many drugs, too much booze, too many birds… too much going on, and we were starting to get bored! Stuart Copeland from The Police was travelling around filming it all, and towards the end, he kept saying, 'Why don't you go and smash this up, or that up?' and eventually we were like, 'Why don't you fuck off? We just wanna sit down for a bit!' It was all getting a bit predictable. He'd try and get us to go into motorway cafes and start throwing the food around, and we were like, 'No, it's fucking childish!' Before then we'd have done it just for a laugh, but it was getting so predictable; everyone was expecting us to do all this stuff all the time. During that tour, we fizzled out. We didn't go out with a bang; rather, we started out with a bang, and then we got bored with it. There was too much going on around us, and it quickly lost its sparkle."

The 'I Hate People' single (b/w 'Let's Break The Law') brought a second Indie No. 1 three months later (No. 46 in the Nationals), before the debut album 'We Are… The League' exceeded all expectations by not only squatting in the Indies like a malignant tumour for twenty-three weeks (and reaching No. 1) but making No. 24 in the Nationals and bothering that chart for three months during the summer of '82. It featured twelve deliciously down 'n' dirty diatribes against the average Joe Public and his mediocre 'ambitions', every last one of them heaving at the seams with huge, rough-hewn choruses, mangled, molten power chords and the obligatory foul language.

"We used to hate all those po-faced political bands. We used to get on best with bands like The Damned, 'cos we were a breath of fresh air for 'em – all those early bands used to hate each other and were at each other's throats as well! We came along, with our bags of speed, and off we went, and we recharged people around us, because the whole music business fucking stunk, it really did. We used to go to Dingwalls just for a fight, just to play up… I can remember being severely beaten up by the bouncers outside Steve Strange's club in Camden! But every night was like that; we were hated everywhere we went, especially by all those sensitive musician types, but we enjoyed every minute of it!

"People bought our records 'cos they could see the funny side of it. I think I can say with my hand on heart that we were the first proper yobbo band, and people loved that two-fingered attitude. We were on a burnout mission; our only master plan as such was to enjoy it while it lasted! Magoo always said, 'Well, if there's a market for rubbish, let's go out and sell it!' We'd turn up with a few songs, take the piss out of everybody, nick as much as we could, indulge in as many illegal substances as we could, and then, 'Thank you and goodnight!'

"It didn't change us one little bit, 'cos we never got fuck all out of it!" he adds, on the subject of their growing notoriety. "We were still on the dole! If anything it made us poorer, in a way, 'cos you'd go down the pub and you'd have to buy everyone beers! We never got there, wherever 'there' was, so it never really mattered; it was all just a natural progression, we were just boys from Tunbridge Wells… there were no TV appearances or anything, we just weren't allowed the necessary breaks.

"I remember we met Billy Connolly at the BBC once. He came up to us and said we were fuckin' great, and we stuck ANWL stickers all over his head! Kenny Everett really backed off though; he was really scared! Billy Connelly knew we were having a bit of fun, but Kenny Everett was really shitting himself! We were larger than life, but that's the sort of people we were; we were larger than life around town as well. But you could've lost us in any pub in Tunbridge Wells really; there were loads of blokes like us. We were just motorcycle riding, punk rocker, misfit skinheads…! It was definitely a Tunbridge thing – we really were a product of the town."

None of that prevented the third single, 'Woman', a sensitive ode to married bliss that also appeared as a limited edition picture disc, topping the Independents yet again in July '82. It was followed in November of the same year by 'For You', which, although not quite as successful as the preceding three singles, remains the band's finest moment, a truly stunning track that not only rocks hard but is subtly shaded with a tremendous pathos. It saw the Anti-Nowhere League briefly expanding to a five-piece line-up with the addition of rhythm guitarist Mark 'Gilly' Gilham, and coming of age in a spectacular fashion.

"I suppose that was the first real song I'd written, and it was about a mate of mine, Jimmy J., that died in the Falklands. 'The Ballad of JJ Decay' (the B-side of 'For You') was written about him as well. Before that, things had just popped into my head and I'd scribble 'em down, but this was the first time I'd sat down and written about a subject.

"I think it was probably the first song I actually meant as well," he adds with a wry chuckle. "I didn't mean the others; they were more like accidents in my head – I'd wake up in the middle of the night looking for a pen and paper. They would arrive every fucking hour; the more I wrote, the more there was."

A second studio album was written, intended for release on WXYZ and to be entitled 'Branded', but the League fell out with their label ("We thought they were trying to manipulate us… they certainly weren't fully behind us"), and the record never saw the light of day. The 'Live In Yugoslavia' album acted as a useful stop-gap release though, reaching No. 2 in the Indies when it was issued by ID Records in November 1983.

The touring and excessive lifestyle was increasingly taking its toll on the band however, and by late 1984 when they recorded the anthemic 'Out On The Wasteland' single, PJ had left, to be replaced – just for that release – by Michael Bettell.

"That was why we stopped the band the first time round," agrees Animal. "We were burning out of control and we would've died, I think. Musically we were into The Pistols and The Ruts or whatever, but what drove us was that we dressed up in motorbike gear, we dressed up in skinhead gear, and we were out of control! It just exaggerated what we were doing, what we were like as people. We drank more booze, we took more drugs, we had more women, we just did more… and more…

"I remember hanging onto Winston who was trying to throw himself out of a hotel window about fifty stories up in New York. 'Oh, my fuckin' head!' he was yelling. 'It fuckin' hurts! I can't take this anymore!' And if I had let go of his arse, he'd have been gone, dead, through the fucking roof below! That was when we knew we had to put the brakes on. We were truly out of control by then. Everywhere we went there were drugs, piles of them, absolutely anything we wanted… especially in New York, and we were just boys from Tunbridge Wells – we had never had so much fun!"

'Out On The Wasteland' also marked a new, more futuristic image for the band, not dissimilar to that made famous by Mel Gibson's 'Mad Max' road warrior films.

"Well, in the early days, people kept saying, 'You're not punk, you're not punk!' We rode motorbikes, but we played punk music; we didn't know what the fuck we were doing really… we weren't interested in categories or anything. With the 'Wasteland' thing, they're all our cars and our bikes and stuff on the cover; they weren't props or anything, so we were just reverting back to the biker thing really, just being ourselves… well, maybe I went over the top a bit! But we were just pulling back from the punk thing really. People were accusing us of not being punk, but we never said we were punk in the first place; it just happened that we came along and got caught up in the same scene as all these other punk bands. The 'Wasteland' thing was a bit self-indulgent, I suppose, but it wasn't that far removed from what we did on Saturday afternoons anyway."

In 1985, the ANWL recruited Jonathon Birch on drums, signed to mainstream metal label, GWR, and released their much-maligned 'The Perfect Crime' album, which saw the band bravely utilising synths, a brass section and even the until-then-undiscovered depths of Animal's more-than-able tonsils. Although an excellent atmospheric rock album in its own right, wonderfully executed and enjoying a slick, spacious production, it was so far removed from the League's former filthy glories as to be unrecognisable.

Deciding they were 'All washed up', they chose to bow out on a high note, and played a farewell show in Tunbridge Wells, a suitably rowdy affair that was recorded for posterity and from which four songs were released by Link as the 'Fuck Around The Clock' 12".

However, prompted by Metallica's aforementioned cover of 'So What?' (Animal even made a guest vocal appearance at the band's 1992 Wembley show) the band reformed in the mid-Nineties. They signed to German label Impact for the 'Pig Iron' CD (1996) and the excellent 'Scum' album, which was a welcome return to form.

"Magoo was always the brains behind the mayhem really. He wanted to keep it simple, keep it to the point; we weren't after any musical acclaim. It's the old reliable recipe, just stick with what you love yourself. Some people are great at being clever, but what's the fucking point of another band doing that for the sake of it? You couldn't really get someone like Oasis writing 'I Hate People', could ya? Once you cross a certain bridge and you become self-indulgent, there's no going back… but we've never gone forward, so it's easy not to go back as well!

"But when other people got involved, as well as Magoo and I, when democracy came in, that was when it all started to fall apart. When we wrote the 'Scum' album, we went back to our old way of working… he'd start playing, I'd start singing; my foot would be tapping, he'd be laughing, and we'd know we were there! That always means we're onto something that's gonna be a little bit of fun…

"The songs on 'Scum' were really good, but we ran out of money. We could have made more of the production, and it could have been better promoted, and that's why it disappeared, which is a bit of a fucking shame really."

1997 saw The League back in Yugoslavia ("The more we go there, the more we like it!"), that resulted in the Impact live album, 'Return to Yugoslavia', and the band have been a strong draw on the punk reformation circuit ever since. As well as heavy touring, a brand new studio album

– possibly even the belated realisation of the long-lost 'Branded' record – is planned for 2004, and as long as there are Nowheres to rage against, it seems the ANWL have sufficient reason for existence.

"I don't think it'll ever be quite the same again, but all we can do is play our songs as best we can, and as long as we have fun, and people turn up and enjoy it, we'll keep doing it. The day I turn up at a show and everybody is stood at the back not giving a shit, is the day I give up and move to Belgrade, never to be seen again. But twenty years ago, I never thought the band would last five minutes anyway! If you told me then that we were going to do as much as we have, I'd have thought you were a fucking lunatic!"

SELECT DISCOGRAPHY:
7"s:
'So What?'/'Streets Of London' (WXYZ, 1981)
'I Hate People' (WXYZ, 1982)
'Woman' (WXYZ, 1982)
'For You' (WXYZ, 1982)
'Out On The Wasteland' (ABC, 1984)

12"s:
'Out On The Wasteland' (ABC, 1984)
'Fuck Around The Clock' (Link, 1986)

LPs:
'We Are The League' (WXYZ, 1982)
'Live In Yugoslavia' (ID, 1983)
'The Perfect Crime' (GWR, 1985)
'Scum' (Impact, 1996)
'Return To Yugoslavia' (Impact, 1997)

AT A GLANCE:
There are many Anti-Nowhere League collections and reissues available, although Captain Oi!'s 2001 CD digipack version of 'We Are… The League' comes highly recommended, as it contains an attractive fold-out poster-style booklet and seven bonus tracks that conveniently round up not only the band's first album but the first four classic singles as well. Anagram's 1990 'Complete Singles' CD compiles all the 7"s and EPs from 'Streets Of London' right through to 'Fuck Around The Clock' and is another good point of embarkation for the curious.

PETER AND THE TEST TUBE BABIES

D espite the amusing name and an often shambolic approach to their careers, Peter And The Test Tube Babies from Brighton have a proven track record in both longevity and musical quality. They're still together today, producing excellent – albeit infrequent – studio albums and never fail to entertain in the live situation.

They were formed in 1978 by "The first punk in Peacehaven", Peter Bywaters, with his school friends Derek 'Del' Greening and Chris 'Trapper' Marchant when they left their first band, The Cornflakes.

"We were originally called Restriction," reveals Del. "Then it got changed to The New Originals, and then we changed it to The Cornflakes, to be a bit more punk. But we were shit, we were doing Jimi Hendrix covers."

Peter actually ended up taking over as manager of The Cornflakes just before the Test Tube Babies began.

Peter And The Test Tube Babies
L–R: Del, Ogs, Peter (on shoulders),
Trapper (Pic: Tony Mottram)

"Purely because I was going to a lot of gigs in Brighton," he explains. "This was in '76 or '77, and there was a punk explosion, bands starting up every week. And soon I was getting The Cornflakes two or three gigs a week, no problem, and they were really enjoying going from practising in someone's garage to actually playing in front of people. But their singer, Simon Hall, didn't like punk! He had to really bite his tongue to go and do these gigs. He was always complaining, 'Oh these people with their hair sticking out everywhere and zips in their clothes'… and I was like, 'Fuckin' hell, it's punk rock, that's what it's all about!' In the end, Del left, and I said, 'What about me and you doing a band?' I'd already written one song of my own…"

Which was entitled 'The Queen Gives Good Blowjobs', effectively setting the tone for his band's patented and gleefully anarchic humour. Several other sensitive ditties such as 'Maniac' and 'Elvis Is Dead' were penned in Peter's dad's garage, before Trapper was enlisted on bass, and the band's first show was booked for October 4th 1978 at the Alhambra with Fan Club (formerly Wrist Action) even though they were still without a drummer.

"Thankfully there was this guy (Trevor Rutherford) at school," laughs Peter. "He wasn't a punk at all, but his dad had a factory where we could practise, and he had a drum kit too, so we got him in. We had one rehearsal on the Sunday and did our first gig on the Tuesday."

"We did four songs or something," adds Del. "Then we played again on the Thursday, supporting Nicky And The Dots at the Richmond. And there was a guy there who was doing the (Brighton compilation) 'Vaultage '78' album and asked us to be on it. It was like bloody Craig David – drummer on Sunday, gig on Tuesday…"

Peter: "Another gig on Thursday… contract on Friday…and we were recording on the

Sunday. So within one week we did our first two gigs and started our recording career!"

"We didn't even have a name," admits Del. "And Dave, the singer from Fan Club, had to write on the chalkboard outside the pub who was playing at the gig, and he billed us as something silly, like Peter And The Packet Of Peanuts or Peter And The Pints Of Lager, or something... but he also asked, 'What about Peter And The Testicles?'

"Then some kid in Peacehaven came up to Peter and said, 'Why don't you write a song about test tube babies?' 'cos that was all that was on the news then – it was 1978, and the first test tube baby, Louise Brown, had just been born – and we just nicked the name from that really."

The newly named Test Tube Babies contributed 'Elvis Is Dead' to the 'Vaultage' album ("We just wanted to piss all the Teds off really," chuckles Peter), a compilation so-called because many of Brighton's alternative bands practised at the Vault, an underground crypt in an old graveyard. It was there that they met Mark Andrew Storr-Hoggins (aka 'Ogs'), who would soon become their first permanent drummer but was then playing with The Plastics, amongst others.

"Ogs used to go to the Alhambra," Del recalls. "There was a night club underneath called 'The Inn Place' at the time, and I used to drink down there too. We both knew that the other was in bands and we got talking, and I told him that our drummer had just pissed off to America, that we had this tour, and he could have all the beer he could drink if he joined! So we did one quick rehearsal and off we went."

"He always denied that he was actually in the band," says Peter. "Fifteen years later he was still saying that he wasn't in the band. 'I'm just standing in 'til their drummer comes back! I'm still waiting for my free beer!'

"But it was a bit like 'Spinal Tap' before we got Ogs on drums. After Trevor, we had Dave Kent, then a mad bloke from Hastings called Danny, then Nick 'Loz' Lozides...

"And for some reason, for about six months whilst Danny was in the band, we actually swapped bass players with Nicky And The Dots. They took Trapper and we took Blotto... don't ask me why, though!"

The track on 'Vaultage' brought them to the attention of Radio 1 DJ John Peel, who offered the band one of his much-sought-after sessions, which happily led to coverage in Sounds and gigs all around the country. As a result the Test Tube Babies were asked to appear on the 1980 'Oi! The Album' compilation by Garry Bushell, to which they contributed two stand-out tracks, '(Wanna) Rob A Bank' and 'Intensive Care'.

"He came to Brighton to interview us; we had a front cover and centre spread in Sounds," explains Del. "He was down in the little tomb we rehearsed in, sat there with his fingers in his ears, writing away on his note pad between songs. And he asked us to go on this album full of second wave punk bands that was apparently going to be called 'Here Comes The New Punk'; he had The Exploited on there, and The Upstarts, and it sounded quite good, so we said we'd do it. It was only the week it came out and we saw it advertised in Sounds, that we found out it was called 'Oi! The Album'. That was the first we heard of the title really, and we thought it was a bit stupid, to be honest.

"Bushell probably did it as a bit of a joke to start with, but it snowballed and got really political, and suddenly we'd be playing places in London and coach loads of skinheads would be turning up. And we'd be on stage, pissed as usual, having a laugh, and these skinheads wanted to hear something really powerful. It didn't really gel, it was like oil and water, and we were just bumbling about onstage!

"Once when we played Skunx, they turned up for me in the van in the afternoon, and I'd been out all night drinking and had just gotten up, so I got in the van in my pyjamas! I played the gig in front of about 500 skinheads in my girlfriend's pink dressing gown!"

"Anyway, then Del saw this classified advert in Sounds," says Peter. "It wasn't even in a box or anything, asking for punk and skinhead bands, so we wrote off... and they sent us a contract.

So we just signed it and sent it back, we didn't take it to a lawyer or anything! Our manager (Nick McGerr) was tearing his hair out, saying, 'You could have at least shown it to me!"

The label in question was No Future, who had already signed up Blitz and The Partisans, and were rapidly making a name for themselves as purveyors of the finest in UK hardcore punk. The Test Tubes' debut single, 'Banned From The Pubs', gatecrashed the Independent Top Ten in early 1982. An energetic tear 'em up in every sense of the phrase, delivered with infectious gusto, it catapulted the band into the limelight, and their second single, 'Run Like Hell' (b/w 'Up Yer Bum'), shot to No. 2, spending over four months in the Indies when it was released late that same summer.

Just like 'Banned From The Pubs' before it, 'Run Like Hell' continued what would become a Test Tube tradition, of setting humorous stories, that any street-wise yob could empathise with, to super-tight and memorable punk rock tunes. But if the lyrics are to be believed, it has to be said that Peter had more than his fair share of bad luck, having been beaten senseless by Teds ('Intensive Care') and taken home by a 'Transvestite', not to mention being 'Blown Out Again' and 'Banned From The Pubs'.

"Well, neither 'Intensive Care' or 'Transvestite' actually happened," he admits. "But in a town like Brighton in 1978, they so easily could have. Thing is, there were so many other bands at the time going on about, 'Fuck the government, fuck the system, and fuck the police', and all that crap, we just let them get on with it. I mean, I was more interested in the price of a pint than politics on any large scale, so I just did something different."

Peter 'Test Tube' Bywaters, 'the first punk in Peacehaven...'
(Pic: Tony Mottram)

The band's relationship with No Future was to be short-lived however, and their debut album was their last release for the label. 'Pissed And Proud', which came out Christmas 1982, had the band glowering from the front cover clutching the obligatory bottles of cheap Merrydown cider, and again made No. 2 in the Indies. Surprisingly, it was a live record, which was quite an unusual thing for a punk band to choose as their first album.

"I didn't really want to do it," reckons Peter. "But it was our manager's idea, 'cos it would be cheaper to make a half-decent live recording than go in the studio and do a proper album!"

"Also, it was 'cos we're really lazy," laughs Del. "We worked it out the other day, and we've done on average one studio album every five years or something like that, haha! The rest have been 'greatest hits' and 'live' stuff. Anyway, most of our material had already been out by then, on the two singles and the compilations, so rather than do an album with only about three new songs on it, the live album was a legitimate way to do a new release, and at the same time capture the whole live vibe of the band."

And it succeeded admirably, with the band's irreverent humour coming across not only in their music but through their between-song banter with the crowd. Although recorded completely live with a proper mobile studio, hence the killer sound quality, the album is actually culled from two different gigs, one at Klub Foot in London, and one in Blackpool.

"It was (our manager) Nick who promoted that Blackpool show," Del elaborates. "It was called 'Up Yer Tower', and the idea was to record and film the whole gig – a bit like Holidays In The Sun, but twenty years earlier – and then there would be an 'Up Yer Tower' album and an 'Up Yer Tower' video. It was a good idea, but it all went wrong; there was so much trouble, we only ended up playing about five songs! There were all these bottles smashing behind us, and we all had glass in our hair. I was playing and I saw this broom from one of the cleaning cupboards flying towards me, and it took every string off my guitar! So I spent the next twenty minutes restringing and tuning my guitar – which doesn't exactly make for a great live album! Which is why we filled in the gaps with the Klub Foot show."

By comparison, the band's sophomore album a year later, 'The Mating Sounds Of South American Frogs', was a slick and accomplished affair, recorded by Barry Sage – who had previously worked with The Rolling Stones. Thankfully even he couldn't smooth off the band's loveable rough edges, and the album, although polished, is still an exercise in drunken youthful anarchy, albeit the tuneful variety. It was the first album to appear on Trapper Records, the label set up by McGerr after his falling-out with No Future, and so-called because "Trapper was the most inept bloke you could ever think of to run a record company!"

"When Nick started the label, he put us in Pink Floyd's studio in Britannia Row," says Del incredulously. "It was massive, and when you went upstairs, they still had that big pink pig up there. It was phenomenally expensive, about £500 a day, maybe more, which was a lot of money in 1983. We had the studio block-booked for a month, and we never used to go. It was always empty; we'd be back in Brighton doing loads of mushrooms and acid! I'd be tripping all night, get up about 4 o'clock in the afternoon, go to the pub, and suddenly remember I should be in the studio doing guitars, and I'd just blow it out and go back to bed.

"I remember being up the studio one day, and I had to go back to Brighton to sign on. It was a £500 a day studio, and I had to go back to sign on to get my £35 a week! The manager wouldn't give me the money for the train fare either, so I had to hitch, and it took me two days! Then when I got there, I thought, 'Bollocks, I ain't going back yet!' So I got out of it for a few more days... and there's this engineer sat there waiting for me while I'm out on a bender."

"And they had a snooker table in there 'n' all, and you know how long a game of that can take," chuckles Peter. "The engineer would stick his head round the door and say, 'We need you now, to do another line of that song', and I'd be like, 'Yeah, all right, I'll be there in a minute! I'm in the middle of a game!"

The album was preceded by the excellent 'Zombie Creeping Flesh' single, which was a slight departure for the band with its horror-themed lyrics and cover, and actually used to launch the Trapper label (that also went on to sign The Fits, with whom The Test Tubes shared the brilliant 'Pressed For Cash' 12") via an ambitious poster and radio campaign and a high-profile gig at the prestigious Brixton Ace.

"Yeah, Nick built this big gig up, and it sold really well," says Del. "In fact, I think it sold out. But the bottom line is, we blew it! I said, 'Where's our catering?' 'Oh, there isn't any!' So we just went to the pub on empty stomachs, and they had to come and find us ten minutes after we were meant to be onstage, and we were pissed out of our heads!

"Even Toot, the roadie (who now works for Status Quo), was pissed up and he tuned the bass an octave too high! He was supposed to be working the dry ice machine as well and he left it running! So the building was full of smoke, and we were all out of tune, and then this ridiculous high-pitched bass came in…"

"And I'd just started going out with this really posh bird," Peter picks up the story. "She was quite a bit older than me, and she came to see us play. There were posters everywhere as she came into London, advertising the gig, making us out to be this big professional band, and we came onstage, with Del and Trap playing something completely different to each other… and then me and Trap stripped off and played the whole gig with our knobs hanging out. And this woman hadn't seen me naked at that point, so needless to say, the relationship foundered."

'The Mating Sounds Of South American Frogs' was the album where The Test Tubes defined their unique sound; Del's dramatic harmony leads in stark contrast to Peter's rough vocal charms. With Trapper's constantly roving bass and Ogs' fluent, dynamic rhythms providing an ever-shifting backdrop upon which the band could unfold their hilarious, sometimes poignant, tales of everyday life. In true Testies tradition, the bizarre title was picked on a whim whilst flicking through sound effect albums in the studio, and the cover photo torn from a book in the library over the road. Yet despite their apparent lack of effort, the album was another huge hit for the band.

"We never actually plan anything, you see," claims Del. "We've never sat down and thought about anything really, not the band's name, not our style, not my guitar sound; it all just happened by accident. We just did the next thing that seemed obvious to us; it's always been like that, ever since the early days. And whenever we were pushed into doing something that was planned, by our management or whoever, we used to fuck it up! Not deliberately, but it was almost a subconscious reaction… 'Oh, there's a bar over there, let's get pissed!' We never had a master plan to be a pissed punk band, we just went with the flow."

'Frogs' spawned three great singles over the course of 1984, 'Blown Out Again', 'Wimpeez' and 'The Jinx', and saw the band undertaking their first proper tours of Europe and America.

"We did twelve shows in the States, and got paid $9 each," sighs Del. "And then we were overweight at the airport with our luggage coming back, 'cos we had this big 'Frogs' backdrop…"

"So we just threw it in a dustbin at the airport!" laughs Peter. "The thing is, it was supposed to be a big tour, and we had plane tickets that were open for a few months, and the plan was that we'd start on the West Coast and work our way across to the East. But it was a really bad winter, and we did all the Californian dates, and Arizona, but then we were s'posed to fly from there to somewhere else… but lots of airports were closed, so the next gig got cancelled. Then, because it was such a shoestring budget, each gig relied on the money from the previous gig to get us there, so it all collapsed after about a dozen gigs. And we were left to our own devices.

"When we got to the airport to go home, I thought, 'Hang on a minute, I ain't fucking going back yet! I'm staying here!' Del and Trapper thought it sounded like a good idea too, so we divvied up what little money there was and all went our separate ways."

Del: "Me and Trap stayed there all over Christmas, and we got a job putting up decorations… so there we were, like fucking Laurel and Hardy, up this ladder, putting up these decorations, after playing a sold-out show to 4000 people at the (Los Angeles) Olympic Auditorium! Trying to raise money to fly back on the 10th 'cos I was signing on two days later!"

Peter: "I stayed with this English guy who worked in a shop on Hollywood Boulevard. His boss needed the shop painting, so I said, 'I can paint that!' Even though I wasn't a fuckin' painter at all. So I ended up painting this shop, and started going out with this really tasty bird who worked there. And I dragged this job out for months, getting paid decent money. I mean, why would I wanna go back to England and sign on? So every time the boss went out, I downed tools, spinning this job out as long as possible!

"And one day I'm in bed with my girlfriend in Hollywood, and I get a phone call from Del saying, 'You better get your fuckin' arse back to England, we've got a European tour starting in three days!' They'd been trying to get hold of me for weeks, 'cos no one knew where I was, I didn't have a mobile phone or anything… so reluctantly I had to leave and come home."

"I remember me and the manager driving down to Victoria Station to pick him up," cackles Del wickedly. "And he was standing there in a poncho with tassles on it, a hat and a neck scarf. We drove past him three times, 'cos we didn't recognise him. We called him Clint Balsawood on that tour!"

"I even had fuckin' cowboy boots on as well," admits Peter. "I came back from America totally Americanised, what an idiot!"

The 'Loud Blaring Punk Rock' album came out next, in July 1985, and went Top Ten in the Indies during a fifteen-week chart run… even though half the songs on the album weren't even written by Peter And The Test Tube Babies.

"Yeah, for a period in the Eighties, we also had another band going on, Walnut And The Wankers," explains Peter. "Walnut is Del's brother, now our roadie, and as a joke, we got this band together, with Del on drums, me singing, Walnut on guitar, and a guy called Squeech on bass. Ogs was off doing something with Crown Of Thorns, this bloody Goth band, at the time. And we did all these really crap songs like 'Pick Your Nose And Eat It' and 'Child Molester'…"

"This guy from Red Rhino phoned us up, and asked if we had any old demo tapes he could release, 'cos he'd give us six grand for them," continues Del. "And we thought, 'Hey, we could buy a van with that!' So we said 'Yes', even though we didn't have any songs. Well, we thought we had the songs to start with, but when we got the tapes down from the attic, there was so much oxide on them, they fell to bits. But the lure of this six grand drove us on.

"So, we re-recorded it all – an eighteen track album, half of it old Test Tube songs that hadn't been released, and the other half were Walnut songs, which I showed Ogs how to play in the studio. Trapper went home, 'cos he had flu, so I played all the bass, and it was just me and Ogs, and I was like, 'When I raise my eyebrows we stop, when they go back down, we start again…!' And that was it, we did the whole album like that, all in one night."

"Then we got all our mates to take a load of speed and do all the backing vocals," says Peter. "We stayed up all night, and mixed it the next morning, took it to Mayking to cut it, and made the album sleeve while we were waiting. Del made up the record label logo, Hairy Pie Records, and drew the labels by hand, and then I went up to Leeds and got our six grand… in cash!"

"And we all went out on the piss with it," laughs Del. "We had all this money in our pockets, bundled up in wraps, and Ogs wanted to buy a motorbike, so we lent him the money, and he lost £200 on the way back on this bike, when one of the wraps fell out of his pocket."

Peter: "We were still signing on at the time, so it seemed like a fortune. By rights, we should have had loads of money off 'Frogs'; we should have had some money from something, but we hadn't seen anything at all… and suddenly we had six grand! It was our biggest pay day to date."

Despite emerging from such off-handed chaos, and containing more than a few blatantly throwaway tracks, 'Loud Blaring Punk Rock' is a fine album that does exactly what it says on the tin. It was another Top Ten Indie hit for the band, as was 'Rotting In The Fart Sack', a five-track 12" for Jungle that appeared soon after and helped finance the recording of the band's next album, the magnificent 'Soberphobia'.

"By then we'd sacked Nick, and we were on our own," says Del. "I'd blown Jungle out by that time as well, 'cos I'd decided that they were useless, so for the first time ever we were actually doing it all for ourselves. I ended up producing it, and I would be there paying the engineer daily, 'C'mon, mate, what about fifty quid for cash?' And actually I did that album for under £4000. We were really focused; we really wanted to make it... good!"

And it was indeed a great record, albeit a rather sombre affair compared to the previous slices of unruly bedlam. Del was really coming into his own as a great guitarist, Peter contributed some – shock, horror! – profound lyrics, and the whole band sounded at the top of their game.

"The thing is, you gotta remember, by the time we did 'Soberphobia' we'd been going for quite a while," says Peter defensively. "And obviously we weren't going to get worse musically, we were going to get better. And I think we did. In fact, I prefer that album to 'Frogs', it was a natural progression. You say it was 'produced', but so what? Don't people want better-produced albums then? One of the main reasons that we sound different to other bands is that so many of them set their parameters and that's it, they never stray from the course they've set out on..."

Whilst reminiscing about the recording of the album at Greenhouse Studios with Noel Thompson, Del recalls a typical Trapper story.

"I remember he went in to do his bass parts, and they were shit, so I phoned him up to bollock him, and his missus told me he couldn't come to the phone, 'cos he was in the bath! And I said, 'His fucking bass sounds like it was recorded in the bath! And it would've helped if he'd played the right notes!' He got a bit more together towards the end, but he was basically a useless bloke!"

"We were all pretty naive, but he was in the premier division!" laughs Peter. "It's a funny story how he got his nickname too. When we all lived in Peacehaven, me, Del, Trapper, and a mate called Simon, used to do everything together. One day we were walking along this track at the back of Peacehaven, and suddenly Trap got down on his knees and put his ear to the ground, and said, 'I think there's horses coming'... and around this corner came about twenty horses. The thing is, we'd seen them anyway; well, everyone else had apart from him! That's how he got the name."

Over the best part of the next two decades, Peter and Del steered The Test Tube Babies through thick and thin, a surfeit of drummers and bassists, albums that were good ('Supermodels', We Bite 1995), bad ('Cringe', SPV 1991) and ugly ('Schwein Lake Live', We Bite 1996). Along the way, they built an incredibly devoted following around the globe, touring everywhere from Japan to Brazil, recorded an album of cheesy pop covers (1990's ingeniously bizarre 'Shit Factory' for SPV),

Peter And The Test Tube Babies
L-R: Ogs, Peter, Trapper, Del
(Pic: Jana)

and even found time to moonlight in some other bands – Del with goth rockers Flesh For Lulu and Peter with the pseudo metal band, The Masked Raiders. But throughout it all, they've never compromised their wonderfully melodic style nor lost their inebriated sense of fun.

"Every December we tour Germany," says Del, providing the perfect example. "We finish in Frankfurt on December 23rd, and fly home on Christmas Eve, with all the money from the tour to pay for the wives' excesses. This one year, Henry, our German manager, had this great idea that we should stay out there and play Christmas Day, 'cos we'd get more money. Peter was well depressed, waking up on Christmas Day in his bunk all alone, and there we were, sat at the back of the tour bus, and he says, 'What are these six red pills?' I said, 'I dunno', and he said, 'I'll take them anyway!' And then all we saw of him for the next four days was this hand hanging limp out the side of his bunk… we just used to take his pulse as we walked past!"

"I have to take a step back sometimes," reflects Peter on a more serious note, "and remind myself that, although what I'm doing is not important, it seems to be more important to other people. And, this might sound bigheaded but we have a little bit of responsibility now. A lot of people think it's funny to see us pissed up all the time, and those people might think that our best gigs are the ones we think were our worst gigs, but some people pay good money to hear us actually play the songs."

"Me and Peter think differently about this," counters Del. "I was sent a tape from a gig in Sweden, from about 1984, I think, and the music is abysmal; we're pissed up, stopping and starting, but the humour is just so funny. We walk onstage and someone introduces us wrong, and we spend twenty minutes tuning up, and Trap's abusing the crowd. We eventually start off with 'Maniac', and Ogs comes in wrong, so we stop and start again… it's half hour before we actually start, but it's hilarious. The complete opposite of what a gig should be! For me, that's what The Test Tube Babies are about!"

Peter: "I'd rather get on and do the songs."

Del: "Be Bon Jovi, you mean?"

Peter: "No, it's hardly Bon Jovi, is it? I'd rather play the songs properly and crack jokes in-between. The music is the main thing."

Del: "It wasn't the main thing when we started though, was it?"

Such minor altercations aside, the pair have stuck together through thick and thin ("We have the same lack of ambition!" quips Del), and, now joined by Paul H. on bass and 'Gay David' on drums, they remain a strong draw wherever they play around the world. But how would they like to be remembered?

"I'd like to be remembered as being memorable!" deadpans Del in typical Test Tube fashion. "Nah, I don't wanna be remembered at all… unless it reflects in our sales, haha! Well, just the fact that we touched a few people around the world is enough for me… what more could we want? Loadsa money, I suppose!"

"In many ways, I don't think we're worthy of our success," says a humble Peter in closing. "We're just lazy; we haven't really tried or worked hard for it. I dunno, I'd like to be remembered as…"

Del: "Fat?"

Peter: "Young, slim and handsome… but that was only the first three years!"

SELECT DISCOGRAPHY:
7"s:
'Banned From The Pubs' (No Future, 1982)
'Run Like Hell' (No Future, 1982)
'Zombie Creeping Flesh' (Trapper, 1983)
'Wimpeez' (Trapper, 1983)
'The Jinx' (Trapper, 1983)
'Keys To The City' (Hairy Pie, 1986)
'When I Fall In Love' (SPV, 1990)
'Supermodels' (Dr. Strange, 1996)
'Fuck The Millennium' (We Bite, 1999) – released as a CD EP by Trapper in the UK

12"s:
'The Jinx' (Trapper, 1983)
'Pressed For Cash' (Trapper, 1984) – split with The Fits
'Rotting In The Fart Sack' (Jungle, 1985)
'Keys To The City' (Hairy Pie, 1986)

LPs:
'Pissed And Proud' (No Future, 1982)
'The Mating Sounds Of South American Frogs' (Trapper, 1983)
'Loud Blaring Punk Rock' (Hairy Pie, 1985)
'Soberphobia' (Dojo, 1987)
'Shit Factory' (SPV, 1990)
'Cringe' (SPV, 1991)
'Supermodels' (We Bite, 1995)
'Schwein Lake Live' (We Bite, 1996)
'Alien Pubduction' (We Bite, 1998)

AT A GLANCE:
For a general overview, the 2001 Anagram CD 'The Best Of Peter And The Test Tube Babies' features twenty-two tracks culled from all periods of the band's colourful existence, and even features an enhanced video clip of 'Moped Lads' filmed in 1983 at the Brixton Fridge. In 2002 however, Captain Oi! undertook an extensive reissue programme, so now it's possible to get definitive CD versions, boosted with bonus tracks and liner notes by Peter, of the band's best albums, 'The Mating Sounds Of South American Frogs', 'Soberphobia' and 'Supermodels'. And anyone brave enough to sample the visual delights of the Test Tube Babies is recommended to check out the brilliant 'Cattle And Bum' DVD (Anagram, 2002).

AD NAUSEAM

 ne of the gnarlier outfits of the period had to be Portsmouth's Ad Nauseam, who formed in 1982 from the remains of two earlier Pompey bands, Birth Trauma and The Annihilates. The band actually started off playing two separate sets with two different vocalists!

"There wasn't any one thing that really prompted me to join a band," admits founding member and vocalist, Barry Coward. "I just think that was what a lot of people my age were doing at the time. The hometown environment had nothing to do with it though; it was the whole punk scene in general that was exciting to me. I can remember hearing 'Realities Of War' by Discharge and thinking 'Fuck me! This is what it's all about!' I took a lot of inspiration from them and the likes of Disorder, Chaos UK, Amebix, and The Subhumans, and we got to play with a lot of those bands ourselves in the end, which was great as we loved every one of them."

Alongside his friends, drummer Mick Bonseir, bassist Steve 'Colonel' Taylor and guitarist Keith Salmon, Barry set about garnering a strong local following for Ad Nauseam by playing in and around Pompey on a regular basis.

"The punk scene in Portsmouth was quite healthy. There weren't too many hardcore bands around, but everyone knew each other, and there was no rivalry – none that I was aware of anyway. I'll always remember piling as many mates as we could into the back of a hired Luton van, pulling the shutter doors down, and travelling miles and miles to play gigs. Sometimes we weren't even on the bill, but we'd turn up and play anyway! We met some great bands that were into the same things as us. There was such great enthusiasm for the punk scene at the time... okay, so there were some arseholes about as well, but the majority of them were good people. At the end of the day, we just wanted to have some fun... after all, that's what it's all about, isn't it?"

Securing themselves a deal with Flicknife Records, Ad Nauseam entered Mekon Studios in London to record 1983's 'Brainstorm' EP. This primitive but punishing four-track single – featuring 'Thatcher', 'Crazy World', 'Don't Vote' and 'Daddy, Daddy' – a quickly sold well over three thousand copies and saw the band making a name for themselves as a fierce live act up and down the country as well as along the south coast. Mail began flooding in from around the world... and they even received some American radio play courtesy of Maximum Rock'n'Roll.

"Well, it wasn't that good, but it's done now and I'm proud of it – no regrets!" states Barry proudly regarding the single. "And as for gigs, my favourite ever moment was at The George Robey, when Jello Biafra (of The Dead Kennedys) was at the front dancing to us! He spoke to me after the gig too, and was a bloody nice bloke! Another time was when we played with The Amebix, and Rob had chicken bones in his hair – brilliant! I have **Ad Nauseam, 1984** such a lot of good memories because of Ad Nauseam. We played **L–R: Brian, Turkee, Wheeler, Barry**

with some brilliant bands and made some great friends, I loved every minute."

But the original incarnation of the band was a short-lived affair that split soon after 'Brainstorm', although it didn't take Barry long to assemble a new Ad Nauseam from the profusion of local musicians. Brian Barnett joined on guitar, Barry 'Baz' Coombes on bass, and a local skinhead who had his roots in the ska and two-tone scenes name of Chris 'Turkee' Calloway took up the vacant drum stool.

"A skinhead in a hardcore punk band... why not?" asks Turkee. "I didn't have a problem with it, and neither did anyone else. There was a really good skinhead/punk scene back then, and never any trouble as far as I know. I was still into the ska thing though, and would still go off to watch all those bands... but look at the punk scene now anyway. Half of the new punk bands play ska beats all the time!"

Baz was soon replaced by Brian Wheeler, and the band undertook shows with the likes of GBH, Disorder, Conflict and The Stupids, recording several demos, including 'Bad Noizeam' and the cracking 1985 effort, 'Five Go Mad'. By this time, Wheeler had left to be replaced by John Haskett, and a lead guitarist had been added to the line-up in the shape of Scott Fury. The new Ad Nauseam was not only musically faster, tighter and more metallic than the band that recorded for Flicknife, but lyrically a lot more light-hearted.

"Maybe we were listening to other musical styles," Barry ponders the more metal direction the band took. "But also all our new members brought their own little bits to Ad Nauseam, and that was the result. We kept moving and moving, 'cos if you stand still... well, you stand still, don't you?"

"Scott Fury was a lazy sod," laughs Turkee, on the subject of their new guitarist. "This was a man who slept twenty-three hours a day – honestly! And we had to literally drag him out of bed all the time, but it was worth the hassle, 'cos what a great lead guitarist he was!

"My favourite gig was when we supported Broken Bones at Basins Night Club in Portsmouth, and we blew them off stage!" remembers the drummer gleefully. "What a night! And the worse was easily when we were meant to play Bournemouth one time, so we packed about twenty or thirty of our mates into the back of our transit van, one very cold February afternoon... I think it was snowing, in fact. We got all the way there, met up with the other bands that were playing, only to find that the landlord had beaten his wife up and had been arrested, so the club had been shut down for the night. We were freezing cold and stuck in Bournemouth with nothing to do.

"Probably the craziest thing we ever did was when we carried all our gear – drums and everything! – two miles to a beach in Southsea to play a party at midnight on the back of a truck. We got so drunk, we didn't play very well at all, and I fell off my stool, right off the lorry, twice! Never mind, eh?"

This definitive version of Ad Nauseam recorded a strictly limited (to 500 copies) 12", 'The Greatest Show On Earth', in Portsmouth's (now demolished) Crystal Room Studios. It was self-released in 1987, to much critical acclaim, with the financial backing being provided by a local musician, Andy Thomas.

Opening with the circus music with which the band began their live shows, it contains eight tracks of speedy and accomplished punk/metal, all given a cheeky innovative twist, and remains the band's crowning glory, as they split up the following year when boredom and frustration set in.

Barry went on to front the thrash metal band, Decimator, with whom he was known as 'Mad Dog', who did two albums for Newcastle label, Neat – 1989's 'Carnage City State Mosh Patrol' and 1993's 'Dirty, Hot And Hungry'. Turkee meanwhile has played in a string of punk and ska bands since Ad Nauseam, and currently drums for traditional ska/reggae band, The Racketeers, and quirky, tuneful punk band Popper.

"I really can't remember why we split up, I think I just got fed up with it all," says Brian. "But shit happens, eh? We were young and gave it everything we had, but more importantly we enjoyed ourselves doing it."

SELECT DISCOGRAPHY:
7"s:
'Brainstorm' EP (Flicknife, 1983)

12"s:
'The Greatest Show On Earth' (Crystal, 1987)

AT A GLANCE:

Despite recording (as well as their single and LP) about eight demos, there has yet to be a thorough Ad Nauseam retrospective CD, although the curious could try contacting Turkee (being sure to enclose sufficient return postage) c/o 17 Andover Rd., Southsea, Portsmouth, Hants., PO4 9QG, England.

BUTCHER

utcher were one of the more obscure second wave punk bands, but that doesn't make their story any less compelling or indicative of the time and the tragedy and triumphs that accompanied it. The band were formed in Bournemouth in August 1981 by bassist Steve 'Snatch' Morgan, who recruited to his cause guitarist Dave John and drummer Rob, both of whom had played with him previously in The Intestines.

The Intestines were probably the first proper punk band from Bournemouth. Having formed in July 1978, they released two singles, the first for Leicester-based company Alternative Capitalists (nowadays known as Sorted Records), the second on their own Inept label. They even made local headlines when they were accused of swearing at the annual Beat Contest, an open-air talent show in the Pleasure Gardens primarily intended for the town's many tourists.

The Butcher line-up was rounded out by vocalist Sid (aka Lawrence Rigler), and, albeit outside of the actual band, their mate, Sharky, who managed them.

"What did we have to rebel against?" ponders Dave, when asked whether or not they were products of their immediate environment. "Bournemouth is a holiday resort and a place that rich people can retire to, but outside the wealthy centre there are poorer areas that suffered the same high unemployment as the rest of the country in the early Eighties. There was no heavy industry, and career opportunities were dominated by seasonal work related to tourism. The town centre was geared solely for the tourists in fact, leaving few places for local youth to go that were not either too expensive or 'smart casual' only. It was easy to gain a perspective on inequality. No regular venues were willing to promote the local punk bands so we had to hire venues and book ourselves.

"And at first there were no other punk bands in the area so The Intestines used to play as the novelty act with vaguely New Wave inspired bands such as Interference, Gooch, Trevor Etc. and The 53 Rumanian Boys, The Animal Haircuts, Go Faster Pussycat Kill Kill Kill, and White Youth In Asia. As time went on, we started to build our own audience... especially after high profile gigs with The Piranhas and UK Subs, and when John Peel played the first single.

"Butcher inherited this audience and built on it. Later we were able to play with bands whose outlook was closer to our own, such as Illegitimate, Annex, Agrovation, Genetic Mistakes, Shock To The System, Self Abuse, Confession of Sin, Big Sleep, Idiom Tribe and Mad Are Sane. The newer bands also started organising their own gigs with us on the bill... Self Abuse used to organise a few gigs with Devon band Cult Maniax."

Sadly, Snatch died just six months after forming the band, aged only seventeen. In January 1982, a mere week after leaving home, he was found dead as a result of mixing too many pills and alcohol. After much soul-searching by the remaining members, he was replaced in April 1982 by a good friend of his, Colin, who had previously played in both Annex and Agrovation.

In August 1982, very aware that if they didn't do it

Butcher, live at the Rooftop, 1984

themselves, it was highly likely that no one else would either, Butcher released their debut single, 'On The Ground' (backed by 'Grow Up, Don't Blow Up'), on Inept. It was recorded live in Misty's eight-track Studio at the Triangle, Bournemouth ("They were later called Harmony Studios, invested in expensive equipment and promptly went bust!"), then mixed and mastered all in one day. No doubt benefiting from such enforced spontaneity, the single captured the band perfectly, the imperfections of the raw recording swept away before a tidal wave of energy and youthful enthusiasm.

It was a thoroughly DIY affair, plagued with problems from start to finish, but the band persevered and handled the whole process from the initial recording of the songs right through to hand-delivering promotional copies to DJs and delivering stock to distributors. The saga of poorly-printed covers and incompetence on the part of the pressing plant, forwarded to the editor by Sharky, was eventually printed in Punk Lives magazine as a word of warning to any other bands thinking of pursuing a similar path to getting their music heard by a wider audience.

As a result of the publicity, and no doubt the single's airing on John Peel's show, 'On The Ground' sold well enough to justify a second pressing, and Butcher were encouraged enough to begin work immediately on the follow-up. Their second single, March '83's 'Stand And Fight' (pressed on red vinyl, and backed by 'Killing Groups'), was recorded at Milborne Port's Monitor Studios. Unfortunately, although technically far slicker than their incendiary debut, it failed to ignite the listener with quite the same excitement.

"We also tried to use our contacts with the distributors to help other local bands," says Dave of their Inept label. "We released cassettes by Confession Of Sin, Big Sleep, and Mad Are Sane. We had to record each tape separately, even cutting out and sticking on the labels. Small Wonder regularly listed them in their adverts in Sounds."

An additional track recorded during the same session as 'Stand And Fight', 'Ain't It Great?', appeared alongside Riot Squad SA, on a flexi-single given away free with London fanzine Chainsaw in Spring 1983, to coincide with an interview they had conducted with the band. The same fanzine also put two Butcher songs – 'Psycho Trend' and 'Get It On' – on another flexi a year later, this time alongside Mornington Crescent and ferocious Dutch hardcore band, BGK.

By 1984, the band were bored with only playing locally, and decided to spread their wings, aided by a decent demo on Inept, the 'Blood Age' cassette, which they sent out to any and every promoter whose address they could coerce from their ever-increasing number of contacts.

"As a result, we started getting gigs further away from Bournemouth, including a festival on the Isle Of Wight with King Kurt, the Richmond Arms in Brighton, the 100 Club in Oxford Street, the Ad Lib Club in Kensington and the Kings Head, Fulham. We supported bands such as Broken Bones, GBH, Angelic Upstarts and Punilux. We played with The English Dogs several times, and they took us on the southern part of one of their tours.

"At first we used to hire mini-buses. On the way to our first gig at the 100 Club the mini-bus broke down on the way, so we had to wait while the hire company sent someone up with another van. We arrived at the club just in time to go on, and had our first review in Sounds as a consequence... where we were described as 'Tuneless and whining'!

"Other times we'd hire full size coaches and sell tickets locally. One time we got banned from the 100 Club after someone who came up on the coach was found to be carrying knives. He had to write a grovelling letter explaining he was behaving independently of the band, that it was his first time in London and where he came from in deepest Dorset knives were vital to his survival, before they let us back."

In 1985, Rot Records included the Butcher songs 'Time Will Tell' and 'Leaves Alive' on their 'A Kick Up The Arse, Volume One' compilation, whilst in 1986, French label 77 Records included 'Holy Messiah (What A Way To Go)' on one of their collections. 77 also expressed an interest in releasing a full album by the band, but failed to come up with the agreed funding for recording. The preparatory demos the band were working on leading up to this ill-fated release eventually saw the light of day as a posthumous cassette, 'Ignite The Thrill', released by Inept in 1988.

In October 1987, a disillusioned Colin left the band, followed soon after by Sid, which spelt the end for Butcher. Colin formed a low-key thrash metal band (briefly known as both Butchered and Battery) with a Japanese student, Naruhiko 'Mocchie' Mochida, that even included ex-Butcher members, Dave and Sid, for a short while. The band split in 1993 when Naru returned home to Japan, where he still plays in the Osaka-based Hoglan.

During the early Nineties, Colin and Dave also contributed to demo recordings by Dark Days, another band managed by Sharky, but eventually Colin channelled all his creative energies into making horror and sci-fi sculptures, and he now has his own shop in London's Camden Lock.

In 1996, Dave joined No Wings Fins Or Fuselage, with whom he recorded three albums before returning to full-time education in 2000. Along with original singer Harry Scrubber, he is currently working on a long-overdue Intestines album with Rob, who owns his own record shop in Bournemouth. Sid, meanwhile, travelled the world, even working for a time in Borneo, but tragically died in a motorcycle accident in Dorset in 1999, aged 37.

SELECT DISCOGRAPHY:
7"s:
'On The Ground' (Inept, 1982)
'Stand And Fight' (Inept, 1983)

AT A GLANCE:
Despite penning many a fine tune, Butcher have never enjoyed an official CD discography release, but Dave has compiled all their recordings onto a CDR, should anyone care to contact him at djohn@bournemouth.ac.uk

CULT MANIAX

O ne of the few punk bands from the extreme Southwest to make an impact on a national level were the Cult Maniax, formed in Torrington in 1978 by vocalist Alan 'Big Al' Mitchell. They still exist – albeit on a casual basis – even today, but are best remembered for their brilliant 'Blitz' single and the trail of chaos they left wherever they played during the early Eighties.

"It was a good scene down in Devon back then, just as rocking as any of the cities," reckons Al. "We'd go and see The Pistols and The Damned in places like Plymouth and Exeter, but the country towns had some good little scenes going too. Before punk came along, I was already into stuff like T-Rex, Bowie and Iggy Pop. I was a little bit older than the rest of the band, and I was already playing acoustic guitar, doing folk and stuff like that.

"The band's first ever show was in late 1978, or early '79, supporting Hawkwind at a festival. Their singer's daughter used to hang around with us, and that's where most of our amps and speakers came from; we got them second-hand from Hawkwind. We used to play with them a lot and that first gig was a little biker's festival above an antique shop in Barnstaple. I think it was just called the Barnstaple Antique Emporium, and it was owned by a load of hippies."

For the earliest Maniax line-up, Al was joined by Rico Sergeant on guitar, Michael 'Foxy' Steer on bass and Paul 'Mildew' Mills on drums. Their first official release was the (early 1982) 'Black Horse' EP, for Next Wave, a four-track affair that, as well as the title track, featured 'Young Anarchists', 'Frenzy' and 'The Russians Are Coming'. A vicious attack on the landlord of Torrington pub the Black Horse, who had previously barred the band from his establishment, it caused a storm of controversy and only sold two hundred copies before it was banned by the Bristol High Court and all remaining copies were seized and destroyed.

"It's a long story," laughs Al. "I wish we never did it, really, but it was basically our old manager, Bunker Brazier, who talked us into it. He had twisted testicles, and had to have an operation to put 'em straight... but I think he had a twisted mind 'n' all!

"When the single came out, my old dear said, 'Oh, for fuck's sake, don't let your old man find out, he'll kill you!' But then he turned on the TV and there we were, being called 'A sick punk band' on the regional news! It was all over the front pages of the local papers. Next Wave was our manager's label, set up for just that EP, but after all that he freaked out a bit and didn't do anything else."

Soon after, the band replaced Rico with Paul Bennett on guitar and released their crowning glory, the superb 'Blitz' (b/w 'Lucy Looe') single, on their own Elephant Rock Records, that went on to sell over 20,000 copies.

"That was banned by the Bristol High Court 'n' all," says Al proudly. "On account of 'Lucy Looe' being all about blow-jobbing! Me and Paul wrote it in less than five minutes whilst we were waiting for Foxy and Mildew to turn up at practise. It seemed a bit stupid banning it after it had sold so many copies though."

Whilst lacking certain production values, both the early releases captured the band's abrasively melodic punk rock and Al's sneering Lydon-esque warble more than adequately, with 'Blitz' an especially memorable moment grimly likening the devastation wreaked by the riots of 1981 to that of burnt-out London during 1942.

"We released the next single too quickly, really, and it flopped a bit," continues Al. "That was the 'Black Mass' EP, which was all about witches... we get a lot of 'em around this way. It was all a laugh but we had this big backdrop with a pentagram on it and everything! We even had people turning up to gigs in black cloaks and stuff... I just thought it was the acid kicking in! To be honest, most of the Eighties was one big blur of noise and colour for me; we were absolutely fucking blitzed all the time."

The Cult Maniax played the length and breadth of the country, from the 100 Club in London, with the Cockney Rejects, to Adam And Eve's in Leeds.

"The most memorable show we ever did was supporting the Anti-Nowhere League at the Top Rank in Plymouth; there must have been three or four thousand people there. But on the way down, we stopped the van for a piss, and we looked over the hedge and there were hundreds of magic mushrooms in this fucking field. So we jumped over the hedge and ate all these magic mushrooms, and by the time we got onstage at the Top Rank, the whole band were tripping their tits off! Anyway, we managed to get the gear into this big dark backstage area, and we were all stoned, and the management comes over and asked anyone who wasn't in the band to go back outside to get their hands stamped, and of course, the whole band walked back outside!

"The drummer from the League came back there later on, and he asked to have a go on our drum kit. So we let him, and he said one of the drums was out of tune, and we all started really

freaking about it, 'cos we were tripping so strong by then. We were like, 'Oh my god, our drums are out of tune', and really panicking!

"Anyway, we managed to get the gear onstage, but halfway through the first song, Paul went mad and did a Pete Townshend and smashed his guitar up; he had to borrow another guitar off one of the other bands, but it wasn't so good. The gig was wicked though; the skinheads went mad, the crash barrier went down, two kids ended up in hospital, and the place got wrecked... but it was a good laugh!

"For another gig in Plymouth, our van fell through at the last minute, and we just couldn't get another one anywhere. In the end we borrowed an open-back truck, and then halfway to Plymouth, a fucking car pulled out in front of us, and the truck somersaulted down the road, with gear and people flying out everywhere like rag dolls! Some of us got taken to hospital in an ambulance; it was a helluva mess! We couldn't play the gig, of course, and all the punks went on the rampage and had a riot 'cos we didn't turn up. One of our crew's still got grit in his face from bouncing along the road in front of the van."

In 1983, American Phonograph released the band's one and only studio album, 'Cold Love', which after the preceding singles was something of a disappointment. Despite some good material, not least of all the furious opener 'Time Bomb City', the release was

Cult Maniax, L-R: Foxy, Paul, Big Al, Mildew
(Pic: Paul Martin)

castrated by a weak mix, too much drums and hardly any guitars.

"We recorded for two weeks down in London," explains Al. "And we were meant to go back the following week to mix it, after we'd all been away on holiday to Belgium. But then the bastard from American Phonograph mixed it without us and started pressing it before we'd even got back. It even had some of the tracks with the drums all backwards on it, all experimental, and it

was crap! It's fucking awful; luckily for him, we never ever saw the guy again!"

On one of the band's forays up north, they impressed Xcentric Noise Records from Hull enough at another Adam And Eve's show in Leeds to sign them up. They released the 'Full Of Spunk' single in August 1984, which made No. 11 in the Indies during a three month chart run. It was closely followed by 'The Amazing Adventures Of Johnny The Duck' single (that was also issued in 12" format) during Christmas '84, and the 'Where Do We All Go?' six-track live 12", June 1985. All sold well, narrowly missing out on the Indie Top Ten, but none were as musically convincing as the earlier, more fiery, Maniax releases.

"Our problem was that we peaked too early, and it was all downhill from there," Al agrees. "For the last few singles we were running out of ideas, and it was all getting a bit experimental. We even had a single released in 1987 as The Vibe Tribe, which was basically the Cult Maniax under a different name, called 'Skylark Boogie', about this big old American car I had, a Buick Skylark; that was on Tribal Records, an offshoot of Elephant Rock. And then we split up in the late Eighties; it had just come to an end really. Things die off eventually, don't they? The spirit had gone; the songs were sounding stale, and... well, we were going to rehearsals and we couldn't stand the sight of each other.

"But it was a good thing in the end, 'cos we wrote some really good songs independently of each other, whilst staying good friends. Paul formed The Whirliebirds, and I started The Sweet Thangs. I actually prefer The Sweet Thangs to the Maniax really. We were just getting in each other's way towards the end; we had very different ideas about where we wanted to take the band."

Despite 'splitting up', the Cult Maniax have played various shows together over the last fifteen years, with Jez 'Fluffy' Evans on bass, "Just for a laugh", including the 1996 Fuck Reading festival at the London Astoria.

Al went on to become a keen historian, particularly regarding Seventeenth Century warfare, and a trained swordsmen, heavily involved with the Sealed Knot. A loveably eccentric character, he's now also the town crier of Torrington, and a bona fide lay preacher. He currently plays with his own two-piece folk outfit, Freeborn Men ("We play all sorts of stuff, based on rebel music throughout the ages!"), but the world hasn't heard the last of The Cult Maniax. "We're even thinking of getting together for a few shows later this year, it should be a good laugh. And it's a good way to get stuff off your chest. The lyrics are a bit dated nowadays, I know that... but they meant something to me when I wrote 'em... after ten pints of cider at least!"

SELECT DISCOGRAPHY:
7"s:
'Black Horse' EP (Next Wave, 1982)
'Blitz' (Elephant Rock, 1982)
'The Black Mass EP' (Elephant Rock, 1982)
'Full Of Spunk' (Xcentric Noise, 1984)
'The Amazing Adventures Of Johnny The Duck' (Xcentric Noise, 1984)

12"s:
'The Amazing Adventures Of Johnny The Duck' (Xcentric Noise, 1984)
'Where Do We All Go?' (Xcentric Noise, 1985)

LPs:
'Cold Love' (American Phonograph, 1983)

AT A GLANCE:

There has unfortunately not yet been a comprehensive retrospective CD of the Cult Maniax, although a rather poor quality 'Live At Leeds' CD was issued by Retch Records in 1997.

CHAPTER NINE

WALES

THE PARTISANS

M uch like far-flung Scotland and Ireland, Wales proudly developed a vibrant and colourful punk subculture despite its relative isolation from the mainly London-centric music industry. And the enthusiastic determination of its protagonists ensured the emergence of some truly great bands that were more interested in creating something positive in their lives than pandering to the whims of the press.

The biggest of the second wave bands to emerge from Wales, The Partisans formed in Bridgend in early 1978, whilst still in their early teens. Their original line-up comprised Phil Stanton on vocals, Rob 'Spike' Harrington on guitar and vocals, Andy Lealand, also on guitar, Mark 'Shark' Harris on drums, and Mark 'Savage' Parsons on bass. When Savage and Phil left, the following year, after playing just one show at a local school, Spike moved to main vocals and Andy's girlfriend Louise Wright joined on bass, completing what is still regarded by many to this day as the 'classic' Partisans line-up.

The band formed after being swept away by the excitement of the earliest punk bands, especially The Clash, the Sex Pistols and The Ramones – even though they had problems getting into many of the gigs they desperately wanted to attend.

"Being fifteen or sixteen was a bit of a disadvantage," reckons Spike. 'We got turned away from some gigs which we really wanted to get into. Nothing like punk had ever happened before, so even dressing mildly differently caused quite a stir.

"You just can't beat the twisted teenage punk angst of the Buzzcocks, but there were some bands like The Desperate Bicycles, and Patrik Fitzgerald, who summed up the whole DIY thing for me. And really early on in Wales there was a band from Cardiff called Victimize. I've still got their pin badge somewhere: 'Fuck The Pistols, I've been Victimized'!"

"The scene was obviously more exciting then as it was all new and fresh," says Andy. "The early Clash gigs were the best I have ever been to. Almost all the punk bands coming out between '77 and '79 had a big influence upon us. As far as I recall there were no local bands that influenced us as such, but there were loads of Welsh bands by around 1981; Foreign Legion (or Dead On Arrival, as they were known back then), Pseudo Sadists, The Oppressed... all of them doing their own thing."

"All the usual first wave punk bands, definitely," agrees Shark of the band's influences. "Not really any of the second wave bands – they were okay but didn't inspire us. We were the only Welsh punk band noticeably active prior to 1980, I think."

It wasn't long before The Partisans did a tape of some of their favourite punk cover songs, and soon after they went to Cardiff's 123 Studios to record their first real demo, which included early versions of tracks that would eventually appear on their debut album. A copy was sent to Sounds, and it made No. 2 in Gary Bushell's playlist that week. Their first singer, Phil Stanton, who was going out with Spike's older sister at the time, and who even co-wrote some of those songs with the band, sent the demo off to Malvern label, No Future, who promptly signed them.

The first release was the double A-side single, 'Police Story'/'Killing Machine', which came out in September 1981, spent twenty-two weeks in the Indie Charts (peaking at No. 5), and earned the band another rave review in Sounds. Although rather throwaway compared to the band's later material, it nonetheless throbs with a barely contained exuberance and intensity, and it's difficult not to succumb to its youthful charm. Garry Bushell was by this time so enamoured with the band, he invited them to appear on his third Oi album, the hugely successful 'Carry On Oi', which was not only an

The Partisans, London 1981
L–R: Spike, Louise, Andy, Shark

Indie hit but made No. 60 in the National Charts too. The band contributed 'Arms Race' and 'No U Turns', two of the stronger tracks on the compilation, and found themselves gigging with other Oi bands such as The Ejected and label-mates Blitz.

"The Oi thing caused some hassle at gigs," reckons Spike. "We were from a place right between Cardiff and Swansea, and there's huge football rivalry between the two. Some punks and skins just used gigs as an excuse to be totally fucking pathetic... no doubt, I'll get a punch in the face for saying that!"

The next release for the band was the '17 Years Of Hell' single, in May 1982. The A-side was a change of pace, a rolling mid-tempo number with an insistent backing vocal, but the two cuts on the flip were more standard fare, tearing along at 100mph and raging against the establishment ('I'm anti-Queen... and I don't wanna live in no Union Jack,' yells Spike on the combustive 'Power And Greed'). It was another Indie hit, this time reaching No. 2 in the chart, but neither band nor label really capitalised on its success with any concerted touring. Half of The Partisans were still at school when their No Future singles were released, and if it hadn't been for Andy's step-father Keith being prepared to hire vans and drive the band around, they probably wouldn't have played any of their early London shows at all. Then, when they did manage to overcome such logistical problems and actually play out of Wales, they had mindless violence to contend with. Not least of all a show in Wolverhampton that deteriorated into one massive brawl.

"No one in the band can be perceived as a 'bovver boy'; we are normal, peace-loving, passive types, and we hate aggressive behaviour... especially when it's unchannelled aggression. All the biggest dickheads are the violent ones. Anyway, that night there was some stupid fuck who obviously wanted Louise's attention, and, having no personality and even less charm, he decided that if he lobbed a glass at her face, hopefully she would fall in love with him or something! I saw it all through the corner of my eye, so I jumped on the guy and the rest of the band joined in, and the whole pub turned into a blood bath. Scary shit, and just the kind of stuff that makes intelligent bands split up."

Indeed, in the face of such stupidity, the band actually broke up during the summer of '82. Andy and Louise had split up themselves by then ("But she's still a really good mate… and oddly enough she's now going out with Sav, our very first bass player," says Spike), with Andy moving to London. He ended up living in a squat with various members of Sex Gang Children, whom he also worked for as a roadie.

In late 1982, to fulfil contractual obligations, The Partisans reformed and recorded their self-titled debut album, which came out in February the following year. Twelve tracks of abrasive, pissed-off punk rock, so tight it squeaked, it was recorded with Andy travelling back to Wales for the day.

"As usual we didn't rehearse before we went into the studio," admits Andy. "I think we just recorded it as if it was a demo, completely live with a few overdubs. It was all done and mixed within eight hours or something; we really had no idea what we were doing, and I don't think we cared that much. We just sent it off to No Future and they released it shortly afterwards."

As well as re-recorded versions of the cuts that appeared on the Oi album (and '17 Years Of Hell'), the standout tracks were the band's theme song, 'Partisans', and the defiantly sneering 'I Don't Give A Fuck'. It was another Top Five Indie hit, and reached the No. 1 spot in the Punk Charts. By this time Louise was rapidly becoming Punk's second most popular pin-up, hot on the heels of Beki Bondage, and just her image on the covers seemingly helped attract the band a few more listeners, although her high speed picking belied her demure looks.

"We all liked The Adverts, and I guess, indirectly, we stole the idea from them, having a girl on bass and stuff," says Andy. "Yeah, the press did focus a little more on her, but we didn't care that much."

"It was whilst listening to records with a friend that I saw a picture of this stunningly attractive young lass on the cover of one of his compilation LPs," admits Lyndon Henstridge, responsible for the excellent unofficial No Future website. "Upon my enquiry, he informed me of the band in which she played, and this was my introduction to The Partisans. Within days, I had purchased their debut LP and was immediately drawn to it. From the opening track to the rather unusual 'Overdose', this was a piece of vinyl well worth the money that I'd paid… and there was the added bonus of more photographs of the lovely Louise!

"The mix of raw power and aggression, blended well with the melodic and tuneful backing music, kept it on my turntable for a couple of weeks. I particularly liked the idea of their self-titled track, something that could be used as their anthem at gigs."

Spike still regards the album favourably, over twenty years on. "I like 'Overdose' from that first album too, even though it's a bit of a Chelsea rip-off! Even quirky songs like 'No Time' were quite catchy, and 'Arms Race' was good 'cos it's unfortunately still 100% appropriate today!"

Despite the album doing so well, the band that actually recorded it did very few gigs, and soon there were yet more changes in The Partisans camp. Louise left for good, and the remaining two members also relocated to London to continue the band as a three-piece. The few shows they played with Spike handling both vocal and guitar duties, with Andy on bass, didn't work out, and they ended up recruiting Dave Parsons to replace Louise.

Relations had also soured with No Future, and a fresh deal was inked with Link Records who signed the band to their new Cloak And Dagger imprint in late '83.

"We insisted on the Cloak And Dagger tag," reckons Andy. "That was our idea 'cos we didn't want to be on an Oi-only label. We were all a bit dubious of Oi music by then, and besides, we had grown up with punk, and Oi had made little real impression on us musically."

The resulting 'Blind Ambition' EP really saw the band come of age, effortlessly shirking off any generic trappings they had inadvertently landed themselves with and embracing a far more tuneful approach. The single just oozes maturity and confidence, especially the title track with its insistent descending verse quite literally exploding into the majestic chorus riff.

However, despite a full marks review in Punk Lives, and mainstream DJ Peter Powell even playing it on daytime Radio One, it failed to set the charts alight in the same way as the band's previous output. In a further effort to break new ground, The Partisans supported Conflict at the Brixton Ace on a bill that was dominated by anarcho bands, and, testament to their crossover appeal, they went down extremely well.

"We liked Crass from the outset," reveals Spike. "And the whole Union Jack/Oi tag was pissing us off a bit, so playing with Conflict seemed the natural thing to do; maybe we should have played with them a lot sooner…!"

Their set was recorded and appeared as one side of their second album, 'Time Was Right', although by the time they recorded the studio side, Dave had left (he went on to join Transvision Vamp, and now plays in Bush!) so Andy played all the bass parts.

"We actually wanted to do a complete studio album," he explains. "But we didn't have enough songs and the record company really wanted to release something as soon as possible, as the whole punk scene was on its last legs. It probably would have taken us another two years just to get our shit together and write some new stuff, so we did that half studio/half live thing."

In fact, the label was in such a rush to get the album out, the mixes that got used on the final cut weren't actually the ones intended for release.

"It was chaos as usual," Andy reveals. "I think we had three days to do that album. The first day was a complete disaster; we had been sold some really bad speed and as a result we recorded everything out of time… we didn't have a clue what was going on, so the next day we redid all the tracks, which went pretty well. On the last day it was the mix, and we all got stoned at the mixing desk, including the producer, and everything sounded fantastic, the levels were perfect… anyway, we were stoned for months afterwards, so nothing sounded weird. It was only when we were straight again that we realised the mixes were all fucked up! Luckily we had done some better mixes of 'I Never Needed You' and 'The Time Was Right', but it was too late – the album had already been released, and the good mixes had disappeared."

Despite all this, 'Time Was Right' remains a miraculously cohesive effort. It opens with a rockier, far more accomplished reworking of 'I Never Needed You', that originally appeared on their debut album, but the similarities between the two records end there. Most of the thrashy speed had been replaced by simple infectious beats and good old-fashioned tunes, harking back to the classic punk bands that influenced the band in the first place.

"Old age!" jokes Shark, as to the reasons behind their change in musical direction. "No, it was just a natural progression as we got older… and we weren't worried about losing fans; we would have done it anyway."

"Everything changes, everything, why shouldn't we?" adds Andy. "As for losing fans, who cares? It's up to them, let them make their own life, isn't it? Not to expect us to live up to their expectations!

"Listen, punk was shit by 1982, and just getting worse by the minute! We stayed 'punk' as far as we were concerned; just 'cos we could play our guitars didn't mean that we were not punk anymore. We just weren't interested in keeping an audience with such a sheep-like attitude!"

Whatever the reasons behind the shift in style, there's no denying that the new Partisans were an infinitely more professional sounding band, and for every die-hard punk they lost through one door, they gained a discerning rock fan in the other.

"Their third single, 'Blind Ambition', was sufficiently different to their previous releases, without being too different," reckons Lyndon Henstridge. "The tracks are much more refined and melodic, whilst maintaining the punk riffs, and it is their best single, if you ask me.

"Their second LP was released at about the same time, and follows the same style as the single. In my opinion, it was better than the first LP, even though it doesn't include the intended cuts of each track. In fact, the title track is my favourite ever Partisans song."

"Forget the live side (it's okay), forget the first album (sounded great then, but doesn't stand the test of time) and go straight to the second Partisans album," enthuses Sean from Rough Trade who rates 'Time Was Right' as his all-time favourite Eighties punk album. "Each track is worth the admission price alone; it has the power, passion and tunes, but most of all it has soul. Over the years I've had to buy this record three times because I keep wearing it out!"

The Partisans, 2001
Clockwise from top left: Spike, Magnus, Andy, Gustav

Despite great reviews across the board and modestly successful sales – it troubled the Indie Top Twenty for a few weeks upon its release during July '84 – the band were slowly and unspectacularly coming apart at the seams.

"After farting around so much with record companies, we just lost interest," says Shark. "I also realized that I had to work to earn a living!"

"We were getting shafted by everyone in the business," sighs Andy. "We couldn't even afford to rehearse in the end, there was no money coming in at all. We didn't split really; there was no official statement or anything – we just lost interest in the whole thing. The so-called punk rock record labels were treating us like mutes, idiots… we just couldn't continue. What was the point of writing new songs for some asshole that was not going to pay us for our efforts?"

"I'm not convinced that we ever wanted to be in a 'proper' band, anyway," adds Spike. "I don't think we knew what it meant, or required from us, and when we started to investigate, we thought 'Fuck this'! The whole punk thing that we grew up with, and what we were doing, became a contradiction, and our enthusiasm for being in a band just got diverted into other interests."

The band went their separate ways; Andy moved to Sweden, Spike became a hospital orderly for a while, before moving home to South Wales, and Shark went to work on the oil rigs before disappearing off to the Far East for several years. Andy and Spike kept in touch though, and in 1989, actually recorded two songs together as Agent Orange ("Spike and I didn't want to cash in on The Partisans name"). The resulting 'Run Go Grab' and 'Eyes Shut', although recorded with a drum machine, were both decent tunes giving a very definite nod towards the duo's beloved Clash.

During the late Nineties, The Partisans got back together as a proper band again, this time recruiting two of Andy's Swedish friends, Magnus Neundorff and Mikael 'Gustav' Gustavsson, and in 2001, American label TKO released the 'So Neat' single.

"I still like to play guitar and write tunes," says Andy. "And Spike writes some good lyrics, although it's more of a project than a reformation. As for what's next, well… I guess we will just put out the odd record every few years or so, and play a few little gigs here and there."

"We carry on doing what we always did because we can," adds Spike. "It's sad, pathetic and sounds really arrogant, but like the song used to go, 'I don't give a fuck'. And what's more, the new songs kick ass!"

The TKO single is excellent, picking up the band's creative thread somewhere around the 'Blind Ambition' period, the CD version including an extra track 'Hysteria', which rates as one of the best songs The Partisans have ever put their name to. And they've just finished working on a brand new album, 'Idiot Nation', but remain as elusive as ever on the live front.

"The world has changed in so many ways in the past twenty years, but it's still the same shits running the show," says Spike in closing. "But if there's still a fifteen year old out there somewhere getting inspired by a song like 'Garageland', good on 'em!

"We never set out to achieve anything, and we haven't, so no regrets there then, I guess! But just to be remembered, for better or for worse, is good enough for me. Oh, and Tony Blair is a cunt. Can I say that?"

SELECT DISCOGRAPHY:
7"s:
'Police Story' (No Future, 1981)
'17 Years Of Hell' (No Future, 1982)
'Blind Ambition' (Link/Cloak And Dagger, 1983)
'So Neat' (TKO, 2001) – also available as a CD EP

LPs:
'The Partisans' (No Future, 1983)
'Time Was Right' (Link/Cloak And Dagger, 1984)
'Idiot Nation' (Dr. Strange, 2004)

AT A GLANCE:
Captain Oi!'s 'The Best Of The Partisans' CD features all the band's Eighties singles, their tracks from the 'Carry On Oi' album, and selected cuts from the debut album. There's a discography, good liner notes, artwork and photos, and even the two Agent Orange demo tracks from 1989… though the band dispute that they were ever intended to be released under The Partisans moniker.

PICTURE FRAME SEDUCTION

I n an era of generic band names, usually prefixed with 'The', Picture Frame Seduction was one of the more imaginative monikers of the early Eighties. Apparently named after a song by US punks KGB, the band were also one of the harder working groups on the circuit. But tucked away in the furthest most corner of Wales, it was difficult to ever be in the right place at the right time as far as the music industry was concerned, so, despite achieving respectable sales, they never attained the kind of popularity afforded The Partisans, despite doing ten times as many shows.

Formed in Haverfordwest, Pembrokeshire in 1978, by original drummer Keith Haynes and vocalist Barrie O'Dare, they played their first show at their school (Sir Thomas Picton) at Christmas of that year. For the gig Keith actually played guitar and they were joined by Robin Folland on bass and stand-in drummer Jonathon 'Griff' Griffiths; at that time, they were known merely as The Frames.

"It was frightening," laughs Keith. "There were loads of kids there, some 300 and we were awful, but everyone just jumped around and eventually started wrecking the place – good fun at the time!"

1979 saw more gigs at The Patch and Tower Hill youth clubs, and the band not only adopted the name P.F.S. but also trimmed to a three-piece for their first demos, recorded in Neyland. Keith played drums, Rob moved to guitar, and the new addition was Tim Horsley on bass and vocals. However, the four-track tape was sadly lost many years ago.

In 1980, another demo was recorded in Saundersfoot, which included an early version of live favourite 'Getcha Rox Off', and the band began playing out regularly all over South Wales. It

Picture Frame Seduction, live 100 Club
(Pic: Paul May)

was also about this time that Keith applied to an ad in Sounds when Discharge needed a new drummer and ended up replacing Tez, if only for a short while.

"I wasn't with them for long," he admits. "I was only sixteen. But the time I was with them was bloody brilliant, we were writing the material for the 'Why?' 12". In the end I went home to Haverfordwest. Then Bambi (Dave Ellesmere, who ended up playing on the 12") came along and I just wanted to go home anyway; the living conditions were shite, the pay was non-existent and the guy who managed Discharge, Mike Stone, was just having a laugh. Discharge sold shitloads and didn't seem to be getting much back. But I was there, and nobody can take that away from me."

In 1981, Picture Frame Seduction recorded another three songs, one of which, (the band's anthem) 'Getcha Rox Off', appeared on Insane Record's 'Demolition Blues' compilation, alongside the likes of The Aborted, The Secluded and The Oppressed, the Cardiff skinhead band fronted by Roddy Moreno, who also ran Oi Records.

"I always liked Roddy Moreno and what his band stood for," says Keith. "We played in Cardiff with them (The Oppressed) once, and they were top lads, a skinhead band with real values... but the audience looked like they were all into the NF, so we gave it to them big time. I was terrified, but who cares! I'm a Swansea fan too, so we thought, 'Let's go down fighting!' And Roddy gave them as much shit as we did.

"We were willing to do anything, at any time. We had a death wish! And that freaked a few other bands out. If it went off at gigs, as it often did, we would have it with whoever wanted it. Just young madness really... we had very few rules, and that was our culture. I remember once we played in Treorchy Youth Club; it was a good gig, and then the whole audience attacked us! We loved it at the time, and they did too. Punk was never peaceful..."

After breaking his arm badly in a car accident, Keith found himself in hospital whilst Griff – who had played drums at the very first Frames gig – stood in for him at the Aberystwyth University Battle of The Bands, organised by the Welsh Anti-Nuclear Alliance. Amongst the judges was none other than Nick Turner of Hawkwind. P.F.S. won, and were invited to record the track 'Nuclear Free Zone', a menacing mid-tempo stomper not dissimilar to Anti Pasti, at Berkshire Studios, for inclusion on a CND benefit album, which never materialised after the label went bust.

Deciding to keep Griff in the band, Keith became the band's main vocalist, and as a four-piece, with 'Getcha Rox Off' getting some regular airplay on John Peel, P.F.S. toured the UK extensively, notching up over 200 shows during the rest of 1982 and '83. Unfortunately not all of them were without incident, with a staunch fan of the band actually being killed after a gig in Whitland.

"That was tragic. He was stabbed in some sort of argument in the train station outside the venue. A few people were arrested for murder that night, but I think it was all dusted over as an accident. He was a big P.F.S. fan, it was very sad. As for what really happened? God only knows, but he died from a stab wound to the heart.

"Yes, I felt responsible because had we not played there he would not have died. I often wonder about things like that. Our actions can lead to all sorts of shit, and there was quite a lot of fighting no matter where we played. Especially when we played with Anti Pasti in Haverfordwest. 600 turned up and there was a huge fight between bikers and punks. All the young punks getting kicked all over the place but giving it the big one back too. We were kids taking on men and fighting for our lives! The same happened when we played with Chron Gen as well... yet more madness, mayhem and confusion! I suppose this piece makes us sound a bit troublesome, but this is what happened, and we ain't Russians so history can't be changed to suit!"

Rob and Tim eventually left ("They were getting edgy") during Christmas 1983, to be replaced by new guitarist, Mark Bozier from Wheathampstead, Hampshire (formerly with Illegal 15 and Honey Bane), and new bassist Steve Parkin, who the band met in a chip shop in Aberaeron.

"He was still at school!" laughs Keith. "He left immediately and ditched his exams to join the band!"

March 1984 saw the release of P.F.S.'s debut single, 'I'm Good Enough For Me' (backed by 'Sabotage The Classes' and 'Fur Queue'), on Lampeter-based Solar Sound Records. Recorded at Llanrhystud, Cardiganshire, and produced by Andrew Hawkey, it sold over 8,000 copies and even reached No. 1 in Sounds' magazine's Welsh Punk Chart.

"It's not brilliant in my opinion, but everyone who writes to us now loves it, especially the

Americans. It was 'GBH influenced', so I'm told. Odd that we were playing this stuff before anyone had heard of GBH! Who I must add were and are a bloody fine band, that admittedly influenced us thereafter. We should have gone with No Future, at least we would've had more sales; everyone bought all the stuff on that label. But it sold well enough regardless..."

A 32-date UK tour was undertaken in support of the single, that took the band from Penzance to Glasgow and back again. There were also additional shows supporting The Varukers, GBH, The Exploited, The UK Subs and even mainstream rockabillies King Kurt!

"Where do you start?" chuckles Keith, when pushed for some live highlights. "Touring with The UK Subs... the rucking... Charlie (Harper, Subs frontman) used to shit in a plastic bag and whack it round your head when you were sleeping! He was living with a young girl band at the time, Debar they were called, from South London. We often crashed there when playing London. Wattie was a top bloke, really helpful, and those Exploited gigs were hectic as fuck. We hated Nazis and the skinheads that were into that used to end up rucking with us... God knows how we didn't all end up dead!

"We were skint and on the road 24/7. All over the place – name a town and we played it... sometimes in front of 50 people, sometimes in front of 600 plus. We even played Ronnie Scott's Jazz Club in Soho with Splodge and The Urban Dogs. The 100 Club was a great venue too; we did that with The Exploited, and also with GBH on a number of occasions. Lemmy (Motörhead bassist/vocalist) came to see us at Dingwalls in London and announced that we were 'Fucking noisy on the old ears'! I bought him a pint of vodka for that; he downed it and staggered off into the night. Jimmy Pursey came to see us at The Old Queens Head in Stockwell; I loved Sham 69, but he didn't like the (in his words) 'Undercurrent of violence that punk gigs stood for'. And that coming from Sham 69! But he came along, checked us out and had the decency to have a beer and a chat."

In 1985, P.F.S. spent three months recording the 'Hand Of The Rider' album at Solar Sound Studios in Lampeter. Produced by Andrew Hawkey again and originally planned as just a 12" for Solar, the record ended up as a sixteen-track album on Dunk from Riot Squad's label Rot, after the band bought the master tapes from Solar following disagreements over the mix. It went on to sell over ten thousand copies, albeit through several unofficial bootlegs by unscrupulous labels both in the US (badly pressed by a Seattle label in 1987) and Australia (where it appeared in 1989 on blue vinyl). As well as the omnipresent 'Getcha Rox Off', the album contained such instant punk classics as 'My Mate Sulphate' and 'Old Soldiers Never Die', an in-your-face thrasher that builds to a climactic and powerful chant of 'Old soldiers never die... only the young ones!'

"As before!" says Keith of the manic bout of touring they undertook to promote the album. "Just a constant day and night thrash around the country. We played with King Kurt again on that tour too; they were off their heads, and we got on very well. I loved their madness. I remember we played in Wales and some girl claimed to have been raped on the stage when they played. More police, more questions, more arrests. It was bollocks, mind you, she was pissed and off her head. Raped? She was so ugly you wouldn't have even hit her to improve her looks. Sad cow!"

However, in 1987, following an appearance the previous year on Rot's 'A Kick Up The Arse, Volume One' compilation with the tracks 'White Lite' and 'My Mate Sulphate', P.F.S. split up. They played farewell shows in Haverfordwest and at the 100 Club in London, supported by The Varukers.

"I'd just had enough," reveals Keith. "So had Griff. Mark was a complete fuck-up due to drugs, he had no sense of responsibility when we played, and Steve wanted 'to go abroad'... he ended up in Newquay, Wales! Griff went to India, and I joined the RAF – honest! And now I'm a trainer for the council. It was just time to move on. Had we had any sense we would have persevered and been the new Manics! Ah, but that's life…"

As with so many other bands in this book though, that wasn't the end of the story, not by a long chalk. Soon after the band's demise, Keith and Rob, along with local Haverfordwest DJ Anthony Laugharne, recorded a benefit single comprising three cover versions ('With A Little Help From My Friends', 'New England' and 'Entertainment USA') and released it on P.F.S. Records, with all proceeds going to charity. Michael Jackson, who owns the rights to all The Beatles' material, refused the band permission to release 'With A Little Help…', and the record made the front pages of several tabloids, but despite the publicity, it flopped. Never really intended as a 'proper' P.F.S. release, it remains an interesting curio.

"That single is mad, not hardcore punk at all…more like some '77 punk fuck-up. Simon Bates even played it on Radio One. The DJ who features on it is dead now; he died in 1989, from muscular dystrophy. It was for him really; it made his life complete being on a record. He died a happy chappy. We used the name P.F.S. and released it on P.F.S. records to get more sales; I don't know what it sold… maybe 2000? But that wasn't the point, we did it for Anthony."

More tragedy followed when guitarist Mark Bozier died in September 1990, aged 26, of a heart attack.

In 2000, Picture Frame Seduction reunited for a 'one-off' gig at The Waterfront in Haverfordwest. The show was recorded for posterity, and eventually released in 2003 as the album 'What's That Hardcore Noise?' by Retch Records. A great little snapshot of an energetic punk band thoroughly enjoying themselves onstage, it even included three new studio tracks recorded by the band, newly reformed with Steve Arthur on bass. With a comprehensive retrospective CD slated on LA label, Grand Theft Audio, and yet more gigs being lined up, it would appear that the Hand of P.F.S. does indeed ride once again.

"Whatever happens, we were there, and we're not afraid to be there today," says Keith. "We know you only get one chance, and we are taking it. We can still pull a huge audience in Wales, especially in the West. People in the punk scene now should realise the hardship we all went through; we took real casualties, real life deaths, as a result of P.F.S. Talk of drive-bys and death in rap songs for spoilt kids making stupid hand gestures makes me laugh, they know fuck all. They are pretenders living a daydream whilst mummy makes their tea. I think we contributed reality; the dream for us was doing it, and not being afraid to get out there and stand up. We took Johnny Rotten's words at face value when he told us to get off our arses! Some fanzines even called us 'The Welsh Pistols', that is either insulting or stupid. We were P.F.S. and still are, people can remember us how they want. That is if they have a mind to remember at all…"

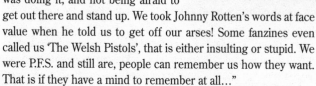

Keith Haynes, vocalist with underrated Welsh punkers, Picture Frame Seduction

SELECT DISCOGRAPHY:
7"s:
'I'm Good Enough For Me' (Solar Sound, 1984)

LPs:
'Hand Of The Rider' (Rot, 1985)
'What's That Hardcore Noise?' (Retch, 2003) – live CD

AT A GLANCE:

The imminent Grand Theft Audio CD looks set to be the definitive P.F.S release, featuring as it does the single, the first album, various unreleased live tracks and even the 1980 demo. The band have also recently reissued that first album themselves, on P.F.S Records, as a limited vinyl run with a new sleeve.

SOLDIER DOLLS

D espite two very strong singles, Soldier Dolls remain one of the more obscure of the Welsh punk bands from the early Eighties, probably because they only played outside of Wales once – and that was their final show! Formed in Cardiff in 1981 (after a short period under the unfortunate moniker of Animation), they played their first gig in September of 1982 – a show they actually gatecrashed rather than be invited to play. This seemed something of a trademark for the band, seeing as decent gigs were few and far between at the time.

"None of us could play a note... and I really mean that, we couldn't even tune our guitars," laughs Fester, recalling those pre-Soldier Dolls endeavours. "We didn't have a drum kit either, and both Evo and I wanted to be the drummer, so we had a pact... whoever got their drums first would be the drummer and the other the singer! Thank God he got his kit first (mine came a few months later), so I ended up singing; he's a fantastic drummer."

The original line-up of Andrew 'Fester' Mae – vocals, Dave 'DKA' Alderman – guitar, 'Slow' Bob Humphries – bass, and Dave 'Evo' Evans – drums, recorded two tapes, the 'Ten Track Sampler' and the 'From The Cradle To The Grave' demos, and it was apparent even from these earliest studio efforts that Soldier Dolls had a lot of potential.

"That original line up was, in my opinion at least, twenty years ahead of its time," reckons Fester. "The music was a mix of hardcore, metal, and pure punk... which seems to be much more popular now than it was back then. The bass player and drummer were really into heavy metal, which helped give the band quite a different sound."

"Musically we were much faster than a lot of other bands, before it was 'trendy' to play so fast," adds DKA. "And we had a big Yank influence as well, especially on my part as the guitar player. We even had a sense of humour... when most people were turning into po-faced fuckers!

"I actually probably prefer that earlier 'Mark 1' period," he admits, with the benefit of hindsight. "It was tighter – maybe more bombastic – and was when we really captured the true spirit of the band. We probably took ourselves too seriously afterwards..."

Soon after the second tape was in the can, Evo and Bob left for musical pastures anew, taking with them much of the metallic edge enjoyed by the band's first incarnation. They were replaced by – respectively – Matt 'Morph' Gray (who eventually ended up playing guitar in The Darling Buds!) and Jamie Richards.

This line-up was the one that appeared on the band's two subsequent EPs and at the majority of the shows they played.

"Another reason why Evo and Bob quit," explains Fester, "was that everywhere we seemed to play, trouble seemed to follow. The skinhead movement was picking up pace and violence came with it, like hand in glove. At one gig some guy in the crowd was spitting at my then-girlfriend. I didn't like it and I jumped off stage and gave him a slap. I thought at the time it was quite justified; however, he was 'in' with all the skins and that was the beginning of the end for tranquillity at our gigs."

"Those gigs were disorganised, violent, rowdy affairs," agrees DKA. "We played to anyone and everyone who would listen: young kids, punks, skins, whoever. I remember being 100% into playing every show possible; logistics and monetary matters weren't a concern back then – we just got up, got stuck in and sweated our balls off for very little reward. Big deal!"

In 1983, Soldier Dolls self-released their debut EP, 'What Do They Know?', on their very own Scream Records. A three-song affair, featuring the tracks 'Gotham City Is Dead' and 'Be Like You' alongside the anthemic title track, it showcased the band's high-speed gruff-vocal approach to decent effect, but they weren't particularly happy with how it turned out and only bothered with a bare minimum of promotion.

Later that year, they recorded their second EP, which was unleashed by Scream late in '84. Partially funded this time around by Revolver/Cartel, who were handling distribution duties, 'A Taste Of Blood' was to be the band's defining moment, and was pressed on an appropriately garish red wax. Their first release to be blessed with a solid, thick sound, all four tracks tore along with a vengeance, but it was on 'Iron Curtain' that Soldier Dolls found an intensity so urgent it was breathtaking.

After hitting such a peak, the only way was down, and the band slowly disintegrated.

"That second line-up, the one on the records, went fairly gradually," confirms Fester. "I think that Jamie, the bass player, really wanted to play guitar; he just got tired of playing bass. So we became a three-piece and I played bass. By that time I was writing all the songs, and I was trying to get a more commercial feel happening. DKA and Morph didn't like the way it was going, so, after playing in Bristol with The Folk Devils, we called it a day. That was late 1985. We all did other things later but for me it was never the same..."

In fact, DKA started up Slowjam with a character named Darren D. (and was actually joined later on by Morph) whilst Fester and Jamie played together in Highway 4, but neither band hit quite the same spot as the raw, youthful angst they had **Soldier Dolls** exorcised whilst in Soldier Dolls. **L-R: DKA, Fester, Jamie, Morph**

Incidentally, all the ex-members now reside abroad, having emigrated to the sunnier climes of Spain and France – and in the case of Fester, Canada – during recent years. DKA, now based in Paris, is currently part of the Warehouse 99 Project, alongside fellow like-minded noise conspirator Herve Marche, whose highly energised and innovative 2003 self-titled CD for Kick & Rush/Chronowax doesn't sound dissimilar to an industrial version of The Stranglers.

DISCOGRAPHY:
7"s:
'What Do They Know?' (Scream, 1983)
'A Taste Of Blood' (Scream, 1984)

AT A GLANCE:
The band have self-released a few CDR collections, but they were never officially distributed and are hence extremely hard to find.

FOREIGN LEGION

T ucked away up in the Welsh Valleys, Merthyr Tydfil's Foreign Legion have survived many ups and downs to become one of the few traditional punk bands remaining in Wales today, even recording their most recent album with punk legend Mick Jones from The Clash. However, when they first got together in 1980, they were originally known as Dead On Arrival, a name they kept until early 1984 when they became aware of the Canadian hardcore band also called D.O.A.

The embryonic line-up was Marcus Howells (previously with Society) – vocals, David Truskie-Thomas – guitar, Alan Powell – bass, and Nigel Clevor – drums.

"It's all really strange looking back; when you were younger it seems you had time for everything, when you get older you don't have time for anything!" reflects Marcus. "We were definitely influenced by our area, we were a product of our environment. All the Merthyr punks, skins and rude boys used to hang out outside Phoenix Records on the Brecon Road area of Merthyr. We all used to check

Foreign Legion, in 1983, when they were still known as D.O.A. L–R: David Truskie–Thomas, Nigel Clevor, Marcus Howells, Alan Powell
(with 'Papa Skin', the band's roadie on the floor, looking up...)

out the new albums by The Clash, the Pistols, The Damned etc. All we wanted to do was form a band.

"Nigel was a very good schoolboy boxer; he saved up all his paper round money to buy his first drum kit. Alan was always up hours before any of the rest of us; he was a member of the Welsh swimming team."

The band's first show was in front of a capacity local crowd at Aberfan Community Centre, and they quietly continued to build a strong following in South Wales until they landed their first big support slot, opening for The Partisans at Trefachen Community Centre.

Their first show outside of Wales was at the Leigh Park Community Centre in Portsmouth, where they played with Acid Attack and Four Minute Warning. Both bands would later join D.O.A. for the 'On The Streets' compilation, which came out through Sane Records (based in North Wales) in summer 1983.

"But the best D.O.A. gig we played was when we played in Swansea Marina, November 1983, supporting UK Subs and The Fits; the place was packed and we went down very well," says Marcus, before adding with a chuckle. "And the worst gig we did was December 1982, at our local church hall. Four support bands had played before us, and we were only into our third song when my bloody H&H PA top packed up, and that was the end of that gig!"

The band recorded their first demo in October 1982, at Tonypandy 4-track studios in Rhondda. Seven songs were recorded; two ('Child Molester' and 'Zyklon B') found their way onto the aforementioned Sane compilation, whilst 'Perfect Society' eventually materialised on Captain Oi!'s 'Oi The Demos' compilation CD in 1989. It's a little rough around the edges to say the least, but there are some decent tunes struggling to get free from the mess, and the bass playing is especially competent.

"Looking back, I wish we had spent more time recording and mixing, but that's the way it is, I guess," sighs Marcus. "Back then we were just excited to get our first demo out on the streets. Roman Jugg from The Damned even bought a copy… but he wouldn't buy the tea for us at the local café!"

In January 1984, Nigel Clevor (who tragically died in 1997) left, to be replaced by Michael Wilding, and in March of that year, as mentioned earlier, they changed their name to Foreign Legion. Three months later and they were playing their first London show, supporting the UK Subs at The 100 Club. They had something of a residency there, appearing a further four times, supporting The Adicts twice, Broken Bones and The Angelic Upstarts.

"What we used to do was write letters out to all the bigger bands and just ask if they ever wanted a support band; we got a lot of great gigs like that. Vice Squad in Hereford, 999 in Cardiff…"

Drummer Michael was soon replaced by Patrick McDermott, but in February 1985, Foreign Legion underwent a major line-up change, leaving Marcus as the only surviving original member, being joined by Helen James on bass, Llyn Murphy on guitar and Paul March on drums.

"That was all because of musical differences," says Marcus of the reshuffle. "David wanted to play stuff like Hanoi Rocks, whilst we wanted to keep the punk sound going."

With a renewed enthusiasm, the band recorded four songs at Studio Cardiff, including the powerful 'Message From Nowhere', which they released themselves on their own Rent-A-Racket label as the 'Trench Line' EP in early 1986. It was distributed by Revolver, and helped their profile immensely, so much so that they played their first show abroad in July of that year, at The Old Warehouse, just outside Le Havre in France, with Pavillone 13 and Burning Ambitions.

Llyn was replaced by Julie on guitar, before the band returned to France for a huge show with Berurier Noir and the Babylon Fighters at the Elysées Montmartre Theatre. Soon after, there were yet more line-up changes, with Andrew Heggy joining on second guitar, only to move to bass when Steven Thomas replaced Julie.

This line-up played several high profile supports, one to Joe Strummer and one to The Alarm, both at their local Dollars nightclub, before splitting in 1988.

"That was one of our favourite gigs in the Eighties, when we supported Joe Strummer in South Wales. We had a great sound, there was a great crowd, and it was brilliant to do it because we are all such big Clash fans. It was a very sad loss for the punk rock world when Joe passed away.

"We split in 1988, because two members just wanted to play rock stuff – and besides, Andy had just had enough."

Marcus tried to keep the band going, recruiting Peter Giles on guitar, and the duo recorded their enjoyable 1989 'Surf City' single for German label, Schlawiner. Ben Stansfield was brought in on drums, and Mark 'Jolly' Williams on bass, and more gigs were undertaken, including shows in France and Switzerland with French band, Kurt. This line-up recorded the 12-track 1990 LP, 'Welcome To Fort Zinderneuf', for Link Records, but eventually split in 1992 because of work and family pressures, playing their 'final show' in Swansea during August of that year.

In November 1999, Foreign Legion reformed with a vengeance. Unlike some reformed bands that are a shadow of their former glories, this reunion was more than justified as the band have not only been far more prolific than they ever were in the Eighties, but their new material is so mature and tuneful as to put the 'old' Foreign Legion to shame. The new line-up of Marcus on vocals, Andrew Heggy on bass, Jolly on guitar and Ben Stansfield on drums released no less than three singles during 2000, and a split LP, 'Cry Of The Legion', with Major Accident for Austrian label, DSS, early 2001. They promoted the split release by touring the US East Coast with Major Accident in February 2001, even hitting the legendary NYC club, CBGB, for a show with Urban Riot, A.P.A. and the Templars. The band were back over to the USA that summer as well, for the Promote Chaos festival in Atlanta, appearing alongside such punk luminaries as The Anti-Nowhere League and The Test Tube Babies.

Upon their return, Frank Busani replaced Jolly on guitar, and the band began work on their excellent 'What Goes Around Comes Around' album, which appeared courtesy of DSS, and was produced by none other than Mick Jones of The Clash. The album is a scintillating fusion of simplicity, melody and passion, that more than stands up to repeated listens.

"I met Mick Jones eight years back at a QPR football match, and eventually gave him copies of our EPs in 2000," reveals Marcus. "A week later, I got a call from him, and he said he liked our stuff. He asked for some live video footage for him to make us a promo video, and he edited three tracks, 'Jump', 'Wake Up' and 'Where's Johnny?' After we did the video, we asked him if he wanted to produce our new album – and he did! We're all over the moon with the work Mick did on it, and we are all so pleased to have worked with him! We had some great days in his studio.

"I would say that, be it old or new Foreign Legion, we've always been 100% into it at all times, and it shows. It's a similar vibe now as it was back when we started;

Foreign Legion, May 2002, Signal Studios, Acton L-R: Frank, Andy, Robin (a member of producer Mick Jones' new band, Carbon/Silicon), Stan (sitting), Marcus, and Mick Jones himself we're all totally committed and age has not changed us or what we want to achieve. We are all so pleased with what we have done in Foreign Legion these last twenty-five years… here's to the next twenty-five! Yes please!"

SELECT DISCOGRAPHY:
7"s:
'Trench Line' EP (Rent-A-Racket, 1986)
'Surf City' EP (Schlawiner, 1989)
'The Years Gone By' (Upstart Productions, 2000)
'Punk Rock Jukebox' (DSS, 2000)
'We Don't Care About Rock'n'Roll ' (Dirty Faces, 2000) – split with District

LPs:
'Welcome To Fort Zinderneuf' (Link, 1990) – later licensed to Venture Records
'Cry Of The Legion' (DSS, 2001) – split with Major Accident
'What Goes Around Comes Around' (DSS, 2002)

AT A GLANCE:
The band have been included on many retrospective compilation CDs, not least of all 'Oi: The Rarities, Volume 2' and 'Pop Oi' (both on Captain Oi! Records), but the best place to experience Foreign Legion would be their latest album, 'What Goes Around Comes Around', a great set of very well-presented punk tunes.

E lsewhere, Impact from Cwmbran self-released their own 7", 'Punk Christmas', and appeared on No Future's 'A Country Fit For Heroes' Volume 2, whilst The Pseudo-Sadists from Swansea appeared on the first instalment of the same compilation with 'Power Schemes'. Although they never released anything officially, Death Patrol were probably the most popular and well-respected Newport punk band, whose guitarist Bryn went on to play with both The Abs and Dr. Bison. Many other noteworthy bands emerged from the demise of the second wave of Welsh punk in the latter half of the Eighties. The politically-charged Classified Protest from Blainau later became the excellent Rectify, who enjoyed great success in Europe, and The Cowboy Killers from Newport were one of the most rabid live bands to ever set foot on a stage. Members of Shrapnel from Neath would later show up in Stockwell and Ten Benson, whilst in the Nineties Four Letter Word from Cardiff even signed to US label BYO and undertook lengthy tours Stateside to promote their criminally underrated albums. And the future of fiery Welsh punk looks safe in the hands of In The Shit who seem to get more intense with each release.

CHAPTER TEN

NORTHERN IRELAND

THE DEFECTS

I solated as it was, the Northern Irish scene developed at its own leisurely pace, a microcosm of the one on the mainland, and trailing it by several years. Whereas the rest of the UK had literally hundreds of bands, a new release seemingly every week during the fertile early Eighties, Northern Ireland struggled to keep up, with only The Outcasts and The Defects being prolific during the period this book is aimed at.

And with its mainstream community split in two by pedantic traditions, it offered up a very different atmosphere to the rest of the UK within which punk could grow. Also, whereas the sheer number of acts on the mainland led inevitably to some inter-band skullduggery as everyone competed for those coveted recording deals, it seems the Irish scene was much closer-knit, out of necessity.

"Northern Ireland was a unique creature," acknowledges Sean O'Neill, co-author (with Guy Trelford) of It Makes You Want To Spit! The Definitive Guide To Punk In Ulster. "It had been starved of visiting live acts and had absolutely no music industry or infrastructure. As a consequence, punk arrived here later than the rest of the UK. Rudi, The Outcasts, Stiff Little Fingers and The Undertones didn't release their debut 45s until the first half of 1978.

"In retrospect, punk provided a third tradition, a new religion, an alternative way of life. During the darkest days of the Troubles, punk brought together kids from both religions to venues where the most important thing was that you were a punk, not which side of the political divide you were born into. Something none of us really thought about at the time.

"The early Eighties Ulster punk scene was set against a backdrop of spiralling troubles, curfews, home-made mortars, car bombs, Maze hunger strikes, security checks as you entered the city centre, Ian Paisley and his 'third force' up mountains in the middle of the night and worst of all… show bands in goddamn flares! Hippies in zips we were not. Northern Ireland needed punk and it became one of the last strongholds in the UK."

"All the punks got on really well," agrees Ian Murdock, vocalist with The Defects. "Both Protestants and Catholics, the only real religion was punk. There was never any rivalry between us and any of the other bands either; both The Outcasts and Rudi let us support them many times. We all hung about together, and musically we just wrote about what we saw… and coming from Belfast we obviously saw different things than what you would see on the mainland."

And seeing as The Outcasts had at least one of their feet firmly planted in the original '77/'78 wave of punk rock, it's safe to say that The Defects were probably the biggest and best of the purely second wave Irish punk bands. They paved the way for the likes of Re'bel, Rabies, Subculture and Stalag 17 (who released a split 12" with Toxic Waste, 'The Truth Will Be Heard', on Mortarhate), and during their brief existence, they released some superb records that married perfectly the sneering melodies of the classic early punk bands with the aggressive intensity of the harder bands that followed.

"I got into punk rock when I was twelve or thirteen, around 1977 or '78," reveals vocalist, Ian 'Buck' Murdock. "The Sex Pistols were the main thing that drew me to the scene. I read about them in all the papers and I loved their 'Fuck off' attitude towards authority; as far as I was concerned, they spoke for my generation."

The band was formed in 1979 in east Belfast, by four friends who shared a mutual interest in punk ("All we did was listen to punk music and look at pictures in magazines," he laughs). As well as Buck on vocals, there was Glenn Kingsmore on drums, Marcus 'Dukie' Duke on guitar, and Gregg Fenton on bass... although Gregg was soon replaced by Jeff Gilmore, who himself was superseded by Gary Smith, the bassist who actually played on all the band's subsequent recordings. Only Jeff had any previous musical experience, having played in a 'family band' called Country Rock.

"We all learnt from each other by just listening to records and learning our favourite songs ... mainly by The Clash," remembers Buck. "The Defects first got together after The Clash played in the Ulster Hall, which was probably 1979. I myself wasn't there, but the rest of the band were, and, needless to say, The Clash blew them away. The first songs The Defects ever learnt were all off the first Clash album.

"We practised in my bedroom at my parents' house! They were not that bothered really... in fact, they were very supportive; my dad even used to take us to gigs in his van!

The Defects L–R: Buck, Gary, Glen
(Pic: Kim Aldis)

Locally we were influenced by Rudi and The Outcasts. I went to see these two bands as much as I possibly could; they played a lot in the Pound Club and the Harp Bar in the late Seventies and early Eighties. We were also very influenced by almost all the national punk bands around at that time."

The Defects made their live debut at the Clonduff Community Centre in east Belfast in August 1979 supporting another local band called Acme. It was Buck's first time ever on a stage, and he dealt with it the way so many other young punk musicians have dealt with it since:

"I drank a bottle of Olde English cider to calm the nerves… but it didn't work as I puked up at the side of the stage! I know that we played 'Anarchy In The UK', 'Janie Jones', and 'White Riot', but I can't remember much else! In fact, our next five or six gigs were also in Clonduff Community Centre."

The Defects were soon supporting their mentors Rudi and The Outcasts, and making a name for themselves around Belfast ("We were young and new," reckons Buck when asked what he thinks they bought that was fresh to the scene). In 1981, after their first demo had failed to secure them a recording deal, they decided to start their own label, Casualty Records, and release their own single, "Because no one else would. We borrowed a thousand quid off my

parents and we recorded the songs at Down Town Radio Studios… the session only lasted four hours and I crashed the van on the way there!"

The resulting EP was a genuine rough diamond, featuring three great tracks – 'Dance ('Til You Drop)', 'Guilty Conscience' and 'Brutality' – that both belied and benefited from the band's youthful inexperience. As well as the euphoric hooks of the A-side, 'Brutality' was a scathing attack on the heavy-handed tactics of the Royal Ulster Constabulary, ending with a vehement chant of 'SS RUC'!

"The cops picked on everybody, it didn't matter whether you were a punk or not," reckons Buck. "Having said that, when they found out about 'Brutality', they hassled us constantly. We were stopped and searched nearly everyday by the army and the police; we had a car with 'Defects Staff Car' on the windscreen, so we

Buck of The Defects, live at The Pound, Belfast, 1980

were very easy to spot! Things have changed a bit now, and I have changed a little also, with age, but I still don't think the police can be trusted not to give you a beating or worse."

"The Defects arrived on the Belfast punk scene like a breath of fresh air," remembers Sean O'Neill. "Their live sound was raw and raucous and they rejuvenated a stagnant local scene, which had been showing signs of burn-out. Prior to their vinyl debut they had already built up a sizable local following and had played some storming gigs around Belfast, including now legendary shows at the Pound. Invariably these gigs involved Buck swinging from the rafters, lots of chaos and their set finishing with their 'signature tune', 'Brutality'. Chants of 'SS RUC' bellowed from the sweaty club situated just on the periphery of Musgrave Street Constabulary. Ironically, the venue has since been demolished and is part of that very same police station!"

The single sold well – two thousand copies, despite being only available in Ireland – and garnered The Defects many positive reviews, eventually bringing them to the attention of Carol Clerk from the Melody Maker music paper, herself a native of Northern Ireland but by then residing in London.

"The first time I ever heard of The Defects was the first time I actually saw them," explains Carol. "They were milling around in a pub called the Queen's Inn with a bunch of mates. I was living in London by then, working for Melody Maker, but I used to come home to Belfast a couple of times a year.

"The Queen's Inn was the only pub in my area; I used to meet up with old friends there and it was always pretty quiet. So when I walked into the lounge during New Year of 1982 and found the place crowded with punk rockers, it was a huge surprise, very exciting. I'd been working with many of the English punk bands since joining Melody Maker two years earlier, and I was naturally intrigued by these young guys with 'The Defects' on the back of their studded leather jackets. I wanted to know why they had suddenly turned the Queen's Inn into a hotbed of punky monkey business!

"Anyway, we all got talking, and Buck, Glenn, Gary and Dukie – The Defects – invited me to come and see a gig they were playing a few nights later. It was at Orangefield School on January 14th 1982; they were supporting The Outcasts. They had this massive enthusiasm, which was very refreshing. They were obviously fans as well as musicians and since they were unsigned, free agents working in Northern Ireland, they were untainted by the sort of peer pressure, label expectation and business anxiety that plagued many of the English bands. The fact that they were so young was also important. They looked great, really fresh and vital, and because they were playing primarily for themselves and their coterie of fans, it was all coming straight from the hip. No airs and graces, no managers or company people telling them how it should sound. They were just themselves, and that was a great thing to experience. Obviously, they were really raw and aggressive and spontaneous, but they liked to chuck in the odd chant… and, crucially, they were poppy too. There's nothing like a good tune, or a nagging hook, no matter what sort of music you're into!"

Carol returned to London straight after and not only wrote a glowing feature about the band for Melody Maker, but also told John Curd all about them. John was the manager of Buck's favourite band, The Anti-Nowhere League, and he ran the Chelsea-based WXYZ Records.

"After that, there was a little bit of to-ing and fro-ing," says Carol, picking up the story. "I think Buck and Glenn came over first on a fact-finding mission… but it all quickly resulted in The Defects signing to WXYZ and moving to London, where they stayed for a couple of years. I saw them quite often, obviously at their own shows, but Buck in particular became a regular visitor to the Melody Maker pub, The Oporto, and he was up for any gigs or 'ligs' that we were going to on whatever evening he should happen to turn up.

"There were all sorts of adventures. The punk bands coming in and out of London were very friendly with one another, and so wherever you went, you would bump into people from The Damned or the UK Subs or The Exploited or the League or Chelsea – the list is endless! And Buck and the other Defects were soon assimilated into the scene. They were really popular with the other groups because they were so loveably down-to-earth… so 'Belfast'. I never heard a bad word said about them by anybody!"

With the backing of a decent label, The Defects were soon playing their first London show, at the 100 Club supporting Chelsea ("To be honest, I was in awe of the whole thing," admits Buck), and then they were on the road with The Anti-Nowhere League for their infamous 'So What?' tour.

"All the gigs on that tour were good," enthuses Buck. "The best was probably Glasgow Apollo… and the worst was Leicester De Montfort Hall – the skinheads who came started a major riot! As for memorable stories… there's so many of them. The ANWL giving Gary the bumps for his birthday on the hard shoulder of the M1, or the vice squad busting into our hotel in Manchester looking for two teenage female runaways just as Winston from The League was coming down the stairs in stockings and suspenders! Oh, and getting mistaken for super-group The Police… (Police drummer) Stewart Copeland was travelling with us 'cos he was filming the tour, and when he got out of the bus first, a crowd gathered, waiting for Sting… but they were cruelly disappointed when four smelly Belfast punks jumped out instead!

"Animal from The League was driving one night when he missed the turn-off; he did a U-turn on the motorway… we thought we were going the right direction on the inside lane, but we were actually going the wrong direction in the outside lane! We only found out when all the lorries coming the other way started flashing at us… we very nearly died a rock'n'roll death!"

To coincide with the tour, WXYZ released the 'Survival' single, in May 1982; a brooding observation on the cutthroat nature of modern materialism. A pounding tom signature underscores a repetitive simplistic riff, making for an almost tribal stomping epic, it was backed by a re-recorded 'Brutality', and spent twenty weeks in the Indies, reaching No. 8 following the success of the 'So What?' stint.

After the tour, The Defects relocated to London ("There was just nowhere to play in Ireland") and undertook more roadwork with their psychotic psychobilly label-mates The Meteors. The band then set about the recording of their one and only album, 'Defective Breakdown', at Jacobs Studios in Surrey; it was released in November of that year to great acclaim.

"We recorded it in this farmhouse in Surrey," recollects Buck. "'Down On The Farm' by the UK Subs was actually written about that place! Rick Wakeman was recording the World Cup music there at the same time, and I heard it morning, noon and night… it even kept us awake as we slept over his studio! So, to get him back, we raided his private bar, and on our last night we had a party. The Meteors were there; Paul Fenech chased the ducks round the yard with a machete! He was pissed on Rick's red wine.

"Given the chance again, I wouldn't have released it quite so soon; I would personally liked to have had another single out before the album. I would also have changed the cover as I never liked it that much. My favourite songs on it are '20th Century' and 'Metal Walls', and compared to other punk albums of its time, I still think it sounds good… but then again, I am biased! We recorded it all pretty much live, with a few overdubs on top; it took us about two weeks altogether."

Opening with a faster, punchier version of their 'Dance' single, and also containing a heavier re-recording of 'Survival', 'Defective Breakdown' is a fine collection of songs that tear along at a frantic pace without ever losing sight of the all-important catchy chorus that throbs indignantly at the heart of each track. Again it performed well, briefly cracking the Indie Top Ten, but, desperately looking for a way to cross his latest signings over to a wider audience, John Curd – by then operating as ID Records – persuaded The Defects to release a cover of Elvis Presley's 'Suspicious Minds' in January 1984.

"Elvis is supposed to be sacrosanct," laughs Carol Clerk. "But he had been dead for long enough that it was okay for other people to cover his songs… within reason! The Defects' cover of 'Suspicious Minds' was capricious, spirited and respectful, and I really liked it. Still do."

Sadly Carol is one of the few loyal fans of the band that does. Although a decent enough single in its own right, it was hardly prime Defects material, with most of their original fire having been all but extinguished by outside interference; it even saw producer Ray Shulman playing keyboards. And, released as it was, just as the second wave of punk was starting its inevitable decline, it sold considerably less than the preceding WXYZ releases.

"God only knows how we were talked into doing it," sighs Buck. "It was the last straw really. Our management just wanted us to get more commercial; I was told not to sing it 'too punky'! We weren't even big Elvis fans, but we had heard Gary Glitter doin' it and for some reason we liked it. It came as no surprise when our die-hard punk fans hated it though."

Thankfully the B-side featured two speedier tracks that were much more in keeping with the band's previous output, but unfortunately even they were hindered by the weedy radio-friendly sound; not enough guitar and too much reverb.

Feeling somewhat powerless and disillusioned with his diminishing control over the band's destiny, Buck left The Defects soon after the release of 'Suspicious Minds'. "Things had soured for quite a while before then though; we had no money, no food, and besides, the songs we were writing were crap. Someone, somewhere, along the way decided we were to move well away from punk... a move that I was not into at all. The band did one more gig supporting 999 without me, with our drummer Glenn singing... although I did rejoin to support The Clash in Belfast – the offer to play with them was just too much to turn down!

"They were dead on too; I spent most of the night in their dressing room. Paul Simonon had the biggest ghettoblaster I had ever seen... and lots of grass! I suppose the band split rather than replacing me because everybody just wanted to get home to Belfast... apart from Dukie, who stayed in London until 2001."

"To be honest, they left more of a gap when they moved to London, particularly in the lives

The Defects, L–R: Glenn, Buck, Dukie, Gary
(Pic: Kim Aldis)

of the fans and friends who had supported them from the outset," reflects Carol, when asked whether the band's demise left a yawning hole in the Belfast music underground. "The Ulster punk scene, like any other movement from Northern Ireland, had to accept that its bands must move to the mainland to achieve any measure of promotion and success. To have denied them that would have been to deny them a shot at a real career. The Defects took the chance, and any resentment would have been as petty as it was jealous and territorial.

"By the time they split, they had not been part of the Ulster punk scene as such for some time, which implies a simply parochial importance. Had they stayed together, by some miracle, I believe it's unlikely they would have gone on to realise their potential anyway. For various reasons, they had run out of steam. It's not my place to explain why but I can say that, apart from Dukie, who remained in London, the band members had individual reasons for wanting to pack it in. There was a certain homesickness and dissatisfaction which, in their various manifestations, were stronger than the group's desire for success. And when that kicked in, then no one was in a position to fulfil whatever potential they might once have had.

"The Defects did what they wanted to do. And when they didn't want to do it anymore, they split. I wish more people in their position would have the balls to call it a day!"

In 1996, Buck resurrected a one-off version of The Defects for a punk festival at the Bath Pavilion. Featuring his brother, Gary, on drums, and two other brothers, Stevie and Colin Boyd, on guitar and bass respectively, they rattled out a set that included several classic punk covers as well as Buck's favourite Defects material. The gig was actually filmed for posterity, and has since been released by Barn End Productions.

Buck now runs a rehearsal studio in Belfast, but still plays locally most weekends with his punk and ska covers band, Doghouse, and he remembers his time with The Defects fondly.

"We were one of the few bands around at the time, and everyone that came to see us always had a really good laugh. We were young, new and fresh; our music was fast and exciting… and there really weren't too many punks in Belfast that didn't have The Defects on the back of their studded jackets at some time or other."

SELECT DISCOGRAPHY:
7"s:
'Dance ('Til You Drop)' (Casualty, 1981)
'Survival' (WXYZ, 1982)
'Suspicious Minds' (ID 1984)

LPs:
'Defective Breakdown' (WXYZ, 1982)

AT A GLANCE:
The 1994 Captain Oi! CD reissue of the 'Defective Breakdown' album also features the eight additional tracks from the band's three singles, making it a virtually definitive Defects discography. With over twenty slices of powerful, tuneful punk, it's a must-have release for any fan of the genre.

THE OUTCASTS

P robably the second biggest punk band overall to hail from Northern Ireland (after Stiff Little Fingers, of course), The Outcasts, as mentioned earlier, formed in early 1977 and released their first single in 1978, so could hardly be strictly termed second wave. But as they were so influential, and much of their recorded output falls within the time constraints of this book anyway, no section on Northern Irish punk could be complete without them.

"During 1976 rumours of punk had been spreading from London," recalls vocalist/bassist Greg Cowan. "We had seen pictures of punks in the tabloids and stories about the Pistols were appearing in the N.M.E. I had a very limited taste in music at this time, namely Alice Cooper and David Bowie, but because of the Bowie connections I'd discovered bands like The Stooges and The Velvets. Getty (aka Colin Getgood), who would have been my best friend at the time, had discovered The New York Dolls and was always banging on about them. My brothers, Martin and Colin, were part of a fashion crowd that hung about clubs in Bangor calling themselves The Young Americans, a mixture of David Bowie's live look and Brian Ferry's 'GI eye patch' period. Getty and I were in a bedroom band that never actually played anywhere but gave us a basic idea about bass and guitar. Then 'Anarchy In The UK' came along and everything changed; it was the

first time we could put a sound to the name Punk.

"After we had torn up our clothes and cut our hair, me and Getty were asked to leave the band we were in but, seeing as we had two guitars, bass and a borrowed drum kit, Colin asked us to join his band. So our first line up was Colin on drums, Martin on rhythm guitar, Getty on lead guitar, me on bass, and a guy called Blair Hamilton doing vocals. Colin named us The Outcasts after being banned from five clubs in one week! Blair left us after a month when he went to live in London.

The Outcasts, 1980, L–R: Colin Cowan, Getty, Greg and Martin Cowan

"Our first gig was in May 1977, in the Lambs Lounge, east Belfast, where Stiff Little Fingers had had their live debut only the week before. To be honest, we weren't ready and must have made an awful bloody noise; we knew nothing about equipment and if Jake Burns (from SLF) hadn't helped us out we wouldn't have been able to play at all. We played about ten of our own songs and about six covers, by The Pistols, Clash, Damned and Ramones... but nobody recognised any of them anyway! There was a big crowd though and they were very forgiving. And because it was in a Loyalist area, at the end of the night the band were supposed to play the national anthem, but when we were told this, three of us bolted, leaving Getty alone on stage. He tried to play it on the guitar but because he was so shite, the regulars all thought he was taking the piss and pelted him with coins!"

Despite such a torrid introduction to live performance, The Outcasts persevered, gradually building themselves a strong and loyal local following. They soon came to the attention of small Irish label, It, who released May 1978's 'Frustration' single. Although hampered somewhat by clunky drumming and a thin production job, the single is a great snapshot of the band's early energy. Of the two B-side tracks, 'Don't Want To Be No Adult' and 'You're A Disease', the latter is the standout cut, boasting a fine, memorable chorus.

"Northern Ireland didn't have any live music scene to speak of so we created our own," says Greg, of the problems they overcame in the beginning. "It gave us a very independent view on things; we created our own gigs where there were none before. We would hire hotels as private parties and then play at them; we were always barred afterwards but by then it was too late!

"And, as a rule, we hated all the other local bands until we got to know them. We assumed we were the only punk band in Belfast and it came as a shock to find that there were others! There was a kind of cartoon violence between the rest and us; the first time we met members of Rudi was at a Runaways concert where we got thrown out for fighting each other. Martin in particular enjoyed terrorising other bands, but not too seriously. Most of our early gigs were a disaster – we couldn't really play and Colin would smash his drum kit up two or three times a night – but after the Harp started and we began touring Ireland, we slowly tightened up.

"The early punk scene in Belfast was more a fashion thing with people standing round looking cool, but after our first single started to get played on the radio we started to get our own following, a much harder crowd. To be a punk in Belfast wasn't easy; it didn't matter which side you were from, you fought your way out and fought your way back home each night. This led to a healthy 'us against the world' attitude for both band and audience."

And it was their fiery attitude that ultimately led to The Outcasts signing with Terri Hooley's seminal Good Vibrations label during the summer of 1978, the first fruit of this union being the 'Justa Nother Teenage Rebel' 7" in November of that year.

"Yes, Terri has always said he hated us musically but liked our attitude! He came to see us play with Rudi after hearing our first single, and offered to release our next record. We didn't actually ever sign to Good Vibrations; Terri never signed anybody as such, you just had to go along with his whims."

The 'Teenage Rebel' 7" (backed by 'Love Is For Sops') saw the band being played several times by John Peel on his popular Radio One show. Soon after its release The Outcasts also appeared, with the lazily anthemic 'The Cops Are Comin'', on a four-band double-7" Good Vibrations sampler entitled 'Battle Of The Bands', alongside Rudi, The Idiot and Spider.

In late 1979, a single, then the band's first album appeared, both entitled 'Self Conscious Over You'.

Featuring re-recorded versions of 'The Cops Are Comin'', 'Love Is For Sops' and 'You're A Disease', alongside a clutch of new songs, the flawed full-length debut showcased The Outcasts' penchant for strong melodies and simple, memorable arrangements, the spirit of first wave punk delivered with the snarling aggression of the second.

Irish punks, Rut, Spud and Trotsky (Pic: Seany Rotten)

"We always hated our first album," laughs Greg. "To be honest, we hated most of our recordings... everything came out sounding more 'pop' than we meant it to. I think 'Prince's Grew Up A Frog' must rate as one of the worst songs ever! And unfortunately it was the first song of ours that I heard played on the radio!"

Another Outcasts track, the measured but lethally effective 'Cyborg', was also featured on another Good Vibrations compilation 7", 1980's 'Room To Move', a joint venture with Energy Records from Southern Ireland, that also saw contributions from Shock Treatment, The Vipers and Big Self. It was to be the band's last release for the label.

"Terri threw us off Good Vibes because he couldn't stand the hassle anymore," admits Greg. "I always looked on the trouble that followed us around as cartoonish, but there was another side to it all. Because of the Troubles, Belfast used to close early back then, so there was a lot of house parties; any time we appeared there would be things broken, people getting beaten up and everybody knew Terri was our manager, so they would all descend on him with the bills etc. Things reached a head when Terri had a Good Vibes party and didn't invite us; we found out and some of his hippie friends got hurt, so Terri wrote us each a letter essentially sacking us."

Just prior to the release of their debut album, Greg suffered a serious road accident that not only set back the promotion of 'Self Conscious…' but also stopped his bass playing in its tracks.

"My car crash happened just before the first album release, and left me in traction for fourteen weeks, meaning that tours of both Ireland and England were scrubbed. It also meant that, because I had screws in my left arm and had to wear a caliper for months afterwards, Gordy Blair joined on bass."

Gordy had previously played with Rudi, and his appointment left Greg free to concentrate on his vocal delivery. Gordy wasn't the only new addition to the band in 1980 either – Raymond Falls, then a sixteen-year old schoolboy, joined as second drummer, bringing a whole new dimension of power to the band's already fierce rhythms.

"We added Raymond on drums because Colin was such a bad drummer, plus he was going out with Raymond's sister. We had all improved musically quite considerably at this stage, except Colin… not that this mattered too much, 'cos Colin was the heart and soul of the band, but it was nice to have a drummer who could play a proper drum roll!"

The new-look Outcasts made their recording debut with the moody, magnificent 'Magnum Force' single, which saw the light of day via their own GBH Records in 1981, and marked the band's coming of age stylistically. Both the A-side title track, and 'Gangland Warfare' on the flip, were superb, with Greg's voice really coming into its own, and the band locked tight behind him, surging and snapping dynamically forward. It was produced by their soon-to-be manager Ross Graham, whom they had met whilst recording the first album.

"John Davies who made 'Shell Shock Rock' (a documentary about the Northern Irish music scene) arrived in the studio whilst we were re-recording 'You're A Disease' for the 'Self Conscious…' album; we just thought he was an old hippie, so didn't take him seriously. Ross was working as his assistant and really took an interest in what we were recording. After Terri dumped us, we set up our own label, GBH, and asked Ross to produce 'Magnum Force', and later on, he took over the management side of things as well."

Soon after the single, in May 1981, The Outcasts did their first well-received John Peel session, during which they performed 'Gangland Warfare', 'The End Of The Rising Sun', 'Programme Love' and 'Machine Gun'.

"The first Peel session came at a brilliant time for us; we had just played a couple of London gigs and were about to head off for our first major tour of France. We drove along Oxford Street heading towards the BBC with the van doors open, screaming at passers-by. It was our first time in a proper studio, but Ross kept interfering, annoying the producer. At some stage Peel arrived, but none of us could think of anything to say so he just left…!"

During the summer of '81, the band changed the name of their label to Outcasts Only, and issued the four-track 'Programme Love' EP. As well as the title track, it included 'Beating And Screaming, Parts 1 And 2', and one of the band's hardest rocking numbers, 'Mania', which also appeared on the best-selling 'Punk And Disorderly' compilation on Anagram.

Spring 1982 saw The Outcasts released their thunderous cover version of The Glitter Band hit 'Angel Face', which ironically featured Greg glowering from the front cover looking anything but angelic! It was backed by a reworking of 'Gangland Warfare', and spent over two months in the Indies charts, peaking at No. 21. However, just when everything seemed to be going right for the band, tragedy struck and Colin Cowan died in a car crash just before the release of the new single.

"Colin's death was devastating;" sighs Greg. "He couldn't really drum but he was the core of the band. He started The Outcasts, he even gave the band its name, and before Ross came along, it was Colin that did all the day-to-day running of stuff and made most of the major decisions. On a more personal level, of course, he was the big brother I'd worshipped since a kid.

"We had a meeting in a park across the road from our parents' house – the band, Mickey Cassidy, Big Tommy, wee Chris and a big carryout. Because there had been such a big turn-out for the funeral, we decided to play a thank you gig at the Harp Bar, and everyone was so positive we decided to keep going."

So, now sadly a four piece, The Outcasts returned to the fray, bloodied but unbowed, with a second Peel session (featuring 'Winter', 'Magnum Force', 'Sex And Glory' and 'Frustration') and the 'Blood And Thunder' album for Abstract, which shot to No. 20 in the Indies just before Christmas 1982.

"We were actually on New Rose, a Parisian label," explains Greg. "But we were licensed to Anagram in England. 'Blood And Thunder' wasn't recorded as an album; it was just everything we had recorded with Ross. Looking back, it sounded better than 'Self Conscious', but we'd lost some of our spark; it's almost like we were trying to appeal to second wave punks instead of just being ourselves."

It was followed by one of their finest releases, 1983's 'Nowhere Left To Run', an atmospheric, doomy rocker that still has the power to send shivers down the spine even now, over twenty years later. The single came in both the 7" format (backed by 'The Running's Over, Time To Pray') and 12", boosted by an instrumental version of the title track and their cover version of 'Ruby'.

The band's next offering saw yet another subtle metamorphosis in style, but again, another convincing and enjoyable one. The 'Seven Deadly Sins' LP, released by New Rose in August 1984, added a distinctly psychobilly tinge to proceedings, so much so in fact that the title track was included on Anagram's pure psychobilly compilation 'Revenge Of The Killer Pussies'. It was also released as a single shortly after the LP appeared, backed by 'Swamp Fever', which managed a month in the Indies, creeping to No. 40.

Running out of creative steam, The Outcasts covered The Stooges' '1969' for their final single before splitting in early 1985.

"It was just time to go," says Greg. "To be honest, I wish we had split a year earlier then we did. When you first start out, you can't believe you're actually doing gigs, then you're releasing records, then touring, a bit of TV, it's all moving up… then when your record company dumps you, the tours dry up and your manager stops returning your calls, it all gets a bit sad.

"It's hard to think of any recordings of ours that I actually like; nothing ever turned out the way we hoped. At the beginning we couldn't play and then, when we could, most of our best songs were already over. But I'm still proud of us as a live band, especially in our later stages."

Greg, Martin and Getty stayed together as a band for a short time using the moniker Time To Pray, but even that folded by 1986. Ray Falls meanwhile joined the army.

In 2003, Greg formed a one-off 'Irish punk supergroup', for want of a better word, alongside members of Rudi and Stalag 17, to play at the book launch of It Makes You Want To Spit! which was part of the Belfast Festival. Their well-received set included half a dozen Outcasts songs.

"I would never reform The Outcasts, nor would any of the rest of the band, but I understand why other bands do get back together. Part of me thinks that when we were kids we were so dead against all the silly old fucks older than us that you kill something when you try and play it years later. But there is the nostalgia thing too, where it's great to go out and listen to all the old songs... plus I miss just being in a band.

"Still, I'm happy that we are remembered at all; we weren't doing things that we thought would be discussed twenty years later. I wish the records had been better, of course, but I still get a kick out of meeting people and being tied into a special time in their lives."

SELECT DISCOGRAPHY:
7"s:
'Frustration' (It, 1978)
'Justa Nother Teenage Rebel' (Good Vibrations, 1978)
'Self Conscious Over You' (Good Vibrations, 1979)
'Magnum Force' (GBH, 1981)
'Programme Love' (Outcasts Only, 1981)
'Angel Face' (Outcasts Only, 1982)
'Nowhere Left To Run' (Anagram, 1982)
'Seven Deadly Sins' (New Rose, 1984)
'1969' (New Rose, 1985)

12"s:
'Nowhere Left To Run' (Anagram, 1983)

LPs:
'Self Conscious Over You' (Good Vibrations, 1979)
'Blood And Thunder' (Abstract, 1982)
'Seven Deadly Sins' (New Rose, 1984) – Mini LP only

AT A GLANCE:
Anagram's 'The Outcasts: Punk Singles Collection' CD (1995) does exactly what the title suggests and collects all the band's singles onto one disc. It comes complete with artwork, liner notes by Mark Brennan and an exhaustive discography. Elsewhere, Captain Oi! have compiled both 'Blood And Thunder' and 'Seven Deadly Sins' onto one CD, and boosted it with several other latter-period single tracks. The CD also features cover art, a discography and several press cuttings.

So, what Northern Ireland lacked in quantity, they more than made up for in quality, and both The Defects and The Outcasts remain extremely influential in punk circles worldwide, having left behind a musical legacy that is still cherished by those that experienced it first-hand.

"When a group of us went to London in the early Eighties, we felt an immense sense of pride having The Outcasts and The Defects painted on our leather jackets," recalls Sean O'Neill fondly. "The same sense of pride we'd previously felt watching The Undertones and Stiff Little Fingers on 'Top Of The Pops'. I can recall our first memorable trip to London vividly. About eight of us caught the Larne to Stranraer ferry and then the overnight train from Scotland to London. On our arrival in Scotland we were singled out from the rest of the passengers by the cops and were subsequently quizzed by special branch officers, which unfortunately took an age and by the time we'd been allowed to proceed, every bloody seat on the train had been taken. We made our way through the train to the rear carriage where we found two completely empty cabins in the mail section. There was no lighting in this carriage, but we had a few candles with us and with the help of a few cases of beer, we made the best of it. We proceeded to occupy both cabins and got rotten drunk. I can recall having to physically restrain one of my mates who was so drunk that he decided he wanted to walk outside on the roof of the train!

"We eventually arrived in London early the next morning, totally wrecked from drinking copious amounts of booze all night. We staggered round to our mate's squat and crashed for a few hours. London was great; we quickly learnt how to bunk the Tubes, then met Peter And The Test Tube Babies down the Kings Road! Charlie Harper even dedicated a song to the Belfast punks the night we saw The UK Subs at Skunx. We saw lots of other great bands too, like The Newtown Neurotics... acts that would never have played Northern Ireland. It has to be remembered that we were coming from an environment where we literally had a ring of steel around the city centre in Belfast. You were searched by the army upon reaching the city and again by security staff in the shops as you entered them. Bands always left us off their tour schedules, so London was like a different world to us. We were throwing our hands in the air as we entered shops there, for God's sake, expecting to be searched... we were that used to it."

Another lifelong love of Irish punk is carried in the heart of Andy Cairns, guitarist/vocalist with hugely successful rock band, Therapy? Having grown up on a small estate in Ballyclare, just outside Belfast, the excitement of punk music was a lifeline he clung to as an escape from the grim drudgery of the locale he grew up in. Through alternative music and global touring, he eventually managed to escape that stifling environment, but ultimately one is defined by one's roots, so when asked to do a long-overdue live DVD with Therapy? the band chose to do it back home in Belfast.

"To a small town like ours, the arrival of punk rock seemed to herald the end of the world," laughs Andy. "To my parents and their friends, who had been born during the Second World War, it was seen as an enormous threat to the society their own parents had striven to rebuild after the conflict. To them, the end was nigh, and soon spiky-haired, glue-sniffing youths would be running riot in the streets, mugging the elderly, burning the Queen and slashing people to pieces with razor blades and safety pins!

"To buy records, any decent records that is, I used to have to get the bus into Belfast on Saturday and go to Caroline Music or Terri Hooley's famous Good Vibrations store on Great Victoria Street. These stores had everything and more that I could want... if I could have afforded it.

"Those trips to the city also opened my eyes to 'real' punks, just like the ones in Sounds and on TV. There were also shops where you could buy leather jackets, Dr. Marten's boots, band T-shirts, studded belts and wristbands. Smithfield Market also had its share of army surplus and various other military pageantry. Indeed it was there that my younger brother, also getting into punk, picked up a replica Luftwaffe uniform as worn by other older punks round Belfast. He hadn't quite bargained on the reception it would get at home though, where my father had lost not only his own dad but also his uncle in Flanders during WW2 at the hands of the Germans!

"The first real big punk gig we all got a chance to go to en masse was the UK Subs, Anti-Pasti and local power-poppers, The Bankrobbers, at Belfast's Ulster Hall," he adds, remembering youthful adventures with his other punk friends from Ballyclare. "Two of our dads drove us up in cars to the show and we spent the whole journey promising them that it would all be okay and, 'Yes, we would be outside at 10.30pm on the dot to be picked up'. We were all fourteen and had school the next day! As we arrived near the venue, the first thing we saw was a group of punks pelting the RUC with bottles, chanting 'SS RUC... SS RUC!' Embarrassingly, our folks dropped us off right at the front door of the venue where we had to undergo the excruciating walk of shame to the back of the queue in the manner of punk bumpkins out for the day!

"Once inside, though, it was fantastic. 'Fresh Fruit For Rotting Vegetables' (by The Dead Kennedys) was on the PA and we were shocked 'cos we never thought there could be so many punk rockers in Northern Ireland, let alone under one roof. The Bankrobbers were booed off, and rightly so, but Anti-Pasti were great and very, very loud. Then The Subs came on and the place went berserk… so much so that frontman Charlie Harper fell off the stage during 'Public Servant' and couldn't be found, leaving Nicky Garratt to fill in on vocal duties for the next few songs.

"After that night, our lot went Subs crazy; we had all the singles and albums on coloured vinyl, hundreds of button badges and shirts, and waited with bated breath for each of their releases. The bubble finally burst with that photo on the cover of 'Keep On Running 'Til You Burn' though, when they inexplicably appeared in New Romantic garb. At the same time Stiff Little Fingers seemed to be using the same stylist when they played 'Listen' on 'Top Of The Pops', with trendy haircuts and P.L.O.-type scarves. What was once the preserve of Spandau Ballet and their ilk had somehow, by osmosis, got to some of our own heroes…"

CHAPTER ELEVEN

SCOTLAND

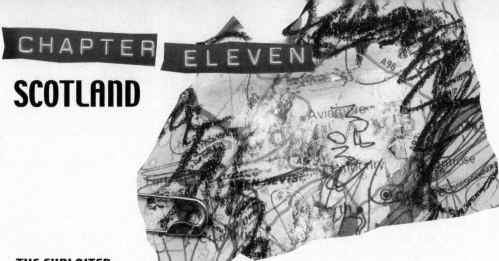

THE EXPLOITED

For many, The Exploited were the quintessential second wave punk band with their senses-searing high-speed outbursts against the system, and wild-eyed frontman Walter 'Wattie' Buchan's perfect red mohican. They were certainly the biggest punk band to ever emerge from Scotland in the Eighties, if not the whole of the UK, and it's safe to say that, with years of continuous touring under their belts and many consistently ferocious albums to their name, their fans still regard them as the biggest and best punk band in the world, even today. Their 2003 album for Dreamcatcher, 'Fuck The System', proves they've not lost their penchant for penning intense, vital material, and their recent tour of South America that saw rioting outside many venues demonstrates that unpredictable danger still rides on their coat-tails.

Formed in Edinburgh in 1979, The Exploited first appeared on Garry Bushell's 'Oi! The Album' compilation with 'Daily News' and 'I Believe In Anarchy', before releasing their first two singles 'Army Life' and 'Exploited Barmy Army' on their own Exploited Records in mid- and late-1980. Both singles were a phenomenal success, with 'Army Life' in particular troubling the Indie Top Twenty for an incredible eighteen months.

The band, whose line-up had settled by that time to include 'Big' John Duncan – guitar, Gary McCormack – bass and 'Dru Stix' (aka Glen Campbell, now sadly deceased) – drums, were already courting controversy even then. Like so many of the hugely popular acts at the time, they were both impulsive and extreme, and quickly loved and hated in almost equal measure by various factions of the punk subculture. Their fans hailed them as influential saviours, their detractors as thugs causing mayhem with songs such as the irresponsible 'Fuck The Mods' or 'Sex And Violence', although even their most ardent critics had to admire the band's formidable musical prowess.

"Yeah, to those of us for whom punk means a little bit more than having a mohican on your head, getting pissed and causing chaos, The Exploited really epitomise a kind of sad cartoon punk, devoid of any real politics or positivity," admits Deek Allan, vocalist with fellow Edinburgh band, Oi Polloi. "That said, however, when we were school kids they did influence us a lot. I remember rushing to buy (their first album) 'Punk's Not Dead' when it came out, and the first song we ever played at our very first practice was an attempted cover of The Exploited's 'SPG'. Their appearance on 'Top Of The Pops' was the talk of everyone in the playground the next day too. Though unluckily for Wattie one of the clerks in the local dole office had been watching it as well, and when he next went in to sign on, he had some explaining to do!

"The first time I went to see them I was actually determined not to like them as I wasn't really impressed by their attitude and preferred the 'anarcho' side of things, but despite that I have to say that musically they were fucking brilliant."

The next Exploited single, 'Dogs Of War', appeared in May 1981, and flew to No. 2 in the Indies, the band having just headlined the sold-out Apocalypse tour across the UK. It was closely followed by a brilliant debut album, the aforementioned 'Punk's Not Dead', a blistering sonic assault that not only topped the Indies but made the National Top Twenty as well. It was immediately apparent that such simplistic, super-intense rants as 'Royalty', 'Cop Car' and 'Dole Q' were inadvertently sating some primal, chaotic urge in the psyche of disenchanted Eighties youth.

Late '81's 'Dead Cities' single even saw the band blasting from TV screens the length and breadth of the country when they appeared on 'Top Of The Pops'. It quickly had the BBC swamped with angry calls from outraged 'normal' folk whose sensibilities had been rudely pogoed upon from a great height by the four colourful yobbos strutting menacingly back and forth on the studio's sound stage.

By the time the superb 'Attack'/'Alternative' double A-side single was released in spring '82, Dru had been replaced behind the kit by Danny Heatley, formerly with The Satellites, and the band were really coming into their own. That summer they unleashed the 'Troops Of Tomorrow' album, which many regard as their crowning glory and is still untouchable as an exercise in high-octane punk rock even today. The songs were much more memorable than on their debut full-length, and Big John's guitar sounded as if it was carved from burning oak.

The title track was a stirring rendition of The Vibrators' classic, and the album cover, depicting the band, armed and dangerous, surrounded by an army of punk mutants rising from the sewers, captured the desperate social atmosphere of the time. 'Disorder' and 'UK82', were even covered – as a medley – to great effect by thrash metal giants, Slayer (with vocals courtesy of rap star Ice T), for the 1993 'Judgement Night' soundtrack.

'Troops...' was of course a runaway success, topping the Indies and managing No. 17 in the Nationals. And in October 1982, the frantic 'Computers Don't Blunder', the band's last release for Secret, actually managed to take the intensity levels a notch higher. However, The Exploited lost considerable momentum when Secret fell apart soon after, and

The ever-popular Exploited, pictured during their 'Troops Of Tomorrow' period L–R: Gary, Danny, Big John, Wattie (Pic: Paul Cox)

the next year was spent looking for a new label, which they eventually found in the shape of Pax, who issued the 'Rival Leaders' EP in late 1983. It was chased up the Indie Charts by the brutal 'Let's Start A War' album, that spliced all its songs with snippets of radio and TV news broadcasts and snarling feedback to create an effective air of foreboding. And, although the band sounded thrashier than ever, it was the brooding mid–tempo 'God Saved The Queen' that was one of the standout cuts. During this period though, The Exploited became an ever–shifting entity as far as line–up was concerned, these recordings the first, and only, to feature Billy Dunn from Livingston band, The Skroteez, on bass.

"There was a lot of aggro between the Edinburgh and Livi punks at the time," recalls Billy. "But a few of the Livi skins were friends with Wattie, and they introduced me to him and I went for the audition. So The Skroteez split up, and most of the people in Livingston fell out with me at the time, but that's the way it goes, I suppose.

"My first Exploited gig was at the Brixton Ace, and Big John was still showing me the songs off the 'Troops Of Tomorrow' album on the way down in the van. I'd only been playing bass for a week, and just before we were meant to go on, I was shitting myself, 'cos I couldn't remember any of the songs! Then someone got knifed in the crowd as we were about to walk onstage, and the gig was stopped by the police, so I was let off the hook.

"The Exploited had been ripped off by Secret before they joined Pax, and then (Pax boss) Marcus Featherby ripped Wattie off as well, and I just got kinda fed up with it all and left."

By the time of 1985's 'Horror Epics', The Exploited featured Wattie's brother Willie on drums and Karl Morris from Xtract on guitar. The punk scene may have been in decline but that didn't stop The Exploited belting out another virulent thrash attack.

"I saw the ad in Sounds after Big John left," explains Karl. "It was my younger brother Ste who persuaded me to call. I was not really into The Exploited but thought, 'What the heck!' I called and Wattie answered, and we set up a date to do an audition; I went up to Edinburgh a couple of times and got the gig! It was a bit nerve-racking meeting Wattie for the first time as I had only seen him on stage, but I got on well with the lads, and when I moved to Edinburgh, I stayed with Willie for quite a while.

"It was a lot of fun in the beginning, going on tour in the UK, then going to Spain and getting thrown in jail for trashing the hotel… that made the Sunday papers! My dad always read the News Of The World and he saw the story about this wild Scottish punk band, and shouts to my mum, 'What's the name of that band our Karl's in?' 'The Exploited,' she replied. 'Bloody hell! He's in jail! It's here in the paper!' My parents had a fit; I wish I could've been a fly on the wall at that moment.

"After we got out, we had to stay in Madrid 'cos we missed our flights back to the UK and we missed the flight to the USA. We stayed in Madrid for about a week living with local punks Speedie and Minola; they fed and housed us until we got our flights sorted, then we flew from Spain to Gatwick, took a bus to Heathrow and got on the flight to Newark. We got off the plane and went to customs, and Willie was the first through. The officer asked him how long he was to be in the US, and Willie replied 'Six weeks'; she looked at his small bag and asked, 'Is this all you brought?' She then started to search the bag; however Willie had not done laundry since we left Scotland and it smelled really bad. The officer looked appalled and sent us all through without looking in another piece of luggage!

"(Bassist) Wayne was at the airport with the tour manager waiting for us; he had managed not to get arrested in Spain and had snuck off to catch the plane. While we were in jail, he was eating space cake, getting drunk and having fun… bastard! And he was the man who started trashing the hotel in the first place.

"We got in the van and went to the first gig. It was in New Jersey and when we got there, the place was full of Marines; I was asked if we were going to play 'Fuck The USA' and I said, 'Maybe!' The Marine grabbed my shirt, almost picking me up off the floor, and screamed in my face, 'Don't play that shit 'cos we are Marines and we will fuck you up!' Needless to say that song was not played in the USA! After that gig, we got back in the van and started the drive to Phoenix, Arizona. 3500 miles and three-and-a-half days of non-stop driving… welcome to America!"

1986 saw The Exploited signing to Rough Justice, the hardcore punk subsidiary of metal label, Music For Nations, the first results of which were the 'Jesus Is Dead' 12" and 'Death Before Dishonour' LP. Both records saw the band taking a slightly more chugging, metallic crossover approach to their inherently aggressive punk rock and managed respectable placings in the Indies, although nothing compared to their early Eighties heyday.

"I remember being in this local pub," chuckles Deek. "It was called the Tap, and all the punks used to hang out there, and bands would play sometimes too. Wattie made a rare appearance which sticks in my mind as this bloke went up to him and said, 'Wattie, don't you think your new album is a bit too metal more than punk?' Wattie headbutted the poor guy in the face, leaving him staggering backwards, covered in blood, and asked, 'Is that punk enough for you then?'"

The band hit their stride once again with the devastating 1990 album, 'The Massacre', by which time Wattie had endured several more line-up changes, this time being joined on guitar by Gordon 'Gogs' Balfour from another Livingston band, The Bayonet Babies.

"I got a call from my mate Billy who also stays in Livi," says Gogs. "He had replaced Gary McCormack on bass about 1983, and although he was no longer in the band, he gave Wattie a call and set up an audition for me. I went along and met the guys, they were fine; it was Smeeks on bass by then, and we had a run-through some of the songs. I played a bit of lead guitar and that was it; we then went round to Wattie's house and had a drink. It was all very informal, just the way I like it.

"Three rehearsals later and I had my first gig with the band, in Antwerp, Belgium. Talk about in at the deep end! There was a lot of material to get through and a lot of guitar solos; luckily I make all my solos up on the spot, so all I had to remember was the riffs, then when I got a nod from Wattie, I was off on a solo – fantastic! Everything went without a hitch and it was a memorable night for me as my first excursion with the band.

"I thoroughly enjoyed playing with The Exploited; I loved all the early stuff, they were a great band with a great image. When I played with them on stage, it was a new musical experience for me; they have a pure spirit in their music. We went from white noise with just a backbeat and Wattie screaming over the top to a sound so clear and so tight, with all the right points being communicated; it was indeed a new sound for me... an extreme, definitely a band of extremes."

And as mentioned earlier, the band are still together and banging out those killer records, with 1996's 'Beat The Bastards' being a particularly potent tour de force. Their vicious live show is as unruly as ever, and Wattie shows no signs of mellowing with age, a manic punk icon with, it would seem, many more years of great music still to come. Oh, and 'Don't Forget The Chaos!'

SELECT DISCOGRAPHY:
7"s:
'Army Life' (Exploited, 1980)
'Exploited Barmy Army' (Exploited, 1980)
'Dogs Of War' (Secret, 1981)
'Dead Cities' (Secret, 1981)
'Don't Let 'Em Grind You Down' (Superville, 1981) – split with Anti Pasti
'Attack'/'Alternative' (Secret, 1982)
'Computers Don't Blunder' (Secret, 1982)
'Rival Leaders' (Pax, 1983)

12"s:
'Britannia Waives The Rules' (Secret, 1982) – three-way split with Infa-Riot and Chron Gen
'Jesus Is Dead' (Rough Justice, 1986)
'War Now' (Rough Justice, 1988)

LPs:

'Punk's Not Dead' (Secret, 1981)
'Exploited Live Onstage' (Superville, 1981)
'Troops Of Tomorrow' (Secret, 1982)
'Let's Start A War' (Pax, 1983)
'Totally Exploited' (Dojo, 1984)
'Horror Epics' (Konexion, 1985)
'Live At The White House' (Suck, 1986)
'Death Before Dishonour' (Rough Justice, 1987)
'The Massacre' (Rough Justice, 1990)
'Beat The Bastards' (Rough Justice, 1996)
'Fuck The System' (Dreamcatcher, 2003)

AT A GLANCE:

The latest album, 'Fuck The System', is as potent an outpouring of pissed-off punk rock as one is likely to hear in this day and age, but for anyone wishing to check out the classic early material, Captain Oi! has reissued the first three studio albums in attractive digipacks. With twenty bonus single and B-side tracks between them, not to mention fold-out posters of the original cover art, they are the perfect overview of the band's glorious salad days. Elsewhere, for a neat snapshot of mid-period Exploited, the Dreamcatcher CD reissue of 'Death Before Dishonour' (2000) conveniently includes both the 'Jesus Is Dead' and 'War Now' 12"s. Also of note on the visual front is the 'Rock'n'Roll Outlaws'/'Sexual Favours' DVD (Cherry Red Films, 2001) that features an in-depth documentary, interviews with Wattie, and a whole live set.

EXTERNAL MENACE

Of all the second wave punk bands from the UK, External Menace are surely the most criminally underrated, despite putting their name to some of the most powerful and instant music of the era and displaying a knack for songwriting far in excess of their tender years. They were formed in Coatbridge, on the Glasgow city limits in 1979 by guitarist John 'Sneddy' Sneddon, and surely the only reason neither of their Eighties singles made the Indie Charts (although they did figure highly in the Sounds Punk Charts of the time) is that they rarely played south of the border.

"I used to listen to a lot of radio from the mid-Seventies onwards, catching the odd early punk tune," explains Sneddy of how it all began for him. "Some of my cousins had learnt guitar and were into

Guitarist Sneddy of the oft-overlooked
External Menace

Lou Reed and stuff; I would sit in on their jam sessions, just listening, and I was hooked. The Ramones were just getting known here with their first album, and I decided that was the kind of thing I liked and wanted to play. I got an old acoustic guitar up together and learnt bar chords by studying Johnny Ramone pictures in the music press. I tried to get a band together for a few years without much success but I managed to learn a few cover songs and even managed to write about a dozen or so of my own."

However, it was only when he met kindred spirit and near-neighbour Wullie Hamill that he made any real headway with forming his own proper band. A band that initially ended up being called The L-Plates in the absence of a better name; they even used a driver's L-plate as their logo!

"We both made our own clothes and got talking about the punk scene, it didn't take long to persuade Wullie to join. Sanz (Sandy Halkett) was next; we met him soon after he moved to our estate. He was only twelve years old, but tall, and had Sham 69 and The Clash painted on his leather bomber jacket. I asked him if he played any instruments and he didn't, but he wanted in, so I showed him some chords and we had ourselves a bassist. And there was a new guy at school, name of Rab Bell, who was a Damned fanatic and was always tapping his hands and feet in class and getting into trouble for it, and he became our drummer; that was our first line-up sorted.

"We rehearsed in Sanz's dad's garage for a few months until complaints from neighbours put a stop to that. Rab and Sanz were naturals, they picked things up really quickly, and before long we had twenty songs, ten covers and ten our own. The first gig we set up was in a local community centre, and we had to play on our own, as the other two bands on the bill didn't turn up! So we did the same set two or three times over, but it was good experience and the gig was a great success."

Rab left after about twenty gigs and the recording of the first demo ("He just couldn't afford his own kit"), the first of over twenty-five line-up changes in the band's existence, and Sneddy ended up helping out another local band The Snap Ons playing bass. When he fell out with his own band over the fact that he was also playing with someone else, he left and joined The Snap Ons as a permanent member. He played on their double A-side single 'Gotta Get Out Of Here'/'Back To '76' before leaving ("Because they didn't wanna write their own material") to reform The L-Plates.

Sneddy suggested a change of name to External Menace, and Derek Paterson, the drummer from The Indicators, a local band that also numbered in their ranks Big John Duncan, who went on to join The Exploited, took Rab's place behind the kit.

"Derek was one big powerful guy with his own style," laughs Sneddy. "He used the sticks back to front to get a really heavy sound, but the way he treated his kit was costing him a new cymbal every month. He had access to even better gear and rehearsal space, and also a gig venue in the shape of a local YMCA; as he was the punk DJ there, we could practice every night if we wanted to. People started arriving from here, there and everywhere to sit in on these rehearsals, and they virtually ended up as mini-gigs.

"We mainly played the usual pub gigs at first, then moved onto nightclubs, the Dingwalls circuit-type stuff, and, thinking about it, a fair amount of outdoor festivals too, mostly organised by an old mate, Willie Sinnott, who lived around the corner. He was an old punk and a talented bassist; he was in Edith And The Ladies, and went on to play with The Shamen, but tragically drowned after their 'Move Any Mountain' single."

It wasn't to be long before the band, who were building a strong local following thanks to their feisty live performances, would be signed up by a label, the Blackpool-based Beat The System Records.

"We recorded an eight-track demo with Derek soon after he joined, but it was our early 1979 tape that got us signed to Beat The System. My mate Bill 'Grumpy' McKinley had moved to Blackpool and was roadie for The Fits; he knew Barry Lights and let him hear the tape.

"Yeah, Barry was a bit tight with cash," he adds laughing. "On Beat The System tours you were lucky to get a bag of chips out of him for your dinner. We lived on cold beans and stuff; it took fifteen years to get any royalty payments out of him at all. But I'm not bitter about it 'cos when a cheque did eventually arrive, it helped pay for the recording of our (1997) 'The Process Of Elimination' album."

In September 1982, External Menace entered Ric Rac Studios in Leeds and recorded their superb debut, the four-track 'Youth Of Today' EP. Its thick pulsing bottom end, driven by some accomplished gurgling bass lines, Sned's abrasive power chords, and Wullie's impassioned bellow, garnered some inevitable comparisons to Scotland's biggest punk export, The Exploited.

'Youth Of Today' was followed in early 1983 by the equally memorable 'No Views' EP, another four cuts of sublimely catchy punk rock. Two tracks, 'What The Hell?' and 'External Menace', were also contributed to Beat The System's 'Total Anarchy' compilation, but changes were afoot before the year was out.

"There was generally a good atmosphere in the band, but nothing lasts forever," sighs Sneddy. "Wullie was causing problems and we eventually had enough and asked him to leave. Tommy Wallace replaced him after a while; Tommy was the singer with Chaotic Youth and they had just split up. I had been mates with Tommy and his brother, Ian, their guitarist, for years, so it seemed like the right move for the time and we did some great gigs together. Probably the best was at the Glasgow Venue with the Test Tube Babies in '83. Tommy left to move to London though, and then we were down to a three-piece."

"My time with External Menace was relatively short, but I had a great time," recalls Tommy. "I must have only done a handful of gigs with them, but remember vividly a lot of rehearsals in Coatbridge, and a lot of drinking in Glasgow! I had already been a fan; Sneddy's guitar style, along with Wullie's powerful vocals, was a fantastic combination.

"I suppose my main reason for leaving was that I had a chance to get a place in London, and being only seventeen and a bit reckless, I made the decision to move, but I was very honoured to have worked with them."

External Menace continued as a three-piece for a while, before Derek left to travel the world as a professional roadie, and he was replaced by Drew Russell, the old drummer of The Snap Ons, who also played with Rough Charm just before they became The Almighty. In 1985, Sneddy's brother Jim joined on bass and Sanz moved to rhythm guitar, but the following year, having undergone such a musical evolution, they decided to change their name.

"We started calling the band something different every gig for a spell to try and get rid of a bad lot of fans that were causing trouble every time we played. We were getting pissed off with all the hassle at gigs and some of the music was not what people wanted to hear anyway; they weren't interested in the ska and reggae touches we had in some of our songs. So we changed the name to Bleedin' Hearts, still playing a lot of Menace material, with some of our newer stuff too, basically just trying out whatever ideas came along."

Sadly Wullie, the band's original singer, was killed in 1987 whilst crossing the M8 motorway at a notorious accident black spot near his home. Also that year, Kevin Taylor joined the band on guitar, and, shortly after, Sanz left, retiring from music altogether ("A shame really, he was a very talented lad; he runs his own newsagents shop now"). By 1991, the band were known as Jett Rink, and undertook a full Scottish tour with The Silencers.

Several years, not to mention line-up and name changes later, and Sneddy relocated to Livingston, moving in with Ian (or John, as he was christened) Welsh, the singer with Livingston punk band Swine Flu and a huge External Menace fan. It didn't take him long to persuade Sneddy to change his band's name back to External Menace once again, before joining them himself as second vocalist for the recording of six new studio tracks that were included on Captain Oi!'s retrospective 'Pure Punk Rock' CD. Then for the next four years Welshy became the band's lead singer with Sneddy providing backing vocals.

"It was a dream come true for me to join my favourite band," recalls Welshy fondly. "Sneddy had been a huge inspiration for me for many years of my life, and I always thought it was criminal that they weren't one of the biggest punk bands to come from the UK; their songs were head and shoulders above most of the competition. So, it was great to finally be able to play alongside him and perform those songs myself."

The 1997 line-up also included Stuart Davis on drums and Billy Dunn on bass, both of whom had been in Swine Flu with Welshy, and both of whom actually started their musical careers in the early Eighties with Livingston punkers The Skroteez. Bobe Copeland was on lead guitar, who was formerly with Self Destruct and went on to play in the Scottish Oi band Baker's Dozen.

The rejuvenated External Menace wasted no time in releasing the excellent 'Seize The Day' EP for French label Negative, and the aforementioned 'The Process Of Elimination' album, which was recorded at Chamber Studios in Edinburgh and appeared through Epistrophy Records from Germany, although Negative handled the CD release and a cassette version later materialised through Poland's Rock'n'Roller Records.

They also contributed tracks to several compilation albums, and two split EPs, one with Recharge (again for Epistrophy), the other with furious Welsh punkers Rectify (for Southampton-based Suspect Device Records); played well-received sets at the first two Holidays In The Sun festivals, in '96 and '97, and toured Europe four times in two years. The UK and European tours in 1998 saw one Criss Damage (aka Chris Baker) behind the kit.

External Menace in Ieper, Belgium, 1997
Front left: Billy, Sneddy, Keith (driver), Welshy, Shawn (roadie), Bob

Predictably enough, things seemed to just be going too smoothly when… "Disaster struck in Den Haag, Holland," sighs Welshy. "It was less than an hour before we were due onstage at a punk festival, on July 4th '98. I went to help two mates who were getting attacked in the street by Dutch football hooligans. I got a metal baseball bat in the face as they ran for cover! I had a broken nose, a fractured eye socket and my upper jawbone was smashed into a hundred pieces; I was lucky to survive. I looked like a purple football!

"The Dutch surgeon said that if the blow had been 2cm higher, my nose would have entered my brain and of course I'd be dead! I now have four metal plates in my face, under the skin, holding it all together. The bastard who did it got five years but was probably out in two! And that was the end of my time in External Menace, as it took me at least two years to recover from all that shit. Where were the Livi bootboys when I needed them?"

"I think for me that our second demo is my least favourite recording," ponders Sneddy. "The quality was poor 'cos the mixing engineer hated us! The sound on the 'Seize The Day' EP is also lacking in balls, basically 'cos we put too much music on a 7" vinyl record.

"The same line-up recorded the 'Process…' album in the very same studio and you can really hear the difference. That was a good line-up but we did too many UK and European tours, too much rehearsing and recording, and we ended up falling out with each other in the end."

However, Sneddy recently reunited with Bobe for External Menace's first ever US tour to promote the Dr. Strange reissue of the 'Process…' album, complete with seven extra tracks and new artwork/layout. It remains, as before, a wonderfully sincere and diverse slice of punk rock, more than capable of speaking to punks of all ages and nationalities.

The other current members are Phil 'Jonah' Jones on bass and Jon Naylor on drums (who took over from Mark Leishman, a long-time friend of Sneddy, several years ago), and after the US tour, External Menace, now based in Manchester, reverted to this three-piece line-up they had existed as until Dr. Strange resurrected interest in the late Nineties incarnation of the band.

"It's nice to get a bit of recognition now and again; it kinda makes it all worthwhile," admits Sneddy. "But really I'd like to be remembered as a band that weren't just out to get as much cash from the punk scene as we could. We shunned record labels, not like some of the bands that were into ripping kids off with overpriced shitty paraphernalia. I think we've made some good catchy meaningful punk rock over the years, and we've hopefully a bit more left in us yet."

SELECT DISCOGRAPHY:
7"s:
'Youth Of Today' (Beat The System, 1982)
'No Views' (Beat The System, 1983)
'Seize The Day' (Negative, 1997)

LPs:
'The Process Of Elimination' (Epistrophy, 1997)

AT A GLANCE:
For early External Menace, look no further than Captain Oi!'s 1995 'Pure Punk Rock' CD, which features all the band's Beat The System recordings, plus various demos from the mid-Eighties, liner notes from Sneddy, and original sleeve art. For latter era EM, the 2004 Dr. Strange reissue of 'The Process Of Elimination' comes highly recommended – not only has the album been remastered, but the CD also includes the 'Seize The Day' EP and the two tracks from the Epistrophy split with Recharge.

THREATS

The Threats from Dalkeith, Midlothian (also famous as the hometown of Fish from Marillion, of all people) may have only done the two early-Eighties EPs, but there was no denying the ferocity of their music, and they certainly left their bootprints all over the road map of Scottish punk rock. And they're back together again today, sounding better than ever, and releasing records so vibrant they certainly show the new breed of punkers a thing or two about intense, catchy songwriting.

Even though their debut single wasn't released until 1982, the band formed as far back as 1979 from the ashes of The Reflectors, boasting a line-up of Joe Amos – vocals, Jim Smith – guitar, Graham Downie – bass, and Gordon 'Gogs' Sinclair – drums. Soon after they adopted the name Threats, Jim and Gogs rethought the band, Jim taking over as guitarist/vocalist with Gogs alongside him on second guitar, recruiting Ian Simpson on bass and moving Joe Amos to drums.

"Hearing The Pistols, Clash and The Damned was all it took," recalls Jim, of his inspiration to form a punk rock band. "It was like a light bulb went on somewhere when we first heard 'Anarchy In The UK'. It gave us a chance to focus all that youthful aggression on somethin' positive and far more enjoyable than just goin' to a fuckin' football game… plus all that disco shit that was goin' on at the time was just... well... aaarrgh!

"I can remember bein' excited all the time; we finally felt like we belonged to somethin' special. And when the second wave kicked in with Discharge and The Exploited etc., we knew this was going to be great. We went to see The Cockney Rejects in Edinburgh, in 1980 I think, and The Exploited were supporting; this was before Wattie even had his mohawk! The Rejects were great but The Exploited were fuckin' amazin'; I thought my head was goin' to burst! Ye see, for a while there, it looked like punk really was dyin'... then bam! It was back, wilder than ever... great!"

Threats, May 2002, in the toilets of CBGBs, New York City, L-R: Jim (on toilet), Gogsy, Davie Metal, Dave Threat (Pic: Bill Caldwell)

Threats recorded their first demo, 'Pacivity', which included embryonic versions of several songs that would later grace their EPs, at Wilf's Planet in Edinburgh in 1979. Although rougher than a prizefighter's knuckles, it revealed the band's confident grasp of arrangement and dynamics, and hinted at great things to come. The title track of the demo was even included on the 'Backlash' compilation put out by Edinburgh label Playlist in 1980.

"Me and Gogs lived next door to each other when we were kids and we got into the whole glam rock thing," Jim explains of the musical influences at work in the band's sound. "Stuff like T Rex, Sweet and Slade... in fact, Slade are still one of my favourite bands. Anything loud and raucous totally appealed to us, and that's when we first started bangin' around with drums and guitars."

The following year, Jim and Gogs parted company with their rhythm section again; enter Martin 'Tin' Tucker on bass and Mick 'Mad Mental' Amos (Joe's cousin) behind the kit. A second demo was recorded, this time in East Kilbride, that saw the band's sound evolving into something harder, faster and more distorted, without losing sight of the solid tunes of 'Pacivity'. The demo eventually brought them to the attention of Rondelet, who released the 'Go To Hell' EP in 1982.

A youthful jolt of pure adrenaline, 'Go To Hell' treads a fine line between the singalong choruses of the first wave punk bands and the chaotic noise favoured by the second. Blessed with a lovely thick bass sound and a lively guitar production (courtesy once again of Wilf's Planet) that literally crackles with pent-up energy, the EP drags you along by your neck from start to finish, and remains to this day one of the great unsung punk releases of the era.

Soon after, Martin was replaced by Dylan on bass, and Threats released the 'Politicians And Ministers' 12", again on Rondelet. Featuring six more tracks of the band's distinctive speedy punk rock, including the anthemic 'Writing On The Wall', the EP didn't hit the listener quite as hard as 'Go To Hell', but was still head and shoulders above most of the competition and subsequently spent over a month in the Indie Charts.

"We never really thought about tryin' to set ourselves apart," reckons Jim. "We just wanted to write some memorable songs, somethin' that people could chant along to. I think we achieved that then, and hope we're still doin' it now! And for me, lyrically, just writing about one thing, like politics, is too restrictive. My head's always got somethin' goin' on inside about things I see around us, and basically if it rattles my cage, I'll write about it..."

But sadly, apart from two tracks ('Go To Hell' and 'Afghanistan') contributed to the Rondelet compilation LP, 'The Only Alternative', that was the end — for a good few years, at least – of new Threats recordings. They toured the UK with Anti Pasti, then went out on their own headlining stint, before finally splitting up in late 1983.

"I left, I just wanted a break from it," sighs Jim. "We were all fed up with it getting harder and harder to get gigs, our record company was shit, and our manager was a right shark. I always thought that, after a bit of a break, we'd get on with it again, fresh and ready to go, but everybody's circumstances changed and it just didn't happen."

Jim reformed the band briefly in 1996, alongside Craig Costello on guitar, Craig Robertson on drums and Gene Clark on bass, but this line-up only got as far as playing two shows in nearby Edinburgh.

"I had been asked a lot of times to reform the band, but I hadn't seen Gogs for years and didn't want to do it without him. A friend of mine Craig Costello, who's an amazin' guitarist, eventually talked me into it in 1996... well, I say he talked me into it, but I actually said 'Yes!' before he'd even finished the sentence! We did a couple of gigs in Edinburgh, which were amazing, but still no sign of Gogs. I did finally meet up with him at last, but he was too busy to do it, and it all fizzled out again – until we got asked to play Holidays In The Sun 2001."

Threats, Jim and Gogs, 1981

After playing H.I.T.S. as a three-piece comprising Jim, Craig Robertson and new bassist, Davy Rosie, Threats released their three-track comeback 7", 'Back In Hell' on Scottish label Intimidation. A fine return to the fray, with the band sounding as if they'd never been away, it even included a new recording of 'Pacivity', the first song the band ever recorded back in 1979.

Gogs finally rejoined in January 2002 ("After I threatened to kill him," laughs Jim), and Craig Robertson was replaced on drums with Davey 'Metal' Pottinger, resulting in the current line-up of Threats. New Jersey label, Punknite, reissued the 'Back In Hell' 7" as a CD, bolstered by three new recordings featuring the new members... including a lively reworking of the excellent 'Politicians And Ministers'. It's great testament to the vision of the original band that their songs have stood the test of time so well, and sound as relevant today as they did twenty years ago.

The CD brought them to the attention of highly respected US punk label, Doctor Strange, who promptly signed the band for their most recent new release, 'Twelve Punk Moves'. A cocky, high-octane affair that takes, and builds upon, all the classic ingredients that made the band's back catalogue so vital, the album features a dozen in-your-face modern punk anthems. Sounding like the true missing link between The Sex Pistols and The Exploited, but given a neat modern twist via American hardcore, it ably suggests that the best may still be to come from these Scottish veterans.

"Threats are a punk band – they play punk rock, and nothin' else!" states Jim defiantly, in closing. "In years to come, if someone plays a Threats song and it makes them want to jump up and down, break things or scream, we've done our job!"

SELECT DISCOGRAPHY:
7"s:
'Go To Hell' (Rondelet, 1982)
'Back In Hell' (Intimidation, 2001)

12"s:
'Politicians And Ministers' (Rondelet, 1982)

LPs:
'Live At CBGBs' (Doctor Strange, 2002)

CDs:
'Back In Hell' (Punknite, 2002)
'Twelve Punk Moves' (Doctor Strange, 2003)

AT A GLANCE:

The 'Demos And Rarities' CD (Doctor Strange, 2003) compiles all the band's early Eighties output, including demos and alternate takes, and comes in a nice, fold-out cover complete with a detailed Threats family tree, making it an essential purchase. That said, the new album, 'Twelve Punk Moves', probably the best thing the band have done to date, also comes highly recommended.

Threats would like to respectfully dedicate their section in this book to the memory of Mick Amos, who died in 1998.

ANTI-SOCIAL

L ivingston is a 'new town' that sprang up between Glasgow and Edinburgh in the Sixties to swallow up the population overspill from the two cities, and, as is so often sadly the case with such hurried communities, little or no thought was given to the psychological needs of its inhabitants. Least of all the unemployed teenagers with nothing to do but listen to punk rock and sniff glue.

"It was just a vast concrete jungle of houses and car parks," confirms Welshy (aka John Welsh), who went on to front Swine Flu (the first Livingston punk band to tour Europe) and eventually External Menace. "One shopping centre and not much else, a really soulless place, and the perfect breeding ground for an army of punk rockers.

"And yes, there was a lot of glue! Livingston was covered in used glue bags back then and nearly all the punks were at it. It was so depressing and insular, and it might have helped contribute to the senseless violence that ruined so many of the gigs. The Livi punks had a notorious reputation everywhere they went, and a lot of it was justified, I'm afraid, which was a real shame, because there were tons of positive people in our scene, but the negative punks seemed to rule by fear."

But from this volatile melting pot of unchannelled aggression emerged an incredible number of punk bands that sadly went largely unrecognised beyond the town limits, let alone south of the border. Great bands such as On Parole and Another Youth never really progressed past the demo stage. And, although the former had the track 'Condemned' included on No Future's 'A Country Fit For Heroes, Volume Two' 12", their music on the whole seems tragically destined to gather dust as forgotten cassettes hoarded away proudly by die-hard fans. Others such as Abuse, Juvenile Delinquents and Disgust, only played live and never committed their material to tape .

One such demo band was Anti-Social, and their guitarist Gordon 'Gogs' Balfour describes just how and why they arrived at such an appropriate moniker.

"In 1979 we started a band that went through more names than we had songs, but the name was important – it was our handle, our statement to everyone, saying exactly what we were about. Some of the earlier band names included Rabies, The Lure, Red Alert, The Blitzed... and finally Anti-Social. It was Anti-Social that summed up where we were and what we were about, so it stuck.

Livi punks, Anti-Social
L-R: Scottie, Cameron, Gogs

"It was our first band that did anything beyond a couple of rehearsals. We were all mates from the same neighbourhood, growing up together, and we were very tight. Unfortunately we were literally very anti-social in our thinking as well as our music... not just towards the established order but everything and everyone! Thankfully we soon blended with other punks in our area; it started with our guitarist helping out another band and before too long we had made some new pals. I think the big Livi scene grew from small factions in small areas all coming together, to drink alcohol basically, when we were all around the age of sixteen or seventeen."

"The first time I saw Gogs was in Rainbow Records, wearing these kids' plastic sunglasses, like Captain Sensible used to wear," laughs Welshy. "He had a chain going from the glasses to his earring, which had a tea bag hanging off it! And to finish off the look, he had 'I don't care' written on his back in huge letters... but he's a superb bloke, and it was a pleasure when I finally played with him in Swine Flu years later."

Gogs was joined in the band by Alan 'Scottie' Scott on vocals, Cameron Stevens on guitar and Gary 'Hainy' Hain on drums. Over the next few years, Anti Social played many suitably chaotic gigs and recorded two fine demos, before splitting in 1982. Scottie and Gogs (who by then had progressed from bass to guitar) formed the Bayonet Babies with Frank Nicol on bass, Alan 'Craney' Cranston on drums and Angus 'Gus' Macrury on rhythm guitar. They were to be one of the more respected Livi punk bands until they split in 1987, even contributing a track, 'I've Got Those Crazy Helicopters In My Head', to the 1986 'Jello Aid' compilation album on Alternative Tentacles.

Gogs went on to join The Exploited, with whom he toured the world and played on 'The Massacre' album, before ending up with Welshy in Swine Flu for their last ever show, supporting NOFX. He currently plays with modern Oi band, Baker's Dozen.

THE SKROTEEZ

T he Skroteez were the first band from the thriving Livingston punk community to have an official release in their own right, 1982's spirited 'Overspill' EP on Square Anarchy Records, but their members were all involved in punk much earlier than that.

"My brother Trevor came back up from London, where he had been squatting with a couple of members of The Ruts, with a copy of the 'Never Mind The Bollocks' album," remembers guitarist William Dall Dunn. "That was in 1977, and I was in the third year at school with my mate Stuart Davies, who also ended up in The Skroteez with me, and as soon as we heard that, that was it. I never left school with any O-levels, but I did have a total knowledge of the chord structures of 'Never Mind The Bollocks'! Every twelve-to-sixteen year old needs some kind of musical style to cling onto as they're growing up, and that was it for me... punk rock!"

Billy and Stuart weren't the only ones to heed John Lydon's call to arms though, and soon Livingston had a punk scene to rival that of nearby Edinburgh and Glasgow.

"We were kinda like a cartel in Livingston. There was only one shop (the aforementioned Rainbow Records, more recently known as Coda, now sadly closed down), that was bringing up all the stuff from England. All the big bands like The Clash, The Damned, Sham 69… and as soon as we heard all that stuff, that provided some form of rebellion for all us bored teenagers who had fuck all to do. We all clubbed together and got cheap guitars from the catalogue for about £30 with a 3W amplifier, and we all thought we were Steve Jones!

"Originally there were only three Livingston punk bands back in the early Eighties - The Skroteez, Glasgow SS (the 'SS' apparently stood for Social Security, and their guitarist Bongo went on to play for Molotov Cocktail) and Ugen Kampf, but gradually there were more and more, and they were all inter-related. If you weren't in one band, you were in another!"

And true to form Billy and Stuart began their musical careers with another local outfit, The Dentz, alongside Adrian 'Dodo' Dowe and Fraser Allen.

"That was in 1980," explains Billy. "We never actually played any gigs, just practised in our bedroom, but that was our apprenticeship, shall we say? And we chose the name because all of our guitars and amps had… hundreds of dents in them!"

The Skroteez materialised as a result of The Dentz imploding, and initially comprised Billy and Stuart, on guitar and drums respectively, with Dave 'Hendo' Henderson handling vocal duties, and Tam Corbett being the first to pick up the bass for them. Tam was later replaced by Tony Aungsoe, and eventually, after the single had been released, by Frank Conway. Their first gig was at their local primary school in late 1980.

"There wasn't a bad crowd for the time. I had a really cheap Kay guitar, and I threw it in the air and kicked it to pieces at the

One of the few line-up shots in existence of The Skroteez
L-R: Hendo, Stu, Tony, Billy

end of the gig. I thought it was brilliant, thought I was some kind of guitar hero. But I crept back into the building when everyone had left, and sneaked back into the room, and there was my guitar lying in bits on the floor – I nearly cried!"

More wanton destruction landed the band, and several more of the Livingston punks, in trouble when they made headlines following a heated showdown with local police after a friend's party. 'The Night The Punks Turned Ugly' screamed the local papers, a phrase that was immortalised forever when another Livingston band, First Offence, took it for the title of their 1983 three-track EP on Chaos Records.

"We were all around a mate's house for his birthday," says Billy. "We were all drinking, and a few of us were sniffing glue, as you do. Anyway, he said, 'Right lads, I'm leaving this flat soon, so you can wreck it if ye want!' So, we went into the bedroom, ripping the mattresses up, setting light to things… and before we knew it, the constabulary turns up. The papers said there were forty punks, but in reality there was only about twenty, and there was a big fight outside with the police. Me and Hendo were chased by this big sergeant around this guy's flat; it was like something out of the Keystone Cops! Round and round the coffee table we went, until this copper rugby-tackled Hendo and I dived out the window!"

Ironically enough, it was just such anarchic behaviour that inadvertently landed The Skroteez their 'record deal'.

"Glue was like the drug of choice for most Scottish punk rockers," he confirms. "And one night I was casually having a wee sniff in somebody's back garden, and I got grabbed into the house by this woman, who sat me down in her living room in the middle of the night and started talking to me about life and stuff. And there I am, stood with my spiky hair and these big red rashes all round my mouth…!

"Anyway, she knew this woman called Heather Badd who worked for a record company, and we had a meeting with her at her house. We were that naive at the time, when she asked me if we had a PA, I thought it was a button on my guitar! She took over as the manager of The Skroteez, and helped us set up Square Anarchy Records and bring out the 'Overspill' EP. I think we got a fish supper and two cans of lager each for that single (laughs)! But it was good; we had letters from all over, even from Australia – not bad for a bunch of plebs."

Featuring three tracks of basic high-energy punk rock, the EP remains highly listenable even today. 'New Town' on the A-side, as the title suggests, was a less than appreciative appraisal of Livingston ("They should blow it all up, or else burn it all down!"), and was backed by 'Who's Law?' and the defiant, aggressive 'Livi Punkz'. Unfortunately it was to be the one and only vinyl release for The Skroteez, who split up when Billy departed to join The Exploited on bass in 1983.

"They got some gigs down south 'cos of the single, and supported The Business at Skunx in London," says Welshy. "The gig was a disaster though as their singer Hendo drank a bottle of whisky before he went onstage. Halfway through the first song, he passed out, fell off the stage and didn't get back up! Gig over!

"At Drifters in Manchester, The Skroteez were supporting The UK Subs when a riot broke out between the Livi punks who'd went down to the gig, and the Manchester punks. Huge glass ashtrays were thrown at each other, tables and chairs used as weapons, pint glasses thrown everywhere… real intense violence. The cops showed up, took one look in the door then quietly closed them and fucked off. Priceless!"

Billy left The Exploited after recording the 'Let's Start A War' LP and 'Rival Leaders' 7", but rejoined them briefly whilst they were promoting their superb 'Beat The Bastards' album in 1996. He undertook three European tours with them in support of the record, including the Dynamo Open Air and With Full Force festivals. Between those stints with The Exploited, he also played with Swine Flu and External Menace (Welshy: "He contributed to both bands big time!") and he's currently with the upbeat and sublimely melodic Assassins. A modern punk band that also number amongst their ranks Gus McCury who was the guitarist on First Offence's 'The Night The Punks Turned Ugly' EP and drummer Iain who played live with The Exploited whilst they were touring their 'The Massacre' album.

"I've had a tremendous time, I wouldn't trade it for anything," reckons Billy. "I'm still good friends with a lot of those guys I played with. And I still love punk rock, especially a lot of the American bands like The Vandals and NOFX, but I'm not a pigeonhole punk rocker; I like everything from Ministry to jazz and reggae dub! Anything that sounds good to me... why be limited by labels?"

SELECT DISCOGRAPHY:
7"s:
'Overspill' EP (Square Anarchy, 1982)

AT A GLANCE:
The Skroteez have never enjoyed a CD release of their material, although the curious might try writing to Billy c/o 37 Craigswood, C-Hill, Livingston, EH54 5EP, Scotland, who may be persuaded to copy them the EP if costs are covered. The Assassins are more than worthy of investigation too.

BARBED WIRE

A s mentioned earlier, alongside The Skroteez and Glasgow SS, Ugen Kampf were one of the earliest Livingston punk bands. They comprised Ralph Tod – vocals, Alan Ramsay – guitar, Graham Hopkins – bass, and Ralph's older brother, Ian – drums, and recorded two impressively tight and energetic demos, the first in 1981, the second in '82. They never enjoyed any official vinyl release in their own right though, which is a minor tragedy as the demos hinted at a tremendous well of potential, especially on the superb track 'Hark', that featured in both sessions. Musical promise that the Tod brothers went on to realise to an extent with their next band, Barbed Wire. They did however have a track, 'Weapons Of War', included posthumously on the 1982 Crass Records compilation, 'Bullshit Detector'.

"The second gig I ever witnessed was a turbo charged set by Ugen Kampf at a local youth club," recalls Welshy fondly. "This was early 1981 and I was only thirteen. I thought they looked great; all dyed, spiky hair, studs, bondage gear etc. And their songs just blew me away; hearing such quality punk rock in the flesh for the first time at thirteen years old was like seeing The Pistols or The Clash in '77! It had the same kind of effect on me anyway; I thought bombs were going off all around me, it felt like I was plugged into the mains! Sounds mad, I know, but it's true. I had a churning in my stomach of pure excitement and it was seeing Ugen Kampf that made me want to be in a punk band of my own."

By the time Ugen Kampf became Barbed Wire in 1984, Ralph was playing bass, with his brother still behind the kit, and they were joined by Paul Henderson (the younger brother of Hendo from The Skroteez) on vocals and Cameron Stevens on guitar. After replying to an ad in Sounds with their two demos, recorded at Wilf's Planet and the Pier House in Edinburgh, the band secured a deal with Welsh label, Oi Records, and released the excellent 'The Age That Didn't Care' album in 1986. Ten storming tracks of rowdy, tuneful punk rock make it one of the overlooked gems of the period.

"The best Barbed Wire gig would have to be one in Edinburgh with Conflict," reckons Ian. "A punk from Livi hit a police officer over the head with an ashtray when we were playing; it turned into a riot and the gig was stopped! As for the worst gig... probably when we played the Duchess

Of York in Leeds – skinheads wrecked the pub as we were playing one of our songs, 'Death And Destruction'!"

Two tracks – 'No Hope' and 'Nazi Briton (Fuck Off)' – from their '85 demo were also included on the 1986 Oi Records compilation, 'This Is Oi'. Then, in 1987, Barbed Wire contributed six songs to a split album on Oi entitled 'Skins 'N' Punks, Volume Four', that they shared with Welsh band The Abnormal. However, they disbanded soon after.

All the ex-members of Barbed Wire are still actively involved with punk rock; Paul Henderson plays guitar for Overspill, Ralph Tod sings for Critikill, and Ian Tod and Cameron Stevens play (drums and guitar respectively) for Chinese Burn.

SELECT DISCOGRAPHY:
LPs:
'The Age That Didn't Care' (Oi, 1986)
'Skins 'N' Punks, Volume Four' (Oi, 1987) – split with The Abnormal

AT A GLANCE:
The excellent 1995 Captain Oi! reissue of 'The Age That Didn't Care' also includes both Barbed Wire tracks from the 'This Is Oi' compilation as well as their songs from the split LP with The Abnormal.

CHAOTIC YOUTH

One of the lesser-known bands from Scotland, Chaotic Youth could certainly have gone onto bigger and better things, if only they'd taken themselves a little more seriously at the time. Like so many of their peers, they formed primarily out of boredom, to 'have a good laugh', but as their recordings prove, they were above-average musicians – for the punk scene at least – with a natural predisposition for a good rowdy tune.

"My dad played guitar in cabaret bands and such like, and was always going on at us from an early age to learn to play," remembers guitarist Ian Wallace. "I was interested in it, but it seemed too hard, I never quite got to grips with it, never really got beyond two chords and gave up. Of course, when punk came along it didn't seem so hard anymore. I had a knackered old amp in my bedroom and a sixties Telecaster copy, and I started making up chords that sounded kinda punk!

"The first ever band we did was just me and my brother, Tommy. We were bored one night, it was sometime around 1978, and we decided to do some songs, and we just made them up as we went along! We called ourselves the Social Dogs, and we got our mate Andy McLaughlin to play bass... except he didn't have a bass, so just used the top two strings of a guitar. We just sat in the room and made loads of tapes – which you really need a high pain threshold to listen to! – and about a year-and-a-half later we managed to get a drummer, Kenny We played one gig at the school and got banned for swearing! I don't think they got the sentiment somehow! And not long after that, Andy left to do another band with Kenny, and me and Tommy were back to square one."

The Social Dogs, with Andy's brother Allan (who later wrote for the New Musical Express under the pseudonym Tommy Udo) making a guest appearance, actually had one of their excruciating bedroom recordings, the track 'Morning Star', appear on the Crass Records demo compilation 'Bullshit Detector, Volume One'.

Eventually Ian and Tommy asked Ricky McGuire, one of Tommy's friends from school, to play bass, and Chaotic Youth were conceived soon after.

"He'd never played before but just copied what the guitar was doing on the top string, but then he really took to it, a real natural, and was playing all wee fiddly bits in no time! I think it was Ricky who knew John (Hamilton), who wanted to be a drummer, so we asked him to join. He'd never played before either, but he took to it naturally as well."

"Ricky saved up to buy a bass guitar, but didn't have enough to buy a case for it, so in the early days our equipment was carried about in cardboard boxes," recalls Tommy. "John was the only one whose family had a car so early rehearsals were held in his garage. However, this didn't last long as John's neighbours were, for some reason, deeply offended by the fantastic musical talent that was oozing out of the garage, and would subsequently call the police to shut us up…"

Probably the main reason for the band's lack of profile was the fact that they never ever played outside of Scotland.

"I remember trying to do gigs was always a hassle," agrees Ian. "We had no equipment of our own, and no van or anything like that. For rehearsals we'd use my dad's amps, and my sister's PA. She was in a rock band at the time, and one of her band members would give us a lift to rehearsal and back in their old van. It was only about a mile away but this van used to break down two or three times there and back. When we did gigs we had to rely on the other bands we were playing with to let us use their gear. To be honest, as far as the gigs went, we treated them more like a night out on the piss; by the time we got onstage we were always really drunk. In fact, at one of the gigs we played with Anti Pasti and the Threats at the Mayfair (in Glasgow, now called the Garage), I was seeing three guitar necks and wasn't quite sure which was the real one! We used to just plug in and hope for the best, and usually it wasn't too bad… well, most folk seemed to like it anyway."

Suitably encouraged, the band entered a local eight-track studio and recorded a ten-song demo, which landed them a place on No Future's 'A Country Fit For Heroes' compilation. Despite having been recorded virtually live, their song 'Whose Bomb?' was a definite highlight of the collection, and garnered the band much interest. They were even offered a UK tour with The Exploited, which unfortunately fell through due to their total lack of transport or equipment.

"We had lots of other gig offers and fanzine interviews after the No Future record," says Ian. "We even had a royalty cheque off them once! It wasn't much, just enough for a few beers, so we went out and got pissed – instead of putting it towards something useful that might help or promote the band!

"We also sent the second demo to No Future, and they didn't like it too much. It was a lot noisier, much more typical of the early Eighties punk sound. We just fell into it all really. Looking back we should've stuck to our guns and played what we wanted, not what we thought everyone else wanted to hear."

Although passed up by No Future, Chaotic Youth soon found themselves signed to Blackpool label, Beat The System, for the excellent 'Sad Society' EP. Again it was Bill 'Grumpy' McInlay, whom Ian credits with landing them the deal. Not only did he do a fanzine called Another Load Of Bollocks, but he roadied for The Fits, who were Beat The System's best-selling act.

"Grumpy basically talked Barry Lights (B.T.S. label boss) into signing us; I don't think he'd even heard us, he just did it to shut Grumpy up, haha! We'd actually split up by the time we recorded it anyway, but got back together to do the single, thought it'd be a laugh. We went down to Blackpool to record it, and did it all in a few hours. It was very rushed, 'cos External Menace were recording their first single the same day. I seem to remember using Sneddy's guitar to record 'cos mine was playing up as usual!

"Anyway, the next thing we knew was Barry Lights was talking about not releasing it 'cos he was unhappy with the mix or something. I only found out that it actually came out after I moved to London and met someone in the record shop I worked at who had a copy!"

The 1982 single featured four tracks – 'Sad Society', 'No Future UK', 'Tip Off (The Police)' and 'Arms Race' – that weren't dissimilar to a more melodic, mid-tempo Exploited in their restrained abrasive power, with Ricky's thick gurgling bass sound a commanding anchor at the centre of the melee. Barry Lights also put a further two songs – 'Out Of Order' and 'Don't Take Their Shit' – recorded during the same session as the single, on his 'Total Anarchy' compilation, which saw the band holding their own alongside other Beat The System signings such as Uproar and Death Sentence.

"We just stopped practising really, lost interest and went our separate ways," admits Ian, on the band's untimely demise. "We never discussed it or anything, but Ricky went off and joined The Fits, and I moved to London, and that was that. Ricky was the only one who wanted to be a musician; I was never really that bothered. I just enjoyed writing songs, and I never thought about 'getting anywhere' with the band... stuff like No Future and Beat The System just sort of happened!

"Tommy went and joined External Menace for a while, and then roadied for Mick Rossi from Slaughter And The Dogs' band, The Duellists. I did a coupla bands in the early Nineties and we did a few gigs and a few demos, but nothing ever came of it. I even did a Chaotic gig for my 40th birthday party, with a few mates. I was the only original member but I was surprised at how good all the songs sounded even now!"

SELECT DISCOGRAPHY:
'Sad Society' EP (Beat The System, 1982)

AT A GLANCE:
Three of the tracks from the 'Sad Society' single appeared on Anagram's 1995 'Beat The System - The Punk Singles' CD, and the 'Total Anarchy' compilation also enjoyed a CD release, through Step-1 in 1996. It's worth noting that 'Tip Off (The Police)', the track from the single that doesn't appear on the Anagram CD, actually appears on the 'Total Anarchy' CD as one of the bonus tracks.

E lsewhere, Patrol from Fife and Intensive Care, who eventually relocated to Crawley, had two tracks each on Volume Two of 'A Country Fit For Heroes', the former even having their early Eighties output recently

Chaotic Youth, live 1982
L-R: Tommy Wallace (vocals), Ian Wallace (background), Ricky McGuire (foreground)
Note the high-tech lighting rig... a torch!

released by Intimidation Records as a red-vinyl 7". Another band freshly exhumed by Intimidation is The Actives, from Dunfermline, who had two EPs ('Riot' and 'Wait And See') and an album ('Kick It Down'), released by Quiet Records in 1983. The (limited to 500 copies) 'Reactivated' LP contains seventeen previously unavailable demo tracks recorded between 1982 and 1986.

The Actives from Dunfermline, an underrated band 'freshly exhumed by Intimidation Records'

THE ACTIVES

D unfermline band The Actives formed in 1980 and issued a mighty fine 7", 12" and LP before fizzling out when band members moved onto other things. Their premature demise was a little disappointing as their releases, and especially some of the demos they recorded between those vinyl releases, captured the aggression of The Exploited, the speed of Discharge and the hooks of GBH.

"I heard the first Ramones album, and then 'Damned, Damned, Damned', and they radically changed what my idea of music was fundamentally about," begins drummer Paul Kirk. "It didn't matter how proficient you were, it was more about the raw energy. Then I discovered the wonders of the John Peel show and would tape his show every night, and try to get the 7" singles that he'd played via Small Wonder Records mail-order in London, or Bruce's in Edinburgh or Muir's in Dunfermline [whose owner, Sandy Muir, was the manager of The Skids at the time]. I was also lucky in

The Actives

that my close friends were also into punk, so we'd exchange tapes and lend each other records and fanzines.

"My home town of Dunfermline had a great live music scene. There was the famous Kinema Ballroom [as seen in the Clash's 'Rude Boy' film] which put on most of the early punk bands like The Clash, Stranglers, Damned, Ultravox, Wayne County, Richard Hell & the Voidoids, Suicide, The Ruts, Rezillos, and Slaughter & the Dogs etc. There were also a few smaller places like the Glen Pavilion, Carnegie Hall Annexe and Belleville Hotel for bands to play. Dunfermline was also home to [the aforementioned] Skids, who were very much the local heroes. They definitely gave the town an extra lift when it came to the punk scene in its early days. Also a band called Delinx, who were really good. They featured Bruce Watson, who went on to Big Country fame."

Four friends from school, The Actives also featured vocalist Lewis Kennedy, guitarist Graeme 'Smed' Smith, and bassist Alan 'Budgie' Burgess, and were inspired to start their own band by local anarcho act The Alternative, who several of them roadied for.

"It just seemed like a natural progression from carrying and helping set up another band's gear to doing it with our own gear," reckons Paul. "We didn't really have any big plans though . . . maybe to get a single out and have John Peel play it. That was about as far as it went. We just enjoyed making a racket, and at the same time trying to get to grips with the rudiments of our chosen instruments. Rat Scabies was my hero, so I *had* to be the drummer – even though I was pretty useless! It didn't seem to matter, and rightfully so."

Predictably enough then, The Actives played their first gig in support of The Alternative, at the Kirkcaldy YMCA in late 1981 ("Some of the crowd seemed to like us which we thought was quite surprising!"), before recording their first demo with John Turner at Palladium Studios in Edinburgh. More gigging and a second demo brought them to the attention of ex-Menace bassist Charlie Casey who landed them a deal with new London label Quiet (also responsible for releases by New Model Army and Red Letter Day etc.). The debut 'Riot' EP was admittedly rough round the edges, but propelled by that abrasive energy so prevalent at the time.

"We went back in to Palladium and recorded and mixed four songs in a day and a half. To our surprise, it was very well received [reaching No. 14 in Sounds magazine's Punk Chart] but in hindsight it could have been much better produced. We were pushed for time, though, not to mention our financial constraints, so we just had to make do. It still sounds okay.

"We played Glasgow, Edinburgh and London to promote it, and lots of smaller venues dotted around Scotland and the north of England. We had some good support slots with the UK Subs, Exploited, Abrasive Wheels and Adicts. The best gig was probably the one with the Wheels in Glasgow though. We played a blinder that night, and it was great to have a seething mass of punks going crazy down the front. The worst gig we ever did was in a small mining town in east Scotland; they hated us and wanted to do us serious harm before, during and after the gig! We were lucky to escape unscathed."

The 'Kick It Down' LP was then rushed out to capitalise on the buzz generated by the EP, but was hindered by a thin boxy sound, albeit one that was in keeping with the traditionally lo-fi aesthetics of the UK82 genre. Once acclimatised to the dinny mix though, there's some hard-hitting punk rock to be had, with harsh vocals reminiscent of Bristol's Court Martial.

"Quiet gave us the princely sum of 250 quid," scoffs Paul, "And we knocked the whole thing out in two days at Palladium. We hated it. The production is atrocious, as is the mastering, which rather than make it sound a wee bit better actually made it sound even worse. None of us play our copies very often, if at all. The demos we did around that time sounded much, much better, so we'd always play them instead."

The band's parting shot – at the time – was the 'Wait & See!' 12", which was recorded during January 1984 at London's Alaska Studios, and was a thoroughly convincing release that saw the band starting to mature into a punk band of considerable power and intellect. Sadly though, they went their separate ways before they could really fulfil that potential.

"Well, the most obvious progression was that we could finally all play our instruments a lot better, which resulted in a much tighter-sounding release. If you compare the 'Riot' EP with 'Wait & See!', you'll hear what I mean. And lyrically, Lewis went from singing about boredom, being on the dole and Thatcherism through to isolation and failed relationships.

"But then he [Lewis] left to go to Spain to work and live, and shortly after, despite us getting a new singer [Rice, previously with Alternative], I was offered the drumming job with Twisted Nerve from Edinburgh. Our last gig was supporting the Toy Dolls who we, as local legend has it, apparently blew off the stage. We were extremely tight by then and could hammer through our set a bit like the Ramones used to. It was at a venue called The Palace in Rosyth, a dockyard town about ten minutes outside Dunfermline."

Paul continued with Twisted Nerve for a while before playing in various short-lived projects and starting his own label, Human Condition Records. After working in the USA and Canada as a production manager, he got married and moved to Japan, where he now runs Hand-Held Recordings and makes music under the moniker Akatombo. Smed went on to play double bass in the popular jazz/blues band Baby Isaac, whilst Lewis and Budgie both chose family life over the pursuit of a musical career.

In 2003, Intimidation Records compiled the band's strongest demo recordings for the first time on vinyl as the 'Reactivated' LP, but there was never any real consideration given by the ex-band members to reforming to promote it. Instead they prefer to be remembered as they were, a young belligerent force to be reckoned with, albeit somewhat overlooked in the grand scheme of things.

"We'd had our fling," concedes Paul. "It was, and still is, a job for the younger generations to get out there and make a racket. But we were – and still are – a very unassuming bunch of blokes, so maybe if people remember a good time whilst watching us play, or have a happy memory related to listening to our vinyl releases, that'd be good. What set us apart from other Scottish/UK bands on the go at that time was how fast our songs were. We played at the same tempo as the early hardcore bands from the U.S. Great fun . . . but knackering if you were the drummer!"

SELECT DISCOGRAPHY:
7"S:
'Riot' EP (Quiet, 1983)

12"S:
'Wait & See!' (Quiet, 1984)

LPS:
'Kick It Down' (Quiet, 1983)
'Reactivate' (Intimidation, 2003)

AT A GLANCE:
Intimidation's 'Reactivate' LP is the album the band would prefer us to remember them by, compiling as it does their demos from '82 and '83, which were actually superior to their vinyl releases.

CHAPTER TWELVE

THE LABELS

RIOT CITY

In keeping with the DIY punk ethic, rather than shop their demos around in search of a deal, many of the second wave punk bands released their earliest records themselves, and literally hundreds of independent record labels sprang up almost overnight. Most of them crashed and burnt as quickly as they had flourished, but some were excessively prolific – albeit for a short time – and played a major part in the scene's development.

Bristol-based Riot City, along with rival company No Future, was probably the label most synonymous with the whole early Eighties hardcore punk vibe, loved by the fans for its consistent output, despised by mainstream industry types who were no doubt appalled at the seeming lack of quality control being exercised. It must have appeared to them, or any casual observer, that almost anyone could pick up a guitar, thrash out a tune and get a record released… but isn't that the essence of punk rock in a nutshell?

Riot City grew from Heartbeat, a label started by Simon Edwards in 1978, the idea for a pure punk offshoot initially kindled when he included Vice Squad on his now-legendary 'Avon Calling' compilation album.

"Much to the disgust of many of the other bands on there!" snorts Simon. "Some of whom actually pulled out when Vice Squad were confirmed for inclusion! I was so fucked off at this attitude towards them that I really wanted to piss these bigoted wankers off by doing more stuff with bands like this… and not long after, Vice Squad recorded a demo, brought it round to me and, of course, I loved it. I took it to Cherry Red, with whom I had just secured a production deal, but they hated it, and said they wouldn't finance it! If only they knew then what they do now!

"So, from that point, I was on my own. I returned to Bristol with the grim news of rejection, but it just so happened that Dave and Shane from Vice Squad had this idea of forming a label totally dedicated to releasing punk bands. And they had already come up with the name Riot City - a reaction to street riots and the blight of frustration that was sweeping the country."

And in early 1981, Riot City was officially launched, with Vice Squad's hugely successful, 'Last Rockers' single being the first release. A true classic in every sense of the word, it stormed the Independent Charts and propelled both band and label into the limelight. Over the course of the next three years, Riot City went on to release almost thirty more singles, eleven albums and various 12"s, by punk bands from the length and breadth of the country, not just Bristol, that sold in total over 200,000 copies. As well as Vice Squad, many stalwarts of the genre, including the Abrasive Wheels, Chaos UK and The Varukers, enjoyed releases on the label, all of which were snapped up by a noise-hungry public.

"It was quite a personal thing," reckons Simon, when asked how he chose the bands he would put out from the slew of demos he received every day. "If I liked the music and thought they came across as good people with a worthy cause, then chances are we would get on. I didn't always agree with their sentiment, but if they put it forward with enough passion and belief then who was I to stand in their way? I had a unique vehicle to give them a voice and in a way felt obliged to let them scream. I always liked the more chaotic approach too, so a few 'loose ones' got through just because I liked their guts."

A perfect example of how Riot City liked to give exposure to rough 'n' ready, upcoming new punk bands was the 'Riotous Assembly' compilation album. The label's first full-length release, it made the Indie Top Ten when it spent two months in the Chart during the summer of 1982.

"Once again the criteria for inclusion wasn't the first ten Pistols soundalikes who contacted us, but more that certain 'They deserve a chance' approach, and that included some that maybe would never get a single deal with us but we still thought that what they sent deserved to be heard."

The cover even consisted not of band photos, but of pictures of Bristol punks taken at an impromptu session in the middle of the city one Saturday morning!

"Ah yes, that was an event to behold," chuckles Simon. "I just put the word out that I would be doing this photo-shoot for the album sleeve down in town outside Virgin, a common meeting place for the Bristol punks, thinking only twenty or thirty would show up – never once expecting the crowds that did actually show! The theme was obviously a 'Riotous Assembly' and that's really what we got! But thankfully we managed to get all the shots done just before the local constabulary decided to join in! It was quite a spectacle, generally good-humoured, and just great to see all those punks together...shame we couldn't use more of the photos on the album really."

The album helped land certain bands, such as Court Martial, The Undead and Resistance '77, a proper deal with the label, whilst other bands such as TDA, Havoc and Dead Katss, promptly vanished without trace after inclusion.

"I always liked the Vice Squad 12" EP of the first two 45s," ponders Simon, when pushed to choose his favourite Riot City releases. "It had a story behind it, and was really the culmination of a number of memorable occasions... the crazy sales that blew us all away... all the great tours... and, best of all, me getting thrown off the stage just after taking the cover photo by an over-zealous bouncer that didn't know who I was and wouldn't listen to any reason! The Cambridge Corn Exchange left its mark on me in more ways than one...

"I always had great affection for Chaos UK too; they were great blokes and Vice Squad hated them which helped satisfy my need to put out records that pissed people off! Especially as it was on a label they helped create in the first place! This is punk rock after all...

"Mayhem's releases were great, although the band never quite matched their recorded intensity live but still I've always wished they could have been bigger. If I had to take two singles to a desert island though, it would be Emergency's 'Points Of View', and Ultra Violent's 'Crime For Revenge', though a close third would be something by The Ejected. I mean, how many times has a beggar asked you for 10p and you've replied 'Nah, not me'?

"But there are no real favourites; there's just too many fine moments across all of the releases. For example, how could I possibly rate 'Sausage, Beans And Chips' by Chaotic Dischord as my favourite? Yet it, and many others, are, to me, utterly indispensable."

Of course, Chaotic Dischord were the project band put together by certain members of Vice Squad primarily to prove a point to Simon that they thought he was signing too many generic thrash bands.

"Yeah that's partly true," he admits. "One boozy night in the Fishponds Full Moon pub, I was given a cassette by Igor, a Vice Squad roadie, who said that Dischord were from Swindon and refused to talk to record labels as they were seen to be the

Simon Edwards of Riot City Records

establishment. It was more nonsense that appealed to me at the time... and as for the music? Well, it was brilliant – just a horrible fuckin' racket, and, of course, I loved it. I was never part of the political side of punk so this stuff was, to me, the antidote – songs that sounded 'politico' but were just the opposite!

"The whole thing blew up in my face when I found out that it was fuckin' Vice Squad. I think it was Rob (Miller, aka The Baron) from the Amebix who told me first, bless him. An hour or so of humiliation passed off with me just laughing out loud at being had! What a tosser I felt! But time would tell a different story when the band actually started selling a lot of records.

"I think you have to be able to take all this stuff on the chin otherwise how tedious would life be? Never did this sort of clowning around ever make me think twice about what I was doing. It was all a part of it; we were all having a blast. We never ever believed that it would have been as good as it was, so still having people writing about it all these years later is extremely flattering."

It wasn't all smiles though, with the label copping a lot of flak from critics, (Sounds journalist) Garry Bushell even referring to it once as the 'dustbin of punk'.

"There was also a lot of shit written about Riot City in Maximum Rock & Roll; Crass even accused me of being 'The back door to EMI, endorsing them and making missiles from my front room'! What utter, utter bollocks! Vice Squad had signed to EMI and had kept the Riot City logo for their EMI releases... an odd thing, yes, but it had nothing to do with my own operation. And, for the record, I thought signing to them was a very bad decision by the Vice Squad management anyway.

"I would have always hoped that the punk ethos would have meant people with strong opinions had to check things out first, then shout out loud afterwards, safe in the knowledge that they were right... not just rant about crap that made no sense! That sort of thing did piss me off, but then I just laughed at it and got on with things that mattered.

"Someone's opinion is just that – their own opinion – and you have to have a broader outlook than that when running a label. I didn't put out records to satisfy critics; they were released because we, the bands and me, wanted to put them out. It's easy to turn around now and say, 'Yeah, but they could have been better produced', or whatever. Well, I'm sure they could have been, but at the time we didn't have an unlimited resource, so we did the best we could with what we had, simple as that. I stand by all the stuff we did, although, sure, if I did some of them now, the approach may well be different."

Inevitably, though, the tsunami that was the second wave of punk rock eventually crashed spectacularly to shore, its implosion not only leaving behind many casualties but also sowing the seeds for the ensuing UK hardcore scene. Riot City were one of many labels left high and dry, exhausted of both funds and inspiration.

"Sales were falling, not just mine but other companies too," sighs Simon. "The second wave was waning and the time felt right to stop while we were just about still ahead. We managed to squeeze out another couple of Chaotic Dischord releases, just for the hell of it, but then it was more a matter of, 'Oh fuck it, that's enough!'

"I suppose I couldn't help but regret it. I'd had such an amazing time doing something that had become a major part of my life; it was rather like losing a close friend. I did wander around wondering what to do next for quite a while!"

For many years, Simon concentrated on his career as a route planner for the AA, content in the knowledge that he helped shape musical history in some small but significant way, but more recently he has returned to the fray with Trash City Records. A scaled-down version of Riot City for the new millennium, the label has so far helped launch A-KO, a stunning melodic metalcore band, on an unsuspecting public.

"The underground movements around the mainstream are still as vibrant as ever," says Simon optimistically. "Hardcore punk seems consistently healthy, producing some fine bands, and the very fact that new labels spring up all the time to continue the campaign, is an important statement and clear evidence that punk rock is as meaningful and relevant now as it ever was. As for me, I'm just bloody proud to have been able to play a part in punk's history."

CHRONOLOGICAL LABEL DISCOGRAPHY:

7"s:

Vice Squad 'Last Rockers' (1981)
Vice Squad 'Resurrection' (1981)
The Insane 'Politics' (1981)
Abrasive Wheels 'Vicious Circle' (1981)
Court Martial 'Gotta Get Out' (1982)
Chaos UK 'Burning Britain' (1982)
Undead 'It's Corruption' (1982)
The Expelled 'No Life, No Future' (1982)
Abrasive Wheels 'Army Song' (1982)
Chaotic Dischord 'Fuck The World' (1982)
Court Martial 'No Solution' (1982)
Chaos UK 'Loud, Political And Uncompromising' (1982)
Mayhem 'Gentle Murder' (1982)
The Ejected 'Have You Got 10p?' (1982)
Undead 'Violent Visions' (1982)
Abrasive Wheels 'Burn 'Em Down' (1982)
The Expelled 'Government Policy' (1982)
Resistance '77 'Nowhere To Play' (1982)
The Ejected 'Noise For The Boys' (1982)
No Choice 'Sadist Dream' (1983)
Emergency 'Points Of View' (1983)
Chaotic Dischord 'Never Trust A Friend' (1983)
Sex Aids 'Back On The Piss Again' (1983)
Mayhem 'Pulling Puppet's Strings' (1983)
Ultra Violent 'Crime For Revenge' (1983)
The Underdogs 'East Of Dachau' (1983)
The Varukers 'Die For Your Government' (1983)
The Ejected 'Push The Button' (1983)
The Varukers 'Led To The Slaughter' (1983)

12"s:

Vice Squad 'Last Rockers'/'Resurrection' (1981)
Chaotic Dischord 'Don't Throw It All Away' (1983)
The Varukers 'Another Religion, Another War' (1984)
Chaos UK 'The Singles' (1984)

LPs:

Various Artists 'Riotous Assembly' (1982)
Various Artists 'Hell Comes To Your House' (1982) – licensed f/Bemisbrain Records, USA
Abrasive Wheels 'When The Punks Go Marching In' (1982)
Chaos UK 'Chaos UK' (1983)
The Ejected 'A Touch Of Class' (1983)
Chaotic Dischord 'Fuck Politics, Fuck Religion, Fuck The Lot Of You' (1983)

The Varukers 'Bloodsuckers' (1983)
Undead 'Killing Of Reality' (1984)
The Ejected 'The Spirit Of Rebellion' (1984)
Chaotic Dischord 'Live In New York' (1984)
Various Artists 'Life's A Riot And Then You Die' (1985)

AT A GLANCE:

Step-1 reissued the must-have 'Riotous Assembly' compilation on CD in 1994, whilst Anagram released – in '93 and '95 respectively – two highly recommended CD compilations, 'Riot City, The Punk Singles' Volumes One And Two. Between the two discs there are almost sixty tracks that provide an ideal overview of the label. Most recently, Anagram have issued a series of well-packaged CDs, 'The Riot City Years', each one concentrating on particularly noteworthy bands, including Vice Squad, Abrasive Wheels, Chaos UK and The Varukers, that released stuff on the label.

NO FUTURE

L ike Riot City, No Future were only very prolific for a short time, but their bands and releases dominated the Independent Charts with gleeful abandonment, and have remained hugely influential to this very day. "It was around about 1980, I think, when I left school and went to work for the Ministry Of Defence in Malvern," begins label co-founder, Chris Berry. "I was in a big open plan office, and I got friendly with this guy, Richard Jones, who, along with Iain McNay of Cherry Red in London, had his own promotions company. He used to put on gigs at the Malvern Winter Gardens, and even used to sell records he would buy from Rough Trade in London on a stall there, and I ended up going along, working on the stall, and enjoying all these bands. Richard taught me a lot about music, and if it hadn't been for him, I would probably still be listening to Led Zeppelin and Pink Floyd… I was quite happy with all that until I was introduced to punk rock.

"One day we were chatting, and we decided to start our own label, and we put an advert in Sounds asking for 'punk and skinhead bands'. At the time that was what excited us, and we thought there was a market for it. Riot City had just started up, and Cherry Red had just had great success with The Dead Kennedys.

"The name, as cheesy as this may sound, came from The Pistols' song. It always used to amaze me when people said The Pistols couldn't play; they were fantastic musicians, that guitar sound was amazing… although they were more rock'n'roll than anything else really.

"Anyway, after that ad, we were swamped with demo tapes. Not only that, but I'd been stupid enough to put my home phone number on the ad, and I still lived at home with my parents, so I'd get in from work, and my mother would have my tea ready… but it would go cold 'cos the phone was always ringing! My parents were very

The Blood, one of the most unruly signings to Malvern-based No Future Records (Pic: Tony Mottram)

accepting really, 'cos I had some really weird and wonderful people ringing up all the time."

The best demo they received was from a New Mills band, Blitz, whose superb four-track 'All Out Attack' debut EP was the label's first release, and was an incredible, unexpected overnight success story.

"The Blitz demo had so much aggression and power, and the sheer sound and presentation of it was far beyond anything else we'd been sent," remembers Chris. "It was ready to go as it was, in fact, 'cos they'd actually bothered to go into a good studio and do a decent recording. Blitz always were a little different from the other bands we worked with; they had their heads screwed on and knew what they were doing and where they wanted to go. Unfortunately, in the end, they started to believe their own hype a bit too much.

"We did one thousand copies to start with, 'cos that's all we thought we'd sell. So we didn't even bother getting any labels pressed, we just used white labels and stamped them. I took them off to London to Rough Trade, and they bought the lot, and said, 'We think you better press some more – and quick!' So we did another two thousand, and they sold all those too, so then we did another five thousand... it all just took off. Garry Bushell picked up on them, and it went from there."

Suddenly able to fund further releases far easier than expected, No Future began snapping up punk talent from all around the country, quickly garnering a strong roster that between them turned out many a much-loved punk classic. The Partisans, a young band from Bridgend in South Wales, were next with their rabid 'Police Story' single, closely followed by Brighton's tongue-in-cheek Test Tube Babies, and their eminently loveable 'Banned From The Pubs' EP.

"We never looked too far ahead; just the next release, the next gig," reckons Chris. "We were too busy trying to look after all these bands we were signing, a lot of whom portrayed this ferocious image, but in person, were quite the opposite – a lot of them were actually very immature. Some of them were literally kids. I remember The Partisans were asked to do quite a big gig in Bristol, with Vice Squad I think, and I had a phone call from one of their parents, and was told that they weren't allowed to go unless there was a chaperone, haha! Their parents just wanted their best interests, obviously, but because of their ages, they were a contractual nightmare.

"Things went badly wrong with The Test Tube Babies in the end though, but that had a lot to do with their manager, Nick McGerr. Looking back he was far more professional than we were, but he took away any fun we might have had working with the band. He would think nothing of driving up to Malvern from Somerset to have a rant! I remember we did a No Future gig at the Lyceum, and Peter slagged me off from the stage for about twenty minutes, which was... well, different! But musically they were brilliant."

One of the label's earliest releases was the 'A Country Fit For Heroes' 12", a low-priced sampler that compiled, much like Crass Record's 'Bullshit Detector' series did, the best tracks from some of the many demos the label had been sent.

"That was Richard's idea really, I have to give him credit for that. There were a lot of bands who had one great song on their demo, but who weren't worthy of a proper deal. We just decided to do a 12" to give some of them some exposure. We did it all on the cheap really – we nicked the front cover photo from a book without crediting the source... and we were really naughty and didn't send out any free copies to the bands! We wanted to keep the cover price as low as possible, so it was all done on the cheap, but it did incredibly well for what it is. Bushell really championed that one."

Several of the bands that appeared on the 12" went on to sign for further releases – The Samples, from Worcester, who Chris actually managed; Attak and The Violators, who were both from the same area as Blitz; Crux from Nuneaton, who went on to do a split 12" with Crash; and the excellent Blitzkrieg, who opened the sampler in fine, electrifying style with 'The Future Must

Be Ours' and then released one further single for the label.

"We used to get on quite well with most of our bands, especially before they got too big; they would treat us quite respectfully 'cos we were putting out their records. I used to like working with Blitz, especially Carl, and I can remember crashing over on his bedroom floor, and talking into the middle of the night and his mum ended up shouting at us! I would have these bands come stay with me, too, and I was still living at home. My mum and dad were always very tolerant of all these mohicans turning up at all hours on our doorstep."

Not all the bands were quite so easy to work with however. "I gotta tell you about The Blood!" laughs Chris, further confirming all the rumours that the band were essentially an unmanageable force of nature. "Bushell put them in touch with us, and we did this brilliant single with them. They came up to the office for a meeting, and they all seemed to be about six feet tall! I first met with them in London at this really dodgy pub, where the landlord had this huge dog and a shotgun behind the bar... and when it was turning-out time, he just used to let the dog out from behind the bar!

"Anyway, they turned up at Adelaide House with at least sixteen cans of lager each, to sign these contracts, and within the first hour, they filled the whole building with cigarette smoke, and drank the bloody lot. I was completely phased by the time they left. One single with them was quite enough!"

After a very prosperous few years, when it seemed that everything pumped out by the label would be snapped up greedily by the record-buying public (Blitz's Voice Of A Generation' album even spending a month in the Top Thirty of the National Charts), No Future's fortunes took a dive in 1984, when Chris hit some serious cash flow problems.

"I think I went a bit loopy really," he confesses. "The music scene was changing, the initial excitement for punk music was waning, sales were dropping... and effectively we were spending more money than we had coming in. Had I known then what I do now, we should have had someone do some financial forecasting – but all we had was a local accountant that just prepared our books. I didn't have anyone telling me, 'No, you can't spend that much in the studio', so I just went and spent it! I was personally convinced that things were going to carry on as well as they had been forever. Soon we owed money to the pressing plants and everything."

One of the things that Chris did to try and stop the rot, perhaps suspecting the label had painted itself into a corner, was start up Future Records, an offshoot where he could release more experimental material.

"I set up Future mainly to release Blitz, when they went all weird. Carl had got involved with Tim Harris, who had previously produced the band, and they did a single, 'Telecommunication', which actually sold very well – it got a lot of air play on Peel and Jensen, but then things went a bit too arty.

"We lost credibility in the eyes of most punks about then, and we definitely lost the support of Bushell. I'd probably had enough too; I was getting tired of it all, and we released a few distinctly dodgy records towards the end that really should have never came out.

"I went on to do Future for quite a long time after, working with a band called And Also The Trees, who were very successful in Europe and did a lot of touring out there. They were kinda like The Cure, and I worked with them for three or four years, but wasn't earning any money when I desperately needed to. In the end, I couldn't even afford to pay the rent. It was a bit of a sad day really, but I went and got a real job; I felt it was time to move on."

Chris now runs a retail business in the Cotswolds with his partner, but still regards his time as a punk rock magnate with philosophical fondness, and has even been contemplating a return to the fray of music management since being interviewed for this book.

"Like I said, we were caught up in the whole thing, and just enjoying the scene, and we were attracting a certain type of band. We didn't really know what we were doing at the time; we were just putting records out. We were only nineteen or twenty or whatever, and we just did what we did. I'm very flattered, and more than a little gobsmacked to be honest, to think that what we did is still regarded as so important."

SELECT CHRONOLOGICAL LABEL DISCOGRAPHY:

7"s:
Blitz 'All Out Attack' EP (1981)
The Partisans 'Police Story' (1981)
Peter And The Test Tube Babies 'Banned From The Pubs' (1982)
Red Alert 'In Britain' (1982)
Blitz 'Never Surrender' (1982)
Attak 'Today's Generation' (1982)
Blitzkrieg 'Lest We Forget' (1982)
The Violators 'Gangland' (1982)
The Insane 'El Salvador' (1982)
Channel 3 'I've Got A Gun' (1982)
The Partisans '17 Years Of Hell' (1982)
Red Alert 'Take No Prisoners' (1982)
The Samples 'Dead Hero' (1982)
Peter And The Test Tube Babies 'Run Like Hell' (1982)
Blitz 'Warriors' (1982)
Attak 'Murder In The Subway' (1982)
The Violators 'Summer Of '81' (1982)
Red Alert 'City Invasion' (1983)
The Wall 'Day Tripper' (1983)
The Blood 'Megalomania' (1983)
Rose Of Victory 'Suffragette City' (1983)

12"s:
Various Artists 'A Country Fit For Heroes' (1982)
Crux/Crash 'Split' (1982)
Various Artists 'A Country Fit For Heroes, Volume 2' (1983)
Screaming Dead 'Night Creatures' (1983)
The Violators 'Die With Dignity' (1983)
Red Alert 'There's A Guitar Burning' (1983)

LPs:
Blitz 'Voice Of A Generation' (1982)
Channel 3 'I've Got A Gun' (1982)
Peter And The Test Tube Babies 'Pissed And Proud' (1982)
The Partisans 'The Partisans' (1983)
Red Alert 'We've Got The Power' (1983)
Attak 'Zombies' (1983)
Channel 3 'After The Lights Go Out' (1983)
Various Artists 'Angels With Dirty Faces' (1984)
Various Artists 'There Is No Future' (1984)

AT A GLANCE:
Captain Oi!'s twenty-four track 'A Country Fit For Heroes' CD (1994) compiles both volumes of the influential compilation 12" onto one disc, complete with original artwork and informative liner notes. Anagram's excellent double-CD 'The History Of No Future' features fifty-four tracks from all the label's best releases, plus cover art, a discography and yet more liner notes, and is thus a convenient and ideal overview.

CLAY

lthough No Future and Riot City boasted the greater number of punk bands, what Clay Records lacked in quantity, they more than made up for with quality, releasing the classic early albums by two of the biggest and most important bands of the genre, Discharge and GBH. "I started out working in London in the mid-Seventies, for Beggars Banquet," begins Mike Stone, who founded the label in Stoke-on-Trent in 1979. "I was actually the first 'outsider' employed by the company, but I was quite instrumental in starting up their label. I was running their shop in North End Road for them, and we had a rehearsal room in the basement; Generation X practised there, so did The Lurkers. They made a right racket, to be honest, but it was an exciting racket, and I ended up managing them. I ran 'em around, getting them gigs and stuff, and I got them signed to Beggars Banquet after a great gig at The Roxy. Their single was the first release on Beggars Banquet – BEG 1. I was in charge of A & R for the label, and signed a lot of bands, including a Mod group called The Merton Parkas.

"To cut a long story short, I left the company the same week that Gary Numan went No. 1 with 'Are Friends Electric?' It's hard to believe now, 'cos it was like a fairy story at the time, but they were on the point of going bankrupt just as Gary topped the charts and saved them! It was totally unexpected. I can still remember him walking into the shop unannounced with a demo in his hand.

"Anyway, I moved to Stoke in 1979, with my girlfriend, who lived up there, and opened a shop, Mike Stone Records, but in the back of my mind I always had the idea of doing a label of my own. I'd been bitten by the bug whilst at Beggars Banquet. The media were saying that punk was dead, but the reality was quite the opposite. From talking to everyone that came into the shop, I could see that the people still wanted to hear punk rock, but the record industry wasn't interested in servicing the demand. I just saw that gap in the market and tried to fill it."

Although the first act signed to the label was a local band, The Plastic Idols, who had an Indie Top Thirty single with 'Adventure' during the summer of 1980, the first release was actually Discharge's visceral 'Realities Of War' EP. It entered the Indie Charts on April 19th 1980, where it remained for forty-four weeks, peaking at No. 5. Despite a rough sound job, the single shook the music scene to its very foundations and established both band and label as major forces to be reckoned with.

Subsequent releases by Discharge were just as formidable, not to mention successful, with each one honing their violent sonic assault ever tighter and sharper. Inevitably Mike released several singles by his beloved Lurkers, as well as also signing such rising young punk stars as GBH and the Abrasive Wheels – the latter having just left Riot City. He also spread his musical wings somewhat by hooking up with bands such as Zanti Misfitz, White Door and The Killjoys, none of whom were anywhere near as successful as the punk bands on the roster.

"In hindsight, I wish I'd just stayed focused on the punk stuff, 'cos I went off the rails a bit at times. I'm still very proud of the punk records I released, but I did some oddball stuff that I'm ashamed I ever put the Clay name to – including a charity record for some bloody horse! The only non-punk band I don't regret working with is Demon, who I think are one of the most underrated rock bands of all time, and I'm still working with them even today. At the time, I was licensing them to Carrere Records, the same label as Saxon, and it wasn't until 'The Plague' (released July 1983, it

Mike Stone, of Clay Records, pictured in front of Mike Stone Records, with Cal from Discharge

reached No. 21 in the Indies) that they were on Clay, but they suited the label in many ways. They were lyrically quite punk for a rock band, if you know what I mean?"

Regardless of the other bands on Clay, Mike has more than guaranteed his place in Punk's Hall of Fame by issuing those aforementioned groundbreaking debuts by Discharge and GBH. Hugely influential records on not only all the punk bands that bloomed in their wake, but also many metal bands who cite these Midland thrash acts as major inspirations. Add into the equation some classic releases by The English Dogs, and some strong offerings from the Abrasive Wheels (albeit none of them as essential as their earlier Riot City output) and you have an impressive canon of work.

"I always paid my bands!" reckons Mike on his dealings with his artists. "I had run-ins with some of them – what label doesn't? But we always worked it out in the end. I got on with most of them; I always tried to be fair. Our relationships were 50/50 friendship/professional – after all, you've got to have a few ground rules!

"Although I went to the States with the Wheels in 1984, to this day I still wish I'd gone over there with Discharge for their first US tour, but I was just too busy. I ran Clay totally on my own, did everything myself. I had a silent partner that financed me to start with, John Spencer, who ran a local haulage company, and he drew a wage for the first year-and-a-half, but then I bought him out."

Sadly though, as with many other independent labels at the time, when Pinnacle went bankrupt in 1984, Clay was dragged down in the ensuing financial chaos.

"I just couldn't withstand the loss," sighs Mike regretfully. "It wasn't that huge a sum of money really, about £25,000, but I'd already banked on it coming in and had spent it on various upcoming projects, so suddenly I had to find £50,000! I tried to keep it all going as best I could, but it was too much to sort out, so in the end I sold it all off to Trojan (who have since been sold themselves to Sanctuary). I even sold them the publishing, which was a big mistake in hindsight, seeing as Metallica and Anthrax have both covered Discharge since, and Slayer have covered GBH, etc., but I got out while I could and paid all my debts."

And although burnt badly by the whole experience, Mike remains admirably optimistic, and remembers the good times fondly.

"But it took me a long time to recover, it was quite a kick in the guts. I moved to Wolverhampton and started Sonic Records, put some Demon stuff out, but that didn't work out too well, and eventually I moved back to Stoke. I still manage Demon and we have our own label, Spaced Out Music, and we've recently remastered their whole back catalogue.

"I suppose the most rewarding thing about the label was being able to put two fingers up at everyone who told me it wouldn't work. The attitude locally was terrible, everyone was laughing at me to start with, so it was fantastic when it all took off and GBH went into the National Top Twenty. It was a dream come true, I couldn't believe it."

SELECT LABEL DISCOGRAPHY:
7"s:
Discharge 'Realities Of War' (1980)
Discharge 'Fight Back' (1980)
Discharge 'Decontrol' (1980)
Discharge 'Never Again' (1981)
GBH 'No Survivors' (1982)
GBH 'Sick Boy' (1982)
The Lurkers 'This Dirty Town' (1982)
Discharge 'State Violence, State Control' (1982)

GBH 'Give Me Fire' (1982)
The Lurkers 'Drag You Out' (1982)
The Lurkers 'Frankenstein Again' (1983)
GBH 'Catch 23' (1983)
Abrasive Wheels 'Jailhouse Rock' (1983)
Abrasive Wheels 'Banner Of Hope' (1983)
Discharge 'Price Of Silence' (1983)
The Lurkers 'Let's Dance Now' (1984)
Abrasive Wheels 'The Prisoner' (1984)
Discharge 'The More I See' (1984)
GBH 'Do What You Do' (1984)
Discharge 'Ignorance' (1985)

12"s:

Discharge 'Why?' (1981)
GBH 'Leather, Bristles, Studs And Acne' (1981)
Discharge 'Warning' (1983)
English Dogs 'Mad Punx And English Dogs' (1983)
The Lurkers 'Final Vinyl' (1984)

LPs:

Discharge 'Hear Nothing, See Nothing, Say Nothing' (1982)
GBH 'City Baby Attacked By Rats' (1982)
GBH 'Leather, Bristles, No Survivors And Sick Boys' (1983)
GBH 'City Baby's Revenge' (1983)
Abrasive Wheels 'Black Leather Girl' (1984)
English Dogs 'Invasion Of The Porky Men' (1984)
Discharge 'Never Again' (1984)
Discharge 'Grave New World' (1986)

AT A GLANCE:

In 1995, Trojan issued 'Clay Punk Singles Collection' CDs by both GBH and Discharge, which were musically fantastic, of course, but thoroughly uninspired on the packaging front. Thankfully, Sanctuary have recently reissued the early Discharge back catalogue, beautifully presented in card sleeves with many extra tracks and enlightening liner notes, whilst in 2002 Captain Oi! gave the early GBH releases the CD reissue treatment they deserve.

BEAT THE SYSTEM

B ased in Blackpool, Beat The System was started by Barry Lights, who then owned One Eleven Records (named after the number of the shop), primarily to help launch The Fits. It went on to release several other well-respected hardcore punk bands, and has been surprisingly influential in its approach and style on some modern labels, not least of all Punkcore in the US.

"One night I went to Jenks and this punk band was on stage called The Fits," remembers Barry. "They were crap really, but Mick, the lead singer, had this energy that reminded me of the Sex Pistols. I mentioned the shop to him and the next thing I knew was the band came in and brought this cassette of three songs they'd recorded. I mean these lads were determined, despite so many people in Blackpool telling them they were shit, so, because I rated the singer, I agreed to manage them and help them shop around for a deal.

"A year later and still no deal, we decided to do it ourselves. The three songs that The Fits came into the shop with had been recorded in 1981 at Manchester Central Sound Studios and a guy called Terry Hampton had produced the tracks. I had already formed Lightbeat Records and Lightbeat Music, so-called because of my stage name from doing lights for a lot of top bands, but I didn't really want punk on this label, so we came up with Beat The System."

That first EP by The Fits was defiantly entitled 'You Said We'd Never Make It', and remains Barry's favourite of all his releases.

"Yes, the first one was special, even though it wasn't the best. I wanted to do a good job for the sleeve so we put a gatefold one out which included all the song lyrics and about eight different photos. We actually stopped up one night gluing them all together! It was just brilliant having that single in my hands; I can remember going down to London to pick up them up, then going round to Rough Trade and selling them a hundred copies."

Uproar, one of the more popular bands on Blackpool's Beat The System Records

That was to be the only release that The Fits did on Beat The System however, as they signed soon after to Rondelet, but Barry hooked up with several other local bands, namely Anti-Social and One Way System, before beginning to sign bands from further afield, such as External Menace and Uproar.

"I didn't really care where the bands were from as long as their music had balls, energy, excitement and good songs," reckons Barry. "They all had a lot to say for themselves, but I think most just wanted to belong somewhere and cop off with punkettes whilst having a good time!

"Somehow the political climate in Britain seems just the same now as it was then... you've got the 'haves' and the 'have-nots'. It did help the bands in a way though, having no work about; all the band members were unemployed, so it gave them plenty of time to practise.

"From the songs they wrote, a lot of the band members thought the group that they were in was their job anyway, and used it to get their message to the people; they all had a point to their lyrics."

The label certainly pulled few punches with its musical output; from the anthemic Oi of local skinheads, Anti-Social, to the blistering noise of Death Sentence, a multi-racial thrash band from the Midlands, every release was noisy, raw and very real.

Unfortunately Barry had to put the label on hold for many years when Pinnacle went bankrupt on him, but in recent times he has resurrected 'Stagebeat Music' to release the likes of the Mycro Chics.

"Punk rock today? Is there such a thing?" ponders Barry in closing. "It's all good music at the end of the day. In 1982, I had The Fits, and their songs... well, some of them... were definitely ahead of their time. I always wanted a band to do commercial punk and go to America. We all want recognition for our work. Bands, artistes and writers all need to make it in the mainstream, just to finance their creativity.

"I always let the bands do it their way though; they were the only ones that knew what they really wanted from their music, so they had full control of artwork and stuff. Most bands want you to keep off, so I've never really been too 'hands on'. Put it this way, if I had to do it all again, I wouldn't change a thing, but it's still nice to know that I can pick a good song or group from nowhere. It's hard to describe, it's just a feeling you get in your gut."

CHRONOLOGICAL LABEL DISCOGRAPHY:
7"s:
The Fits 'You Said We'd Never Make It' (1981)
One Way System 'Stab The Judge' (1982)
Anti-Social 'With Another Punk' (1982)
External Menace 'Youth Of Today' (1982)
External Menace 'No Views' (1982)
Death Sentence 'Death And Pure Destruction' (1982)
Anti-Social 'Made In England' (1982)
Anti-Social 'Official Hooligan' (1982)
Chaotic Youth 'Sad Society' (1982)
Uproar 'Rebel Youth' (1982)
Uproar 'Die For Me' (1983)
Post Mortem 'Post Mortem' (1983)

LPs:
Various Artists 'Total Anarchy' (1982)
Uproar 'And The Lord Said Let There Be...' (1983)

AT A GLANCE:
In 1995, Anagram released the twenty-five track 'Beat The System: Punk Singles Collection' CD, whilst in '96 Step-1 reissued the 'Total Anarchy' compilation on CD, complete with ten bonus tracks. Between them, the two discs give a comprehensive overview of Beat The System's early Eighties output.

Elsewhere, Secret had an incredibly strong roster that included The Exploited, The Business and Infa-Riot; WXYZ released great records by the Anti-Nowhere League, The Meteors and The Defects; Rondolet worked with Anti Pasti, Special Duties and Riot Squad; Inferno in Birmingham unleashed The Varukers, Dead Wretched and Criminal Class; and Pax gave us strong material from The Mau Maus and The Exploited. Bands tended to flit from label to label far more frequently than they do now, but at various points in their careers, Anagram was home to One Way System, Vice Squad and The Angelic Upstarts; Flicknife played host to Erazerhead, Ad Nauseam and Major Accident; Razor had The Adicts, Chron Gen and Newtown Neurotics; and Fall Out offered up Broken Bones, The Enemy and Action Pact.

CAPTAIN OI!

I n more recent years, one label has become synonymous with top quality punk reissues – Captain Oi!, the brainchild of Mark Brennan, ex-bassist with The Business and all-round punk historian extraordinaire. He can always be counted on to furnish the listener with not just great music, but also lovingly compiled booklets and as many bonus tracks as can fit onto the disc. Every release is a labour of love and that always shows in the final product.

"I did Link first with Lol (Pryor), who managed The Business," says Mark of his earliest forays into running a label. "He'd had previous experience, having already done Syndicate and Wonderful World, and I'd worked in studios before who'd done stuff for his labels, so it seemed a logical step to pair up. We wanted to do stuff for the newer bands, so the first album we did was 'Oi! The Resurrection' and we had bands like Section 5, Vicious Rumours, and Renegade, mixed in with the old, like The 4-Skins and The Business… 'cos that was the only way we could get the stores to take them.

"Anyway, we went on to put out over 200 albums! Including some ska and psychobilly stuff, but then our sales started falling off, about the same time CDs were coming out. Back then I couldn't for the life of me think who would want to buy punk rock on CD!

"We were doing Dojo Records at the same time, as part of Castle, and I didn't like a lot of things we were putting out; it wasn't really my cup of tea. Then one day we had the VAT man come down, and he had all this paperwork with him. I remember, when he went home, I chucked it all in the bin, and thought to myself, 'I really don't wanna do this much longer. It isn't fun anymore"

Whilst Lol decided to continue with the expansion of Dojo, Mark took a sabbatical and turned to writing for the likes of Record Collector. Which is where he had the idea for Captain Oi!, a collector's label where he could exhume and restore some of his favourite classic out-of-print titles.

"I was finding that there was nothing for me to buy, and I figured that there must be other people out there in the same boat. So, if I released something that I wanted to buy myself, I should be able to sell a few, and that's what's happened ever since. Some of them don't do so well, but I love everything I put out, and I won't put any more or less effort into a Dickies album that's gonna sell fifteen thousand copies to, say, a Magnificent album that might only sell a thousand. We've made a few mistakes along the way, but it ain't through lack of trying."

To start with, Mark only really planned on re-releasing maybe twenty of his favourite records, but since then he has pumped out over 300 CDs and 100 LPs, every one of them handled with the same attention to detail that garnered such a glowing reputation in the first place to the point where the Captain Oi! version of any release is now widely regarded as the definitive one.

"Originally, years ago, there was a label called Ace Records, which was mainly rockabilly, old doo-wop stuff, and blues," reveals Mark. "I'd never heard of 95% of what they put out, but I looked at their CDs and thought, 'Christ, there's really been some love put into this!' And I wanted to be the Ace Records of retro punk rock, taking classic artists and pressing it up as best as possible.

"A young fan has little chance of tracking down, let alone affording, obscure early singles by all these bands," he adds, on the subject of the ultra-rare bonus material he always manages to unearth to round off his CDs. "So I want to try to at least let them hear it. But a lot of other labels just don't give a shit. There's so much stuff out there under the banner of punk rock that's piss-poor, and it sits in the stores forever, and when you try to go and sell them a decent version, they don't take it, because the damage is already done. It's like the old saying goes; it's very hard to get a good name, but very easy to get a bad one."

In recent years, Captain Oi! has even taken to releasing brand new studio albums, albeit only by a specific type of band, proving that Brennan's not just about nostalgia and helping in the process to ensure the continuing survival of his beloved punk scene. The future as well as the past seems safe in his capable hands.

"If you look at the newer bands we've done, they all have a retro feel anyway," reckons Mark. "Like Argy Bargy, a modern Oi band. And it makes sense for bands like Special Duties and Cockney Rejects to put out new albums with us, 'cos it's the home of their old stuff too, but we're not geared up to brand new bands. We haven't got the right press people, to book adverts and allocate tour support. I did all that with Link, and I don't really wanna go down that road again. I'll re-release them though, no problem, if they come and see me in twenty years' time!"

PUNK LIVES

Although the backbone of the punk scene throughout the ages has traditionally been underground fanzines, lovingly crafted in bedrooms around the world, for just over a year, beginning back in mid-1982, there was even a glossy mag hitting high street stores solely devoted to it. Punk Lives was the spiky-haired equivalent of heavy metal's Kerrang!, and did much to popularise the second wave. Although earlier issues appeared 'slapped together' and were more biased towards posters than in-depth journalism, each issue improved on the one preceding it, despite such nonsense as a regular 'Hunky Punk Of The Month'. It became a much-needed monthly lifeline for young punks stranded in the more remote areas of the country that had little or no access to gigs and, pre-Internet, few ways to tap into the underground network.

"Before Punk Lives, there was a magazine called Punk's Not Dead," reveals its editor Alf Martin. "It was published by a company called Morgan Grampian who also owned Sounds, Record Mirror, Kerrang! and the music industry magazine, Music Week. I was then editor of Record Mirror and Kerrang! and, although the punk mag sold over 70,000 copies as a 'one-off' put together by various people on the above magazines, Morgan Grampian refused to let us produce another one. The chairman objected to the content!

"I decided punk wasn't dead, left the company and started Punk Lives from my home, basically, with my wife trying to sell adverts and deal with all the correspondence and a whole bunch of freelance writers or enthusiasts who wanted to contribute. We actually produced twelve issues but only eleven were published because, basically, we ran out of money and couldn't continue."

Towards the end of its short existence, Punk Lives was even featuring bands such as The Mob and Newtown Neurotics on its covers, and the reviews were becoming increasingly critical and trustworthy. For all its apparent trivialisation of the scene, it was certainly a valuable source of information, and it's a shame that it never had chance to evolve fully, because who knows what it may have blossomed into?

"Create a movement and pretty soon, it's got its own glossy magazine!" scoffs Kim Igoe of Action Pact. "But having worked with (the assistant editor) Mick, on his Panache fanzine, I feel I can vouch for its integrity. The only other publication championing the cause of second wave punk was Sounds, but they tended to favour the acts of the beer 'n' fags mentality. I found Punk Lives to be crucial, in that it focused on the more positive bands. It was the perfect antidote to the nonsense being spouted by the likes of Garry Bushell."

"At the time I thought Punk Lives was a good thing," reckons Tommy Couch from One Way System. "Just because it gave us more info on a growing scene. In hindsight maybe it was an attempt to cash-in, but in Fleetwood at that time, being such a small town, any news on punk was good news!"

Other bands are a little less complimentary in their appraisal.

"When you were young, it was good to finally read about your favourite band and have these posters to put on the bedroom wall," begins Paul Hoddy (Broken Bones). "But looking back at it, it was really detrimental because some of the bands believed the hype, got ideas above their station and started to release shit rock'n'roll records with full colour pictures of themselves on the front covers. I don't know why they didn't just stick to fanzines, as they were (and still are) the best way to find out about a band."

"Half of it was okay, the other half was dismal," reasons Colin from GBH. "Bands you'd never heard of, non-punk bands... even a pen pals page! But maybe it got across to a few new people. They put me on the cover of one of them; trouble was, there was a free gift of a packet of Dentyne given away with that issue, so I had a big pack of chewing gum stuck on my cheek!"

"You had to target the various punk audience elements, without letting yourself down," explains the aforementioned assistant editor Mick Mercer, who was also contributing to ZigZag and Melody Maker at the time. "So I kept to the same level of humour and didn't dumb down my opinions... although you would naturally find yourself making some of your opinions more blatant. Without wishing to annoy too many people, the average punk fan at that time didn't necessarily desire richly intelligent, informative and imaginative copy. We only had a certain audience to aim at, and to try and please all of them was never going to be easy."

Mick himself has mixed feelings about the second wave of punk, some of which manifested itself in his writing at the time.

"Mainly I loved how fortunate I was to have the best musical band and the best character band of the era, both living up the road from me. That was Dead Mans Shadow and Action Pact. It was good to interact with them and see how they developed. Musically, very few of the bands from this second generation made what people still regard as exciting records. Some, like The Varukers and The Expelled,

The Straps, live at the Music Machine, 1980 (Pic: Lynn Werner)

had a few good singles, but few had anything you could call a recognisable style, or any aura of real excitement and creativity.

"I hated the sheer predictability of most of it. The banality of the foul and useless Oi bands was actually mirrored by a lot of the anarcho and pseudo-anarcho bands simply lumbering around. Maybe 5% of all the bands had a genuine sense of direction, the rest were just some weird, if logical, extension of the scene itself being so big. I also hated the media coverage in the music papers, which seemed to assume there was nothing good involved, and so people generally didn't want to dip a toe into the spiky waters to find out for themselves."

HOLIDAYS IN THE SUN

Many of the second wave punk bands have reformed since the late Nineties as a direct (or at least indirect) result of the Holidays In The Sun festivals, either having been asked to play or encouraged by the new-found interest in their music. The brainwave of one Daz Russell (who used to book all the hardcore shows at Birmingham's legendary Mermaid venue in the Eighties), H.I.T.S. was started in 1996 with the able assistance of his then-wife Jennie.

"After he'd done a really successful punk all-dayer in Bath, Daz had this idea to do a weekend punk festival in a seaside resort and call it Holidays In The Sun!" explains Jennie, when asked about the origins of the phenomenon. "I thought he was absolutely fucking mad at first. He wanted to do it in Brighton, but the Brighton Centre would have none of it, so half jokingly I suggested Blackpool… it's a bit cheesy and a bit punk rock. He phoned the Winter Gardens there and they were well up for it, so he booked it. It all got a bit out of hand though, as the word got out, with bands asking for silly money and stuff, and it was a bit of a financial disaster. So, after that, we owed loads of people money, but it was a really great time and everybody loved it, so we decided to continue."

And the rest, as they say, is history, with the event growing in both reputation and size, and most recently even changing its name to Wasted, as part of an ambitious plan to give the festival a facelift ensuring its survival long into the future.

"The best thing is the people, though, definitely," says Jennie enthusiastically. "They come from all over the world, even places like Israel, Australia and Japan; it makes for a brilliant atmosphere. It's like one big family, that's what I love about it. There's some people there that probably only see two bands all weekend 'cos they're just chilling with folks they haven't seen since the year before. It's like one big party. And the punters see bands that they either wouldn't or couldn't, so it broadens their horizons as well."

Of course, the H.I.T.S. festivals have a reputation for being about pure nostalgia, and if a band is to thrive, as well as just survive, they have to cross over to a newer younger audience as well. More power to Daz and Jennie then for booking as many young, upcoming bands as they can, but the event is still dominated by the older bands, a fact not overlooked by its critics.

"I've only been to one," says Garry Bushell. "I hate festivals anyway, but this was just a nostalgia fest. 40-year-old punks with beer guts are just as sad as the old Teddy Boys we used to take the piss out of. Still, I guess you won't get mugged down memory lane…"

John Igoe of Dead Mans Shadow is even more damning in his condemnation. "I'm afraid that I find such exercises to be total bollocks. The whole thing is a parody of the original punk ethic and designed to line pockets… but what will they do next? A punk summer season at Butlins?

"When I was in DMS, we used to scoff at all those old buzzards like The Stones, still treading the boards. It was a great time during the punk era, but it's over. If you want to play, then try something different, but don't turn it into a laughing stock!"

"Well, I thought that H.I.T.S. was just revelling in the past the first time we played it; in fact it was like being in a time warp!" says Beki Bondage, bringing some balance to the argument. "There's nothing wrong with that as long as you give the present and future a chance too. Some of the original bands are almost like tribute bands now, they haven't moved forward at all. There were lots of bad things about punk the first time round as well as good, so you have to keep improving things. Last year's H.I.T.S. was particularly good tho', as there were loads of different people there; older punks who'd been around since the beginning and new kids who'd seen Offspring on TV and were curious about where it all came from."

"Just look at how many people turn up, I think that speaks for itself," agrees Andy from Demob. "And there's a lot of young kids there who never got chance to see these great bands first time around… these bands who helped influence all their favourite bands of today, like Blink 182 or whatever. Old fans, young fans, it doesn't matter… if your music is good enough, it will appeal to everyone. Punk rock is pretty much ageless, and it will endure. As long as people want to express themselves, there will be punk rock."

"It used to bother me when we got slagged off," sighs Jennie. "People saying that we don't pay bands or that we treat them really badly, when we don't. We've had bad times, but hasn't everybody? And we have owed people, but we've always paid them. What really pisses me off is that most of the people who slag us off have never even been. It's like, if somebody comes, and they don't like it, and they have a really shit time, then I'm sorry to hear that, but it's fair enough, but most of the shit we get comes from people who've never been, who know nothing about it in the first place."

"It's an easy criticism to say that the whole thing is an irrelevance just because a certain number of reformed bands are appearing, whatever their motives," John Finch from Lunatic Fringe rightly points out. "But anyone who bothers to read the list of bands typically playing would also see that they could watch more new (and therefore more relevant?) bands in one day than they could probably see in a month in their hometown.

"The surreal nature of the event appeals to me too. It's like entering an alternative seaside world wherein all, or almost all, of society consists of postcard punks for three days. Yes, there are some valid criticisms concerning this type of event, but ultimately, no-one is forced to attend, and I'm sure that anyone who feels that strongly about them can always go out and create some kind of viable alternative for themselves."

"The H.I.T.S. festivals are excellent," reckons Chiz, of Septic Psychos infamy. "There is a good mix of old and new bands, and there are some really great bands from overseas who we would probably never see if it wasn't for these festivals. I've also travelled to some places for H.I.T.S. gigs that I would never have gone to otherwise – East Berlin, Spain's Basque region, East and West USA… punk rock, beer and travel, you can't beat it! These gigs bring everyone together… year by year we're turning into one big happy family!"

And through such festivals, and the bands that cite the period as a major influence, the spirit of UK82 shall endure. Just as the first wave bands eventually imploded, so did the second, coming apart messily at the seams as bands split up and labels went under. The initial buzz of the scene diminished as it grew over-saturated with increasingly generic acts, but, as anyone who was there will tell you, it was an exciting and special time for underground music that will live on in our hearts forever.

APPENDIX THREE

RELATED WEBSITES

www.abh.8k.com
www.abrasivewheels.net
www.angelicupstarts.co.uk
www.antinowhereleague.com
www.artofthestate.co.uk
www.attak.co.uk
www.blitzwarriors.com
www.broken-bones.co.uk
www.captainoi.com
www.cherryred.co.uk
www.cockneyrejects.net
www.deadline-uk.com
www.deathrock.com
www.demobpunk.com
www.discharge.uk.com
www.mysite.freeserve.com/drongosforeurope
www.drstrange.com
www.punkjunkies.com
www.the-gonads.co.uk/
www.hiddentalentbooking.com
www.householdnamerecords.co.uk
www.inflammablematerial.co.uk
www.instantagony.co.uk
www.intimidationrecords.co.uk
www.londonpunks.co.uk
www.mickmercer.com
www.mmzine.co.uk
www.neurotics.org.uk
www.members.tripod.com/nihilismontheprowl
www.lthenstridge.freeserve.co.uk/NoFuture
www.onewaysystem.co.uk
www.pictureframeseduction.com
www.punkbands.com
www.punkcore.com
www.punkinscotland.co.uk
www.punkoiuk.co.uk
www.punktastic.com
www.records.razor-blades.com
www.redalert1.co.uk
www.resistance77.co.uk
www.geocities.com/runnin_feart
www.theskeptix.com
www.special_duties.surf3.net/

www.step1music.com
www.testtubebabies.co.uk
www.thethreats.co.uk
www.tkorecords.com
www.tonymottram.com
www.thetoydolls.com
www.ukdecay.co.uk
www.uksubs.com
www.varukers.co.uk
www.vicesquad.org.uk
www.worldwidepunk.com

APPENDIX FOUR

UPDATED DISCOGRAPHIES

(significant releases by the bands in the book since *Burning Britain* was first published in 2004):

THE 4-SKINS
'Turning The Past Into The Present' 7" (Randale/Clockwork Firm, 2009) – *split with Evil Conduct*
'The Return' CD/LP (Randale, 2010)

ABRASIVE WHEELS
'Nothing To Prove' CDEP (S.O.S., 2007)
'Skum' CD/LP (Crashed Out, 2009)

THE ADICTS
'Rollercoaster' CD/LP (SOS, 2004)
'Life Goes On' CD/LP (I Used To Fuck People Like You in Prison, 2009)
'All The Young Droogs' CD/LP (DC-Jam, 2012)

ANGELIC UPSTARTS
'The Dirty Dozen' CD/LP (I Hate People, 2011) – *split with Crashed Out*

ANTI-NOWHERE LEAGUE
'Kings & Queens' CD/LP (Captain Oi, 2005)
'The Road To Rampton' CD/LP (Nowhere, 2007)
'This Is War' 7" (Papagajuv Hlasatel, 2011)

BROKEN BONES
'No One Survives' 7" (Doctor Strange, 2004)
'Time For Anger, Not Justice' CD/LP (Doctor Strange, 2005)
'Death Walks The Streets' 7" (Doctor Strange, 2009)
'Fuck You And All You Stand For!' CD/LP (Rodent Popsicle, 2010)

THE BUSINESS
'Mean Girl' MLP/MCD (Bad Dog, 2008)
'Don't Give A Fuck' 7" (I Used To Fuck People Like You In Prison, 2009) – *split with Control*

COCKNEY REJECTS
'Unforgiven' CD/LP (G&R, 2007)
'East End Babylon' CD/LP (Cadiz, 2012)

THE DEFECTS
'Demos & Live' LP (Antisociety, 2010)
'Revelator' 12" (Punkerama, 2011)
'Riot Free Zone?' 7" (Punkerama, 2013)
'Politicophobia' CD/LP (Punkerama, 2013)
'Hill Street' CDEP (Punkerama, 2013)

DEMOB
'If It Ain't Punk, It Don't Rock' CD/LP (Amber, 2004)

THE DESTRUCTORS
'Punk Singles Collection' CD (Captain Oi, 2006)
'Politika' CD (Rowdy Farrago, 2010)
'11.11.11. In Memoriam' CD (Rowdy Farrago, 2011)
'Ragnarok 12.12.12' CD (Rowdy Farrago, 2012)
'Pow! That's Kill Music Vol 2' CD (Rowdy Farrago, 2012)
'The Sublime, The Perverse, The Ridiculous' CD (Rowdy Farrago, 2013)

As Destructors 666:
'Many Were Killed, Few Were Chosen' CD (Rowdy Farrago, 2007)
'Malleus Maleficarum' MCD (Rowdy Farrago, 2008)
'Pow! That's Killmusik 666, Volume One: Revision' CD (Rowdy Farrago, 2009)

Since Allen Adams reformed The Destructors in 2007 as Destructors 666 (reverting back to just The Destructors in 2009), the band have released a huge amount of music, including numerous EPs and split releases, with only a taster listed above. For the full updated discography, the reader should visit www.destructors666.com.

DISCHARGE
'Beginning Of The End' 7"/CDEP (Thunk, 2006)
'Disensitise' CD/LP (Vile, 2009)
'Propaganda Feeds' 7" (HG Fact, 2011)

DRONGOS FOR EUROPE
'Barcode Generation' CD/LP (Puke N Vomit, 2004)
'Hope And Glory' 7" (Puke N Vomit, 2004)
'Hotline To Hades' CD/LP (Punk Shit, 2005)
'Dance When Maggie's Dead' 7" (DFE, 2007)
'Cage The Rage' CD/LP (DFE, 2010)
'Messed Up' 7" (DFE, 2012)

ENGLISH DOGS
'Tales From The Asylum' CDEP (Self-released, 2008)
'Get Off My Fucking Moon' 7" EP (Self-released, 2011)
'The Dog Sick EP' CDEP (Anti-Acoustic League, 2012) – *split with Sick On The Bus*
'Punk Fucking Rock' 7" (Chaosphere/Dog City, 2013) – *split with Clockwork Boys*
'We Did, We Do, We Always Fucking Will' CD (N.D.R., 2014)

EXTERNAL MENACE
'Early Demos EP (1979 – 1982)' 7" (Loud Punk, 2011)
'Coalition Blues' LP (Dirty Punk, 2013)

THE FITS
'Lead On' 7" (self-released, 2013)

FOREIGN LEGION
'Death Valley' CD/LP (Durty Mick, 2007)
'Salute To The Boys' 7" (KB, 2012) – *split with Riot Company*
'Clockwork Kids Still Alive!' 7" (Rusty Knife, 2012) – *split with Cervelli Stanki*
'Light At The End Of The Tunnel' CD/LP (KB, 2013)

GBH
'Cruel & Unusual' CD/LP (Idol, 2004)
'Perfume And Piss' CD/LP (Hellcat, 2010)

INSTANT AGONY
'One Man Army' 7" (Puke N Vomit, 2005)
'Exploitation' CD/LP (Be Afraid, 2007)

THE OUTCASTS
'Vive Lyon!' CD (Spit, 2011)

PETER AND THE TEST TUBE BABIES
'A Foot Full Of Bullets' CD/LP (Locomotive, 2005)
'Very Disaster!!!' CD/LP (Anfibio, 2011) – *split with Reazione*
'Split' 7" (Oi! The Boat, 2012) – *split with Penny Cocks*
'Piss Ups' CD/LP (Randale, 2012)

RED ALERT
'Excess All Areas' CD/LP (Captain Oi, 2005)
'Split' CD/LP (Red Giants, 2010) – *split with Produzenten Der Froide*
'We Stand As One' 10"/MLP (Steeltown, 2013) – *split with Loudmouth & Halbstarke Jungs*

RESISTANCE 77
'Songs For A Nanny State' CD/LP (Captain Oi, 2006)
'True Punk & Oi Will Never Die' 7" (Camden Town, 2006)

THE SEPTIC PSYCHOS
'Rotten And Rancid' CD/LP (Dirty Old Man/Weird, 2010)

SENSA YUMA
'Safe Sound & Insane' CD/LP (Mass Productions, 2007)
'Kickin & Screamin' CD/LP (Mass Productions, 2011)

SOLDIER DOLLS
'Soldier Dolls' CD/LP (Longshot, 2006)

THE STRAPS
'The Punk Collection' CD (Captain Oi, 2005)

THREATS
'God Is Not With Us Today' CD/LP (Doctor Strange, 2006)

TOY DOLLS
'Our Last Album?' CD/LP (Secret, 2004)
'Another Bleedin' Best Of' CD/LP (Secret, 2011)
'The Album After The Last One' CD/LP (Secret, 2012)

UK SUBS
'Violent State (live)' CD/LP (Dirty Punk, 2004)
'666 Yeah' 7" (Jet 13, 2006)
'Warhead' MCD/MLP (Jet 13, 2008)
'Work In Progress' CD/LP (Captain Oi, 2010)
'Product Supply' 7" (Time & Matter, 2011)
'XXIV' CD/LP (Captain Oi, 2013)

THE VARUKERS
'Hellbound' MCD/MLP (Asylum, 2005)
'1984 – 2000' double-CD (Anti-Society, 2013)

VICE SQUAD
'Defiant' CD/LP (STP, 2007)
'London Underground' CD/LP (Last Rockers, 2009)
'Punk Rock Radio' CD/LP (Last Rockers, 2011)

ABOUT PM PRESS

PM Press was founded at the end of 2007 by a small
collection of folks with decades of publishing, media, and
organizing experience. PM Press co-conspirators have
published and distributed hundreds of books, pamphlets,
CDs, and DVDs. Members of PM have founded enduring
book fairs, spearheaded victorious tenant organizing campaigns, and worked
closely with bookstores, academic conferences, and even rock bands to deliver
political and challenging ideas to all walks of life. We're old enough to know what
we're doing and young enough to know what's at stake.

We seek to create radical and stimulating fiction and non-fiction books, pamphlets,
T-shirts, visual and audio materials to entertain, educate and inspire you. We
aim to distribute these through every available channel with every available
technology — whether that means you are seeing anarchist classics at our bookfair
stalls; reading our latest vegan cookbook at the café; downloading geeky fiction
e-books; or digging new music and timely videos from our website.

PM Press is always on the lookout for talented and skilled volunteers, artists,
activists and writers to work with. If you have a great idea for a project or can
contribute in some way, please get in touch.

PM Press
PO Box 23912
Oakland, CA 94623
www.pmpress.org

FRIENDS OF PM PRESS

These are indisputably momentous times—the financial system is melting down globally and the Empire is stumbling. Now more than ever there is a vital need for radical ideas.

In the six years since its founding—and on a mere shoestring—PM Press has risen to the formidable challenge of publishing and distributing knowledge and entertainment for the struggles ahead. With over 250 releases to date, we have published an impressive and stimulating array of literature, art, music, politics, and culture. Using every available medium, we've succeeded in connecting those hungry for ideas and information to those putting them into practice.

Friends of PM allows you to directly help impact, amplify, and revitalize the discourse and actions of radical writers, filmmakers, and artists. It provides us with a stable foundation from which we can build upon our early successes and provides a much-needed subsidy for the materials that can't necessarily pay their own way. You can help make that happen—and receive every new title automatically delivered to your door once a month—by joining as a Friend of PM Press. And, we'll throw in a free T-shirt when you sign up.

Here are your options:

- **$30 a month** Get all books and pamphlets plus 50% discount on all webstore purchases

- **$40 a month** Get all PM Press releases (including CDs and DVDs) plus 50% discount on all webstore purchases

- **$100 a month** Superstar—Everything plus PM merchandise, free downloads, and 50% discount on all webstore purchases

For those who can't afford $30 or more a month, we're introducing **Sustainer Rates** at $15, $10 and $5. Sustainers get a free PM Press T-shirt and a 50% discount on all purchases from our website.

Your Visa or Mastercard will be billed once a month, until you tell us to stop. Or until our efforts succeed in bringing the revolution around. Or the financial meltdown of Capital makes plastic redundant. Whichever comes first.

The Day the Country Died: A History of Anarcho Punk 1980-1984

Ian Glasper

ISBN: 978-1-60486-516-5
$24.95   496 pages

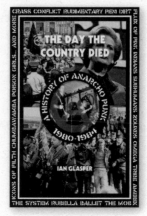

The Day the Country Died features author, historian, and musician Ian Glasper (*Burning Britain*) exploring in minute detail the influential, esoteric, UK anarcho punk scene of the early Eighties. If the colorful '80s punk bands captured in *Burning Britain* were loud, political, and uncompromising, those examined in *The Day the Country Died* were even more so, totally prepared to risk their liberty to communicate the ideals they believed in so passionately.

With Crass and Poison Girls opening the floodgates, the arrival of bands such as Zounds, Flux of Pink Indians, Conflict, Subhumans, Chumbawamba, Amebix, Rudimentary Peni, Antisect, Omega Tribe, and Icons of Filth heralded a brand new age of honesty and integrity in underground music. With a backdrop of Thatcher's Britain, punk music became self-sufficient and considerably more aggressive, blending a DIY ethos with activism to create the perfectly bleak soundtrack to the zeitgeist of a discontented British youth.

It was a time when punk stopped being merely a radical fashion statement, and became a force for real social change; a genuine revolutionary movement, driven by some of the most challenging noises ever committed to tape. Anarchy, as regards punk rock, no longer meant "cash from chaos." It meant "freedom, peace, and unity." Anarcho punk took the rebellion inherent in punk from the beginning to a whole new level of personal awareness.

All the scene's biggest names, and most of the smaller ones, are comprehensively covered with new, exclusive interviews and hundreds of previously unseen photographs.

"The oral testimony assembled here provides an often-lucid participant's view of the work of the wider anarcho-punk milieu, which demonstrates just as tellingly the diversity as well as the commonality by which it was defined. The collection hints at the extent to which—within a militant antiwar, anti-work, anti-system framework— the perception and priorities of the movement's activists differed: something the movement's critics (who were always keen to deride the uniformity of the 'Crass punks') rarely understood."
—Rich Cross, *Freedom*

Punk Rock: An Oral History

John Robb
with a foreword by Henry Rollins

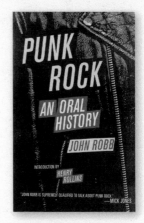

ISBN: 978-1-60486-005-4
$19.95   584 pages

With its own fashion, culture, and chaotic energy, punk rock boasted a do-it-yourself ethos that allowed anyone to take part. Vibrant and volatile, the punk scene left an extraordinary legacy of music and cultural change. John Robb talks to many of those who cultivated the movement, such as John Lydon, Lemmy, Siouxsie Sioux, Mick Jones, Chrissie Hynde, Malcolm McLaren, Henry Rollins, and Glen Matlock, weaving together their accounts to create a raw and unprecedented oral history of UK punk. All the main players are here: from The Clash to Crass, from The Sex Pistols to the Stranglers, from the UK Subs to Buzzcocks—over 150 interviews capture the excitement of the most thrilling wave of rock 'n' roll pop culture ever. Ranging from its widely debated roots in the late 1960s to its enduring influence on the bands, fashion, and culture of today, this history brings to life the energy and the anarchy as no other book has done.

"Its unique brand of energy helps make it a riot all its own."
—*Harp* magazine

"John Robb is a great writer… and he is supremely qualified in my opinion to talk about punk rock."
—Mick Jones, The Clash

"John Robb is as punk rock as The Clash."
—Alan McGee

The Story of Crass

George Berger

ISBN: 978-1-60486-037-5
$20.00   304 pages

Crass was the anarcho-punk face of a revolutionary
movement founded by radical thinkers and artists
Penny Rimbaud, Gee Vaucher and Steve Ignorant.
When punk ruled the waves, Crass waived the rules
and took it further, putting out their own records,
films and magazines and setting up a series of
situationist pranks that were dutifully covered by the
world's press. Not just another iconoclastic band,
Crass was a musical, social and political phenomenon.

Commune dwellers who were rarely photographed and remained contemptuous
of conventional pop stardom, their members explored and finally exhausted the
possibilities of punk-led anarchy. They have at last collaborated on telling the
whole Crass story, giving access to many never-before seen photos and interviews.

*"Lucid in recounting their dealings with freaks, coppers, and punks, the band's voices
predominate, and that's for the best."*
— *The Guardian*

*"Thoroughly researched… chockful of fascinating revelations… it is, surprisingly, the
first real history of the pioneers of anarcho-punk."*
— *Classic Rock*

*"They (Crass) sowed the ground for the return of serious anarchism in the early
eighties."*
— Jon Savage, *England's Dreaming*

Spray Paint the Walls:
The Story of Black Flag

Stevie Chick

ISBN: 978-1-60486-418-2
$19.95   432 pages

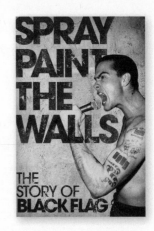

Black Flag were the pioneers of American Hardcore, and this is their blood-spattered story. Formed in Hermosa Beach, California in 1978, for eight brutal years they made and played brilliant, ugly, no-holds-barred music on a self-appointed touring circuit of America's clubs, squats and community halls. They fought with everybody: the police, the record industry and even their own fans. They toured overseas on pennies a day and did it in beat-up trucks and vans.

Spray Paint the Walls tells Black Flag's story from the inside, drawing on exclusive interviews with the group's members, their contemporaries, and the bands they inspired. It's the story of Henry Rollins, and his journey from fan to iconic frontman. And it's the story of Greg Ginn, who turned his electronics company into one of the world's most influential independent record labels while leading Black Flag from punk's three-chord frenzy into heavy metal and free-jazz. Featuring over 30 photos of the band from Glen E. Friedman, Edward Colver, and others.

"Neither Greg Ginn nor Henry Rollins sat for interviews but their voices are included from earlier interviews, and more importantly Chuck Dukowski spoke to Chick—a first I believe. The story, laid out from the band's earliest practices in 1976 to its end ten years later, makes a far more dramatic book than the usual shelf-fillers with their stretch to make the empty stories of various chart-toppers sound exciting and crucial and against the odds."
—Joe Carducci, formerly of SST Records

"Here is an exhaustive prequel to, followed by a more balanced re-telling of, Rollins' Get in the Van *journal, chronicling Flag's emergence in suburban Hermosa Beach, far from the trendy Hollywood scene (Germs, X, etc.) and how their ultra-harsh, hi-speed riffage sparked moshpit violence—initially fun, but soon aggravated by jocks and riot police. Greg Ginn, their aloof guitarist/slave-driver/ideologue dominates in absentia. Gradually, he fires everyone but Rollins, yet, his pan-American shoestring SST empire is relentlessly inspirational. A gory, gobsmacking read."*
—Andrew Perry, *MOJO*

"Chick's analytical and in-depth biography of the progenitors of SoCal Hardcore builds up to a page-turning, scene-setting climax… Chick does a fine job of detailing the importance, influence and dedicated touring ethic of the band. Not to mention finally laying to rest the ludicrous but long-running Stalinesque punk rock opinion that of all Flag's diverse career output, only the material before Rollins joined was of any value."
—Alex Burrows, *Classic Rock*

Dead Kennedys: Fresh Fruit for Rotting Vegetables, The Early Years

Alex Ogg
with illustrations by Winston Smith
and photographs by Ruby Ray

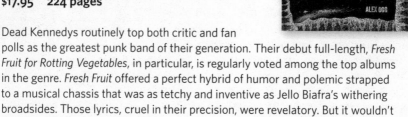

ISBN: 978-1-60486-489-2
$17.95 224 pages

Dead Kennedys routinely top both critic and fan polls as the greatest punk band of their generation. Their debut full-length, *Fresh Fruit for Rotting Vegetables*, in particular, is regularly voted among the top albums in the genre. *Fresh Fruit* offered a perfect hybrid of humor and polemic strapped to a musical chassis that was as tetchy and inventive as Jello Biafra's withering broadsides. Those lyrics, cruel in their precision, were revelatory. But it wouldn't have worked if the underlying sonics were not such an uproarious rush, the paraffin to Biafra's naked flame.

Dead Kennedys' continuing influence is an extraordinary achievement for a band that had practically zero radio play and only released records on independent labels. They not only existed outside of the mainstream but were, as V. Vale of *Search and Destroy* noted, the first band of their stature to turn on and attack the music industry itself. The DKs set so much in motion. They were integral to the formulation of an alternative network that allowed bands on the first rung of the ladder to tour outside of their own backyard. They were instrumental in supporting the concept of all-ages shows and spurned the advances of corporate rock promoters and industry lapdogs. They legitimized the notion of an American punk band touring internationally while disseminating the true horror of their native country's foreign policies, effectively serving as anti-ambassadors on their travels.

The book uses dozens of first-hand interviews, photos, and original artwork to offer a new perspective on a group who would become mired in controversy almost from the get-go. It applauds the band's key role in transforming punk rhetoric, both polemical and musical, into something genuinely threatening—and enormously funny. The author offers context in terms of both the global and local trajectory of punk and, while not flinching from the wildly differing takes individual band members have on the evolution of the band, attempts to be celebratory—if not uncritical.

"We have a sense of humor and we're not afraid to use it in a vicious way if we have to. In some ways, we're cultural terrorists, using music instead of guns."
—Jello Biafra of the Dead Kennedys